PUBLIC INTEREST RULES OF INTERNATIONAL LAW

The Ashgate International Law Series

Series Editor: Alex Conte, OECD, Paris

The Ashgate International Law Series brings together top-quality titles, principally in the area of public international law but also in private international law, under the label of a single international series. Each title represents work which is the result of high-level research, aimed at both the professorial and postgraduate academic market as well as the expert practitioner.

Also in the series

Terrorism, War and International Law
The Legality of the Use of Force Against Afghanistan in 2001
Myra Williamson
ISBN 978-0-7546-7403-0

A Dual Approach to Ocean Governance
The Cases of Zonal and Integrated Management
in International Law of the Sea
Yoshifumi Tanaka
ISBN 978-0-7546-7170-1

Public Interest Rules of International Law

Towards Effective Implementation

Edited by

TERUO KOMORI

Chiba University, Japan

KAREL WELLENS

Radboud University Nijmegen, The Netherlands

ASHGATE

Published by
Ashgate Publishing Limited
Wey Court East
Union Road
Farnham
Surrey, GU9 7PT
England

Ashgate Publishing Company
Suite 420
101 Cherry Street
Burlington
VT 05401-4405
USA

www.ashgate.com

British Library Cataloguing in Publication Data
Public interest rules of international law : towards effective implementation. -- (The Ashgate international law series)
1. International law. 2. Public policy (International law)
I. Series II. Komori, Teruo. III. Wellens, Karel.
341'.04-dc22

Library of Congress Cataloging-in-Publication Data
Public interest rules of international law : towards effective implementation / edited by Teruo Komori and Karel Wellens.
p. cm. -- (Ashgate international law series)
Includes bibliographical references and index.
ISBN 978-0-7546-7823-6 (hardback) -- ISBN 978-0-7546-9617-9 (ebook)
1. Public interest law. 2. Human rights. 3. Environmental law, International. I. Komori, Teruo. II. Wellens, Karel.
K118.P82P83 2009
341--dc22

2009019772

ISBN: 978-0-7546-7823-6 (hbk)
ISBN: 978-0-7546-9617-9 (ebk)

Mixed Sources
Product group from well-managed forests and other controlled sources
www.fsc.org Cert no. SA-COC-1565
© 1996 Forest Stewardship Council
FSC

Printed and bound in Great Britain by
MPG Books Group, UK

Contents

PART III COORDINATION OF LEGAL REGIMES AND SYSTEMS IN THE IMPLEMENTATION PROCESS

List of Tables

Notes on Contributors

Editors

Teruo Komori, Emeritus Professor of Chiba University, former Professor of Hokkaido University, Graduate School of Law, Law of Treaties, International Public Policy.

Karel Wellens, Professor of the Radboud University of Nijmegen, Faculty of Law, Law of International Organization, General Theory of International Law.

Contributors

AGO Shin-ichi, Professor of Kyushu University, Graduate School of Law, Visiting Professor of Victoria University, Canada, International Labor Law, International Economic Law.

Kern Alexander, Chair in Corporate and Financial Market Law, University of Zurich Law Faculty, and Senior Research Fellow in International Financial Regulation, The Centre for Financial Analysis and Policy, University of Cambridge. Professor of Zurich University, International Banking Regulation.

Masahiko Asada, Professor of Kyoto University, Graduate School of Law, Law of International Disarmament.

Shuichi Furuya, Professor of Waseda University, Law School, International Criminal Law, Law of Extradition.

Takeo Horiguchi, Associate Professor of Hokkaido University, Graduate School of Public Policy, International Environmental Law.

Nobuyuki Kato, Professor of Hokkaigakuen University, Faculty of Law, International Remedies.

Mari Koyano, Professor of Hokkaido University, Graduate School of Law, International Environmental Law, International Public Policy.

Vitit Muntarbhorn, Professor of Chulalongkorn University, Thailand, Special Rapporteur of the United Nations Human Rights Commission, International Human Rights.

OTA Ikuko, Professor of Hiroshima City University, Faculty of International Studies, International Human Rights, International Public Policy.

Hironobu Sakai, Professor of Kyoto University, Graduate School of Law, United Nations Law.

Akira Sakota, Professor of Otaru University of Commerce, Department of Law, Law of Outer Space, State Responsibility.

Akiho Shibata, Professor of Kobe University, Graduate School of International Cooperation Studies, International Environmental Law, Antarctic Law.

TERAYA Koji, Associate Professor of University of Tokyo, Graduate Schools for Law and Politics, International Human Rights, General Theory of International Law.

Marie-Claire Cordonier Segger, Director of the Centre for International Sustainable Development Law (CISDL), Canada; Fellow of the Lauterpacht Centre for International Law, University of Cambridge; and Chair of the International Law on Sustainable Development Partnership (CISDL, International Law Association and International Development Law Organisation).

Introduction

Teruo Komori

Changing Character of International Law

The central theme in traditional international law was to strike a balance between rights and duties among States as subjects of international law. Even general international rules, which are regarded as binding the international community as a whole, were not created to protect general interests (i.e., interests going beyond the individual parties), but only the interests of each party, or of all parties combined.[1] In this regard, it is not wrong to say that rules of international law had the same character as those of private law in domestic legal systems.

The procedures of dispute settlement in traditional international law also had the same character. Only parties whose rights or interests were damaged were qualified to have recourse to dispute settlement procedures. Disputes were settled among parties involved. To what extent the violation of international rules affect the international community as a whole was not an issue to be contended. Thus within the traditional international law, how effective rules of international law were depended on the degree of commitment by parties and on the means of dispute settlement available by parties.

In recent years, however, many international laws have been created to protect the interests of the global community including future generations like the multilateral treaties for international environmental protection. In addition, many other legal issues such as the protection of international human rights, the restraint of use of force, the application of humanitarian law, the utilization of high seas and outer space and the maintenance of the international financial order, are considered to be issues to which the international community as a whole should cooperatively respond. In this sense, it is possible to say that international rules embodying those issues are creating the legal order protecting the public interests of the international community as a whole. It is certainly undeniable that there are still differences of views among States concerning which interests should be regarded as public interests, how they should be institutionalized, and how they should be implemented. Those differences of views, however, are concerned not with making rules balancing the interests of individual parties but with deciding which interests should be regarded as public interests and how international public order should be institutionalized.

1 Cassese 1990, 12.

Such formation of institutions protecting the public interests of the international community has brought changes to the legal process prevailed in the traditional framework of international law. The method of combining framework convention with its protocol in treaty making and adopting non-binding commitment like declarations are increasingly used to induce States to be members of those institutions. Actors participating in those regimes are diversified due to the fact that activities of NGOs and corporations are linked to those of intergovernmental organizations. Dispute settlement mechanisms are also becoming complex. Thus, the formation of those institutions in international society, lacking central government delegated with public power to govern, has brought diversity and complexity into legal processes of international law and coincidentally caused the phenomenon of so-called fragmentation of international legal order.

It seems impossible to characterize those changes and phenomenon found in the legal processes of present international law relevantly within the framework of traditional international law, which has been essentially based on consent of States and has had the character of private law. In order to characterize those changes properly in the framework of present international law, it seems rather necessary to reconstruct a theory of international law putting more emphasis on the public interest aspect of rules of international law. And this theoretical reconstruction of international law incorporating the concept of public interest into its framework seems to be relevant to the application and the interpretation in practice of international rules having those diversified characters.

Approaches to Diversity and Complexity of the International Legal Process

Various Other Approaches

Various approaches have been taken by international lawyers and political scientists to comprehend and respond to those phenomena and problems. First of all, with regard to how we should characterize the phenomenon of fragmentation of the international legal system, a negative view of the phenomenon has emphasized that it is a consequence of political struggle for competence, particularly among international tribunals, and recognizes that it should be solved by way of a politics of tolerance and pluralism.[2]

On the other hand, most of the international lawyers who have responded affirmatively to it deal with the problems roughly form the following two groups of perspectives. One group deals with the problems in light of how and to what extent the phenomenon has changed the concepts and theory of traditional international law, and the other focuses on the analysis of the operational process of institutions in light of how the compliance with the rules is secured or what problems are disturbing their implementation.

2 Koskenniemi and Leino 2002, 574–579.

Some of the studies from the former perspective include those by Rosario Huesa Vinaixa and Karel Wellens focusing on the influence of source upon fragmentation of international law;[3] the study by Pauwelyn arguing the conflict of norms caused by fragmentation;[4] the study by Dekker focusing on the influence that governance or legal pluralism have toward the institutions and concept of international law;[5] and a series of works organized by Kingsbury and Krisch that try to reconstruct the operation of governance systematically under the concept of global administrative law by focusing on the feature that their operations are administrative.[6]

In case of the studies from the latter perspective, most deal with compliance or implementation processes of multilateral environmental treaties as the object,[7] but there are other studies dealing individually with the implementation process of international human rights treaties,[8] the verification system of disarmament treaties,[9] or with the implementation process of various regulatory regimes together.[10] Although there are differences in their concerns or in their focuses of analysis, they have similar structure in that they first describe the procedures securing compliance by the parties, non-compliance mechanism and how those mechanisms are used, and then argue the practical function of those mechanisms for securing compliance and effectiveness of institutions and their legal implication in international law.

The Distinctive Approach of this Book

In contrast to those studies, this book tries to deal with the operational processes of legal institutions protecting the public interests of the international community from the following two concerns. Our first concern with the analysis of operational processes is that, as in other studies, it is necessary to look at the operation of diversified procedures to judge whether or not they are working. In practice, it is almost impossible to expect the automatic application of those procedures because there is no administrative and judicial organ exclusively undertaking the application of rules, and the interests of parties often conflict with their implementation. In addition, it is necessary to analyze the operation of rules in order to know which procedures are useful for achieving the goals of institutions.

The second concern is that there are some substantive problems that were not determined at the time of their decision-making but have arisen later in the

3 Huesa Vinaixa and Wellens 2006.

4 Pauwelyn 2003.

5 Dekker and Werner 2004.

6 Kingsbury 2005.

7 Victor 2005.

8 Alston and Crawford 2000.

9 Avenhaus 2006.

10 Szasz 1999, Ulfstein, Marauhn and Zimmermann 2007.

operational process, such as the amendment of measures or coordination between legal institutions. As regards public institutions and policies embodying a wide range of regulations, it is generally difficult to comprehend the entire structure of those institutions and policies without analyzing the operation of their implementation process: in the operational process, factors and problems which were not predicted at the time of decision-making and go beyond the sphere of applying existing rules may come into play. In the process, key issues to be argued include what the justificatory and feasible solution are, and therefore how appropriately institutions or parties can respond to those problems in terms of how the public interest of the international community is closely related to the effectiveness of institutions. Thus, problems to be dealt with in the operational process are not restricted to those of complying with provided procedures in a treaty.

Moreover, the fact that contemporary institutions protecting the public interests of the international community are adopted in the form of a treaty or agreement of some type or other raises the problem of how the parties of a treaty can apply the rules and measures taken under the treaty to non-parties in order to achieve the goal of institutions. Also in this context, substantive arguments to justify the application of those rules and measures to non-parties are particularly essential. This is why this study draws much attention to the role of legitimacy in the operational processes of institutions.

Legal institutions examined here extend to such various spheres of law as international environmental law, the protection of human rights including labour rights, the restraint of the use of force, humanitarian law, laws of Antarctic and outer space, and rules for the maintenance of international financial order in which the adoption of substantive measures plays an important part in their operation.

In the examination of the operational process of those institutions, this book particularly looks into the processes concerning how measures are legitimized or justified. Even in the MEAs (Multilateral Environmental Agreements), in which non-confrontational and facilitative procedures are important mechanisms for securing compliance, it is indicated that legitimacy constitutes an important factor in the decision of measures when the problems become complex and parties are in dispute.[11] Other arguments include that it is essential to shift the basis of assessment on how a procedure is working from a logic of consequences to a logic of appropriateness which links to the formation of norm consciousness.[12] Factors of that kind seem to play a more important role in institutions in which non-compliance mechanisms are not well organized because there may be situations in which it will be necessary to take measures not stipulated in the treaties against the parties, or it will become necessary to require third States of treaties to take some measures.

If this approach is taken, then as a next step it is necessary to examine how relevant it is in securing the effectiveness of institutions, though the point is

11 Brunnée 2007, 389.

12 Mitchell 2005, 79–81.

closely related to how we construct the concept of effectiveness. As regards the effectiveness of institutions, it is often contended that where the procedures adopted to achieve the goals of institutions are not working or where deviation from institutional rules are not solved through dispute settlement mechanism, those institutions and rules lack effectiveness or are irrelevant.[13] With regard to the institutions and rules protecting international public interests, however, it is one thing to state analytically that they are lacking effectiveness and another to state as a matter of evaluation that they are irrelevant in the sense that they are not necessary. Those contentions are correlated but different in character and therefore must be dealt with separately.

First, when institutions protecting international public interests have problems with their procedures for responding to non-compliance but their goals are still valid, the issues to be argued are about how those institutions can solve the problems or what measures shall be taken for achieving the goals, but not about whether or not they are irrelevant. In other words, the key issue is what are the effective procedures or responses to be taken. Therefore, if you contend that an institution is irrelevant because its procedures are ineffective, you have to put forward effective procedures replacing those you contend ineffective. If the procedure you believe effective is not proved to be effective in reaching the goal of the institution, it is not a meaningful replacement in the process. In this regard, it is possible to say that the operational processes of the institutions protecting international public interests consist of two processes, one of applying the provided procedures in an effective way and one of searching for a new effective procedure if there is a problem with the existing one.[14]

Secondly, when arguing the effectiveness of institutions, it is necessary to consider on what factors those views base their concept of effectiveness and in what context those factors are applied because the judgment of whether or not an institution is effective may depend on those factors and contexts in which it is applied. According to political theories of constructivism, legitimacy and justification play an important role when measures to be taken are in dispute.[15] Oran Young has also argued that the concept of effectiveness is diversified according to the objectives of institutions.[16] This shows that the validity of assumptions on which positivistic theories relied in the analysis of effectiveness are also questioned.

This study is an attempt to examine the operational process of institutions from the perspective stated above. And this is at the same time a study to look into the impact that factors in the operational process have given to the framework of international law and a study as well to rethink the concept of the effectiveness of law through the examination of operational processes.

13 Brunnée and Toope 2002, 274.

14 Brunnée 2006, 402.

15 Brunnée and Toope 2002, 277–278.

16 Young 1994.

Structure of the Book

In organizing the contents of this book, the writer of each chapter selected a subject within their specific sphere of research that is closely concerned with the perspective stated above. Moreover, in order to restrict the topic to the examination of operational processes, two conditions have been imposed on the argument in each chapter.

First, the judgment of whether the interest that an institution protects is an international public interest should be confirmed by the fact that the provisions or preamble of a treaty or a convention utilize terms such as 'general interest' or 'community interest of the international community'. In particular we regard an interest as internationally public in those cases where an institution aims at achieving the common goal of the international community as a whole or in a case where non-compliance by a Party with provisions of the institution inevitably gives rise to damage in some manner to any other Parties. Secondly, in a case where the perception that the interest an institution protects is international public interest is being challenged, we discuss how the institution responds to the challenge within the regime but do not argue the issue from the perspective of a new framework of primary rule *de lege ferenda.*

This book consists of four parts.

Part I: Theoretical Aspects of the Implementation Processes

Part I examines the theoretical aspects of the implementation processes of institutions protecting the public interests of the international community.

In Chapter 1, 'General Observations', Wellens explores the theoretical framework issues that are necessary to analyze the functions of the rules protecting public interests by examining the conceptual framework of public interest rules, the impact of the public interest nature of the rules on various aspects of the implementation process, and the impact of the public interest nature of the rules on various aspects of the enforcement process.

In Chapter 2, 'Diversification of Implementation Processes and Changing Concepts of Effectiveness', Komori analyzes how the implementation processes of institutions protecting public interests have been diversified and as a theoretical implication of such diversification he indicates that the concept of effectiveness of rules should be dealt with from a process-based approach but not from the factor-based approach that traditional legal theories have adopted.

In Chapter 3, 'Multifaceted Conceptions of Implementation and Human Rights Approach', Teraya Koji deals with the issue of implementation from the perspective of the role human rights play therein. He emphasizes the important role that legitimacy or justice, the integrity of various norms and the social conditions play in securing the implementation of international rules and therefore criticizes the dominant theory characterized as judicial positivism. Then he tries to demonstrate that a human rights approach is the most suitable for building a more comprehensive implementation theory. However, he argues that this does not mean the denial of judicial positivism because it still has significance in making relevant norms clear. Thus he concludes that the conception of implementation is not unitary but multilayered and that a human rights approach serves to elaborate the multilayered structure of implementation.

Part II: Diversity and Complexity of Institutionalized Implementation Process

Part II deals with the diversities and complexities of institutionalized implementation processes in practice.

In Chapter 4, 'UN Reform 2005 and Beyond: Conceptualization, Institutionalization and Implementation', Muntarbhorn examines the United Nations (UN)-related reforms initiated by the 2005 Summit of Heads of Government which adopted a variety of measures to re-energize the body from the perspective of whether the rules of the game have changed. While he admits that the normative elements, such as State sovereignty, prohibition of use of force, self-defence and other essentials of international peace and security under the UN Charter are, for the most part, left untouched, he considers that the rules of the game have been changing with a 'slight variation on a theme': the reforms introduce the notion of the State's 'responsibility to protect' its citizens, failing which the UN should act more proactively to do so. The 2005 reforms set into motion some restructuring at the institutional level, but leave untouched the apex of the system – the UN Security Council and the General Assembly. The UN Economic and Social Council is to become more of a coordination–cooperation forum for development issues. The new institutions include the UN Human Rights Council and Peace-building Commission. He also takes into account the new Democracy Fund as well as ongoing reforms in the domain of management and administration by interlinking those reforms with the practical angle of how they are being implemented to date. He concludes that neither angelic, nor demonic, the truth behind the UN (on most accounts) is that it is only as good as its member States intend it to be.

In Chapter 5, 'Legitimization of Measures to Secure Effectiveness in UN Peacekeeping: The Role of Chapter VII of the UN Charter', Sakai clarifies how the measures taken by the UN in its Peacekeeping Operations have been justified, mainly through considering the meaning of the effectiveness concept in those Operations. He focuses on so called 'robust' UN Peacekeeping Operations since the end of the twentieth century, in which limited use of force is authorized under Chapter VII. The effectiveness of the implementation of their new and diversified mandate may bring legitimacy to the introduction of Chapter VII into those activities, in re-shaping their fundamental conduct principles.

In Chapter 6, 'Security Council Resolution 1540 and International Legislation', Asada argues that we should characterize the rule-making activity in the form of a resolution by the Security Council within the framework of the United Nations Charter.

In Chapter 7, 'Proportionality as a Norm of Application for the Precautionary Principle: Its Significance for the Operation of the Precautionary Regime for Land-based Marine Pollution in the North-West Atlantic', Horiguchi explores the significance of proportionality in the implementation of the OSPAR Convention, which is arguably one of the most important precautionary environmental regimes to date. He first draws attention to the fact that although it is pointed out that the proportionality between a goal and a means is a limiting factor for the application of the precautionary principle in general, it has been seldom examined empirically. Thus he examines whether and how the consideration of proportionality is institutionalized in actual decision-making of precautionary measures, focusing on the development of international regulations for land-based marine pollution under the OSPAR Convention. He also argues that such institutionalization can enhance the effectiveness of the precautionary regime, rather than undermine it.

In Chapter 8, 'The Role of Diplomatic Protection in the Implementation Process of Public Interests', Kato deals with the role that the customary law of diplomatic protection plays in the protection of individuals and the public interests of the international community. He indicates that with the development of human rights norms, diplomatic protection is increasingly deemed to have the function of protecting injured nationals' rights, and to be more effective than the implementation mechanisms of human rights instruments. And he argues that as the mechanism that a State other than an injured State can invoke responsibility in the violation of obligations *erga omnes* is recognized in the law of State responsibility, but nevertheless has not yet been established, diplomatic protection exercised by an injured State is liable to have a dual role to protect its own nationals and to safeguard public interests.

Part III: Coordination of Legal Regimes and Systems in the Implementation Process

Part III deals with the coordination of legal regimes and systems that are in conflict with each other in their implementation processes.

In Chapter 9, Effective Implementation of Intersecting Public International Regimes: Environment, Development and Trade Law, Cordonier Segger examines how to coordinate the implementation of various rules when economic, social, and environmental regimes intersect.

In Chapter 10, 'Effective Implementation of International Environmental Agreements: Learning Lessons from the Danube Delta Conflict', Koyano tries to give some hints on how we answer the question of how to ensure the effective implementation of MEAs by conducting a case study of the management processes of the Danube Delta conflicts under several MEAs. She discusses the characteristics of the implementation processes of MEAs in terms of three principal factors, i.e., the method of ensuring implementation, involvement of non-State stakeholders and coordination between relevant international agreements. The characteristics found in these processes are: interactive dialogues consisting of fact-finding, persuasion through multilateral consultation, active involvement of NGOs at various levels and complementary interaction between multiple processes. From those processes she draws such lesson as the usefulness and limits of interactive dialogue, active roles of NGOs, and the significance of practical coordination between overlapping MEAs in the process of interactive dialogue on certain conditions.

In Chapter 11, 'Principle of Complementarity in Reality: Who Actually Applies It in What Way under the ICC System?', Furuya explores the principle of complementarity of the ICC system as one of the rules determining the allocation of cases between international and national jurisdictions. In contrast with extant research, which has mainly relied on the interpretation of the Rome Statute, particularly the notions of 'unwillingness' and 'inability' in Article 17, he attempts to focus on the reality of the principle and illustrates that the principle is actually invoked by the Prosecutor in an earlier stage of proceedings of the ICC when he decides whether a situation is to be preliminarily examined and officially investigated. He also examines the practice of the so-called 'self-referral', by which a situation is referred to the Prosecutor by the States where the alleged crimes were committed. In so doing, he demonstrates that the prosecutorial strategy of the self-referral has shifted the factors to be evaluated from the 'unwillingness' and 'inability' of the state concerned to the gravity of crimes in question.

In Chapter 12, 'Implementation of Article VI of the1967 Outer Space Treaty: The Responsible State and Appropriate State for Private Space Activities', Sakota examines the issue of the determination of the responsible/appropriate State in the Article VI of 1967 Outer Space Treaty. He concludes firstly that the meaning of 'responsibility' in this Article is 'obligation' rather than legal responsibility for internationally wrongful acts, and secondly, on the basis of the analysis of the registration practices of space objects that with regard to the operation of a functional space object the responsible/appropriate State might be the State of nationality of the owner/operator of the object and conversely with regard to the launch activity of a space object that State might be the State of location of the launching.

In Chapter 13, 'How to Design an International Liability Regime for Public Spaces: The Case of Antarctic Environment', Shibata tries to highlight the issue of the process of coordination and interaction between domestic legal regimes of prospective Contracting Parties and the Antarctic environmental liability regime during its negotiation and even after its adoption. On his examination, he suggests the possible ways and means to make this coordination process progress in order to operationalize the Antarctic Environmental Liability Regime.

Part IV: Diversification of Actors in the Implementation of International Public Interests

Part IV deals with the issues arising from the diversification actors in the implementation of international public interests.

In Chapter 14, 'International Economic Law and the Basel Committee on Banking Supervision – an Alternative Form of International Law-Making?', Alexander examines the role of the Basel Committee on Banking Supervision in influencing the development of public international law norms of banking law and regulation. In doing so, he analyzes the Committee's flexible and informal decision-making processes and how it represents a new form of international economic and financial lawmaking that is a response to the liberalization and deregulation of the global economy. He specifically analyzes the Basel Capital Accord; how it represents an alternative form of international economic law; and how it is implemented and enforced through official sector and private market incentives and sanctions. He argues that because the Accord has been adopted by most countries it has become a general principle of public administrative law and thus constitutes a source of public international law and therefore should be an international public policy concern because its decision-making process is controlled by the G10 developed countries with little input from developing and emerging market countries. He concludes with some observations on how the Basel Accord reflects a broader trend in international economic norm building in the global economy.

In Chapter 15, 'Corporate Social Responsibility and its Implications for Public International Law', Ago Shin-Ichi discusses the concept of CSR (corporate social responsibility), indicating that it leads us to an important finding, namely that an interesting development is taking place in international law, and in international labour law, in particular. More specifically, he argues that attaching legal importance to the 'quasi'- or 'para'-legal phenomenon of the CSR forces us to reconsider the traditional frame of reference, including the basic presumption that the subjects of international law are States. Moreover, he foresees the trend towards diversifying the international legislative processes. In doing so, he also strengthens the argument that a 'process-based approach' is required in evaluating the current situation within international law.

In Chapter 16, 'Privatization of Childcare as a Way of Implementing Young Children's Rights: The Recommendations of the Committee on the Rights of the Child and their Implications for Japan', Ota examines the privatization of childcare services from the viewpoint of the optimal implementation of young children's rights. Focusing on two recommendations adopted by the Committee on the Rights of the Child, a monitoring body of the UNCRC, she argues that the documents have contributed to ensuring the effective implementation of the UNCRC in two points: first, they have complemented the early design of its implementation by assisting parents and State parties to fulfill their obligations; second, they have helped to clarify the interpretation of Article 3 (the best interests of the child) of the Convention. Then, as a case study of the domestic implementation of this Convention, she examines some implications of the ongoing changeover of day-nursery services to the form of private consignment in Japan.

In conclusion, Wellens abstracts the following four points from this study. First, the diversification of the implementation process, whether institutionalized or not, is undeniable and could be an indication that the process is developing on its own. While on the one hand object and purpose of a particular public interest rule may be fuelling this diversification, the principle of mutual supportiveness has the potential of producing cross-fertilization and of bringing more consistency in the process.

Second, as to conscious efforts made to stimulate a process of harmonization, coordination of legal regimes and systems in the implementation process will certainly continue to play an important role, while the diversification of actors inevitably requires conscious efforts in order to reduce disharmony in the process.

Third, the incremental or more advanced stage of harmonization reaches its limits when the object and purpose of the public interest rule, in order to maintain its effectiveness, calls for common but differentiated responsibilities. Even the most effective judicial system for enforcement of human rights is in need of a framework to clarify the way domestic courts apply the European Convention on Human Rights and the European Court's case law and how they apply domestic law in harmonization with the European body of human rights law.

Fourth, the process of implementation of public interest rules through the use of third-party countermeasures could develop on its own and will be subject to a certain process of cross fertilization, but one has to admit that the emerging constitutionalization of the enforcement function under general international law has not been matched by a corresponding development of institutional safeguards against the exercise of improper or arbitrary use of third-party countermeasures.

And finally he concludes that the picture presented in this book indicates that both development on its own with cross-fertilization and conscious efforts of harmonization are taking place. Object and purpose of the public interest rule once again appears to be among the decisive factors in this regard. That is another reason why measuring effectiveness of the process cannot be uniform. The principle of mutual supportiveness undoubtedly provides us with the best chance to meet the main challenge faced by the school of constitutionalism, namely to turn the interconnection, *as a matter of fact*, of cross-sectorial issues relating to armed conflict, the environment, development and human rights, into *a matter of law.* More frequent utilization of the principle of mutual supportiveness both *ex ante* and *ex post*, could certainly improve the degree of effectiveness required by the public interest nature of the rules we have analyzed.

References

Alston, P. and Crawford, J. (eds) (2000), *The Future of UN Human Rights Treaty Monitoring* (Cambridge: Cambridge University Press).

Avenhaus, R., Kyriakopoulos, N., Richard, M. and Stein, G. (eds) (2006), *Verifying Treaty Compliance* (Berlin: Springer).

Brunnée, J. and Toope, S. (2002), 'Persuasion and Enforcement: Explaining Compliance with International Law', *Finnish Yearbook of International Law* 13.

Brunnée, J. (2006), 'Multilateral Environmental Agreements and the Compliance Continuum', in *Multilateral Governance of Global Environmental Change* (Cambridge: Cambridge University Press).

Brunnée, J. (2007), 'Compliance Control', in Ulfstein, Marauhn and Zimmermann (eds).

Cassese, A. (1990), *Human Rights in a Changing World* (Cambridge: Polity Press).

Dekker, I. and Werner, W. (eds) (2004), *Governance and International Legal Theory* (Leiden: Martinus Nijhoff Publisher).

Huesa Vinaixa, R. and Wellens, K. (eds) (2006), *L'Influence Des Sources sur L'Unité et la Fragmentation du Droit International* (Bruxelles: Bruylant).

Kingsbury, B. et al. (eds) (2005), 'The Emergence of Global Administrative Law', *Law & Contemporary Problem* 68:3 and 4.

Koskenniemi, M. and Leino, P. (2002), 'Fragmentation of International Law? Post-modern Anxieties', *Leiden Journal of International Law* 15:574–579.

Mitchell, R. (2005), 'Flexibility, Compliance and Norm Development in Climate Regime', in Hovi, Stokke and Ulfstein (eds).

Pauwelyn, J. (2003), *Conflict of Norms in Public International Law* (Cambridge: Cambridge University Press).

Stokke, O., Hovi, J. and Ulfstein, G. (eds) (2005), *Implementing the Climate Regime* (London: Earthscan).

Szasz, P. (ed.) (1999), *Administrative and Expert Monitoring of International Treaties* (New York: Transnational Publishers).

Ulfstein, G., Marauhn, T. and Zimmermann, A. (eds) (2007), *Making Treaties Work* (Cambridge: Cambridge University Press).

Victor, D. et al. (eds) (1988), *The Implementation and Effectiveness of International Environmental Commitments* (Laxenburg: International Institute for Applied Systems Analysis).

Young, O. (1994), *International Governance* (Ithaca: Cornell University Press).

PART I
Theoretical Aspects of the Implementation Processes

Chapter 1
General Observations

Karel Wellens

Introduction

This book is about the implementation of rules that are protecting public interests of the international community. Its focus is on process-based concepts of effectiveness in international law. My contribution consists of general observations on some theoretical issues.

First, a conceptual framework will be laid out. Then, we will turn to the impact of the public interest nature of the rules on various aspects of the implementation and enforcement process.

International legal discourse has always been faced with the dialectics between facts and norms. Recently, the dynamics of the international legal order brought about an irreversible focus on the implementation and enforcement of primary rules, both in state practice and in doctrine. The two major trends in contemporary international law – its humanization and the focus on its enforcement – are not only irreversible but largely intertwined.

Indeed, rules protecting public interests of the international community occupy a prominent place in modern international law. The general approach to international law has a great impact on the processes involving this category of rules.

The degree to which public international law (PIL) is perceived as capable of governing the use of power is reflected in a more transactional or more normative approach. With regard to public interest rules the normative has already put aside the transactional to a large extent. The ongoing debate about the comprehensive,[1] important[2] or limited[3] role attributed to *ius cogens* norms is an echo hereof.

With regard to public interest rules, constitutionalism comes in as a theory that analyzes the interaction between the source of the authority of power and the best way of controlling its exercise: its basic premise is that 'the *international community is a legal community*. A legal community is governed by rules and not (only) by power'.[4]

1 Orakhelashvili 2006.
2 Tams 2005b.
3 Shelton 2006a, 291–323.
4 Peters 2006, 579–610 at 586.

The distinction between the international society and the international community is of paramount importance.

The 'international society is the aggregate of its members, the sovereign States that interact in the international arena as unitary, hermetic and co-equal units'.[5]

The 'international community represents a normative entity characterized by shared norms and undertakings' and it is 'grounded politically on common values'.[6] Its members 'share a feeling of responsibility and have a common interest to protect and promote the referent values'.[7] The prescriptive setting of the international community 'contains an indivisible net of values at national and international level'.[8]

The international society rests upon 'contractual symbiosis interested in the external manifestation of sovereignty emanating from identifiable and unitary sources', whereas members of the international community 'interpret phenomena according to their value matrix and respond accordingly'.[9] The present state of PIL necessarily implies the co-existence, also in terms of implementation and enforcement, of the law of co-existence, the law of cooperation and the law of solidarity, the latter protecting public interests of the international community.[10]

The instruments and mechanisms for ensuring effective implementation have to vary according to the nature of the primary rule.

Any analysis of the implementation/enforcement process of our rules has to take into account a number of other structural factors: the conventional or customary origin of the rules, conflict of norms, the object and purpose of particular rules (prohibitive, prescriptive or permissive), autonomous enforcement within and the degree of cross-fertilization between various branches as well as the permanent interaction between the various actors involved.

The public interest nature of the rules qualifies the impact of these factors and affects the traditional notions of jurisdiction and aspects of state responsibility.

Conceptual Framework

Rules Protecting Public Interests: Sensu Stricto and Sensu Lato

We are not referring to the international community's obvious public interest in the implementation of 'ordinary' rules of PIL by States and other subjects.

How can we identify rules that are protecting (the) public interests of the international community? The actual terms of a treaty may indicate that the

5 Tsagourias 2006, 211–240 at 215.
6 Tsagourias 2006, 212 and 214.
7 Tsagourias 2006, 215.
8 Tsagourias 2006, 231.
9 Tsagourias 2006, 219 and 220.
10 Wellens 2005, 775–807 at 804.

conventional rules are aimed at protecting such an interest. Near-universality and lack of contestation by non-parties are additional elements in this regard. When the conventional rule finds its counterpart in customary law, the public interest nature of this customary rule is beyond doubt.

If a rule does not explicitly claim to be protecting such an interest, the qualification has to be found in the substantive content, the very object and purpose of the rule.

Although public interest rules may be said to embody universal values, a main distinction presents itself. Indeed, the public interest objective may be of fundamental or less fundamental importance to the international community.[11] Hence, there are public interest rules *sensu stricto* and *sensu lato*.

In the *sensu lato* (*s.l.*) category 'balancing the interest' is inherent in the rule-setting and thus also in the implementation process, whereas in the *sensu stricto* (*s.s.*) category, the balancing has occurred in the formulation of the primary rule and resulted in the *absolute prevalence of the interest of the international community*.

The category *s.s.* comprises not only peremptory norms but also non-derogeable human rights (HR) and the 'intransgressible' principles of international humanitarian law (IHL).[12] At stake are the 'non-fragmentable protection of community interest',[13] the integral safeguarding of the interest *s.l.* of the 'international community'.

The category *s.l.* comprises for instance (certain) rules in international environmental law, international criminal law and international trade law. Public interest rules *s.l.* mainly operate within the 'international society'.

Whereas the qualification 'public interest' is irreversible for the *sensu stricto* category, this is not necessarily the case for *sensu lato* rules. For instance the rule on state immunity is clearly in the interest of the 'international society (of States)' but may be eroded through developments of the public interest of the 'international community'.

The main consequences of the distinction *sensu stricto/sensu lato* are to be found in several aspects of their implementation and enforcement process.

Because of their absolute nature, public interests rules *s.s.* are not 'rules of thumb or presumptions subject to adjustments with a view to optimal result'.[14] Hence the question whether there is room for differential rules, differential responsibilities and thus differential implementation and enforcement, has to be answered in the negative, although they may be qualified in scope.[15]

Because of the structural deficiencies at the international community level, the exclusion of differentiation for public interest rules *s.s.* will affect the effectiveness

11 Case T. 253/02.

12 Legality of the Threat or Use of Nuclear Weapons, Advisory Opinion of 8 July 1996, ICJ Reports (1996), 226 at 257, §79.

13 Orakhelashvili 2006, 83.

14 Koskenniemi 2007, 1–30 at 14.

15 Such as the main general norms of IHL: Orakhelasvhili 2006, 68.

of their (collective) implementation and enforcement. The non-derogeability of peremptory norms and of certain HR and IHL norms extends to the consequences arising from their violation.[16]

Public interest rules *s.l.* do allow derogation clauses or disconnection clauses between a number of States parties, even though *inter sese* agreements are 'often used as a technique' for 'more effective implementation of the original treaty between a limited number of treaty parties'.[17]

Differential rules and responsibilities are an ever-increasing feature of international trade and environmental law, derogable HR law, and the law of arms control.[18]

The Notion of Effectiveness

Our focus is on whether the public interest rules have been implemented in an effective way; we do not doubt the adequateness of the primary rules as such.

Is a good record of compliance necessary for regimes to be effective? Raustalia and Slaughther have pointed out that regimes can be effective even if compliance is low.[19]

Effectiveness is a multifaceted notion and it is bound to have a different scope although a similar role in various relevant branches of international law. The way of measuring effectiveness varies significantly while recent studies have convincingly shown attempts to chart compliance empirically and analytically are fraught with methodological difficulties.[20]

In international criminal law, the effectiveness of the implementation by States of their obligation to prosecute particular crimes will be measured by 'the absence of trials led by this Court' according to the ICC Prosecutor.[21]

In the area of arms control it is generally accepted that there is no 100 per cent guarantee of compliance whereas the CITES embargo system was credited with 'an almost 100% success rate' in bringing about compliance,[22] through its system of enforcement measures for 'persistent non-compliance'.[23] The sanctions-

16 Orakhelasvhili 2006, 243.

17 A/CN.4/L.682/Add.1, Fragmentation of International Law: Difficulties Arising from the Diversification and Expansion of International Law. Report of the Study Group of the International Law Commission. Addendum. Appendix. Draft Conclusions of the Work of the Study Group. Finalized by Marti Koskenniemi, of 2 May 2006, §31.

18 Recent research has shown that differential treatment has been effective in enhancing compliance: Rajamani 2006.

19 Gilligan 2006, 935–967 at 940.

20 Viljoen and Louw 2007, 1–34 at 32.

21 As cited by Kleffner 2006, 79–104 at 86.

22 Sand 2006, 259–272 at 266.

23 Mrema 2006, 201–227 at 208.

based approach was taken 'because of its lack of resources to support capacity-building'.[24]

Bianchi has skilfully identified the difficulties of assessing the effectiveness of the Security Council (SC) anti-terrorist measures.[25]

A satisfactory degree of effectiveness can only be achieved by a more intrusive and systematically applied supervisory mechanism[26] as the law of arms control has shown.

Various factors have an impact on the effectiveness of the implementation process: assistance *ex ante* to induce compliance (legal obligation for developed States to provide financial and technical assistance under the Montreal and Kyoto Protocols) or *ex post* to restore compliance (SC with regard to international peace and security); the soft-law nature of the instruments containing public interests rules *s.l.*; the classification of primary obligations as bilateral, of an interdependent nature or as collective obligations of an integral type. The indivisibility or *erga omnes* nature of, for example, WTO obligations has an impact on standing and countermeasures.[27]

Proliferation of norms 'may pave the way to inconsistencies which may negatively reverberate on effectiveness',[28] especially when the drafters of the primary rules are using the implementation process on an experimental basis in order to solve such inconsistencies.[29] Such multifunctionality of the implementation process is available for public interest rules *s.l.* only.

Effectiveness plays an important role in the enforcement debate. 'International jurisprudence suggests that (conventional) enforcement regimes are more likely to be exclusive if they are effective'.[30] But this still leaves the question whether conventional enforcement regimes are also more effective if they are exclusive *vis-à-vis* extra-conventional means of enforcement.

Moreover, the perception by States of the degree of effectiveness reached within a particular regime may induce States to have recourse to dispute settlement procedures (DSP) in lieu of non-compliance procedures (NCP).[31]

24 Reeve 2006, 134–178 at 159.

25 Lack of adequate parameters, lack of uniform legislative solutions at the domestic level, lack of an effective supervisory mechanism to ascertain the correctness of auto-reporting although in this last regard some institutional improvements have been made recently: Bianchi 2006, 881–919 at 884, 893, 898, 900–902.

26 Bianchi 2006, 903.

27 Gazzini 2006, 723–742.

28 Bianchi 2006, 914.

29 Raustalia and Victor 2004, 277–309 at 302.

30 Tams 2005b, 277.

31 Ulfstein 2007, 116–133 at 121.

The Notion of Implementation

Implementation 'covers all relevant laws, regulations, policies and other measures and initiatives that Contracting Parties adopt and or take to meet their obligations'.[32]

The notion of implementation is broader than compliance with rules: cooperation means working together, not just carrying out legal rules on an individual State basis.

In the process of implementation an attempt is made to reconcile effectiveness, legality and legitimacy.

Involvement of private actors in the process of implementation may enhance its effectiveness, but entails the risk of affecting the public interest drive approach, thus creating new problems in terms of legitimacy.[33]

Reciprocity does not play a significant role, or no role at all in the implementation process of public interest rules, because of the non-synallagmatic nature of the underlying obligations. However, the absence of (strict) reciprocity makes it more difficult to anticipate long-term difficulties of implementation.

A variety of mechanisms are used in the implementation process. There is self-assessment through reporting by States Parties followed by scrutiny through a review conference or special treaty bodies such as in the areas of environmental and human rights. A complaint or a full-fledged violation procedure may also be available to individual victims and/or other States Parties.

While universality of a treaty would normally be conducive to implementation, a broad, virtually universal membership of a monitoring body does not always guarantee more effective implementation as the case of the Codex Alimentarius Commission dealing with the global regulation of GMOs illustrates.[34]

Formalized agreements 'raise the reputation costs of non-compliance'.[35] Soft law instruments may thus be perceived as hardly suitable for the implementation of public interest rules, but their implementation may very well score high on the effectiveness index.

The use of DSP for a dispute over the mere interpretation of a public interest rule, without this process implying a violation by another Party, can be an important means of enhancing the effectiveness of implementation by both Parties at a later stage.

The Notion of (Non-)compliance

In general terms, compliance refers to the fulfilment by the Contracting Parties of their obligations, while non-compliance may take several different forms.

32 Mrema 2006, 213.

33 Peters 2006, 593.

34 Krisch 2006, 247–278 at 260.

35 Bell 2006, 373–412 at 386.

The 'soundness of the whole treaty regime' is important for effective compliance: this requires clear-cut obligations, a transparent compliance control mechanism, and clarity about the consequences of non-compliance, the cost of which should be higher than the benefits of compliance.[36] The compliance regime may be 'an explanatory factor for state (non-) participation in international environmental treaties'.[37]

All public interest rules *s.l.* have internal built-in and external incentives towards compliance.

Room for Flexibility?

Because of their integral nature and hence their claim to absolute and unconditional implementation,[38] public interest rules *s.s.* do not allow 'a degree' of compliance or 'flexible' implementation.[39] The object and purpose of public interest rules *s.s.* do not tolerate non-compliance to be used as an intermediate form for direct state responsibility as a result of direct violations such as in the law of arms control, environmental law and trade law.

Drafters of public interest rules *s.l.* may opt for intentional flexibility in compliance through mechanisms such as emission trading in the Kyoto Protocol which can not only endanger the effectiveness of the compliance system but also 'the environmental effectiveness of the whole regime'.[40] In arms control agreements, however, new techniques of governance have been 'developed in order to *increase* [my italics] the effectiveness; they are seeking "to avoid the 'all or nothing' approach" and aiming at achieving a "reasonable level of compliance" instead'.[41] Comments by HR bodies indicate 'the *degree of compliance* [my italics] by the State concerned'.[42]

Although the ICJ in Gabickovo[43] did not need to determine the existence of a principle of approximate treaty application, it 'spoke convincingly in favour of a flexible implementation of the treaty'.[44]

---

36 Preface by Beyerlin 2006, VII. See also Viljoen and Louw 2007, 12–17 who add the length of time to deal with a complaint of non-compliance and a well-reasoned decision.

37 Kolari 2006, 874–879 at 876.

38 Yearbook International Law Commission (1958), Vol. II, 27–28.

39 See for instance Article 1 of the Chemical Weapons Convention: 'Each State Party to this Convention undertakes never under any circumstances…'.

40 Kolari 2006, 878.

41 Marauhn 2006, 243–272 at 246.

42 Zimmermann 2007, 15–47 at 26.

43 Gabcikovo-Nagymaros Project (Hungary/Slovakia), Judgment, ICJ Reports (1997), 1 at 53, §76.

44 Skubizewski 1999, 475–483 at 479.

Non-compliance in its Various Forms

With regard to public interest rules *s.l.* there is *capacity-based non-compliance*. Lack of financial resources or of technical expertise and an ill-equipped domestic legal toolbox play a role in MEAs, in the implementation of SC freezing orders or of other anti-terrorist measures such as immigration and border control.[45]

A second and third form of non-compliance have in common their intentional nature, but they still have to be distinguished from each other.

Intentional non-compliance may be simply rooted in bad faith: acts of genocide as well as other violations of *ius cogens* norms can only occur intentionally.

Different in scope and objective is what Cogan has aptly called 'operational *non-compliance*', the major benefit of which is to ensure 'that the international legal system retains its effectiveness', although this is bound to vary 'with the nature of the breach and the primary rule at issue'.[46] This is used to bridge 'the enforcement gap created by inadequate community mechanisms of control'.[47]

The different responses by the international community towards the NATO intervention in Kosovo and the military action against Iraq clearly demonstrate the limits of such an 'effectiveness bonus'.

Procedural Responses to Non-compliance

How have States responded, at the procedural, institutional level to the phenomenon of both capacity-based and intentional non-compliance?

Choosing NCP or DSP is 'at least partially, due to the difference in the underlying rights being protected'.[48]

Active treaty 'management' aims at ensuring 'the observance of international rules' and this 'independently of breaches'.[49] It 'has established itself as central to compliance strategies'[50] in the areas of HR, environmental protection and arms control.

In cases of capacity-based non-compliance, NCPs of a non-adversarial nature have been put in place. In environmental law a heavy emphasis is placed on 'justificatory discourse'[51] 'allowing compliance issues to be addressed in a multilateral context rather than through bilateral dispute settlement procedures'.[52] Non-confrontational 'compliance control promises to show more efficacy in

45 Bianchi 2006, 897–898.
46 Cogan 2006, 189–210 at 205.
47 Cogan 2006, 191.
48 Zimmermann 2007, 47.
49 Tams 2007b, 391–409 at 393.
50 Brunnée 2007a, 373–390 at 373.
51 Brunnée 2007b, 1–23 at 18.
52 Ulfstein 2007, 117.

practice than that of taking merely repressive measures'[53] through facilitating future compliance. The same goes for the political NCPs in the law of arms control[54] where DSP has never played a major role.[55]

Decisions of NCPs are not final 'in the sense of res judicata' and 'may therefore be seen as less intrusive on State sovereignty',[56] except of course in the area of arms control where they typically include verifications and inspections,[57] with the CWC being unique in having the 'most intrusive verification regime established so far'.[58] Such intrusive compliance controls however depend on the willingness of States and their capability 'of enforcing compliance if the controls lead to the result that there is gross non-compliance'.[59]

In HR law, on-site investigations by monitoring bodies may perform a preventative or a reactive function.[60]

In cases of intentional non-compliance or violations, judicial or quasi-judicial enforcement of an adversarial nature is a 'primary form of law enforcement'.[61]

The Relation Between NCP and DSP

The relation between NCP and DSP is best described as one of a complex and delicate co-existence. They co-exist for instance in the Ozone Layer Convention (Article 11) and in arms control.[62] In environmental law, NCPs supplement DSP bodies with more facilitative quality,[63] while judicial 'pronouncements serve rather to elucidate important principles than to achieve a concrete and detailed settlement by themselves'[64] because it is difficult, if not impossible to allocate responsibility for harm to specific actors.[65] In HR and IHL law, there is complementarity as well between courts and Truth and Reconciliation Commissions (TRCs).

Is it always true that reference to a DSP is 'a last resort in the event a compliance system fails?'[66] The concerns that trigger a DSP may partly overlap with those of a NCP.[67]

53 Beyerlin 2006, VII.
54 Paulus 2007, 351–372 at 366.
55 Marauhn 2007, 251.
56 Ulfstein, Marauhn and Zimmermann 2007, 3–12 at 10.
57 Marauhn 2007, 257.
58 Tabassi 2007, 273–300 at 273.
59 Oeter 1997, 101–169 at 168.
60 Kicker 2007, 91–111 at 101– 102 and Brunnée 2007a, 379.
61 Tams 2007b, 394.
62 Marauhn 2007, 257.
63 Ulfstein, Marauhn and Zimmermann 2007, 9.
64 Paulus 2007, 363.
65 Paulus 2007, 365.
66 Reeve 2007, 158.
67 Chinkin 1998, 123–140 at 132.

The question has been raised whether 'a party to a dispute (can) continue with the bilateral dispute resolution procedures under Article 11 (of the Ozone Layer Convention) although another self-designated party has commenced the institutional procedures relating to non-compliance'.[68]

Koskeniemmi has pointed out that 'the compliance procedure should be dropped because their objectives differ and they may frustrate the adjudicatory process'[69] while others do not consider this to be a legal impediment.[70]

Formal DSPs are provided for in most MEAs, but they have remained unused,[71] exception made of course for the OSPAR case.

In case of recourse to extra-treaty DSP it should be made 'useful for and not disruptive of treaty implementation'.[72]

Impact of Non-compliance

Non-compliance does not only undermine the primary rules which are breached, but also the 'assumption that states must comply with international law'.[73] On the other hand, the Court's pronouncement that *prima facie* non-compliance justified by the defendant State based on 'exceptions or justifications contained within the rule itself' rather confirms than weakens the rule[74] is *a fortiori* applicable to public interest rules.

Although the impact of utilising NCP and DSP may overlap to the extent that they both necessarily imply (NCP) or contain (DSP) a determination that a State has failed its obligations, Koskenniemi rightly pointed to the 'deformalisation of State responsibility'.[75]

Endemic non-compliance by one or several of the State Parties would be a manifestation of the failure of the special regime; relevant general law would then, once more, become applicable.[76]

---

68 Chinkin 1998 at 133: questions raised by Koskenniemi.

69 Chinkin 1998 at 133: question raised by Koskenniemi. Article 16 of the Kyoto Protocol and Decision I/7 of the Meeting of the Parties to the Aarhus Convention only contain a without prejudice clause.

70 Fitzmaurice and Redgwell 2000, 35–65 at 58.

71 Brunnée 2006, 14, note 62.

72 Paulus 2007, 372.

73 Cogan 2006, 204.

74 Military and Paramilitary Activities in and against Nicaragua (*Nicaragua v United States of America*), Judgment, ICJ Reports (1986), 14 at 98, §186.

75 Koskenniemi 2007 at 13, note 55.

76 A/CN4/L.682/Add.1 at 8, §16.

Enforcement in its Various Forms

Enforcement may be defined as an 'act of compelling compliance with the law'.[77] It denotes 'measures of ensuring the observance of rules *on the international plane*' which are 'prompted *by a previous case of non-observance*'.[78] It can be an incentive to encourage compliance, but also 'a form of collective disapproval' of the breach of norms.[79]

As enforcement is a 'fairly complex activity',[80] some useful distinctions could be made, although international law enforcement consists mostly of a combination of various forms.[81]

Formal and Informal Enforcement

Formal enforcement or hard enforcement exists where there is a 'body with the authority and the capacity to consider claims brought by a representative range of interested parties and to grant relief through the direct imposition of pre-announced and salient sanctions for non-compliance'.[82] The International Criminal Court (ICC), European Court of Justice (ECJ), European Court of Human Rights (ECHR) and Inter-American Commission on Human Rights (IACHR) would qualify, while under this criterion the International Court of Justice (ICJ) and World Trade Organization Dispute Settlement Body (WTO DSB) would not.[83] There is an obvious link at stake with the balancing of the public interests protected by the primary rule and the interests of individual victimized parties.

Informal enforcement or soft enforcement is based 'on reputational effects and the threat of retaliation' and it remains subject to state control.[84] Modern arms control agreements and environmental agreements come within this category.[85] An example is a public statement made after an on-site investigation carried out by the expert body.[86]

Public interests rules *s.s.* seem to require formal enforcement, whereas a combination of formal and informal enforcement may be more tailored to the needs of public interest rules *s.l.*

77 Black's Dictionary 2004 at 569.
78 Tams 2007b, 392.
79 Brunnée and Toope 2002, 273–295 at 276.
80 Bianchi 2006 at 895.
81 Scott and Stephan 2006 at 17.
82 Scott and Stephan 2006, 4.
83 Scott and Stephan 2006, 10, 113, 116 and 114.
84 Scott and Stephan 2006, 9 and 4.
85 Scott and Stephan 2006, 151–153.
86 Kicker 2007, 107.

Informal mechanisms may be more effective in some cases, although formal enforcement 'may diminish the effectiveness of informal incentives that motivate compliance'.[87]

In the law of arms control, challenge inspections – which have not taken place yet – may be triggered 'by a situation which has given rise to concern that there is already a violation'[88] and are coming close to enforcement.

In international environmental law, different types of obligations 'may require different types or a different mix of compliance instruments'.[89] The choice seems to be mainly between 'managerial and sanction-oriented models'.[90]

The Kyoto Protocol NCP 'is the only one that explicitly declares its goal to be to facilitate, promote and *enforce* compliance with the Protocol'. The compliance body has both a 'facilitative' and an 'enforcement'[91] branch and there is a shift away from the managerial towards the enforcement.[92] There is also the gradual hardening 'towards enforcement of the practice of the Montreal Protocol NCP Committee[93] which has issued several cautions that suspension of the right to trade in ozone-depleting substances might be considered'.[94]

Problems 'of third-party verification may explain why international environmental agreements do not use formal enforcement'.[95]

Traditional means of enforcement can always be brought back on the agenda[96] once the effectiveness of non-traditional ones is perceived as weakening. It may become more common, as MEAs 'incorporate mores stringent restrictions on States' activities',[97] and it brings with it the requirement of 'due process assurances' throughout the process.[98]

International trade law and human rights law, except of course for the ECHR and the IACHR, provide an intermediate form of enforcement.[99]

International criminal law foresees formal enforcement by both international and domestic courts. It has been rightly pointed out that the lack of direct enforcement does not prevent the ICC to have some deterrent effect.[100]

87 Scott and Stephan 2006, 21.
88 Marauhn 2007, 266.
89 Sach 2006, IX–XI at X–XI.
90 Brunnée 2006, 10.
91 Brunnée 2006, 19 and 20.
92 Kolari 2006, 877.
93 Brunnée 2006, 21.
94 Ulfstein 2007, 130.
95 Scott and Stephan 2006, 153.
96 Marauhn 2007, 267.
97 Ulfstein 2007, 132.
98 Ulfstein 2007, 127–128.
99 Scott and Stephan 2006, 157–166.
100 Gilligan 2006, 953.

Systemic and Non-systemic Enforcement

Another major distinction is the one drawn by Tams between systemic and non-systemic enforcement.[101]

Systemic enforcement is provided by a particular treaty regime. Here the *de minimis* rule seems to be applicable as a result of the material breach criterion.[102]

Non-systemic enforcement is provided by general international law where, under the law of state responsibility rules, only serious breaches of obligations under peremptory norms entail particular, additional consequences.

States often rely on non-systemic enforcement when they perceive the systemic mechanisms as less developed: 'Western States could have instituted ICJ proceedings, pursuant to Article IX, against Yugoslavia in order to verify their assertion. The fact that they did not, but instead relied on self-help suggests that in their view, judicial recourse did not exclude extra-conventional means of responding against alleged acts of genocide'.[103] The outcome of the Bosnia Genocide case seems to support the choice made at the time.

Another example of non-systemic enforcement is the potential use by the ICC of its competence over war crimes in international armed conflicts with regard to chemical weapons the use of which is prohibited by the Chemical Weapons Convention (CWC).[104]

'*Quasi-systemic enforcement*' arises when the enforcement is provided by the treaty but the actual process is carried out by a body outside the treaty. Examples include the role of the SC with regard to the Nuclear Non-proliferation Treaty (NPT) or the CWC[105] and under the Genocide Convention.

Three Main Avenues of Enforcement

Finally, three main forms or avenues of enforcement can be distinguished.

There is the *direct recourse open to individuals* against infringement of their rights. There is *institutional enforcement* of international obligations within the framework of an IO. And there is *decentralized enforcement* through domestic courts and the taking of countermeasures[106] to which we return later. Naturally, the degree of effectiveness of these different modalities varies.

---

101 Tams 2005b, 395–396.

102 See for instance Article XII, 4 of the CWC Convention dealing with cases of particular gravity, although there is no agreement between the States Parties on the exact scope of this term: Tabassi 2007, 296.

103 Tams 2005b, 295.

104 Tabassi 2007, 298.

105 Tams 2007b, 405.

106 Tams 2005b, 6.

Common Features

However the fact remains that in all cases non-compliance with the obligation aimed at preserving and protecting global community goods does not necessarily have a direct detrimental impact on an individual State party. It rather affects the treaty community of States as a whole (obligations *erga omnes partes*).

Collective obligations benefit from collective enforcement.[107] In this regard, participation of non-State actors in the enforcement process is increasing.

The efficiency of HR monitoring depends to a large extent 'on shadow reports submitted by NGOs'.[108] Other examples of '*public private partnerships*' can be found in WTO trade litigation and in the Prototype Carbon Fund within the Clean Development Mechanism of the Kyoto Protocol.[109]

This significant development, a trend which 'erodes *the public-private split* on the international plane' and because 'it integrates the transnational civil society into the fabric of international law'[110] may contribute to constitutionalization.

The enforcement of public interest rules *s.l.* could benefit from a system of provisional approval of incentives towards compliance, provided corrective actions are being taken to rectify specified minor non-compliances within a certain time. Final approval would be postponed until major non-compliances are corrected.[111]

At a general level, NCPs face a dual danger. The interests of the international community as a whole may not be taken fully into account during the facilitative and friendly settlement,[112] and the procedures may become ineffective, so that real differences will be converted 'to the detriment of upholding collective obligations or interested third party interests'.[113]

The Necessary Link between Primary and Secondary Rules

Three approaches may be discerned with regard to the relationship between primary public interest rules *s.s.* and secondary rules.

According to one view, an automatic linkage between the breach of a fundamental rule and the applicability of special secondary rules must be deemed out of the question because 'the array of conceivable sanctions is so different

107 *Ireland v United Kingdom* (Application A/5310/71), Judgment of 18 January 1978, Series A, no. 25, §239.

108 Peters 2006, 592.

109 Peters 2006, 592.

110 Peters 2006, 593.

111 Similar to the certification of forest management operators: Meidinger 2006, 47–87 at 71. See also the mechanisms of the Kimberley process.

112 Chinkin 1998, 130.

113 Koskenniemi as referred to by Chinkin 1998, 131.

in nature and gravity'.[114] The position is clear: 'the substantive superiority of a specific rule and the legal consequences deriving from its breach should remain separate'.[115]

An intermediate position consists of doubting the link because of the uncertainties in state practice. The fact that a separate regime of state responsibility for violations of public interest rules *s.s.* does not come about leads to a search for emerging fragments of specificity, in an attempt to reconstruct, to save what is left of the original idea.

And there is the third, persuasive view that such a separate regime not coming about has and could not have prevented the inherent comprehensive legal effects of the peremptory nature of the primary rules on the secondary rules.[116]

Effects of peremptory norms have to be considered and accepted in a consolidated and integral manner because they supplement the role of the primary norms in safeguarding the interests of the international community.[117]

It is the 'character of primary norms which determines the nature of secondary rules'[118] because there is 'symbiotic relationship'.[119]

When creating primary rules, States draft tailor-made secondary rules on compliance and enforcement to suit the relevant subject-matter.

This inherent link is underlined for instance in the following definition of universal jurisdiction: 'the power of national courts to institute proceedings against an individual or individuals who have allegedly committed a serious crime sanctioned by international law on the sole basis of the character and the severity of that crime under international law'.[120]

Jenks has aptly observed that 'international procedural law should react to changes in substantive law'.[121]

The distinction between primary and secondary rules, between substantive and procedural protection seems, generally, to be fading away, although progress is slow and not without difficulty.

The ICJ's judgment in the DRC Rwanda case demonstrated the negative impact the disconnection between primary and secondary rules, between the substantive and the procedural provisions of the Genocide Convention can have on the effective enforcement of a public interest rule *s.s.*, in spite of the Applicant combining the role of injured State and of an agent for the international community. After the SWA and East Timor cases the Court missed another opportunity to follow a new

114 Tomuschat 2006, 425–442 at 429.
115 Tomuschat 2006 at 430.
116 Orakhelasvhili 2006, *passim*.
117 Orakhelasvhili 2006, 578.
118 A/CN4/L.682, §420.
119 Dyzerhaus 2005, 127–166 at 130.
120 Rozakis 2005, 318.
121 Jenks as referred to by Benzing 2006, 369–408 at 376.

judicial policy and to close the structural community interest gap at the operational level of enforcement.

Judge Owada rightly pointed out that the amended language of Article IX did not create additional 'new substantive obligations' but did 'create a new procedural scope to the jurisdiction of the Court' by including 'within the Court's purview' the 'obligation flowing to the State parties under general international law'.[122]

Tribunals must safeguard community interests *s.s.* 'not only in terms of substance but also at the jurisdictional level' and must 'adopt methods of interpretation and application of a jurisdictional instrument which support [the] enforcement [of public interest rules *s.s.*] rather than obstructing it'.[123]

The complementarity between general and special secondary rules gave rise to complex problems in cases involving the violation of primary public interest rules *s.s.*, as the issue of complicity for acts of genocide in the Bosnia case has demonstrated.

Balancing Public Interests and the Interests of Individual Victimized Parties

In most cases, violations of public interest rules *s.s.* or non-compliance with public interest rules *s.l.* lead to the identification of the injured State; its consequential rights are, under the systemic/non-systemic enforcement distinction, provided for either in a particular treaty or in the general state responsibility regime. We focus on the individual as the victimized party, whose rights have been saved by the without prejudice clause in Article 33, 2 of the ILC.

There is a growing tendency to explore and establish a variety of mechanisms and procedures to protect the interests of the individual victim within the wider context of the enforcement of public interests rules. It may suffice to indicate a few examples.

One way of achieving a certain balance between the interests of the international community and those of the individual victim is bringing to justice individual perpetrators who have committed serious or grave breaches of public interest rules *s.s.*

The practice and expectation of impunity for violations of HR and IHL are among the fundamental obstacles to the observance of these bodies of law.[124] The controversy over impunity through the adoption of national amnesty laws seems slowly to be decided in favour of the exercise of criminal jurisdiction. The granting of amnesty for crimes under common Article 3 would undermine the right of other

122 Application of the Convention on the Prevention and Punishment of the Crime of Genocide (*Bosnia and Herzegovina v Serbia and Montenegro*) Judgment of 26 February 2007, Separate Opinion of Judge Owada, §73.

123 Orakhelasvhili 2006, 490 and 508.

124 UN Commission on Human Rights resolution 2002/79, preamble, adopted on 25 April 2002.

States to exercise universal jurisdiction.[125] The more frequent recourse to TRCs is another, but this time soft way of enforcing HR and IHL by monitoring the perpetrator's accountability for past abuses towards both the local community and individual victims.

Furthermore, for victims of serious abuses (in particular war crimes, crimes against humanity and genocide) a right to reparation, including compensation for damages resulting from these abuses is emerging.[126] Indications of this development are the following.

The ILA Committee on Compensation for Victims of War has proposed a Model Statute for *Ad Hoc* Compensation Commission to the 2008 ILA Conference in Brazil.[127]

On 16 December 2005 the United Nations General Assembly (UNGA) adopted Basic Principles and Guidelines on the Right to a Remedy and Reparation for Victims of Gross Violations of International Human Rights Law and Serious Violations of International Humanitarian Law. The UNGA did not create new obligations but identified mechanisms, modalities and procedures and methods for the implementation of existing obligations in case of *gross and serious* violations.[128] Victims do have the right of equal and effective access to justice and to adequate, effective and prompt reparation for harm suffered. The first right is of course the most common mechanism for individuals to enjoy in an effective way the rights directly granted to them by the international legal order.[129]

It is important to note that these rights do not follow from the duty to respect and to ensure respect for HR and IHL. They could only result from the violation of a primary public interest rule having direct effect and granting individual rights.[130]

The basic principles and guidelines are without prejudice to existing general or special rules of PIL providing for the right to a remedy and reparation for victims of *all* violations of HR and IHL.[131]

In international environmental law, however, a draft article providing for individual cause of action before domestic courts for breaches of binding

125 See Special Court for Sierra Leone, *Prosecutor v Morris Kallon*, Case no. SCSL-2004-15-PT, 15 March 2004.

126 S/2005/60, International Commission of Inquiry on Darfur. Report to the Secretary-General, 25 January 2005, §597.

127 ILA Committee on Consequences for Victims of War, Report submitted to the 2008 ILA Rio de Janeiro Conference, 500–518.

128 General Assembly resolution A/RES.60/147 adopted on 16 December 2005, preamble.

129 d'Argent 2005, 27–55 at 47. On the divergences from and innovations compared with traditional forms of reparation see d'Argent 2005, 47–53.

130 See convincingly d'Argent 2005, 43–45.

131 A/Res. 60/147, §26.

provisions was considered by the ILA Committee on Transnational Enforcement of Environmental Law as not reflecting existing international law.[132]

In the law of arms control the Ottawa Convention is the first 'treaty banning a weapon to require that assistance be provided to the weapon's victims'.[133]

And there is also the tendency to 'replace a system of diplomatic protection based on the international minimum standard by a system of inter-state enforcement based on the erga omnes character of international human rights standards'.[134]

The role of diplomatic protection should not be overlooked either in preserving the rights of individual suspects in the fight against terrorism, where even prompt action by the State of nationality may be required as became clear in recent CFI cases.[135]

Impact of the Public Interest Nature of the Rules on Various Aspects of the Implementation Process

Broadly Defined Principle of Complementarity

A broadly defined principle of complementarity has the potential to stretch well beyond its ICC context,[136] as a 'catalyst for compliance'.[137] As a matter of fact it already covers a broad range of relationships and activities.

It operates between treaty based and *erga omnes* enforcement rights, between State and non-State enforcement,[138] between treaty bodies and States on the permissibility of reservations to treaties,[139] and between regional HR systems and the UN machinery[140] in the monitoring of compliance with HR law.

Complementarity presents itself in the combination, the duality of State and individual criminal responsibility, as expressed for instance in Article 25, §4 of the ICC Statute, and this 'in spite of the compartmentalized approach'.[141]

---

132 ILA Committee on Transnational Enforcement of Environmental Law, Final Report, submitted to the 2006 ILA Toronto Conference, p. 2 and annex I.

133 Lawand 2007, 324–347 at 328.

134 ILA Committee on International Human Rights Law and Practice, Interim Report on the Relationship between General International Law and International Human Rights Law, submitted to the 2006 ILA Toronto Conference, p. 3, Preliminary findings, §4.

135 Case T. 253/02, *Chafiq Ayadi v Council of the European Union* (2006) ECR [2006] II-2199-2200, §141 and 2202–2203, §§149–150.

136 Fassbender 2006, 73–77 at 73.

137 Kleffner 2006, 80.

138 Tams 2005b, 268.

139 Yearbook of the International Law Commission (1997), Vol. II, Part Two, §87.

140 Buergenthal 2006, 783–807 at 792.

141 Cançado Trindade 2005, 253–269 at 258.

It has also found expression in the rule requiring exhaustion of local remedies before having access to HR bodies[142] or before resorting to diplomatic protection.

The rationale for the principle of complementarity is the need to enhance the effectiveness of the implementation of public interest rules for instance between the international and domestic legal orders. It operates both ways: its supervisory element has to do with capacity-based and intentional non-compliance while its positive component is reaching out to domestic jurisdictions to fulfil their own role in the process.[143]

On the other hand, effective implementation does not necessarily require the double use of the collective security system and state responsibility. States do not invoke state responsibility in lieu of SC responses, unless the system has not provided them with a positive result.[144]

With regard to the ICC Gioia rightly warned that the delicate balance between the international and national jurisdictions 'should not be achieved to the detriment of the fundamental purpose of having in place an effective system of prevention and punishment of the crimes covered by the Statute'.[145]

The ICJ's activity in the *Bosnia Genocide* case complements that of the ICTY in the achievement of international justice.[146]

General international law complements particular treaty regimes through the principle of systemic integration pursuant to Article 31(3)c of the Vienna Convention on the Law of Treaties which brings us to the process of interpretation.

The Process of Interpretation

The effectiveness of the implementation process partly depends on the right choices made when interpreting a rule; public interest rules are not different in this respect although they do raise a number of specific issues.

The existence of public interest rules is a new legal situation 'not without effects on the traditional manner of interpreting certain aspects of other principles of international law'.[147] It makes the *systemic integration* under Article 31(3)c particularly relevant. The judgment in the *Oil Platforms* case demonstrated how it may contribute to the enforcement of a peremptory norm. The principle of systemic integration 'goes further than merely restate the applicability of general international law in the operation of particular treaties. *It points to the need to take*

142 Kleffner 2006, 99, note 57.

143 Kleffner 2006, 83 and 86.

144 Forteau 2006, 485.

145 Gioia 2006, 105–113 at 111.

146 Application of the Convention on the Prevention and Punishment of the Crime of Genocide (*Bosnia and Herzegovina v Serbia and Montenegro*) Judgment of 26 February 2007, Separate Opinion of Judge Tomka, §73.

147 Torres Bernardez, 286.

into account the normative environment more widely [my italics]'.[148] The last is particularly relevant to the interpretation of public interest rules.

Public interest rules reflect 'the current interests and concerns of the international community as a whole'.[149]

Does the irreversibility of their qualification as public interest rules *s.s.* allow an *evolutive interpretation*? The answer appears to be positive: one cannot even exclude that, because of their peremptory and non-derogable nature, the normal limits of such an evolutive interpretation may be crossed. The extraterritorial scope of the obligation to prevent and to punish the crime of genocide is a case in point.[150]

On the other hand, one cannot resort to an evolutive interpretation in order to increase the ability to implement and enforce public interest rule *s.l.* A State 'in *no way incurs evolutionary and indeterminate duties.* A State cannot incur unknown obligations whether for the future or even the present'.[151] But public interest rules should neither be interpreted in a manner restricting 'to the greatest possible degree the obligations undertaken by the Parties' as the ECHR ruled.[152]

Approximate treaty application produces less implementation but is to some extent inevitable for public interest rules *s.l.*

Given the public interest nature *s.s.* of rules, the object and purpose test occupies a prominent place in their interpretation. However, the different outcome of using the test in the recent ICJ case law with regard to substantive (*Wall* opinion) and procedural (DRC *Rwanda*) provisions calls for caution in this regard.

The Exercise of Jurisdiction

The 'choice of the frame determines the decision',[153] hence the question arises how the exercise of jurisdiction by various actors relates to the effectiveness of the implementation of public interest rules.

Extraterritorial Jurisdiction

Modern international law 'requires States to show a special interest if and when they act extraterritorially'.[154]

---

148 A/CN4/L.682, §415.

149 Torres Bernardez 2005, 286.

150 Application of the Convention on the Prevention and Punishment of the Crime of Genocide, Preliminary Objections, Judgment, ICJ Reports (1996), 595 at 616, §31.

151 Gabcikovo-Nagymaros Project (Hungary/ Slovakia), Judgment, ICJ Reports (1997), 1 at 123. Separate opinion Judge Bedjaoui, §14. See also Scott and Stephan, The Limits at 188, qualifying this as 'enforcement creep'.

152 *Wemhoff v Germany*, Judgment of 27 June 1968, Series A no. 7 at 23, §8.

153 Koskenniemi 2007, 3.

154 Tomuschat 2005, 220.

As the limits of 'domestic jurisdiction' are being felt rather soon when attempts are made to enforce public interest rules *s.s.* domestic courts tend to resort to the exercise of extraterritorial jurisdiction, which traditionally has been instrumental in protecting mere individual interests of the State.

In those cases, extraterritorial jurisdiction is not exercised as a normal implementation mechanism but as a rather exceptional, temporary measure until such time as efficient national and international mechanisms will be made available to provide victims of a violation of public interest rule *s.s.* with a course of action.

International judicial and quasi-judicial bodies on their part have followed a double track. One way is to confirm that public interest rules are capable of being applied extraterritorially, for example when dealing with violations of HR and IHL as the Court did in the *Wall* opinion, the *DRC Uganda* and in the *Bosnia Genocide* cases.

The other approach would consist in bringing extraterritorial exercise of 'jurisdiction' or of 'control' by States within the realm of their own jurisdiction: this way these bodies are able to extend their protecting function beyond the territory of a contracting Party.

Universal Jurisdiction

Another significant development is the growing exercise of universal jurisdiction in case of violations of public interests rules *s.s.* I agree with Van Alebeek that the 'principle of (universal) jurisdiction should now be seen as having its theoretical basis in the concept of erga omnes obligations'.[155]

The exercise of universal jurisdiction is based on an international community prosecutorial interest and puts 'domestic courts at the service of the international community'.[156] It is the judicial expression of solidarity within the international community when faced with (serious) violations public interest rules *s.s.*

The divergence of views – both within courts and in doctrine – on the precise relationship between the primary public interest rule *s.s.* and the exercise of universal jurisdiction is reflected in the controversy over the merely permissive or mandatory nature of such exercise.

Orakhelashvili rightly pointed out that 'the duty to prosecute and universal jurisdiction are two separate, though interconnected and mutually supportive consequences of the ius cogens nature of the crime'.[157]

The obligation to respect and to ensure respect for HR and IHL includes the duty to prosecute and also supports the concept of complementarity[158] in the search for the protection of public interests *s.s.* of the international community.

155 Van Alebeek discussing the Pinochet case, as cited by Tams 2005b, 9.

156 Tomuschat 2005, 220.

157 Orakhelashvili 2006, 299.

158 General Assembly Resolution A/Res/60/147, §§3 and 4.

Indeed, the 'international community leaves it to the individual State to prosecute isolated crimes' through the exercise of universal jurisdiction, whereas the ICC is called upon to deal with 'pattern of breaches of the law in situations' where this 'amounts to an en-bloc rejection of standards of civilized behaviour'.[159]

It is still controversial 'whether current international law recognizes a civil counterpart to the universal criminal jurisdiction with regard to international crimes'.[160] At present, conventional and customary law does not seem to contain a legal obligation as to for instance a *ius cogens* exception to state immunity.[161] As recent case law shows, the debate on this is still wide open.[162]

The (Potentially) Ambivalent Role of Domestic Courts

Domestic courts act as *de facto* 'international courts' to implement rules of PIL and 'play a key role in the enforcement of the international value system',[163] but there is limited room for judicial control over international enforcement of public interest rules.

The role of domestic courts is potentially ambivalent: their performance may be instrumental towards effective implementation, but judicial considerations of good governance, rule of law, lack of legitimacy may also hamper the process.

Domestic courts may deny direct effect to public interest rules, creating a buffer against their more effective implementation as an alternative mechanism to the disappearance of veto rights at the enforcement stage.[164]

An intermediate position may consist in taking into account the opinion of the world community not to control the domestic judicial outcome but as 'respected and significant confirmation' of own conclusions[165] or to use international law to 'creatively support the existence of a domestic rule' even in cases involving public interest rules *s.s.*[166]

The third approach is to grant direct effect without any change at all because of the 'internal' effectiveness of the process, as the recent case law of the CFI has amply illustrated. Public interest rules *s.s.* leave no room for such changes anyway. Moreover, a suggestion was recently made to amend SC resolutions so that they

159 Tomuschat 2005, 240.

160 Giegerich 2006, 203–237 at 209.

161 Giegerich 2006 at 217.

162 Nolte 2006, 373–383 and Flauss 2006, 385–415. See also of course the Al-Adsani case before the ECtHR: Al-Adsani. The United Kingdom (Application No. 35763/97), Judgment of 21 November 2001.

163 De Wet 2006, 611–632 at 629.

164 Krisch 2006, 262–263.

165 Justice Kennedy in the Roper case as cited by Douglas-Scott 2006, 629–665 at 656.

166 Saul 2007, 213–224 at 217 discussing the Abassi case.

'request Member States to incorporate them into their domestic legislation and compel the courts to enforce and implement them'.[167]

According to primary interest rules such as HR treaties, a special status in national constitutions undoubtedly has a positive impact on the effective domestic compliance with international judicial decisions.[168]

The potentially ambivalent role of domestic courts with regard to public interest rules *s.l.* was illustrated in the aftermath of the ICJ Avena orders and judgment, as the decision to submit a dispute to the ICJ apparently did not represent a commitment by the State 'to require its own courts to implement any decisions that the ICJ might take'.[169]

This is in sharp contrast with WTO dispute settlement decisions which 'are in most cases factually decisive for domestic administrative action', as the cost of non-compliance would simply be too high.[170]

The most far reaching measure domestic courts can apply in their contribution to the implementation of public interest rules is to use their power to set aside conflicting national measures.

Because of their nature public interest rules *s.s.* do not tolerate inconsistencies between domestic and international case law, which with regard to ordinary rules of PIL may be viewed as triggering reflection and progress.

Impact of the Public Interest Nature of the Rules on Various Aspects of the Enforcement Process

The availability and use of instruments and mechanisms to enforce public interest rules is crucial, but the collective nature of the interest under protection gives rise to particular problems. Various aspects of a procedural nature deserve mention here.

The fact that a claimant State had been 'individually affected by the conduct against which' it complains does not therefore 'disqualify him from acting in the general interest'.[171] The *East Timor* and *DRC Rwanda* cases are relevant here.

Also with regard to public interest rules *s.l.* such an action cannot be excluded 'either to prevent the other party from acting as a 'free-rider' or out of concern for the threat against the environment represented by the violation'.[172]

The collective interest under protection may also be invoked in favour of alleviating or even shifting the burden of proof.

167 S/PV.5474, 22 June 2006 at 26: Representative of Ghana.

168 Buergenthal 2006, 804.

169 Scott and Stephan 2007, 197.

170 Krisch and Kingsbury 2006, 1–13 at 4.

171 Tams 2005a, 723–728 at 726.

172 Ulfstein 2007, 121.

Taking formal note of a refusal by a party to judicial proceedings to divulge the contents of unedited documents would normally entail 'to shift the onus probandi or to allow a more liberal recourse to inference',[173] whereas findings under a NCP could in a subsequent DSP only be rebutted by clear and convincing evidence.[174]

The duality of individual and state responsibility – which 'continues to be a constant feature of international law'[175] – does not necessarily rule out that the proof of intent could in both cases be inferred from a pattern of conduct and from a combination of surrounding circumstances as the Applicant and some judges argued in the *Bosnia Genocide* case.[176] When the victim or a third State is unable to furnish direct proof, 'a more liberal recourse to inferences of fact and circumstantial evidence'[177] should be allowed.

A more strict and rigorous application of complicity to violations of public interest rules *s.s.* would not only clarify the respective responsibilities of States in complying with such rules, but it would also enhance their enforcement. This may be achieved either by lowering the required threshold from sharing the intent to mere knowledge[178] or by imposing a rebuttable presumption of intent on the State providing aid or assistance: it would then have to prove its unawareness of the potential use of that assistance.

In the *Bosnia Genocide* case the ICJ went the other way as it allowed the Federal Republic of Yugoslavia (FRY) to benefit from a presumption of unawareness.[179]

Judge *ad hoc* Lauterpacht's observation in the earlier stages of the same case that the imposition of an arms embargo could be seen 'as having in effect called' on Members of the UN, 'to become in some degree supporters of the genocide

---

173 Application of the Convention on the Prevention and Punishment of the Crime of Genocide (*Bosnia and Herzegovina v Serbia and Montenegro*) Judgment of 26 February 2007, Dissenting Opinion Vice-President Al-Khaswaneh, §35 supporting the Applicant's view on this aspect.

174 Beyerlin, Stolland and Wolfrum 2006, 359–369 at 369.

175 Application of the Convention on the Prevention and Punishment of the Crime of Genocide (*Bosnia and Herzegovina v Serbia and Montenegro*) Judgment of 26 February 2007, §173.

176 Application of the Convention on the Prevention and Punishment of the Crime of Genocide (*Bosnia and Herzegovina v Serbia and Montenegro*) Judgment of 26 February 2007, §373 and Dissenting Opinion Vice-President Al-Khaswaneh, §42.

177 The Corfu Channel Case (merits) *United Kingdom v Albania*, Judgment of 9 April 1949, ICJ Reports (1949), 4 at 18.

178 Application of the Convention on the Prevention and Punishment of the Crime of Genocide (*Bosnia and Herzegovina v Serbia and Montenegro*) Judgment of 26 February 2007, Declaration of Judge Keith, §7 and Dissenting Opinion of Judge Mahiou, §125.

179 Application of the Convention on the Prevention and Punishment of the Crime of Genocide (*Bosnia and Herzegovina v Serbia and Montenegro*) Judgment of 26 February 2007, Declaration Judge Bennouna at 2.

activities',[180] is an important reminder of complicity by abstention or omission: the question of the existence of a general duty to enforce public interest rules will be dealt with later.

The (Hesitant) Role of (Regional) International Courts: 'The Policy of Deference'

International courts and tribunals (ICTs) are there to serve the interests of the international community, but they are hesitant to use the variety of instruments at their disposal to protect these interests: the (*proprio motu*) indication of provisional measures to prevent the aggravation of the dispute, the use of their fact-finding powers to supplement the material submitted by the parties (which the Court could have done in the *Bosnia Genocide* case), allowing intervention on behalf of the public interest and the way they handle the standard of proof.[181]

In cases of public interest rules *s.s.* no margin of appreciation is left to States, and there is no possibility of derogation for instance based on principles of proportionality.

In cases of public interest rules *s.l.* where there is a reduced (HR) or wider (environmental law) margin of appreciation, ICTs have to assess whether the State conduct was proportionate to the objective stated and whether the conduct had been effective in achieving that objective.[182]

It is at this juncture that deference and abstention come into play, especially in cases of institutional enforcement of public interest rules when active cooperation of regional or universal ICTs is required.

Their hesitation also manifests itself through a policy of 'deference' when they are not exercising to the full extent their judicial duty to settle the dispute over the compliance with public interest rules. The dispute remains 'without any final decision by the court based on the applicable law and without the resolution of the substantive claims before the court'.[183]

Such a policy must be squarely placed against the background of their relationship with domestic courts. Mutual influence through standard legal relationships and more subtle political channels can 'enhance the effectiveness of

---

180 Application of the Convention on the Prevention and Punishment of the Crime of Genocide, Provisional Measures, Order of 13 September 1993, ICJ Reports (1993), 325 at 441, §102.

181 See further Benzing 2006.

182 See also Shelton 2006b, 4–11.

183 Burke-White, 'Double-edged Tribunals: The Domestic Political Effects of International Courts in the Enforcement of International Criminal Law', paper presented at the 2007 Oslo Conference on The New International Law, on file with the author, 3.

the transnational legal system'.[184] The principle of complementarity can be seen at work here.

Through their legal as well as political impact on domestic courts, ICTs are able 'to ensure state compliance with underlying substantive legal obligations'.[185] The mere threat of international adjudication may 'alter the cost-benefits analysis towards (non-)compliance by the target State'.[186]

Cross-fertilization between ICTs through various forms of judicial dialogue gives reason for concern when, as a result, deference or abstention become a more frequent feature of judicial policy in the enforcement of public interest rules.[187]

Europe is proud to possess an *ius commune* of HR,[188] a body of fundamental public interest rules, but how is this reflected in the process of their judicial enforcement? Both domestic and regional courts have resorted to the use of rebuttable presumptions, as part of their policy of deference. HR protection procedures provided by international organizations are presumed to be 'equivalent' but rebuttal is possible when that protection is 'manifestly deficient'.[189] Cases where the implementation of SC sanctions may be frustrated by the application of a peremptory norm figure prominently here. The equivalent protection test applies to both substantive and procedural protection of HR.[190]

Such presumptions carry the risk of seriously affecting the first level of enforcement as envisaged by the drafters of the primary rules.[191]

The *Bosphorus* case has demonstrated deferential policy even between the ECHR and the ECJ, in spite of the former being entrusted with the task of reviewing, if need be, compliance by the latter with higher rules of public interest such as the need to provide equivalent protection of ECHR rights.[192]

Although *res judicata* operates only with regard to the parties to the case, a judicial policy of deference and abstention is bound to have an *erga omnes* effect.

184 Burke-White, 'Double-edged Tribunals: The Domestic Political Effects of International Courts in the Enforcement of International Criminal Law', paper presented at the 2007 Oslo Conference on The New International Law, on file with the author, 12–13.

185 Burke-White, 'Double-edged Tribunals: The Domestic Political Effects of International Courts in the Enforcement of International Criminal Law', paper presented at the 2007 Oslo Conference on The New International Law, on file with the author, 2.

186 Burke-White, 'Double-edged Tribunals: The Domestic Political Effects of International Courts in the Enforcement of International Criminal Law', paper presented at the 2007 Oslo Conference on The New International Law, on file with the author, 4–5.

187 See for instance on this more negative aspect of cross-fertilization, Douglas-Scott 2006, 640–652.

188 Douglas-Scott 2006, 665.

189 *Bosphorus Hava Yollari Turzm ve Ticaret Anonim Sirketi v Ireland* (Application no. 45036/98), Judgment of 30 June 2005, §155 and 156.

190 De Wet 2006, 622.

191 For a contrary view see Bianchi 2006, 916.

192 Douglas-Scott 2006 at 638.

Enforcement through the State Responsibility Regime

The role state responsibility plays in various branches also varies depending on the particularity of the public interest the primary rules protect. But for instance the fact that state responsibility 'has never played a prominent role in arms control law' did not prevent various 'state responsibility' responses – ranging from 'retorsion, across suspension, withdrawal and termination to collective sanctions under chapter VII to have been inserted in arms control agreements as enforcement strategies'.[193]

Breaches of peremptory norms are objective wrongs as they constitute an offence against the community interest.[194] Because of their absolute and unconditional nature there is no possibility of invoking circumstances precluding wrongfulness (Article 26 of the ILC) and they may not be affected by the taking of countermeasures (Article 50(1)). The impossibility of invoking a circumstance precluding wrongfulness in order to justify a violation of fundamental obligations of the collective security system is not yet positive law.[195]

Conversely, essential interests of the international community as a whole can be protected through the invocation of necessity (Article 25(1)b) as well.

The fact that Article 48 of the ILC articles involves a matter of progressive development 'is justified since it provides a means of protecting the community interest'.[196]

The Determination of a Violation

The international community is indispensable in attributing a public interest nature to primary rules. It thus seems only logical that the same international community must acknowledge that there has been a (serious) violation of such rules before other than injured states can take lawful measures or countermeasures. States' responsibility cannot be presumed and auto-interpretation by individual States would cause serious problems in the enforcement of public interest rules.

Article 40 of the ILC articles does not lay down any procedure for such a determination.

However, there is no requirement of prior assessment by a third party 'of whether the target States has actually committed a wrongful act'.[197] Special Rapporteur Arangio-Ruiz has in vain tried to solve this structural deficiency once and for all. The acceptance of his proposals would have remedied 'a core structural weakness of international law', but there is a 'growing network of treaties, that

193 Marauhn 2007, 251.

194 Sir Robert Yennings as referred to by Orakhelasvhili 2006, 71.

195 Forteau 2006, 19, 397–398 and 483.

196 ILC commentary as cited by Gaja 2005b, 137.

197 Tams 2005b, 20.

require dispute resolution prior to taking countermeasures',[198] most importantly within the WTO DSB.

Collective Responses?

Redress for breaches of absolute obligations 'becomes a matter of collective or institutionalised action' under Article 60(2)a of the Vienna Convention on the Law of Treaties.[199] A 'requirement of collective action has not been accepted in international practice'.[200]

As to collective action, there is little point in suspending or terminating treaties aimed at the protection of public interests *s.l.* and the state responsibility regime 'provides no generalized normative system by which States parties to a multilateral treaty may act as collective entity'.[201]

As to the institutionalized action, Article 89 of Protocol I to the Geneva Conventions and Article VII of the Genocide Convention provide us with examples of quasi-systemic enforcement by endowing the SC with the role of guarantor of compliance. On the other hand it is interesting to note that 'the very rationale of arms control agreements is to develop mechanisms avoiding the need to resort to the Security Council'.[202]

Serious breaches of public interest rules *s.s.* are 'likely to be addressed by the competent international organizations including the Security Council and the General Assembly'.[203] However, law enforcement does not as a rule come within SC powers, competences and functions. At most one can say that is the SC's prerogative or duty to enforce the Charter and customary law based prohibition for States to undertake actions when these constitute a threat to the peace, breach of the peace or act of aggression. Except for Article 51, the UN Charter, is 'silent on enforcement rights of other actors' apart from the SC.[204] The victim State has no real role to play: its interests stay at the background of the collective action.[205]

State practice provides us with a number of examples where States have taken countermeasures 'although the matter had been addressed by the Security Council'.[206]

198 O'Connell 2005, 49–62 at 56 and 57.
199 Tams 2005b, 62.
200 Tams 2005b, 240.
201 Ulfstein, Marauhn and Zimmermann 2007, 5–6.
202 Marauhn 2007, 272.
203 Crawford 2002, 248.
204 Tams 2005b, 261.
205 Forteau 2006, 167.
206 Tams 2005b, 267.

The Taking of Countermeasures

When it comes to responses to breaches of public interest rules, the parallelism between the law of treaties and the state responsibility regime is incomplete because of Article 54 of the ILC articles.

The taking of countermeasures by other than injured States as a response to a serious violation of a public interest rule *s.s.* is along the lines of the concept of operational non-compliance referred to earlier.

Whether States can take countermeasures in such circumstances is 'one of the most controversial issues in the law of state responsibility'.[207]

Article 54 has been aptly described as 'unduly restrictive and unfortunate'[208] and 'a dramatic example of indecisiveness'.[209] The lack of support by States for an explicit recognition of such a right to take countermeasures is to blame. However, 'to the majority of States, such a provision would have been acceptable'.[210]

The principle of solidarity is not only at the very origin of the primary public interest rules but is also important in the process of their enforcement. Hence, the legal basis for a right to take countermeasures has to be found in the legal injury to the subjective rights collectively granted: the *ius omnium* has been injured by the breach of such a collective obligation.[211]

Tams's convincing conclusion that 'present-day international law recognizes a right of all States, irrespective of individual injury, to take countermeasures in response to large-scale or systematic breaches of obligations erga omnes'[212] is supported by an extensive analysis of relevant state practice and of comments on the ILC draft articles.

The Institut de Droit International decided to contribute to the evolution left open by Article 54 through the adoption of a resolution along the same lines at its Krakow session, provided of course, 'there is widespread acknowledgment within the international community of the existence of a breach'.[213]

The protests following the Estai incident, although countermeasures were not invoked, showed the international community's reluctance[214] to accept countermeasures to enforce public interest rules *s.l.*, especially when, under the principle of proportionality, other 'forms of international cooperation have proved more effective' in the enforcement process.[215]

---

207 Tams 2005b, 14.
208 Tams 2005b, 311.
209 Tomuschat 2006, 434.
210 Tams 2005b, 247–248.
211 Barboza 2005, 7–22 at 21.
212 Tams 2005b, 250.
213 Gaja 2005b, 148.
214 Guilfoyle 2007, 68–82 at 75.
215 Guilfoyle 2007, 68–82 at 75.

In cases where the enforcement has been multilateralized, such as in the Genocide Convention and in Protocol I, the right of third states to take countermeasures is suspended until the mechanisms provided for have proven to be ineffective.[216]

Is There a General Duty to Enforce Public Interest Rules?

The discussion about the existence of such a duty is taking place with regard to various public interest rules. The growing trend towards the acceptance of this duty may turn out to be irreversible.

Because the duty of cooperation provided for in Article 41, 1 of the ILC articles possibly reflects a gradual development, the international community may have a legitimate expectation, stopping short of a legal duty, that States make representations to another State in order to protect the community interest and use their influence to promote compliance. The non-use of 'undeniable influence' may amount to the breach of a conventional duty of prevention.[217]

The primary obligation not 'to take conduct that would result in a breach' may 'be extended by the norm to cover also conduct that is required to prevent a breach by other states'.[218] According to the UN General Assembly the obligation to respect and ensure respect for HR and IHL includes *the duty to prevent violations*.[219]

Article 1 of the Genocide Convention explicitly provides for the duty to prevent genocide, which is an 'overriding legal imperative' whenever 'there is a serious danger of its occurrence of which the State is or should be aware'.[220]

The Court ruled that a State has to take all measures 'within its power', as the obligation to prevent genocide is 'an obligation of conduct and not one of result'.[221]

Several judges took a different view. As the obligations under the Genocide Convention are *ius cogens*, there is no room for measures 'within its power'. The duty to prevent is not an obligation regarding the means but one regarding the end.[222]

---

216 Hillgruber 2006, 265–293 at 279–280.

217 Application of the Convention on the Prevention and Punishment of the Crime of Genocide (*Bosnia and Herzegovina v Serbia and Montenegro*) Judgment of 26 February 2007, §438.

218 Gaja 2005a, 31–35 at 35.

219 General Assembly Resolution A/RES/60/147, §3.

220 Application of the Convention on the Prevention and Punishment of the Crime of Genocide (*Bosnia and Herzegovina v Serbia and Montenegro*) Judgment of 26 February 2007, Joint Declaration of Judges Shi and Koroma, §5.

221 Application of the Convention on the Prevention and Punishment of the Crime of Genocide (*Bosnia and Herzegovina v Serbia and Montenegro*) Judgment of 26 February 2007, §430.

222 Application of the Convention on the Prevention and Punishment of the Crime of Genocide (*Bosnia and Herzegovina v Serbia and Montenegro*) Judgment of 26 February

Even when States called upon the SC pursuant to Article VIII, 'this does not mean that the States Parties to the Convention are relieved of the obligation to take such action as they can to prevent genocide from occurring'.[223]

There seems to be no compelling reason why this reasoning should not apply to calls for institutional enforcement of other public interest rules, as part of the emerging general duty of prevention.

The duty of prevention fits within an approach of international relations based on universal solidarity; state responsibility for omission is established in order to safeguard the international community's fundamental interests. This duty applies to the international community as a whole; it is an obligation *erga omnes*.[224]

Developments in customary international criminal law have also been significant. The *duty to fight impunity* as a possible emerging general law rule already 'finds expression in the jurisprudence constante of the Interamerican Court'.[225]

There is an increasingly widespread rejection of granting amnesty for serious crimes under international law and a growing acceptance of the corollary *erga omnes* obligation to punish certain international crimes.[226] The duty to prosecute is a 'necessary corollary to ius cogens crimes'.[227]

The *obligation not to recognize as lawful* a situation created by a serious breach has given rise to a debate about its legal basis,[228] its substance[229] and its potential scope of application.[230]

2007, Separate Opinion Judge Ad Hoc Kreca, §§117 and 119 and Declaration Judge Skotnikov, p. 10.

223 Application of the Convention on the Prevention and Punishment of the Crime of Genocide (*Bosnia and Herzegovina v Serbia and Montenegro*) Judgment of 26 February 2007, §427.

224 Application of the Convention on the Prevention and Punishment of the Crime of Genocide (*Bosnia and Herzegovina v Serbia and Montenegro*) Judgment of 26 February 2007, Separate Opinion Judge Ranjeva, §§1, 2 and 4.

225 Cançado Trindade 2005, 257.

226 As this was stressed by Judge *Ad Hoc* Van den Wyngaert in Case concerning the arrest Warrant of 11 April 2000 (*Democratic Republic of the Congo v Belgium*), Judgment of 14 February 2002, ICJ Reports (2002), 3 at 166, §46.

227 Orakhelasvhili 2006, 299.

228 Legal consequences of the Construction of a Wall in the Occupied Palestinian Territory, Advisory opinion of 9 July 2004, ICJ Reports (2004), 136 at 216, Separate Opinion of Judge Higgins, §§37–38.

229 Legal consequences of the Construction of a Wall in the Occupied Palestinian Territory, Advisory opinion of 9 July 2004, ICJ Reports (2004), 136 at 232, Separate Opinion of Judge Kooijmans, §44.

230 Talmon 2006, 99–125 at 125. This is confirmed by an analysis of state practice: Christakis 2006, 127–166. In case of genocide the obligation may rather be a positive one of recognition, Christakis 2006, 128.

At the same time, the traditional instrument of recognition is undergoing a shift towards a normative approach, as 'a tool to promote the values of the international community'.[231]

Conclusion

Public interest rules *s.s.* and, to a lesser extent, public interest rules *s.l.* require uniform interpretation and application.[232] It is here that the structural deficiencies of the international legal system show most clearly.

The international community 'lacks institutions mandated to initiate the judicial enforcement of community interests'.[233]

It is true that the rule of consent to its jurisdiction 'severely restricts the effectiveness of ICJ enforcement'[234] of public interest rules but this does not justify excessive reliance on it as in the *DRC Rwanda* case. This was another 'touch of the Court's own infallibility in its reasoning' which is difficult to accept.[235]

Admittedly it is true that the Court 'did not refrain from commenting on events threatening community interests even where it found that it did not have prima facie jurisdiction'.[236]

That the 'major change of political sentiment' considered necessary by Rosenne to allow judicial action before the ICJ in order to enforce public interest rules[237] is something for the distant future, renders a shift in the ICJ's judicial policy all the more urgent.

In the meantime, the role of individual States remains crucial. Hence the importance of the emergence under customary law of duties for States to exercise universal jurisdiction in appropriate cases, to prevent breaches of public interest rules by other States and non-state actors and of the right to take unilateral countermeasures as a response to serious breaches. These duties and rights are component elements not so much of state sovereignty as of States' responsibility to protect the public interest of the international community.

The implementation and enforcement of public interest rules also requires consistency. The incremental cross-fertilization between various branches such as 'international human rights law to assist in transnational enforcement of

231 Tierney 2006, 1–19 at 13.

232 Orakhelasvhili 2006, 72.

233 Benzing 2006, 372.

234 Tams 2005b, 160.

235 Application of the Convention on the Prevention and Punishment of the Crime of Genocide (*Bosnia and Herzegovina v Serbia and Montenegro*) Judgment of 26 February 2007, Declaration Judge Skotnikov, p. 3.

236 Benzing 2006, 380.

237 As cited by Orakhelasvhili 2006, 523, note 34.

international environmental law'[238] could be useful here. A prime example is the Aarhus Convention containing procedural environmental rights for the individual, leading to its qualification as a semi-human rights and semi-environmental convention.[239]

An increased NGO participation would relieve part of the tension between wide support from the various segments of the international community during the drafting process of the primary rules and the under-representation of the same segments at the subsequent enforcement stage, the exception being NGO involvement in the enforcement process of the Ottawa Anti-Personnel Mines Convention.

Finally, one of the questions this research project has to address is the one raised by Harlow: should the process of implementation of public interest rules be free 'to develop on its own, possibly subject to a process of cross fertilization in the context of globalization?' or alternatively 'should conscious efforts be made to stimulate a process of harmonization?'[240]

As 'throughout its history, the development of international law has been influenced by the requirements of international life',[241] it is not unlikely that the structural deficiencies of the international legal order will turn out to be of a temporary nature only, as nowadays there is a marked shift to formal enforcement in various branches.

References

Books, Articles and Chapters in Books

Barboza, J. (2005), 'Legal Injury: The Tip of the Iceberg in the Law of State Responsibility?', in Ragazzi (ed.).

Bell, C. (2006), 'Peace Agreements: Their Nature and Legal Status', *American Journal of International Law* 100, 373–412.

Benzing, M. (2006), 'Community Interests in the Procedure of International Courts and Tribunals', *The Law and Practice of International Courts and Tribunals* 5, 369–408.

Beyerlin, U., Stoll, P.T. and Wolfrum, R. (2006), 'Conclusions Drawn from the Conference on Ensuring Compliance with MEAs', in Beyerlin, Stoll and Wolfrum (eds).

238 ILA Report of the 70th Conference, held in New Delhi, 2–6 April 2002 (London 2002), 825–857 at 830.

239 Koester 2007, 179–217 at 214.

240 Harlow 2006, 187–214 at 187.

241 Reparations for Injuries suffered in the Service of the United Nations, Advisory Opinion, ICJ Reports (1949), 174 at 178.

Beyerlin, U., Stoll, P.T. and Wolfrum, R. (eds) (2006), *Ensuring Compliance with Multilateral Environmental Agreements. A Dialogue between Practitioners and Academia* (Leiden: Martinus Nijhoff Publishers).

Bianchi, A. (2006), 'Assessing the Effectiveness of the UN Security Council's Anti-terrorist Measures: The Quest for Legitimacy and Cohesion', *European Journal of International Law* 17, 881–919.

Brunnée, J. (2007a), 'Compliance Control' in Ulfstein, Marauhn and Zimmermann (eds).

Brunnée, J. (2007b), 'Enforcement Mechanisms in International Law and International Environmental Law', in Beyerlin, Stoll and Wolfrum (eds).

Buergenthal, T. (2006), 'The Evolving International Human Rights System', *American Journal of International Law* 100, 783–807.

Cançado Trindade, A.A. (2005), 'Complementarity between State Responsibility and Individual Responsibility for Grave Violations of Human Rights: The Crime of State Revisited' in Ragazzi (ed.).

Chinkin, C.M. (1998), 'Alternative Dispute Resolution under International Law' in Evans (ed.).

Christakis, T. (2006), 'L'Obligation de non-reconnaissance des situations créées par le recours illicite à la force ou d'autres actes enfreignant des règles fondamentales', in Tomuschat and Thouvenin (eds).

Cogan, J. (2006), 'Non-compliance and the International Rule of Law', *Yale Journal of International Law* 31, 189–210.

Crawford, J. (2002), *The ILC's Articles on State Responsibility. Introduction, Text and Commentaries* (Cambridge: Cambridge University Press).

d'Argent, P. (2005), 'Le Droit de la Responsabilité internationale complété? Examen des Principes Fondamentaux et Directives concernant le Droit à un Recours et à Réparation des Victimes de Violations Flagrantes du Droit internationale des Droits de l'Homme et de Violations Graves du Droit International Humanitaire', *Annuaire Français de Droit International* 51 27–55.

Douglas-Scott, S. (2006), 'Tale of Two Courts: Luxembourg, Strasbourg and the Growing Human Rights *Acquis*', *Common Market Law Review*, 629–665.

Evans, M. (ed.) (1998), Remedies in International Law: The Institutional Dilemma (Oxford: Hart Publishing).

Fassbender, B. (2006), 'Comments on Chapters 1 and 2 of Frédéric Mégret and Gerben Kor', in Fassbender, Mégret and Kor (eds).

Fassbender, B., Mégret, F. and Kor, G. (eds) (2006), *Complementary Views on Complementarity* (Cambridge: Cambridge University Press).

Flauss, J.F. (2006), 'Compétence Civile Universelle et Droit International Général', in Tomuschat and Thouvenin (eds).

Forteau, M. (2006), *Droit de la Sécurité Collective et Droit de la Responsabilité Internationale de l'Etat* (Paris: Pedone).

Gaja, G. (2005a), 'Do States Have a Duty to Ensure Compliance with Obligations Erga Omnes by other States?' in Ragazzi (ed.).

Gaja, G. (2005b), 'Report on Obligations and Rights Erga Omnes in International Law', *Annuaire de l'Institut de Droit International* 71(I), 137.

Gazzini, T. (2006), 'The Legal Nature of WTO Obligations and the Consequences of Their Violation', *European Journal of International Law* 17 (2006), 723–742.

Giegerich, T. (2006), 'Do Damages Claims Arising from Jus Cogens Violations Override State Immunity from the Jurisdiction of Foreign Courts?', in Tomuschat and Thouvenin (eds).

Gilligan, M. (2006), 'Is Enforcement Necessary for Effectiveness?', *International Organization* 60, 935–967.

Gioia, F. (2006), 'Comments on Chapter 3 of Jann Kleffner' in Kleffner (ed.).

Guilfoyle, D. (2007), 'Interdicting Vessels to Enforce the Common Interest: Maritime Countermeasures and the Use of Force', *International & Comparative Law Quarterly* 56, 68–82.

Harlow, C. (2006), 'Global Administrative Law: The Quest for Principles and Values', *European Journal of International Law* 17, 187–214.

Hillgruber, C. (2006), 'The Right of Third States to Take Countermeasures', in Tomuschat and Thouvenin (eds).

Kleffner, J. (2006), 'Complementarity as a Catalyst for Compliance', in Kleffner (ed.).

Kleffner, J. (ed.) (2006), *Complementary views on Complementarity: Proceedings of the International Roundtable on the Complementary Nature of the International Criminal Court* (The Hague: Asser Press).

Koester, V. (2007), 'The Convention on Access to Information, Public Participation in Decision-Making and Access to Justice in Environmental Matters (Aarhus Convention)', in Ulfstein, Marauhn and Zimmermann (eds).

Kolari, T. (2006), 'Book Review', *European Journal of International Law* 17, 874–879.

Koskenniemi, M. (2007), 'The Fate of Public International Law: Between Technique and Politics', *The Modern Law Review* 70, 1–30.

Krisch, N. (2006), 'The Pluralism of Global Administrative Law', *European Journal of International Law* 17, 247–278.

Krisch, N. and Kinsgbury, B. (2006), 'Introduction: Global Governance and Global Administrative Law in the International Legal Order', *European Journal of International Law* 17, 1–13.

Lawand, K. (2007), 'The Convention on the Prohibition of the Use, Stockpiling, Production and Transfer of Anti-Personnel Mines and on Their Destruction (Ottawa Convention)', in Ulfstein, Marauhn and Zimmermann (eds).

MacDonald, R.S.J and Johnston, D.M. (eds) (2005), *Towards World Constitutionalism. Issues in the Legal Ordering of the World Community* (Leiden: Martinus Nijhoff Publishers).

Marauhn, T. (2007), 'Dispute Resolution, Compliance Control and Enforcement of International Arms Control Law', in Ulfstein, Marauhn and Zimmermann (eds).

Mrema, E.M. (2006), 'Cross-cutting Issues Related to Ensuring Compliance with MEAs', in Beyerlin, Stoll and Wolfrum (eds).

Nolte, G. (2006), 'Universal Jurisdiction in the Area of Private Law – the Alien Tort Claims Act', in Tomuschat and Thouvenin (eds).

O'Connell, M. (2005), 'Controlling Countermeasures' in Ragazzi (ed.).

Oeter, S. (1997), 'Inspection in International Law. Monitoring Compliance and the Problem of Implementation in International Law', *German Yearbook of International Law* 28, 101–169.

Orakhelashvili, A. (2006), *Peremptory Norms in International Law* (Oxford: Oxford University Press).

Paulus, A. (2007), 'Dispute Resolution', in Ulfstein, Marauhn and Zimmermann (eds).

Peters, A. (2006), 'Compensatory Constitutionalism: The Function and Potential of Fundamental International Norms and Structures', *Leiden Journal of International Law* 19, 579–610.

Ragazzi, M. (ed.) (2005), *International Responsibility Today: Essays in Memory of Oscar Schachter* (Leiden: Martinus Nijhoff Publishers).

Rajamani, L. (2006), *Differential Treatment in International Environmental Law* (Oxford: Oxford University Press).

Raustalia, K. and Victor, D. (2004), 'The Regime Complex for Plant Genetic Resources', *International Organization* 58, 277–309.

Reeve, R. (2006), 'The Convention on International Trade in Endangered Species of Wild Fauna and Flora (CITES)', in Ulfstein, Marauhn and Zimmermann (eds).

Rozakis, C. (2005), *Annuaire de l'Institut de Droit International* 71(I).

Sand, P. (2006), 'Sanctions in Case of Non-compliance and State Responsibility: *pacta sunt servanda* – Or Else?', in Beyerlin, Stoll and Wolfrum (eds).

Saul, M. (2007), 'Book Review', *European Journal of International Law* 18, 213–224.

Scott, R.E. and Stephan, P.B. (eds) (2007), *The Limits of Leviathan: Contract Theory and the Enforcement of International Law* (Cambridge: Cambridge University Press).

Shelton, D. (2006a), 'Normative Hierarchy in International Law', *American Journal of International Law* 100, 291–323.

Shelton, D. (2006b), 'Subsidiarity and Human Rights Law', *Human Rights Journal* 27, 4–11.

Skubizewski, K. (1999), 'Respect for Treaties', in Yapko and Boumedra (eds).

Tabassi, L. (2007), 'The Convention on the Prohibition of the Development, Production, Stockpiling and Use of Chemical Weapons and on Their Destruction (Chemical Weapons Convention)', in Ulfstein, Marauhn and Zimmermann (eds).

Talmon, S. (2006), 'The Duty not to Recognize as Lawful a Situation Created by the Illegal Use of Force or Other Serious Breaches of a Ius Cogens Obligation: An Obligation without Real Substance?', in Tomuschat and Thouvenin (eds).

Tams, C. (2005a), 'Book Review', *German Yearbook of International Law* 48, 723–728.

Tams, C. (2005b), *Enforcing Obligations Erga Omnes in International Law* (Cambridge: Cambridge University Press).

Tams, C. (2007), 'Enforcement' in Ulfstein, Marauhn and Zimmermann (eds).

Tierney, S. (2006), 'Questioning Authority: The Normative Challenge in Forging an International Community', in Warbrick and Tierney (eds).

Tomuschat, C. (2005), 'Provisional Report on Universal Criminal Jurisdiction with Regard to the Crime of Genocide, Crimes Against Humanity and War Crimes', in *Annuaire de l'Institut de Droit International* 71(I).

Tomuschat, C. (2006), 'Reconceptualizing', in Tomuschat and Thouvenin (eds).

Tomuschat, C. and Thouvenin, J.M. (eds) (2006), *The Fundamental Rules of the International Legal Order* (Leiden: Koninklijke Brill).

Torres Bernardez, S. (2005), *Annuaire de l'Institut de Droit International* 71(I), 286.

Tsagourias, N. (2006), 'International Community, Recognition of States, and Political Cloning', in Warbrick and Tierney (eds).

Ulfstein, G. (2007), 'Dispute Resolution, Compliance Control and Enforcement in International Environmental Law', in Ulfstein, Marauhn and Zimmermann (eds).

Ulfstein, G., Marauhn, T. and Zimmermann, A. (2007), 'Introduction', in Ulfstein, Marauhn and Zimmermann (eds).

Ulfstein, G., Marauhn, T. and Zimmermann, A. (eds) (2007), *Making Treaties Work. Human Rights, Environment and Arms Control* (Cambridge: Cambridge University Press).

Viljoen, F. and Louw, L. (2007), 'State Compliance with the Recommendations of the African Commission on Human and Peoples' Rights 1994–2004', *American Journal of International Law* 101, 1–34.

Warbrick, C. and Tierney, S. (2006), Towards an International Legal Community? The Sovereignty of States and the Sovereignty of International Law (London: British Institute of International Law).

Wellens, K.C. (2005), 'Solidarity as a Constitutional Principle: Its Expanding Role and Inherent Limitations', in MacDonald and Johnston (eds).

De Wet, E. (2006), 'The Emergence of International and Regional Value Systems as a Manifestation of the Emerging International Constitutional Order', *Leiden Journal of International Law* 19, 611–632.

Yapko, E. and Boumedra, T. (1999), *Liber Amicorum Mohammed Bedjaoui* (The Hague: Kluwer Law International).

Zimmermann, A. (2007), 'Dispute Resolution, Compliance Control and Enforcement in Human Rights Law', in Ulfstein, Marauhn and Zimmermann (eds).

Official Documents and Others

ICJ Reports.
A/CN4/L.682 .
A/CN.4/L.682/Add.1, 2 May 2006.
A/RES.60/147.
S/2005/60.
S/PV.5474, 22 June 2006.
Black's Dictionary 2004.
Yearbooks International Law Commission .
Chemical Weapons Convention.
UN Commission on Human Rights Resolution 2002/79.
Special Court for Sierra Leone, *Prosecutor v Morris Kallon*, Case No. SCSL-2004-15-PT, 15 March 2004.
ILA Report of the 70th Conference, held in New Delhi, 2–6 April 2002.
ILA Committee on Consequences for Victims of War, Report submitted to the 2008 ILA Rio de Janeiro Conference..
ILA Committee on Transnational Enforcement of Environmental Law, Final Report, submitted to the 2006 ILA Toronto Conference.
ILA Committee on International Human Rights Law and Practice, Interim Report on the Relationship between General International Law and International Human Rights Law, submitted to the 2006 ILA Toronto Conference.
Case T. 253/02, *Chafiq Ayadi v Council of the European Union* (2006).
Yearbook of the International Law Commission (1997).
Wemhoff v Germany, Judgment of 27 June 1968, Series A No. 7.
Ireland v United Kingdom (Application A/5310/71), Judgment of 18 January 1978, Series A No. 25.
Al-Adsani. The United Kingdom (Application No. 35763/97), Judgment of 21 November 2001.
Bosphorus Hava Yollari Turzm ve Ticaret Anonim Sirketi v Ireland (Application No. 45036/98), Judgment of 30 June 2005

Chapter 2
Diversification of Implementation Processes and Changing Concepts of Effectiveness: From a Factor-based to a Process-based Approach

Teruo Komori

Introduction

Over the last 50 years, many treaties have been adopted whose object and purpose are to secure the application of some standards in the international community as a whole, such as rules of the various conventions on human rights or of treaties that seek to protect global interests like multilateral environmental agreements (hereinafter MEAs). Compared with other international laws that aim primarily at coordinating the reciprocal interests among States and therefore have the character of private law,[1] it is possible to say that institutions embodied in these legal instruments have the character of public law in the sense that they protect the public interests of the international community.

The formation of laws purporting to protect the public interests of the international community has changed, in various aspects, the framework of traditional international law that has had the character of private law. One of these aspects is that in treaties protecting international public interests, diversified procedures necessary for achieving the goals of treaties have been adopted. For example, in the UN system of maintaining peace as well as in the ICC, because restraining the violation of rules and solving the dispute according to those rules plays an important role in the maintenance of that international order, emphasis is put on the role of enforcement and dispute settlement procedures. However, in MEAs in which progressive and sustainable responses are sought, emphasis is put on non-adversarial and facilitative procedures. Institutions for the protection of human rights seem to have both aspects.

With regard to the diversification of compliance procedures, many studies draw attention to the compliance procedures in MEAs.[2] MEAs have diversified the compliance procedures for securing the objectives of treaties and have made

1 Lauterpacht 1927, Cassese 1990, 12.

2 Victor 1998, Stokke 2005, Ulfstein, Marauhn and Zimmermann 2007.

the implementation process complex in three ways. First, because it is impossible to apply uniform rules to parties who have significant differences in their capacity to implement such rules it seems unfair to impute the responsibility for non-compliance to those who do not possess the capacity. Second, it is necessary to provide mechanisms that respond to the changing situations, due to the uncertainties involving changes of environmental conditions and technology. Third, unlike domestic administrative institutions, there are no treaty organs in an international sphere that possess enough resources to implement the regulations of treaties autonomously. Therefore, the implementation of international institutions has to be coordinated with the implementation mechanisms in the domestic sphere in many aspects. In this way, the implementation processes of MEAs have become more complex than those of traditional international law.

It seems that the phenomena of diversification of compliance procedures and of the complexity of implementation processes have impacted not only on the conception of effectiveness and factors constituting the conception of effectiveness, but also on the understanding of the relationship between effectiveness and legitimacy on which the validity of institutions is based.

It is generally understood that the matter of legitimacy of an institution is discussed in the course of the law-making and the effectiveness of an institution is judged by how effectively a procedure of dispute settlement is applied when Parties deviate from Party rules. With regard to the institutions of environmental protection, however, it is often inevitable to respond flexibly to a changing situation in the implementation processes because the regulative standards are goal-oriented and the implementation processes are complex. This means that the distinction between law-making and the application of law becomes blurred as both become intertwined.[3]

Moreover, the adoption of new rules and measures enhancing the operation of institutions must be secured even when the parties hold opposing views. Consequently in cases in which agreement by consent cannot be reached, it becomes necessary to justify it as a public measure of the institution by relying on some kind of legitimacy.[4]

Similar situations in which the decision-making in the implementation process must be justified can be seen in other institutions protecting the public interests of the international community. Taking the UN system of maintaining peace, for example, how the PKO or other humanitarian activities can be justified as legitimate within the framework of the UN Charter has been a key issue because it is hard to have recourse to ex-systemic rights of the use of force recognized in traditional international law and, in addition, it is unwise to marginalize the UN in the maintenance of peace.[5]

3 Kingsbury 2007, 68.
4 Bodansky 2007, 713.
5 Coicaud 2001, 291.

Moreover, institutions protecting the public interests of the international community are usually adopted in the form of a treaty. So, if parties to the treaty try to achieve the treaty goal worldwide, they are required to argue how principles and rules provided in the treaty are applied *de jure* or *de facto* to non-parties to it. In this regard, in any institution, normative justification to ground the generalization of principles and rules has great significance for the worldwide achievement of treaty goals.

However, seemingly in most studies on the implementation processes of treaties the main focus has been put on the explanation of the means in terms of how effective the procedures provided for in treaties has been in securing compliance with rules rather than on an examination of how the dynamics of the implementation processes are constructed. It is only recently that a focus was put on the role legitimacy plays in the implementation process in studies of MEAs.[6]

In order to clarify the dynamics of the implementation processes of institutions protecting the public interests of the international community, this chapter examines, in the light of the above theoretical concern, various structural features of complexity in the implementation process in the second section and operational features of the implementation process in the third section.

Structural Features of Implementation Processes

The construction of procedures in institutions possessing a public law nature is complex not only in the sense that procedures applied in the international sphere are different institution-by-institution and Party-by-Party, but also in the sense that the implementation process in the international sphere is linked to and coordinated with the domestic legal system. Due to space limitations, this chapter mainly examines features of MEAs, making some comparisons with those of other institutions.[7]

Diversities of Procedures in the International Sphere

Procedures in the implementation processes in the international sphere as provided for by treaties are dispute procedures, compliance control procedures, enforcement and prior consultation. Which of them is considered to play a more important role in the implementation process depends on the nature of each institution. The institution of maintaining peace, which must respond to each case of rule violation separately, explicitly adopts dispute settlement procedures and enforcement. On the other hand, the institutions of environmental protection, which are required to have developmental and administrative responses to the non-compliance or rules,

6 Bodansky 2007, Brunnée and Toope 2002, 286–289.

7 Brunnée 2007, 388–390.

seem to put more weight on compliance control procedures as implementation mechanism.

Dispute Settlement

As is indicated by Andreus Paulus, the development of dispute settlement is far from uniform. The role that judicial adjudication plays is very different from issue to issue.[8]

In MEAs there are two possible ways that parties can solve disputes among themselves by using classical types of dispute settlement. One is where the key issue in a dispute is concerned with the interpretation or application of treaty provisions. The Framework Convention on Climate Change (FCCC) provides in Article 14(1) that in the event of a dispute between any two or more parties concerning the interpretation of the Convention, the parties concerned shall seek a settlement of the dispute through negotiation or any other peaceful means of their choice. Thus parties can submit a dispute between themselves to the International Court of Justice (ICJ) by special agreement or unilaterally if the opposing parties have made a declaration of recognizing its compulsory jurisdiction provided for in Article 14(2). A similar provision is also laid down in Article 27 of United Nations Convention on Biological Diversity.

In general, settlement of a dispute over the interpretation or application of conventions by judicial adjudication has an important role in the maintenance of order prescribed by those conventions. However, in MEAs in which non-compliance with substantive rules is likely to cause damage globally and therefore must be primarily prevented, the classical types of dispute settlement in which parties are restricted to the parties concerned with the dispute and a case is solved *post hoc* do not occupy a central role in the maintenance of order.

Another possible way in which classical dispute settlement procedures can be used is where parties can make a claim for the reparation for damages caused by the violation of rules of a convention. As was indicated by Koskenniemi, making a claim for the damages based on the rules of State responsibility is not excluded if the non-compliance with rules entails the responsibility of a State.[9] However, considering that in practice the element of fault still constitutes a requisite condition in the judgment of the responsibility of a State even when the case contains an equivocal issue, it is legally difficult to impute State responsibility to States that intend to comply with the rules of a convention or to States that lack the capability to comply with the rules of a convention.

8 Paulus 2007, 352.

9 Koskenniemi 1992, 108–111.

Compliance Control

MEAs seem to place emphasis on procedures that enhance compliance in their implementation process. This is not only because damage caused by non-compliance is likely to extend globally, but also in order for these institutions to achieve their goals, they need to take certain factors into consideration, including responsiveness to changing situations, differences in capabilities between parties and flexibility in the decision-making of measures pursuant to the provisions of treaties.

According to the Procedures and Mechanisms relating to Compliance under the Kyoto Protocol, compliance procedures are divided into facilitative measures and enforcement measures. Facilitative measures have two functions. One is to provide advice and facilitation in implementing the Protocol to all parties in Annex I and Annex II, and the other is mainly to promote compliance with their commitment under the Protocol by parties in Annex II, taking into account the principle of common but differentiated responsibilities and respective capabilities as contained in Article 3, paragraph 1, of the Convention.[10] The second measure to enhance compliance by developing countries is very important in inducing them to become parties to the Convention. However, it is helpful to the countries that intend to enhance their compliance capabilities but not for the countries that have no such intention.

On the other hand, enforcement measures are applied to a Party in Annex I that is not in compliance with (a) its quantified emission limitation or reduction commitment under Article 3, paragraph 1, of the Protocol; (b) the methodological and reporting requirements under Article 5, paragraphs 1 and 2, and Article 7, paragraphs 1 and 4 of the Protocol and (c) the eligibility requirements under Articles 6, 12 and 17 of the Protocol.[11]

Enforcement measures applied under the Compliance Procedures of the Kyoto Protocol are declaration of non-compliance and development of a plan. If the Party is not in compliance with the enforcement measures within three months of the determination of non-compliance, or such longer period that the enforcement branch considers appropriate, it has to submit to the enforcement branch for review and assessment a plan that includes: (a) an analysis of the causes of non-compliance by the Party; (b) measures that the Party intends to implement in order to remedy the non-compliance and (c) a timetable for implementing such measures within a time frame.[12]

The adoption of these enforcement measures in compliance procedures under the Kyoto Protocol has meant that that this non-compliance system has shifted its character from managerial control to enforcement.[13] Nevertheless, considering

10 FCCC/CP/2001/Add.3, 67.

11 FCCC/CP/2001/13/Add.3, 68.

12 Part XV, FCCC/CP/2001/Add.3, 75.

13 Werksman 2005, 23.

the kind of enforceable measures and the purpose of the enforcement provided in it, that it shall aim at the restoration of compliance to ensure environmental integrity and shall provide for an incentive to comply,[14] it seems to show that the functions of measures used for enforcement are diversified and therefore the distinction between functions of compliance procedures and enforcement is becoming unclear.

Moreover, in the implementation of these facilitative and enforcement measures, the main mechanism controlling these measures is the information control function by monitoring systems integrated into treaty regimes. Monitoring is a mechanism through which international organizations or treaty organs can control the compliance of treaties and the maintenance of order by obligating the parties to submit a report on how they have complied with treaties. Types of monitoring are divided into either legal review or factual review, and the methods used in factual review are diversified. In MEAs, the task of monitoring is rather on the factual review and therefore the gathering of enough information of sufficient quality to form a judgment is necessary.[15]

Enforcement

I start my argument with the questions of why the legal definition of enforcement is necessary and, if it is necessary, how it should be defined. Tam commented on the role of enforcement in the summary of *Making Treaties Work*,[16] and begins his argument by questioning a definition of enforcement as the process of ensuring observance of laws. He takes this definition from a prominent online dictionary to which he thinks most writers and practitioners would agree.

Tam questions this definition because he thinks that it is rather broad so as to distinguish enforcement from other forms of ensuring the observance of rules, such as managerial approaches, often labeled 'compliance control'. And he puts forward his own definition of enforcement comprised of three elements: measures for ensuring the observance of rules *on the international plane*, attempts to ensure the observance of rules *prompted by a previous case of non-compliance* and the conduct aiming at *bringing the target State back into compliance*.[17]

Unlike Tam's definition of enforcement, my understanding of the question of why the legal definition of enforcement is necessary is that, because enforcement measures can be enforced against the target States contrary to their will, when taking them against those States it is required to satisfy some qualifications to justify them, particularly if they are being taken as sanction. Thus, the definition of enforcement measures is necessary to distinguish measures that do not need justification from those that do need it. And if this understanding is correct, then

14 Part V (6), FCCC/CP/2001/Add.3, 69.

15 Morita 2000, 156–158.

16 Ulfstein, Marauhn and Zimmermann 2007, 391–400.

17 Tam 2007, 391–393.

what is required in the definition is to define measures enforceable against the target States contrary to their will on the basis of non-compliance but not to define the effect that those measures have on the implementation. Moreover, as enforcement in the implementation process is considered as a procedure, it must be defined in terms of form or procedure.

Generally, enforcement measures are anticipated to have the effect of ensuring the observance of rules. Even the argument relying on game theory seems to be based on the same assumption.[18] But as is shown by Tam's deliberate use of terms 'attempts to ensure' and 'aiming at bringing', I think the fact that enforcement measures aim at ensuring the observance of rules does not necessarily mean that they can really ensure it. Therefore, it is possible to say that measures adopted in a treaty and the conditions to justify their use can vary in accordance with the enforcement strategy of a treaty including so-called 'soft' and 'hard' measures and also with the qualification of enforcement in general international law.

The 'hardest' enforcement measures are military action by air, sea or land force or economic sanctions that the UN Security Council may take to maintain or restore international peace and security. In the case of gross violations of human rights, there may be a possibility that measures provided for in Articles 41 and 42 of the UN Charter are taken. But they cannot be taken straightforwardly from the fact that rules of international human rights are violated, but because the violation is determined to constitute a threat to the peace of breach of the peace, in Article 39. In human rights conventions there is no provision that allows a case to be brought before judicial adjudication except in the case of the regional conventions like the European Convention for the Protection of Human Rights.

In MEAs, most of the procedures are for securing compliance control and the systemic enforcement measures adopted in treaties are 'softer' ones. Under the 1992 Annex V of the Montreal Protocol, the following measures might be taken in respect of non-compliance with the Protocol in accordance with the applicable rules of international law concerning the suspension and operation of a treaty. These include (b) issuing cautions and (c) suspension of specific rights and privileges under the Protocol including those concerned with industrial rationalization, production, consumption, and trade, transfer of technology, financial mechanism and institutional arrangements. In the Aarhus Convention of 1998, Annex (g) refers to the suspension, in accordance with the applicable rules of international law concerning the suspension of a treaty, of the special rights and privileges accorded to the Party concerned under the Convention.[19]

Although the expressions of both provisions in the two annexes are similar, Koester indicates that both provisions are not the same in their substance because he interprets them to mean that the scope of the special rights and privileges suspended under the Aarhus Convention is restricted to such rights accorded specifically to that part under the Convention as membership of bureau, chairmanship of

18 Downs, Rocke and Barsoon 1996, 379–406.

19 ECE/MP.PP/2/Add.8.

subsidiary bodies and so on.[20] This interpretation seems to show that how 'hard' or how 'soft' the enforcement measures in MEAs are depends on treaties.

Prior Consultation

Prior consultation procedures have become increasingly important with the increase in environmental risk caused by industrial activities and also with the development of environmental impact assessment systems in domestic administrations.

The types and functions of prior consultations vary depending on the character of the treaties. The application of prior consultation procedures in the international sphere extends from the institutions of non-navigational use of international watercourses to the institutions of preventing marine pollution, which aim at the protection of interests of the international community.[21]

Take, for example, the Convention for the Prevention of Maritime Pollution by Dumping of Waste and Other Matter (London Dumping Convention, 1972), which provides in Article 5(2):

> A Contracting Party may issue a special permit as an exception to Article 4 (1) (a), in emergencies, posing unacceptable risk relating to human health and admitting no other feasible solution. Before doing so the Party shall consult any other country or countries that are likely to be affected and the Organization which, after consulting other parties, and international organizations as appropriate, shall, in accordance with Article 15 promptly recommend the Party the most appropriate procedures to adopt.

The same provision is adopted in the Protocol to the London Dumping Convention, Article 8(2), and OSPAR Convention Annex 2, Article 9. As is laid out in these articles, this prior consultation procedure is used in order that the Organization may recommend an exceptional measure that is in principle prohibited when risk to human health in emergencies is unacceptably high.

Koyano, who has examined the functions of this procedure in treaties by conducting interviews with people working in various treaty organs, demonstrates that the procedure has an administrative function in the implementation of treaties.[22]

Links to Domestic Legal Systems in Implementation Processes: The Role of Domestic Systems

In the implementation processes of international public interests institutions, domestic legal and administrative systems play a significant role for two reasons.

20 Koester 2007, 211.

21 Koyano 2006, 132–160.

22 Koyano 2006, 206–250.

First, they play an important role because treaty organs engaging in the implementation of treaties are not provided with enough competence and resources to operate in the implementation of treaties. A Party of a treaty is in general required to enact domestic law in accordance with it so as to implement it, but the implementation of domestic law having incorporated a treaty is *prima facie* within the preview of a Party. A treaty organ is not entrusted with the power to conduct monitoring by itself within the territory of parties except for the IAEA and the treaty organs for disarmament and the prohibition of weapons.[23] In particular, the administration of permitting and monitoring industrial activities that have an important role in controlling compliance is forced to be delegated to domestic administration systems. That domestic implementation process plays an important part in the institutions of international public interests is related not only to the matter of competences but also to the matter of resources available to ensure the operation of procedures. Even with regard to the operation of the monitoring system, governmental organs of parties or NGOs must collect necessary information in order that COP or other treaty organs can review the reports submitted by parties. This is even more so with regard to the financial mechanisms whose financial resources depend on the provision by parties and other funds.

Second, domestic administrative systems play a key role in implementation regimes because international regulations are addressed not only to States but also to corporations and natural persons or possibly to the domestic economic and social system. Therefore, in order for the institutions to be effective, implementation regimes must be effective in controlling State parties and subjects other than States as well.

As described above, however, treaty organs are not generally competent to monitor within the territory of parties. Even the jurisdiction of the ICC is complementary to national criminal jurisdiction. Effective regulation of the activities by corporations and natural persons within the territory of a Party needs a law that makes the regulation of them explicit and gives specific organs the competence to implement it.

Thus, in the entire implementation process of institutions of international public interests, domestic systems carry out a primary part of operations and also contribute in some manner to their operation in the international sphere.

Diversification in the Integration of Treaty Rules into Domestic Law

There are also differences in the way that each State integrates treaty rules into its domestic legal system. These differences arise partly because the impact that treaty provisions have on domestic legal systems are different owing to the difference of types of regulation in treaties, and partly because the structure and character of domestic legal systems differ from State to State.

23 Avenhaus 2006.

With regard to what impact treaties have on domestic legal systems, typologically there are three types of treaties in the light of how they regulate domestic legal systems.[24] The first type is a treaty that obligates States to secure the result laid out in the treaty but leaves the method of integrating it into the domestic legal system to each State. The FCCC and the Kyoto Protocol fall into this category, which cannot provide for the rules and means in treaties for achieving their goals. Then second type are treaties that obligate a State to coordinate the differences between the standards set in a treaty and its domestic law in order to achieve full realization of its object promptly and progressively. Most human rights conventions fall into this category. The third type of treaty obligates States to introduce the rules and standards of a treaty directly into domestic law without giving discretion to each State in order to maintain the integrity of a treaty. The reason why a treaty needs to maintain its integrity in this case may be because it provides States with the same rights and competences exerted within their territory or because treaty rules are applied to nationals and non-nationals. Among MEAs, the Montreal Protocol and CITES belong in this category because their standards are very clearly stipulated and easily integrated into domestic law.

Thus the differences in structure and character in domestic legal systems influence the structure of the implementation processes. Particularly with regard to the treaties belonging to the first category, the construction of an implementation regime is susceptible to variation according to the differences in the legal and economic systems of a State. Therefore, whether or not a State is in compliance with a treaty rule is often unclear due to these differences in the mechanism for integrating treaties into domestic systems.

Operational Features of Implementation Processes

Compliance procedures in institutions embodying international public interests have been diversified in order to facilitate compliance by parties and to secure the effectiveness of such institutions. However, as Hovi and Ulfstein point out, there are a number of weaknesses in the Kyoto compliance regime that might make it weak,[25] and it is not certain that compliance procedures can automatically secure the effectiveness of institutions. How effectively those regimes work in practice depends on how treaty organs and parties respond to the problems they are facing in their implementation processes.

The problems these institutions are faced with in their implementation processes can be divided into two groups if we examine them from a theoretical viewpoint of how the concepts of effectiveness and legitimacy interact in those processes. The first group of problems is concerned with how implementation regimes are constructed so as to facilitate the procedures in pursuance of the treaty

24 Yamamoto 1994, 113.

25 Hovi, Stokke and Ulfstein 2005, 11.

provisions, which is theoretically characterized as a matter of justification by laws. The second is concerned with how to adopt new rules and measures during the process of responding to changing situations when there is a conflict of views between a treaty organ and parties. In dealing with the second group of problems it is often difficult to apply provisions of treaties. In this process the adoption of a measure or a new rule needs justification in some manner and thus the conceptual distinction between the application of rules and rule-making becomes blurred. This process may be theoretically characterized as an adaptation process in which the justification or persuasion of a decision is essential.

Activities for Enhancing the Effectiveness of Institutional Procedures

There seem to be three phases of activities in the implementation process that are necessary for controlling institutional procedures so as to secure the effectiveness of treaties. The phases are, first, constructing a regime to implement the procedural operations; second, reviewing how effective the operations are and third, creating the factual and environmental conditions to enhance their operation.

Construction of an Implementation Regime

In general, in order to make institutional procedures work, a treaty institution organizes an implementation regime to operate them. In MEAs, treaty organs of a so-called COP model are composed of the COP/MOP (Conference of the Parties/Meeting of the Parties) as a supreme organ, a Scientific Committee and a Compliance Committee as subsidiary bodies.

The COP as a central organ in the implementation regime, according to Ulfstein, has three functions. These are, first, the competence at the internal level of an institution such as adopting rules of procedures, financial regulations and budget establishing subsidiary bodies and secretariat; second, a power of substantive decision-making such as the adoption of new substantive commitments and third, the competence at the external level such as the conclusion of an agreement with UNEP or the State hosting the secretariat and meeting of the parties.[26]

Along with the establishment of treaty organs, the most important function of COP in the implementation process is to secure compliance with treaty rules by monitoring whether parties are in compliance with them or by building the capacity of developing States. In order to make these procedures work, it is indispensable to secure resources and materials sufficient enough to operate them. What is important for monitoring is to gather information about the activities of parties and to have the ability to review them.

At present in MEAs, these functions are mostly carried out by the treaty organs of a treaty and the international governmental organizations hosting the secretariat of treaties. And with regard to the mandate of capacity building, it is undertaken by

26 Ulfstein 2007, 880–885.

the Global Environmental Facility which designates the UNDP, UNEP and World Bank as its implementing agencies. In addition, gathering information necessary for monitoring and reviewing is conducted under the cooperation of international organizations above as well as informal networks or information sources like the International Network for Environmental Compliance and Enforcement (INECE) and non-governmental organizations (NGOs). Thus, how treaty organs are working is related to how they can cooperate with external organs including NGOs and how they can avoid the problems created by that cooperative relationship.[27]

Examination of Effects

Two factors are relevant in the examination of the effects of an implementation regime of an institution. One is a matter of criteria to review its effectiveness and the other is a matter of procedures to be used in the enhancement of its effectiveness.

The first criteria on which the examination should be based are multiple because characters of institutions are various and procedures used in implementation regimes are diversified and complex. Therefore the significance of a criterion depends on the character and the purpose of an institution.

In institutions of human rights protection, for example, it is essential to enhance human rights standards within the territory of the parties by adopting monitoring systems and at the same time to remedy the violation of human rights in the States, because addressing violations of human rights leads to securing equality in the application of human rights standards. Moreover, human rights standards are conceptually and not quantitatively constructed. Therefore, to harmonize the interpretation of these standards may be an important factor for securing the effectiveness of human rights treaties. In this regard, it seems to be problematic that the Human Rights Committee tends to focus on systemic considerations and nevertheless has problems in its capacity to process the reports from parties.[28]

In institutions of environmental protection, aspects and factors by which the effectiveness of institutions are measured are diversified because implementation processes are complex and the standards applied are often different according to groups of parties. As an example, the complete compliance with the reporting obligations by all parties does not necessarily secure the effectiveness of an institution. Funding for capacity-building does not always bring results.[29] And even if the goal is achieved, it may not be as a result of the compliance with treaty rules.[30]

Second, it is necessary to examine which procedures are more effective in the implementation process. Traditionally, whether or not treaty rules were enforceable was an important criterion to judge the effectiveness of a treaty. In MEAs, the

27 With regard to the problems by NGOs, see Raustiala and Victor 1988, 666–667.

28 Crawford 2000, 8.

29 Raustiala and Victor 1988, 674.

30 Raustiala and Victor 1988, 670.

effectiveness of institutions is often judged not in terms of maintaining the *status quo* but in terms of whether their goals are being achieved. In this respect, more effective measures are those that can induce the autonomous compliance with rules by parties. It is pointed out that in responding to cases of non-compliance with rules, sometimes enforcement measures work and sometimes informal type of commitments prove more effective.[31] This shows that the choice of measures in implementation processes need to be flexible.

Enhancing Awareness

For the prevention of non-compliance it is necessary to encourage and enhance the autonomous compliance with rules by parties. Thus enhancing the normative awareness of parties on the issue of what should be done and encouraging parties to have accurate information on the situation are essential for that purpose.

Efforts to enhance normative awareness are conducted at various levels. One of them is the activities of international organizations and governmental organs taking the form of 'enlightenment' and education. For the purpose of raising awareness and publicity within the territory of parties, UNEP Guidelines not only advise parties to take into consideration the institutional framework to promote education for the general public but also propose the training of public prosecutors, judges and administrators to enhance enforcement ability within the territory of parties.[32]

Raising awareness is conducted also by corporations and by NGOs. Activities in the form of Corporate Social Responsibility and Global Compact, which rely on market mechanisms to secure their implementation, are meaningful for raising awareness in the sense that a greater number of the general public can have the opportunity to commit themselves to the compliance with the standards of environmental protection.[33]

31 Raustiala and Victor 1988, 685.

32 UNEP Guideline on Compliance with and Enforcement of Multilateral Environmental Agreements, 2001, paragraphs 41 and 43. A more specific and considered view has been put forward by Dr. John Barker on the basis of his experience as an adviser in the reform of the legal system of Malawi. See his paper entitled 'Reflections on Good Governance and the Role of the International Community', addressed by John Barker at the Conference of the Pan African Lawyers Union, Abujia, Nigeria (4–5 July 2005).

33 See Ago, Chapter 15 of this book, 'Corporate Social Responsibility and its Implications for Public International Law'.

Justifying Measures Taken in the Implementation Process

Adaptation to Changing Situations and Features of Justification

There are cases in the implementation process of a treaty in which parties disagree about which measure should be taken in case of non-compliance with a rule or about what commitment they should decide upon in the change of circumstances. Or there is a case, such as that of PKO or of the regulation of terrorist activities in the UN, where the issue at stake is concerned with the legal possibility of deciding a measure beyond the method of treaty interpretation provided for in Article 31 of the Vienna Convention on the Law of Treaties. In those cases, if any positive decision cannot be made because of disagreement among parties, it is likely to be considered that the treaty or the organization may have lost its effectiveness and consequently its legitimacy.[34]

In those instances, what types of measures are legitimate depends on the character of measures taken and the character of the public interests the treaty protect. The difference of the character of measures has much to do with whether it is an *ad hoc* response to a violation of a rule or whether the measure is to be applied continuously. And the difference of the character of public interests is related as to whether it is a public interest *sensu stricto* or a public interest *sensu lato.*[35]

As an example of rules protecting public interests *sensu stricto*, it is not permissible for Member States or the UN organ to amend the rule on the restraint on the use of force provided for in Article 2(4) of the UN Charter in responding to an event which may be determined as breach of the peace unless the Security Council failed to act. In this case, how States can respond must be argued in terms of whether a measure is justifiable systemically or ex-systemically as an exception to the framework of the UN Charter.

On the other hand, in multilateral environmental treaties, which introduce the combination of a framework Convention and its Protocol and in this sense provide rules protecting public interests *sensu lato*, it is not exceptional to change rules and to adopt measures which are not based on the consent of all the parties. In practice, it is rather exceptional in MEAs to bring conflicts concerning the application and interpretation of rules to adjudication and most of the problems with which parties are in conflict are processed in the form of negotiation or the adoption by deliberation of new commitments in COP/MOP. Accordingly in this process of negotiation and decision-making, procedural equity which assures the participation of all the parties in that process and the legitimacy of a claim within the framework of a treaty that is usually required in the law-making process becomes a key issue in the process. And most of the decisions rely on the concept of implied powers to authorize them.

34 Gray 2007, 157.

35 See Wellens, Chapter 1 of this book, 'General Observations', 16.

Thus, in the implementation processes of institutions, including MEAs, factors of effectiveness and legitimacy intersect when there are uncertainties in the process or opposing views among parties. In order to deal appropriately with those problems, it seems necessary to make clear what aspects of legitimacy are at stake and what matters of legitimacy are concerned.

Context in which Legitimacy is a Stake

There are various contexts in which legitimacy becomes a key issue in deciding which measure is appropriate within the framework of a treaty. In the following section, I will discuss four contexts in which legitimacy is a key issue.

1. Legitimacy of an Action as an Exception

As shown by the failure at the Security Council, there is a case in which views differ between parties concerning whether a measure decided in pursuance of the authorized procedure should be taken or whether a measure based on substantive legitimacy should be recognized.

In this case, it seems, how this difference should be resolved has much to do with the nature of the issue in conflict. Take, for example, the Kosovo case in which whether or not humanitarian intervention was justifiable was disputed on the basis of opposing views about the legitimacy of such a course of action. The reason the issue became controversial was because the use of force in this case was based on the grounds that use of force within the UN is legitimate either when it is authorized by the Security Council resolution under Chapter 7 of the Charter or when parties can have recourse to it as self-defense under Article 51. Conversely, the view insisting that the use of force in that case was legitimate was based on the ground that the use of force for the purpose of humanitarian protection is justified and therefore substantively legitimate when the UN failed to act pursuant to the legitimate procedure.

However, these opposing views contain complex considerations, so it is necessary to take those considerations into account when deciding which course of action should be chosen. As regards the view justifying humanitarian intervention under some qualified circumstances, it takes into consideration such factors as the fact that the system of the restraint of the use of force under the UN Charter operates asymmetrically between a State having provoked and a State being provoked, and that the failure of the UN to act in case of gross violations of human rights and humanitarian disaster degrades the legitimacy of the procedures provided under the Charter. But this view does not consider it desirable to marginalize the UN in the maintenance of peace. Therefore, it tries to justify the use of force for humanitarian protection as an exception.[36]

36 Franck 2002,174–191, Coicaud 2001, 256–293.

On the other hand, concerning the view denying the use of force in the name of humanitarian intervention, the argument that the use of force should be based procedurally on the authorization of the Security Council resolution is nevertheless intertwined with various substantive considerations. These are the possibility of applying a double standard in the justification of the use of force, the additional damage caused by the use of force for humanitarian intervention and the argument that recognizing an exception to the law itself completely undermines the legal system itself. In this view, a reform plan to waive the veto power is proposed in order to solve the imperfection of legitimate procedures.[37]

In this respect, it seems possible to say that this difference of views in terms of whether procedural legitimacy or substantive legitimacy should be given priority is combined with the opposition of substantive considerations on how the dysfunction of legitimate procedure should be dealt with.[38] Thus the real issue to be argued in this case is not how the UN should be reformed for the future but how the UN should act to save victims of the imminent armed conflict and to control it during the time until the UN is reformed. Therefore it seems what measure is legitimate in this case is closely related to the legitimacy of substantive considerations on which each view is based.

2. Procedural Equity

The issue concerning the legitimacy-deficit of a decision-making procedure has been argued from various points of view. One is related to the distorting influence that the one-state–one-vote system based on the concept of sovereign equality has on decision-making, and the other is related to matters of representation-deficit that are concerned with the fact that all the Parties and stake-holders are not permitted to participate equally in the decision-making.[39] From the second perspective, the measures determined in the decision-making process in which all the parties are not represented are treated also as lacking substantive legitimacy for the reason that they do not reflect the interests of all the Parties in an appropriate way even if they protect the public interests of the international community.

Procedural equity, which is the concept used in MEAs to secure impartial participation in the decision-making process, is important in relation to securing the effectiveness of treaties for two reasons. One is that the Parties are more likely to respect a decision if they subscribe to its terms than if they are driven reluctantly into observance by means of a majority decision,[40] and the other is conversely that equal participation may be useful to avoid the de-legitimating effects of a lack of participation.[41]

37 Joyner 2002, 609–612.

38 This point is more clearly made by Roberts 2008, 205–206.

39 Bodansky 2007, 705–722, Buchanan 2003, 40–41.

40 Depledge 2005, 93.

41 Bodansky 2007, 717.

In the negotiating process in the COP of the Kyoto Protocol, a consensus method was adopted to realize procedural equity. This was because it was considered that the method would resolve the limitation caused by the traditional consensus system in the implementation of the treaties protecting public interests and facilitate the formation of new commitments. At the same time, as a means to secure procedural equity the COP adopted procedural rules including a one-party–one-vote rule, a two-thirds quorum rule for decision-making, a document must be circulated in advance rule, a translation requirement rule, a standard meeting hours rule and a no more than official meetings rule.[42]

It has been pointed out that these procedural rules were effective in accommodating the views of small minorities in consensus when parties enlisted in Annex I have urgent need for consensus.[43] However, these procedural rules, on the other hand, were used as a strategic means to block decision-making in order to pursue political objectives[44] and consequently various procedural tools that the organizers of the negotiation can wield to help secure a consensus in order to overcome the threat of procedural blockage have been developed.[45]

This use of procedures as a strategic means and counter tool in the decision-making process suggests that the consensus method adopted to secure equity through consensus is not always useful for the effectiveness of the treaties protecting international public interests. The main purpose of adopting legitimate procedural rules is to realize equity in consensus but not to block the decision-making in the negotiation process. In this respect, it appears that whether the procedures are effective in realizing equity in the decision-making has much to do with the deliberative substances of the negotiation.

3. Legitimacy in the Distribution of Interests and Burden-sharing

Taking into consideration the fact that there are differences among parties in their capacity to implement a treaty, treaties protecting international public interests recognize the differential treatment in terms of rights and duties, the distribution of responsibility or in some other manner. What type of differential treatment is adopted, and what kinds of influence the differential treatment gives to other parties depend on the object and nature of the institutions.

As an example of differential treatment, the International Covenant on Economic, Social and Cultural Rights provides in Article 2(1):

> Each State Party to the present Covenant undertakes to take steps individually and through international assistance and cooperation, especially economic and technical, to the maximum of its available resources, with a view to achieving

42 Depledge 2005, 80–81.
43 Depledge 2005, 94.
44 Depledge 2005, 84.
45 Depledge 2005, 97–101.

> progressively the full realization of the rights recognized in the present Convention by all means, including particularly the adoption of legislative measures.

This type of differential treatment is adopted to provide parties with discretion in their undertaking to achieve the full realization of the rights and not to give effects to the legal status of other parties because the Convention aims at enhancing the level of standards in every State Party without prejudice to other parties' rights.

On the other hand, the principle of differential treatment among the parties to the Kyoto Protocol has complex functions. As the penetrating examination by Rajamani shows, the conceptualization of this principle is connected with various factors such as difference in capability, historical acts of environmental degradation by industrial States, the necessity of economic and social development in the developing States, intergenerational equity and attainability of the quantitative goal.[46] And at the same time, the principle influences other parties because it is combined with the distribution of responsibilities among parties in Annex 1 and Annex 2 in the reduction of gas emission. Therefore, in case it is impossible to achieve its goal, it seems necessary to consider which factors should be emphasized in the process of achieving consensus.

Considering that so many factors are intertwined, I think it is very difficult to achieve consensus only by deliberation. However, generally speaking, I think it is necessary to understand that the Kyoto Protocol requires industrial countries to undertake mitigation commitments and developing countries, to the extent possible given their respective capabilities and development priorities, to cooperate with industrial countries in helping them reach their commitments. Moreover it is necessary to take action in keeping with the objectives and purposes of the regime.[47] Finally, it is also necessary to organize a regime to prevent free-riding. In the case of the FCCC, it is very likely that non-compliance by some States damages the international community as a whole.

Last but not least, daring to refer to the theoretical basis of the legitimacy of differential treatment, I do not think that the principles of common but differentiated responsibilities should be based on the Aristotelian conception that justice requires the dissimilar to be treated dissimilarly.[48] My point is that the concept of equality in current international law, on the contrary, is based on another aspect of the concept of justice that requires equals to be treated alike without regard to factual differences and also that the FCCC regime was adopted by a one-nation–one-vote procedure based on this conception of sovereign equality. I am of the view that, taking into account that members of the international community are interdependent in the protection of the global environment, the question of what types and to what extent differential treatments are legitimate should be discussed

46 Rajamani 2006, 71–88.

47 Rajamani 2006, 254–255.

48 Rajamani 2006, 254.

on the basis of what factors justify the differential treatment within the framework of objects and purposes of the regimes but not on the basis of the conception that the dissimilar should be treated dissimilarly. The conception of justice that requires equals to be treated alike, which focuses on an element of commonality but not an element of difference, still has a very strong function in the process of international law-making.

4. Legitimacy of the Perceptions about Normative Implication and Risk

The perception that continuing the current situation of gas emission will cause a risk on a global scale to the subsistence of human beings or the natural environment constitutes the fundamental basis of the validity of the Vienna Convention for the Protection of the Ozone Layer and the FCCC.

Moreover, it is essential to demonstrate that this perception is based on the scientific evidence in order for these institutions to be characterized as institution of international public interests. Equally, States insisting that the perception is not proved by scientific evidence must demonstrate that their own view is scientifically evidenced because whether or not there is a risk on a global scale is a matter to be judged by reference to scientific evidence and not a matter to be decided by majority rule. Therefore, the factors that ground the legitimacy of a decision in the implementation process will be different depending on whether the decision is related to the change of a rule based on the change of scientific fact or to the change of rules concerning the distribution of interests among parties.

On the other hand, in the case of the International Convention for the Regulation of Whaling (ICRW) and CITES, the legitimacy of a decision or a measure adopted in the implementation process has been argued within the context of two issues. One is whether a decision is endorsed by scientific evidence and the other is whether or not a decision has relied on an object that is different from the object and purpose provided for in those treaties. In practice, critics of the moratorium on commercial whaling by the International Whaling Commission (IWC) claim that the IWC, in adopting the moratorium, acted contrary to the ICRW for two reasons: that first, the moratorium is inconsistent with the Convention's stated purpose, namely, 'to make possible the orderly development of the whaling industry', and second, the decision lacked a scientific basis, as required by the Convention.[49]

Of these two issues, the latter concerning the interpretation of the treaty object is more difficult to deal with because it is linked to the political activities trying to realize the idea of 'preservationism', which denies the killing of animals for consumptive use and recognizes only non-consumptive use like whale watching.

The opposition between the preservationism and conservationism recognizing consumptive use within a limit is seen in any sphere of environmental protection. In the implementation process of CITES and ICRW in which this opposition influences their operations, a voting method instead of a consensus method is

49 Bodansky 2007, 713.

adopted as a decision-making procedure in the COP of CITES and IWC. But how strongly this opposition influences the decision is different between the COP of CITES and IWC. In COP 10 of CITES in 1995, it became possible to list down the African Elephant from Annex 1 to Annex 2 after long and intentional efforts to solve the conflict in the COP rooted in this opposition between the conservationism and the preservationism through deliberations based on scientific evidence.[50] On the other hand in IWC, concerning the interpretation of the treaty object, the opposition between two groups persists without having a common understanding about the role of scientific evidence.

The difference between these two examples indicates that making a decision according to the majority rule without solving the difference in interpretation of a treaty object undermines its effectiveness and legitimacy as well. Therefore, to secure the effectives and legitimacy of a decision in the implementation process, I think it is necessary not to allow one's ideas or beliefs to intrude but to think seriously about the philosophical, political, social and scientific backgrounds against which each viewpoint is argued.[51]

Concluding Remarks: Towards Process-based Concepts of Effectiveness

I have described how the introduction of institutions protecting international public interests into the sphere of international law has changed its procedures and its implementation process. This raises various normative implications in international law, such as the possibility of constructing a theory of public order in the international community, or the possibility of organizing a theory of global administrative law.[52]

Here, as a concluding remark on the theoretical aspects of the issue, I will focus on how the changing concept of effectiveness and factors endorsing effectiveness due to diverse compliance procedures and the complexity of implementation are related to securing effectiveness of institutions.

According to the most prevalent view in international law, the effectiveness of law denotes that the law is enforceable and a remedy of the violation of the law is to be made in some manner. Therefore, in international law, establishing procedures to seek peaceful settlement of disputes and institutionalizing a mechanism to enforce rules has been considered to be important for securing the effectiveness of international law. And this conception of effectiveness has been applied to institution-building in many treaties. Unless the rules of an institution can secure effectiveness in this sense, they are often regarded as lacking effectiveness and consequently as losing their legitimacy or validity.

50 Sakaguchi 2006, 258–259.

51 Gillespie 2005.

52 Kingsbury 2005.

Contrary to this view, Young argues that effectiveness has various dimensions. According to his view, effectiveness is figured as a dependent variable, which means that it is a character varied by some other factors.[53] Then he identifies six different dimensions of effectiveness: effectiveness as problem solving, effectiveness as goal attainment, process effectiveness, constitutive effectiveness and evaluative effectiveness. Moreover, according to him, the effectiveness of each dimension has a relationship with other in some manner, but this is not a linear relationship. Therefore, an institution is judged to be effective in one dimension but not in others.[54]

As is clear with MEAs, institutions protecting international public interests are not necessarily institutions aiming at maintaining *status quo*. In institutions such as those for the protection of human rights, the restraint of the use of force and the protection of humanitarian laws, it is essential to secure the compliance with the established rules, whereas in most MEAs, it is important to respond effectively to changing situations. Accordingly, which procedures are effective or what type of implementation regime is most effective for the full realization of institutions may depend on the character and object of each institution. Moreover, which dimension of effectiveness is relevant to the assessment of effectiveness of an institution may be different according to the institution at hand. If an institution is not effective in a dimension of effectiveness most relevant to it, it is considered to be ineffective. But if it is, it may not be a major problem that the institution has some problems with other less relevant dimensions of effectiveness.

Thus, the concept of effectiveness applied to institutions protecting international public interests does not need to be simple or uniform. Taking into account that there are various dimensions of effectiveness, it is important in order to secure effectiveness of an institution to construct an implementation regime that adapts to the dimension of effectiveness most relevant to it.

Moreover, the fact that dimensions of effectiveness vary means that how institutions are made effective may also vary. As is shown earlier, 'hard' enforcement measures, which may be effective in restoring international non-compliance, are not always effective to non-compliance caused by the lack of capability. And where the legitimacy of a measure is at stake, solving problems by deliberation is more effective in inducing compliance by parties.[55] This seems to imply that when creating law, we have to draw greater attention to what kinds of means are available and what type of implementation processes can be established.

53 Young 1994, 142.

54 Young 1994, 140–160.

55 Brunnée and Toope 2002, 274.

References

Alston, P. and Crawford, J. (eds) (2000), *The Future of UN Human Rights Treaty Monitoring* (Cambridge: Cambridge University Press).

Alston, P. and Crawford, J. (eds) (2008), *Human Rights, Intervention, and the Use of Force* (Oxford: Oxford University Press).

Avenhaus, R., Kyriakopoulos, N., Richard, M. and Stein, G. (eds) (2006), *Verifying Treaty Compliance* (Berlin: Springer).

Barker, J. (2005), 'Reflections on Good Governance and the Role of the International Community', Paper at the Conference of the Pan African Lawyers Union, Abuja, Nigeria.

Bodansky, D., Brunnée, J. and Hey, E. (eds) (2007), *The Oxford Handbook of International Environmental Law* (Oxford: Oxford University Press).

Bodansky, D. (2007), 'Legitimacy', in Bodansky, Brunnée and Hey (eds).

Brunnée, J. and Toope, S. (2002), 'Persuasion and Enforcement: Explaining Compliance with International Law', *Finnish Yearbook of International Law* 23, 286–289.

Brunnée, J. (2007), 'Compliance Control', in Ulfstein, Marauhn and Zimmermann (eds).

Buchanan, A. (2003), *Justice, Legitimacy, and Self-determination – Moral Foundations for International Law* (Oxford: Oxford University Press).

Cassese, A. (1990), *Human Rights in a Changing World* (Cambridge: Polity Press).

Coicaud, J. and Heiskanen, V. (eds) (2001), *The Legitimacy of International Organizations* (Tokyo: United Nations University Press).

Coicaud, J. (2001), 'International Democratic Culture and its Sources: The Case of Collective Security and Peacekeeping Operations in 1990s', in Coicaud and Heiskanen (eds).

Crawford, J. (2000), 'The UN Human Rights Treaty System: A System In Crisis', in Alston and Crawford (eds).

Depledge, J. (2005), *The Organization of Global Negotiations – Constructing the Climate Change Regime* (London: Earthscan).

Downs, G., Rocke, D. and Barsoon, P. (1996), 'Is the Good News about Compliance Good News about Cooperation?' *International Organization* 50:3, 379–406.

Franck, T. (2002), *Recourse to Force* (Cambridge: Cambridge University Press).

Gillespie, A. (2005), *Whaling Diplomacy* (Cheltenham: Edward Elgar).

Gray, C. (2007), 'A Crisis of Legitimacy for the UN Collective Security System?' *International & Comparative Law Quarterly* 56, 157–170.

Holzgrefe, J. and Keohane, R. (eds) (2003), *Humanitarian Intervention* (Cambridge: Cambridge University Press).

Hovi, J., Stokke, O. and Ulfstein, G. (eds) (2005), 'Introduction and Main Findings', in Hovi, Stokke and Ulfstein (eds).

Joyner, D. (2002), 'The Kosovo Intervention: Legal and a More Persuasive Paradigm', *European Journal of International Law* 13:3, 597–619.

Kingsbury, B. (2007), 'Global Environmental Governance as Administration', in Bodansky, Brunnée and Hey (eds).

Kingsbury, B., Krisch, N. and Stewart, R. (2005), 'The Emergence of Global Administrative Law', *Law and Contemporary Problems* 68:3 and 4, 15–61.

Koester, V. (2007), 'The Convention on Access to Information, Public Participation in Decision-Making and Access to Justice in Environmental Matters', in Ulfstein, Marauhn and Zimmermann (eds).

Koskenniemi, M. (1992), 'Breach of Treaty or Non-compliance? Reflections on the Enforcement of the Montreal Protocol', *Yearbook of International Environmental Law* 3, 108–111.

Koyano, M. (2006), *Kokusai Kankyouhou ni okeru Jizen Kyougi Seido* (original in Japanese) (*Prior Consultation Procedures in International Law: The Evolution as an Implementation Process of Legal Institutions*) (Tokyo: Yushindo Press).

Lauterpacht, H. (1927), *Private Law Sources and Analogies of International Law* (London: Longmans).

Morita, A. (2000), *Kokusai Control no Riron to Jissai* (original in Japanese) (*International Control: Theory and Practice*), (Tokyo: Tokyo University Press).

Paulus, A. (2007), 'Dispute Resolution', in Ulfstein, Marauhn and Zimmermann (eds).

Rajamani, L. (2006), *Differential Treatment in International Environmental Law* (Oxford: Oxford University Press).

Raustiala, K. and Victor, D. (eds) (1988), *The Implementation and Effectiveness of International Commitments* (Cambridge: MIT Press).

Roberts, A. (2008), 'Legality Verses Legitimacy: Can Uses of Force be Illegal but Justified', in Alston and Crawford (eds).

Sakaguchi, I. (2006), *Global Environmental Governance and the Process of Regime Development: CITES, NGOs, and States* (original in Japanese) (Tokyo: Kokusai Shoin Press).

Stokke, O., Hovi, J. and Ulfstein, G. (eds) (2005), *Implementing the Climate Regime* (London: Earthscan).

Tam, C. (2007), 'Enforcement', in Ulfstein, Marauhn and Zimmermann (eds).

Ulfstein, G., Marauhn, T. and Zimmermann, A. (eds) (2007), *Making Treaties Work* (Cambridge: Cambridge University Press).

Ulfstein, G. (2007), 'Treaty Bodies', in Bodansky, Brunnée and Hey (eds).

Werksman, J. (2005), 'The Negotiation of a Kyoto Compliance System', Stokke, Hovi and Ulfstein (eds).

Wheeler, N. (2000), *Saving Strangers – Humanitarian Intervention in International Society* (Oxford: Oxford University Press).

Yamamoto, S. (1994), *Kokusaiho* (original in Japanese) (*International Law*) (Tokyo: Yuhikaku Press).

Young, O. (1994), *International Governance: Protecting the Environment in a Stateless Society* (Ithaca: Cornell University Press).

Chapter 3
Multifaceted Conceptions of Implementation and the Human Rights Approach

TERAYA Koji*

Introduction

Implementation is one of the most important phases in the realization of international law. Without implementation, international law is thought to be tantamount to meaningless marks on paper. International lawyers have tried to answer the question as to how states can be bought to observe international law. The commonly held assumption that international law has always been less strictly observed than domestic law throws into question its very status as a part of law. Notably, Louis Henkin attempted to respond to such a blind belief by arguing that 'almost all nations observe almost all principles of international law and almost all of their obligations almost all of the time',[1] but without empirical evidence and a cogent theory, this statement runs the risk of turning into yet another blind belief. One must raise the question as to whether strict observance is in fact desirable. If so, in what sense is it desirable? Before that, one must also raise the prerequisite question: what does observance mean?

If one can find a dominant conception of 'observance' or any common denominator among the various usages of the term, it refers to the condition whereby acts or situations are in accordance with the norms of international society. Presupposing a dichotomy between facts and norms, this conception regards observance as the absence of any discrepancy between a state's actions and international norms.

It can be said that this simple conception is mainly associated with legal positivism,[2] especially in conjunction with statism, in terms of their emphasis on the separation of facts and norms. Hans Kelsen's pure theory, which attempts to establish law as a science, adopts the position of methodological dualism to separate norms from facts. According to Kelsen, it is irrelevant to the concept of law whether or not people actually behave in such a manner as to avoid legal

* This chapter is part of a research project supported by the Nomura Foundation for Social Science.

1 Henkin 1979, 47.

2 This doctrine assumes a great variety of claims and thus the precise explanation needs more investigation.

sanction and whether or not legal sanction is actually carried out, while law is a coercive order providing coercive measures as sanctions. The concepts of validity and efficacy are sharply separated.[3] John Austin, a different type of positivist, argues that laws or rules, properly so called, are species of commands.[4] Again, this presupposes the separation of facts from norms.

Other theories are also concerned with the observance, whether or not they employ the term or its related terms. The issue inevitably arises when they discuss the question of what international law is and should be. The sharp distinction between fact and norm is not always dominant in these theories, but they can be interpreted within the framework of the fact–norm distinction. Natural law theory, usually regarded as the opposite position to positivism, finds the source of law in nature, but this is nature not as fact but as obligation, thereby retaining the distinction between the two realms in the same way as legal positivism. The above common presupposition is also compatible with the comprehensive theory of M.S. McDougal, who, from a different angle, focuses on formal authority and effective control in conceptualizing international law as a combination of these two.[5] It can be argued that policy-oriented goals belong to the status of 'ought'. Political realism, in general, has little to say about law, but this is because it believes that law is not such a useful tool for achieving national interest. This also presupposes that its usefulness, even with its limited role, lies in the accordance of law with fact. For Hans J. Morgenthau, international law is situated in restraints on power.[6] He inaugurated the instrumentalist approach to international relations,[7] a position that shows a similar distinction between fact and norm.

This static framework and conception of observance, however, overlook the features of 'observance' which they attempt to elucidate. Fundamental problems arise if we adopt this simple conception. Firstly, we confront the issue of bad laws. Simply aiming for the accordance of laws with facts would allow even bad laws to qualify for the observance of international law, a position at odds with a tradition in existence since the time of Socrates. Observance would be merely formal and, according to this tradition, such observance would be meaningless. It is widely recognized that legal positivism does not concern itself with the legitimacy or justice of norms. 'Justice', if any, is assumed to be already contained in each rule, and this position does not allow for questions as to why we should obey such a rule. Legal theorists who wish to regard law as entailing justice will argue that the observance is not desirable if the relevant rules lack legitimacy or are unjust, but this claim comes not from the definition of observance, but from their other basic positions. This controversy endangers the foundations of observance. In addition,

3 See his numerous books including, Kelsen 1942, Lecture I; 2006 (originally 1949), 18–20.

4 Austin 1995 (originally 1983), 21.

5 McDougal 1953, 181 ff.

6 Morgenthau 1985, Chapters 14, 15.

7 Koskenniemi 2000, 28.

one should consider the fact that norms that are both just and legitimate would promote positive action in a more effective manner. It may be an exaggeration to say that observance is impossible without a norm's legitimacy, but it is also safe to say that greater legitimacy will lead to higher levels of observance in the long run.

Secondly, the above simple idea cannot adequately account for the coherence, or in Dworkin's terms 'integrity',[8] of various international norms. If each rule exists in an isolated form, conflicts would be left without any coordination or possibility of cooperation towards their resolution. This is similar to the idea of primary rules without secondary rules in the usage of H.L.A. Hart.[9] He conceives of law as the union of primary and secondary rules, arguing that law is not just a type of rule that requires human beings to do or abstain from certain actions and are concerned only with actions involving physical movement or change. For Hart, the primary rules are separate, without any identifying common mark, static with no means of adapting to changing circumstances, and inefficient in maintaining themselves in the face of various social pressures.[10] The secondary rules are thus required to create or vary duties or obligations. This well-known argument concerns how to recognize law without suggesting its contents, but if justice or legitimacy is emphasized, as argued in the above first point, their integrity also becomes an issue. An invariant point is desirable or necessary to provide a common mark, to respond to changing circumstances and to maintain law in an efficient manner. Demonstrating the integrity of various norms will continue to provide the justifiable scope and meaning of each international norm as a legal process. Because various constructions exist for that purpose, it will be discussed which are more helpful than others.

Thirdly, this conception does not explain the social conditions for observance of international law, an issue which is often regarded as beyond the scope of legal studies. This position reveals its naivety in international society in cases where international law has been violated. One is left able only to call vociferously for states to observe the existing rules of international society. Such violations can only be labeled as injustices by recalling such concepts which holders of this position have expelled from the legal sphere. A policy-oriented approach, for example, is more conscious of social conditions. Bearing in mind that law continues to function within society, one should not overlook the social preconditions for the observance process.

Bridging the gap between fact and norm remains one possible conception of observance, and thus a more comprehensive framework should be developed with this idea as a starting point. 'Implementation', in line with the main focus of this book, seems a more suitable term to cover the wide range of issues above, while 'observance' presupposes the traditional framework based on the relationship of

8 Dworkin 1986.

9 Hart 1961, Chapter V.

10 Hart 1961, 90–91.

right and duty[11] and connotes the element of enforcement. 'Implementation' is conceivable with multifaceted aspects. In other words, implementation is not just conceived of as a monistic notion of the accordance of facts with norms between states, but also involves the consideration of other factors such as the *raison d'être* of law and the social conditions of implementation. These factors can be dealt with separately, but when one discusses implementation and associated issues as a whole, they should be thought of as closely connected to each other.

Many approaches claim their own utility in concern with the above objectives. This chapter focuses on human rights as one such approach. This may sound strange, because human rights are usually thought of as forming a specific area within international law. Frequent reference to the importance of human rights usually relates to its substantive aspect among international norms. Nevertheless, it can also be an approach which provides more coherence to all the areas of international law, and the observance of norms can be judged from the perspective of human rights. Human rights are often regarded as an approach in the context of environmental law.[12] International economic law has also begun to consider the relationship between human rights and international trade.[13] This can be extended to international law in general. Much has been discussed on the implementation to human rights law,[14] but less discussion from the human rights approach itself.[15] The ideal of human rights has a special power to promote the implementation of relevant actors and enjoys a unique status in the multifaceted conception which follows. This, in turn, explains why frequent mention is made of the 'humanization' of international law, which Professor Karel Wellens describes as one of the major trends in contemporary international law.[16]

Providing Legitimacy to States as Producers of International Law

Human Rights as Rootedness of States

Once the role of legitimacy or justice is recognized in the observance of international law, one finds that this role is characterized in different ways by a number of theories and perspectives. Among them, a human rights perspective provides a unique role for legitimacy for states, which are still the main actors in international society and the producers of international law. The relative decline in their status

11 See Introduction to this book, 1. See also UNEP, paras. 9, 38.

12 See, for example, Boyle and Anderson 1996.

13 See, for example, Cottier, Pauwelyn and Bürgi (eds) 2005.

14 For example, Alston and Crawford 2000.

15 The project of global administrative law takes a different path (see the Introduction to this book), but one of the main normative bases is also protection rights. Kingsbury, Krisch and Stewart 2005, 45–48.

16 See Wellens, Chapter 1 in this book. Generally, Meron 2006, especially at xv.

has not changed entirely the situation in which international laws are produced. It is important to remember that states can be regarded not only as international actors, but also as legal phenomena themselves if seen from a different angle. States therefore need some source for their legitimacy. Legitimacy can be interpreted in a number of ways and, as Professor Teruo Komori has demonstrated, becomes an issue in different phases in the implementation process.[17] This chapter focuses, from the human rights perspective, on the 'rootedness' component of legitimacy.[18] If law and states do not have a basis in a justifiable historical origin, they cannot maintain the quality of authenticity. The search for rootedness requires further investigation into the background of international law.

Human rights seem to be the most important element in judging the rootedness of a state. In social contract theory, as is well known, individuals have natural rights, and in order to live a life for 'the time, which Nature ordinarily alloweth men to live',[19] they make a contract to establish state power. The core *raison d'être* of the state is to provide safety to individuals in the community. It is simply logical that this should apply not only to its internal acts but also to the state's external acts, such as concluding peace treaties, although the originators of social contract theory made little mention thereof.

By the nineteenth century, states had enlarged their jurisdiction to include economic and social matters and, in accordance with this enlargement, rights had also to be extended to include both economic and social rights. Not only socialism but also capitalism recognized the interests of the non-bourgeois in its attempts to mitigate the socialist movement, with this recognition of interests finding expression in notions of '(human) rights'. One can find here a clear connection between public interest and rights endowed by the state. More importantly, it is necessary to emphasize that economic and social welfare are key matters in protecting classical rights, as recent studies have shown the inseparability of economic and social rights on the one hand, and civil and political rights on the other. This is because, in the age of globalization, the public interest is realized through international cooperation.

Relying on social contract theory might be criticized on the grounds that it is just an hypothesis, or at best something lost in the immemorial past. However, its hypothetical character does not preclude its appeal, because the question here is how we reach to the powerful norm to secure states' compliance, and for that purpose, the quality of norms is relevant. Moreover, it is a misunderstanding to

17 See especially Chapter 2 in this book.

18 This element must corresponds to 'pedigree', which T.M. Franck, in his influential studies on the legitimacy in international law, mentions as one of the components of legitimacy. According to Franck, pedigree 'pulls toward rule compliance by emphasizing the deep rootedness of the rule or the rule-making authority'. See Franck 1990, 94. He uses this term especially in relation to the cultural and anthropological dimensions, but I do not confine 'rootedness' to this usage.

19 Hobbes 1991 (originally 1651), Chapter XIV, especially at para. 64.

think that the social contract does not actually exist. For instance, the right of self-determination in Article 1 of the International Covenant on Civil and Political Rights (ICCPR) realizes an essential part of the theory. The right to development is its economic version. Current peace-building efforts among failed states are nothing more than the building nation state which European countries achieved in the modern age. Also in immigration control, we find expression of the social contract: immigrants try to make a contract for living in a new society. The historical 'contract' survives while the political membership continually changes.

The Limit of States' Action in the International Sphere

Even if the modern states rarely think back to their rootedness, the above logic buttress their law and rules and their implementation and, in turn, constrains them as a background theory. This is widely recognized in the realm of domestic law by, for example, constitutional law studies, but there is no reason to distinguish the external actions of the state from its internal actions. A state's actions should here include external actions. Thus, human rights have a role to play in the limiting of states' actions at the international sphere as well as at the domestic sphere.

Concluding a treaty can be regarded as part of the process of implementing international norms. Treaties furnish bases and guidelines for numerous rules and policies. Therefore, the inclusion of *jus cogens* into the Vienna Convention on the Law of Treaty, which applied to all treaties, has had a great impact in all states. As shown in the *Barcelona Traction* case (1970),[20] the following concept of obligation *erga omnes* demonstrates a similar impact in the form of structure of right and duty.

Moreover, one can find extended use of *jus cogens* in the discussion of State Responsibility (Article 40 and 41 of the 2001 draft).[21] Beyond the limited domain of validity, this use makes *jus cogens* more influential in the continuous process of implementation, because state responsibility brings each state act directly into question. The concept of international crimes of State in Article 19 of the 1996 Draft on State Responsibility was deleted, but this does not mean the idea has been diminished.[22]

Human rights norms are notable enumerations of such hierarchical norms. Compared with other enumerated norms agreed between states, such as the prohibition on aggression, human rights are explained by the very *raison d'être* of the state. In fact, human rights and humanitarian consideration are the main

---

20 ICJ 1970, paras. 33, 34.

21 Articles 42 and 48 are also relevant. See Crawford 2002, 245–260, 276–280.

22 What the Special Rapporteur thought unnecessary is the language of 'crime' and 'delict'. See Crawford 1999, 443. Criticisms of the deletion are found in, for example, Abi-Saab 1999; Pellet 1999.

concerns in the discussion of *jus cogens*.[23] Unlike some interpretations,[24] this does not mean that all human rights are *jus cogens* or other related norms, but it is certain that their core overlaps with hierarchical norms. Non-derogable rights provided in human rights treaties such as Article 4 of the ICCPR give one demarcation for distinguishing the core from other parts.[25] These rights, which are non-derogable even in a state of emergency, and thus have priority even over the existence of the state, are the very rights which motivate the people to establish the state by contract. In other words, they are the roots of states.

Human rights work to define the limits of the states' actions. Implementations incompatible with theses norms are invalidated. Beyond the context of validity, human rights provide the code of conduct for states, as shown in the context of state responsibility.

Providing Integrity to International Norms

Conflicts and Cooperation between International Norms and Human Rights

The static notion of observance as bridging the gap between fact and norm has little concern with the integrity of norms, because it is enough to confirm that each individual situation is in accordance with each specific rule. However, implementing each rule is more dynamic in the process of international law as an entire system. The integrity of the whole is clearly revealed in considering the purpose of the norms, a position which accords with the contemporary trend in applying the concepts of human rights to international norms. Human rights demonstrate the purpose of law, in line with the rootedness issue considered above. The following discussion will show this function of human rights, considering cooperation and conflict with major international norms such as democracy, peace, economy and environment.

Democracy has enjoyed precedence among international norms, especially since the 1990s. The right of self-determination (Common Article 1 of the ICCPR and IESCR) and the rights of political participation (Article 25 of the ICCPR) express this value in the language of human rights.

However, as studies in constitutional law frequently point out, human rights are persistently threatened by the will of the majority. International lawyers tend to assume that democratic states respect human rights, because they usually focus on despotic states' infringements of human rights in the international sphere. But, this masks an intrinsic conflict between democracy and human rights.[26] NGOs

23 Meron 2006, 201–207.

24 Judge Tanaka's opinion in ICJ 1996, 298; ECJ, Case T-306/01; Case T-315/01.

25 See Chapter 1. This emphasis does not mean that these concepts are the same. See Teraya 2001, 917–941.

26 Crawford 1994, 115; Teraya 2007.

make this conflict more complicated, despite being regarded as promoters of international democracy. Indeed, they are so influential that one cannot disregard the significance of their role, as shown in the implementation of human rights treaties, and their opinions make world politics more democratic by presenting viewpoints other than the official government position. The category, however, merely defines these organizations as not part of the government, and there is considerable variety among them. For instance, it is said that influential NGOs are located disproportionately in Europe and the US, and that they tend to emphasize civil and political rights more than they should.[27] The answer to the question whether democracy is compatible with the protection and promotion of human rights, depends on the specific conditions of each case.

Peace has been a formative value in the history of international law. The venerable topic of international law, as found in various civilizations, concerns laws of war, and Grotius, the so-called 'Father of International Law', in his book 'On the Law of War and Peace' was trying to put and end to 'war, such as even barbarous races should be ashamed of'.[28] Traditionally, 'coexistence', as well as being a common aim, has been one of the main purposes of international law, defining international law as an instrument for the regulation of a pluralistic, heterogeneous society.[29] Without international safety, human rights are hardly possible. One could even speak of a 'right to peace'.[30] The language of 'human security' invoked these days[31] is a sort of human rights/humanitarian interpretation of security.

There are problems however concerning the very term 'peace'. Peace has come to require more and more, and some of the requirements contradict each other. One influential idea is Galtung's concept of 'positive peace'. Galtung conceived of the absence of structural violence as 'positive peace', this being distinct from the less satisfactory 'negative peace', the mere absence of personal violence.[32] From this viewpoint, peace is not just a state of non-violence. Discussions of human security by the UN[33] reflect this conception. This raises the status of human rights, but it could easily lead, contrary to the author's intention, to incessant challenges to the principle of the non-use of force, in the name of human rights. Contradictions arise between human rights and international peace.[34] The use of force for humanitarian purposes has come to be regarded as more legitimate, especially after the end of

27 Onuma 2005, 186–189.

28 Grotius 1925 (originally 1625), 20.

29 Weil 1983, 4190–420. See also Friedmann 1964, 60–62.

30 Although a vague provision, see, for example, Article 23 of the African Charter on Human and Peoples' Rights.

31 http://www.mofa.go.jp/policy/human_secu/index.html.

32 Galtung 1969, 183ff.

33 For example, Commission on Human Security 2003.

34 Schachter 1991, 117–126, 331–332.

Cold War, culminating in the intervention in Kosovo in 1999, which is legally unjustifiable under the UN Charter.[35]

In the ICJ advisory opinion on legality of threat or use of nuclear weapons (1996), some of the proponents claims the illegality of the use of nuclear weapons, arguing that it would violate the right to life as provided in Article 6 of the ICCPR. The ICJ denied the deduction from the Covenant, but this is because it acknowledged the need to refer to the applicable *lex specialis*, namely, the law applicable in armed conflict.[36] This reference is also not decisive in judging the legality of the threat or use of nuclear weapons, but it represents a typical example of the human rights approach and the connection of human rights with peace as public interest *sensu lato*.

Economic development and the environment are not as imperative as the interests just discussed, but these relatively new interests, sometimes regarded as the object of the 'international law of co-operation',[37] are the prerequisite values for all human rights in the sense that all states' actions, including protecting human rights, rely on financial resources. The right to development is one of the expressions in the language of human rights.

The nature of economic development leads to unavoidable conflicts with human rights, as in the case of, for example, the right to property versus the expropriation of land for the building of a dam. The *Nibutani Dam* case[38] in Japan presents a more complicated example, where the rights of the Ainu ethnic minority were also an issue because the land involved in the dam construction was for them a holy place. Economic development must also take equality into consideration. The right to development is enjoyed not only by individuals but also by groups, but it is quite unimaginable that every member of a group gains the same amount of economic benefit. One should also be aware of questions of developmental dictatorship and human rights violations in this context.

As demonstrated above, while human rights correspond with other international norms in line with their legitimate power discussed in earlier, they do stir up irreconcilable conflicts. Certainly, public interests such as democracy, peace, economic development and the environment are noble values for international society to purse. However, a desire for democracy that excludes minorities is merely totalitarianism, and peace without human rights is nothing more than the silence of the grave. Public interests cannot be sought after in an all-out manner. Without limitation, they become an obstacle to the process of implementation of the international rules which embody those interests. Human rights clarify the compromising point in transboundaries. The human rights approach submits international norms as a set in a dialectic process and contribute to their implementation.

35 Franck 2002, 134–173; Komori 2004, 8–30.

36 ICJ 1996, para. 25.

37 Friedmann 1964, 62ff.

38 Sapporo District Court, 27 May 1997.

Constitutional Character of Human Rights

It is worth inquiring as to why human rights have the quality of providing integrity to international norms. This chapter finds the key in the constitutional character of human rights. The concept of 'constitution' is a multi-sense term, but, as a stating point, one can turn to Allott's definition: '[a] constitution is a structure-system which is shared by all societies'.[39] A constitution is important from a number of perspectives, but in this context, the significant feature is its ability to bind a range of norms together in a structure-system. The constitution makes possible the willing and acting of the uniquely constituted, which is equivalent to personality for a person.[40] While Johnston identifies ten propositions definitive of the term 'constitutionalism', he thinks that only three of them can be applied to international law; 'a constitution is fundamental law', 'a constitutional amendment requires special, rather onerous, legislative procedures', 'the ethical core of constitutionalism is a bill of rights that guarantees legal protection to individuals and minorities from the threat of tyrannical rulers, elites, and majorities'. The first two propositions apply to the UN Charter thanks to its obviously high legal status and the difficulty of its being amended. The third proposition applies to the core of civil rights.[41] Whether one agrees with this categorization or not, the concept has certainly multiple meanings which lead to the following question: in what sense are human rights constitutional?

Firstly, the constitutionality of human rights is directly connected to that of the domestic legal order. Consideration of constitutionality originates in the domestic order and, in the modern age, the particular focus concerns the balance of power and right.[42] Compared with domestic constitutions, the UN Charter, although certainly assuming a constitutional character in any sense, is engaged indirectly through the constitutions of individual states, which are not necessarily the same constitution as the UN Charter. While an international constitution is not necessarily the same as that of a specific state,[43] sharing the same would provide a stronger constitutional character. Human rights can provide the hinge for the two. It has been said that the UN Charter excels at 'the intention to get out of the fog of the indistinct constitutional rhetoric by turning to one visible document'.[44] However, the constitutional structure does not mean such a discernable character in the stipulation but intrinsic backbone inherent in the stipulations and its relevant norms. It is not proper to mention the UN Charter as a whole, including some technical stipulations, has constitutional character.

39 Allott 1990, 167. See also de Wet 2006, 52–53.

40 Allott 1990, 133.

41 Johnston 2005, 17–18. Other descriptions of enumeration, more specifically in the domestic sphere, are shown in Henkin 1994, 41–42.

42 An historical overview is furnished by McIlwain 1947.

43 Fassbender 2005, 848–849.

44 Fassbender 2005, 848–849.

Secondly, the constitutionality of human rights can be ascribed to the fact that they express a structure-system relevant to any substantive value rather than to specific substantive values. Contrary to popular belief, human rights are not of a kind with such values as peace, environment and economy. As Professor Wellens argues,[45] these values should be separated into at least into two categories. Otherwise, one cannot balance conflicting or disparate interests in the implementation process. We can take this discussion one step further. From the viewpoint of this chapter, public interests *sensu stricto* have their qualification by enjoying constitutional status. A distinction should be made between values as a continuum of importance on the one hand, and the controlling structure-system presiding over those values on the other hand. Thanks to this latter character, human rights can provide a standard to judge various international interests. This is the role which states' sovereignty has long played in traditional international law. In other words, regarding human rights as a constitution for the world brings a paradigm shift, even if not completely, from states' sovereignty to human rights. International law is now being re-conceptualized from a human rights perspective.

This constitutional change continues progressively with the accumulation of various legal documents and practices, overcoming the genetic limitations of each document.[46] Connecting each interest and rule to human rights makes its implementation more effective. The UN Charter and human rights treaties play a paramount role in the process, though they are not always decisive. For instance, states are able to opt out of human rights treaties because they are the type of treaty which states have the discretion to conclude and abrogate. Being dependent on states' discretion is not compatible with human rights. In addition, not all states ratify important human rights treaties and states parties do not always observe these norms. However, it is also true that human rights treaties do provide practical means to criticize violating states, and more states are participating in this regime. Human rights are not always decisive, but they function as one of the strongest norms in both international and internal society. Indeed, human rights have been the central drive to bringing hierarchy and constitution into international norms.[47]

Having said that, this constitutional character does not lead to the claim that the human rights perspective is the best, all the time and in any situation. The limits of human rights come from human rights' character, which originally aimed at allowing people to live 'the time, which Nature ordinarily alloweth men to live'. While this effect is so strong as to be a virtual 'political trump'[48] in Dworkin's sense, the scope is quite limited, because modern states and present international law are more concerned with matters that do not require such political trumps. The role of human rights is usually minor in rather technical matters such as the delimitation

45 See Chapter 1 in this book. See also his argument on a constitutional principle: Wellens 2005, 802–804.

46 See Henkin 1994, 44–51.

47 de Wet 2006, 57–64.

48 Dworkin 1977, xi.

of national boarders. Economic human rights are unlikely to be referred to the interpretation of specific articles in WTO treaties, because economic values are usually realized in macroeconomic measures. The human rights approach changes its effectiveness in each context. The scope of the 'political trump' tends to become inflated because human rights talk becomes more powerful. The expansion itself is not improper, but one should realize that there are different types of human rights discourse.

Providing Social Conditions for Observance

Rule of Law, Democracy and Human Rights

In addition to the normative conditions discussed above, one should consider the social conditions to implementation. Sociological investigation is vital in order to make norms work. Also in this discussion, the human rights approach bears a unique importance. Remembering that the state is a legal construction,[49] it is indirect to ensure implementation by exercising influence on states. Reality lies in the existing individuals and the societies as they gather. The effectiveness of the human rights approach exists in influencing each individual directly. This is frequently mentioned with regard to war criminals, but it can be placed in the broader context of international law.

While normative analysis demonstrates the influence of the quality of norms over an effective implementation, sociological investigation brings the quality of individuals and their societies into question. Generally speaking, it may be said from within the Kantian tradition[50] that democratic states are more favourable towards the observance of international law. Democratic governance requires the rule of law in a state, and this respect for law in the domestic sphere must be more easily extended to external relations. Officials would not invoke 'double standards' in esteeming only their own domestic law, even if their real behavior is the opposite. Transparency in governance, in accordance with publicity in Kant's thought,[51] plays an important role in preventing governments from behaving in a deceptive manner. The quality of society ensures states to implement international norms in due process.

Human rights and democracy based on those rights contributes to build up and maintain such a society. The right of self-determination (Article 1 of the ICCPR) and the rights of political participation (Article 25 of the ICCPR) express directly the values of democracy so that they serve the implementation of international

49 Notably, Hans Kelsen proposed such an idea. See, for example, Kelsen 1934, 117–127; Kelsen 2006 (originally 1949), 181ff.

50 His republican constitutionalism is not the same as democracy, but is compatible with the basic contemporary understanding of democracy (Russett 1993, 4).

51 Kant 1992 (originally 1795), 101–103. See also the first Preliminary Article.

law. To make such democracy substantial, it is necessary to protect freedom of expression (Article 19 of the ICCPR), and freedom of peaceful assembly (Article 21 of the ICCPR), freedom of association (Article 22 of the ICCPR). The right to information that those rights presuppose makes it the government and related bodies transparent. Persons unfavourable to governments should receive legal protection such as freedom from arbitrary detention (Article 9 of the ICCPR), the right to a fair trial (Article 14 of the ICCPR) and, more fundamentally, the right to life (Article 6 of the ICCPR) and freedom from torture (Article 7 of the ICCPR).

Not only civil and political rights but also economic, social and cultural rights are crucial for the quality of society favourable to implementing international law in a just and effective manner. People enduring hardship in the provision of their daily food do not enjoy the 'luxury' of keeping watch on their state's actions in the international sphere. The sacrifice of human rights to a developmental dictatorship should be rebutted by Sen's argument that the general statistical picture does not yield any clear relationship between economic growth and political and civil rights and, rather, 'no substantial famine has ever occurred in any country with a democratic form of government and relatively free press'.[52] The right to an adequate standard of living (Article 11 of the International Covenant on Economic, Social and Cultural Rights (ICESCR)) and the right to health (Article 12 of the ICESCR) are important rights. The right to education (Article 13 of the IESCR) should also be mentioned, since those rights are concerned with personal and spiritual development, such as freedom of expression, and are vain without the support of this right.

The Limitations of Democracy

In general, democratic societies are thought to be in favour of the appropriate implementation of international law, but this is not necessarily true all the time. Also in this context, one should bear in mind that it is possible for democracy itself to conflict with human rights. In this hard case, human rights play the role of a brake.

One can find a clear example in the use of force. While the claim that 'democracies do not fight each other' merits careful scrutiny,[53] it is certain that this claim does not apply to war between democratic states and non-democratic states and, more notably, to the 'war on terror'. The bombing of Afghanistan subsequent to 9/11 (2001) and the more problematic Iraq War (2003) were not prevented by democracy. On the contrary, not a few commentators would say that democracy, or its derivative form of patriotism, defended US foreign policy at that time. The 'war on terror' cannot stop itself. While the US Supreme Court acknowledged the violation of Common Article 3 of the 1949 Geneva Conventions in the *Hamdan*

52 Sen 1999, 92.

53 Details are investigated, for example, in Russet 1993.

case (2006),[54] Congress, where the majority will is regarded as being embodied in a democratic system, passed the Military Commission Act of 2006, which confirmed the US foreign policy.[55] The concept of human rights provides the brake necessary to prevent any escalation, especially for victims, in this case the civilians in Afghanistan and Iraq. Terrorists, whether in fact or allegedly, also have the right to a fair trial and other rights.

Refugees and stateless persons are another example. It is difficult for the majority to accept a minority group that does not belong to their own community, especially when their entry raises difficult social issues such as labour and security. Relevant international norms may be put at risk.

As is frequently pointed out, the momentum for the present esteem in which human rights is held began to develop during the Second World War, when the Allies clearly set human rights as their purpose of war against the Axis. After the war, the UN came to include human rights norms in its Charter. Nonetheless, democracy and fascism bear similar characteristics in their emphasis on the many and unity. To put it differently, democracy today can only be endorsed by its considering human rights.

It is worth reconfirming that democracy is the midway point to appropriate implementation; human rights are more decisive.

Determinacy of Human Rights and the Positivist Contribution

The Significance and Modes of Clarifying Human Rights Norms

The above discussion focuses more on attention to the multifaceted conceptions of implementation rather than the static interpretation as the bridging gap between fact and norm. To bear relevance to international reality, the conception of implementation should be more than accordance of norms with facts at the inter-state level. This conception is mainly associated with legal positivism. This does not mean, however, that theories based on the static conception do not make any contribution to implementation. It is a mistake to believe that the static conception is totally replaced by new ideas. Claiming a clear separation of fact and norm contributes so much that it gives determinacy to norms through traditional interpretative techniques. Norms without definite meaning cannot provide a guideline for relevant actors, even if they thoroughly intend to implement those norms. Furthermore, third parties whose task it may be to judge legality or legitimacy cannot play their role, either. Not only the existence of norms but also their determinacy is important.[56]

54 Supreme Court of the United States, 2006 548 US 557, 67–68.

55 Military Commissions Act of 2006, 2006.

56 In a human rights context, Merrills 1996, 34–38.

Two types of international forums play an important role in determining human rights norms. One of them comprises the human rights bodies of international human rights treaties such as the ICCPR and the ICESCR. When the conditions are satisfied, they deliver their views concerning to individual communications and investigate reports from States Parties and make general comments. For example, General Comment 3 adopted by the Committee of the ESCR,[57] had such a great impact on the interpretation of progressive obligation of state parties provided in Article 2(1) of the ICESCR that the whole obligation would not be interpreted as being merely progressive. This is one of the core documents that criticize the dichotomy between civil and political rights on the one hand and economic, social and cultural rights on the other hand. This kind of interpretations goes beyond the domain of international human rights law narrowly defined. The suggested indivisibility of human rights brings the lives of human individuals into a wider context and includes economic and social problems, which are not necessarily regarded as a proper concern of human rights. It furnishes a firm positivistic basis with policy-oriented rights and concepts such as the right to development, the right to peace and human security. By this means, rights-based analysis becomes possible.

The importance of this kind of international forum is also clear when one considers that this interpretation would not have been submitted without the Committee on Economic, Social and Cultural Rights, which was established in 1985.

The other type comprises more general bodies such as the General Assembly and the Security Council of the United Nations. For instance, the Security Council determines a 'threat to the peace, breach of the peace or act of aggression' (Article 39 of the UN Charter) by recognizing serious violations of human rights.[58] When the General Assembly or the Secretary General denounces humanitarian crises, they unavoidably employ terms such as 'violation' and 'human rights'. In short, organs not based on human rights treaties also show an active engagement in clarifying the meaning of human rights in each context, relating it to general international law.

This type of forum is more significant for the human rights approach, because, as Brownlie notes,[59] excessive focus on human rights often leads to the erroneous impression that there is an independent area of 'international human rights law'. Even if specific systems exist to protect and promote human rights, they cannot detach themselves from international law in general. The protection and promotion of human rights is achieved not only by human rights systems but also by other general systems. This will, in turn, effect on the rationale of general international law with the constitutional character of human rights.

---

57 E/1991/23, Annex III, 1990.

58 See Chapter 5.

59 Brownlie 1998, 65–66.

The Scope of Useful Determinacy

It is usually understood that determinacy of norms is required for their implementation, but there is here an inevitable element of degree. Not only general clauses, but also other concrete clauses leave room for interpretation, because the drafters cannot be expected to make allowance for all future cases. A more fundamental sceptism comes from the idea that the essential attitude expressed in human rights is not compatible with positivism, the mainstream of international law study. Koskenniemi thus suggests that '[b]y remaining in the periphery, in the field of largely subconscious private, moral-religious experience that defies technical articulation, human rights may be more able to retain their constraining hold on the way most people, and by extension most states, behave'.[60] Human rights are not the only norms to consider the compatibility of idealistic emotion and realistic reason, but they should do so more than other norms if one remembers their historical role in modern revolutions.

However, this does not lead to the conclusion that the determinacy of norms is unnecessary for their implementation. The question of how a system should be established is different from the question as to why people are motivated to do so. It is not inconceivable that people with human rights ideals, without losing their integrity, can be excellent positivists at the same time. A more common scenario is one where different persons in a group, with different ideas, cooperate with each other. In addition, the question of degree is unavoidable, though one should not overestimate this characteristic. The degree of determinacy can vary from context to context. The level of determinacy appropriate to a relatively political institution is not the same as that required by a judicial institution. In general, the former brings a broad conception of human rights into its system, while the latter is more concerned with a strict definition of the relevant terms. Therefore, two positions requiring different levels of precision in the definition of norms should not be regarded as opposing each other. Rather, they comprise two poles separating countless middle points along a continuum.

Concluding Remarks

This chapter demonstrates the significance of the human rights approach to the implementation of international law.

I have emphasized that the conception of implementation is not unitary but multifaceted. Besides the static conception of implementation, a mere accordance of norms with facts in the inter-state relation, one needs to consider other factors such as justice, legitimacy and various social conditions. As an extension of the static idea, these elements enrich our conception of implementation as a whole system. This means that implementation itself is subject to interpretation, and

60 Koskenniemi 1990, 1962.

thus reinterpreted, implementation will assure the usefulness and cooperation of a variety of methodologies including the legal positivism, philosophical approaches, jurisprudential analysis and sociological investigation. A positivistic approach, and approaches which focus on other factors, are in fact complementary in developing a theory about the implementation of international law, as are the different conceptions of implementation.

Another emphasis is on the significance of human rights for the multifaceted conceptions of implementation just mentioned. This focus succeeds in explaining the legitimacy of states and international law more than other possible approaches. It also provides the integrity for norms at the global level and some perspective on social conditions of implementation. This is not contingent. While traditional international law emphasizes sovereign states and their *pacta*, human rights take their position in the opposite side to this political entity and, at the same time, legitimate it at the foundation. For this reason, the human rights approach is distinctive in both reinterpreting and enriching the traditional conception of implementation.

References

Books, Articles and Chapters in Books

Abi-Saab, G. (1999), 'The Uses of Article 19', *European Journal of International Law*, 10:2, 339–351.

Allott, P. (1990), *Eunomia: New Order for a New World* (Oxford: Oxford University Press).

Alston, P. and Crawford, J. (eds) (2000), *The Future of UN Human Rights Treaty Monitoring*, (Cambridge: Cambridge University Press).

Austin, J. (1995 (originally 1983)), *The Province of Jurisprudence Determined* (Cambridge: Cambridge University Press).

Bauer, J.R. and Bell, D.A. (eds) (1999), *The East Asian Challenge for Human Rights* (Cambridge: Cambridge University Press).

Boyle, A. and Anderson, M. (eds) (1996), *Human Rights Approaches to Environmental Protection* (Oxford: Clarendon Press).

Brownlie, I. (1998), *The Rule of Law in International Affairs: International Law at the Fiftieth Anniversary of the United Nations* (The Hague: Martinus Nijhoff Publishers).

Byers, M. (ed.) (2000), *The Role of Law in International Politics: Essays in International Relations and International Law* (Oxford: Oxford University Press).

Cottier, T., Pauwelyn, J. and Bürgi, E. (eds) (2005), *Human Rights and International Trade* (Oxford: Oxford University Press).

Crawford, J. (1994), 'Democracy and International Law', *British Yearbook of International Law* 64, 113–133.

Crawford, J. (1999), 'Revising the Draft Articles on State Responsibility', *European Journal of International Law* 10:2, 435–460.

Crawford, J. (2002), *The International Law Commission's Articles on State Responsibility: Introduction, Text and Commentaries* (Cambridge: Cambridge University Press).

Dworkin, R. (1977), *Taking Rights Seriously* (Cambridge, Massachusetts: Harvard University Press).

Dworkin, R. (1986), *Law's Empire* (Cambridge, Massachusetts: Belknap Press of Harvard University Press).

Fassbender, B. (2005), 'The Meaning of International Constitutional Law', in MacDonald and Johnston (eds).

Franck, T.M. (1990), *The Power of Legitimacy among Nations* (New York: Oxford University Press).

Franck, T.M (2002), *Recourse to Force: State Action Against Threats and Armed Attacks* (Cambridge: Cambridge University Press).

Friedmann, W. (1964), *The Changing Structure of International Law* (London: Stevens and Sons).

Galtung, J. (1969), 'Violence, Peace, and Peace Research', *The Journal of Peace Research* 1969:3, 167–191.

Grotius, H. (1925 (originally 1625)), *De jure belli ac pacis libri tresi*, trans. F.W. Kelsey (Oxford: Clarendon Press).

Hart, H.L.A. (1961), *The Concept of Law* (Oxford: Clarendon Press).

Henkin, L. (1979), *How Nations Behave: Law and Foreign Policy*, 2nd ed. (New York: Columbia University Press).

Henkin, L. (1994), 'A New Birth of Constitutionalism: Genetic Influences and Genetic Defects', in Rosenfeld (ed.).

Hobbes, T. (1991 (originally 1651)), *Leviathan*, R. Tuck (ed.) (Cambridge: Cambridge University Press).

Johnston, D.M. (2005), 'World Constitutionalism in the Theory of International Law', in Macdonald and Johnston (eds).

Kant, I. (1992 (originally 1795)), *Zum ewigen Frieden: Ein philosophischer Entwurf* (Hamburg: Felix Meiner Verlag).

Kelsen, H. (1934), *Reine Rechtslehre* (Leipzig: Franz Deuticke).

Kelsen, H. (1942), *Law and Peace in International Relations* (Cambridge, Massachusetts: Harvard University Press).

Kelsen, H. (2006 (originally 1949)), *General Theory of Law and State*, with a new introduction by A.J. Treviño (New Brunswick: Transaction Publishers).

Kingsbury, B., Krisch, N. and Stewart, R. (2005), 'The Emergence of Global Administrative Law', *Law and Contemporary Problems* 68:3&4, 15–61.

Koskenniemi, M. (1990), 'The Pull of the Mainstream', *Michigan Law Review* 88, 1946–1962.

Koskenniemi, M. (2000), 'Carl Schmitt, Hans Morgenthau, and the Image of Law in International Relations', in Byers (ed.).

Komori, T. (2004), 'Public Policy Aspects of International Disputes in International Law', *The Journal of International Law and Diplomacy* 103:2, 1–30 [in Japanese].

Macdonald, R.St.J. and Johnston, D.M. (eds) (2005), *Toward World Constitutionalism: Issues in the Legal Ordering of the World Community* (Leiden: Martinus Nijhoff Publishers).

McDougal, M.S. (1953), 'International Law, Power, and Policy: A Contemporary Conception', *Recueil des cours* 82, 137–258.

McIlwain, C.H. (1947), *Constitutionalism: Ancient and Modern*, rev. ed. (Ithaca, New York: Cornell University Press).

Merrills, J.G. (1996), 'Environmental Protection and Human Rights: Conceptual Aspects', in Boyle and Anderson (eds).

Meron T. (2006), *The Humanization of International Law* (Leiden: Martinus Nijhoff Publishers).

Morgenthau, H.J. (1985), *Politics among Nations: The Struggle for Power and Peace*, revised by Thompson, K.W. (Boston: McGraw-Hill).

Sen, A. (1999), 'Human Rights and Economic Achievements', in Bauer and Bell (eds).

Onuma, Y. (1998), *Jinken, Kokka, Bunmei* [Hunam Rights, States, Civilizations] (Tokyo: Chikumashobō) [in Japansese].

Onuma, Y. (2005), 'A Transcivilizational Perspective on Global Legal Order in the Twenty-first Century: A Way to Overcome West-centric and Judiciary-centric Deficits in International Legal Thoughts', in MacDonald and Johnston (eds).

Pellet, A. (1999), 'Can a State Commit a Crime? Definitely, Yes!' *European Journal of International Law* 10:2, 425–434.

Rosenfeld, M. (ed.) (1994), *Constitutionalism, Identity, Difference, and Legitimacy: Theoretical Perspectives* (Durham: Duke University Press).

Russett, B. (1993), *Grasping the Democratic Peace: Principles for a Post-Cold War World* (Princeton: Princeton University Press).

Schachter, O. (1991), *International Law in Theory and Practice* (Dordrecht: Martinus Nijhoff Publishers).

Teraya, K. (2001), 'Emerging Hierarchy in International Human Rights and Beyond: From the Perspective of Non-derogable Rights', *European Journal of International Law* 12:5, 917–941.

Teraya, K. (2007), 'For the Rights of "Nobodies": Theoretical Response to the Globalizing Tension between Human Rights and Democracy', *Victoria University of Wellington Law Review* 38:2, 299–316.

Weil, P. (1983), 'Towards Relative Normativity in International Law', *American Journal of International Law* 77, 413–442.

Wellens, K. (2005), 'Solidarity as a Constitutional Principle: Its Expanding Role and Inherent Limitations', in MacDonald and Johnston (eds).

de Wet, E. (2006), 'The International Constitutional Order', *International and Comparative Law Quarterly* 55:1, 51–76.

Official Documents and Others

ICJ Report.

Commission on Human Security, *Human Security Now*, 2003.

Committee of Economic, Social and Cultural Rights, *General Comment 3* (E/1991/23, Annex III, 1990).

European Court of Justice, The Judgments of Court of First Instance, judgments of 21.9.2005.

European Court of Justice, Case T-306/01 (*Ahmed Ali Yusuf and Al Barakaat International Foundation v Council of the European Union and Commission of the European Communities*).

European Court of Justice, Case T-315/01 (Yassin Abdullah Kadi v Council of the European Union and Commission of the European Communities).

International Court of Justice, Judge Tanaka's opinion in South West Africa Case Second Phase, Judgment, ICJ Reports 1966.

International Court of Justice, Barcelona Traction, Light and Power Company, Limited, Judgment, I.C.J Reports 1970.

International Court of Justice, Legality of the Threat or Use of Nuclear Weapons, Advisory Opinion, ICJ Reports 1996.

Sapporo District Court, The Nibutani case: 27 May 1997, 1598, *Hanrei Jihō*, 33–55 [Japanese] (details of the case and an extract of the judgment can be read in English in (1998) *Japanese Annual of International Law*, 41, 92–95).

Supreme Court of the United States, *Hamdan v Rumsfeld, Secretary of Defense, et al.*, decided 29 June 2006, 548 US 557.

Military Commissions Act of 2006, Public Law 109-366-OCT.17,2006.

Internet-based Documents

Ministry of Foreign Affaires of Japan, Human Security, http://www.mofa.go.jp/policy/human_secu/index.html.

United Nations Environment Programme, *Guidelines on Compliance with and Enforcement of Multilateral Environmental Agreements*, http://www.unep.org/DEC/docs/UNEP.Guidelines.on.Compliance.MEA.pdf.

PART II
Diversity and Complexity of the Institutionalized Implementation Process

Chapter 4
UN Reform 2005 and Beyond: Conceptualization, Institutionalization and Implementation

Vitit Muntarbhorn

Introduction

Born out of human ideals based upon 'We the Peoples', and the consequences of the Second World War, the United Nations (UN) has now passed its half-century mark. It is impossible to envisage a world without the UN today and it is constantly in the news. Yet it is immersed in an ambivalent image. At times a saviour, a developer, a protector, a motivator, an arbiter. At times a bureaucratizer, a desensitizer, a procrastinator, an obstructer. Public perceptions and understanding of the organization vary from the appreciative to the depreciative, from the benign to the maligned. There is perhaps an element of truth behind all of this, while, of course for some commentators, there is room for further polarization – from maleficent exaggeration to beneficent realization. In reality, more often than not, the UN is only as good as the member States enable it to be.

Throughout the years, talk of reform has been in the air periodically.[1] It was, however, the year of the Summit of Heads of Government – 2005 – which adopted a reform package with far-reaching changes which are still being implemented today. That Summit adopted the Outcome Document which restructured the UN on key fronts, while leaving untouched key components of the system.[2] The package was inevitably a political compromise leaving much to be desired. On a constructive front, it opened a window of opportunities for more effectiveness in several areas, while leaving untouched other areas. The challenge today is not to backtrack or regress, but to drive forward and progress.

Have the rules of the game changed? The 2005 reforms introduce some restructuring at the institutional level, but leave untouched the apex of the system – the UN Security Council. The new institutions analyzed below include the UN Human Rights Council and the Peace-building Commission. The normative

1 There is a myriad of literature on UN reforms. For a bibliography, see: www.unreformabibliography.htm.

2 General Assembly Res. A/60/L/1, *2005 World Summit Outcome*, 20 September 2005.

elements, such as State sovereignty, prohibition of use of force, self-defence and other essentials of international peace and security under the UN Charter are, for the most part, left untouched. However, there is a 'slight variation on a theme': the reforms introduce the notion of the State's 'responsibility to protect' its citizens, failing which the UN should act more proactively to do so. The notion itself can be seen as an incremental shift, which hopefully will press the UN to take actions more effectively and expeditiously. It remains to be seen how it will be implemented, but the evidence, to date, suggests a modest development, heavily influenced by the quid quo pro of international politics.

Conceptualization

The founding document of the UN – the UN Charter – laid down the aims and objectives behind the organization, the main ground rules for operations, and the organs behind the system. The inspiration for international peace and security were complemented by human rights, democracy and development. Yet the main organs of the system have always reflected the presence of governments, and where it mattered most, those who won the Second World War.

At the apex of the system there is the Security Council – a 15-member body, the only UN organ with the power to adopt sanctions if needed. The predominance of the five victors of the War is manifested by their permanent seats as well as their power to veto resolutions. A more representative body is the General Assembly in which all members of the UN have a seat, but it lacks the power to take binding decisions in matters beyond its internal administration. To the side, there is the Economic and Social Council, a body vested with the role of motivating economic and social development; perhaps its most famed offshoot before the 2005 reform was its offspring – the Commission on Human Rights. The latter was decommissioned in 2005 as a result of its 'credibility deficit', leading to the establishment of the Human Rights Council discussed below. Before the 2005 reform, there also existed the Trusteeship Council, which helped with the decolonization process. It has now been abolished, since much of the decolonization has been achieved, rendering that body redundant. On the judicial side, there is the International Court of Justice, which acts as the World Court, principally a forum for inter-State adjudication.

Conceptually, the 2005 Reform consolidates the nexus between peace, security, human rights and development by emphasizing that they are interlinked and mutually reinforcing. Interestingly, the Outcome Document highlights four pillars for more detailed commitments and reinforcement: development, peace and collective security, human rights and the rule of law, and strengthening the UN.

Under the pillar of development, there is emphasis on overcoming poverty and fulfilling the Millennium Development Goals which, at the turn of the millennium, established key targets such as reducing those in absolute poverty – with less than one dollar income a day – by half by 2015. This entails concretizing a global partnership for development, financing for development, domestic resource mobilization, investment, debt cancellation and management, equitable trade, responsive global decision-making, south–south cooperation, education, rural and agricultural development, employment, environmental protection, health care, gender equality, scientific and technological development, actions to address migration from a development perspective, and meeting regions with special needs, especially Africa.

The pillar of peace and collective security is tackled under the Outcome Document by emphasizing the need for cooperation, pacific settlement of disputes, prohibition of the use of force under the UN Charter, anti-terrorism, peace-keeping, peace-building (by setting up the new Peace-building Commission discussed below), and setting the framework for sanctions, countering transnational organized crime, and protecting women and children in armed conflicts.

The pillar of human rights helps to strengthen the various entities linked with the promotion and protection of human rights, such as the office of the UN High Commissioner for Human Rights and the various human rights treaty bodies, addressing the issue of internally displaced persons and refugees, upholding the rule of law and democracy, with special emphasis on children's rights, human security and the promotion of a culture of peace among cultures, civilizations and religions.

Perhaps the most catalytic conceptual change from the Outcome Document which interrelates between human rights and the UN system, especially the Security Council, is the recognition of the notion of 'the responsibility to protect' populations from egregious human rights violations. Where the nation State fails to act, there is all the more reason for the UN to act with a possible graduation of measures ranging from non-binding measures to sanctions, impliedly establishing parameters for State sovereignty as a relative and non-absolute notion. The 'responsibility to protect' concept is expressed as follows:

> 138. Each individual State has the responsibility to protect its populations from genocide, war crimes, ethnic cleansing and crimes against humanity. This responsibility entails the prevention of such crimes, including their incitement, through appropriate and necessary means. We accept that responsibility and will act in accordance with it. The international community should, as appropriate, encourage and help States to exercise this responsibility and support the United Nations in establishing an early warning capacity.
>
> 139. The international community, through the United Nations, also has the responsibility, to use appropriate diplomatic, humanitarian and other peaceful means, in accordance with Chapters VI and VIII of the Charter of the United Nations, to help protect populations from genocide, war crimes, ethnic cleansing and crimes against humanity. In this context, we are prepared to take collective action, in a timely and decisive manner, through the Security Council, in accordance with the Charter, including Chapter VII, on a case-by-case basis and in cooperation with relevant regional organizations as appropriate, should

> peaceful means be inadequate and national authorities are manifestly failing to protect the populations from genocide, war crimes, ethnic cleansing and crimes against humanity….[3]

There has thus been a paradigm shift, inviting the Security Council to be more resolute in taking actions against key violators. The notion of 'the responsibility to protect' has been tested since the Outcome Document particularly in situations of armed conflicts and turbulent flashpoints, such as the violations in Sudan *vis à vis* the people of Darfur.[4] And 'the jury is still out' concerning the implementation process and its impact.

With regard to the pillar aimed at strengthening the UN, several institutional reforms have taken place as a result of the Outcome Document, and these are referred to below. This has been necessary, given the changing nature of UN operations. As noted by the report of the UN Secretary-General titled 'Investing in the United Nations for a Stronger Organization Worldwide' (2006):

> Today's United Nations is vastly different from the Organization that emerged from the San Francisco Conference more than 60 years ago. Its normative work remains important and substantive. In the past decade, however, it has undergone a dramatic operational expansion in a wide range of fields, from human rights to development. Most notable has been a fourfold increase in peacekeeping. The United Nations today has a wide range of missions, a $5 billion peacekeeping budget and 80,000 peacekeepers in the field – including more than twice as are employed at Headquarters in New York. The United Nations, in short, is no longer a conference-servicing Organization located in a few headquarters locations. It is a highly diverse Organization working worldwide to improve the lives of people who need help.
>
> Such a radically expanded range of activities calls for a radical overhaul of the United Nations Secretariat – its rules, structure, systems and culture. Up to now, that has not happened. The staff members of the Organization – its most valuable resource – are increasingly stretched. Our management systems simply do not do them justice.
>
> Previous reform efforts, while generating some significant improvements, have sometimes addressed the symptoms rather than the causes of the Organization's weaknesses, and have failed to adequately address new needs and requirements.[5]

3 General Assembly Res.A/60/L/1, *2005 World Summit Outcome*, 20 September 2005.

4 For example, Security Council Res. 1674(2006), April 2006.

5 UN 2006b, ii.

A conceptual shift advocated by the Outcome Document pertains to the call for more effectiveness, efficiency and accountability on the part of the UN. In the lead-up to the Summit, various scandals involving UN personnel propelled the need for administrative reforms within the UN. One example can already be seen from these reforms introduced to complement the thrust of the Outcome Document:

> Disclosures ranging from the findings of the Independent Inquiry Committee into the United Nations Oil-for-Food Programme to the absolutely impermissible acts of sexual exploitation by some of our peacekeepers in the field have all too clearly demonstrated the need for a more rigorous, enforceable set of rules and regulations, and tougher sanctions. In response, during the course of 2005 (the UN Secretary General) introduced a number of changes aimed at correcting the situation and giving senior management the tools necessary to ensure that all employees of the Organization adhere to the highest standards. In particular, the United Nations has:
>
> - Established a dedicated Ethics Office, approved by Member States.
> - Promulgated strengthened rules to ensure protection against retaliation for those who report misconduct through a new 'whistleblower' protection policy.
> - Put in place more stringent requirements for financial disclosure and declaration of interests, covering broader categories of senior officials and the entire procurement staff.
> - Established strict guidelines for the acceptance of pro bono services from private-sector companies.
> - Implemented a comprehensive set of measures to prevent sexual exploitation in field missions, investigate allegations and hold perpetrators accountable; over the past 14 months, in response to such violations more than 100 individual United Nations staff and peacekeepers have either been dismissed or expelled and a number of entire military units have been repatriated.[6]

The reforms on the administrative and budgetary front are ongoing and will be tested by how they are able to mobilize a huge bureaucracy to reinvent itself in terms cost-effectiveness and efficacy.

There is also currently the issue of how to make the UN more cohesive and reduce overlaps and wastage. Thus the call for 'One UN', now with pilot schemes to marshal UN resources in a convergent manner and propel UN agencies to take a more integrated approach at the national level, in terms of programming anchored to the ground level, particularly in the humanitarian field.[7]

6 UN 2006b, 5.

7 UN 2006a.

Institutionalization

The Security Council

The 2005 package perpetuated some of the status quo while initialing some seminal changes. First, it left untouched the Security Council. Throughout the years, there have been many suggestions for reforms of the Council to make it more representative and democratic. Yet, they have all faltered for lack of political will and blockage particularly from the permanent members of the Council.

Interestingly, prior to the Summit, the high level of panel of experts set up by the UN Secretary-General to submit ideas for UN reform offered a set of possible changes to broaden the composition of the Council from the current 15 members to 24 or 25 members. These would have opened the door to more access by other countries to the Security Council as follows:

> 250. The Panel believes that a decision on the enlargement of the Council…is now a necessity. The presentation of two clearly defined alternatives, of the kind described below as models A and B, should help to clarify – and perhaps bring to resolution a debate which has made little progress in the last 12 years.
>
> 251. Models A and B both involve a distribution of seats as between four major regional areas, which we identify respectively as 'Africa', 'Asia and Pacific', 'Europe' and 'Americas'. We see these descriptions as helpful in making and implementing judgements about the composition of the Security Council, but make no recommendation about changing the composition of the current regional groups for general electoral and other United Nations purposes. Some members of the Panel, in particular our Latin American colleagues, expressed a preference for basing any distribution of seats on the current regional groups.
>
> 252. Model A provides for six new permanent seats, with no veto being created, and three new two-year term non-permanent seats, divided among the major regional areas….
>
> 253. Model B provides for no new permanent seats but creates a new category of eight four-year renewable-term seats and one new two-year non-permanent (and non-renewable) seat, divided among the major regional areas…
>
> 254. In both models, having regard to Article 23 of the Charter of the United nations, a method of encouraging Member States to contribute more to international peace and security would be for the General Assembly, taking into account established practices of regional consultation, to elect Security Council members by giving preference for permanent or longer-term seats to those States that are among the top three financial contributors in their relevant regional area to the regular budget, or the top three voluntary contributors from their regional

area, or the top three contributors from their regional area to the United Nations peacekeeping missions.[8]

But it was not to be.

The Peace-building Commission

On another front, the General Assembly has been left untouched. Interlinking between the Security Council and the General Assembly, a new organ of the UN has now been established as a result of the 2005 reform: the Peace-building Commission. In substance, it is an intergovernmental advisory body which is mandated to tackle post-conflict situations and help regenerate the country, rather than an organ that can act preventively before a conflict takes place. The purposes of the Commission are listed as follows by the Security Council Resolution 1645(2005) based upon the Outcome Document:

> 2…
>
> a) To bring together all relevant actors to marshal resources and to advise on and propose integrated strategies for post-conflict peace-building and recovery;
>
> b) To focus attention on the reconstruction and institution-building efforts necessary for recovery from conflict and to support the development of integrated strategies in order to lay the foundation for sustainable development;
>
> c) To provide recommendations and information to improve the coordination of all relevant actors within and outside the United Nations, to develop best practices, to help to ensure predictable financing for early recovery activities and to extend the period of attention given by the international community to post-conflict recovery.[9]

It is directed by an Organizational Committee of 31 members as follows (each with a two-year renewable term):

- seven members of the Security Council, including permanent members;
- seven members of the Economic and Social Council, elected from regional groups;
- five top providers to UN budgets;

8 UN General Assembly Doc. A/59/566, *A More Secure World: Our Shared Responsibility: Report of the High Level Panel on Threats, Challenges and Change*, December 2004.

9 Security Council Res. 1645(2005), December 2005.

- five top providers of military personnel and civilian police to UN missions;
- seven other members, bearing in mind regional groupings.

The country-specific meetings of the Commission are to have representatives from the country under consideration, countries in the region engaged in post-conflict process, various contributors to military and other resources, various UN representatives, and regional and international financial institutions. It is serviced by a Peace-building Fund and a related Office.

The Economic and Social Council

On another front, there is the presence of the Economic and Social Council. The 2005 reform adjusted the Council to become a more proactive development forum, particularly to coordinate the realization of the Millennium Development Goals. As per the Outcome Document, the following is envisaged:

> a) Promote global dialogue and partnership on global policies and trends in the economic, social, environmental and humanitarian fields. For this purpose, the Council should serve as a quality platform for high level engagement among Member States and with the international financial institutions, the private sector and civil society on emerging global trends, policies and action and develop its ability to respond better and more rapidly to development in the international economic, environmental and social fields;
>
> b) Hold a biennial high-level Development Cooperation Forum to review trends in international development cooperation, including strategies, policies and financing, promote greater coherence among development partners and strengthen links between the normative and operational work of the United Nations;
>
> c) Ensure follow-up of the outcomes of the major United Nations conferences and summits, including the internationally agreed development goals, and hold annul ministerial-level substantive reviews to assess progress, drawing on its functional and regional commissions and other international institutions, in accordance with their respective mandates;
>
> d) Support and complement international efforts aimed at addressing humanitarian emergencies, including natural disasters, in order to promote an improved, coordinated response from the United Nations;
>
> e) Play a major role in the overall coordination of funds, programmes and agencies, ensuring coherence among them and avoiding duplication of mandates and activities.[10]

10 General Assembly Res. A/60/L/1, *2005 World Summit Outcome*.

The Human Rights Council

As already noted, with the demise of the Commission on Human Rights, the Outcome Document was instrumental in setting a new human rights body – the Human Rights Council. A smaller body than previous Commission (47 seats in lieu of the previous 53), the Council now falls under the supervision of the General Assembly rather than the Economic and Social Council and is vested with the power of promoting universal respect for human rights, addressing situations of violations, making recommendations thereon, and fostering coordination and mainstreaming of human rights within the UN system. Unlike the previous Commission, which only met for some six weeks per year, the Council is a standing body with the possibility of meeting throughout the whole year.

In its first year of work, it has been evident that the voices from the South, such as the Asian and African Group, and the Organisation of Islamic Conference, have exercised great weight in the functioning of the Council. The Council has addressed very specifically the issue of Israeli actions in the Occupied Palestinian Territories and Southern Lebanon. Of late, it has also taken up the issue of the plight of people affected by the violence, such as in Darfur.[11] The beginnings of the implementation process of the work of the Council are dealt with below.

Other Innovations

Beyond the above innovations, the Outcome Document introduced other changes. Interestingly, a Democracy Fund, with contributions from 28 member States from the North and South, has now been established in response to the Document's statement that 'democracy is a universal value based on the freely expressed will of people to determine their own political, economic, social and cultural system and their full participation in all aspects of their lives'.[12] The Fund has been placed under the UN Fund for International Partnerships (UNFIP) and is supervised by an Advisory Board, a Programme Consultative Group (PCG) and the Office of the UN Democracy Fund. The Fund's work has been endorsed by the 2006 Ministerial Meeting of the Communities of Democracy, the 14th Summit of the Non-aligned Movement and the 6th International Conference of New and Restored Democracies.

With regard to strengthening the UN as part of the reform, work is ongoing – on reform of the secretariat and management. Some of the reforms have already been referred to, such as the setting up an Ethics Office, and others are referred to below in relation to the implementation process.

Other strands of reform emerging from the 2005 Outcome Document include:

11 For example, Human Rights Council Res. A/HRC/4/L.7/Rev.2 (March 2007) on Darfur.

12 General Assembly Res. A/60/L/1, *2005 World Summit Outcome*, para. 135.

- deletion of Chapter XIII of the Charter concerning the now defunct Trusteeship Council and references to the Council in Chapter XIII;
- deletion of references to 'enemy States' in Articles 53, 77 and 107 of the Charter;
- and request to the Security Council to consider the mandate of the Military Staff Committee of the UN.

Implementation

The Security Council

Given the recent nature of the reform package from 2005, it may be somewhat premature to assess the implementation process, especially from the angle of outcome and impact. Yet, some observations can be made even at this rather early stage.

With regard to the Security Council, the notion of 'the responsibility to protect' has been tested particularly in regard to its impact on the Darfur situation.[13] While the Council has pushed for the presence of UN peacekeepers together with troops from the African Union in Darfur, there has been a test of wills between members of the Security Council and the Sudanese authorities which have delayed deployment of UN troops. From the angle of accountability, it is worth noting that the Council has been ready to transfer individuals to the International Criminal Court for trial for egregious human rights violations perpetrated in the Darfur context. However, in substance, the Council itself has not opened the door to a more representative body – a more democratic body within itself.

The Peace-building Commission

With regard to the Peace-building Commission, pilot projects are already being implemented particularly in two countries in Africa. To date, the Commission has chosen Burundi and Sierra Leone for attention and has helped to mobilize resources to aid the two countries. In the process, it has carried out country visits to be apprised of the situation and to brief the Security Council and the General Assembly on developments. The Chairman's Summary of the Burundi Country-specific Meeting of the Peace-building Commission in December 2006 exemplifies some of the key issues at the ground level as follows:

> 4. Members of the Commission also welcomed the importance placed by the Government on initiating immediate action in the areas of combating corruption, professionalization of security forces and small arms reduction, strengthening

13 Security Council Res. 1674(2006), April 2006.

> the rule of law, the justice system, and the fight against impunity, and support for the establishment and functioning of the Land Commission….
>
> 8. Members of the Commission noted the Government's concerns about human rights abuses and its commitment to address these concerns, including gender equality issues, and highly recommend the support be provided urgently to the Government's plan to establish an independent national human rights commission and to develop transitional justice mechanisms. Such support should accelerate building up national capacities for both the promotion and protection of human rights.[14]

A parallel report from a field mission to Sierra Leone noted the following concerns: youth unemployment, good governance, justice sector and security sector reform, capacity building, regional dimensions of peace consolidation. The recommendations from the mission included the following:

> 29. The mission and the Government of Sierra Leone agreed on the need to develop an integrated strategic framework for the Peace-building Commission's medium term engagement with the country….
>
> 30. It was agreed that the integrated strategic framework for peace-building will build on and strengthen existing frameworks, such as poverty reduction strategy paper and the peace consolidation strategy rather than replace them.[15]

There would be opportunities to tap resources from the Peace-building Fund.

The Economic and Social Council

With regard to the Economic and Social Council, the focus on its work as the primary development forum and its link with the Millennium Development Goals provides fresh purpose to a rather docile arm of the UN.

The Human Rights Council

On the matter of the Human Rights Council, operationally, the first year of the Council (2006–2007) was spent on evolving its programme of work. In June 2007, it adopted the text of its President which structured its operations in four areas: the introduction of the Universal Periodic Review (UPR), the setting up of the Human Rights Council Advisory Committee, the revamping of the previous individual

14 Chairman's Summary of the Burundi Country-specific Meeting of the Peace-building Commission, 12 December 2006.

15 General Assembly and Security Council Doc. A/61/901-S/2007/269, May 2007.

communications system to become a new complaints procedure, and the review of the Special Procedures of the UN, particularly the adoption of a Code of Conduct to shape their work.[16]

The UPR is a new process whereby the record of all countries on human rights is to be reviewed by the Human Rights Council.[17] It is based upon an intergovernmental process with interactive and cooperative dialogue between the country being reviewed and the Council, leading possibly to technical cooperation. It is prospected that each country will be reviewed every four years. The country will be asked to submit a report of no more than 20 pages, to be supplemented by information human rights treaty bodies and UN special procedures and other UN sources compiled by the Office of the UN High Commissioner for Human Rights (OHCHR) and additional inputs from other stakeholders summarized by the OHCHR. Guidelines are due to be prepared on this soon. After discussions in the Council, the Council can make recommendations with which the country under review agrees and other recommendations (with which the country does not necessarily agree) together with the comments of the State concerned. Where a country fails to follow up, there may be further measures adopted by the Council in regard to non-cooperation.

The President's text formulates the UPR system as follows:

> 2. Modalities
>
> The modalities of the review shall be as follows:
>
> - The review will be conducted in one Working Group, chaired by the President of the Council and composed of the 47 member States of the Council. Each member State will decide on the composition of its delegation;
> - Observer States can participate in the review, including in the interactive dialogue;
> - Other relevant stakeholders can attend the conduct of the review of the Working Group;
> - A group of three rapporteurs, selected by drawing lots among the members of the Council and from different Regional Groups (troika) will be formed to facilitate each review, including the preparation of the report of the Working Group. OHCHR will provide the necessary assistance and expertise to the rapporteurs;
> - The concerned country may request that one of the rapporteurs be from its own Regional Group and may also request the substitution of a rapporteur in only one occasion;
> - A rapporteur may request to be excused from its participation in a specific review process;

16 Human Rights Council: Institution Building: President's Text, 18 June 2007.

17 For developments, see International Service for Human Rights (ISHR) and Friedrich Ebert Stiftung (FES) (2006).

- Interactive dialogue between the country under review and the Council will take place in the Working Group. The rapporteurs could collate issues or questions to be transmitted to the State under review to facilitate its preparation and focus the interactive dialogue, while guaranteeing fairness and transparency;
- The duration of the review will be three hours for each country in the Working Group. Additional time of up to one hour will be allocated for the consideration of the outcome by the Council plenary;
- Half an hour will be allocated for the adoption of the report of each country under review in the Working Group;
- A reasonable time frame should be allocated in between the review and the adoption of the report of each State in the Working Group;
- The final outcome will be adopted by the plenary of the Council.[18]

The outcome of the review is provided for as follows:

1. Format of the outcome

A report consisting of a summary of the proceedings of the review process; recommendations and/conclusions; and voluntary commitments.

2. Content of the outcome

UPR is a cooperative mechanism. Its outcome could include, inter alia:

- Assessment in an objective and transparent manner of the human rights situation in the reviewed country, including positive developments and challenges faced by the country;
- Sharing of best practices;
- Emphasis on enhancing cooperation for the promotion and protection of human rights;
- Provision of technical assistance and capacity-building in consultation with and with the consent of the country concerned;
- Voluntary commitments and pledges made by the country reviewed.

3. Adoption of the outcome

- The reviewed country should be fully involved in the outcome;
- Before the adoption of the outcome by the plenary of the Council, the State concerned should be offered the possibility to present replies to questions or issues that were not sufficiently addressed during the interactive dialogue;
- The State concerned and the member States of the Council, as well as observer States, will be given the opportunity to express their views on the outcome of the review before the plenary takes action on it;
- Other relevant stakeholders will have the opportunity to make general comments before the adoption of the outcome by the plenary;

---

18 Human Rights Council: Institution Building: President's Text, 18 June 2007.

- Recommendations that enjoy the support of the State concerned will be identified as such. Other recommendations, together with the comments of the State concerned thereon, will be noted. Both will be included in the outcome report to be adopted by the Council.

F. Follow-up to the review

- The outcome of UPR, as a cooperative mechanism, should be implemented primarily by the State concerned and, as appropriate, by other relevant stakeholders;
- The subsequent review should focus, inter alia, on the implementation of the preceding outcome;
- The Council should have a standing item on its agenda devoted to UPR;
- The international community will assist in implementing the recommendations and conclusions regarding capacity-building and technical assistance, in consultation with and with the consent of the country concerned;
- In considering the UPR outcome, the Council will decide if and when any specific follow-up would be necessary;
- After exhausting all efforts to encourage a State to cooperate with the UPR mechanism, the Council will address, as appropriate, cased of persistent non-cooperation with the mechanism.[19]

Previously under the Commission on Human Rights, there was a sub-commission comprised of a group of experts that could advise on human rights issues as well as help screen individual communications addressed to the UN. The system has been reformed, with a new body taking the place of the sub-commission. The new Human Rights Council Advisory Committee will be composed of 18 experts to act as a think-tank to the Council, with seats allocated geographically. The Committee is to advise on thematic issues, at the request of the Council, and it is not to adopt resolutions. It is to meet up to two sessions for a maximum of 10 working days a year. A number of members from the Committee will also help to screen cases under the new complaints system set up to receive communications from individuals concerning human rights violations.

With regard to the new complaints procedure, it builds upon the previous procedure known as the '1503' after the resolution that established it decades ago. The 1503 was a confidential procedure for individuals to complain of key human rights violations; the procedures enabled the Commission on Human Rights to dialogue confidentially with the State complained against to rectify the situation. There was no binding sanction, and the main criterion for acting on the complaint was that of a consistent pattern of gross and reliably attested human rights violations. The new complaint procedures adhere to this criterion while building upon the specifics including the following:

---

19 Human Rights Council: Institution Building: President's Text, 18 June 2007.

> B. Admissibility criteria for communications
> A communication related to a violation of human rights and fundamental freedoms, for the purpose of this procedure, shall be admissible, unless:
>
> - It has manifestly political motivations and its object is not consistent with the Charter of the United Nations, the Universal Declaration of Human Rights and other applicable instruments in the field of human rights law; or
> - It does not contain a factual description of the alleged violations, including the rights which are alleged to be violated; or
> - Its language is abusive. However, such communication may be considered if it meets the other criteria for admissibility after deletion of the abusive language; or
> - It is not submitted by a person or a group of persons claiming to be the victim of violations of human rights and fundamental freedoms or by any person or group of persons, including NGOs acting in good faith in accordance with principles of human rights, not resorting to politically motivated stands contrary to the provisions of the Charter of the United Nations and claiming to have direct and reliable knowledge of those violations. Nonetheless, reliably attested communications shall not be inadmissible solely because the knowledge of the individual is second hand, provided they are accompanied by clear evidence; or
> - It is exclusively based on reports disseminated by mass media; or
> - It refers to a case that appears to reveal a consistent pattern of gross and reliably attested violations of human rights already being dealt with by a special procedure, a treaty body or other United Nations or similar regional complaints procedure in the field of human rights; or
> - The domestic remedies have not been exhausted, unless it appears that such remedies would be ineffective or unreasonably prolonged.
>
> The National Human Rights Institutions (NHRIs), where they are established and work under the guidelines of the Principles Relating to Status of Nations Institutions (the Paris Principles) including in regard to quasi-judicial competence, can serve as effective means in addressing individual human rights violations.[20]

The complaints are to be vetted by two working groups, the first tier being the working group on communications drawn from the Human Rights Council Advisory Committee. If the case passes the vetting by that group, it then goes to the Working Group on Situations composed of government members drawn from each regional group in the Council. A novelty of this procedure is that the complainant will be informed by the Council that the complaint has been received.

20 Human Rights Council: Institution Building: President's Text, 18 June 2007.

The complainant and the State in question will also be informed of the final outcome. Various options are open as a response to the complaint:

- Discontinue considering the situation when further consideration or action is not warranted;
- Keep the situation under review and to request the State concerned to provide further information within a reasonable amount of time;
- Keep the situation under review and appoint an independent and highly qualified expert to monitor the situation and report back to the Council;
- Discontinue reviewing the matter under the confidential procedure in order to take up public consideration of the same;
- Recommend to OHCHR to provide technical cooperation, capacity-building assistance or advisory services to the State concerned.[21]

Perhaps the most heated debate in the package concerned the issue of Special Procedures – a system of UN monitors/investigators on human rights, acting pro bono and in an independent capacity, such as Special Rapporteurs, Special Representatives of the UN Secretary-General and Working Groups; many are appointed from the academia and civil society. Until the package, there were just over 40 Special Procedures covering themes such as the sale of children, and country situations such as Belarus and the Democratic People's Republic of Korea (DPRK). Some countries wished to abolish the country mandates where they had been established without the consent of the country in question; there were four mandates of this kind – on Cuba, Myanmar, Belarus and DPRK. In the package under the President's text, two were abolished – the mandate on Cuba and Belarus, but the other two remained on the basis of their being mandates with an obligation to report to the UN General Assembly. Both the Myanmar and DPRK mandates fell into this category as they both have UN General Assembly resolutions behind them, requesting them to report to the UN General Assembly, in addition to reporting to the UN Commission on Human Rights, and now, by extension, to the Human Rights Council. With regard to future mandates, the compromise reached in the Council to establish country mandates through country-related resolutions repudiated the initial suggestion from some governments to use a two-thirds majority rule, but opted for sponsorship of such resolutions preferably by at least 15 member countries of the Council.

Another controversial move from some States was to impose a Code of Conduct on the work of the Special Procedures. The latter had always felt that such a Code was unnecessary as the Special Procedures already had operational guidelines guiding their work in the form of their manual of operations. However, in the end, a Code was adopted by the Council, although much modified from its more stringent original draft. The thrust of the Code adopted through the President's text includes the following components:

21 Human Rights Council: Institution Building: President's Text, 18 June 2007.

- There is an umbrella provision urging all States to cooperate with the Special Procedures, as well as to provide information in a timely manner and to respond to communications from the Special Procedures (concerning allegations of human rights violations).
- The provisions of the Special Procedures' manual should be in consonance with the Code.
- Mandate holders are to act in an independent capacity and refrain from using their position for private gain.
- They should cross-check to the best extent possible the facts before sending communications to the country in question.
- Letters of allegation to be sent to the country in question should not be exclusively based on reports disseminated by mass media and mandate holders should only resort to urgent appeals 'in cases where the alleged violations are time-sensitive in terms of involving loss of life, life-threatening situations or either imminent or ongoing damage of an extremely grave nature to victims that cannot be addressed in a timely manner by the procedure concerning letter of allegation'.
- Field visits by mandate holders should be conducted with the consent, or at the invitation of the State concerned, and be prepared in close collaboration with the Permanent Mission of the State concerned.
- Mandate holders are to communicate with concerned governments through diplomatic channels.
- They are accountable to the Human Rights Council.[22]

With regard to the recommendations and conclusions of the mandate holders, which may also be interlinked with how they conduct their press conferences, Article 13 of the Code stipulates as follows:

> Mandate holders shall:
> a) While expressing their considered views, particularly in their public statements concerning allegations of human rights violations, also indicate fairly what responses were given by the concerned State;
> b) While reporting on a concerned State, ensure that their declarations on the human rights situation in the country are at all times compatible with their mandate and the integrity, independence and impartiality which their status requires, and which is likely to promote a constructive dialogue among stakeholders, as well as cooperation for the promotion and protection of human rights;
> c) Ensure that the concerned government authorities are the first recipients of their conclusions and recommendations concerning this State and are given

22 Human Rights Council: Institution Building: President's Text, 18 June 2007.

> adequate time to respond, and that likewise the Council is the first recipient of conclusions and recommendations addressed to this body.[23]

Some of the provisos above may give rise to problems of interpretation and implementation. For instance, in view of the independent nature of the work of mandate holders, if the latter criticize a country for a poor human rights record, is this 'likely to promote a constructive cooperation' with the government in question as one of the stakeholders? The final proviso may also impede the manner and content of how mandate holders may wish to externalize their concerns. For instance, the stipulation that the Council is to be the first recipient of conclusions and recommendations may cause delays since the Council may not be 'sitting' at the time when those conclusions and recommendations are to be made. The Code itself suffers from the undercurrent of some countries which wish to exert more control over the work of the Special Procedures. During the discussions leading to the President's text, some governments were even putting forward the possibility of setting up an Ethics Committee composed of government representatives to vet the work of the Special Procedures. This issue remains an unfinished agenda that may reappear; it will test the independence of the Special Procedures to advocate on behalf of the victims. Moreover, the Code remains weak on the need to have States responding cooperatively with the special procedures. In reality, many countries still refuse to invite mandate holders into the country – or simply decline to respond to their requests for entry. The call by the mandate holders to have standing invitations to visit has only responded to by some. On another front, some countries refuse to cooperate with the mandate holders by failing to respond to their communications and/or by ignoring their recommendations. The devil is, of course, in the details.

On another front, the next phase will be to see how the Council can address situations in a broader manner – broader than the to-date concentration on Israel and the Occupied Palestinian Territories. In future, the UPR also will begin, and the mandates of the Special Procedures will be reviewed in due course.[24]

---

23 The draft resolution on the Code was tendered by Algeria: Human Rights Council Res. A/HRC/5/L.3/Rev.1, June 2007.

24 The mandates of the Special Procedures are to be reviewed in future; pending that, mandate holders remain in their position, subject to the six-year maximum for their terms. See also General Assembly Res. 60/251, March 2006, which states that the Human Rights Council 'shall assume, review and, where necessary, improve and rationalize all mandates, mechanisms, functions and responsibilities of the Commission on Human Rights, in order to maintain a system of special procedures, expert advice and a complaint procedure; the Council shall complete this review within one year after the holding of its first session'.

The Democracy Fund

Meanwhile, the Democracy Fund is beginning its operations. An update of its work (May 2007) notes as follows:

> First Round of Projects
> 1303 projects were received online amounting to US$447 million. The proposals were examined and shortlisted by the PCG and submitted to the Board, who recommended 125 projects to the Secretary General (SG). The SG approved a package worth US$36 million, covering all regions. The largest share has been allocated to Sub-Saharan Africa (37%). Over 60% of recommended projects were submitted by civil society organizations, 24% by UN agencies and 14% by governmental or regional organizations, most often in partnership with one another. Funded projects promote civic education, electoral support and political parties (28%), democratic dialogue and constitutional processes (26%), civil society empowerment (16%), accountability, transparency and integrity (16%), human rights and fundamental freedoms (9%) and access to information (6%). Disbursement was implemented during the first quarter of 2007).[25]

The Fund has also held meetings with many partners, such as the African Governance Forum and the Inter-Parliamentary Union. Incidentally, it does not promote a particular model of democracy.

Concluding Remarks

From the angle of improvement of UN operations and management, recent reforms from 2006 include the following:

- adopting new accountancy standards and granting the Secretary General limited budgetary discretion;
- delivery of the Secretary General's High Level Panel on UN System-wide Coherence in relation to development, humanitarian assistance and the environment with the message of 'delivering as one' for a more coherent UN structure at the country level;
- strengthening the internal controls of the UN procurement system and establishment of a new unit to improve vendor diversification;
- in 2007, reform on the Administration of Justice at the UN, setting up a decentralized system of administration of justice in two tiers and with a decentralized office of the Ombudsman;
- in 2007 reform to unify the security management system.

25 UNDEF Latest Update 2007.

Much also depends upon implementation through a more cohesive system at the national and local level. Thus the 'one UN' approach is being tested in various countries in the humanitarian field. The Outcome Document also opens the door to more collaboration with regional organizations and a broad range of stakeholders at the national level, including civil society and the private sector.

Yet, in retrospect, it may seem ironic that the incisive words of 'We the Peoples', entrenched semantically in the UN Charter, pose perhaps the greatest challenge still to the UN as a system – for the organization remains primarily an inter-governmental body, with few channels for civil society participation. None of the major organs of the UN draw directly from the populations at large. There is no Assembly of the Peoples, and access of non-governmental organizations and related actors to the UN is more often than not limited to those which are accredited to the UN.

Thus the 2005 Reform can only be seen as a small though significant packaged beginning. It remains a modest affair when set against the backdrop of what the UN could represent from the prism of 'We the Peoples'. The real institutional revolution will never take place in the UN unless it can make the quantum leap to become less of a (United?) Forum for States, and more of a Society of Nations (beyond States). Intractable perhaps; impossible maybe; there remains the yearning that that pinnacle of international organizations should embody, indeed personify, more meaningfully the aspirations, representation and participation 'of the peoples, by the peoples and for the peoples'.

References

Books, Articles and Chapters in Books

International Service for Human Rights (ISHR) and Friedrich Ebert Stiftung (FES) (2006), *A New Chapter for Human Rights: A Handbook on Issues of Transition from the Commission on Human Rights to the Human Rights Council* (Geneva: ISHR and FES).

Official Documents and Others

UN (2006a), *Delivering as One: Report of the Secretary General's High Level Panel* (New York: UN).

UN (2006b), *Investing in the United Nations for a Stronger Organization Worldwide* (New York: UN).

Internet-based References

UN Reforms <http://www.unreformabibliography.htm>.

Chapter 5
Legitimization of Measures to Secure Effectiveness in UN Peacekeeping: The Role of Chapter VII of the UN Charter

Hironobu Sakai

Introduction

One of the main purposes of the United Nations is the maintenance of the international peace and security, and this purpose should undoubtedly reflect one of the most important of public interests in the international community.[1] Although the United Nations introduced this system as a means to achieve collective security, it is a well-known fact that it could not operate during the Cold War period. The system did not function well partly because of the political, ideological and military confrontations between United States and Soviet Union, and partly because there existed too great a disproportion of military and economic capabilities among nations in the contemporary world. Despite this difficulty in the field of international peace and security, the United Nations has succeeded in creating a unique peacekeeping function in order to compensate for the dysfunction of the collective security system.[2] In examining the effectiveness of these peacekeeping operations, this chapter analyzes the functioning of the system that regulates them.

UN peacekeeping forces have been utilized in various disputes since the Suez Crisis,[3] when the international community first paid great attention to them. Many of the disputes to which the peacekeeping operations have been dispatched are interstate conflicts; their purpose has been to act as a buffer between parties in dispute, with the mandate of monitoring ceasefire and separation of forces, and building enough confidence between the hostile parties to enable a peaceful

1 Since the regime of the UN collective security theoretically obliges States to act in the interest of a common value, the preservation of peace (Wolfrum 2006, 1093).

2 Virally 1972, 483.

3 On historical overview of UN peacekeeping operations during the Cold War, Durch (ed.) 1993. For the effectiveness of traditional UN peacekeeping operations during the Cold War, Leurdijk 1988, 311–317.

settlement of the dispute.[4] Moreover, the fundamental principles of the operations have been constructed through the accumulated experience of their activities, in concert with rules of general international law.[5] It is important in this regard to note that UN peacekeeping has been looked upon not as an action under Chapter VII of the UN Charter, but as non-compulsory character, unlike the collective security system.[6]

After the Cold War, however, UN peacekeeping changed greatly.[7] Many international disputes took on the character of civil wars and the mandate of the activity expanded correspondingly. For example, under Chapter VII of the UN Charter, UN peacekeeping forces intervened in former Yugoslavia conflicts as well as in the Somali crisis. These two peacekeeping forces, the UN Peacekeeping Force (UNPROFOR) and the second UN Operation in Somalia (UNOSOM II), could not effectively carry out their mandate and ended in a failure; consequently, the UN peacekeeping operation as a whole temporarily entered a dark period in the latter 1990s. Since the end of the 1990s, UN peacekeeping forces have maintained an especially close relationship with the activities of multinational forces, and UN peacekeeping operations have been deployed in many places again under Chapter VII of the UN Charter.

This chapter will first confirm the mandate and fundamental principles of traditional peacekeeping operations, and then, in considering the background and the appearance of peacekeeping under Chapter VII of the UN Charter after the Cold War, examine how current peacekeeping operations have renewed the system and (re)arranged their fundamental principles in order to effectively carry out their new mandate.

---

4 Higgins applies 'peacekeeping' to the operations in which personnel owing allegiance to the United Nations are engaged in military or paramilitary duties; and/or carrying weapons for their own defence in the pursuit of duties designated by the United Nations as necessary for the maintenance or restoration of peace (Higgins 1969, ix). See also: Franck 1985, 168.

5 United Nations Emergency Force: Summary Study of the Experience Derived from the Establishment and Operation of the Force, U.N.Doc.A/3943, paras. 154–193; Siekmann 1991, 3–7.

6 *Certain Expenses of the United Nations (Article 17, paragraph 2, of the Charter), Advisory Opinion of 20 July 1962, I.C.J. Reports 1962*, 171–172. With regard to this point, UN peacekeeping operations require the consent of the State parties. For the consent of States concerned in traditional UN peacekeeping operations, Manin 1971.

7 Fetherston 1994, 20–44.

Significance and Limitations of Traditional UN Peacekeeping Operations

Mandate and Fundamental Principles of Traditional Peacekeeping Operation

During the Cold War, traditional UN peacekeeping performed a key role as part of the main function of the United Nations. It is beyond doubt that this operation has replaced the UN collective security system, which could never fulfill its function due to the confrontation between the superpowers, and has contributed to the settlement of disputes by restraining the escalation of conflicts.[8] UN peacekeeping forces and military observer missions have been sent to conflict areas in the public interest of the international community for controlling small-scale armed conflicts, while receiving personnel, material and financial supports from UN member states (for the concept of peacekeeping, see Diehl 1993, 4–14). In this sense, UN peacekeeping has taken on the character of a public system in maintaining international peace and security, and has also acquired legitimacy within the UN system itself owing to its legality with respect to the rules of the UN Charter.[9]

The mandate of traditional peacekeeping includes the deployment of military units to local areas with the agreement of the countries concerned for controlling conflicts, preventing situations from deteriorating and contributing to a peaceful settlement of disputes through the neutral character of the UN. The operations cannot be mandatory due to their neutral character under non Chapter VII, and therefore offer limited help towards the achievement of 'passive peace' as a buffer between the disputing parties. The fundamental principles of peacekeeping theoretically reflect the character of such activities, and have been clarified through practice. These are known to include three main principles: the consent principle, the neutrality and impartiality principle, and the self-defence principle. Typically, traditional peacekeeping operations work as follows: the peacekeeping forces obtain the consent of the countries concerned for deployments to the respective areas and to perform military operations such as ceasefire monitoring from a neutral and even-handed position, using force only for self-defence.[10]

On what conditions could these fundamental principles be formed and why could such traditional peacekeeping operations make certain contributions to the maintenance of international peace and security during the Cold War? First, traditional peacekeeping only targeted small armed conflicts between states. Moreover, the conflicts did not relate directly to the interests of the superpowers but generally occurred in marginal regions. This means that the parties involved could be easily identified and any contingent collisions could be avoided as much as possible through the established chain of command and control and by the parties to the conflicts through exercising effective control over their respective

8 But Cassese 1986, 226–227, points out that it 'may turn out to be counter-productive' as well.

9 Skjelsbaek 1990, 63–65.

10 Suy 1998, 548–558.

territories. However, the ability of the peacekeeping forces to respect these fundamental principles in a civil war was quite limited, as was made very clear during the civil war in Congo in the 1960s.[11]

Second, it should be pointed out that the mandate of traditional peacekeeping was limited to the exercise of the interposed and neutral functions, such as ceasefire monitoring. The main purpose of this activity is to deploy forces in the area between the parties in dispute and to defuse the tensions between them. Therefore, it does not involve engaging the disputing parties as an enemy or assuming military power as a means of solving the problem. In addition, traditional peacekeeping does not interfere in the domestic affairs of the parties. Instead, it builds confidence for a peaceful settlement of the dispute by temporarily maintaining a tranquil situation. This activity aims only at the achievement of 'passive peace' without any armed clashes.[12]

These basic conditions – the character of the dispute, the content of its mandate and the values which should be realized through it for the international community – may have been affected as the situation changed, and this evolution could have influenced the application of the fundamental principles that regulate UN peacekeeping activities.[13] The situation actually came to pass with the end of the Cold War.

Changes in the Nature of Disputes after the Cold War and Difficulties for the UN Peacekeeping in its Aftermath

Transformation and Evaluation of UN Peacekeeping UN peacekeeping experienced a crisis during the conflicts in the former Yugoslavia and the Somali civil war in the first half of the 1990s. In each of these two cases the dispute was in the nature of a civil war and humanitarian aid was indispensable due to the deterioration of the living environment of the resident populations.[14] In addition, the mandate of the peacekeeping operations in these crises exceeded the basic aim of reducing combat and maintaining peace, and also included political settlement of the dispute itself.[15] For effective performance of a mandate expanded in such a manner, it was necessary to consider the use of military enforcement measures based on Chapter VII. The UN peacekeeping operations in the former Yugoslavia as well as in Somalia were among the first instances.

11 Abi-Saab 1978.

12 Malitza 1987, 239.

13 The changing values in international community after the end of the Cold War, as will seen later, may reflect the enlargement of the concept 'threat to peace' in the area of international security, especially under Chapter VII of the UN Charter. For the enlargement of the concept and its influence on the UN peacekeeping functions, Österdal 1998; Sorel 1995, 3–57.

14 Roberts 1995, 7–28.

15 Kühne 1993, 51.

In these operations, stronger measures were needed for accomplishing the mandate, especially to ensure the security of the personnel and workers engaging in humanitarian activities. These were military actions based on Chapter VII of the UN Charter, and brought about a collision with the self-defence principle, on which traditional peacekeeping operations are generally based. For example, UNOSOM II developed as a 'peace enforcement' activity in the Somali civil war and was authorized to take military action under Chapter VII to secure ceasefire monitoring, the transportation of humanitarian goods and to disarm the parties.[16] Since broadly authorized to take military action under Chapter VII, as a result of the expansion of its mandate, without any consent of the parties concerned, UNOSOM II itself became involved as a party in the armed conflict.[17] In the former Yugoslavia conflict, while a main purpose of invoking Chapter VII in the relevant resolutions about UNPROFOR was to secure the safety and freedom of movement of UNPROFOR personnel, the expansion of its mandate without any regard to the intention of the parties concerned created an increasing possibility of military action by UNPROFOR, and UNPROFOR finally became a party concerned in the armed conflict, as in the case of UNOSOM II.[18]

Many of conflicts after the Cold War, as seen in former Yugoslavia and Somalia, have been of the nature of civil war, where non-state entities are parties concerned and the international community has been specially requested to handle the humanitarian issues (Abi-Saab 1995, 7). At first, UN peacekeeping forces tried to deal with these situations by revising the fundamental principles governing their activities. The validity of their activities was still based on the United Nations system and they aimed at securing the effectiveness of their operations by partly revising the traditional fundamental principles. However, the objective conditions that would be the main factors in securing their effectiveness, i.e., the preconditions for the application of the traditional fundamental principles – conflicts between states, consent and the cooperation by the parties concerned, and the effective control of the territories by parties concerned, etc. – have unfortunately been lost. Finally, permission for military action under Chapter VII was requested by multinational forces as a means to secure the effectiveness in performing their mandate and for securing the safety of their personnel. This shows a 'subcontracting' to multinational forces or regional organization forces

16 White 1994, 158. For peace enforcement unit, Agenda for Peace. Preventive Diplomacy, Peacemaking and Peace-Keeping. Reports of the Secretary-General pursuant to the Statement adopted by the Summit Meeting of the Security Council on 31 January 1992, U.N.Doc.A/47/277-S/24111, para.44.

17 For the reality and evaluation of UNOSOM II, Durch 1997, 326–351.

18 On the use of force by UNPROFOR, see Christakis 1996, 151–186. For the applicability of the fundamental principles in these cases, Meijer 1994, 63–87; Brown 1994, 559–602.

through Chapter VII.[19] While the validity of the activities under the United Nations system as well as the effectiveness of the performance of the mandate in these 'subcontract' operations was attempted through Chapter VII, the reality is that effective control over these operations did not depend upon the UN but on the leading participating states of the multinational forces.[20]

From UN Peacekeeping Forces to Multinational Forces

Thus, it was seen in the middle of the 1990s that the exercise of forcible military measures was important for the security of the personnel in peacekeeping operations and to effectively secure the observance of the parties to the peace agreement. Furthermore, it became clear that the UN unfortunately lacked the will and ability to actively exercise mandatory power under Chapter VII in most intra-state conflicts.[21] It is against such a background that multinational military activities appeared in the later 1990s.[22]

It is possible and necessary to distinguish the two kinds of multinational forces operations. One is an operation to secure the implementation of a peace agreement through the use of force under Chapter VII of the UN Charter. A typical example is the Implementation Force (IFOR) and the Stabilization Force (SFOR), which deployed under the leadership of the North Atlantic Treaty Organization (NATO) in Bosnia-Herzegovina after the conclusion of the Dayton Peace Agreement. This operation premised the possibility of the use of force under Chapter VII as a means of implementing the agreement depending on the consent to it by the parties to the agreement. It is also important in this regard to note that whether an action by force was impartial was judged not by the parties but with reference to equal implementation of the Agreement and to equal securing of it by the multinational forces.[23]

The second type is the kind of a multinational force similar to the UN peacekeeping force used for humanitarian purposes, e.g., the Multinational Protection Force in Albania in April 1997 and the Mission interafricane chargée de surveiller l'application des Accords de Bangui (MISAB), deployed in the Central African Republic in August 1997. Both these forces began to operate as the background in the humanitarian crisis as well as disorder in the respective

---

19 Weiss (ed.) 1998. For the differences between a multinational forces or 'coalitions of the willing' approach and a regional forces approach, both of which are decentralized approach to enforcement action, Wilson 2003, 89–106.

20 Lagrange 1999, 52.

21 Berdal 1993, 31.

22 In this case, the mandates of multinational forces which are authorized to use force may also include peacekeeping tasks so that the concept of peacekeeping and these multinational forces might not always fully distinguishable (Blokker 2005, 15).

23 Sarooshi 1999, 272–281.

areas, and the impartiality of their activities, which were aimed at improving the humanitarian situation, was particularly emphasized.[24]

It should be noted that UN peacekeeping operations respected their traditional essential principles again and restricted their own mandate to the original ones because of the failure in Somalia and in the former Yugoslavia. Therefore, they shared the mandate in maintaining international peace and security with multinational forces within the framework of the UN Charter. While multinational forces were to be deployed when the use of force should be required to perform their mandate under Chapter VII, UN peacekeeping operations were sent only when they did not have to use the force to implement their mandate.

It is not a coincidence that the actions of the multinational forces gained precedence over UN peacekeeping operations at that time. The main reason multinational forces were on the rise was because the UN peacekeeping forces did not have any means for the effective implementation of their own mandate, in spite of their diversification after the Cold War.[25] In addition to this factor, however, there were also positive factors that favoured the use of multinational forces.

First, the tendency of some regional organizations to look for opportunities to exercise a peacekeeping function has surfaced, particularly in the 1990s. NATO, for instance, originally a military alliance for collective self-defence against the communist bloc countries, has reconsidered its *raison d'être* after the Cold War structure collapsed, and has turned to the exercise of peacekeeping functions in order to maintain the peace of Europe as a whole. This transformation by NATO of its security policy led to its military activities in Bosnia-Herzegovina.[26] The European Union has also made efforts to improve its peacekeeping functions by making political and diplomatic integration one of its objectives and by establishing an original standby force system. This effort was realized as the Operation Artemis in the Democratic Republic of Congo in 2004.[27]

Second, some states had their own interests in regional conflicts, along with the will and ability to send their troops as leading countries within the multinational forces. In the Albanian crisis, Italy – fearing a refugee outflow into its own territory – initiated the dispatch of a multinational force for the restoration of order and humanitarian purposes there[28]. In the Central African Republic, France,

24 Kritsiotis 1999, 534–535; Castillo 1998, 246–252.

25 It may be rather safer to say that '[A]d hoc multinational or regional organizations' capabilities to deploy military forces are sometimes more effective tools to ensure compliance or provide robust peacekeeping' (Smith 2002, 101).

26 For the change of NATO's strategy in 1990s, Rearden 1995, 71–92; Gazzini 2001, 412–415. See also: Leurdijk 1994, which describes the operations by NATO in Yugoslavia.

27 Bagayoko 2004, 101–116.

28 Letter dated 27 March 1997 from the Permanent Representative of Italy to the United Nations Addressed to the Secretary-General, U.N.Doc.S/1997/258. But see also Kostakos and Bourantonis 1998, 56.

a former colonial power, made an effort to repress the civil war with the aid of some francophone African countries.[29] Since the end of the 1990s, the number of civil war has increased and the deterioration and aggravation of the situation in Africa has forced former colonial powers to deploy their troops and has thus led to the intervention through multinational forces in these conflicts.[30]

It is important to note that such multinational forces have been set up through Security Council resolutions referring to Chapter VII, which authorizes the use of force. This point is crucial because 'peacekeeping' by multinational forces might pose a challenge to the public interests of the international community if the arbitrariness of states participating in those forces interfered in the implementation process, without the authorization by the Security Council (SC). Having been established to implement the mandate that the UN peacekeeping forces should have implemented, the multinational forces have been authorized to use force under Chapter VII, through which these operations have been able to secure the effectiveness of accomplishing the mandate and to procure the legitimacy of their activities within the UN system.[31]

The Role of Chapter VII of the UN Charter in Peacekeeping and Its Evaluation

Emergence of the UN 'Robust' Peacekeeping

While multinational force activities developed in the later half of the 1990s, UN peacekeeping operations began to decline. UN peacekeeping, however, has developed again since the end of the 1990s. Moreover, one of the main features of the current UN peacekeeping forces is that their activities are based on Chapter VII.[32] The situation raises two questions: why are the UN peacekeeping operations back in the spotlight at this time, and whether the link between Chapter VII of the UN Charter and UN peacekeeping should be regarded as the same situation UN peacekeeping found itself in during the first half of the 1990s, i.e., peace enforcement action.

29 Mbadinga 2001, 23–24.

30 Especially for the recent intervening activities by powerful states to African states during the first half of the 1990s, Berdal 1998, 49–79.

31 Sarooshi 1999, 233, though this 'authorization model' in multinational forces has some problems, in particular on the control by the Security Council over their operations (Blokker 2000, 560–567).

32 Main 'robust' UN peacekeeping operations under Chapter VII of UN Charter are as follows; UNAMSIL; UNTAET; MONUC; UNMIL; UNOCI; MINUSTAH; ONUB; UNMIS. The Brahimi Report also calls for more robust rules of engagement in operations involving intra-state conflicts, but notably it still deals with UN peacekeeping operations under non Chapter VII (Report of the Panel on United Nations Peace Operations, U.N.Doc. A/55/305-S/2000/809). See also Williams and Bellamy 2007, 6–10.

With regard to the new UN peacekeeping operations falling under Chapter VII, it is necessary to examine their development with reference to their relationship with the multinational forces. As we have seen, one of the crucial conditions that permit multinational forces to deploy in conflict areas is that a leading country has material national interest in the conflict and also has a strong willingness to exercise its own military capabilities on the ground. Therefore, a multinational force would not necessarily be established promptly if a leading country did not have sufficient interest in sending in its troops, even if it had the military capacity to manage the multinational force. It is also difficult for just a few countries to indefinitely manage the force in accomplishing its multidimensional mandate, because of the militarily and financially heavy burdens, even after the multinational force has been deployed successfully. Various suggestions have been made to improve this situation – regional problems should be left to the region and regional peacekeeping forces should be promoted by regional organizations with financial and technical help from the international community. Moreover, UN peacekeeping forces should be used to share the heavy burden of the military activities by the multinational forces with the international community as a whole. To accomplish its multidimensional mandate, the UN peacekeeping needs to employ 'robust' means like the multinational forces themselves and this easily leads to a common understanding in the international community that a new UN peacekeeping force should be authorized to use force under Chapter VII.[33]

However, it is necessary to pay attention to the fact that this type of UN peacekeeping has certain features that are different from the UN peace enforcement activities that developed in the first half of the 1990s, though they do have in common the fact that the actions were authorized under Chapter VII: military action beyond self-defence. In the case of recent peacekeeping forces, for instance, all parties concerned usually set out the speed and area of troop deployment and the timetable for the peacemaking process in the peace agreements, which clearly provide for the roles of the peacekeeping force, such as Disarmament, Demobilization and Rehabilitation (DDR), to accomplish this relatively new mandate. This means that no fresh mandate should be given to the UN peacekeeping forces without the consent of the parties to the dispute, in order to prevent the mandate from expanding incrementally with the evolution of the situation.[34] It can be pointed out, moreover, that one of the features is that the parties concerned agree in peace agreements or in any peace negotiating process that the UN peacekeeping force deployed in the conflict area be able to conduct any action under Chapter VII. In this case, the parties give a general consent to the UN peacekeepers for the use of force beyond self-defence when they face with any

33 Bellamy, Williams and Griffin 2003, 211–229.

34 Isselé 2001, 794–795.

obstruction to the accomplishment of their mandate or any violation of the peace agreement.[35]

Appraisal of Chapter VII of UN Charter in UN Peacekeeping

Most 'robust' UN peacekeeping operations are authorized to take military action under Chapter VII of the UN Charter.[36] It should be asked whether and, if any, how this fact has influenced on the application of the fundamental principles of traditional UN peacekeeping operations to the respective cases.

As for the consent principle, while there are some cases to which this principle did not apply, such as the UN Iraq–Kuwait Observer Mission (UNIKOM) and the UN Transitional Authority in Eastern Slavonia, Baranja and Western Sirmium (UNTAES), the peculiarities of these cases should be considered. UNIKOM was an activity under the special situation of the Gulf War in which the UN exercised military and non-military enforcement measures against Iraq under Chapter VII.[37] In the case of UNTAES, there is the background that the Croatian government had opposed the prolongation of any interim rule by the UN for a transitional period until the area in question was incorporated into Croatia again.[38] Thus, in these two missions, Chapter VII of the UN Charter was invoked to deal with their respective circumstances. Apart from these exceptions, it should be kept in mind that in most recent UN peacekeeping operations, the parties concerned must give their consent not only to the deployment of the missions in the field but also to the content of their mandate and its manner of implementation. They have given their prior consent to the use of force by the UN peacekeeping forces under Chapter VII through the peace agreement. This means that the occurrence of local military actions by the UN peacekeepers, if any, would not constitute the collapse of the cease-fire agreement as a whole.[39]

The impartial nature of recent UN peacekeeping operations implies not only a passive meaning of non-interference to the domestic affairs of local countries but also a positive meaning of reasonable performance of the mandate provided in the peace agreements. The principle of impartiality may be interpreted in such

35 The Lome Peace Agreement (U.N.Doc.S/1999/777, Annex) for UNAMSIL, the Lusaka Ceasefire Agreement (U.N.Doc.S/1999/815, Annex) for MONUC, the Accra Peace Agreement (U.N.Doc.S/2003/850, Annex) for UNMIL, the Linas-Marcoussis Agreement (U.N.Doc.S/2003/99, Annex) for UNOCI, are respectively concluded to that effect.

36 UNMEE is an exceptional operation. It provided sufficiently robust rules of engagement, but for a Chapter VI mission. U.N.Doc.S/RES/1320 (2000). Romses 2001, 119.

37 U.N.Doc.S/RES/687 (1991), op.para. 5; U.N.Doc.S/RES/689 (1991), op.para. 2; Report of the Secretary-General on the Implementation of Paragraph 5 of Security Council Resolution 687 (1991), U.N.Doc.S/22454, para. 16.

38 U.N.Doc.A/50/757-S/1995/951, Annex, para.1; U.N.Doc.S/RES/1037 (1996). Gray 1996, 265–269.

39 Sakai 2004, 237–278.

a way to be adapted to the legal execution and effective implementation by UN peacekeeping operations as an expansion of their mandate of the DDR and so on.[40]

Thus, the introduction of Chapter VII of the UN Charter has in fact influenced these principles of traditional UN peacekeeping. Nevertheless, it must be the self-defence principle on which Chapter VII has had the most crucial influence among three fundamental principles. According to the traditional principle, self-defence includes in the strict sense protection of the security of the personnel and in its wider sense the minimum military action necessary to implement its mandate.[41] The reason why Chapter VII has been invoked in the relevant resolution of recent UN peacekeeping is to permit the expanded scope of self-defence in both the strict and wider sense. While in the strict sense the main object of the self-defence is to protect the lives of personnel, it is also important to secure the safety and freedom of movement of personnel, as well as to protect civilians from physical dangers that have been present in the recent UN peacekeeping. Therefore, there is a tendency for the use of force by UN peacekeepers to expand not only to the personnel of the mission but also to civilians in the conflicts and for the UN to justify these activities by Chapter VII rather than dealing with them within the limits of self-defence. In the wider sense, it originally includes an element that may broaden the possibility of military action as the expanded mandate of the UN peacekeeping operation, and this element has operated and actualized the use of force in the recent development of UN peacekeeping.[42]

Securing the Effective Implementation of the Mandate under Chapter VII of the UN Charter

Reasons for Introducing Chapter VII of the UN Charter The reason Chapter VII of the UN Charter has been referred to in Security Council resolutions, under which UN peacekeeping operations are established, is not because they have tried to exclude any consent of the parties concerned or to give a compulsory character to the operations. In any UN peacekeeping operation, the exclusion of consent by the parties concerned through the application of Chapter VII, especially to its territorial deployment, has been limited to extremely exceptional cases. Thus, nearly all recent UN peacekeeping operations under Chapter VII have respected the consent principle regarding their activities and have not changed into actions

40 On the relations between the principle of impartiality and the UN peacekeeping operations, Tsagourias 2007, 478–481. After the end of the Cold War, the UN peacekeeping operations were expected to be more ‘impartial’ than ‘neutral’, ‘in the sense that it was expected to develop certain standards which it applied equally to all parties’ (Aksu 2003, 94).

41 Von Grünigen 1978, 138.

42 Cox 1999, 239–273. For the use of force by UN peacekeeping force in general, Findlay 2002.

that are involuntary in character with respect to the parties concerned.

Then why has UN peacekeeping organized again under Chapter VII of the UN Charter? Three reasons are suggested.

First, UN peacekeeping operations have been under pressure by necessity to strengthen their military response toward any harmful acts against the security of their personnel. In the process of verifying whether the parties are observing the peace agreements, UN peacekeeping forces have sustained attacks with great frequency. This is partly because the parties concerned may be so diverse in a dispute that those who are not in favour of implementing the peace agreement may prevent the peacekeepers from performing their mandate, and partly because the instructions to observe the peace agreement given by leaders of the parties concerned cannot reach the rank and file if the chain of command and control is weak. It is natural for the troop-contributing countries to request that the UN provide a legal basis to secure the safety of UN peacekeeping personnel likely to be exposed to such dangers. Most African countries, especially those in which UN peacekeeping forces are deployed, have strongly demanded that the UN authorize its peacekeeping forces to use the force under Chapter VII of the UN Charter to protect the personnel sent by them. In other words, when troop-contributing countries call upon the UN not to take any military action, Chapter VII would not be necessarily referred to in the establishment resolution of a UN peacekeeping operation. Thus, in deciding to participate in the UN Mission in Eritrea and Ethiopia (UNMEE), the Netherlands, which was expected to be a main troop-contributing country, assumed that this mission would be an operation that was not under Chapter VII due to the public reaction to Chapter VII that originated with the tragedy in Srebrenica.[43]

Second, it is significant that the objectives of UN peacekeeping force have expanded. The mandate of recent UN peacekeeping has become so diversified, including the support of humanitarian assistance activities, that it has also covered the protection of personnel and workers engaged in such activities. In addition, civilians have become more involved in domestic armed conflicts, which has generated a large amount of refugees and internally displaced persons. In the face of such a situation, UN peacekeeping operations have fulfilled such mandates as the protection, return and resettlement of refugees and internally displaced persons. The UN peacekeeping operations, thus, have to use force in order to repulse attacks by the powers opposed to such activities and to protect the workers engaged in the humanitarian assistance activities as along with the civilians, including refugee and internally displaced persons. Since such expansion of objectives for the protected persons could cause tensions between the self-defence principle and the use of force for the protection of civilians, Chapter VII was used to expand the legal limits for the use of force.[44]

43 Sakai 2002, 56–57; Both 2000.

44 McNamara 2006, 199.

Third, situations have arisen in which recent UN peacekeeping forces have acquired the authority to use force under Chapter VII of the UN Charter by fulfilling the mandate and its means of implementation by a preceding multinational force. Today, most multinational forces or regional organizational forces have some relationship with UN peacekeeping forces.[45] There are many cases where the main troop-contributing countries have some historical, political and economic relation to the conflict regions to which their own troops are dispatched, and they usually have the military capability to promptly deploy their military troops to the conflict areas and to repress and control the armed conflicts. Therefore, in the first stage, multinational forces may be immediately deployed upon the outbreak of armed conflict in order to confine it, with the result that the parties to a dispute may conclude a cease-fire agreement, some provisions of which the multinational forces would implement through the use of force until the UN peacekeeping forces come and succeed them. These activities by multinational forces under Chapter VII, in spite of achieving the intended effect on conflicts at the early stage, require support of the international community as a whole in the long term as much of the burden falls on the troop-contributing countries. This is because a lot of personnel, as well as material and financial resources, must be poured into these activities to operate them effectively, even with the legal justification by Chapter VII of the UN Charter. Therefore, the deployment of UN peacekeeping forces, which enjoy the trust of the international community, is requested in such cases. It is preferable for the UN peacekeeping forces to have a mandate and means of implementation similar to that of the multinational forces, so that a smooth adjustment from the preceding multinational to the UN peacekeeping forces may be accomplished.[46] Thus, authorization for the use of force under Chapter VII must be obtained from perspective of maintaining the continuity of their activities.

Evaluation of the Introduction of Chapter VII

As mentioned above, the necessity for effective implementation of the mandate exists in the background that the action under Chapter VII of the UN Charter has been introduced into UN peacekeeping operations. The problem is how such an action has been made use of and what role it has played under Chapter VII.

It can be confirmed that the introduction of an action under Chapter VII shares a close relationship with the changes and diversification of the mandate of UN peacekeeping operations. While the main role of traditional peacekeeping is to observe and monitor ceasefire agreements as a buffer between the parties, the mandate for recent UN peacekeeping operations is related to nation-building activities, such as dispute management, governance, law enforcement activities,

45 As the deployment of multinational forces followed by UN peacekeeping forces, for instance, INTERFET (UNTAET), ECOMIL (UNMIL), ECOMICI (UNOCI).

46 The transition from INTERFET to UNTAET is a good example (Colley 2002, 65–70).

etc. The interest of the international community in UN peacekeeping has shifted from the maintenance of 'passive peace' to the creation and achievement of 'positive peace'.[47] In other words, the shift in viewpoint towards regarding peace as the public interest of the international community has synchronized with the introduction of peacekeeping action under Chapter VII of the UN Charter parallel to the recent enlargement of the threat to peace.[48]

In recent peace or cease-fire agreements, the parties usually give their comprehensive consent to the content of the nation-building program, such as the DDR, separation of powers, national reconciliation and presidential and parliament elections, etc. on one hand, and on the other increasingly agree to authorize the UN peacekeeping forces, intended to monitor and perform such programs, to use force under Chapter VII in order to implement the agreements, as well as to restore law and order. In recent UN peacekeeping operations, action under Chapter VII of the UN Charter has been permitted only for certain limited purposes and not comprehensively and arbitrarily. It should be noted that the parties agree, in advance, on the purposes and the method of achieving them. Such general agreements concerning the nation-building program and the means of its implementation can be confirmed in several recent cases in Africa, such as Sierra Leone, Liberia, Côte d'Ivoire and the Democratic Republic of Congo. In fact, the current situation is that the main contents of the peace agreements, the reduction of the conflicts among nations and the shift from ceasefires to the nation-building process, have been achieved through fulfillment of mandate by UN peacekeeping forces, with limited military action.

Slightly different from those operations, action under Chapter VII of the UN Charter may be referred to in resolutions establishing UN transitional authorities. This refers to the permission for military action by the multinational forces in the case of Kosovo (KFOR) and the permission for military action by the United Nations Transitional Authority for East Timor (UNTAET).[49] From a different viewpoint, however, it is also possible to regard it as the role of Chapter VII to deal with certain problems peculiar to the transitional administration,[50] since such an administration by the UN and the consent of the ruled to its participation in the political process, along with its role in dispute management and nation-building, are indispensable.[51] These cases show that the UN transitional authority has tried to base the source of its power to enact laws and apply them to the population on Chapter VII, if they do not consent to such an administration, but only with the consent of a former ruling government.[52] However, it should not be overlooked

47 White 2002, 161–165. On the relationship between UN peacekeeping operation on the one hand, and nation building and so on, on the other, Azimi and Lin 2006.

48 Schrijver 2006, 9–10; Wellens 2003, 53.

49 On the analysis of these Transitional Administrations, Stahn 2001, 105–183.

50 Ruffert 2001, 613–631; Matheson 2001, 83–85.

51 Generally, see Fox 2004, 69–84.

52 De Hoogh 2001, 1–41.

that the transitional authority has also made great efforts to involve the population in the political process in order to obtain the consent of the ruled.[53] Thus, action under Chapter VII is used as a means for procuring the validity of the transitional administration and practical attempts have been made to secure the actual consent of the inhabitants by reflecting their will in the political process.[54]

Thus, action under Chapter VII of the UN Charter may contribute to secure the effectiveness of UN peacekeeping operations, namely, the performance of their mandate by the military action and the implementation of the peace agreements. At the same time, Chapter VII of the UN Charter in itself may provide UN peacekeeping operations with legal validity and legitimacy, e.g., the legality of the military action and the validity of the UN transitional administration, instead of the implied power doctrine, on which traditional UN peacekeeping has long relied for its lawfulness.[55] It is true, in principle, that the understanding and the consent by the parties concerned are crucial so that UN peacekeeping operations may succeed in the accomplishment of their mandate. To secure their effectiveness and legitimacy, however, Chapter VII of the UN Charter has an extremely important significance in recent UN peacekeeping operations, since in this case Chapter VII should work well and complement the consent by the parties concerned, and should play a decisive part in establishing the legitimacy of 'robust' UN peacekeeping operations through the effective implementation of their complicated mandate with their possible use of force.[56]

Concluding Remarks

Traditional UN peacekeeping operations have not been considered compatible with action under Chapter VII of the UN Charter. This is because traditional UN peacekeeping operations fulfill their mandate by requiring consent by the parties concerned and restricting their mandate to suspending armed conflicts and relieving the tension between the parties. During the Cold War period, any mandatory enforcement under Chapter VII of the UN Charter was excluded, both on theoretical grounds as well as on the practical and security ones of carrying out such a mandate effectively.

It is true that a change in the character of international disputes after the Cold War and the diversification of the mandate of UN peacekeeping operations corresponding to it have brought about certain revisions to the character of the peacekeeping operations and the fundamental principles of their activities. The

53 Salamun 2004, 146.

54 On the limits of Chapter VII on this subject and the necessity of the participation of the population in the political process, Smyrek 2006, 221–222.

55 For the comprehensive consideration of the legal basis of UN peacekeeping operations, Orakhelashvili 2003, 485–523.

56 Gray 2007, 157; Frowein 2003, 122–123.

introduction of Chapter VII of the UN Charter in these operations aimed to secure effective implementation of the mandate parallel to its diversification. From this viewpoint, a re-interpretation of fundamental principles of the peacekeeping operations has been requested, especially as a means to achieve certain objectives relating to permission for the use of force under Chapter VII. Action under Chapter VII has been regarded as a vehicle to secure the implementation of peace agreements, to secure and protect the safety of peacekeeping personnel and of workers engaged in humanitarian relief efforts, and of civilians who are experiencing humanitarian crisis or are the victims of physical violence.[57]

UN peacekeeping operations have expanded their mandate beyond the eradication of armed conflicts to the maintenance of basic conditions to achieve peace. The design for the new UN peacekeeping operations system through the diversification of their mandate has attempted to realize its objectives of effective implementation through the possible use of force. However, difficulties have been expected in uniting Chapter VII of the UN Charter, which is basically of a coercive character, with UN peacekeeping, which gives importance to consent by the parties to a dispute.[58] It is certainly a dilemma that peace through the nation-building should be realized by the use of force, which is clearly contradictory to peace. These difficulties may have been resolved through comprehensive agreements by the parties concerned to the content of the peace agreements and the means for their implementation. It is on the consent and cooperation of the parties that the main measures for securing the effectiveness of the implementation should be based. However, it should be also noted that the UN peacekeeping forces have been authorized to accomplish their mandate by the use of force under Chapter VII, depending on the circumstances around them.

On the one hand, the international community is able to override the non-intervention principle and to get involved in the conditions for achieving peace, which have expanded even to political, economical and social factors. On the other hand, for the purposes of establishing the infrastructure for achieving those conditions and for protecting UN personnel and civilians, a limited use of force has been permitted to UN peacekeeping forces. Both are objectives that the UN Charter aims to attain from the viewpoint of achieving the public interests of the international community as a whole. The introduction of action under Chapter VII in UN peacekeeping operations shows the new ideas of conferring legitimacy on them as well as of securing the effectiveness of their work by the international community.

57 Månsson 2005, 503–519.

58 Lagrange 2005, 86–92; Ben Achhour 2005, 128.

References

Abi-Saab, G. (1978), *The United Nations Operations in the Congo* (Oxford: Oxford University Press).

Abi-Saab, G. (1995), 'United Nations Peacekeeping Old and New: An Overview of the Issues', in Warner (ed.).

Aksu, E. (2003), *The United Nations, Intra-State Peacekeeping and Normative Change* (Manchester: Manchester University Press).

Ando, N., Nakamura, O. and Ida, R. (eds) (2004), *International Organizations in the 21st Century: Lessons and Prospects* (Toshindo) (in Japanese).

Azimi, N. and Lin, C.L. (eds) (2001), *The Reform Process of United Nations Peace Operations. Debriefing and Lessons* (London: Kluwer Law International).

Azimi, N. and Lin, C.L. (eds) (2002), *The United Nations Transitional Administration in East Timor (UNTAET). Debriefing and Lessons* (Leiden: Martinus Nijhoff Publishers).

Azimi, N. and Lin, C.L. (eds) (2006), *United Nations as Peacekeeper and Nation-Builder. Continuity and Change – What Lies Ahead?* (Leiden: Martinus Nijhoff Publishers).

Bagayoko, N. (2004), 'L'opération Artémis, un tournant pour la politique européenne de sécurité et de defense?' *Afrique contemporaine* 209, 101–116.

Bellamy, A.J., Williams, P. and Griffin, S. (2003), *Understanding Peacekeeping* (Cambridge: Polity).

Ben Achour, R. (2005), 'Des opérations de maintien de la paix aux opérations d'imposition et de consolidation de la paix', in SFDI (ed.).

Berdal, M.R. (1993), *Whither UN Peacekeeping? An Analysis of the Changing Military Requirements of UN Peacekeeping with Proposals for its Enhancement* (Oxford: Oxford University Press).

Berdal, M. (1998), 'Peacekeeping in Africa, 1990–1996: The Role of the United States, France and Britain', in Furley et al. (eds).

Blokker, N. (2000), 'Is the Authorization Authorized? Powers and Practice of the UN Security Council to Authorize the Use of Force by "Coalitions of the Able and Willing"', *European Journal of International Law* 11:3, 541–568.

Blokker, N. (2005), 'The Security Council and the Use of Force – On Recent Practice' in Blokker and Schrijver (eds).

Blokker, N. and Schrijver, N. (eds) (2005), *The Security Council and the Use of Force. Theory and Reality – A Need for Change?* (Leiden: Martinus Nijhoff Publishers).

Boisson de Chazournes, L. and Gowland-Debbas, V. (eds) (2001), *The International Legal System in Quest of Equity and Universality. Liber Amicorum Georges Abi-Saab* (Leiden: Martinus Nijhoff Publishers).

Both, N. (2000), *From Indifference to Entrapment. The Netherlands and the Yugoslav Crisis 1990–1995* (Amsterdam: Amsterdam University Press).

Brown, D. (1994), 'The Role of the United Nations in Peacekeeping and Truce-Monitoring: What are the Applicable Norms', *Revue belge de droit international* 27:2, 559–602.

Cassese, A. (ed.) (1978), *United Nations Peace-Keeping. Legal Essays* (The Hague: Sijthoff & Noordhoff).

Cassese, A. (1986), *International Law in a Divided World* (Oxford: Oxford University Press).

Castillo, M. (1998), 'L'Opération Alba: une réussite pour l'ONU, un bilan mitigé pour l'Union européenne et l'UEO', *Annuaire française de droit international* 44, 243–261.

Christakis, T. (1996), *L'ONU, le Chapitre VII et la crise yougoslave* (Paris: Montchrestien).

Colley, F. (2002), 'A View from the Multi-National Force', in Azimi and Lin (eds).

Cox, K.E. (1999), 'Beyond Self-Defense: United Nations Peacekeeping Operations & the Use of Force', *Denver Journal of International Law & Policy* 27:2, 239–273.

Diehl, P.F. (1993), *International Peacekeeping* (Baltimore: The Johns Hopkins University Press).

Dupuy, P.M., Fassbender, B., Shaw, M.N. and Sommermann, K.P. (eds) (2006), *Völkerrechts als Wertordnung. Common Values in International Law. Festshrift für / Essays in Honour of Christian Tomuschat* (Kehl: N.P.Engel Verlag).

Dupuy, R.J. (ed.) (1998), *Manuel sur les organisations internationales*, 2e éd. (Leiden: Martinus Nijhoff Publishers).

Durch, W.J. (ed.) (1993), *The Evolution of UN Peacekeeping. Case Studies and Comparative Analysis* (New York: St. Martin's Press).

Durch, W.J. (1997), 'Introduction to Anarchy: Humanitarian Intervention and "State-Building" in Somalia', in Durch (ed.).

Durch, W.J. (ed.) (1997), *UN Peacekeeping, American Politics, and the Uncivil Wars of the 1990s* (London: MacMillan).

Fetherston, A.B. (1994), *Towards a Theory of United Nations Peacekeeping* (New York: St. Martin's Press).

Findlay, T. (2002), *The Use of Force in UN Peace Operations* (Oxford: Oxford University Press).

Fox, G. H. (2004), 'Democratization', in Malone (ed.), 69–84.

Franck, T.M. (1985), *Nation Against Nation. What Happened to the U.N. Dream and What the U.S. Can Do About It* (Oxford: Oxford University Press).

Frowein, J. Abr. (2003), 'Issues of Legitimacy around the United Nations Security Council', in Frowein et al. (eds).

Frowein, J. Abr., Scharioth, K., Winkelmann, I. and Wolfrum, R. (eds) (2003), *Verhandeln für den Frieden. Liber Amicorum Tono Eitel* (Berlin: Springer).

Furley, O. and May, R. (eds) (1998), *Peacekeeping in Africa* (Aldershot: Ashgate).

Gazzini, T. (2001), 'NATO Coercive Military Activities in the Yugoslav Crisis (1992–1999)', *European Journal of International Law* 12:3, 391–435.

Gray, C. (1996), 'Host-State Consent and United Nations Peacekeeping in Yugoslavia', *Duke Journal of Comparative and International Law* 7:1, 241–270.

Gray, C. (2007), 'A Crisis of Legitimacy for the UN Collective Security System?', *International and Comparative Law Quarterly* 56:1, 157–170.

Higgins, R. (1969), *United Nations Peacekeeping 1946–1967. Documents and Commentary, I. The Middle East* (Oxford: Oxford University Press).

Hoogh, de A.J.J. (2001), 'Attribution or Delegation of (Legislative) Power by the Security Council? The Case of the United Nations Transitional Administration in East Timor (UNTAET)', *The Yearbook of International Peace Operations* 7, 1–41.

Isselé, J.P. (2001), 'La métamorphose des opérations de maintien de la paix des Nations Unies', in Boisson de Chazournes and Gowland-Debbas (eds).

Kostakos, G. and Bourantonis, D. (1998), 'Innovations in Peace-Keeping: The Case of Albania', *Security Dialogue* 29:1, 49–58.

Kritsiotis, D. (1999), 'Security Council Resolution 1101 (1997) and the Multinational Protection force of Operation Alba in Albania', *Leiden Journal of International Law* 12:3, 511–547.

Ku, C. and Jacobson, H.K. (eds) (2002), *Democratic Accountability and the Use of Force in International Law* (Cambridge: Cambridge University Press).

Kühne, W. (ed.) (1993), *Blauheme in einer turbulenten Welt. Beiträge internationaler Experten zur Fortentwicklung des Völkerrechts und der Vereinten Nationen* (Baden-Baden: Nomos).

Kühne, W. (1993), 'Völkerrecht und Friedenssicherung in einer turbulenten Welt: Eine analytische Zusammenfassung der Grundprobleme und Entwicklungsperspektiven' in Kühne (ed.).

Lagrange, E. (1999), *Les opérations de maintien de la paix et le Chapitre VII de la Charte des Nations Unies* (Paris: Montchrestien).

Lagrange, P. (2005), 'Sécurité collective et exercice par le Conseil de sécurité du système d'autorisation de la coercition', in SFDI (ed.).

Leurdijk, D.A. (1988), 'The Expediency and Effectiveness of UN Peace-Keeping Operations', *Netherlands International Law Review* 35:3, 311–317.

Leurdijk, D.A. (1994), *The United Nations and NATO in Former Yugoslavia. Partners in International Cooperation* (Netherlands Atlantic Commission).

Malitza, M. (1987), 'The Improvement of Effectiveness of United Nations Peacekeeping Operations', in UNITAR (ed.).

Manin, P. (1971), *L'Organisation des Nations Unies et le maintien de la paix. le respect du consentement de l'État* (Paris: LGDJ).

Malone, D.M. (ed.) (2004), *The UN Security Council. From the Cold War to the 21st Century* (Boulder: Lynne Rienner Publishers).

Månsson, K. (2005), 'Use of Force and Civilian Protection: Peace Operations in the Congo', *International Peacekeeping* 12:4, 503–519.

Matheson, M. (2001), 'United Nations Governance of Postconflict Societies', *American Journal of International Law* 95:1, 76–85.

Mbadinga, M. I. (2001), 'The Inter-African Mission to Monitor the Implementation of the Bangui Agreement (MISAB)', *International Peacekeeping* 8:4, 21–37.

McNamara, D. (2006), 'Peace Operations and Civilian Protection', in Azimi and Lin (eds).

Meijer, I.C. (1994), 'UN Peace-Keeping Forces: The Conditions of Change', *Leiden Journal of International Law* 7:1, 63–87.

Orakhelashvili, A. (2003), 'The Legal Basis of the United Nations Peace-Keeping Operations', *Virginia Journal of International Law* 43:2, 485–524.

Österdahl, I. (1998), *Threat to the Peace. The Interpretation by the Security Council of Article 39 of the UN Charter* (Iustus Förlag).

Papacosma, S.V. and Heiss, M.A. (eds) (1995), *NATO in the Post-Cold War Era: Does It Have A Future?* (London: Macmillan).

Rearden, S. L. (1995), 'NATO's Strategy: Past, Present, and Future', in Papacosma and Heiss (eds).

Rikhye, I.J. and Skjelsbaek, K. (eds) (1990), *The United Nations and Peacekeeping. Results, Limitations and Prospects: The Lessons of 40 Years of Experience* (London: Macmillan).

Roberts A. (1995), 'From San Francisco to Sarajevo: The UN and the Use of Force', *Survival* 37:4, 7–28.

Romses, R. (2001), 'View from the Field: United Nations Missions' Responses', in Azimi and Lin (eds).

Ruffert, M. (2001), 'The Administration of Kosovo and East-Timor by the International Community', *International and Comparative Law Quarterly* 50:3, 613–631.

Sakai, H. (2002), 'The Role of Troop-Contributing Countries in UN Peacekeeping: Dutch Experiences in the UN Mission in Ethiopia and Eritrea (UNMEE)', *Gaimusho Chosa Geppo* 2002–3, 35–77 (in Japanese).

Sakai, H. (2004), 'Functions of the Principle of Consent in UN Peacekeeping Operations', in Ando, Nakamura and Ida (eds) (2004), 237–278 (in Japanese).

Salamun, M. (2004), *Democratic Governance in International Territorial Administration* (Baden-Baden: Nomos).

Sarooshi, D. (1999), *The United Nations and the Development of Collective Security. The Delegation by the UN Security Council of its Chapter VII Powers* (Oxford: Oxford University Press).

Schrijver, N.J. (2006), 'The Future of the Charter of the United Nations', *Max Planck Yearbook of United Nations Law* 10, 1–34.

SFDI (ed.) (1995), *Le Chapitre VII de la Charte des Nations Unies* (Paris: Éditions A. Pedone).

SFDI (ed.) (2005), *Les metamorphoses de la sécurité collective. Droit, pratique et enjeux stratégiques* (Paris: Éditions A. Pedone).

Siekmann, R.C.R. (1991), *National Contingents in United Nations Peace-Keeping Forces* (The Hague: Martinus Nijhoff Publishers).

Skjelsbaek, K. (1990), 'UN Peacekeeping: Expectations, Limitations and Results: Forty Years of Mixed Experience', in Rikhye and Skjelsbaek (eds).

Smith, E.M. (2002), 'Collective Security, Peacekeeping, and ad hoc Multilateralism', in Ku and Jacobson (eds).

Smyrek, D.S. (2006), *Internationally Administered Territories – International Protectorates?* (Berlin: Duncker & Humblot).

Sorel, J.M. (1995), 'L'élargissement de la notion de menace contre la paix', in SFDI (ed.).

Stahn, C. (2001), 'The United Nations Transitional Administrations in Kosovo and East Timor: A Final Analysis', *Max Planck Yearbook of United Nations Law* 5, 105–183.

Suy, E. (1998), 'Peace-Keeping Operations', in Dupuy (ed.).

Tsagourias, N. (2007), 'Consent, Neutrality/Impartiality and the Use of Force in Peacekeeping: Their Constitutional Dimension', *Journal of Conflict & Security Law* 11:3, 465–482.

UNITAR (ed.) (1987), *The United Nations and Maintenance of International Peace and Security* (The Hague: Martinus Nijhoff Publishers).

Virally, M. (1972), *L'organisation mondiale* (Paris: Librairie Armand Colin).

Von Grünigen, M. (1978), 'Neutrality and Peace-Keeping', in Cassese (ed.).

Warner, D. (ed.) (1995), *New Dimensions of Peacekeeping* (The Hague: Martinus Nijhoff Publishers).

Weiss, T.G. (ed.) (1998), *Beyond UN Subcontracting. Task-Sharing with Regional Security Arrangements and Service-Providing NGOs* (London: Macmillan).

Wellens, K. (2003), 'The UN Security Council and New Threats to the Peace: Back to the Future', *Journal of Conflict & Security Law* 8:1, 15–70.

White, N.D. (1994), 'U.N. Peacekeeping – Development or Destruction?' *International Relations* 12:1, 129–158.

White, N.D. (2002), *The United Nations System. Toward International Justice* (Boulder: Lynne Rienner).

Williams, P.D. and Bellamy, A.J. (2007), 'Contemporary Peace Operations: Four Challenges for the Brahimi Paradigm', *The Yearbook of International Peace Operations* 11, 1–28.

Wilson, G. (2003), 'UN Authorized Enforcement: Regional Organizations versus "Coalitions of the Willing"', *International Peacekeeping* 10:2, 89–106.

Wolfrum, R. (2006), 'Solidarity amongst States: An Emerging Structural Principle of International Law', in Dupuy, Fassbender, Shaw and Sommermann (eds).

Chapter 6
Security Council Resolution 1540 and International Legislation*

Masahiko Asada

Introduction

In *The National Security Strategy of the United States of America* of 2002, the United States declared that: '[t]he gravest danger our Nation faces lies at the crossroads of radicalism and technology'.[1] 'Radicalism' stands for terrorism, and 'technology' for weapons of mass destruction (WMD); so the declaration is meant that the gravest threat lies in the nexus between terrorism and WMD, that is, the proliferation of WMD to terrorists.[2]

Such perception is not specific to the United States alone; it has widely been shared by the international community. In December 2004, The Report of the High-level Panel on Threats, Challenges and Change also declared the need for '[u]rgent short-term action … to defend against the possible terrorist use of nuclear, radiological, chemical and biological weapons'.[3] In the same year, the United Nations (UN) General Assembly adopted a resolution on the '[m]easures to prevent terrorists from acquiring weapons of mass destruction'.[4]

---

* The research on which this chapter is based has been funded by the 21st Century COE program of Kyoto University Graduate School of Law as well as the Matsushita International Foundation.

1 White House 2002, preface.

2 In fact, the *National Security Strategy* continues as follows: 'Our enemies have openly declared that they are seeking weapons of mass destruction, and evidence indicates that they are doing so with determination. The United States will not allow these efforts to succeed' (*ibid.*). In *National Strategy for Combating Terrorism* in 2003, the United States also declared that: 'Weapons of mass destruction pose a direct and serious threat to the United States and the entire international community. The probability of a terrorist organization using a chemical, biological, radiological, or nuclear weapon, or high-yield explosives, has increased significantly during the past decade' (White House 2003a, 9).

3 *A More Secure World: Our Shared Responsibility*, A/59/565, 2 December 2004, 43, para. 135.

4 A/RES/59/80, 3 December 2004. This was the third such resolution of the UN General Assembly since 2002. See A/RES/57/83, 22 November 2002; A/RES/58/48, 8 December 2003; A/RES/60/78, 8 December 2005; A/RES/61/86, 6 December 2006.

Thus, the global threat has rapidly been shifting from one originating from States to one from terrorists. Notwithstanding, the traditional measures in this field remain not adequate or not adequately implemented to counter the new threat. The traditional approach of multilateral treaties on WMD has primarily been aimed at the prevention of proliferation of such weapons to States. In addition, the few provisions that exist in those treaties having something to do with WMD terrorism are sometimes not so elaborate, nor have they been so well implemented as they should be. Thus, there are gaps in the relevant treaty laws. On the other hand, the threat perception of WMD terrorism has grown rapidly, particularly since the 11 September 2001 (9/11) terrorist attacks as well as the ensuing anthrax incidents in the United States in 2001, which led to the above-mentioned warning in *The National Security Strategy*.

Given the urgent need for action to counter the new threat with effective measures as well as the hard fact that there are gaps in the existing laws, the only way out must have been to utilize the legally binding resolution of the Security Council, if one recalls that multilateral treaty making always takes time particularly in the military–security related fields. Against such a backdrop, the UN Security Council adopted Resolution 1540 in April 2004.

However, whether such a way of resorting to Security Council resolutions is permissible under the UN Charter is another question. Moreover, even if it is permissible (not prohibited), whether it is desirable from a legitimacy point of view would be questioned. Irrespective of its permissibility and desirability, if it is inevitable for the Security Council to legislate, what are the conditions for such international legislation to be legitimate? These are the questions that the present chapter tries to address.

With such questions in mind, it first examines the content and significance of Resolution 1540. It then takes up Council Resolution 1373 of 2001 as the first attempt of international legislation with similar objectives of combating terrorism. Subsequently, a general consideration is given to the conditions for legitimate international legislation in the light of the drafting process of Resolution 1540. Finally, the chapter concludes by emphasizing the importance of the rule of law and legitimacy in international legislation by the Security Council, if it is to be truly effective.

Content and Significance of Security Council Resolution 1540

On 28 April 2004, the United Nations Security Council adopted Resolution 1540 under Chapter VII of the UN Charter unanimously.[5] Although an earlier initiative

5 The co-sponsors of the draft Resolution were the United States, the United Kingdom, France, Russia, Spain, Romania and the Philippines.

is sometimes referred to as the first precursor to the Resolution,[6] it is widely recognized that it originated from former US President George W. Bush's call for a 'new antiproliferation resolution' at the UN General Assembly in September 2003. He stated that:

> That [antiproliferation] resolution should call on all Members of the United Nations to criminalize the proliferation of weapons of mass destruction, to enact strict export controls consistent with international standards and to secure any and all sensitive materials within their own borders. The United States stands ready to help any nation draft these new laws and to assist in their enforcement.[7]

This call of the US President was reiterated in his seven-point initiative made on 11 February 2004 at the National Defense University. He proposed as the second item of his initiative 'a new Security Council resolution requiring all states to criminalize proliferation, enact strict export controls, and secure all sensitive materials within their borders'.[8]

The Resolution, as adopted by the Security Council, requires that all States shall:

(1) 'refrain from providing any form of support to non-State actors that attempt to develop, acquire, manufacture, possess, transport, transfer or use nuclear, chemical or biological weapons and their means of delivery' (para. 1);
(2) 'in accordance with their national procedures, ... adopt and enforce appropriate effective laws which prohibit any non-State actor to manufacture, acquire, possess, develop, transport, transfer or use nuclear, chemical or biological weapons and their means of delivery, in particular for terrorist purposes, as well as attempts to engage in any of the foregoing activities, participate in them as an accomplice, assist or finance them' (para. 2);
(3) 'take and enforce effective measures to establish domestic controls to prevent the proliferation of nuclear, chemical, or biological weapons and their means of delivery, including by establishing appropriate controls over related materials ...' by developing security, physical protection, and border and export controls (para. 3).

---

6 Merav Datan refers to the fact that in early 2003 the United Kingdom circulated a non-paper within the European Union, drawing lessons from the Counter-Terrorism Committee (CTC) established by Security Council Resolution 1373, and the idea of a Counter-Proliferation Committee was put forward for discussion and found general favour within the EU (Datan 2005, 48).

7 A/58/PV.7, 23 September 2003, 11.

8 White House 2004.

These requirements were adopted as 'decisions' under Chapter VII of the UN Charter, and thus legally bind all members of the United Nations.[9] At the same time, the Resolution set up a Committee (the 1540 Committee) of the Security Council, composed of the 15 Council members and supported by governmental experts, to monitor the implementation of the Resolution and, to that end, called upon States to present a report on the implementation of the Resolution (para. 4). Moreover, as was referred to in President Bush's statement at the UN General Assembly, the Resolution invited States in a position to do so to offer assistance, in response to specific requests, to the States lacking the infrastructure, experience or resources (para. 7).

How could we assess these provisions? First, the above measures, particularly those contained in the first three operative paragraphs (decisions), are aimed at filling the gaps that have existed in the WMD-related treaties. The latter treaties were not drafted having (fully) in mind the threat of proliferation of WMD to non-State actors; and in terms of the means of delivery of WMD, there exists no global treaty regulating their development, production or possession.[10] Under such circumstances, the Resolution was adopted as a product of the urgent necessity arising from a new security threat of WMD terrorism. Indeed, during the deliberation on the evolving draft of the Resolution, a number of States pointed out the urgent need to fill the gaps.[11] In the Resolution, the term 'non-State actor' is defined rather narrowly as 'individual or entity, not acting under the lawful authority of any State in conducting activities which come within the scope of this resolution', which shows what was the central concern of the drafters of the Resolution.

Second, it should be recognized that the measures contained in paragraph 2 are not all new. A comparable set of measures or the like can be found in national implementation provisions of the WMD treaties. Article VII of the Chemical Weapons Convention (CWC) is a case in point. It provides for the States Parties' obligation to prohibit natural and legal persons from undertaking any activity prohibited to a State Party under the Convention, including enacting penal

9 Professor Daniel H. Joyner, however, argues that Resolution 1540 is null and void of legal effect, because it was adopted under Chapter VII rather than under Articles 11 and 26 of the UN Charter, the latter, according to him, being the authoritative basis for the creation of new non-proliferation law (Joyner 2007, 489–518).

10 The SALT and START treaties, which have limited or reduced the number of strategic arms, including ballistic missiles, are (essentially) bilateral treaties between the United States and the Soviet Union/Russian Federation. The Guidelines for the Missile Technology Control Regime (MTCR) of 1987 and the International Code of Conduct against Ballistic Missile Proliferation (ICOC) of 2002 both aimed at preventing and curbing the proliferation of certain categories of missiles, are not legally binding.

11 See, e.g., S/PV.4950, 22 April 2004, 3 (Philippines), 3 (Brazil), 5 (Algeria), 8 (France), 9 (Angola), 12 (UK), 14 (Romania), 20 (Peru), 21 (New Zealand), 25 (Singapore); S/PV.4950 (Resumption 1), 22 April 2004, 5 (Mexico), 7 (Norway), 8 (Republic of Korea), 10–11 (Jordan).

legislation with respect to such activity.[12] However, it has continuously suffered from poor implementation. As of November 2006, almost ten years after the CWC's entry into force, only 40 per cent of the States Parties had legislation covering all key areas of the Convention.[13] With this, one might ask what would be the effect of adopting a resolution containing similar obligations – will they produce greater results?

To this, it may be argued that a legally binding resolution of the Security Council could have more political weight than a treaty, precisely because the Council is the most powerful political organ of the United Nations in the maintenance of international peace and security. It could be expected that although the net content of obligations is similar, those in a legally binding Council resolution would be respected more and implemented better than those in a treaty, particularly if the insufficient implementation of treaty obligations is due to a lack of political will.[14]

For the cases where the cause of insufficient implementation is attributable to the lack of infrastructure, experience or resources, the Resolution has provided for an apparatus that would accelerate the assistance for the implementation of the obligations under the Resolution. The 1540 Committee set up by the Resolution may be expected to function as a clearinghouse for capacity building that coordinates the exchange of offers and requests for such assistance. The Committee's task also includes the compilation of States' reports on their implementation of the Resolution.[15] By doing so, the Committee could monitor and hopefully improve the Resolution's implementation.

Third, one cannot fail to point out another added value of the Resolution. Through the binding Security Council resolution, non-States Parties to the WMD treaties are equally obliged along with the States Parties thereto to take the relevant steps, as if they were parties to them. During the drafting of the Resolution, India voiced a concern by saying that it will 'not accept any interpretation of the draft resolution that imposes obligations arising from treaties that India has not signed or ratified, consistent with the fundamental principles of international law and the

---

12 Exact wording of the relevant part of the Article is as follows: 'Each State Party shall, in accordance with its constitutional processes, adopt the necessary measures to implement its obligations under this Convention. In particular, it shall: (a) Prohibit natural and legal persons anywhere on its territory or in any other place under its jurisdiction as recognized by international law from undertaking any activity prohibited to a State Party under this Convention, including enacting penal legislation with respect to such activity'.

13 'Update National Implementation' 2006, 33. See also Asada 2006, 32–33.

14 During the Council debates, however, assurances were given that the Resolution does not *ipso facto* authorize enforcement action against States that fail or are unable to comply with the obligations imposed by the Resolution. See, e.g., S/4950, 3 (Philippines), 15 (Pakistan), 17 (US).

15 See <http://disarmament2.un.org/Committee1540/report.html>, accessed on 29 May 2007.

law of treaties'.[16] This and similar other concerns were somewhat accommodated in certain paragraphs of the Resolution which, for instance, affirm the importance for 'all States Parties' to WMD treaties to implement them fully, or call upon all States to promote the universal adoption and full implementation of WMD non-proliferation treaties 'to which they are parties'.[17] Nevertheless, they do not change the fact that the Resolution does oblige non-States Parties to the CWC, for instance, to take the kind of national measures that the States Parties to it are supposed to take.[18]

Be that as it may, the measures that States are required to take under the Resolution are not as clear as those under the CWC. Paragraph 2 of Resolution 1540 requires all States to adopt and enforce 'appropriate effective laws' to prohibit non-State actors to manufacture, develop or use WMD. With such an ambiguous requirement,[19] it cannot be said with conviction that it would lead to universal enactment of truly effective regulative laws; for it is difficult to determine in concrete cases whether the obligation under that paragraph is fulfilled or not in the first place. This is, however, an inevitable result of some States' resistance to a move to write out a detailed prescription in the Resolution, a resistance made in view of the undiminished sovereignty to which they attach great importance.[20]

Fourth, paragraph 3, unlike paragraph 2, contains a new set of measures that are not usually found in WMD treaties. They concern security, physical protection, and border and export controls and, unlike paragraphs 1 and 2, cover not only WMD themselves but also the 'related materials'.[21] These measures are important because of their preventive nature. Prevention is particularly important in the WMD terrorism context, because their use in terrorism would surely result in a devastative situation. National implementation provisions of WMD treaties as

---

16 S/PV.4950, 24.

17 See the fifth preambular paragraph and operative paragraph 8(a) of Resolution 1540. See also the eleventh preambular paragraph. They reflect the changes introduced by the sponsors to clarify their intention regarding the concerns expressed by others. See S/PV.4950, 18 (US); S/PV.4956, 28 April 2004, 3–4 (Pakistan).

18 Still, it should not be forgotten that what Resolution 1540 emphasizes is not those WMD treaties per se but the relevant national legislation and other regulations and controls that provide the basis for action against non-State actors (van Ham and Bosch 2007, 15).

19 See S/PV.4950, 28 (Switzerland). See also 'Keeping WMD from Terrorists: An Interview with 1540 Committee Chairman Ambassador Peter Burian' 2007, 22–23. For other problems raised on Resolution 1540, see Lavalle 2004, 428–435; Talmon 2005, 188–190.

20 For an argument that the Resolution does not prescribe specific legislation, which is left to national action by States, see S/PV.4956, 3 (Pakistan). See also S/PV.4950, 24 (India); S/PV.4950 (Resumption 1), 7 (Kazakhstan).

21 The term 'related materials' is defined by the Resolution as: 'materials, equipment and technology covered by relevant multilateral treaties and arrangements, or included on national control lists, which could be used for the design, development, production or use of nuclear, chemical and biological weapons and their means of delivery'.

well as paragraph 2 of Resolution 1540, both containing obligations to enact penal legislation, would contribute to the *ex post facto* punishment of WMD terrorists, but not necessarily[22] to the prevention of such terrorism. In that sense, measures provided for in paragraph 3 would have the potential of greatly enhancing terrorism prevention preparedness, if properly implemented.[23]

The importance of this aspect of the Resolution will become more apparent if one thinks of the inherently limited effect of the activities of export control groups. The Nuclear Suppliers Group (NSG), an informal (not legally formed) export control group established in 1975, for instance, requires its members to exercise restraint in the transfer of nuclear and nuclear-related items in certain cases in accordance with their national laws and practices.[24] While its 45 members are supposed to have an effective national export control system, many other States in the international community are not, notwithstanding the fact that the latter States may contribute to the transfer of such items in one way or another. In fact, the illicit trafficking activities by the Pakistani metallurgist A.Q. Kahn and his network used Malaysia, United Arab Emirates (Dubai) and other countries with little or no nuclear-related activities in order to provide nuclear weapon-related items and technologies to such end-users as Iran, Libya and North Korea.[25] Nevertheless, it is not deemed conceivable to invite or admit the former kind of countries to the Group, because of the proliferation risks that the sensitive information sharing among such wider membership may entail, as well as the fact that they are not considered to be 'nuclear suppliers'.

By this Resolution, all UN members are legally obliged[26] to '[e]stablish, develop, review and maintain appropriate effective national export and trans-shipment controls' over WMD and their means of delivery as well as related materials, including appropriate laws and regulations to control export, transit, trans-shipment and re-export, and 'establishing and enforcing appropriate criminal or civil penalties for violations of such export control laws and regulations' (para. 3(d)). No treaties can obligate States to establish such a national export control

22 Of course, penal legislation could have a certain deterrent effect.

23 Peter Crail states that the provisions in paragraph 3 are 'the most important from a nonproliferation standpoint' for the same reason (Crail 2006, 368).

24 See 'Guidelines for Nuclear Transfers', INFCIRC/254/Rev.8/Part 1, 20 March 2006; 'Guidelines for Transfers of Nuclear-Related Dual-Use Equipment, Materials, Software, and Related Technology', INFCIRC/254/Rev.7/Part 2, 20 March 2006.

25 See *Nuclear Black Markets* 2007, 65–91.

26 Some States argued that since Article 25 of the UN Charter provides that all decisions of the Security Council shall be accepted and carried out by the Member States, there is no need to invoke Chapter VII of the UN Charter. The co-sponsors of the Resolution responded by saying that the draft resolution is placed under Chapter VII in order to underline the seriousness of their response to the issue, and because they are dealing with what is clearly a threat to international peace and security, and because they are levying binding requirements. See S/PV.4950, 4 (Brazil), 5 (Algeria), 31 (Indonesia); *ibid.*, 7 (Spain), 8–9 (France), 12 (UK), 17 (US).

system so extensively, so quickly and so effectively. Although no time line is given for the implementation of these obligations, if they are implemented within a reasonable time period, considerable effects could be expected in the field of export control without compromising sensitive information.[27]

Resolution 1373 as the First International Legislation by the Security Council

As outlined above, the approach that Resolution 1540 has taken has opened a new horizon to counter WMD terrorism. As a new approach, however, it is not free of criticism. Speaking generally of the Security Council, while it could act swiftly and effectively when needed, it should be cautious not to resort to its extremely powerful means too easily. Speaking specifically of Resolution 1540, it could be asked whether the Security Council has the international legislative power and, if so, on what conditions it could be exercised.

Although 'international legislation'[28] is a very equivocal term, it is used here as meaning the establishment of legal rules of general application to abstract situations, binding all (UN member[29]) States without their separate consent to be bound by them, and usually intended to remain in force for an indefinite period.[30] Since every Security Council decision (adopted under Chapter VII) binds all member States under Article 25 of the UN Charter without their separate consent, the key here is the general nature of the content of the rules concerned, that is, the aspect of establishing new rules of conduct of general application, independent of any specific situation.

According to a generally held view, the collective security system of the United Nations is a system in which the Security Council is to respond to a *specific*

27 In this sense, a Security Council resolution that levies similar requirements without sensitive information sharing accompanied is a clever means to attain the same objectives.

28 There is no established definition of 'international legislation'. It has, however, generally referred to the making of multilateral treaties, while, in a more strict sense, referring to the formulation, by a majority vote, of international legal rules of general application to abstract situations. For the traditional concept of 'international legislation', see, e.g., Hudson 1931, xiii–xviii; McNair 1933–1934, 178; Jessup 1956, 203; Skubiszewski 1965–1966, 198–201; Skubiszewski 1968, 509.

29 The Security Council addresses a growing number of Security Council resolutions, including Resolution 1540, to 'all States' rather than 'all Member States' of the United Nations. However, non-UN member States are not bound by the Charter or the resolutions.

30 Edward Yemin's definition is close to ours. According to him, 'legislative acts have three essential characteristics: they are unilateral in form, they create or modify some element of a legal norm, and the legal norm in question is general in nature, that is, directed to indeterminate addressees and capable of repeated application in time'. Yemin 1969, 6. See also Happold 2003, 596–601; Lavalle 2004, 415; Joyner 2007, 511.

situation by imposing sanctions on the subjects that have given rise to such a situation, after determining it as a threat to the peace, breach of the peace or the act of aggression, in order to maintain or restore international peace and security.[31] The task of the Council in this respect has been characterized as a 'police function'.[32] It is not what the drafters of the UN Charter had specifically in mind as part of collective security system, if not expressly prohibited by the Charter, that the Security Council establishes such rules of general application as would normally be made by a multilateral treaty.[33]

It is true that the Council has recently broadened the scope of measures to be taken under Chapter VII, particularly under Article 41, of the Charter.[34] They include such measures as the establishment of the International Criminal Tribunals for the former Yugoslavia (ICTY) and for Rwanda (ICTR),[35] as well as the creation of the United Nations Compensation Commission (UNCC) to process claims and pay compensation for losses resulting from Iraq's invasion of Kuwait, the establishment of the United Nations Iraq–Kuwait Boundary Demarcation Commission to demarcate the international border between Iraq and Kuwait, and the imposition of disarmament obligations on Iraq.[36] But they all can be understood as part of the measures taken in response to a specific situation being a threat to the peace or breach of the peace and, as such, within the traditional purview of the powers and functions of the Security Council.

By way of contrast, Resolution 1540 was *not* adopted in order to respond to a certain specific situation, but to respond to a generally perceived threat of WMD terrorism and lay down rules of general application for that.

Resolution 1540 was not an entirely new phenomenon, however. Resolution 1373, adopted unanimously on 28 September 2001, some two weeks after 9/11, can be seen as a precedent and probably the first such precedent in this respect.[37] After

---

31 See, e.g., Frowein and Krisch 2002, 709; Zemanek 1999, 636–637; Happold 2003, 599–600; Lavalle 2004, 412. Hans Kelsen, who accepts the concept of the Security Council creating new law, recognizes such law making for 'the concrete case' only (Kelsen 1951, 295, 446).

32 See Frowein and Krisch 2002, 705, 707, 709.

33 Professor D.W. Bowett argues that: 'the [Security] Council does not "legislate": it enforces Charter obligations' (Bowett 1997, 80). Professor Martti Koskenniemi contends that: 'No doubt, it is not possible to conceive the Security Council as a legitimate global law-maker' (Koskenniemi 2005, 74). Professor Georg Nolte, referring to the possible role of the Security Council as a world legislature, describes it as 'a role for which it was not designed' (Nolte 2000, 322). See also de Brichambaut 2000, 275–276; Marschik 2005, 7; Arangio-Ruiz 2000, 628–629; *ICJ Reports 1971*, 294, para.115 Dissenting Opinion of Judge Sir Gerald Fitzmaurice to the Advisory Opinion on Namibia.

34 See generally de Wet 2004, 338–368.

35 S/RES/827(1993), 25 May 1993; S/RES/955(1994), 8 November 1994.

36 See S/RES/687(1991), 3 April 1991.

37 Talmon 2005, 176. Professor Talmon also refers to Resolutions 1422 and 1487 on the International Criminal Court as often overlooked examples of Security Council

reaffirming its unequivocal condemnation of the 9/11 terrorist attacks, the Security Council reaffirmed in the preamble of Resolution 1373 that 'such acts [referring to the 9/11 terrorist attacks], like any act of international terrorism, constitute a threat to international peace and security'. This phrase may be viewed as showing that the Resolution was a response to the specific incident of 9/11, as it is exactly the same as a phrase found in the preamble of Resolution 1368 adopted on the day following the 9/11 attacks. However, the content of the operative paragraphs of Resolution 1373 is so general as to be usually found in an anti-terrorism treaty. The Resolution provides, for example, the obligations of all States to prevent and suppress the financing of terrorist acts, and to criminalize the willful provision or collection of funds with the intention that the funds should be used in order to carry out terrorist acts (para. 1); and to refrain from providing any form of support to entities or persons involved in terrorist acts, and to deny safe haven to those who finance, plan, support, or commit terrorist acts (para. 2). These are decisions made under Chapter VII without referring to any specific situation or specific entity. That they would normally be provided in a treaty can be ascertained by the fact that they largely mirror what is contained in the 1999 International Convention for the Suppression of the Financing of Terrorism (Terrorist Financing Convention).[38]

The Terrorist Financing Convention, entering into force in April 2002, was not in force in September 2001 when Resolution 1373 was adopted. What's more, it was at that time only four States that had already ratified the Convention, which requires 22 ratifications for the entry into force; and there was a strong demand for the earliest possible effectuation of the *content* of the Convention by any means. Such a demand seems to have led to the adoption of a legally binding Security Council resolution containing largely the same content.[39] Put another way, given the scarce number of ratifications, the Security Council decided to 'forcibly' bring into force part of the content of the Convention, and to make it universally applicable to all (UN member) States. While this may have been viewed as a questionable exercise, such concern must have been minimized by the fact that the UN General Assembly's Sixth Committee and the General Assembly itself had already adopted a resolution with the text of the Terrorist Financing Convention annexed, without a vote.[40] In that sense, Resolution 1373 was not entirely new international legislation. Perhaps that is why there was little criticism voiced against the Resolution for the reason that it was international legislation by the

legislation (Talmon 2005, 177–178). According to Axel Marschik, the United States initiated negotiations on a draft resolution that was to become Resolution 1540 in view of the success of the Resolution 1373 regime (Marschik 2005, 16). See also note 6 above.

38 Happold 2003, 594. See also Schrijver 2004, 58; Guillaume 2004, 543.

39 Indeed, paragraph 3(d) of the Resolution calls upon all States to become parties as soon as possible to the relevant international conventions relating to terrorism and, in that context, specifically refers to the Terrorist Financing Convention.

40 A/54/PV.76, 9 December 1999, 8.

Security Council, and the adoption of the Resolution was widely welcomed by the UN member States.[41]

Resolution 1540 and the Problems with International Legislation by the Security Council

How then could we assess Resolution 1540 from the perspective of international legislation? As already seen, the Resolution was adopted under Chapter VII of the UN Charter and binding all UN member States. In its preamble, it affirms that: 'proliferation of nuclear, chemical and biological weapons, as well as their means of delivery', *in general*, 'constitutes a threat to international peace and security'. This affirmation comes from a passage of the Presidential Statement[42] made at the Security Council summit meeting held on 31 January 1992 as a general statement and with no specific situation in mind. The measures contained in operative paragraphs are also general in nature, as we have already seen earlier. Thus, Resolution 1540 has set forth legal rules of general application and can be called as international legislation.

Most of these features of Resolution 1540 are shared by Resolution 1373. But the content of the latter Resolution largely reflected that of an already adopted multilateral treaty yet to enter into force. In contradistinction, Resolution 1540, though part of the measures contained in it can be traced back to a *political* document of G8 Kananaskis Summit of 2002,[43] is entirely new international legislation. That is partly why during the drafting of the Resolution, criticisms were made and concerns were expressed in terms of the competence of the Security Council regarding international legislation.

If one sums up the problems with international legislation by the Security Council, as found in the relevant statements made during the drafting of Resolution 1540 and as compared with normal multilateral treaty-making, the following three aspects may be identified. The first problem concerns the formulation of legal rules by a limited number of States. Namibia, for instance, stated that '[it] recognizes that there are gaps in the existing multilateral legal instruments which need to be filled. However, such gaps can be filled by multilateral negotiated instruments and should not be filled by the Council measures, which are unbalanced and selective,

41 Talmon 2005, 177, 187–188. For somewhat contrastive views on Resolution 1373 from an international legislation perspective, see Szasz 2002, 905 and Happold 2003, 607–610.

42 The Presidential Statement states that: 'The proliferation of all weapons of mass destruction constitutes a threat to international peace and security' (S/23500, 31 January 1992, 4).

43 'Statement by G8 Leaders: The G8 Global Partnership against the Spread of Weapons and Materials of Mass Destruction', Kananaskis, 27 June 2002.

as they represent only the views of those who drafted them'.[44] Likewise, Iran said that '[t]he United Nations Charter entrusted the Security Council with the huge responsibility to maintain international peace and security, but it does not confer authority on the Council to act as a global legislature imposing obligations on States without their participation in the process'.[45]

International legislation by the Security Council means that only 15 members of the Security Council could establish by a majority vote general rules that legally bind 192 members of the United Nations; and the vast majority of States of the international community would be bound by the resulting rules without participating in their drafting process. Among the 15 members are included five permanent members who have the veto power, with which they could block any rules that are contrary to their national interest. The 15 members might also possibly include States that are not very suitable for the drafting of international legislation in certain specific fields in terms of motivations or capabilities. It is true that these apply to all and any legally binding Council resolutions. But the influence is qualitatively different in the case of international legislation because of its general and perpetual applicability.

Second, the lack of treaty negotiation process also poses problems. Nepal rather harshly held that 'the Security Council lacks competence in making treaties. We are afraid that the Council, through this draft resolution, is seeking to establish something tantamount to a treaty by its fiat. This is likely to undermine the intergovernmental treaty-making process and implementation mechanisms'.[46] In the case of treaty, it may be expected that conflicting interests between States or groups of States are ironed out through negotiations, resulting in a satisfactorily balanced text of rules overall. The same cannot perhaps be expected of the legislation by the Security Council, where the five permanent members have a dominant power not only politically but also procedurally. As a result, it may be questionable whether the rules enacted by the Council, while legally binding on all UN members in formal terms, are placed on a firm basis in the international community as a whole. This aspect of the problem may, in turn, affect their actual implementation and compliance. If they are not well implemented or complied with despite their legally binding nature, that might further adversely affect the legally binding force of the Security Council decisions in general.

Third, the denial of the freedom of acceptance may raise a question. Cuba maintained that 'international legal obligations … must not be imposed upon [UN] Member States without their participation and their sovereign acceptance, through the signing and ratification of the corresponding treaties and agreements that have been negotiated multilaterally'.[47] From a slightly different perspective, India declared, as mentioned earlier, that it would 'not accept any interpretation of

44 S/PV.4950 (Resumption 1), 17.

45 S/PV.4950, 32.

46 S/PV.4950 (Resumption 1), 14.

47 S/PV.4950, 30.

the draft resolution that imposes obligations arising from treaties that India has not signed or ratified, consistent with the fundamental principles of international law and the law of treaties'.[48] In the case of treaty, States have the freedom of whether to join or not to join the treaty, irrespective of their participation in the treaty-making process. With such a freedom, they could safeguard their national interest and sovereign rights. However, the Security Council legislation would not allow such sovereign freedom: it necessarily binds all UN member States without exception,[49] whether one likes it or not. Thus, the States' ultimate sovereign guarantee of not being bound by what they have not consented to becomes flimsy.

Admittedly, by joining the UN, its member States have 'agree[d] to accept and carry out the decisions of the Security Council' (Article 25 of the UN Charter). In that sense, it cannot be said that they are bound by what they have not consented to. However, it may be questioned whether that agreement in Article 25 can be said to naturally extend to the Security Council's power to enact international legislation. To take India, which has stayed out of the NPT regime, for example, the 40-year long problem would promptly be resolved if the Security Council adopts a legally binding resolution to the effect that all UN member States, except for the five recognized nuclear-weapon States, shall not receive, or manufacture or otherwise acquire nuclear weapons or other nuclear explosive devices. Its substantive desirability (denuclearization of India and a few others) aside, such a course of action would destroy the very foundation of the treaty law order that bases itself on the consent of each State to be bound by a treaty. This is what India warned about during the drafting of Resolution 1540, as shown above.

At the same time, however, what Professor Barry Kellman says contains some truth. He argues that: 'If a matter of international peace and security requires implementation of obligations that, in another context, might be the substance of a treaty, the Security Council can (and, according to the charter process, should) trump the treaty-making process. One reason for this trump of authority is precisely because the Security Council is better able to shear away extraneous considerations from the treaty negotiation process and make decisions more quickly that have more direct and exclusive bearing on resolving the security threat. When the issue arises to the most important category of concerns (war and peace), the process is not meant to epitomize participatory democracy of sovereign states; it is meant to get the job done'.[50]

Professor Christian Tomuschat supports the idea of international legislation by the Security Council in more general terms by saying that:

48 S/PV.4950, 24.

49 Axel Marschik views Article 48, paragraph 1, of the UN Charter as allowing States to be exempted from the application of the new legally binding rules established by a Security Council resolution (Marschik 2005, 26).

50 Kellman 2004, 159.

> The wording 'threat to the peace' was chosen precisely with a view to permitting the Security Council to take precautionary action well before an armed attack occurs. If prevention is the philosophical concept underlying Article 39 [of the UN Charter], then it must also be possible that the Security Council, in a more *abstract* manner, without having regard to the particular nature of a regime, outlaws certain activities as being incompatible with fundamental interests of the international community [emphasis added].

He also maintains that:

> the Security Council is not confined to taking preventive measures with regard to country-specific situations that threaten international peace. It must also be deemed empowered to enact *general* regulations prohibiting or restricting certain activities which, regardless of who is the author, are susceptible of putting in jeopardy international peace through the effects they are likely to produce[51] [emphasis added].

If such is the case and we have to accept international legislation by the Security Council despite the various problems discussed above, we should at least consider the conditions to be met as brakes, lest the Council should exercise its Chapter VII power too much in trumping the treaty-making process.

Resolution 1540 and the Conditions for Legitimate International Legislation by the Security Council

Although it is impossible to identify all such conditions precisely, it is possible to enumerate relatively important elements. They can be categorized into two groups: substantive and procedural. From a substantive perspective, the subject matter of international legislation by the Security Council must concern, first of all, an essential, common interest of States or of the international community as a whole. Second, it must also be related to issues that have to be tackled with urgency. The first condition can be derived from the fact that Council decisions legally bind *all* UN members *without* requiring individual consent to be bound by them, while the second stems from the fact that the Council legislation establishes legal rules *without* following the normal treaty-making processes.

Of these two conditions, the importance of the latter was particularly emphasized during the Council discussions leading to the adoption of Resolution 1540. For instance, the United Kingdom, after referring to the threat posed by WMD terrorism, said that '[i]t is clear that in the face of this urgent threat only the Security Council can act with the necessary speed and authority. My delegation

51 Tomuschat 1993, 344, 345. See also Tomuschat 1995, 92–94; Harper 1994, 149. For different viewpoints, see literature cited in note 33 above.

believes that, in such circumstances, not only is it appropriate for the Security Council to act, it is imperative that it do so. The Council has a responsibility to respond to this threat to international peace and security'.[52]

Among the Non-Aligned, Singapore, while sharing the concerns expressed by other delegations, supported the draft resolution by stating as follows: 'Singapore understands many of the concerns expressed here in this debate by some of the other delegations. For example, they question whether the Security Council can assume the role of treaty-making or of legislating rules for Member States. We agree that a multilateral treaty regime would be ideal. But multilateral negotiations could take years, and time is not on our side. Urgent action is needed'.[53] Likewise, Switzerland said that: '[i]n principle, legislative obligations, such as those foreseen in the draft resolution under discussion, should be established through multilateral treaties, in whose elaboration all States can participate. It is acceptable for the Security Council to assume such a legislative role only in exceptional circumstances and in response to an urgent need'.[54]

From a procedural point of view, it is important, in order for the Security Council's role of international legislation to be accepted as legitimate, that both the decision-making procedure and the composition of the Security Council are seen as fair and representative. In terms of the decision-making procedure of the Council allowing its permanent members to exercise veto power, it is worth noting that Security Council Resolutions 1373, 1540 and 1673, the last resolution extending the mandate of the 1540 Committee for two years, were all adopted unanimously.[55] It seems that there exists or is emerging an unwritten rule among the Council members that those Council resolutions that function as international legislation should be adopted by unanimous consent. Strictly and legally speaking, there is no requirement that certain types of resolutions must be adopted by unanimous consent. However, in order for a legislative resolution to be seen as legitimate, to be respected and implemented, and thus to be effective, it is quite important that its sponsors, and particularly those permanent members that are sponsors, try to gain unanimous consent to the adoption of the resolution. During the debate on the eventual Resolution 1540, Spain stated that '[w]e believe that, since the Council is legislating for the entire international community, this draft resolution should preferably, although not necessarily, be adopted by consensus'.[56] And in fact, efforts were made to get unanimous consent to the draft.

In the time after the first draft was circulated within the P-5 members in October 2003, extensive consultations were made and resulted in several

52 S/PV.4950, 11.

53 S/PV.4950, 25.

54 S/PV.4950, 28.

55 S/PV.4385, 28 September 2001, 2; S/PV.4956, 2; S/PV.5429, 27 April 2006, 2.

56 S/PV.4950, 7. Delegations emphasized the importance of the unanimous adoption of Resolution 1540 in their statements following the adoption. See, e.g., S/PV.4956, 2 (France), 5 (US), 6 (Russia), 7 (UK), 8 (Spain), 9 (Romania).

important modifications. For instance, paragraph 10 of the Resolution underwent significant transformations. It provided in the December 2003 draft (para. 6) that the Security Council calls upon all States 'to cooperate to prevent, and if necessary *interdict*, shipments that would contribute to the proliferation of nuclear, chemical or biological weapons and their means of delivery'[57] (emphasis added). 'Interdict' was a term that tends to remind people of counter-proliferation and Proliferation Security Initiative (PSI)[58] type of measures, and thus was deleted from the paragraph in March 2004 to read that the Security Council calls upon all States 'to take cooperative action to prevent illicit trafficking in nuclear, chemical or biological weapons, their means of delivery, and related materials'.[59] It was only then that China, as the last member of the P-5, agreed to the draft resolution.[60]

A revised draft was circulated to the non-permanent members of the Council on 23 December 2003. Although the consultations continued strictly among the P-5 members until March 2004,[61] the statement by Pakistan, a non-permanent member of the Council at that time, delivered after the adoption of the Resolution, attests the intensity and seriousness of the efforts that were made to obtain unanimous consent. It said that '[w]e appreciate the serious efforts made by the sponsors of the draft resolution to accommodate our major concerns and those of other States. The draft resolution was revised three times. That enabled Pakistan to support the resolution'.[62] During the consultations, Pakistan had raised a number of doubts, questions and concerns about the draft resolution from a historical, legal and political perspective.[63] The consultations and debates seem to have contributed to alleviating some of these concerns and doubts, leading to the adoption of the Resolution with unanimity. One may be able to see these extensive consultations and debates in the same light as multilateral treaty negotiations, as a process to adjust differences in interests among States.[64]

Still, unanimity among the Council members may not be enough. For a resolution adopted unanimously by the Security Council to be truly legitimate, its composition must also be representative. This is the second aspect of the procedural

57 Datan 2005, 48–50.

58 Former US President George W. Bush announced the establishment of the PSI during a speech in Krakow, Poland, on 31 May 2003. The PSI is a program under which the US and certain of its allies bestow upon themselves the authority to interdict shipments of WMD-related cargoes and seize such cargoes that are identified at sea, in the air or on land. For the basic program of the PSI, see White House 2003b. The PSI is said to be 'an activity, not an organization' (Bolton 2005, 400).

59 'Draft Resolution on Non-Proliferation, March 24, 2004' 2004, 33, para. 8.

60 Datan 2005, 50; S/PV.4950, 6 (China).

61 Marschik 2005, 16.

62 S/PV.4956, 3.

63 S/PV.4950, 15.

64 This may remind us the argument made by Professor Jonathan I. Charney that rather than State practice and *opinio juris*, multilateral forums often play a central role in the creation and shaping of contemporary international law (Charney 1993, 543 *et seq.*).

conditions for a legitimate legislative resolution. However, the representativity of the Security Council is not only an extremely complicated question in itself[65] but also is beyond the purview of this chapter. It will limit itself to stating the following facts in this regard. First, it is simply impossible to reach an agreement on the composition of the Security Council that would satisfy all UN members. If a truly representative body is an objective, it may well end up with the conclusion that the General Assembly is the right forum to legislate. However, not only does the Assembly not have the power to adopt a resolution legally binding all UN member States,[66] such possibility was overwhelmingly rejected at the San Francisco Conference that adopted the UN Charter.[67]

Under such circumstances, a second best approach would be to make efforts to listen to and incorporate as many opinions of the UN members as possible beyond the Security Council[68] in order to reflect 'the general will of the world community' in the legislation.[69]

The desirability of such efforts was expressed especially by New Zealand and seven other States in relation to Resolution 1540. They argued that: 'the draft resolution will not succeed in its aim without the support and acceptance of Member States. Such acceptance requires the Council to dispel any impression of negotiations behind closed doors or that a small group of States is drafting laws for the broader membership without the opportunity for all Member States to express their views'.[70] Thus, they requested an open debate. The opportunity for open debate was provided on 22 April 2004. In that debate, as many as 36 non-members of the Council were invited and expressed their views on the draft resolution,[71] which included Ireland representing 34 EU member and other States as well as Malaysia representing 116 Non-Aligned Movement States. Even modification of the draft was made, based on the views expressed. Thus, it is submitted that in legislating through Resolution 1540 the Security Council provided the international community of States with the opportunity to incorporate their views in the Resolution. It did so in terms of both substance and procedure – an endeavor to draw up rules reflecting the general will of the world community as a whole.[72]

---

65 On this question, see, e.g., Schrijver 2007, 127–138.

66 There are few exceptions, such as those on the admission of a State to membership in the UN and on the expelling of a member from the UN, where a General Assembly resolution has a legally binding effect.

67 *Documents of the United Nations Conference on International Organization* (United Nations Information Organizations, 1945), vol. 9, 70, 346–347.

68 The United Kingdom stated after the adoption of Resolution 1540 that 'Throughout the discussion of the resolution, the sponsors sought to work closely with Council members and, perhaps uniquely, with the wider United Nations membership' (S/PV.4956, 7).

69 Szasz 2002, 905.

70 S/PV.4950, 21 (New Zealand).

71 S/PV.4950, 2; S/PV.4950 (Resumption 1), 2.

72 Such an opportunity also served as a means to clarify the meaning and implications of certain specific provisions of the Resolution.

Some commentators tend to downplay the importance of the public debate held in the Council as an occasion to vent off steam.[73] However, even so, what is important is that the UN members in general feel that they have participated in the drafting of the Resolution and some of their views, however trivial, were incorporated in the final product.

Conclusion

Faced with the new threat of WMD terrorism, the international community has responded with a new approach of international legislation through Security Council resolutions. The traditional approach of multilateral treaties on WMD has primarily been aimed at the prevention of proliferation of such weapons to States and not to non-State actors, except for national implementation measures in certain WMD treaties. Moreover, the implementation of such national implementation measures has generally been poor as well. Thus, there have been obvious gaps both in law and in reality there.

Ideally, a new multilateral treaty should be drafted to counter the new threat. However, the urgent and grave nature of the threat emanating from the nexus of terrorism and weapons of mass destruction does not allow time for such a course of action. Thus, the trump card of binding Security Council resolution was played. Resolution 1540 was adopted, following the example of Resolution 1373. It may be said that these resolutions have also opened up the possibilities of international legislation in other fields. As Dr. Stefan Talmon describes, 'the Security Council has entered its legislative phase'.[74]

The motivation, objective and substantive provisions aside, it should be borne in mind that an easy resort to international legislation through Security Council resolutions involves fundamental problems. If the 15 Council members enact international legislation for the international community without broad outside support, it might not be complied with or implemented, thereby weakening the binding power of Chapter VII resolutions of the Security Council in general. This would be a serious blow to the UN collective security system as a whole. Moreover, a frequent resort to the binding Council resolutions in place of multilateral treaty-making or treaty-amendment processes could also become a serious threat to the international legal order that is increasingly based on multilaterally negotiated treaties and agreements. Last resort should be made with caution.[75]

73 Marschik 2005, 23.

74 Talmon 2005, 175. See also Alvarez 2003, 874.

75 On this point, Japan argued during the deliberation of the draft of Resolution 1540 that: 'In adopting a binding Security Council resolution under Chapter VII of the United Nations Charter, the Security Council assumes a lawmaking function. The Security Council should, therefore, be cautious not to undermine the stability of the international legal framework' (S/PV.4950, 28). See also S/PV.4950 (Resumption 1), 8 (Republic of Korea).

As far as Resolution 1540 is concerned, a number of non-member States of the Security Council had the opportunity to express their views, and some of their views were reflected in the Resolution in one way or another. As a result of such and other endeavors, the Resolution was adopted unanimously and has been implemented with a relatively good record, at least as compared with the implementation record of the corresponding obligations under the CWC, for instance. According to the Report of the 1540 Committee to the Security Council presented on 25 April 2006, 129 States have submitted their national reports on the implementation of the Resolution to the Committee by the end of its two-year term (April 2006).[76] Most of the remaining 62 States are from the three regions of Africa, the Caribbean and the South Pacific,[77] and many of them are not parties to the BWC and/or CWC.[78] They share the problems of insufficient understanding, lack of capacity and different national priorities.[79] This shows the importance of the outreach, assistance and cooperation activities of the 1540 Committee. In this respect, it seems promising that Resolution 1673, extending the Committee's mandate for two years with the emphasis given to such activities, was adopted unanimously on 27 April 2006.[80]

However, reporting cannot be equated with the implementation of the required measures as such. In fact, according to a statistical analysis of the national reports under Resolution 1540, the key 84 States identified as particularly relevant for the implementation of the Resolution have, on average, established less than one-third of the 382 legislative and enforcement mechanisms required under Resolution 1540 to prevent WMD proliferation to non-State actors; even P-5 members of the Security Council have established less than half of the mechanisms, except for the United States.[81] This not only shows that a lot more needs to be done in all senses, but it also uncovers the fact that even a Security Council resolution adopted under Chapter VII might not fully be respected if it is too ambitious and too demanding.

76 The number was as at 20 April. In response to the Committee's examination of the first national reports, 79 States provided additional information. S/2006/257, 25 April 2006, 7, para. 14.

77 S/2006/257, 25 April 2006, 7, para. 15. See also United Nations 2007.

78 Bosch and van Ham 2007, 218.

79 S/2006/257, 3.

80 This resolution was proposed by the President of the Security Council, because there had been agreement among all 15 members of the Council on the adoption of the resolution. For the work of the 1540 Committee, see Bosch and van Ham 2007, 209–212.

81 According to the author of the analysis, to some extent this assessment underestimates the measures that States currently have in place, as nearly every State included information in its report for which the Committee required clarification in order to determine that particular provisions had been fulfilled (Crail 2006, 356, 369, 370, 371). A matrix consisting of 382 measures was created by the Committee's governmental experts to identify which provisions of the Resolution a State has fulfilled (see Crail 2006, 369, 389–399).

Still, the enactment by India in June 2005 of the 'Weapons of Mass Destruction and Their Delivery Systems (Prohibition of Unlawful Activities) Act 2005' and by Pakistan in September 2004 of 'Export Control on Goods, Technologies, Material and Equipment related to Nuclear and Biological Weapons and their Delivery Systems Act, 2004',[82] is to be noted as among the major achievements of the Resolution, though the degree of the Resolution's influence may be different between the two Acts, and depending, of course, on the actual implementation of the respective legislation by them. It should be recalled that the two States are among those which expressed strong reservations about international legislation by the Security Council during the drafting of Resolution 1540.

It should also be recalled that during the deliberation of the draft for Resolution 1540 a number of statements were made to the effect that: 'draft [resolution] does not preclude multilateral agreements on the subject', and that 'consideration by the Council of this issue should be on a temporary basis and for a specific, limited time until an internationally ratified agreement can be concluded'.[83]

All these statements seem to show the deep-rooted reluctance (and perhaps suspicion as well) of certain quarters of the international community, particularly among the members of the Non-Aligned Movement, to accept international legislation by the Security Council as a replacement for a multilaterally negotiated treaty, even where an urgent necessity requires exceptional measures.

In the final analysis, a new thinking is necessary to effectively respond to a new, urgent and grave threat to the international community. In that sense, Resolution 1540 is welcome. This does not, however, mean that everything is allowed if it is effective to deal with such a threat. Not only from the viewpoint of legitimacy, which guarantees the long-standing effectiveness, but also from that of the rule of law in the international community, it seems of fundamental importance to establish the kind of understandings that we discussed in this chapter, if international legislation by the Security Council is destined to become inevitable in the future and is to be well implemented.

References

Books, Articles and Chapters in Books

Alvarez, J.E. (2003), 'Hegemonic International Law Revisited', *American Journal of International Law* 97:4, 873–888.

---

82 S/AC.44/2004/(02)/62/Add.1, 18 January 2006, 2–4, paras. 2–5; S/AC.44/2004/(02)/22, 5 November 2004, 4–5.

83 S/PV.4950, 3 (Philippines); S/PV.4950 (Resumption 1), 2 (Egypt). See also S/PV.4950, 5 (Algeria), 15 (Pakistan), 21 (New Zealand), 28, 29 (Switzerland); S/PV.4950 (Resumption 1), 4 (Malaysia on behalf of NAM), 15 (Nigeria), 17 (Namibia); S/PV.4956, 4 (Pakistan), 9 (Philippines). Cf. S/PV.4950 (Resumption 1), 7 (Australia).

Arangio-Ruiz, G. (2000), 'On the Security Council's "Law-Making"', *Rivista di Diritto Internazionale* 83:3, 609–725.

Asada, M. (2006), 'Bio-Terrorism and National Implementation of the Biological Weapons Convention', *Kyoto Journal of Law and Politics* 3:1, 25–36.

Bolton, J.R. (2005), 'The Bush Administration's Forward Strategy for Nonproliferation', *Chicago Journal of International Law* 5:2, 395–404.

Bosch, O. and van Ham, P. (2007), 'UNSCR 1540: Its Future and Contribution to Global Non-Proliferation and Counter-Terrorism', in Bosch and van Ham (eds).

Bosch, O. and van Ham, P. (eds) (2007), *Global Non-Proliferation and Counter-Terrorism: The Impact of UNSCR 1540* (Washington, DC: Brookings Institution Press).

Boulden, J. and Weiss, T.G. (eds) (2004), *Terrorism and the UN: Before and After September 11* (Bloomington: Indiana UP).

Bowett, D.W. (1997), 'Judicial and Political Functions of the Security Council and the International Court of Justice', in Fox (ed.).

de Brichambaut, M.P. (2000), 'The Role of the United Nations Security Council in the International Legal System', in Byers (ed.).

Byers, M. (ed.) (2000), *The Role of Law in International Politics: Essays in International Relations and International Law* (Oxford: Oxford UP).

Charney, J.I. (1993), 'Universal International Law', *American Journal of International Law* 87:4, 529–551.

Crail, P. (2006), 'Implementing UN Security Council Resolution 1540: A Risk-Based Approach', *Nonproliferation Review* 13:2, 355–399.

Datan, M. (2005), 'Security Council Resolution 1540: WMD and Non-State Trafficking', *Disarmament Diplomacy* 79, 47–55.

Delbrück, J. (ed.) (1995), *Allocation of Law Enforcement Authority in the International System* (Berlin: Duncker und Humblot).

Fox, H. (ed.) (1997), *The Changing Constitution of the United Nations* (London: B.I.I.C.L.).

Frowein, J.A. and Krisch, N. (2002), 'Introduction to Chapter VII', in Simma (ed.).

Guillaume, G. (2004), 'Terrorism and International Law', *International and Comparative Law Quarterly* 53:3, 537–548.

Ham van, P. and Bosch, O. (2007), 'Global Non-Proliferation and Counter-terrorism: The Role of Resolution 1540 and Its Implications', in Bosch and van Ham (eds).

Happold, M. (2003), 'Security Council Resolution 1373 and the Constitution of the United Nations', *Leiden Journal of International Law* 16:3, 593–610.

Harper, K. (1994), 'Does the United Nations Security Council Have the Competence to Act as Court and Legislature?', *New York University Journal of International Law and Politics* 27:1, 103–157.

Hudson, M.O. (1931), *International Legislation*, Vol. I (Washington, DC: Carnegie Endowment for International Peace).

Jessup, P.C. (1956), 'Parliamentary Diplomacy: An Examination of the Legal Quality of the Rules of Procedure of Organs of the United Nations', *Recueil des Cours*, 89, 181–320.

Joyner, D.H. (2007), 'Non-proliferation Law and the United Nations System: Resolution 1540 and the Limits of the Power of the Security Council', *Leiden Journal of International Law* 20:2, 489–518.

Kellman, B. (2004), 'Criminalization and Control of WMD Proliferation: The Security Council Acts', *Nonproliferation Review* 11:2, 142–161.

Kelsen, H. (1951), *The Law of the United Nations: A Critical Analysis of Its Fundamental Problems* (London: Stevens & Sons).

Koskenniemi, M. (2005), 'International Legislation Today: Limits and Possibilities', *Wisconsin International Law Journal* 23:1, 61–92.

Krieger, D. and Ong, C. (eds) (2004), *Disarmament: The Missing Link to an Effective Non-Proliferation Regime* (Santa Barbara: Nuclear Age Peace Foundation).

Lavalle, R. (2004), 'A Novel, If Awkward, Exercise in International Law-Making: Security Council Resolution 1540 (2004)', *Netherlands International Law Review* 51:3, 411–437.

Marschik, A. (2005), *The Security Council as World Legislator?: Theory, Practice and Consequences of an Expansion of Powers*, IILJ Working Paper 2005/18 (New York: Institute for International Law and Justice, New York University).

McNair, A.D. (1933–1934), 'International Legislation', *Iowa Law Review* 19, 177–189.

N.A. (2006), 'Update National Implementation' *Chemical Disarmament* 4:4, 33.

N.A. (2007), 'Keeping WMD from Terrorists: An Interview with 1540 Committee Chairman Ambassador Peter Burian' *Arms Control Today* 37:9, 21–24.

Nolte, G. (2000), 'The Limits of the Security Council's Powers and its Functions in the International Legal System: Some Reflections', in Byers (ed.).

Nuclear Black Markets: Pakistan, A.Q. Khan and the Rise of Proliferation Networks (2007) (London: International Institute of Strategic Studies).

Recueil d'études de droit international en hommage à Paul Guggenheim (1968) (Genève: Faculté de droit de l'Université de Genève).

Schrijver, N. (2004), 'September 11 and Challenges to International Law', in Boulden and Weiss (eds).

Schrijver, N. (2007), 'Reforming the UN Security Council in Pursuance of Collective Security', *Journal of Conflict and Security Law* 12:1, 127–137.

Simma, B. (ed.) (2002), *The Charter of the United Nations: A Commentary*, 2nd ed. (Oxford: Oxford UP).

Skubiszewski, K. (1965–1966), 'Enactment of Law by International Organizations', *British Year Book of International Law* 41, 198–274.

Skubiszewski, K. (1968), 'New Source of the Law of Nations: Resolutions of International Organizations', in *Recueil d'études de droit international en hommage à Paul Guggenheim.*

Szasz, P.C. (2002), 'The Security Council Starts Legislating', *American Journal of International Law* 96:4, 901–905.

Talmon, S. (2005), 'The Security Council as World Legislature', *American Journal of International Law* 99:1, 175–193.

Tomuschat, C. (1993), 'Obligations Arising for States without or against Their Will', *Recueil des Cours* 241, 195–374.

Tomuschat, C. (1995), 'Discussion', in Delbrück (ed.).

United Nations (2007), *United Nations Seminar on Implementing UN Security Council Resolution 1540 in Africa*, ODA Occasional Papers No. 12 (New York: United Nations).

de Wet, E. (2004), *The Chapter VII Powers of the United Nations Security Council* (Oxford: Hart).

Yakpo, E. and Boumedra, T. (eds) (1999), *Liber Amicorum Judge Mohammed Bedjaoui* (The Hague: Kluwer).

Yemin, E. (1969), *Legislative Powers in the United Nations and Specialized Agencies* (Leyden: Sijthoff).

Zemanek, K. (1999), 'Is the Security Council the Sole Judge of Its Own Legality?', in Yakpo and Boumedra (eds).

Official Documents and Others

A/54/PV.76, 9 December 1999.

A/58/PV.7, 23 September 2003.

A More Secure World: Our Shared Responsibility, A/59/565, 2 December 2004.

A/RES/57/83, 22 November 2002.

A/RES/58/48, 8 December 2003.

A/RES/59/80, 3 December 2004.

A/RES/60/78, 8 December 2005.

A/RES/61/86, 6 December 2006.

Documents of the United Nations Conference on International Organization (United Nations Information Organizations, 1945), vol. 9.

'Guidelines for Nuclear Transfers', INFCIRC/254/Rev.8/Part 1, 20 March 2006.

'Guidelines for Transfers of Nuclear-Related Dual-Use Equipment, Materials, Software, and Related Technology', INFCIRC/254/Rev.7/Part 2, 20 March 2006.

ICJ Reports 1971.

S/23500, 31 January 1992.

S/2006/257, 25 April 2006.

S/AC.44/2004/(02)/22, 5 November 2004.

S/AC.44/2004/(02)/62/Add.1, 18 January 2006.

S/PV.4385, 28 September 2001.

S/PV.4950, 22 April 2004.

S/PV.4950 (Resumption 1), 22 April 2004.

S/PV.4956, 28 April 2004.

S/PV.5429, 27 April 2006.

S/RES/687(1991), 3 April 1991.

S/RES/827(1993), 25 May 1993.

S/RES/955(1994), 8 November 1994.

'List of National Reports by Submitting Member States' <http://disarmament2.un.org/Committee1540/report.html>.

'Statement by G8 Leaders: The G8 Global Partnership against the Spread of Weapons and Materials of Mass Destruction', Kananaskis, 27 June 2002.

White House (2002), *The National Security Strategy of the United States of America*, September 2002.

White House (2003a), *National Strategy for Combating Terrorism*, February 2003.

White House (2003b), 'Fact Sheet: Proliferation Security Initiative, Statement of Interdiction Principles', 4 September 2003.

White House (2004), 'President Announces New Measures to Counter the Threat of WMD', 11 February 2004.

Chapter 7
Proportionality as a Norm of Application for the Precautionary Principle: Its Significance for the Operation of the Precautionary Regime for Land-based Marine Pollution in the North-West Atlantic

Takeo Horiguchi

Introduction

As recognized in Principle 15 of the Rio Declaration on Environment and Development (1992) (hereinafter Rio Declaration) and many international environmental agreements concluded afterwards, *precaution* is one of the most important regulatory concepts in contemporary international environmental law.[1] In recent academic literatures, authors' focus has gradually shifted from its definition and legal status (i.e., whether it is a norm of customary international law or not) to its implementation. How should we manage uncertain risks and protect our environment in an anticipatory manner? In carrying out this difficult task, however, it seems that the concept of precaution, in and of itself, does not tell us very much. For example, Cameron and Abouchar say that three common elements can be derived from its formulations in different international instruments: (1) regulatory inaction threatens non-negligible harm; (2) there exists a lack of scientific certainty on the cause and effect relationship and (3) under these circumstances, regulatory inaction is unjustified.[2] While this kind of conceptual core suggests a basic approach for addressing environmental issues, it does not actually provide us with substantive guidance as to what to do in such a situation. If we understand this concept in a simple and strong way, to suggest that regulation is required to eliminate possible risks at all costs, this principle will incoherently prohibit the

---

1 Principle 15 of the Rio Declaration states as follows: In order to protect the environment, the precautionary approach shall be widely applied by States according to their capabilities. Where there are threats of serious or irreversible damage, lack of full scientific certainty shall not be used as a reason for postponing cost-effective measures to prevent environmental degradation.

2 Cameron and Abouchar 1996, 45.

very measures that it requires, as taking precautionary measures has their own risks.[3] In order to avoid such a paralysis, we need some balancing tests at least.

In this regard, it becomes frequently argued that concept of *proportionality* provides us with this kind of test for application of precaution. For example, according to the Communication from the European Commission on the Precautionary Principle (2000) (hereinafter the 2000 EC Communication), proportionality is one of the general principles of risk management, which could limit the application of precaution even outside European Law. It states that 'the measures envisaged must make it possible to achieve the appropriate level of protection. Measures based on the precautionary principle must not be disproportionate to the desired level of protection and must not aim at zero risk' (p. 18). It also states that 'risk reduction measures should include less restrictive alternatives which make it possible to achieve an equivalent level of protection' (p. 18). Moreover, although it is a separate principle from proportionality, it mentions a principle of 'examination of the benefits and costs of action or lack of action' and states that 'a comparison must be made between the most likely positive or negative consequences of the envisaged action and those of inaction in terms of the overall cost to the Community, both in the long- and short-term. The measures envisaged must produce an overall advantage as regards reducing risks to an acceptable level' (p. 19). Thus the proportional relation between a means and a goal is said to be required for the application of precaution. In this article, I use the word 'proportionality' to mean such relation between a means and a goal.

Against this background, some authors have started pointing out the interaction between precaution and proportionality,[4] but generally speaking, its significance for regulation has not been sufficiently explored in most of the existing literatures. There are two reasons why I believe so. Firstly, it has been rarely clarified empirically whether and how concept of proportionality works in actual operation of precautionary regimes.[5] As the concept of proportionality is seldom formulated in relevant environmental conventions, we need to look at the operation of the regimes to understand its influence on the application of precaution. Secondly, as I will show in the next section, the significance of such a balancing test has been usually explored as an element of a due diligence obligation to prevent environmental harms. But in the operation of precautionary environmental regimes, Contracting Parties rarely invoke state responsibility for other Parties' breach of relevant obligations. Rather, their main concern is enhancing effectiveness of the regimes (i.e., promoting their common interest), and therefore it probably deserves to be examined whether the interaction of precaution and proportionality has any importance in this context as well.

---

3 Sunstein 2007, 123–134.

4 See Marr 2003, 35–40; de Sadeleer 2002, 167–172.

5 In this chapter, a 'precautionary regime' means a regime which adopts precautionary principle or approach as a guiding principle for their regulation.

In this chapter, I will attempt to address the above-mentioned problems and to make some progress in understanding the significance of proportionality for the application of precaution by examining operation of a precautionary regime. After exploring briefly how international lawyers have considered the relationship between precaution and proportionality, I will examine whether and how considerations of proportionality are institutionalized in actual decision-making processes for precautionary measures and consider their significance for the effectiveness of an environmental regime, focusing on the development of international regulation for land-based marine pollution (LBMP) under the Convention for the Protection of the Marine Environment of the North-East Atlantic (1992) (hereinafter the OSPAR Convention), which is no doubt one of most developed and most experienced precautionary environmental regimes today.

Precaution, Proportion and Proportionality

Two Types of Proportion in Relation to Precaution

One could say that the notion of proportion is inherent within any legal system. In relation to the concept of precaution in international environmental law, at least two types of proportion have been discussed in academic literature.

The first type concerns the relationship between the significance of risk or magnitude of possible harm, and the level of scientific uncertainty which justifies preventive actions. For example, Handl points out that '(t)oday, it should be axiomatic that the greater the risk of harm threatened, the lower the evidentially burden concerning source-specific causal linkage and injurious trans-boundary environmental impact'.[6] Similarly Freestone states that 'some sort of balancing test is implicit in the formulation discussed above; the greater the possible risk to the environment, the greater the level of scientific uncertainty which may be acceptable for the precautionary principle to become engaged'.[7] Thus it is maintained that the level of scientific uncertainty that could be tolerated for taking precautionary measures should be proportional to the gravity of possible harm.

Authors, however, have recently started to discuss another type of proportion in relation to precaution.[8] This second type concerns the relationship between a means and a goal, namely that the means should be proportionate to the goal it is designed to achieve. In contrast to the first type of proportion, it does not directly address elements of scientific uncertainty or environmental risks which constitute the conceptual core of precaution, yet it is thought to be useful in mitigating any excesses that might arise by application of precaution. Today, this second type of proportion is generally called the 'principle of proportionality'.

6 Handl 1991, 77.

7 Freestone 1991, 33.

8 Marr 2003, 35–40; de Sadeleer 2002, 167–172.

Using proportion in this sense is certainly influenced by the development of the principle of proportionality in EU law, as authors who discuss this type of proportion usually refer to the EU's practice.[9] On the European level, it is widely admitted that the principle of proportionality consists of three tests to co-ordinate conflicting interests, although there is some disagreement on the precise contents of those tests, i.e., appropriateness (or suitability), necessity and proportionality in a narrow sense.[10] For example, in relation to trade-restrictive environmental measures, Ziegler explains these tests as follows:

> (a) whether a measure is genuinely aimed at or reasonably justified for the attempted objective,
>
> (b) whether the measure is essential or necessary for the attainment of the objective, implying that it has to be the least trade-restrictive measure available among several alternatives, and
>
> (c) whether the improvement in environmental quality is proportionate to the restriction of trade resulting from this measure.[11]

But one should be cautious to argue that this principle has been already established in general international law as well.[12] Rather, it is safe to say that this kind of proportion has been established only in certain fields of international law, such as law of armed conflicts, human right, international trade and state responsibility (i.e., countermeasures). And even if this principle is well established in international environmental law, it is not self-evident that the above-mentioned tests are required. We need cautious examination in this regard.

Precaution as a Rule or a Principle

Before examining whether and how the principle of proportionality functions as a norm for the application of precaution, it should be understood why the different types of proportion have been discussed by international lawyers. In my view, the recent shift in commentators' interest on proportion is not only a result of the development of the EU law, but also closely connected with their understanding of how precaution should be characterized as a norm, i.e., as a *rule* or as a *principle*. According to Ronald Dworkin, whose distinction between rules and principles has been generally referred to by international environmental lawyers, a principle 'states a reason that argues in one direction, but does not necessitate a particular decision' as a rule and 'ha(s) a dimension that rules do not – the dimension of

9 Marr 2003, 36; de Sadeleer 2002, 168–169.

10 Ziegler 1996, 96–103; Craig and De Burca 2003, 372.

11 Ziegler 1996, 97–98.

12 See Higgins 1994, 236.

weight or importance'.[13] On the basis of this distinction between a rule and a principle, one could understand more clearly the difference between the two types of proportion mentioned above.

Although the first type of proportion may work as a limiting factor for the application of precaution as a principle as well, the authors who mention this kind of proportion intend to suggest that it mainly functions to formulate precaution as a rule of general international law as an extension of the traditional no-harm rule. Although usually called a principle, the no-harm rule has been actually theorized as a rule, whose violation would provide a basis for invoking state responsibility for damages caused by trans-boundary pollution.[14] In other words, it is theorized as an obligation of due diligence to prevent environmental harms.

Against this background, proportion in the first meaning provides logic, which serves to argue that this traditional rule may also cover uncertain risks in proportion to their gravity. This norm might be called a rule of precautionary action whose violation would be a basis for invoking state responsibility of polluting states.

However, apart from difficulties in setting the threshold of damage in the face of uncertainty, this line of argument would need to confront a simple question: Is there any real need to characterize precaution as a separate rule from the traditional no-harm rule? One might say that precaution is just a new label for the existing norm. Indeed, the authors who point to this first type of proportion recognize this problem. For example, Handl admits that the no-harm rule can cover uncertain risks, but he concludes in the end that there is no new norm of international law called 'precaution'.[15] In contrast, Freestone argues that precaution is a norm of international law, but he also admits that sometimes it is very hard to distinguish precaution from the no-harm rule (i.e., the duty of prevention).[16] These arguments imply that it is not easy to formulate precaution as a rule, and even if it is possible, it is hard to characterize it as a separate rule from the no-harm rule.[17]

---

13 Dworkin 1977, 47. This distinction has been frequently criticized in jurisprudence literatures. For example, Raz 1972, 825–842. While examining these criticisms is beyond scope of this chapter, what is to be noted here is that most authors who characterize precaution as a principle refer to the Dworkin's distinction and so it could be presumed that those authors share the same view as Dworkin's.

14 This is sometimes called the 'classical approach' or 'Trail Smelter approach'. For example, Riphagen 1980, 344–345. As a literature which explicitly characterizes the no-harm rule as a rule, see also Beyerlin 2007, 439.

15 Handl 1991, 78–79.

16 Freestone 1991, 30. Freestone points out that in weakest formulations of precaution 'it would be difficult to distinguish from the preventive principle which is already well known to international environmental law', while he suggests that a reversal of burden of proof is its strongest form.

17 It is true that some authors have tried to characterize precaution as a rule. For example, Beyerlin 2007, 440; Trouwborst 2006, 296. It seems to me that the better understating is that the rule those authors formulate is not direct effect of precaution, but

By contrast, the second type of proportion, namely the principle of proportionality, does not provide the logic to extend the application of the no-harm *rule* to cover uncertain risks, but rather assumes that precaution is firmly established as a different kind of norm, namely a *principle* and as a competing principle proportionality is expected to limit its application. The authors who discuss this type of proportion generally emphasize that precaution is a *principle* rather than a *rule* and suggest that there is an interaction or competition with other principles in its application.[18] Strictly speaking, those competing principles consist of two different kinds of norms. One is a principle which aims to realize non-environmental values and could be applied depending on specific contexts of application of precaution. Principles of Sustainable Development (e.g., sustainable use) or principles of the Law of Sea (e.g., freedom of the high seas) are good examples. Another is a principle which aims to secure some balance of interests and could be applied in every case when a precautionary measure is decided. Therefore, it is arguably characterized as a norm of application for precaution in general. Proportionality is now regarded as one of the latter kind of competing principles, which would provide a good reason to argue against adoption of excessively stringent precautionary measures. Thus, it provides a logic of limitation, rather than a logic of extension for the application of an existent norm. In this sense, the shift of authors' interest in proportion means that they have started recognizing that it is more important to explore the implementation of precaution than to discuss its legal status as a rule of customary international law.

Moreover, it could be argued that this shift reflects the general trend of development of international environmental law, namely from application of law of state responsibility to development of regulatory regimes. It is very hard to formulate a principle as a specific duty, but it provides some guidance for states' rule-making or interpretation of rules for promoting common interest.[19] Thus principles can be seen as norms that are designed to influence decision-making, mainly in the environmental regulatory regimes, within which they are stipulated in relevant instruments as regulatory guidance. Although this does not mean that precaution as a principle has no significance in international litigation,[20] it is within those regulatory regimes that precautionary decision-making is usually made, and this is a reason why I focus on regimes' operations in order to explore the function of the principle of proportionality.

In contrast to the former kind of competing principles, however, the principle of proportionality is rarely formulated in relevant environmental conventions and its significance for regulation has not been sufficiently explored empirically in the existing literatures. Whether and how does proportionality work in the

outcome of reinterpretation of the no-harm rule in light of precaution as a principle. As an argument supporting this understanding, see Birnie and Boyle 2002, 120.

18 See, *inter alia*, Marr 2003, 35–45.

19 See Beyerlin 2007, 437.

20 In this regard, see Birnie and Boyle 2002, 120.

actual operation of precautionary regimes? Let us turn to address this question by examining the OSPAR regime.

Evolution of a Precautionary Regime for LBMP in the North-East Atlantic

Precautionary principle and evolution of the OSPAR regime for LBMP

Sources of marine pollution are mainly human activities on land. These activities encompass many socio-economic sectors, such as industry, forestry, agriculture, transportation, urban development and tourism.[21] Although these activities could first and foremost cause water pollution along coasts of polluting states themselves, and so one may say that LBMP is basically a domestic issue, it is now widely recognized that those pollutants move across artificial boundaries of jurisdiction and contaminate the water of other states or the high seas, especially in a closed or semi-closed sea. Thus international regulations for LBMP have been developed for some regional seas, while there is no global convention in this environmental field, though the non-binding Global Programme of Action for the Protection on the Marine Environment from Land-Based Activities (hereinafter the 1995 Global Programme) was adopted in 1995.[22]

In the 1970s an international agreement for LBMP was concluded for the North-East Atlantic,[23] but the concept of precaution was unfamiliar at the time. Rather, it followed the traditional approach to marine pollution, generally called the 'assimilative approach'. This approach is based on the following premises: the marine environment has a capacity to assimilate pollutants and avoid occurrence of harmful effect; this capacity is not finite and the limit of the capacity can be scientifically established and allocated to concerned states.[24] Importantly, the approach assumes that even if the limit is crossed over, there would be ample time to deal with the contamination without serious environmental degradation. It also provides a basis for arguing that it should be assumed that emission of substances is safe unless it could be scientifically proven that it would cause environmental harm.[25] In this sense, one may call it *economically oriented*, as scientific uncertainty would work in favour of states or people who pursue economic interests.[26]

It should be noted, however, that this was not the only approach endorsed in the past for LBMP. To be more exact, the characteristic of the older regulations

---

21 For example, see paras. 17.18 and 17.19 of Agenda 21, adopted on 13 June 1992. As to sources and effects of LBMP, see also Hassan 2006, 11–36.

22 United Nations Environmental Programme (UNEP) 1995.

23 Convention for the Prevention of Marine Pollution from Land-Based Sources, adopted on 4 June 1974 (hereinafter Paris Convention).

24 See Pravdic 1985, 295.

25 See MacDonald 1995, 266.

26 As to characteristics of assimilative approach in general, see Hey 1992, 308.

should be called an *alternative concept*.[27] This means that parties had a choice between the assimilative approach based upon scientific monitoring on conditions of marine environment as a receptor of wastes, or adopting another approach, which focused on minimizing the generation of harmful substances at their source. While the former approach was mainly adopted by the UK or Ireland whose coastal water was not severely contaminated thanks to ocean currents, the latter was mainly endorsed by European continental countries which asserted that it was a more effective way to prevent LBMP and had a less adverse effect on competitive conditions of concerned states as it called for uniform emission standards.[28] Thus there was a disagreement on an appropriate approach to the prevention of LBMP and this often prevented the parties from adopting effective common measures.

This situation was gradually changed when the *precautionary principle* (*Vorsorgeprinzip*) was proposed by West Germany as a new regulatory concept for marine pollution in North Sea Ministerial Conferences in 1980s. The Bremen Declaration of the first Ministerial Conference (1984) declared that the states were '*conscious* that damage to the marine environment can be irreversible or remediable only at considerable expense and over long periods and that, therefore, coastal states and the EEC must not wait for proof of harmful effects before taking action' (para. A7).[29] Although this paragraph did not explicitly refer to 'precaution', there is no doubt that it reflected essence of *Vorsorgeprinzip*. In fact, the same guideline was reaffirmed as 'the principle of precautionary action' for LBMP in the London Declaration of the second Ministerial Conference (1987) (para. 16.1).[30]

The proposal for this new regulatory concept was based on the recognition that the assimilative approach was not sufficiently efficacious for pollution prevention[31] and aimed at overcoming the stalemate caused by disagreement on a basic approach

27 See Winter 1988, 266; Hohmann 1994, 190.

28 Saetevik 1988, 42.

29 The text of the Bremen Declaration is reprinted in Freestone and Ijlstra 1990, 61–89.

30 The text of the London Declaration is reprinted in Freestone and Ijlstra 1990, 40–60.

31 A German report on environmental issues in North Sea, titled *Umweltprobleme der Nordee* (1980), explains as follows why new concept of precaution is needed: 'a successful environmental policy has to be guided by the principle of precautionary action. ... Mechanisms which determine the limits of environmental capacity are still largely unknown. Environmental policy therefore has to prevent adverse ecological developments, without having the opportunity to be guided only by already established impacts on the marine environment when specific measures have to be taken'. Cited in Freestone 1991, 21–22.

This insufficiency of assimilative approach was already recognized at the beginning of 1980s, in particular for highly dangerous substances. For example, the Parties of the old Paris Convention agreed to adopt the standstill principle as an interim measure for management of mercury. This principle, which required states not to increase concentration of mercury in marine environment, was endorsed partly because it was concerned that

to prevent pollution. As a result, endorsement of a *cumulative concept*, which demanded that uniform emission reduction measures and environmental quality standards should be combined, replaced the *alternative concept*. For example, while the Bremen Declaration provides that a strict limitation of emission of pollutants at source should be imposed if the state of knowledge is insufficient (para. C9), so minimization of emission is basically favoured under scientific uncertainty, it also demands that the adopted emission control should be tightened if environmental monitoring shows that the quality of environment is insufficient (para. C11). This cumulative concept was reaffirmed in para. 15.2 of the London Declaration and preamble of the Hague Declaration of the third Ministerial Conference (1990).[32] One of the main consequences of recognizing the cumulative concept is that inaction by states is no longer justified by lack of scientific proof on the assimilative capacity exceeded by harmful substances. Indeed, in the North Sea Declarations, significant reduction in the emission of harmful substances was agreed. For instance, the London Declaration demanded states to 'take measures to reduce urgently and drastically the total quantity of such substances reaching the aquatic environment of the North Sea, with the aim of achieving a substantial reduction (of the order of 50%) in total inputs from these sources between 1985 and 1995' (para. 16.2).

After these Declarations, the concept of precaution has been formally incorporated into not only the North-Eastern Atlantic regime, which covers the North Sea, but also the Mediterranean Regime and the Baltic Regime as well.[33] Moreover, as paragraph 9 of the 1995 Global Programme refers to precaution as a necessary approach to marine pollution,[34] precautionary regimes are expected to be developed for other regional areas as well. Under these precautionary regimes, emission reduction at source is required to prevent pollution in face of scientific uncertainty. But there is wide concern that the excessive reduction of emissions could cause serious economic loss or disadvantage for regulated states. In this regard, those regimes have adopted standards of Best Available Techniques (BAT) and Best Environmental Practices (BEP) as a means for emission reduction of

mercury pollution would seriously worsen before an appropriate qualitative standard would be agreed. See Paris Commission (PARCOM) 1980, para. 43.

32 The text of the Hague Declaration is reprinted in Freestone and Ijlstra 1990, 3–39.

33 Article 2(2)(a) of the OSPAR Convention; preamble of the Protocol for the Protection of the Mediterranean Sea against Pollution from Land-Based Sources, amended on 7 March 1996 (hereinafter amended Athens Protocol 1996); Article 3.2 of the Convention on the Protection of the Marine Environment of the Baltic Sea (hereinafter Helsinki Convention 1992).

34 The 1995 Global Programme states that '... to protect the marine environment from LBS (=Land-Based Sources) in the context of sustainable development it is necessary to apply preventive, precautionary and anticipatory approaches so as to avoid degradation of the marine environment, as well as to reduce the risk of long term or irreversible adverse effects upon it' (para. 9a).

harmful substances, and one may plausibly suppose that some consideration of proportionality is institutionalized under the relevant processes. Does the concept of proportionality actually exert influence in the decision-making processes for determining those standards? And how?

Proportionality in Decision-Makings on Precautionary Measures: BAT and BEP

BAT and BEP as 'Effective' and 'Appropriate' Standards BAT and BEP are the main regulatory tools for pollution prevention within the OSPAR Convention for LBMP (Article 2(3)b1 and Appendix I).[35] BAT is defined as 'the latest stage of development (state of the art) of processes, of facilities or of methods of operation which indicate the practical suitability of a particular measure for limiting discharges, emissions and waste' (Appendix I, para. 2). As for BEP, the OSPAR Convention defines it as 'the application of the most appropriate combination of environmental control measures and strategies' (Appendix I, para. 6).[36]

These standards aim at reducing and minimizing the input of harmful substances at source, without depending upon the assimilative capacity of the marine environment which is supposed to be determined scientifically in advance of emission control. In this sense, they could be regarded as standards that could be agreed based on the concept of precaution,[37] although the specific content of those standards needs to be determined subsequently for each socio-economic sector and each harmful substance. It is this decision-making process for the elaboration of those standards where some consideration of proportionality between a means and a goal is institutionalized.

First and most importantly, one could argue that these specific standards should be effective and in this sense appropriate to marine environmental protection.[38] Here 'effective' means 'efficacious for environmental protection' in terms of the substance of the given measures. In order to avoid confusion with the term 'effectiveness', which means in this article actual implementation of relevant norms, the word 'appropriateness' will be used to mean being 'effective' or 'efficacious'. A main deficiency of uniform emission reduction is that it dose not necessarily guarantee pollution prevention when volume of emissions are too large or emissions are concentrated too much in limited areas. This is another

35 Similarly, Article 5(4) of the revised Athens Protocol and Article 3(3) of the Helsinki Convention provide for the application of BAT and BEP. See also para. 26 (a)(i)a of the 1995 Global Programme.

36 Almost identical definitions of BAT and BEP could be found in other instruments as well. Annex IV, paras. 2 and 6 of the revised Athens Protocol and Annex II, para. 1 of regulation 2 and para. 1 of regulation 3 of the Helsinki Convention.

37 In the 1990 Hague Declaration, North Sea States agreed that 'the application of precautionary principle requires the application of the Best Available Technology in order to minimize discharges of wastes and residues' (para. 25).

38 For example, see OSPAR Commission 2003 (para. 5.2 of section III).

reason why the *cumulative concept* becomes accepted as an appropriate regulatory guideline. In this regard, 'the nature and volume of the discharges and emissions concerned' (for BAT) or 'the scale of use' (for BEP) is listed as one of factors to be considered when elaborating those standards.[39] Moreover, if it becomes apparent that application of these standards does not result in acceptable level of protection, additional measures should be taken or the standards should be redefined.[40]

Indeed, when several possible means are examined for determining BAT or BEP, their appropriateness is an essential factor to be considered. For example, an OSPAR Commission's publication on 'Best Available Techniques for the Emulsion Polyvinyl Chloride Industry' mentions in the conclusion several techniques as Best Technology mainly referring to their appropriateness (i.e., being 'effective'). Based on this publication, OSPAR Recommendation 99/1 on the Best Available Techniques for the Manufacture of Emulsion PVC (e-PVC) is adopted and it states as follows: 'as a minimum standard, the techniques outlined in paragraphs 3.4–3.18 below, or *equally effective measures*, should be applied to the relevant stages of manufacture of e-PVC in all new plant. An important aim of these techniques is the elimination of VCM emissions, as far as possible' (para. 3.2). Although the OSPAR convention does not explicitly define it, it is plausible to think that BAT or BEP's 'best' implies 'most effective'.[41] One may doubt whether adopting the *most* effective measure is a component of proportionality, and it is not clear whether certain range of effectiveness can be regarded as 'most effective', what is to be noted here is that it is obvious that ineffective (i.e., inappropriate) measures are extremely difficult to be defined or maintained as specific BAT or BEP.

Non-environmental Factors Secondly, socio-economic factors are explicitly required to be considered in the elaboration of those standards. This point was actually contentious, especially for BAT, and it was sometimes argued that most advanced technological standards should be applied regardless of its economic cost.[42] It is true that these standards are basically oriented toward the minimization and elimination of inputs of harmful substances,[43] but given the subsequent development of criteria for the determination of BAT and BEP, it is

39 Para. 2(e) and para. 7(c) of Appendix I of the OSPAR Convention.

40 Paras. 4 and 9 of Appendix I of the OSPAR Convention.

41 Recent international instruments tend to define clearly 'best' as 'most effective' at least for BAT. See Article 2(11) of Council Directive 96/61/EC of 24 September 1996 concerning integrated pollution prevention and control and Article 5 f(iv) of the Convention on Persistent Organic Pollutants, adopted on 22 May 2001.

42 Nollkaemper points out that BAT was traditionally defined strictly in terms of its technological availability and was often contrasted with the concept of the best practical means which demands consideration of their economic availability. Nollkaemper 1993, 131–132.

43 Clean technologies or non waste technology are generally favored for BAT, if it is available and availability of less polluting substitutes have to be examined when deciding BEP. Para. 1 and para. 7(b) of Appendix I of the OSPAR Convention.

no longer possible to argue that they should be determined without considering socio-economic factors. For example, the 'economic feasibility' of techniques is now explicitly recognized as one of the factors to be considered in elaborating BAT.[44] Similarly, 'social and economic implications' is listed as a criterion for determination of specific BEP.[45] Furthermore, it is recognized that what constitutes a BAT or BEP will change with time in light of not only changes in scientific understanding or knowledge, but also changes in economic and social factors.[46] Thus, non-environmental factors are obviously included in those standards.[47]

The Role of 'Cost-effectiveness' However, how to balance environmental interest with non-environmental interest is not necessarily very certain. As I mentioned above, different words are used to indicate the non-environmental factors: 'economic feasibility' for BAT and 'social and economic implications' for BEP. While 'economic feasibility' is decided by examining whether measures could be economically accepted by relevant industries, and in this sense it is distinguished from unlimited balancing of cost and benefit,[48] what 'implication' exactly means is not clear. Indeed, consideration of socio-economic factors is required by several different concepts in the OSPAR regime. For example, the revised Strategies of the OSPAR Commission (2003) (hereinafter the 2003 Strategy),[49] which was adopted as a guideline for developing regulations, explicitly states that application of BAT or BEP to combat eutrophication should take account of their 'cost-effectiveness' in addition to 'feasibility' (para. 3.5b(iii) of section II). Similarly, the 2003 Strategy states that most 'cost-effective' measures should have the highest priority for hazardous substances (para. 5.5 of section III), while it also states that measures for those substances should be selected considering 'an assessment of the advantages, disadvantages and effectiveness of proposed measures' (Para. 5.5c of section III).

Considering the different concepts used, it is not always easy to clarify how socio-economic factors should be considered in decision-making for precautionary measures in the OSPAR regime. But one could plausibly suggest two points in this regard. Firstly, as the 2003 Strategy suggests, the requirement of 'cost-effectiveness' is generally mentioned in relation to selection of several effective measures or setting priority. Indeed, it is required to examine all available options before defining the specific standards in the OSPAR regime. For BAT, 'comparable

---

44 Para. 2(c) of Appendix I of the OSPAR Convention.

45 Para. 7(g) of Appendix I of the OSPAR Convention.

46 Paras. 3 and 8 of Appendix I of the OSPAR Convention.

47 The 1995 Global Programme cautiously notes that BAT is understood to include socio-economic factors for the purpose of the Programme. Moreover, it mentions 'economic costs and benefits' as one of criteria for assessing effectiveness of strategies or measures. See United Nations Environmental Programme (UNEP) 1995, 15–16.

48 Nollkaemper 1996, 162.

49 OSPAR Commission 2003.

processes, facilities or methods of operation which have recently been successfully tried out' shall be especially considered.[50] Regarding BEP, inclusive categories of possible measures are generally listed in related annexes or appendixes.[51] In the best available techniques reference documents (BREFs), which are prepared for European integrated pollution prevention and are referred to in the OSPAR regime as well, possible techniques are comprehensively examined including their socio-economic impact.[52] As a result of such comprehensive assessment and the requirement of 'cost-effectiveness', it must be quite difficult for certain measures to be defined as BAT or BEP, if there is another measure that is equally effective but obviously less costly. But this point is not very clear in the actual decision making within the OSPAR regime.

Secondly, while 'cost-effectiveness' mainly concerns choice among possible measures that are equally efficacious, it seems that there is a room for consideration on benefit and cost of selected effective measures in examining 'economic feasibility' or 'social and economic implication', because the lowest possible cost may still be very high. Besides the requirement of cost-effectiveness, it is often stated that costs and advantages are to be considered in relevant guidelines, as I mentioned above. For another example, in the introductory remarks for a specific BAT, the BREFs explicitly mention that some balancing between cost and advantage of measures are inherent in BAT.[53] This requirement of general consideration of the costs and benefits of the given measures is reflected in the differentiation of regulation between existing plants and new plants. For example, in the OSPAR Recommendation on the Best Available Techniques for the Manufacture of Emulsion PVC of 1999,[54] while the recommended BAT would be applied for new plants from 1 January 2000, it prescribes for existing plants as follows: '... the competent authorities of the Contracting Parties should draw up, in consultation with the plant operators, an improvement programme so as to ensure that the plant performs at increasingly high standards, taking into account the criteria listed in paragraph 2 of Appendix 1 of the OSPAR Convention (Best Available Techniques). From 1 January 2004 the same standards should apply to existing plant as to new plant' (para. 3.3).

One can plausibly argue that this paragraph suggests that even if the described BAT was appropriate and less costly than other options, it was thought that applying these standards immediately to existing plants was too costly, at least on 1 January 2000, due to their adverse effect on their operation or investment costs, and therefore less stringent interim standards were allowed to be applied for those plants in order to improve gradually their performance.

50 Para. 2(a) of Appendix I of the OSPAR Convention.

51 Para. 6 of Appendix I of the OSPAR Convention.

52 See generally European Integrated Pollution Prevention and Control Bureau 2005.

53 For example, see European Commission 2001, 132.

54 The OSPAR Commission 1999.

In sum, it is arguable that BAT and BEP are institutionalized to include some consideration of proportionality in the decision-making process for determining specific precautionary measures, even if the principle of proportionality itself is rarely mentioned explicitly. For deciding specific BAT or BEP standards, possible options should be widely examined and as a result of the examination, it is very hard for inappropriate (inefficacious) or excessively costly measures to be identified or maintained as specific standards. Moreover, in setting priority between several effective options, cost-effectiveness is widely required, although whether this requirement functions as a test of necessity is not very certain in the actual decision-making of the regime. Even if it is possible to argue that the tests of appropriateness, necessity and proportionality in a narrow sense are explicit or, at least implicit in decision-making in the OSPAR regime, it seems that decision-makers are not required to pursue the most proportional measures. Rather, consideration of proportionality demands avoidance of excessiveness or obvious disproportion between a means and a goal in deciding precautionary measures.

Proportionality and the Effectiveness of the Precautionary Regime

Proportionality and Legitimacy of the Precautionary Regime

In the text of the OSPAR Convention, we can find the term 'proportionality' nowhere. Moreover, the precautionary principle is formulated without the requirement of cost-effectiveness, which is now widely mentioned as an element of precautionary principle in other international instruments such as the Rio Declaration. Despite these facts, why is the consideration of proportionality institutionalized under the precautionary OSPAR regime? One may argue that such consideration could undermine precautionary environmental protection. This argument is mainly based on the fact that socio-economic interests generally tend to be given more weight than environmental interests.[55] It is true that environmental interests, especially long-term ones, should be given proper weight, as the 2000 EC Communication emphasized.[56] But naturally this point does not automatically lead to the conclusion that we should not consider non-environmental interests in deciding precautionary measures. Such a conclusion is obviously inconsistent with the concept of sustainable development, which calls for reconciliation between

55 This point has been often mentioned to emphasize incompatibility between precaution and traditional cost–benefit analysis, as the economic accounting methods involved in the latter are biased in that they discount the long-term losses inherent in environmental degradation. See Trouwborst 2006, 249.

56 See European Commission 2000, 18. The Communication also importantly states that '[e]xamination of the pros and cons cannot be reduced to an economic cost–benefit analysis. It is wider in scope and includes non-economic consideration' (19).

environment and socio-economic development and is now generally endorsed as a fundamental goal of the contemporary international community.

Rather, it might be argued that consideration of the proportionality between a means and a goal would enhance the effectiveness of the precautionary regimes. One possible explanation on this point is that since the principle of proportionality is now widely recognized in domestic public law and EU law, international standards without taking account of such proportionality could have difficulty in being implemented domestically. This seems especially true for the OSPAR regime, all of whose parties are European countries where principle of proportionality is relatively well established. But this explanation depends on the feature of certain legal systems and that might be a limit of its explanatory force. Moreover, one can argue that even if the principle of proportionality is well established in some legal systems, its components are not always clear or identical.

Another possible explanation is related to the legitimacy of the precautionary regime. Regarding the effectiveness of international regimes, authors frequently focus on the significance of peculiar procedures for international supervision, such as state reporting systems or non-compliance procedures.[57] It is true that these 'soft enforcement' procedures are frequently useful for promoting compliance and development of relevant rules, but given that those procedures are not almighty, and a strong enforcement mechanism is inherently lacking in the international community, enhancing the legitimacy of regimes is more fundamentally important for their effectiveness. Especially regarding specific BAT and BEP standards, voluntary implementation is essential, as those standards are usually adopted by the non-binding recommendation. In this regard, *state consent* has been traditionally an important source of legitimacy of international institutions, but this source is gradually losing its prominent role, mainly for two reasons.[58] First, relevant decision-making is no longer necessarily based on state consent. As for decision-making on measures in the OSPAR regime, states generally have to seek consensus, but if it is found to be unattainable, there is a room for majority voting.[59] Second, regulation of the precautionary regimes is increasingly influential on non-state actors. Especially for LBMP, targets of regulation encompass almost the whole of human activity, from the operation of gigantic industrial facilities to the daily life of urban people. In light of this situation, state consent alone does not seem to be a strong source of the regime's legitimacy, especially for non-state actors. Against this background, other sources of legitimacy as well need to be pursued for enhancing the effectiveness of regimes. In this regard, authors often focus on *process* as a source of legitimacy. Public participation is a good example, and this too is a current trend in the development of the OSPAR regime for LBMP, as will be mentioned below.

57 As a recent work examining such procedures and enforcement systems in international regimes, see Ulfstein, Marauhn and Zimmermann 2007.

58 See Bodansky 2007, 712–714.

59 Article 13(1) of the OSPAR Convention.

However, there is another possible source of legitimacy: *outcome*, or it is better to say, *efficacy*.[60] If a given regime is expected to be more efficacious for achieving environmental protection than other regimes or unilateral action of states, there is a good reason for states to obey decisions made in that regime. Then a question arises: How could such expectations be generated? It is in this context where institutionalizing regulatory principles has significance. One could argue that consistent decision-making with basic environmental principles such as precaution would positively influence a regimes' legitimacy, because such decisions could efficaciously promote regimes' goals.[61] In case of precautions, the reason it was proposed as a new regulatory concept for regulation of LBMP was that the traditional assimilative approach was thought to be insufficient for the prevention of pollution. Thus consistency with precaution could arguably enhance regimes' legitimacy, because such regimes would be expected to protect environment more efficaciously than other possible regimes that are inconsistent with it.

But what makes the matter more complicated is that the concept of sustainable development is now recognized as an over-arching goal of international environmental regimes, and this concept calls for the reconciliation between environmental interests and socio-economic interests. Therefore pursuing environmental interest only is inconsistent with the fundamental goal to be achieved and radical application of precaution would raise serious doubt about the regime's legitimacy.[62] Indeed, precaution is often regarded and utilized as such an *environment-oriented* concept as it may be invoked to claim a ban of certain activities or zero-risk policy even without taking into account relevant socio-economic interests.[63] This frequently gives rise to concerns about overregulation or paralysis of economic activities. For example, having showed concern about adopting the precautionary principle as regulatory guidance for LBMP, the UK has consistently emphasized that BAT should not impose excessive cost.

Considering the basic structure of the precautionary legal order, these concerns are not without reason. Under the traditional assimilative approach, the general duty to prevent pollution aims to protect the rights of parties to use assimilative capacity as a resource. In this sense, the duty is inherent in the traditional right of states. By contrast, under the concept of precaution, the duty is based on the public interest to protect marine ecosystem, which is external to the right to use

60 See Bodansky 2007, 718–721.

61 Of course, this does not mean that consistent decision-making with the environmental principles is the only factor for enhancing efficacy of regimes. Rather, scientific expertise is more frequently suggested as an important factor. See Bodansky 2007, 718–721.

62 Although it is not related to LBMP, the whale conservation regime seems to have been facing this problem.

63 For example, Handl points out that essence of precaution might be economic utilitarian, but this concept also seems to be underlain by preservationist view which recognizes inherent value of environment. See Handl 1991, 78.

assimilative capacity. Therefore, it might ultimately delegitimize the use of the sea for waste disposal and consequently restrict socio-economic activities to significant degree.[64] Together with the vagueness of the content of precaution, this could provide a plausible reason against the legal authority of precaution.

As consideration of proportionality ensures some balancing between environmental interests and non-environmental interests, a consistent operation of precaution with the principle of proportionality would be expected to realize the goal of sustainable development more efficaciously than an inconsistent one. In fact, this point is recognized within the OSPAR regime. For example, just after stating that measures should be taken to encourage green chemistry to support sustainable development, the 2003 Strategy emphasizes that cost-effective measures should have priority and measures should be developed in the light of requirements laid down in the definition of BAT and BEP in the OSPAR Convention (para. 5.5 of section III). In this sense, it is possible to argue that consistency with proportionality would enhance the legitimacy of the precautionary regimes in terms of efficacy and consequently contributes to their effectiveness. As mentioned in the previous section, authors have often regarded such a balancing test as an element of due diligence obligation.[65] This kind of argument focuses on standard of state responsibility, but given that promoting common interest is usually a more central concern within environmental regulatory regime, it is also important to explore its influence on effectiveness of the regimes.

Does Proportionality Really Function in the Precautionary Regime?

It is to be noted that the OSPAR regime for LBMP has developed several regulatory arrangements that could serve in enhancing this function of proportionality. First of all, relevant information as to proportionality of measures is to be constantly exchanged and collected within the regime. For example, working groups were established for point and diffuse sources of pollution and they have reviewed and developed BAT/BEP measures. For defining specific BAT/BEP, lead countries are designated, which prepare relevant background papers and draft resolutions. In this process, relevant information is collected from other contacting parties and non-state actors, such as industry or NGOs. Moreover, relevant works done in other forums like EU or other regimes are widely referred to.[66] Thus under

64 In fact, the Contracting Parties of the OSPAR Convention agreed in the Sintra Statement (1998) that in principle waste disposal was no longer legitimate use of the sea. See the next subsection below.

65 For example, see Nollkaemper 1996, 74.

66 A guideline adopted for preparation for BAT description states as follows: 'Work started within OSPAR on the preparation of a new OSPAR BAT Description, or the revision of an existing BAT Description should take into account any relevant information from related work being carried out or envisaged in the framework of Council Directive 96/61/ EC on integrated pollution prevention and control (EC BAT Reference Documents; IPPC/

the leadership of certain countries, information which is necessary to decide proportional measures would be stored up, which surely enhances the efficacy of the regime.[67]

Secondly, the general goal of the regime has been more elaborated by setting environmental quality objectives or long-term emission reduction targets. These objectives or targets could mitigate the difficulty in assessing the appropriateness of precautionary measures. For example, the Sintra Statement adopted in ministerial conference of OSPAR Parties in 1998 states,

> we agree to prevent pollution of the maritime area by continuously reducing discharges, emissions and losses of hazardous substances (that is, substances which are toxic, persistent and liable to bioaccumulate or which give rise to an equivalent level of concern), *with the ultimate aim of achieving concentrations in the environment near background values for naturally occurring substances and close to zero for man-made synthetic substances. We shall make every endeavour to move towards the target of cessation of discharges, emissions and losses of hazardous substances by the year 2020. We emphasize the importance of the precautionary principle in this work.*[68]

Whether this aim is realistic or not, it clarified a long-term target which provide more definite basis for assessing appropriateness of specific precautionary measures. For example, there has been recognition that EC's BAT is not necessarily appropriate for OSPAR's BAT, because the aims of regulation are not identical between them.[69] Regarding environmental quality objectives, they would provide basis for assessing appropriateness of existing BAT/BEP standards, as explained above.

Thirdly, by setting priorities on substances to be regulated, efficient use of regulatory resources has been secured to some degree. In this regard, OSPAR

BREF) or from other international organisations dealing with BAT for the sector'. The OSPAR Commission 2004 (Sec. 1, para. 3 of Appendix I).

67 For example, as to the emulsion PVC, the UK was designated as a lead country and required to prepare an elaborated draft of background document and an outline for draft recommendation in 1997. The delegation of UK informed Programmes and Measures Committee of OSPAR (PRAM) that it obtained useful information from industry, but more information would be needed from Contracting Parties to achieve further progress in the work. Consequently, PRAM urged Contracting Parties to provide the UK with relevant information, which would provide basis for subsequently adopted background document and recommendation. See Programmes and Measures Committee of OSPAR (PRAM) 1998a (para. 5.32–5.34). As an evidence of similar process on a specific BEP standard, see Working Group on Diffuse Sources of OSPAR (DIFF) 1998 (para. 6.4–6.6). See also OSPAR Commission 2004 (para. 6 of Appendix I).

68 OSPAR Commission 1998, 2.

69 See Meeting of the Hazardous Substances Committee of OSPAR (HSC) 2001 (para 10.2(d)).

List of Substances of Possible Concern (2002, updated in 2006) and OSPAR List of Chemicals for Priority Action (2004, updated in 2007) have been adopted so far. These lists would serve for allocation of limited regulatory resources toward emission minimization of high-risk substances.

Nevertheless, one might still doubt whether proportionality really functions under a situation of scientific uncertainty. This is a fundamental difficulty inherent in the precautionary regimes, but at least the following points should be noted in this regard. First, decisions on specific BAT and BEP will be reviewed periodically.[70] In the 1997/98 OSPAR Action Plan, it is stipulated that all descriptions of BAT/BEP should be reviewed every ten years at the latest.[71] This is based on the premise that these decisions might turn out to be wrong or insufficient in light of new information or technology. In this sense, precautionary measures are basically provisional and not to be maintained longer than necessary.

Second, as I have already mentioned, the concept of proportionality does not require decision-makers to pursue the *most* proportional measures but to avoid excessiveness or obvious disproportion. In this regard, Nollkaemper suggests that 'the marginal test of proportionality between costs and e.g. emission reduction implied in BAT requirements submittedly leave some limited room for exception to be made in the case of the high costs and little risk reduction'.[72] While it is to be doubted whether 'marginal' is appropriate modification, this suggestion is basically right in that it is not proportion, but disproportion which actually matters.

Third, non-state actors are now admitted to exert some influence upon decision-makings on developing precautionary measures. Paragraph 5.6 of Section 1 of the 2003 Strategies states that

> the Commission and Contracting Parties, individually or jointly, will endeavour to maintain and develop further a constructive dialogue with regard to hazardous substances with all parties concerned, including producers, manufacturers, user groups, authorities and environmental NGOs. This should ensure that all relevant information, such as reliable data on production volumes, use patterns, emission scenarios, exposure concentrations and on properties of substances, is available for the work of the Commission in connection with this strategy.

Such arrangement could be explained as a reinforcement of the regimes' legitimacy by relying on other possible source of legitimacy, namely public participation.

In sum, even if consideration of proportionality between a means and a goal undermined precautionary environmental protection, it might be due to inappropriate weight given to environmental interests, but not due to balancing with non-environmental interests itself. Rather, it could enhance the legitimacy of

70 See again paras. 3 and 8 of Appendix I of the OSPAR Convention.

71 See Programmes and Measures Committee of OSPAR (PRAM) 1998b (para. 3.8 a).

72 Nollkaemper 1996, 92.

the regime, as it possibly serves to generate expectations that the regime would be more efficacious for achieving sustainable development than otherwise. In the OSPAR regime, this function of proportionally is ensured to some degree by several regulatory arrangements, which might serve to make proper decisions and deal with difficulty derived from scientific uncertainty.

Conclusion

In relation to the concept of precaution in international environmental law, the notion of proportion was often referred to for the logical extension of the traditional no-harm rule to address uncertain risks and to argue that a rule which mandated precautionary actions has been established under general international law. But now authors' focus has gradually moved towards another type of proportion that concerns the relation between a means and a goal, and thus would limit the application of precaution as a competing principle. This change reflects not only the development of EU law, but also the general trend of development of international environmental law, namely from the application of the law of state responsibility to the development of regulatory regimes, and also reflects the shift of authors' interest from the legal status of precaution toward its implementation. Issues that remained to be explored are whether and how such considerations of proportionality exert influences on actual precautionary decision-making and the effectiveness of the precautionary regime.

In this chapter, I focused on the precautionary OSPAR regime for LBMP, which seeks to minimize the input of substances under scientific uncertainty and showed that the consideration of proportionality has been institutionalized in the decision-making process for determining specific BAT and BEP standards. It is safe to conclude that inappropriate or too-costly measures are to be hardly defined as specific BAT or BEP standards and cost-effectiveness is widely required to set priorities between possible effective options. This institutionalization of the balancing test between a means and a goal not only removes some difficulty in domestic implementation for several contracting parties where principle of proportionality is well established, but also positively effect the legitimacy of the precautionary regime, as it ensures certain balancing against non-environmental interests, required to realize the overall goal of sustainable development and thus could generate states' expectation that the regime is generally more efficacious than otherwise for achieving that ultimate goal. In this sense, together with the several arrangements for making proper decisions, it is possibly argued that consistent consideration of proportionality between a means and a goal could rather enhance the effectiveness of the precautionary regime.

When Dworkin's distinction between rules and principles has been referred to by international environmental lawyers, only one aspect of the principles' characteristic has been often highlighted in order to overcome the issue of the elusiveness of precaution: a principle 'states a reason that argues in one direction, but does not necessitate a particular decision'. But when authors' interests shift from the legal status of precaution to its implementation, another closely related aspect of principles suggested by Dworkin, namely interaction with other principles, is needed to be focused and analyzed more thoroughly as well. While it is still important to elaborate the conceptual core of precaution itself, defining competing principles in decision-making processes is also necessary to understand the significance of *principles* in contemporary international law where public interests have been recognized and balancing relevant interests becomes one of the main regulatory issues. As this article attempts to show by analyzing the operation of the OSPAR regime, it seems that among possible competing principles, proportionality could play a significant role, because it is possibly relied on in every context where means-and-goal relationship matters, though this concept is rarely mentioned explicitly in relevant instruments and actual decision-making. Whether this conclusion is peculiar to the OSPAR regime, which is largely affected by the development of EU law, remains to be explored, but considering that the goal of sustainable development is globally endorsed and BAT and BEP are regarded as precautionary tools to combat LBMP in the 1995 Global Programme, such a balancing test will be surely developed even outside Europe. Needless to say, it should be also needed to examine precautionary regimes which address other environmental issues. Further analysis on proportionality or other competing principles is strongly required not only to clarify the limit of precaution, which is essential to establish its normative scope and consequently its normative status, but also essential to design effective precautionary regimes to pursue the goal of sustainable development for future generations.

References

Books, Articles and Chapters in Books

Beyerlin, U. (2007), 'Different Type of Norms in International Environmental Law: Policies, Principles and rules', in Bodansky, Brunnée and Hey (eds).

Birnie, P. and Boyle, A. (eds) (2002), *International Law and the Environment*, 2nd edition (Oxford: Oxford University Press).

Bodansky, D. (2007), 'Legitimacy', in Bodansky, Brunnée and Hey (eds).

Bodansky, D., Brunnée, J., and Hey, E. (eds) (2007), *The Oxford Handbook of International Environmental Law* (Oxford: Oxford University Press).

Bothe, M. (ed.) (1980), *Trends in Environmental Policy and Law* (International Union for Conservation of Natural Resources).

Cameron, J. and Abouchar, J. (1996), 'The Status of the Precautionary Principle in International Law', in Freestone, and Hey (eds).

Churchill, R. and Freestone, D. (eds) (1991), *International Law and Global Climate Change* (London: Graham & Trotman).

Craig, P. and De Burca, G. (eds) (2003), *EU Law*, 3rd edition (Oxford University Press).

Dworkin, R. (1977), 'Is Law a System of Rules?', in Dworkin (ed.).

Dworkin, R. (ed.) (1977), *The Philosophy of Law* (Oxford: Oxford University Press).

Freestone, D. (1991), 'Precautionary Principle', in Churchill and Freestone (eds).

Freestone, D. and Hey, E. (eds) (1996), *The Precautionary Principle and International Law: The Challenge of Implementation* (The Hague: Kluwer Law International).

Freestone, D. and Ijlstra, T. (eds) (1990), *The North Sea: Perspectives on Regional Environmental Co-operation* (London: Graham & Trotman Martinus Nijhoff).

Handl, G. (1991), 'Environmental Security and Global Change: The Challenge to International Law', in Lang, Neuhold and Zemanek (eds).

Hassan, D. (2006), *Protecting the Marine Environment from Land-based Sources of Pollution* (Aldershot: Ashgate).

Hey, E. (1992), 'The Precautionary Concept in Environmental Policy and Law: Institutionalizing Caution', *Georgetown International Environmental Law Review* 4, 303–318.

Higgins, R. (1994), *Problems and Process* (Oxford: Oxford University Press).

Hohmann, H. (1994), *Precautionary Legal Duties and Principles of Modern International Environmental Law: The Precautionary Principle: International Environmental Law between Exploitation and Protection* (M. Nijhoff/Graham & Trotman, Kluwer).

Lang, W., Neuhold H. and Zemanek K. (eds) (1991), *Environmental Protection and International Law* (London: Graham & Trotman).

MacDonald, J.M. (1995), 'Appreciating the Precautionary Principles as an Ethical Evolution in Ocean Management', *Ocean Development and International Law* 26, 255–286.

Marr, S. (2003), *The Precautionary Principle in the Law of the Sea: Modern Decision Making in International Law* (Leiden: Martinus Nijhoff Publishers).

Nollkaemper, A. (1993), *The Legal Regime for Transboundary Water Pollution: Between Discretion and Constraint* (M. Nijhoff/Graham & Trotman, Kluwer).

Nollkaemper, A. (1996), 'Balancing the Protection of Marine Ecosystems with Economic Benefits from Land-based Activities: The Quest for International Legal Barriers', *Ocean Development and International Law* 27, 153–176.

Pravdic, V. (1985), 'Environmental Capacity – Is a New Scientific Concept Acceptable as a Strategy to Combat Marine Pollution?', *Marine Pollution Bulletin* 16:7, 295–296.

Raz, J. (1972), 'Legal Principles and Limits of Law', *The Yale Law Journal* 81, 823–854.

Riphagen, W. (1980), 'The International Concern for the Environment as Expressed in the Concept of the "Common Heritage of Mankind" and of "Shared Natural Resources"', in Bothe (ed.).

Sadeleer, de N. (2002), *Environmental Principle: From Political Slogans to Legal Rules* (Oxford: Oxford University Press).

Saetevik, S. (1988), *Environmental Cooperation between the North Sea States: Success or Failure?* (London: Belhaven Press).

Sunstein, C.R. (2007), *Worst-Case Scenarios* (Cambridge, Mass.: Harvard University Press).

Trouwborst, A. (2006), *Precautionary Rights and Duties of States* (Leiden: M. Nijhoff).

Ulfstein, G., Marauhn, T. and Zimmermann, A. (eds) (2007), *Making Treaties Work* (Cambridge: Cambridge University Press).

Winter, G. (1988), 'Der Schutz der Nordsee als problem internationaler Übereinkommen und EG-Richtlinien', *Natur und Recht* 88, 265–272.

Ziegler, A.R. (1996), *Trade and Environmental Law in the European Community* (Oxford: Clarendon Press).

Official Documents and Others

European Commission (2000), *Communication from the European Commission on the Precautionary Principle*, COM(2000)1.

European Commission (2001), *Integrated Pollution Prevention and Control, Reference Document on Best Available Techniques in the Pulp and Paper Industry 2001*, <http://www.p2pays.org/ref/13/12193.pdf>.

European Integrated Pollution Prevention and Control Bureau (2005), *IPCC BREF Outline and Guide 2005*, <http://eippcb.jrc.es/pages/FActivities.htm>.

Meeting of the Hazardous Substances Committee of OSPAR (HSC) (2001), *Summary Record*, HSC 01/12/1-E.

OSPAR Commission (1998), *Sintra Statement*, Annex 45 of Summary Record (OSPAR 98/14/1-(A-B) -E).

OSPAR Commission (1999), *OSPAR Recommendation on the Best Available Techniques for the Manufacture of Emulsion PVC of 1999*, OSPAR Recommendation 99/1.

OSPAR Commission (2003), *2003 Strategies of the OSPAR Commission for the Protection of the Marine Environment of the North-East Atlantic*, OSPAR 03/17/1-E, Annex 31.

OSPAR Commission (2004), *Revised Guidelines for the Preparation for the preparation of draft OSPAR Background Documents and draft OSPAR measures, including guidance for the collection and assessment of data and information for draft background documents*, <http://www.ospar.org/documents/dbase/decrecs/agreements/04-01e_guidance%20background%20docs%20and%20measures.doc>.

Paris Commission (PARCOM) (1980), *Adoption of a 'Standstill Principle' for Mercury Concentration in Water*, PARCOM Agreement 80-03e.

Programmes and Measures Committee of OSPAR (PRAM) (1998a), *Summary Record*, PRAM 98/15/1-E.

Programmes and Measures Committee of OSPAR (PRAM) (1998b), *The1997/98 OSPAR Action Plan*, PRAM 98/3/2.

United Nations Environmental Programme (UNEP) (1995), *Global Programme of Action for the Protection of the Marine Environment from Land-Based Activities*, UNEP(OCA)/LBA/IG2/7.

Working Group on Diffuse Sources of OSPAR (DIFF) (1998), *Summary Record*, DIFF 98/19/1-E.

Chapter 8
The Role of Diplomatic Protection in the Implementation Process of Public Interests

Nobuyuki Kato

Introduction

This chapter provides an overview of the role the customary institution of diplomatic protection plays in the implementation of international law from the perspective of the protection of public interests. The chapter consists of two parts. The first part deals first with the traditional function and effectiveness of diplomatic protection for the protection of private individuals, and then with the influences of human rights norms on diplomatic protection. The second part examines the contemporary potential of that customary institution for ensuring public interests, especially in the light of the International Law Commission (ILC)'s recent codification efforts. Finally a brief concluding comment is added.

Function of Diplomatic Protection in the Protection of Individuals

Legal Fiction in the Mechanism of Diplomatic Protection and its Functions

Classical Formulation The role that diplomatic protection has traditionally played and the legal fiction contained in the mechanism of international protection of private individuals was clearly expressed by the Permanent Court of International Justice in the *Mavrommatis Palestine Concession* case (1924). The Court held as follows: 'By taking up the case of one of its subjects and by resorting to diplomatic action or international judicial proceedings on his behalf, a State is in reality asserting its own rights – its right *to ensure, in the person of its subjects, respect for the rules of international law*. The question, therefore, whether the present dispute originates in an injury to a private interest, which in point of fact is the case in many international disputes, is irrelevant from this standpoint. Once a State has taken up a case on behalf of one of its subjects before an international tribunal, in the eyes of the latter, the State is the sole claimant' (emphasis added).[1] This often-quoted passage represents the quintessence of diplomatic protection in its classical sense that, although at the

1 PCIJ Series A, Judgment 2, 12.

outset there is a dispute between the responsible State and a foreign individual, in the process of the espousal of his/her claim by the State of nationality, the dispute is 'merged'[2] or 'transformed'[3] into an international claim from one State *vis-à-vis* another State. Still in 1970 the International Court of Justice (ICJ) reaffirmed in the judgment of the *Barcelona Traction* case, 'within the limits prescribed-by-international law, a State may exercise diplomatic protection by whatever means and to whatever extent it thinks fit, for it is its own right that the State is asserting'.[4] In other words, it makes clear that the claimant in the inter-State context of diplomatic protection is not the injured private person, but the national State. The passage of the *Mavrommatis* case also makes clear that diplomatic protection exercised by a national State plays *the role of ensuring respect for the rules of international law*,[5] that is, the role of implementing or enforcing international law (*mise en oevre du droit international ou de la responsabilité internationale*).[6]

Recent trends As the judgment in the *Mavrommatis* case implies, the mechanism of international protection of private persons by means of diplomatic protection is based upon *the legal fiction* that an injury suffered by an individual is regarded as an injury to that individual's national State, thus entitling the national State to espouse the claim at the international level.[7] There arises the question nowadays, however, whether diplomatic protection is a procedure for the protection of the individual's human rights or a mechanism for the protection of the interest of the State exercising diplomatic protection.[8] Emphasizing the necessity for taking into account of the distinction between primary and secondary rules of international law, J. Dugard, the Special Rapporteur on the Diplomatic Protection in the ILC contends that '[a]s the international personality of the individual is incomplete, owing to the limited capacity of the individual to assert his or her rights, the fiction inherent in the *Mavromatis Palestine Concessions* case is *the means* employed by international law – a secondary rule – *to enforce the primary rule, which protects the undoubted right of the individual*' (emphasis added).[9] The Commentary to the Draft Articles on Diplomatic Protection (2006) states, '[a] State does not "in reality"

2 Borchard 1915, 356–57.

3 Kooijmans 2004, 1976.

4 ICJ Reports 1970, 44, para. 78.

5 This phrase has sometimes been emphasized by publicists, e.g., Garcia-Amador 1984, 87.

6 Dominicé 2004-1, 81; See, generally, Rousseau 1983, 97ff.

7 Vermeer-Künzli 2007-1, 38. Scelle has acrimoniously criticized the classical legal theory based upon the 'novation fictive' in diplomatic protection as what States attempted to justify 'par des *subterfuges* pseudo-juridiques'. Scelle 1933, 335–36. The problem of the legal fiction in diplomatic protection is recently addressed and analyzed extensively by such eminent scholars as Vermeer-Künzli 2007-1, Pellet 2007-1, and Karazivan 2006.

8 Dugard Report 2006, 3, para. 3.

9 Dugard Report 2006, 4, para. 3.

– to quote Mavrommatis – assert its own right only. "In reality" it also asserts the right of its injured national'.[10] The fiction was, the Commentary continues, 'no more than a means to an end, the end being the protection of the rights of an injured national' and today 'the situation has changed dramatically'.[11] The Special Rapporteur has also pointed out that diplomatic protection is an instrument which allows the State to become involved in the protection of the individual and that the ultimate goal of diplomatic protection is the protection of the human rights of the individual, and that in this sense, diplomatic protection and human rights law complement each other.[12]

Whereas the term 'diplomatic protection' in its broad meaning can be used to cover various actions by States or other international legal subjects to protect a private person,[13] the term in its narrow sense is limited to representations or demands that are made under a *claim of right* by a national State.[14] Diplomatic protection in the latter sense is deemed to be one mode of *invocation* of State responsibility by an injured State against the responsible State for an internationally wrongful act. The ILC also adopted such a strict approach to the notion of diplomatic protection to confine the scope of its codification and to be consistent with the Draft Articles on State Responsibility. In describing the 'salient features' of diplomatic protection, Article 1 ('definition and scope') of the Draft Articles on Diplomatic Protection adopted by the ILC after the second reading in 2006 provides that: 'For the purposes of the present draft articles, diplomatic protection consists of the invocation by a State, through diplomatic action or other means of peaceful settlement, of the responsibility of another State for an injury caused by an internationally wrongful act of that State to a natural or legal person that is a national of the former State with a view to the *implementation* of such responsibility' (emphasis added). According to the commentary to this text, '[d]iplomatic protection is the procedure employed by the State of nationality of the injured persons *to secure protection of that person* and to obtain reparation for the internationally wrongful act inflicted' (emphasis added).[15]

While the corresponding Article 1 of the Draft Articles provisionally adopted in 2004 mentioned 'a State adopting in its own right the cause of its national' in diplomatic protection,[16] the commentary states that the formulation of the final draft

10 ILC Report 2006, 25, para. 3.

11 ILC Report 2006, 25, para. 4.

12 Dugard Report 2006, 4, para. 3.

13 Geck 1987, 110; Geck 1960, 381; Kiss 1969, 690–91. Dupuy distinguishes '*protection diplomatique contentieuse*' from '*protection diplomatique non contentieuse*'. Dupuy 2002, 130–31.

14 Dunn 1932, 20.

15 ILC Report 2006, 24, para. 2.

16 ILC Report 2004, 17, para. 59. The text of Article 1 of the 2004 Draft Articles is just the same as Article 1, paragraph 1 of the Draft Articles provisionally adopted in 2002. ILC. Report 2002, 167. Storost remarks that with this formulation the 'representative

article of 2006 'leaves open the question whether the State exercising diplomatic protection does so in its own right or that of its national – or both'.[17] How to construct the claim of diplomatic protection has been disputed in the teachings of publicists.[18] It is without doubt, however, that this revision of the formulation reflects a growing tendency in general to recognize the injured individual as a holder of the *claim* (*prétention*; *Anspruch*) of diplomatic protection.

Already in the same year as the *Mavrommatis* judgment, Umpire Parker held in *Administrative Decision No. V* that 'the *control* of the United States over claims espoused by it ... is complete', but that 'the generally accepted theory formulated by Vattel, which makes the injury to the national an injury to the nation and internationally therefore the claim a national claim which may and should be espoused by the nation injured, must not be permitted to obscure the realities or blind us to the fact that the ultimate object of asserting the claim is to provide reparation for the private claimant, whose rights have at every step been zealously safeguarded by the United States'.[19] Even Borchard, who propounded the theory of 'merger of the private claim into the national claim of the State' in the mechanism of diplomatic protection,[20] which has long been maintained by the majority of publicists, fully acknowledged, however, 'the fact that in practice the private individual is the essential prosecutor and beneficiary of the claim, and that his State, while having a public interest in all its citizens and in the presentation of their rights against invasion abroad, actually appears in most cases in a representative character only'.[21] It has more recently been asserted that, when exercising diplomatic protection, the State rather enforces individuals' rights, not its own rights.[22] Not a few academic authors, especially of European continental countries, have increasingly contended either that both material rights of the individual and of the State besides the exclusive procedural right of the latter to implement the material rights are contained, or that although the State has the exclusive procedural right, the material right is vested only in the individual.[23]

From the above-mentioned state of affairs, it can safely be confirmed that diplomatic protection is a secondary rule of customary international law for implementing State responsibility to secure protection of an injured private person,

model' (*Vertretungsmodell*) supported by some writers was rejected clearly by the majority of States. Storost 2005, 24.

17 ILC Report 2006, 26, para. 5.

18 Bleckmann 2001, 344.

19 UNRIAA, 7, 153.

20 Borchard 1915, 356–57.

21 Borchard 1930, 361.

22 Gaja 2003-2, 374.

23 Vicuña 2000, 633–34; Geck 1987, 112; Doering 1981, 139; Doering 1996, 14–15; Doering 1999, 371–72; Schwarze 1986, 430; Brunner 1983, 37, 104; Dominicé 2004-2, 729–45; Dominicé 2004–1, 77–9; Bennouna 1998, 245–50; Forlati 2007, 92; and more classically, for example, Koessler 1945, 189; Dahm 1961, 253–56; Dahm 1963, 1–22; O'Connell 1965, 116–21.

and that the legal fiction intrinsic to the mechanism of diplomatic protection is being increasingly considered to function to serve in the interests of the injured persons who have only limited capacity to assert their own rights, rather than in the interests of the espousing national State. The artificial character of the legal fiction that the injury suffered by the individual is treated as if it constituted an injury to the national State is severely criticized today by some writers, who consider that the fiction has lost its relevance.[24] Considering that the individual does not have sufficient power in the international legal sphere[25] and that the national State has the ability to implement international norms, however, '[a]bandoning the legal fiction now would be', as Vermeer Künzli remarks, 'premature and not in the interests of the individual'.[26]

Effectiveness of Diplomatic Protection and the Law of Human Rights

Effectiveness of Diplomatic Protection in the Protection of Individuals

As to the protection of individuals in international law, it has been discussed whether the developments in the field of human rights law have rendered diplomatic protection obsolete.[27] In its first report on diplomatic protection, the Special Rapporteur, John R. Dugard concludes in this respect as follows: 'Contemporary international human rights law accords to nationals and aliens the same protection, which far exceeds the international minimum standard of treatment for aliens set by Western Powers in an earlier era. It does not follow that these developments have rendered obsolete the traditional procedures recognized by customary international law for the treatment of aliens. Although individuals today enjoy more international remedies for the protection of their rights than ever before, *diplomatic protection remains an important weapon in the arsenal of human rights protection*. As long as the State remains the dominant actor in international relations, the espousal of claims by States for the violation of the rights of their nationals *remains the most effective remedy for the promotion of human rights*. Instead of seeking to weaken this remedy by dismissing it as an obsolete fiction that has outlived its usefulness, every effort should be made to strengthen the rules that comprise the right of diplomatic protection' (emphasis added).[28]

The main objective of diplomatic protection today is ultimately to remedy an injury or damage done to an individual, just as in the case of human rights protection mechanisms. The effectiveness of the remedies offered by the mechanisms for individual complaint under human rights conventions within the framework of

24 Salmon 2001, 904; Dominicé 2004-2, 742–43.
25 Bleckmann 2001, 344.
26 Vermeer-Künzli 2007, 68.
27 Garcia-Amador 1958, 435–36.
28 Dugard Report 2000, 10, para. 32.

the United Nations has been far from ideal. At a regional level the European Convention of Human Rights has represented a model for success, but other regional systems for the protection of human rights have not been able to replicate the same degree of effectiveness. Moreover, there is still no regional convention in Asia, where the majority of the world's population live.[29] On the other hand, as E. Milano points out rightfully, 'the customary nature of [diplomatic protection] and its associated legal regime make its application potentially universal. Furthermore, states will tend to take more seriously a claim from another state, rather than a claim from an individual to a human rights monitoring body. More importantly, the very fact that the claim of the individual is espoused by the state and that the state represents the legal actor in an action of diplomatic protection will enable the state of nationality to bring the claim before a number of judicial bodies that could not otherwise be accessible for the individual'.[30] The effectiveness of diplomatic protection compared with that of human rights mechanisms from the viewpoint of the complaining State's behavior has often been mentioned, for example, by Judge Kooijmans, when he wrote, 'States hardly ever make use of their procedural rights under human rights conventions if no political interest of a more general nature is at stake'.[31]

Therefore, '[u]ntil the individual acquires comprehensive procedural rights under international law, it would be a setback for human rights to abandon diplomatic protection'.[32] Rather, the law of diplomatic protection is expected to serve an effective tool of human rights protection. In this sense the institution of diplomatic protection can play an important role in the protection of human rights under contemporary international law.[33]

Influence of the Law of Human Rights on Diplomatic Protection

Originally the law of diplomatic protection and that of human rights protection rested upon two essentially distinct premises[34] and developed basically in different historical contexts from each other. The latter law of human rights developed as a comprehensive and inclusive set of international rights of the individual *vis-à-vis* the State, irrespective of the nationality of that individual.[35] Today, however, it is generally accepted that the law of diplomatic protection by its own contents has been gradually influenced and modified by developments in human rights law. In the context of State responsibility, most injuries to foreigners that in the past would have been characterized as 'denial of justice' are now subsumed as human

29 Dugard Report 2000, 8, para. 25; Milano 2004, 88–89.

30 Dugard Report 2000, 89.

31 Kooijmans 2004, 1978.

32 Dugard Report 2000, 9, para. 29.

33 Tinta 2001, 366.

34 Cançado Trindade 1983, 39. See also Kokott 1996, 47.

35 Milano 2004, 87. See also Tiburcio 2001, 66–69.

rights violations.[36] Already nearly a quarter of a century ago, attention was paid by R. Lillich to the fact that increasingly a number of prominent scholars had began to acknowledge the value, and sometimes even the inevitability, of blending international human rights with the treatment of aliens law.[37] Lillich himself also noted the gradual infusion of international human rights norms into the law of State responsibility for injuries to aliens[38] and thus the relevancy of the former in, *inter alia*, clarifying and strengthening the law of the treatment of aliens.[39] According to L. Condorelli, the law of human rights has influenced the fundamental rules of diplomatic protection in a significant manner because the contents of 'minimum standard of treatment' that each State has the right to claim against the responsible State in favour of its nationals on the basis of general international law are today just derived from principles concerning human rights.[40]

In the recent *Case Concerning Ahmadou Sadio Diallo* (*Republic of Guinea v Democratic Republic of the Congo*), in which the Guinean government alleged violations of human rights – specifically arbitrary arrest without charge which would constitute a violation of the 1948 Universal Declaration of Human Rights, and violation of the victim's right to a fair trial under the 1966 International Covenant for Civil and Political Rights – under the heading of diplomatic protection, the ICJ held in its judgment on the Preliminary Objections (2007) as follows: 'Owing to the substantive development of international law over recent decades in respect of the rights it accords to individuals, the scope *ratione materiae* of diplomatic protection, originally limited to alleged violations of the minimum standard of treatment of aliens, has subsequently widened to include, *inter alia*, internationally guaranteed human rights'.[41] Immediately after such a general comment on the present state of affairs on diplomatic protection, the Court continues, '[i]n the present case Guinea seeks to exercise its diplomatic protection on behalf of Mr. Diallo in respect of the DRC's alleged violations of his rights as a result of his arrest, detention and expulsion, that violation allegedly constituting an internationally wrongful act by the DRC giving rise to its responsibility. It therefore falls to the Court to ascertain

---

36 ALI Restatement 1987, §711, Comment (a). Carbonneau has criticized the approach of this revised Restatement (Third), because, *inter alia*, human rights considerations literally 'engulf' the whole of §711 provisions, engendering disequilibrium rather than fusion, and the attempted synthesis of the law of State responsibility for injury to aliens and human rights norms results in a considerable downplaying of a set of legal rules of the latter that has been proven to be of unquestioning utility in the past. But he does not deny that the latter law is supported by human rights norms and he also suggests the mechanism of diplomatic protection is far more effective than human rights system. Carbonneau 1984, 117–23.

37 Lillich 1983, 26.

38 Lillich 1984, 122.

39 Lillich 1983, 27–29.

40 Condorelli 2003, 20.

41 Judgment of 24 May 2007, 17, para. 39.

whether the Applicant has met the requirements for the exercise of diplomatic protection'.[42]

If human rights also include 'protection against denial of justice', as the ICJ in the *Barcelona Traction* case has mentioned,[43] it follows that the institution of diplomatic protection applies to human rights violations, for the denial of justice has been one of the main causes of diplomatic protection both traditionally and contemporarily. Paulsson demonstrates that the elements of Article 6(1) of the European Convention on Human Rights, Article 14(1) of the International Covenant on Civil and Political Rights, and Article 8 of the American Convention on Human Rights are recurrent features in the various instances of denial of justice.[44] The above-mentioned *Case Concerning Ahmadou Sadio Diallo* can be regarded as only one of many examples which show that 'the mechanisms of [diplomatic protection] represent the most obvious strategy to seek legal protection before the Court for the individual's human rights'.[45] It is pointed out, as can be easily confirmed from three recent ICJ cases[46] brought against the United States for violations of the right to notification under Article 36 of the Vienna Convention on Consular Relations, that the link between human rights and diplomatic protection is becoming more and more recurrent in applicant States' litigating strategies before the ICJ.[47] Apart from one case which was removed from the list, the Court's judgment on its part did not explicitly recognize the violation of 'human rights' of the individuals concerned in these cases so far, although in *LaGrand* case it recognized the existence of individual rights for the detained person to notification under the Vienna Convention (in addition to the rights accorded to the sending State).[48] The judgment of the *Ahmadou Sadio Diallo* case is the precedent that ostensively affirmed the exercise of diplomatic protection for the violation of human rights for the first time, and seems to constitute a landmark in this respect.

The ILC reaffirms that the protection of human beings by many means of international law, including consular protection, resort to international human rights treaties mechanisms, diplomatic protection, and so on, is today one of the principal goals of the international legal order, and that when the protection of foreign nationals is in issue, diplomatic protection, which is the remedy with the longest history and has a proven record of effectiveness, is an obvious redress

42 Judgment of 24 May 2007, 17–18, para. 40.

43 ICJ Reports 1970, 47, para. 91.

44 Paulsson 2005, 133–34.

45 Milano 2004, 109.

46 *Case Concerning the Vienna Convention on Consular Relations* (*Paraguay v US*) (which was removed from the list at last by the request of Paraguay), *LaGrand Case* (*Germany v US*), and *Case Concerning Avena and Other Mexican Nationals* (*Mexico v US*).

47 Milano 2004, 119.

48 ICJ Reports 2001, 494, para. 77; 497, para. 89.

to which States should give serious consideration.[49] That seems to be the reason why the ILC has inserted Article 19 ('recommended practice')[50] as the exercise of progressive development in the Draft Articles on Diplomatic Protection.

Relevancy and Effectiveness of Diplomatic Protection in the Protection of Public Interests

Diplomatic Protection and Obligations Erga Omnes

As to the relationship between diplomatic protection and human rights law, however, a further relevant question should be addressed on the distinction between obligations in the field of diplomatic protection and obligations *erga omnes*, that is, 'obligations owed to the international community as a whole', whose objective is by its very nature to protect 'public interests' in its strict sense. Articulating basic interests and needs as well as fundamental values of the international community as a whole, *erga omnes* norms are essential elements of the international public order.[51]

In its famous *obiter dicta* of the judgment in the *Barcelona Traction* case, the ICJ held as follows: '[A]n essential distinction should be drawn between the obligations of a State towards the international community as a whole, and those arising *vis à vis* another State in the field of diplomatic protection. By their very nature the former are the concern of all States. In view of the importance of the rights involved, all States can be held to have a legal interest in their protection; they are obligations *erga omnes*'.[52] 'Obligations the performance of which is the subject of diplomatic protection are not of the same category. It cannot be held, when one such obligation in particular is in question, in a specific case, that all States have a legal interest in its observance. In order to bring a claim in respect of the breach of such an obligation, a State must first establish its right to do so'.[53] The judgment further went on to say: 'With regard more particularly to human rights,... it should be noted that these also include protection against denial of justice. However, on the universal level, the instruments which embody human

---

49 Commentary to Article 19 of the Draft Articles on Diplomatic Protection, ILC. Report 2006, 95, para (2).

50 Article 19 stipulates as follows:

A State entitled to exercise diplomatic protection according to the present draft articles, should: (a) Give due consideration to the possibility of exercising diplomatic protection, especially when a significant injury has occurred; (b) Take into account, wherever feasible, the views of injured persons with regard to resort to diplomatic protection and the reparation to be sought; and (c) Transfer to the injured person any compensation obtained for the injury from the responsible State subject to any reasonable deductions.

51 Delbrück 1998, 18.

52 ICJ Reports 1970, 32, para. 33.

53 ICJ Reports 1970, para. 35.

rights do not confer on States the capacity to protect the victims of infringements of such rights irrespective of their nationality'.[54]

These passages *apparently* exclude diplomatic protection from obligations *erga omnes*.[55] In other words, the Court's *dicta* can be understood to imply, at least at first sight, that as the mechanism of diplomatic protection functions only in a bilateral relationship between one State and another, so that the latter mechanism could not be relevant for *the primary rules* of obligations *erga omnes*, that is, obligations owed to the international community as a whole, which is regarded by its nature to serve public interests. Actually some commentators contend that the two kinds of obligations and mechanisms should be strictly separated in the light of the *dicta* in the *Barcelona Traction* case.[56] It cannot be denied from the Court's ruling that human rights instruments at the global level do not confer on States the capacity to protect the victims of human rights infringements regardless of their nationality.

But as mentioned above in the preceding section, the international minimum standard of nationals abroad in the field of diplomatic protection is deeply influenced by the development of human rights norms. Therefore the distinction in the *dicta* of the *Barcelona Traction* case 'should not be seen as a distinction concerning *the primary rules*, on the one hand, protecting foreign nationals, on the other, protecting all other human beings; rather, the distinction lies in the nature of the state's action under general international law, one providing diplomatic protection to a national, the other providing for a third party action to protect all substantive human rights' (emphasis added).[57] Moreover, it should be added that in certain circumstances, a national State of an injured person can be 'a third party' in this sense, to protect substantive human rights. The distinction of international norms into two classes in the *Barcelona Traction* case – even if it being not definitive – might appear to consist in one only enforceable bilaterally and another enforceable *bilaterally and by third party States*.[58]

On the Proposal for a State's Duty of Diplomatic Protection in Case of Grave Breach of a Jus Cogens *Norm*

In his first report on diplomatic protection, the Special Rapporteur, J. Dugard, proposed a noteworthy article as one of progressive development which provides: 'Unless the injured person is able to bring a claim for such injury before a competent international court or tribunal, the State of his/her nationality has *a legal duty* to exercise diplomatic protection on behalf of the injured person upon

54 ICJ Reports 1970, 47, para. 91

55 Forcese 2006, 391.

56 Gaja 2003-1, 65–66; Pergantis 2006, 363–364; Forlati 2007, 94. As to Gaja's view, see also ILC Yearbook 2000-I, 43–44, paras. 60–61.

57 Milano 2004, 138.

58 Charney 1989, 71.

request, if the injury results from a grave breach of a *jus cogens* norm attributable to another State' (Article 4, paragraph 1; emphasis added, except Latin words). This obligation of the State of nationality is to be relieved under three conditions stipulated in paragraph 2 of the same Article.[59]

While fully recognizing that this proposed approach is clearly in conflict with the traditional view and involves an exercise in progressive development rather than codification, the Special Rapporteur contends that it cannot, however, be dismissed out of hand as it accords with the principal goal of contemporary international law – the advancement of the human rights of the individual rather than the sovereign powers of the State.[60] According to his report, it is not unreasonable to require a State to react by way of diplomatic protection to measures taken by a State against its nationals which constitute a grave breach of a norm of *jus cogens*. 'If a State party to a human rights convention is required to ensure to everyone within its jurisdiction effective protection against violation of the rights contained in the convention and to provide adequate means of redress', he continues, 'there is no reason why a State of nationality should not be obliged to protect its own national when his or her most basic human rights are seriously violated abroad'.[61]

This bold proposal was, however, not accepted by the ILC, and was at last deleted from the final draft articles. The questions raised against the proposal are, *inter alia*, as follows: first, that the duty was limited to when such a request was made by the injured person, contradicts the principles of State responsibility under which, if *jus cogens* is affected, not only the State of nationality, but all States, should have the right and the duty to protect the individual; and second, in such circumstances as a grave breach of a *jus cogens*, it is not the rights and interests of nationals alone, but those of the international community as a whole.[62] Thus, according to the Special Rapporteur's concluding remarks, 'the general view was that the issue was not yet ripe for the attention of the Commission and that there was a need for more State practice and, particularly, more *opinio juris* before it could be considered'.[63]

It should not be overlooked, on the other hand, that Dugard's proposal enjoyed the support of certain writers, of some members of the Sixth Commission and of the

59 Paragraphs 2 and 3 provided as follows:

2. The State of nationality is relieved of this obligation if:

(a) The exercise of diplomatic protection would seriously endanger the overriding interests of the State and/or its people;

(b) Another State exercises diplomatic protection on behalf of the injured person;

(c) The injured person does not have the effective and dominant nationality of the State.

3. States are obliged to provide in their municipal law for the enforcement of this right before a competent domestic court or other independent national authority.

60 Dugard Report 2000, 32, para. 87.

61 Dugard Report 2000, 33, para. 89.

62 ILC Report 2000, 157–58, paras. 453–55.

63 ILC Report 2000, 158, para. 456.

International Law Association.[64] A commentator strongly supports the introduction of Article 4 *de lege ferenda*, partly because, among other reasons, it would have helped create a more comprehensive system of accountability for the responsibility of states to take up cases of nationals victim to the gravest violations of human rights.[65] It should be noted that those questions raised against the proposal do not throw doubts about the *right* of a national State to exercise diplomatic protection in a grave violation of a *jus cogens* norm. Th. Giegerich affirms that a State whose nationals are among the victims of a *jus cogens* violation is entitled, pursuant to the traditional standards of customary international law, to exercise diplomatic protection for its nationals, demand compensation in their favour and use reprisals, if necessary, to enforce its demand.[66] Whether it should be recognized *de lege ferenda* as a duty or not, diplomatic protection can be exercised by a national State as an effective means to implement the international norm. In this case the national State would be deemed to perform a double function (*dédoublement fonctionnel*), to protect its nationals as the injured State and to pursue the public interest as a member of the international community as a whole.

Invocation of State Responsibility in Case of Violation of Obligations *Erga Omnes* and Diplomatic Protection

The ILC Articles on State Responsibility

Diplomatic protection is not separate from State responsibility: a State acting on behalf of one of its nationals is invoking State responsibility.[67] In other words, diplomatic protection is one of the modalities of the implementation or *mise-en-oeuvre* of State responsibility. Part Three of the 2001 Articles on Responsibility of States for internationally wrongful acts deals with the implementation of State responsibility. Chapter I (Articles 42–48) of Part Three deals with the invocation of State responsibility by other States and with certain associated questions.[68] Central to the invocation of responsibility is the concept of the 'injured State'. This is the State whose individual right has been denied or impaired by the internationally wrongful act or which has otherwise been particularly affected by that act. This concept is introduced in Article 42 ('Invocation of responsibility by an injured State').[69] Article 48 ('Invocation of responsibility by a State other than an injured

64 ILC Report 2000.

65 Milano 2004, 96–97. As to the term 'accountability' in its broadest sense, see Brunnée 2005, 22.

66 Giegerich 2006, 234.

67 ILC Report 2000, 86, para. 286.

68 ILC Report 2001, 292.

69 ILC Report 2001, 293. The text of Article 42 (Invocation of responsibility by an injured State) is as follows:

State') deals with the invocation of responsibility by States other than the injured State acting in the collective interest. It complements the rule contained in Article 42. A State which is entitled to invoke responsibility under Article 48 is acting not in its individual capacity by reason of having suffered injury, but in its capacity as a member of a group of States to which the obligation is owed, or indeed as a member of the international community as a whole.[70]

When the obligation owed to the international community as a whole is breached, any State other than an injured State may claim from the responsible State (a) cessation, assurances and guarantees of non-repetition, and (b) performance of the obligation of reparation in the interest of the injured State or of the beneficiaries of the obligation breached (Article 48, paragraph 2). The ILC admits in the Commentary that this provision of (b) involves a measure of progressive development, but that it is justified since it provides a means of protecting the community or collective interest at stake.[71] According to Article 48, paragraph 3, however, the requirements for the invocation of responsibility under not only Article 43, but also Articles 44 ('Admissibility of claims')[72] and 45 ('Loss

---

A State is entitled as an injured State to invoke the responsibility of another State if the obligation breached is owed to:

(a) That State individually; or

(b) A group of States including that State, or the international community as a whole, and the breach of the obligation:

(i) Specially affects that State; or

(ii) Is of such a character as radically to change the position of all the other States to which the obligation is owed with respect to the further performance of the obligation.

70 ILC Report 2001, 319. The text of Article 48 (Invocation of responsibility by a State other than an injured State) is as follows:

1. Any State other than an injured State is entitled to invoke the responsibility of another State in accordance with paragraph 2 if:

(a) The obligation breached is owed to a group of States including that State, and is established for the protection of a collective interest of the group; or

(b) The obligation breached is owed to the international community as a whole.

2. Any State entitled to invoke responsibility under paragraph 1 may claim from the responsible State:

(a) Cessation of the internationally wrongful act, and assurances and guarantees of non-repetition in accordance with article 30; and

(b) Performance of the obligation of reparation in accordance with the preceding articles, in the interest of the injured State or of the beneficiaries of the obligation breached.

3. The requirements for the invocation of responsibility by an injured State under articles 43, 44, and 45 apply to an invocation of responsibility by a State entitled to do so under paragraph 1.

71 ILC Report 2001, 323, para. 12.

72 The text of Article 44 (Admissibility of claims) is the following:

The responsibility of a State may not be invoked if:

(a) The claim is not brought in accordance with any applicable rule relating to the nationality of claims;

of the right to invoke responsibility')[73] are to apply both to Article 42 and Article 48.[74] Therefore, there arises a difficult question of interpretation.

It has been pointed out and criticized by some writers that the requirements in Article 44, in particular paragraph (a) on the rules of nationality of claims present 'acute problems'[75] or 'an insurmountable obstacle for the success'[76] of a State wishing to invoke responsibility under Article 48. In addition, the applicability of Article 45 means, they argue, that an injured state itself may block invocation of responsibility under Article 48, even when the obligation breached is owed to the international community as a whole.[77] It is thus contended by one author that the room left for enforcement of *erga omnes* human rights obligations beyond the traditional mechanisms of diplomatic protection is minimal.[78] If those requirements should really apply to the invocation of State responsibility for an obligation *erga omnes*, such rules are at least contrary to the following suggestion expressed in the ILC in the year previous to the adoption of the 2001 Articles on State Responsibility: 'Under international law, obligations concerning human rights were typically obligations *erga omnes*. Any State could request cessation of the breach, whether the persons affected were its own nationals, nationals of the wrongdoing State or nationals of a third State. Thus, any requirement of nationality of claims appeared to be out of context when human rights were invoked.... The ICJ in its famous dictum in *the Barcelona Traction* case, indicated that only the State of nationality could intervene in cases of diplomatic protection, but in human rights cases, any State could do so'.[79] Indeed, Article 48 is deemed to be a 'deliberate departure'[80] from the much criticized decision in the 1966 *South West Africa* cases[81] holding that a State may not bring legal proceedings to protect the rights of non-nationals, whose view has to be qualified in the light of the articles

(b) The claim is one to which the rule of exhaustion of local remedies applies and any available and effective local remedy has not been exhausted.

73 The text of Article 45 (Loss of the right to invoke responsibility) is the following: The responsibility of a State may not be invoked if:

(a) The injured State has validly waived the claim;

(b) The injured State is to be considered as having, by reason of its conduct, validly acquiesced in the lapse of the claim.

74 As to the terminological ambiguities between 'serious breaches of obligations under peremptory norms of general international law' (Articles 40 and 41) and 'the breach of obligations *erga omnes*' as well as the coincidence of the two categories of obligations in the ILC Articles on State Responsibility, see Sicilianos (2002), 1140–41.

75 Scobbie 2002, 1213.

76 Milano 2004, 106.

77 Scobbie 2002, 1213.

78 Milano 2004, 107.

79 ILC Report 2000, 145, para. 422.

80 ILC Report 2001, 321, para. 7, footnote 766.

81 Judgment of 18 July 1966 (Second Phase), ICJ Report 1966, 4ff.

on State Responsibility.[82] Any meaningful explanation in this respect cannot be found in the ILC Commentary on Article 48, paragraph 3.[83] It is thus very natural that the 2001 Articles on State responsibility be much criticized in this respect. In short, as Pergantis comes to the point, 'the completely illogical conclusion' is led that 'the non-injured States are always precluded from invoking responsibility under Article 48, since they do not fulfil the nationality requirement!'[84]

The ILC Draft Articles on Diplomatic Protection

On the other hand, the ILC Commentary to the Draft Articles on Diplomatic Protection offers the explicit interpretation that Article 48(1)(b) is not subject to Article 44 of the 2001 Articles on State Responsibility and that nor is it subject to the Draft Articles on Diplomatic Protection.[85] Thus, a State other than the injured State can invoke the responsibility of another State if the obligation breached is owed to the international community as a whole, without complying with the requirements for the exercise of diplomatic protection.[86] According to Vermeer-Künzli, 'the ILC "overlooked the friction" between invocation *erga omnes* under Article 48(1)(b) and the rules on diplomatic protection, it apparently tried to remedy this situation with a simple statement in the Commentary to the Draft Articles on Diplomatic Protection'.[87] In her recent article Vermeer-Künzli has made clear the essential distinction between the two mechanisms and strongly maintains the non-applicability of the requirements under diplomatic protection to the former mechanism of invocation *erga omnes*.[88] She convincingly explores the relationship between the two mechanisms and their *parallel existence*.[89]

82 ILC Report 2006, 87.

83 The Commentary merely states that the Articles of 43 to 45 are 'to be read as applicable equally, *mutatis mutandis*, to a State invoking responsibility under article 48'. ILC Report 2001, 324, para. 14.

84 Pergantis 2006, 365.

85 Commentary to Article 16, ILC Report 2006, 87, footnote 245. Draft Article 16 is a saving clause in order not to affect other treaty mechanisms of protection for individuals, which reads as follows: 'The rights of States, natural persons, legal persons or other entities to resort under international law to actions or procedures other than diplomatic protection to secure redress for injury suffered as a result of an internationally wrongful act, are not affected by the present draft articles'.

86 ILC Report 2006, 87.

87 Vermeer-Künzli 2007-2, 564.

88 Vermeer-Künzli 2007-2, 577–81. She argues the ILC evidently had no intention to subject invocation under Art 48 to the rules on diplomatic protection. Vermeer-Künzli 2007-2, 556.

89 It was a difficult question of interpretation of what meaning Article 48, paragraph 3 really has and how this paragraph should be constructed. From the perspective of objective approach of interpretation based on text, if that provision has any meaning, diplomatic protection must be one mode of 'invocation of responsibility by a State other than an

Kokott argues for the exercise of 'diplomatic protection' by a State other than a national State, in other words, non-applicability of the rules on nationality of claims in the case of violation of fundamental human rights norms which constitute obligations *erga onme.*[90] But such a claim by a third State would be regarded as invocation *erga onmes* rather than as diplomatic protection in its strict sense. Because in this case, as she herself notes, a State is invoking State responsibility not as an injured State, but as a member of the international community as a whole.[91] Vermeer-Künzli underscores the simultaneous existence of the invocation of State responsibility *erga omnes* on the one hand, and diplomatic protection on the other, in the interest of enhancing protection of individuals against violations of peremptory norms. For example, a violation of the prohibition on torture may be claimed either by exercising diplomatic protection on behalf of a national or invocation *erga omnes*.[92] These two mechanisms should be regarded as co-existent, complementary and yet as distinct. Logically speaking, the invocation *erga omnes* by any State should play a primary role in principle because of the nature of the violated obligation. But compared with the latter means, which is not yet firmly established in international law, diplomatic protection is much more effective due to its long-standing recognition in customary international law and with its connection to the injured person.[93] Th. Giegerich seems to take the same view in this regard when he says that in a case where a State whose nationals are among the victims of a *jus cogens* violation is certainly specifically affected by this violation, in the sense of the ILC's Articles [on State Responsibility], the State – as an injured State – is *at the same time* entitled, pursuant to the traditional standards of customary international law, to exercise diplomatic protection for its nationals.[94] In spite of practical defects arising from the discretionary right of a national State in its exercise that the exercise depends basically on the ability and willingness of that State,[95] the *complementary* role that diplomatic protection can play in violation of obligations *erga omnes* should not be overlooked.

---

injured State' when the obligation *erga omnes* is breached under Article 48. Otherwise, the paragraph 3 would be totally meaningless, because the invocation of responsibility to which Article 44 (that requires the rule of nationality of claims and the rule of exhaustion of local remedies) applies is nothing but the mechanism of diplomatic protection. Vermeer-Künzli seems to regard this provision to be a dead letter, and thus have answered to this difficult problem of interpretation. She argues that the words '*mutatis mutandis*' in the commentary (mentioned, *supra* note 83) should be taken seriously, but application *mutatis mutandis* would not be interpreted to be the same as non-applicability.

90 Kokott 1996, 54–61.

91 Kokott 1996, 49–50.

92 Vermeer-Künzli 2007-2, 579.

93 Vermeer-Künzli 2007-2, 580–81.

94 Giegerich 2006, 234.

95 Kokott 1996, 47–48.

Concluding Remarks

The legal fiction traditionally intrinsic to diplomatic protection perhaps functioned – in spite of a discretionary right of the State – to protect nationals injured by another State in violation of minimum standards at a time when individuals did not have international legal capacity to bring their own claims in international law. In former times diplomatic protection was frequently exercised and even abused by States, through State practice of which the customary rules on the preconditions for the exercise of diplomatic protection were developed and established. Not a few cases of State responsibility have been submitted to ICJ on the ground of a violation of a State's own rights in which diplomatic protection is 'absorbed' at the same time, but the Court has not posed the questions of nationality of claims and exhaustion of local remedies, 'without theorization'.[96] States do have the ability and motivations to protect their nationals. To quote Vermeer-Künzli, '[s]ince … a claim brought on behalf of a state usually carries more weight than one brought on behalf of individuals, states should not feel restrained to exercise diplomatic protection if they have an interest in improving the human rights situation of their nationals abroad'.[97]

Today the international minimum standards of aliens have been deeply influenced by international human rights norms, some of which constitute obligations *erga omnes*, and which serve public interests. Especially in cases in which international public interests (of human rights protection) should meet with a State interest, diplomatic protection has been and will be a powerful, effective tool for the implementation of international law, as States have vehemently acted to protect their nationals, for instance in the recent ICJ cases concerning violations of the Vienna Convention on Consular Relations. In the light of the 2001 Articles on State responsibility, on the other hand, the mechanism for 'a State other than an injured State' to invoke responsibility in the violation of obligations *erga omnes* is being recognized as a progressive development, but not yet established. In such a present state of law, 'an injured State', usually a national State, is complementarily entitled and has potential to safeguard public interests through the invocation of State responsibility, that is, through the mechanism of diplomatic protection under customary international law. Although many problematic issues remain to be resolved[98] and, more fundamentally, 'a serious identity crisis for diplomatic protection'[99] is not easy to overcome, Dugard's 'dual approach', which tries to combine a human rights-oriented approach with considerations of effectiveness,[100] seems to be basically acceptable, as far as it means that diplomatic protection plays a role *complementary* to human rights protection mechanisms.

96 Pellet 2007-1, 1374.

97 Vermeer-Künzli 2006, 350.

98 Pellet 2007-2, 1133–55.

99 Pergantis 2006, 354–97.

100 Pergantis 2006, 394–95.

References

Books, Articles and Chapters in Books

Abi-Saab, G. et al. (eds) (1998), *Boutros Boutros-Ghali Amicorum Discipulorumque Liber*, I (Bruxelles: Bruylant).

Battagline, G. et al. (eds) (Comitato promotore) (2004), *Studi di Diritto Internationale in Onore de Gaetano Arangio-Ruiz* (Napoli: Editoriale Scientifica).

Bennouna, M. (1998), 'La protection diplomatique, un droit de l'Etat?', in Abi-Saab et al. (eds).

Bernardini, P. et al. (eds) (2004), *Liber Amicorum Claude Reymond. Autour de l'arbitrage* (Paris: Editions du Juris-Classeur).

Bernhardt, R. (ed.) (1981), *Encyclopedia of Public International Law* 1 (Amsterdam: North-Holland).

Bernhardt, R. (ed.) (1987), *Encyclopedia of Public International Law* 10 (Amsterdam: North-Holland).

Bleckmann, Albert (2001), *Völkerrecht* (Baden-Baden: Nomos Verlagsgesellschaft).

Borchard, E.M. (1915), *The Diplomatic Protection of Citizens Abroad or the Law of International Claims* (New York: Banks Law Pub. Co. 1919; William S. Hein & Co., Inc. Reprint 2003).

Borchard, E.M. (1930), 'The Access of Individuals to International Courts', *American Journal of International Law* 24, 359–65.

Brunnée, J. (2005), 'International Legal Accountability through the Lens of the Law of State Responsibility', *Netherlands Yearbook of International Law* 36, 21–56.

Brunner, N. (1983), Die Frage nach dem Anspruch des Bürgers auf diplomatischen Schutz (Bern: Peter Lang).

Caemmerer, E. von, et al. (Hersg.) (1963), *Vom Deutschen zum Europäischen Recht. Festschrift für Hans Dölle* (Tübingen: Mohr).

Cançado Trindade, A. (1983), *The Application of the Rule of Exhaustion of Local Remedies in International Law* (Cambridge: Cambridge University Press).

Carbonneau, T. (1984), 'The Convergence of the Law of State Responsibility for Injury to Aliens and International Human Rights Norms in the Revised Restatement', *Virginia Journal of International Law*, 25:1, 99–123.

Charney, J. (1989), 'Third State Remedies in International Law', *Michigan Journal of International Law* 10, 57–101.

Condorelli, L. (2003), 'L'evolution du champ d'application de la protection diplomatique', in Flauss (dir.).

Corten, O. et al. (2007), *Droit du pouvoir, pouvoir du droit* (Mélanges offerts à Jean Salmon) (Bruxelles: Bruylant).

Dahm, G. (1961), *Völkerrecht, III* (Stuttgart: W. Kohlhammer).

Dahm, G. (1963), 'Die Subsidiarität des internationalen Rechtsschutzes bei völkerrechtswidriger Verletzung von Privatpersonen', in Caemmerer, E. von, et al. (Hersg.) II, 1–22.

Delbrück, J. (1998), '"Laws in the Public Interest" – Some Observations on the Foundations and Identification of *erga omnes* Norms in International Law', in Götz, Selmer and Wolfrum (Hrsg.), 17–36.

Doering, K. (1981), 'Local Remedies, Exhaustion of', in Bernhardt (ed.).

Doering, K. (1996), 'Handelt es sich bei einem Recht, das durch diplomatischen Schutz eingefordert wird, um ein solches, das dem die Protektion ausübenden Staat zusteht, oder geht es um die Erzwingung von Rechten des betroffenen Individuums?', in Ress and Stein (Hrsg.).

Doering, K. (1999), *Völkerrecht. Ein Lehrbuch* (Heidelberg: C.F. Müller Verlag).

Dominicé, Ch. (2004-1), 'Regard actuel sur la protection diplomatique', in Bernardini et al. (eds).

Dominicé, Ch. (2004-2), 'La prétention de la personne privée dans le systeme de la responsabilité internationale des Etats', in Battagline et al. (eds) (Comitato promotore) II.

Dunn, F. (1932), *The Protection of Nationals. A Study in the Application of International Law* (Baltimore: Johns Hopkins Press; New York: Kraus Reprint Co., 1970).

Dupuy, P.-M. (2002), *Droit international public*, 6e édition (Paris: Dalloz).

Flauss, J.-F. (dir.) (2003), *La Protection Diplomatique. Mutations Contemporaines et Pratiques Nationales* (Bruxelles: Bruylant).

Forcese, C. (2006), 'The Capacity to Protect: Diplomatic Protection of Dual Nationals in the "War on Terror"', *European Journal of International Law* 17:2, 369–94.

Forlati, S. (2007), 'Protection diplomatique, droits de l'homme et reclamations «directes» devant la Cour internationale de justice – Quelques réflexions en marge de l'arrêt Congo/Ouganda', *Revue Générale de Droit International Public* 111:1, 81–116.

Francescakis, Ph. (dir.) (1969), *Encyclopédie juridique. Répertoire de droit international* 2 (Paris: Jurisprudence Générale Dalloz).

Gaja, G. (2003-1), 'Droits des Etats et droits des individus dans le cadre de la protection diplomatique', in Flauss (dir.).

Gaja, G. (2003-2), 'Is a State Specially Affected When its Nationals' Human Rights Are Infringed?', in Vohrah et al. (eds).

Garcia-Amador, F.V. (1958), 'State Responsibility. Some New Problems', *Recueil des Cours* 94, II, 369–461.

Garcia-Amador, F. (1984), *The Changing Law of International Claims* (New York: Oceana Publications).

Geck, W. (1960), 'Diplomatischer Schutz', in Schlohauer and Hans-Jürgen (Hergs.).

Geck, W. (1987), 'Diplomatic Protection', in Bernhardt, R. (ed.).

Giegerich, Th. (2006), 'Do Damages Claims Arising from Jus Cogens Violations Override State Immunity from the Jurisdiction of Foreign Courts?', in Tomuschat and Thouvenin (eds).

Götz, V., Selmer, P., Wolfrum, R. (Hrsg.) (1998), *Liber amicorum Günther Jaenicke – Zum 85. Geburtstag* (Berlin: Springer).

Karazivan, N. (2006), 'Diplomatic Protection: Taking Human Rights Extraterritorially', *Canadian Yearbook of International Law* 44, 299–352.

Kiss, A.-Ch. (1969), 'Protection diplomatique', in Francescakis (dir.).

Koessler, M. (1945), 'Governmental Espousal of Private Claims before International Tribunals', *University of Chicago Law Review* 13, 180–94.

Kohen, G. (ed.) (2007), *Promoting Justice, Human Rights and Conflict Resolution through International Law (Liber Amicorum Lucius Caflish)* (Leiden: Martinus Nijhoff).

Kokott, J. (1996), 'Zum Spannungsverhältnis zwischen nationality rule und Menschenrechtsschutz bei der Ausübung diplomatischer Protektion', in Ress and Stein (Hrsg.).

Kooijmans, P. (2004), 'Is the Right to Diplomatic Protection A Human Rights?', in Battagline, et al. (Comitato promotore), III.

Lillich, R. (1983), 'The Current Status of the Law of State Responsibility for Injuries to Aliens', in Lillich (ed.).

Lillich, R. (ed.) (1983), *International Law of State Responsibility for Injuries to Aliens* (Charlottesville: University Press of Virginia).

Lillich, R. (1984), *The Human Rights of Aliens in Contemporary International Law* (Manchester: Manchester University Press).

Milano, E. (2004), 'Diplomatic Protection and Human Rights before the International Court of Justice: Re-fashioning Tradition?', *Netherlands Yearbook of International Law* 35, 85–142.

O'Connell, D. (1965), *International Law* (London: Stevens & Sons Limited).

Orrego Vicuña, F. (2000), 'Interim Report on "the Changing Law of Nationality of Claims"', *ILA Report*, 69th Conference (London), 631–47.

Paulsson, J. (2005), *Denial of Justice in International Law* (Cambridge: Cambridge University Press).

Pellet, A. (2007-1), 'La seconde mort d'euripide Mavromatis (1)? Notes sur le projet de la C. D. I. sur la protection diplomatique', in Corten et al.

Pellet, A. (2007-2), 'Le projet d'articles de la C.D.I. sur la protection diplomatique: une codification pour (presque) rien', in Kohen (ed.).

Pergantis, V. (2006), 'Towards a "Humanization" of Diplomatic Protection?', *Zeitschrift für ausländisches öffentliches Recht und Völkerrecht* 66, 351–97.

Ress, G. and Stein, T. (Hrsg.) (1996), *Der diplomatische Schutz im Völker- und Europarecht* (Baden-Baden: Nomos Verlagsgesellschaft).

Rousseau, Ch. (1983), *Droit international public* (Paris: Sirey).

Salmon, J. (dir.) (2001), *Dictionnaire de droit international public* (Bruxelles: Bruylant).

Scelle, Georges (1933-IV), 'Règles générales du droit de la paix' *Recueil des Cours* 46, 327–704.

Schlohauer, H.-J. (Hergs.) (1960), *Wörterbuch des Völkerrechts* 1 (Berlin: Verlag Walter de Gruyter & Co.).

Schwarze, J. (1986), 'Rechtsschutz Privater bei völkerrechtswidrigen Handeln fremder Staaten', *Archiv des Völkerrechts* 24:4, 408–33.

Scobbie, I. (2002), 'Invocation of Responsibility for the Breach of "Obligations under Peremptory Norms of General International Law"', *European Journal of International Law* 13:5, 1201–20.

Sicilianos, L.-A. (2002), 'The Classification of Obligations and the Multilateral Dimension of the Relations of International Responsibility', *European Journal of International Law* 13:5, 1127–45.

Storost, Ch. (2005), *Diplomatischer Schutz durch EG und EU?* (Berlin: Duncker & Humblot).

Tiburcio, C. (2001), *The Human Rights of Aliens under International and Comparative Law* (The Hague: Martinus Nijhoff Publishers).

Tinta, M. (2001), 'Due Process and the Right to Life in the Context of the Vienna Convention on Consular Relations: Arguing the LaGrand Case', *European Journal of International Law*, 12, 363–66.

Tomuschat, Ch. and Thouvenin, J.-M. (eds) (2006), *The Fundamental Rules of the International Legal Order. Jus Cogens and Obligations Erga Omnes* (Leiden: Martinus Nijhoff Publishers).

Vermeer-Künzli, A. (2006), 'Exercising Diplomatic Protection: The Fine Line Between Litigation, Demarches and Consular Assistance', *Zeitschrift für ausländisches öffentliches Recht und Völkerrechts* 66, 321–50.

Vermeer-Künzli, A. (2007-1), 'As If: The Legal Fiction in Diplomatic Protection', *European Journal of International Law* 18:1, 37–68.

Vermeer-Künzli, A. (2007-2), 'A Matter of Interest: Diplomatic Protection and State Responsibility *Erga Omnes*', *International and Comparative Law Quarterly* 56:3, 553–82.

Vicuna, O.F. (2000), Interim Report on the Changing Law of Nationality of Claims, ILA Report, 69th Conference.

Vohrah, L. et al. (eds) (2003), *Man's Inhumanity to Man. Essays on International Law in Honour of Antonio Cassese* (The Hague: Kluwer Law International).

Official Documents and Others

ALI Restatement (1987), American Law Institute, Restatement of the Foreign Relations Law of the United States, Third.

Dugard Report (2000), United Nations General Assembly, First Report on Diplomatic Protection by John Dugard (A/CN. 4/506).

Dugard Report (2006), United Nations General Assembly, Seventh Report on Diplomatic Protection by John Dugard (A/CN. 4/567).

ICJ Reports, International Court of Justice, Reports of Judgments, Advisory Opinions and Orders.

ILA Report, International Law Association, Conference Report.

ILC Report, United Nations, Report of the International Law Commission.

ILC Yearbook, Yearbook of the International Law Commission.

PCIJ Series A, Publications of the Permanent Court of International Justice, Series A (Judgment).

UNRIAA, United Nations, Reports of International Arbitral Awards.

PART III
Coordination of Legal Regimes and Systems in the Implementation Process

Chapter 9

Effective Implementation of Intersecting Public International Regimes: Environment, Development and Trade Law

Marie-Claire Cordonier Segger[1]

Introduction

To achieve the diverse public interests of the international community, it is important to secure coordination and coherence among legal regimes and systems in the process of treaty implementation. To ensure that legal systems are able to be 'mutually supportive', rather than the rules of one regime frustrating effective implementation of another regime, balanced means must be found to address inevitable intersections and overlaps.

Focusing on examples from relatively recent trade, development and environment treaty instruments, this chapter argues that where regimes intersect, increased effectiveness can be supported by three principal types of process changes. First, problems can be identified and resolved through the use of innovative procedures such as sustainability impact assessment, inter-agency consultation and public participation, during the negotiation and implementation of trade treaties. Second, synergies and solutions can be built into trade and other treaties by agreeing on substantive rules and new institutions which ensure that regime objectives can be 'mutually supportive' and which set conditions for 'interlocking' of regimes. Third, and as an underlying condition, States can agree on key 'public interest' objectives that the international community holds in common, such as the promotion of

---

1 The author is grateful to the British Chevening Award, the International Development Research Centre and the Social Sciences and Humanities Research Council of Canada for their generous support for this research. This chapter shares thoughts with the author's work in Gehring and Cordonier Segger 2005; Cordonier Segger and Leichner Reynal 2005; Cordonier Segger 2006, and other earlier research. Thanks and acknowledgements are due to Brittany A. Krupica, MPhil & LL.B. (Cantab), B.A. Hons (Wheaton), CISDL Legal Researcher, and Alexandra Harrington, DCL cand (McGill), LL.M. (Albany), J.D. (Albany), CISDL Senior Manager (interim) and CISDL Associate Fellow, for their excellent insights and legal editing skills. The views expressed in this chapter are personal views based on academic research, not in any way intended to reflect the position of the Canadian Government.

sustainable development, in order to provide clarity in treaty interpretation and prevent the priorities of one regime from simply overriding others.

As such, this chapter provides a brief discussion of sustainable development as a global 'public interest' objective that is reflected in an increasing number of trade agreements. It examines new procedural solutions that increase coordination among disparate legal regimes and systems, and considers the incorporation into trade treaties of substantive measures to encourage 'mutually supportive' trade, environment and social development policies and laws, as well as 'inter-locking mechanisms' which mediate between trade, environment and social development regimes.

Trade, the Environment and Development: Conflict or Compatibility?

The rules of trade treaties can intersect with other international regimes established to achieve environment and development objectives.[2] Such overlaps between international trade, environment and social regimes can present certain problems for States in the effective implementation of treaty commitments, particularly when States cleave to the 'spirit' rather than simply the 'letter' of environmental and social regimes.

It is often reiterated that there has never been a WTO dispute on a measure taken pursuant to a multilateral environmental or human rights agreement. The evidence for this proposition is less than straightforward, however. WTO members often attempt to defend trade-related measures in WTO disputes by highlighting social and environmental policy objectives enshrined in other international treaties, including multilateral environmental agreements (MEAs). Though direct conflicts of legal obligations may be rare, the rules of a trade treaty do appear to have the potential to constrain – or even frustrate – efforts to adopt domestic or international rules which implement competing social and environmental commitments. To illustrate, the doubly suspended case of *EU v Chile in the ITLOS/Chile v EU in the WTO* provides an example of how economic, social and environmental objectives and regimes can overlap without exactly supporting each other.

The *Chile – Swordfish Case* concerned the legitimacy of Chilean measures to limit the unsustainable exploitation of a fishery. It was brought simultaneously before the WTO dispute settlement body, established under the Dispute Settlement Understanding of the Agreements Establishing the World Trade Organization, and the International Tribunal for the Law of the Sea (ITLOS), established under the United Nations Convention on the Law of the Sea (UNCLOS).

Swordfish are a migratory 'straddling stock' of the Pacific Ocean. For more than 10 years, Spanish fishing trawlers were engaged in controversy with the conservation authorities of Chile and other Pacific States over sustainable development of the swordfish fisheries of the South Pacific. Chilean fisheries management authorities

2 Gehring and Cordonier Segger 2005.

in the ports could not always prove that undersized swordfish brought in for trans-shipment had been caught in Chilean territorial waters, and repeated violations of conservation rules were crippling Chilean enforcement efforts in the ports. Authorized by the Chilean Fishery Law,[3] Chile enacted a prohibition against Spanish trawlers unloading swordfish in Chilean ports. The EC asserted that since 1991 when the law came into force, the Chileans had effectively closed their ports, *inter alia* for trans-shipment, to Spanish trawlers carrying swordfish, preventing them from reaching their markets in a timely manner,[4] and noted that this was inconsistent with Articles V and XI of the GATT 1994. On 12 December 2000, the Dispute Settlement Body (DSB) established a WTO Panel.[5]

On 19 December 2000, Chile initiated proceedings at the ITLOS,[6] submitting and therefore requesting a declaration, that the EC had *inter alia* violated its obligations under UNCLOS Articles 64 (cooperation in ensuring conservation), 116–119 (conservation of the living resources), 297 (dispute settlement) and 300 (good faith and no abuse of rights). Chile alleged that their ports were closed simply because swordfish were consistently being harvested by the Spanish in violation of conservation measures. While the EC counterclaimed, both countries faced significant consternation. Essentially, claims on the same facts had begun to proceed in two completely distinct legal regimes – and it was quite conceivable that the EC would win in one forum, while Chile would win in the other.

In 2001, the EU and Chile reached a settlement to resolve the swordfish dispute providing both access for EU fishing vessels to Chilean ports and bilateral and multilateral scientific and technical co-operation on conservation of swordfish stocks.[7] As a result of this arrangement, the cases before the WTO and the ITLOS were suspended in 2001, 2003, 2005 and 2007 respectively.[8] An agreement to negotiate a multilateral framework for joint sustainable development of the fishery has not yet been concluded, and the pending cases remain unresolved.[9] Trade negotiators, legal scholars and international relations theorists have yet to fully

---

3 Chile Ley General de Pesca y Acuicultura, Art. 165 as consolidated in Supreme Decree 430 of 28 September 1991, and extended by Decree 598 of 15 October 1999.

4 Orellana 2002.

5 WTO, *Chile – Measures affecting the Transit and Importing of Swordfish*, <http://www.wto.org/english/tratop_e/envir_e/envir_backgrnd_e/c5s1_e.htm>.

6 *Case Concerning the Conservation and Sustainable Exploitation of Swordfish Stocks in the South-Eastern Pacific Ocean v European Communities*, ITLOS, <http://www.oceanlaw.net/cases/swordfish1.html>.

7 See 'EU and Chile Settle WTO/ITLOS Swordfish Dispute', 24 January 2001; 'EU and Chile Reach an Amicable Settlement to End WTO/ITLOS Swordfish Dispute (Brussels)', Europa <http://europa-eu-un.org/articles/cs/article_2230_cs.htm>. See also Orellana 2001.

8 WTO, <http://www.wto.org/english/tratop_e/dispu_e/cases_e/ds193_e.htm>.

9 WTO,<http://www.wto.org/english/tratop_e/dispu_e/cases_e/ds193_e.htm>; Cabrera and Gehring 2001 (online).

understand the implications of this apparently direct 'conflict of regimes' in public international law.

Distinct Communities for Trade, Environment and Social Development

One explanation for such 'conflicts' can be found by combining both law and international relations perspectives. In essence, three distinct (and nearly mutually exclusive) communities can be identified. One focuses on the rules and disciplines to secure increased economic growth (including trade and investment liberalization, competition and financial markets), the second focuses on environmental protection and preservation (including nature conservation and trans-boundary pollution), and the third focuses on social development (including human rights, health and development assistance). Each community is governed by a distinct international regime consisting of a set of multilateral treaties and institutions, and following separate schedules of international negotiations and conferences. These systems tend to undertake implementation differently, securing treaty compliance through diverse international mechanisms such as complaints enforcement procedures, non-compliance committees or tribunals with appellate bodies.[10] Each relies upon the distinct systems of principles and rules enshrined in their own field of law, with differing concepts of legitimacy.[11] In an iterative process, these principles and rules have emerged from and in turn have influenced three correspondingly specialized sets of domestic public laws.[12] Some might even describe each system as 'self-contained'.[13]

10 Hafner 2000, 'Risks Ensuing from Fragmentation of International Law', UN Doc. ILC(LII)/WG/LT/L.1/Add.1: 24, included as Annex to International Law Commission, Report on the Work of its Fifty-Second Session (1 May–9 June and 10 July–18 August 2000), Official Records of the General Assembly, Fifty-Second Session, Supplement No. 10 (A/55/10) (2000). See also (7 May 2004) 'Function and Scope of the *lex specialis* Rule and the Question of 'Self-Contained Regimes' ILC(LVI)/SG/FIL/CRD.1 and (4 May 2004) Add.1. See United Nations A/RES/58/77 General Assembly 8 January 2004 Fifty-Eighth Session Agenda Item 152 Resolution Adopted by the General Assembly on the Report of the Sixth Committee (A/58/514) *Report of the International Law Commission on the Work of its Fifty-Fifth Session*: ILC <http://www.un.org/law/ilc/sessions/56/56sess.htm>. In the International Law Commission, not all members felt that fragmentation was a reason for concern. It was also suggested that 'the proliferation of rules, regimes and institutions might strengthen international law'.

11 Brunnée and Toope 2002, 1–23.

12 Brunnée and Toope 2000, 19 –74.

13 It is the opinion of this author that such a characterization would be an error. See WTO Appellate Body in the case of *US – Standards for Reformulated and Conventional Gasoline* (20 May 1996), WTO Doc. WT/DS2/AB/R, which states that the WTO Agreements are not to be read in clinical isolation from public international law.

Explaining Intersections of Rules and Regimes

Our understanding of the operations of such systems themselves, and how these are perceived in general international law and international relations, is evolving. Two approaches can be used to describe the evolving relationships (and potential overlaps) between trade, environment or social development rules. Each provides a distinct explanation of how each of these systems might constrain or strengthen the effectiveness of implementation processes in the others, leading to different theories of how such overlaps might be resolved.

From one perspective, States could be perceived as independent and equal sovereign unitary actors that only enter into accords when these suit their domestic interests. Each treaty is described almost as a private law contract between States. From this viewpoint, an examination of potential 'conflicts' between such contracts focuses only on actual incompatibility of specific obligations in the treaties, where the provisions of two different treaties regulate the same subject matter at the same time, and one provision is directly opposed to the other. Briefly, as noted by Ronald Dworkin, in the law there are legal rules, policies and principles – rules being the most specific and binding.[14] Rules can be held horizontally against another, or even held horizontally against a legal policy or principle.[15] When two direct, specific rules cannot be met concurrently, one must necessarily be deemed invalid. This can be called a 'conflict of legal norms'. In international law, as Hans Kelsen explains, legal rules (or 'norms') can be divided into four types: (i) prescriptive, (ii) prohibitive, (iii) exempting or (iv) permissive norms.[16] When, for example, two contrary prescriptive norms, or a prescriptive and prohibitive norm, stand directly against each other (so that it is impossible to obey one without breaking the other), a State is caught in a 'conflict of norms'. As Joost Pauwelyn observes in his study of conflicts of norms in WTO law, international trade treaties might aim to regulate or might be applied to the same subject matter as other treaties, and while in such situations obligations may accrue, they might also conflict.[17] When direct conflicts do occur, an adjudicator would normally be expected to apply the rules of the *Vienna Convention on the Law of Treaties*, which reflect the customary international law that governs such situations.[18] These rules include interpreting the respective provisions in light of the overall object and purpose of the treaty, and in accordance with the doctrines of *lex specialis*, and *lex posteriori*, among others.[19] One obligation, if these rules were followed strictly by both Parties, would simply trump the other, and the State would disregard its obligations

14 See generally, Dworkin 1978.

15 Dworkin 1978.

16 Kelsen 1996, 1.

17 Pauwelyn 2003.

18 *Vienna Convention on the Law of Treaties* (May 23, 1969) 1155 U.N.T.S. 331, 8 I.L.M. 679, which reflects the customary norms of international law in this area.

19 *Vienna Convention on the Law of Treaties*, Art. 30.

under the 'losing' treaty (even if this action incurred State responsibility). Such situations of 'direct conflict' are rare, as States are not usually so specific in drafting international legal obligations that alternative means of implementing treaty obligations are impossible. In addition, States that are Parties to one or more overlapping treaties normally make special efforts to ensure, in the drafting and implementation processes, that obligations are consistent with one another. Still, in a situation where States have acceded to a treaty regime (as for developing countries in the WTO) regulators might only discover overlaps after accession. Further, and far more frequently, in bi-lateral or regional trade and investment agreement negotiations, bargaining power between Parties is often far from equal. In such situations, a State may find itself obliged to accept trade disciplines which constrain implementation of other commitments made in environmental, human rights or other sustainable development related treaties.

However, a focus on treaties as 'contracts' and on specific legal overlaps of treaty obligations as 'conflicts' does not necessarily convey the full picture. A second broader and more nuanced perspective, which takes complexities faced by such States and other actors in international law and policy, could be preferable. As noted by John Vogler,[20] regimes are 'sets of implicit or explicit principles, norms, rules and decision-making procedures around which actors' expectations converge in a given area of international relations'.[21] From this perspective, regimes govern specific issue areas[22] and as such, are 'specialized arrangements that pertain to well defined activities, resources or geographical areas and often involve only some subset of the members of international society'.[23] Such a viewpoint focuses on the emergence, evolution and effects of normative communities in international law, reinforced by 'epistemic communities' which share scientific information and data.[24] International regimes often coalesce around international treaty commitments. They evolve and 'deepen' over time,[25] as maintained by Stephen Toope and Jutta Brunnée, through interactions between states and non-state actors, shaping and being shaped by the norms and rules, knowledge and networks generated by the regime.[26] From this perspective, the law between States evolves as the regimes evolve, and more actors than just States are engaged in

20 Principles can be defined as beliefs of fact causation and rectitude, norms as standards of behaviour defined in terms of rights and obligations, rules as specific prescriptions or proscriptions for action, and decision-making procedures as prevailing practices for making and implementing collective choice. See Vogler 2000, 20–43.

21 See especially Ruggie 1983; and, generally, Krasner 1983.

22 Vogler 2000, 20–43.

23 Young 1989, as cited in Vogler 2000, 23.

24 Young 1989, as cited in Vogler 2000, 23. See also Brunnée and Toope 2002, 1–23. See also Brunnée 2002, 1–52.

25 See Brunnée and Toope 2000, 19–74. See also Brunnée and Toope 2002, 105–159.

26 See Brunnée and Toope 2002, 105–159. See also Brunnée and Toope 2002, 1–23.

its implementation.[27] Considerable evidence exists to support this view. Indeed, in order to ensure implementation and adaptability to changing conditions in the implementation process, Parties to sustainable development related treaties often make commitments to respect a binding dispute settlement or compliance procedure, to continue negotiations and to periodically undertake monitoring. For example, Parties to the 1992 *United Nations Convention on Biological Diversity* and the 1992 *United Nations Framework Convention on Climate Change* essentially established framework agreements, which agree upon certain common objectives and then commit to develop more detailed and specific protocols through regular Conferences of the Parties (COPs). Such processes allow the Parties to take new developments in science and technology into account and to react to changing political conditions. Similarly, the Parties to the 1994 *Marrakesh WTO Agreements* established a binding dispute settlement mechanism, a trade policy review mechanism and a continual negotiations process. And in many human rights treaties, Parties set up complaints mechanisms through optional protocols or other instruments, or establish commissions and binding regional courts with a mandate to rule on the conduct of member States. The incremental process of regime-building in all three fields of international law is based on the efforts of States, but also engages inter-governmental and non-governmental institutions through capacity building programmes, financing mechanisms, monitoring systems and other activities. In the absence of such cooperative efforts and procedures, treaties might be ratified but compliance would be slow and even ineffective. As such, from this second perspective, treaties in economic, environment and social fields of international law and policy evolve as 'systems' rather than simply 'contracts'. International law can be seen as systems of law and institutions which may intersect and overlap, covering the same subject matter.

Implications of Intersections between Regimes

Taking these considerations into account, the *Chile – Swordfish Case* and other similar situations in trade law can be understood not as a conflict of norms, as such, but rather as an uncomfortable intersection between international legal regimes.

It is not surprising that we should come to this. Global and regional regulation of economic, environmental and human rights issues continues to expand. For instance, emerging international social and environmental regimes now employ a wide variety of economic instruments, and trade regimes have been agreed to discipline States' use of health, environmental and consumer safety standards. Parties to international treaties seek to develop robust domestic measures to achieve their economic, environmental and social objectives and these efforts are

27 This theory has several implications. For example, it suggests that it may be undesirable for States to try to negotiate a seemingly strong international treaty without first going through a careful, incremental process of regime-building, as States might simply assent with no intention of complying. See also Brunnée and Toope 2002, 1–23.

monitored by international compliance or dispute settlement bodies which can interpret treaty obligations without requiring further consent of the Parties. As new domestic and international programmes and policies are developed and put into practice, they become more likely to overlap with the laws and policies for compliance and enforcement of other new or existing regimes.

Such overlaps can lead to lack of coherence, contradictory programming, waste of resources, loss of credibility, and fragmentation. This point deserves highlighting. The problem for State decision-makers is often *not* a theoretical 'conflict of laws', but rather the waste of resources from running several competing programmes for treaty implementation, along with actual barriers to effectiveness engendered by lack of consultation, cooperation and policy coherence between related international or national institutions in the implementation process. Such intersections also affect other actors than States, when institutions, NGOs, firms and others seek to act in accordance with different requirements placed upon them by international organizations, or non-State actors work to implement treaty rules in one area by sacrificing agreed norms in the other. Classic examples include the demarcation of a wildlife reserve carried out in a way that ignores the human rights of the tribal peoples living within its boundaries, or the implementation of a trade rule in a way that weakens environmental standards. The effectiveness of all regimes suffers.

Depending on the degree of inter-agency cooperation in the country and the extent to which the negotiating schedules of different treaties contradict each other, negotiators of one regime may not even be aware of the developments in a different field. If they are, the Parties to one regime might undertake negotiations to clarify relationships with another overlapping regime. Dispute settlement bodies may even be requested to balance different treaties and domestic objectives. However, in the absence of explicit overarching common public interest objective to provide a balance, States and other actors may not always trust and accommodate new developments in other areas of international law. One flashpoint involves overlaps between global and regional trade law and social and environmental regimes. In many cases, the Parties to a trade treaty differ from the Parties to an environmental or human rights accord. State A is a member of Treaty 1 on trade, while State B is a member of Treaty 1 on trade, Treaty 2 on the environment and Treaty 3 on human rights. In some circumstances, the non-Parties may even seek to constrain, for instance through the rules of a new trade regime, the use by another State of measures that might otherwise be more effective in achieving the objectives of an environmental or social regime. Such 'constraints' and 'restrictions' take place at a minimum of two levels. First, the rules, policies and institutions of an international trade regime can overlap with those of international environmental and social regimes, directly constraining the use of international trade measures by States party to another treaty. These situations are likely very rare, but may occur. Secondly, and perhaps more common, international trade rules can constrain or restrict the domestic measures taken by the Parties to implement international environmental and social treaty objectives. These domestic restrictions may then be communicated (in the iterative processes of the regimes themselves) among States, affecting the next round of international commitments and the treaty implementation.

Such intersections between parallel trade, environment and social development rules and regimes have become the topic of a growing body of legal and international relations research.[28] The issue is not simply between trade and environment regimes. Indeed, concerns regarding overlaps between trade and human rights regimes have even led to inter-governmental bodies making formal submissions to trade negotiations.[29]

Addressing the Intersections of Trade, Environment and Social Regimes

Recent treaties from environmental and social regimes, all of which commit to sustainable development as an objective, contain provisions which can intersect with the provisions of trade law. With regards to the first 'level' of intersection mentioned above, the rules of an international trade regime can overlap with other international environmental and social regimes, directly constraining the use of international trade measures by States. WTO Members have undertaken discussions and have even mandated negotiations to resolve the relationship between WTO rules and the provisions of certain multilateral environmental agreements (MEAs).[30] WTO communications claim that while in general, MEAs 'are to be encouraged', the WTO Committee on Trade and Environment 'has wrestled with the issue of how to address the trade provisions which several of these agreements contain.'. This Committee has argued that 'A possible source of conflict between the trade measures contained in MEAs and WTO rules could be

28 See Francioni 2001. See also Kirton and Maclaren 2002. For related global policy debates, see, e.g.,WTO Secretariat 2000 and Proceedings of the WTO High Level Symposium on Trade and Environment, Geneva, 15–16 March 1999 and WTO High Level Symposium on Trade and Development, Geneva, 17–18 March 1999.

29 See, e.g., (26 November 1999), 'The Substantive Issues Arising in the Implementation of the International Covenant on Economic, Social and Cultural Rights: Statement of the United Nations Committee on Economic, Social and Cultural Rights to the Third Ministerial Conference of the World Trade Organization', E/C.12/1999/9, adopted by the 47th Meeting, Twenty-First Session, which states 'the Committee urges WTO to undertake a review of the full range of international trade and investment policies and rules in order to ensure that these are consistent with existing treaties, legislation and policies designed to protect and promote all human rights. Such a review should address as a matter of highest priority the impact of WTO policies on the most vulnerable sectors of society as well as on the environment'.

30 World Trade Organization 2004, *Environment Backgrounder: The Relationship Between MEAs and the WTO* (Geneva: WTO), WTO <http://www.wto.org/english/tratop_e/envir_e/envir_backgrnd_e/c5s1_e.htm>.

the violation by MEAs of the WTO's non-discrimination principle'.[31] Several of the most venerable (and broadly ratified) MEAs fall into this category. The 1973 *Convention on International Trade in Endangered Species of Flora and Fauna 1973* (CITES)[32] contains trade measures to prevent Parties from allowing illegally harvested species to enter international commerce. The 1997 *Montreal Protocol on Substances that Deplete the Ozone Layer* to the 1985 *Vienna Convention for the Protection of the Ozone Layer*[33] contains trade measures to prevent Parties from trading with non-Parties in goods that either contain or were produced using prohibited ozone depleting substances. The 1989 *Basel Convention on the Control of Transboundary Movements of Hazardous Wastes and their Disposal*[34] contains trade measures to prevent developed country Parties (or States with which they trade) from illegally disposing of hazardous wastes in the territories of developing country Parties. Such provisions, which on their face appear to violate non-discrimination and national treatment obligations in trade law, among others, have generated a great deal of international debate in the trade community, just as the trade rules (and certain early decisions of the GATT and WTO) have generated debates in the environmental community.

More recent sustainable development related treaties provide two particularly illustrative examples. In a first example, many trade treaties contain provisions related to Standards and Phytosanitary (SPS) standards. These standards cover some of the same subject matter as certain health and environment related provisions of the 2001 *Cartagena Protocol on Biosafety* to the 1992 *United Nations Convention on Biological Diversity* (UN CBD).[35] The Protocol focuses on the safe use of potentially risky biotechnology[36] and operationalizes the precautionary approach[37] with regard to living modified organisms (LMOs). The final text of

31 World Trade Organization (2004), *Environment Backgrounder: The Relationship Between MEAs and the WTO* (Geneva: WTO), WTO <http://www.wto.org/english/tratop_e/envir_e/envir_backgrnd_e/c5s1_e.htm>.

32 *Convention on International Trade of Endangered Species and Wild Fauna and Flora*, 3 March 1973, 993 U.N.T.S. 243, T.I.A.S. No. 8249, 12 I.L.M. 1085 (1973).

33 *Montreal Protocol on Substances that Deplete the Ozone Layer*, 17 September 1987, 1522 U.N.T.S. 3, 26 I.L.M. 154 (entered into force 1 January 1989).

34 *Basel Convention on the Control of Transboundary Movements of Hazardous Wastes and Their Disposal*, 22 March 1989, 1673 U.N.T.S. 57, I.L.M. 28: 649 (entered into force 5 May 1992).

35 *United Nations Convention on Biological Diversity*, 5 June 1992, I.L.M. 31: 822.

36 See Arts. 1, 2 and 19 of the CBD, and see Art. 1 of the *Cartagena Protocol on Biosafety to the United Nations Convention on Biological Diversity* (entered into force 29 January 2000), I.L.M. 39: 1027.

37 Principle 15 reads: 'In order to protect the environment, the precautionary approach shall be widely applied by States according to their capabilities. Where there are threats of serious or irreversible damage, lack of full scientific certainty shall not be used as a reason for postponing cost-effective measures to prevent environmental degradation'. See *Agenda 21* (14 June 1992), I.L.M. 31: 874.

the Preamble actually states, in two apparently contradictory clauses, that on one hand, the treaty shall not be interpreted as implying a change in the rights and obligations of a Party under any existing agreements, while also recognizing, on the other hand, that this recital is not meant to subordinate the Protocol to other international agreements.[38] The procedures contained in the Protocol require both risk assessment and risk management.[39] In the Protocol, and in Annex III which contains guidelines for risk assessments under the Protocol,[40] Parties have agreed that they have a right to use the principle of the precautionary approach, basing their decision concerning the importation of an LMO on the desire of the Party to protect the environment or health.[41] In particular, the Protocol states that '[l]ack of scientific knowledge or scientific consensus should not necessarily be interpreted as indicating a particular level of risk, an absence of risk, or an acceptable risk'.[42]

In the Protocol,[43] it appears clear that provisions on precaution allow importing Parties to shift the burden of compiling evidence on the safety of an LMO to the exporter, which often has access to more information about the LMO that they seek to export.[44] This 'permissive norm' could easily overlap with the 'prohibitive' SPS provisions in a trade agreement. Indeed, SPS provisions could be used to restrict measures aimed at controlling trade in LMOs: in the case of food safety[45] and regulations to protect the environment.[46] Under SPS exceptions in many trade agreements, the burden of proof falls on the Party enacting a precautionary measure. This Party may be required to defend its measure – in a dispute settlement mechanism of the trade regime – by demonstrating that the measure and its application are transparent, *science-based*, made in a predictable and timely manner, and strictly necessary for the protection of human, animal and plant

---

38 Cartagena Protocol on Biosafety, *supra* note 35. See Pythoud and Thomas 2002, 39.

39 Cartagena Protocol on Biosafety, *supra* note 35, Arts. 15 and 16.

40 Cartagena Protocol on Biosafety, *supra* note 35, Annex III.

41 IUCN 2003, para. 340.

42 Cartagena Protocol on Biosafety, *supra* note 35, Annex III at 3, 4.

43 In the *Hormones* dispute, the Appellate Body did not take a position on the status of the precautionary principle in international law, but it noted that it found reflection, *inter alia*, in Art. 5.7 of the SPS Agreement. It found that to the extent it is not explicitly incorporated in Art. 5.7, the principle does not override the provisions regarding risk assessment contained in Art. 5.1 and 5.2 of the SPS Agreement. See *EC Measures Concerning Meat and Meat Products (Hormones)* (13 February 1998), WTO Doc. WT/DS26/AB/R, WT/DS48/AB/R.

44 Cartagena Protocol on Biosafety, *supra* note 35, Art. 15(2).

45 These apply to risks from additives, contaminants, toxins or disease-causing organisms. SPS measures are defined in Annex A of the *WTO Agreement on the Application of Sanitary and Phytosanitary Measures* (SPS Agreement).

46 For example, regulations to avoid the spread of GMOs, their breeding with wild relatives, or negative effects on wild animals, might be considered measures taken to prevent or limit damage from the entry, establishment or spread of pests. See WTO SPS Agreement, *supra* note 44, at Annex A:1.

health.[47] Occasions in which a 'precautionary approach' can be used are often time-bound, exceptional and limited provisional measures. This overlap on the issue of whether precaution can or cannot be used by a Party to the UNCBD Cartagena Protocol in deciding whether to permit the importation of an LMO could lead to a situation like the one described above in the *Chile – Swordfish Case*, where one regime is used against the other, with potentially conflicting findings at worst, and a chilling effect at least. Indeed, at certain stages of the WTO *EC – Approval and Marketing of Biotech Products Case*, the European Community and its Members argued for application of the precautionary principle, as reflected in the UNCBD Cartagena Protocol, to respect limits on the importation of certain biotechnology products.[48] Unsurprisingly, the WTO Panel dispute settlement body, which focuses on trade law obligations within the trade regime, was not convinced.

In a second example, provisions concerning subsidies, antidumping and countervailing duties in trade agreements can be linked to the subject matter of regimes which specifically permit or recommend the use of economic instruments to reduce greenhouse gas emissions. The 1992 *United Nations Framework Convention on Climate Change* (UNFCCC) contains provisions stating an intention not to unjustifiably or arbitrarily restrict international trade[49] and similar provisions are repeated in the 1997 *Kyoto Protocol*.[50] States were clearly aware that measures taken under these treaties hold the potential to restrict trade if not carefully crafted. Climate change is an externality which, so far, has not been internalized in production processes, input costs, consumer choices and energy markets.[51] Analysis suggests that the 1997 *Kyoto Protocol* can serve as an important

47 Many trade agreements require burdensome risk assessment procedures, and limit the use of SPS measures to 'appropriate levels' of sanitary or phytosanitary protection. Even provisional measures, similar to those defined in Art. 5.7 of the SPS Agreement, *supra* note 44, still place burdens of proof on the precautionary Party.

48 Panel Report, *European Communities – Measures Affecting the Approval and Marketing of Biotech Products*, WT/DS291/R, WT/DS292/R, WT/DS293/R, circulated 29 September 2006. The Panel found that the EC had applied a de facto moratorium on biotech products from June 1999 and August 2003, violating WTO SPS Annex C(1)(a), and Art. 8. Further, EC member State safeguard measures were deemed to violate Arts. 5.1 and 2.2 of the SPS Agreement as they were not based on risk assessments satisfying the definition of the SPS Agreement and were therefore presumed to be maintained without sufficient scientific evidence. For commentary, among many excellent papers on this topic, see Winham, G.R. (2003), 'International Regime Conflict in Trade and Environment: The Biosafety Protocol and the WTO', *World Trade Review* 2:2:131–155.

49 *United Nations Framework Convention on Climate Change*, 9 May 1992, I.L.M. 31: 849 which states, at Art. 3.5, that 'Measures taken to combat climate change, including unilateral ones, should not constitute a means of arbitrary or unjustifiable discrimination or a disguised restriction on international trade'.

50 *Kyoto Protocol to the United Nations Framework Convention on Climate Change*, 10 December 1997, (1998), I.L.M. 37: 22, Art. 2.3.

51 Assuncao 2000.

mechanism to correct climate policy failures, supporting internalization of climate change externalities,[52] but it is also clear that the Protocol faces major challenges and restrictions and that it will be very difficult to implement the accord in a timely and effective manner. How might the provisions of the *Kyoto Protocol*, or special domestic norms that are set in place to implement the Protocol, conflict with trade provisions related to subsidies, antidumping and countervailing duties? A subsidy can be defined as a financial contribution or benefit conferred by a government to domestic industries.[53] Any of these measures might be needed by Annex 1 Parties to the *Kyoto Protocol* in order to provide emissions reduction incentives for domestic firms.[54] These incentives could be investigated and challenged under measures on subsidies which seek to disallow such forms of support.[55] *Kyoto Protocol* measures could be deemed discriminatory, if subsidies and tax incentives caused 'adverse effects to the interests of other members'.[56] The WTO *Agreement on Subsidies and Countervailing Measures* contains exceptions for a one-time subsidy introduced to offset increases in production costs of firms adjusting to new environmental regulations.[57] Further, a subsidy might be characterized as 'specific', and hence found non-actionable, if there were objective and legally enforceable criteria

---

52 The *Kyoto Protocol* commits Annex 1 Parties to the *United Nations Framework Convention on Climate Change* (UNFCCC) to reduce their overall greenhouse gas emissions by at least 5.2 per cent below 1990 levels in the commitment period 2008 to 2012 (Art. 3, para. 1). Reduction and limitation targets vary among Parties (see Annex B). See *Kyoto Protocol, supra* note 49.

53 More specifically, it can take the form of direct transfers or loan guarantees, fiscal incentives such as tax credits, provision of goods and services other than general infrastructure, or direct payments to a funding mechanism. Definitions of a 'subsidy' in regional or bi-lateral trade agreements are often similar to the definition in the 1994 *WTO Agreement on Subsidies and Countervailing Measures*, at Art. 1.

54 For example, subsidy scheme could promote the use of emission-free renewable energy or could seek to reduce fossil energy consumption. It is conceivable that in key economic sectors significantly open to foreign trade, several subsidy schemes currently envisaged to reduce specific industries' emissions would run against trade rules.

55 Trade agreements provide for aggrieved parties to the accord, on behalf of competitors from their countries who are affected by unfair subsidies, to initiate determinations of subsidies and injuries, leading to investigations and potentially, duties, with provisions for dispute settlement and a Joint Committee.

56 A trade agreement may state that subsidies might be invalid if they are: 1) granted specifically to a particular firm or industry within a country, 2) linked to exports of the subsidized good, 3) contingent upon use of domestic over imported goods, or 4) found to cause 'adverse effects' to foreign competitors. Subsidy schemes aimed at reducing greenhouse gas emissions would likely be considered 'specific', falling under the first criteria. In addition, while proving 'adverse effects' can be complicated, it may not prevent parties from initiating a dispute on behalf of competitor producers if they estimate the subsidy impairs their market share or discriminates against their exports.

57 See *WTO Agreement on Subsidies and Countervailing Measures* in WTO (1999), 172, Art. 8.2(c).

governing eligibility for, and the amount of, the subsidy and if eligibility were automatic for any company meeting the criteria.[58] If eligibility for, and the amount of, a subsidy were directly linked to concrete criteria, such as energy efficiency or intensity, the measure may be pardoned under trade rules. However, depending on how the subsidy is crafted and applied, the risk of inconsistency also exists, particularly if all energy were found to be a 'like-product' in spite of different production and processing methods (i.e., energy produced from clean or renewable sources, versus energy produced from fossil fuels).

These 'intersections' demonstrate the risk of fragmented, non-integrated international law making. Beyond strict rules on conflicts of laws, a common public interest framework, or objective, may provide a more nuanced manner to more forward and strike the appropriate balance between economic, environmental and social development considerations in such instances.

Sustainable Development as a 'Public Interest' Objective of International Law

Sustainable development, as an overarching common 'public interest' objective affirmed on myriad occasions by the international community, may provide a useful 'bridging concept' in instances of regime intersection. In many of the most rapidly evolving new international regimes, including the WTO, States have jointly and explicitly committed to a common objective of sustainable development, using different formulations depending on the treaty and sector. Where overlaps or even conflicts between economic, social and environmental rules and regimes are possible, treaties and dispute settlement decisions may use States common 'sustainable development objective' to guide decisions and accommodations at the interstices.

It is not clear that sustainable development itself, as a concept, has the character or status of a customary norm of international law.[59] But neither is it void of all meaning or normative value in international law. Rather, it can be argued that the concept of sustainable development has a dual nature in international law.[60]

58 This is the case for the *WTO Agreement on Subsidies and Countervailing Measures*, *supra* note 52, at Art. 2.1(b), which states that these criteria need to be neutral, economic in nature and horizontal in application.

59 See Lowe 1999, 36. See also Boyle and Freestone 1999, 16–18.

60 While 'sustainable development' as such, may not be a customary principle of international law, it has been suggested that one of the principles of international law related to sustainable development includes a 'principle of integration', as proposed in the 2002 International Law Association's *New Delhi Declaration on Principles of International Law Related to Sustainable Development*, see International Law Association 2002, 209–216. See also Cordonier Segger and Khalfan 2004, 45–50. And see French 2005, 51.

First, from a more traditional legal perspective, sustainable development is an explicitly recognized objective of many international treaties, both at the global and regional levels, including many international trade treaties.[61]

In the 2001 *Doha Declaration*, States declared: 'We strongly reaffirm our commitment to the objective of sustainable development, as stated in the Preamble to the Marrakesh Agreement'.[62] This is echoed in reports of the WTO Panel and Appellate Body, which directly address the concept of sustainable development in world trade law. The WTO Appellate Body found, at note 107 in the *US – Shrimp Case*, that '[t]his concept has been generally accepted as integrating economic and social development and environmental protection'.[63] Further, the WTO Panel found, at note 202 in the *US – Shrimp Case, Recourse to Article 21.5 by Malaysia*,[64] that 'the concept is elaborated ... so as to put in place development that is sustainable ... that "meets the needs of the present generation without compromising the ability of future generations to meet their own needs"'. Four implications of these definitions are noteworthy for world trade law. First, the WTO Appellate Body and Panel adopted the most commonly accepted definition[65] of sustainable development, which refers to the needs of both present and future generations. Second, they described sustainable development as an objective for trade law, rather than as a customary principle of environmental law. Third, they noted that the concept involves 'integration'. Fourth, they explicitly recognized 'social

61 For discussion in the context of the trade and sustainable development debate, see, among others, Gehring and Cordonier Segger 2005. See also French 2005, 168–211. Since 1994, sustainable development has been a specific objective of the WTO. As noted in the (1994) *Marrakesh Agreement Establishing the World Trade Organization*, 15 April 1994, 1867 U.N.T.S. 154, I.L.M. 33: 1144, Preamble 'Recognizing that their relations in the field of trade and economic endeavour should be conducted with a view to raising standards of living ... *while allowing for the optimal use of the world's resources in accordance with the objective of sustainable development*, seeking both to protect and preserve the environment and to enhance the means for doing so in a manner consistent with their respective needs and concerns at different levels of economic development' (Emphasis added), WTO <http://www.wto.org/english/docs_e/legal_e/legal_e.htm>.

62 See *Ministerial Declaration, Ministerial Conference* – Fourth Session, Doha, Qatar (14 November 2001), WTO Doc. WT/MIN(01)/DEC/W/1, at para. 6. In the Dworkinian sense, such an 'objective' can also be called a 'policy'. Dworkin 1978, 22, where he argues that a policy is 'that kind of standard that sets out a goal to be reached, generally an improvement in some economic, political or social feature of the community (though some goals are negative, in that they stipulate that some present feature is to be protected from adverse change)'.

63 *United States – Import Prohibition of Certain Shrimp and Shrimp Products* (6 November 1998), WTO Doc. WT/DS58/AB/R, at note 107.

64 *United States – Import Prohibition of Certain Shrimp and Shrimp Products, Recourse to Article 21.5 by Malaysia* (15 June 2001), WTO Doc. WT/DS58/RW, at note 202.

65 See World Commission on Environment and Development (1987), *Our Common Future* (Oxford: Oxford University Press) [hereinafter the Brundtland Report].

development' as an element to be integrated, along with economic development and environmental protection.[66] In international law, sustainable development can be considered part of the 'object and purpose' of a growing number of treaties and therefore directly relevant in the interpretation of their provisions.[67] To achieve a sustainable development 'treaty objective' of this type, emerging principles of customary law might be reflected in treaties or even used by Courts. One such principle might involve integration of regimes, sometimes labeled a 'sustainable development principle'. The Permanent Court of Arbitration, in its Arbitral Award for the *Arbitration Regarding the Iron Rhine ('Ijzeren Rijn') Railway (Belgium v Netherlands)* 24 May 2005, may provide an example of use of this 'integration' principle. In this case, The Netherlands, which had created nature reserves along the path of the historic 'Iron Rhine' railway line, sought to prevent its reactivation. Belgium argued that the upgrading of the Iron Rhine Railway was part of a shift from road to rail transportation, assisting in the reduction of greenhouse gases, in order to contribute to sustainable development. Neither country wished to be responsible for costly assessment and mitigation measures. The Tribunal found that while Belgium's transit rights were secure, environmental concerns needed to be taken into account in development and hence the costs of the environmental measures would need to be *integrated* into Belgium's project. In its reasoning, the Tribunal refers to the 'notion … of sustainable development', and at para. 59, states that:

> [e]nvironmental law and the law on development stand not as alternatives but as mutually reinforcing, integral concepts, which require that where development may cause significant harm to the environment, there is a duty to prevent, or at least mitigate such harm. ... This duty, in the opinion of the Tribunal, has now become a principle of general international law. This principle applies not only

66 The social element was later also highlighted in the outcomes of the 2002 World Summit for Sustainable Development, which concluded, in the *Johannesburg Plan of Implementation*, at para. 140 (c), that there was a need to 'promote the full integration of sustainable development objectives into programmes and policies of bodies that have a primary focus on social issues' noting that, '[i]n particular, the social dimension of sustainable development should be strengthened …' See *2002 Johannesburg Declaration*, and *2002 Johannesburg Plan of Implementation, Report of the World Summit on Sustainable Development*, Johannesburg (South Africa) (4 Sept. 2002), UN Doc. A/CONF.199/20, at 140(c), WSSD <http://www.un.org/esa/sustdev/documents/WSSD_POI_PD/English/POIToc.htm>.

67 This Treaty is widely recognized as reflecting the customary international law norms of treaty interpretation and states that a 'treaty shall be interpreted in good faith in accordance with the ordinary meaning to be given to the terms of the treaty in their context and *in the light of its object and purpose*'. *Vienna Convention on Law of Treaties*, May 23, 1969, 1155 U.N.T.S. 331; 8 I.L.M. 679 (1969), at Art. 31(1).

> in autonomous activities but also in activities undertaken in implementation of specific treaties between the Parties.[68]

This reasoning may be an example of a *lex ferenda* customary law principle at work, one that requires States to integrate environmental considerations into social and economic development planning (*et à l'envers*). It may, of course, also be simply a means of applying the duty not to cause wide environment's harm. The objective is sustainable development, while the principle used by the Court to achieve it involves integration. Analysis of such cases, as they are resolved, can help to interpret and understand the meaning of sustainable development in international law, including world trade law.

Second, as an important 'public interest' objective of the international community, it is possible that States' common commitments to sustainable development can directly facilitate the reconciliation and integration of norms concerning socio-economic development and protection of the environment. As argued by Vaughan Lowe, the objective appears to have served as an 'interstitial norm' of this type in the *Gabcikovo-Nagymaros Case* at the International Court of Justice, where it was found that:

> Throughout the ages, mankind has, for economic and other reasons, constantly interfered with nature. In the past, this was often done without consideration of the effects upon the environment. Owing to new scientific insights and to a growing awareness of the risks for mankind – for present and future generations of pursuit of such interventions at an unconsidered and unabated pace, new norms and standards have been developed, set forth in a great number of instruments during the last two decades. Such new norms have to be taken into consideration, and such new standards given proper weight, not only when States contemplate new activities but also when continuing with activities begun in the past. *This need to reconcile economic development with protection of the environment is aptly expressed in the concept of sustainable development.*[69] *(Emphasis added)*

In instances where trade liberalization rules (or other economic development norms) intersect with environmental or social norms, a public interest commitment to sustainable development could be used to denote the Parties' intention to secure balanced, mutually supportive and integrated outcomes. This view is in keeping with the consensus of over 180 States, in the 2002 *Johannesburg Plan of Implementation* (JPOI), which addresses challenges related to globalization, trade

---

68 *Iron Rhine ('Ijzeren Rijn') Railway Case (Belgium v the Netherlands)* (2005), <http://www.pca-cpa.org/ENGLISH/RPC/BENL/BE-NL%20Award%20240505.pdf>, at 59, 114, (Permanent Court of Arbitration) (Arbitrators: Judge Rosalyn Higgins, President, Professor Guy Schrans, Judge Bruno Simma, Professor Alfred H.A. Soons, Judge Peter Tomka).

69 *Gabcikovo-Nagymaros Project (Hungary v Slovakia)*, [1997] I.C.J. Rep. 7 at 78.

and investment rules,[70] and also calls attention to the need for further development of the underlying institutional framework for sustainable development. In the JPOI at paragraph 139, States noted the need to:

> (a) Strengthen … commitments to sustainable development;
>
> (b) Integrat[e] the economic, social and environmental dimensions of sustainable development in a balanced manner; …
>
> (d) Strengthen … coherence, coordination and monitoring; …
>
> (f) Increas[e] effectiveness and efficiency through limiting overlap and duplication of activities of international organizations, within and outside the United Nations system, based on their mandates and comparative advantages.[71]

At paragraph 140, States noted in particular the need to:

> (b) Strengthen collaboration within and between the United Nations system, international financial institutions … and the World Trade Organization … Strengthened inter-agency collaboration should be pursued in all relevant contexts … to support, in particular, the efforts of developing countries …
>
> (c) Strengthen and better integrate the three dimensions of sustainable development policies and programmes …[72]

As such, sustainable development can be seen as a public interest objective of WTO law, aiding in the interpretation of trade law obligations where these need to integrate social development and environmental protection, in the interest of development that can last, for the benefit of present and future generations. The objective may also play an 'interstitial' normative role in trade and other sustainable development treaty law, encouraging the reconciliation or 'mutual supportiveness' of economic development and trade obligations where these overlap with social development and environmental protection norms.

---

70 The Johannesburg Declaration, in para. 14, states 'Globalization has added a new dimension to these challenges ... benefits and costs of globalization are unevenly distributed, with developing countries facing special difficulties in meeting this challenge'. See *2002 Johannesburg Declaration*, and *2002 Johannesburg Plan of Implementation*, *supra* note 65. See, for commentary, Gehring 2004.

71 See *2002 Johannesburg Plan of Implementation*, *supra* note 65 at 139.

72 See *2002 Johannesburg Plan of Implementation*, *supra* note 65 at 140.

Sustainable Development in World Trade Law

To accommodate the overlaps between legal systems and regimes, States use both informal and formal negotiations to debate the social, economic and environmental consequences of obligations in each regime. Such debates can take place in the World Trade Organization, and in the international decision-making bodies of other trade, investment and financial law forums.[73] They will also, most likely, play out in the dispute settlement bodies of these forums, mainly through clarification and interpretation of the 'exceptions' to the trade rules.[74]

However, a second option is also emerging. Some States are taking the 'sustainable development' objective of world trade law seriously, developing a more integrated approach. There is work being undertaken to elaborate and operationalize, through new processes, a world trade law that can deliberately promote sustainable development. This work focuses on opening 'windows' or general exceptions and reservations in trade obligations, but also on reforming the evolving international rules in each substantive area of trade law (trade in goods, trade in services, subsidies, intellectual property rights, sanitary and phytosanitary standards, technical barriers to trade, agriculture, textiles, investment law and competition law, *inter alia*). For example, in WTO negotiations on environmental goods and services, it could be possible to reduce tariffs on agricultural waste based biofuels such as ethanol and biodiesel, of which developing countries such as Costa Rica are principal producers.[75] Such a trade liberalization measure may have potential to deliver both environmental and development benefits. If changes in these specific rules could affect the environment or social development, new trade rules can be designed to contribute directly to the objective of sustainable development in each area. Such an agenda can be developed through decisions of trade tribunals, which have a role to play in interpreting international trade law,[76] but will especially be elaborated through negotiations of the Parties to international trade agreements at the global, regional and bi-lateral levels. The use of new procedures, such as sustainability impact assessment, might contribute substantially to the effectiveness of the negotiations, the eventual measures and the future implementation of the accords.

---

73 Such debates may also take place in international social development institutions such as the International Labour Organization, the World Health Organization, etc.

74 Such questions might also be addressed in the compliance mechanisms of multilateral environmental agreements (MEAs), or in international human rights tribunals (such as the European Court of Human Rights, or the Inter-American Court of Human Rights).

75 Singh 2005. Online: <www.iisd.org/pdf/2005/trade_environmental_goods.pdf>; Barria et al. 2003.

76 While there is no *stare decisis* in the WTO, one does find that previous Appellate Body decisions to have persuasive authority. See Bhala 1998/99, 845 –956; Bhala 2000/2001, 873 –978; and Fadzil and Rani, online: *Malayan Law Journal* <http://www.mlj.com.my/free/articles/rozlinda&harris2.htm>.

Future International Trade Negotiations and Sustainable Development

While adjudication of disputes is part of treaty implementation and also serves to clarify the rules agreed to in a treaty, it is not the only way that regimes evolve and deepen. Negotiation processes are used to change and develop a regime, affecting its rules and how they are implemented through both formal rule changes and the development of informal guidelines or understandings which may later be described as subsequent treaty practice in the interpretation of international legal obligations. Members of the WTO explicitly agreed to consider certain sustainable development aspects of world trade law in the new round of negotiations launched in Doha, Qatar, in 2001.[77] First, the WTO Members at para. 6 of the Ministerial Declaration's Preamble stressed that the multilateral trading system and efforts towards environmental protection *and* sustainable development 'can and must' be mutually supportive. Second, the Doha Declaration makes a procedural change to negotiations in para. 51 which instructs the Committee on Trade and Environment and the Committee on Trade and Development to 'each act as a forum to identify and debate developmental and environmental aspects of the negotiations, in order to help achieve the objective of having sustainable development appropriately reflected'. It is, arguably, this procedural change which will have the most significant impact in the future, as the WTO and its members seek to better understand this commitment in negotiations. However, this is still far from an integrated sustainable development agenda.

In the 2001 Doha Ministerial Conference, agreement was also reached to commence negotiations on certain aspects of the WTO/MEA relationship, though not to negotiate a solution to conflicts which oppose MEA parties and non-parties.[78] Paragraph 31(i) and (ii) of the *Doha Ministerial Declaration* launches negotiations on trade and environment in several areas, including (i) the relationship between WTO rules and trade obligations set out in Multilateral Environmental Agreements (MEAs); and (ii) procedures for information exchange between MEA secretariats and relevant WTO committees, including criteria for granting observer status, among other issues.[79] Whilst conversations are taking place, progress at the global level has been very, very slow.

---

77 See Cordonier Segger and Gehring 2005.

78 Members agreed to clarify the relationship between WTO rules and MEAs, with respect to those MEAs which contain 'specific trade obligations' (STOs). The outcome of those negotiations must be limited to the applicability of WTO rules to conflicts between WTO Members who are parties to an MEA: WTO <http://www.wto.org/english/tratop_e/envir_e/envir_backgrnd_e/c5s3_e.htm>.

79 Members are attempting to reach common understandings, on the basis of two complementary approaches: the identification of STOs in MEAs; and a more conceptual discussion on the WTO–MEA relationship. WTO <http://www.wto.org/english/tratop_e/envir_e/envir_backgrnd_e/c5s3_e.htm>.

Sustainable Developments in New Regional and Bi-lateral Trade Treaties

States have also set sustainable development as an objective of several regional and bi-lateral trade treaties. Putting this commitment into practice may prove challenging. However, the objective is by no means impossible to achieve. A few potentially useful provisions can be briefly surveyed.

Sustainable Development Objectives Recognized in Trade Treaty Preambles

The Preamble of the 1994 *North American Free Trade Agreement* between the Government of Canada, the Government of the United Mexican States, and the Government of the United States of America (NAFTA) states that 'The Government of Canada, the Government of the United Mexican States and the Government of the United States of America, resolved to … promote sustainable development; … have agreed as follows …'[80] This commitment is also found in the preambles of the *Canada–Chile Free Trade Agreement*,[81] the *Canada–Costa Rica Free Trade Agreement*, the *Chile–United States Free Trade Agreement*, and the *Peru–United States Free Trade Agreement*. It is also found, in Spanish, in the *Bolivia–Mexico Free Trade Agreement*. These explicit joint resolutions set the promotion of sustainable development as a shared objective of these trade agreements, among other priorities. But how does one render this objective operational? What kinds of provisions, in a regional or bi-lateral trade agreement, can be included to promote sustainable development?

Exceptions for Social Development and Environmental Measures

One of the ways to provide for mutual supportiveness between trade liberalization, social development and environmental protection regimes is to ensure that one regime does not actually conflict with the other, or unduly constrain the adoption of legitimate measures to deliver on the commitments of the other. An 'exceptions' provision is commonly included in trade treaties modeled on the GATT Article XX, providing space for certain legitimate government measures which trade policies might otherwise inadvertently limit or constrain.[82] As such, if an otherwise inconsistent measure can be shown (by the Party claiming the exception) to fall under certain limited exceptions and also to comply with a 'chapeau', which requires that it does not result in arbitrary or unjustifiable discrimination and does

80 See Preamble: *North American Free Trade Agreement* (NAFTA), adopted 1 January 1994, I.L.M. 32:289, 605 treaty text, <http://www.sice.oas.org/trade/nafta.asp>.

81 *Canada–Chile Free Trade Agreement*, Canada, Chile, 5 December 1996, http://www.international.gc.ca/trade-agreements-accords-commerciaux/agr-acc/chile-chili/menu.aspx?lang=en, at Preamble (entered into force 5 July, 1997).

82 *General Agreement on Tariffs and Treaties 1994*, April 1994, <http://www.wto.org/english/docs_e/legal_e/legal_e.htm>, at Art. XX.

not constitute disguised protectionism, it can be permitted by the trade agreement. For instance, in the WTO *US – Shrimp Case*, it was not clear whether living natural resources could fall within the scope of Article XX(g), but by referring to a common objective of sustainable development to assist in interpreting the meaning of the exception, the Panel and Appellate Body eventually found that it did. These provisions clarify that the Parties intend to give more policy space to their regulators, in the interest of environmental and natural source conservation measures. Such space may be helpful to ensure a 'mutual supportiveness', or at least to prevent one priority (trade) from almost always overriding the other, in spite of limited exceptions.

Specific exceptions may also be provided in certain chapters of the trade agreements, responding to concerns that have been identified in global debates or impact assessments. For instance, the WTO has raised concerns about the need for flexibility for regulators in the area of services.[83] And indeed, a set of specific exceptions is provided in the *Canada–Chile FTA*. Subject to a 'chapeau', this Agreement provides exceptions for 'measures necessary to secure compliance with laws or regulations that are not inconsistent with the provisions of this Agreement, including those relating to health and safety and consumer protection'.[84] Furthermore, Parties often include extremely specific reservations in each chapter of a regional or bi-lateral trade treaty. Such reservations can even exempt entire sectors of health, education or other social development regulations from the trade disciplines. In addition, Parties may include actual 'conflicts clauses' in trade agreements, whereby the rules of prior treaties related to the environment (for instance) are given explicit preference by the Parties in the event of a conflict between the regimes, as will be discussed further below.

Parallel Cooperation Agreements on Environmental and Social Matters

A second approach to ensure that a trade agreement contributes to sustainable development was pioneered with the *North American Free Trade Agreement* (NAFTA) and has continued to be developed in other trade agreements. This approach involves developing 'value-added' cooperative agreements during trade treaty negotiations, typically addressing labour and environment issues. Some trade agreements contain 'chapters', which also refer to further cooperation strategies or agreements, while others are negotiated with parallel social or environmental 'side agreements'.[85]

---

83 WTO Council for Trade in Services, Ministerial Decision on Trade in Services and the Environment, Decision on Trade in Services and the Environment, S/C/M/1, adopted 1 March 1995, S/L/4.

84 *Canada–Chile FTA*, *supra* note 80, at Art. G-01.

85 See Cordonier Segger 2002. See also Cordonier Segger and Leichner Reynal 2005; Barcena 2002.

With regards to social development and labour rights, the first side agreement was the *North American Agreement on Labour Cooperation* (NAALC), which commits to 'improve working conditions and living standards' in all parties, to 'protect, enhance and enforce basic workers' rights', through eleven core labour principles.[86] A Commission for Labour Co-operation (Ministerial Council and Secretariat, assisted by National Administrative Offices [NAOs] in each country) is established[87] and the NAALC provides for a complaints process,[88] and also a compliance mechanism in the event that an arbitral panel finds a persistent pattern of failure by a country to effectively enforce its labour law.[89] If a country fails to correct the problem, the panel may impose a fine, with certain caps. A similar model is used by the 1997 *Canada–Chile Labour Cooperation Agreement* (CCLCA). Under the CCLCA, Parties commit to maintain and improve labour standards, to effectively enforce their labour law and other guarantees[90] and to create a Commission for Labour Cooperation structured similar to the one in the NAALC.[91] The CCLCA has two main components: a Cooperative Work Program and a procedure for handling issues of concern, in a way that is similar to the NAALC.[92] The *Canada–Costa Rica Labour Cooperation Agreement* (CCRLCA) has certain differences. Administratively, the CCRLCA is much simpler, and does not include provisions for national secretariats, evaluation committees of experts or panel rosters, in order to be simpler to implement for a Party with less administrative capacity. In terms of scope and coverage, all three agreements cover eleven principles and rights. However, the CCRLCA obligations, in Annex 1, are directly related to the 1998 *ILO Declaration on Fundamental Principles and Rights at Work*, which came into

86 NAFTA, *supra* note 79, at Art. 1.

87 NAFTA, *supra* note 79, at Arts. 8–9, 12, 15 and 21. See NAALC Secretariat, <http://www.naalc.org>. See in particular: Commission for Labour Cooperation (2000), *Comparative Guide to Labour and Employment Laws in North America. Labour Relations Law in North America* (Washington: NAALC).

88 See Banks 2002.

89 NAFTA, *supra* note 79, at Arts. 23–26, 27–29, 37–39. For a summary of disputes to date under the NAALC, see Human Rights Watch, <http://www.hrw.org/reports/2001/nafta/nafta0401-05.htm>.

90 See First Annual Report: Canada–Chile Agreement on Labour Cooperation (July 1997–June 1998), <http://www.labour-travail.hrdc-drhc.gc.ca/doc/ialc-cidt/eng/e/backen.htm#background>.

91 See First Annual Report: Canada–Chile Agreement on Labour Cooperation (July 1997–June 1998), <http://www.labour-travail.hrdc-drhc.gc.ca/doc/ialc-cidt/eng/e/backen.htm#background>.

92 See Ministerial Council (2000 December), *Report on the Three-Year Review of the Canada–Chile Agreement on Labour Cooperation* <http://www.labour-travail.hrdc-rhc.gc.ca/psait_spila/aicdt_ialc/2003_2004/report_english.htm>.

effect after the *Canada–Chile LCA* and the NAALC. Furthermore, the CCRLCA does not provide for monetary fines.[93]

The *Chile–US FTA* provides a slightly different model. It includes a Labour Chapter 18 which lays out a cooperative agenda to promote worker rights.[94] In the accord, Parties agree that it is inappropriate to weaken or reduce domestic labour protections to encourage trade or investment, and requires that Parties shall effectively enforce their own domestic labour laws; a cooperative mechanism is provided specifically to promote respect for the principles embodied in the 1998 *ILO Declaration on Fundamental Principles and Rights at Work* and compliance with *ILO Convention 182 on the Worst Forms of Child Labour*. The Labour Chapter is subject to the dispute settlement provisions of the *Chile–US FTA* with high standards of openness and transparency, including open public hearings, public release of legal submissions by parties, a special roster of labour or environmental experts for disputes in these areas and rights for interested third parties to submit views. The emphasis is put on the promotion of compliance through consultation, joint action plans and trade-enhancing remedies, but the enforcement mechanism also includes monetary penalties.[95]

Environmental agreements/chapters seek to facilitate cooperation on environmental protection objectives, including the strengthening of environmental laws and regulations. An early model is the *North American Agreement on Environmental Cooperation* (NAAEC) between Canada, Mexico and the United States, which has been well documented in academic literature.[96] NAAEC objectives are assigned to an institution, the Commission for Environmental Cooperation (CEC), which is served by a Secretariat and governed by the Tri-partite Council of Environment Ministers that works to promote environmental cooperation among the Parties.[97] If a persistent pattern of non-enforcement of environmental laws is identified, a factual report process also exists.[98] With

93 Communication with Dale Whiteside (Deputy Director, Strategic Trade Policy, Department of Foreign Affairs and International Trade, Government of Canada, 26 June 2003, on file with authors).

94 *United States–Chile Free Trade Agreement*, Chile, United States, 1 January 2004, <http://www.ustr.gov/trade-agreements/free-trade-agreements/chile-fta/final-text> at Art. 18.

95 USTR, *Summary of Chile–US Free Trade Agreement* <http://www.ustr.gov/regions/whemisphere/samerica/2002-12-11-chile_summary.pdf>.

96 *North American Agreement for Environmental Cooperation* (NAAEC), adopted 1 January 1994, I.L.M. 32:1480, treaty text available online, http://www.cec.org>. See Cordonier Segger 2005, above 1, 183 –222 and Deere and Esty 2002. See also de Mestral 2003.

97 Specifically, the Council has a co-operative work plan based on priority areas, including: establishing limits for specific air and marine pollutants; environmental assessments of projects with trans-boundary implications; and, reciprocal court access for damage or injury resulting from trans-boundary pollution.

98 See Alanis Ortega 2002 and Wilson 2002.

guidance from its Joint Public Advisory Committee, the CEC has become a strong inter-governmental voice in North America for the environment.[99] Elements of the NAAEC, and certainly the CEC itself, demonstrate the usefulness of a credible institution as part of any regional regime that seeks to harmonize environment and trade objectives. Modeled on the NAAEC, the *Canada–Chile Agreement on Environmental Cooperation* (CCAEC) also provides a framework for bilateral cooperation on environmental issues.[100] The CCAEC provides a commission for environmental cooperation, the provision of environmental information and a joint public advisory council process.[101] It establishes national secretariats to implement its mandate and recognizes prior commitments under other environmental agreements. The annexes, which phase in the application of the Agreement to Chilean environmental law, led to a comprehensive and valuable revision of environmental law in Chile.[102] The *Canada–Costa Rica Environmental Cooperation Agreement* focuses more on environmental information exchange and capacity building in the area of environmental enforcement and monitoring,[103] with a stronger focus on access to environmental information and capacity building for environmental policy and law-makers.[104] Rather than an enforcement process, it includes provisions granting rights to request information from any party on the effective implementation of environmental law in its territory and the duty to respond publicly to this request.[105]

The *Chile–US FTA* provides, in Chapter 19 (Environment), for the establishment of an Environmental Affairs Council[106] and a common, detailed work programme on specific topics.[107] As with the labour chapters, the *Chile–US FTA* and the *Peru–US FTA* both include provisions which permit access to the FTA dispute settlement

99 Additional details on the North American Commission for Environment Cooperation are available at <http://www.cec.org>.

100 Bowcott, A., Manager, Environment Canada, International Relations Canada, and Canada's Chief Negotiator for the Canada–Chile, Canada–Costa Rica, Canada–Central America Environmental Side Agreements (Series of interviews, January–April, 2003, notes on file with the author).

101 Durbin 2000.

102 The *Agreement on Environmental Cooperation between the Governments of Canada and the Republic of Chile*, 36 I.L.M. 1196, adopted 6 February 1997, Arts. 2 and 10, sections 1 and 2. Treaty text is available online, <http://www.sice.oas.org/trade/chican_e/chcatoc.asp#environ>.

103 Gitli and Murillo 2002.

104 See the *Agreement on Environmental Cooperation between the Government of Canada and the Government of the Republic of Costa Rica*, adopted 23 April 2001, treaty text available, <http://www.sice.oas.org/Trade/cancr/English/enve.asp>.

105 See the *Agreement on Environmental Cooperation between the Government of Canada and the Government of the Republic of Costa Rica*, adopted 23 April 2001, treaty text available, <http://www.sice.oas.org/Trade/cancr/English/enve.asp> at Art. 9.

106 *US–Chile FTA*, *supra* note 93, at Art. 19.3.

107 Corbin 2003, 119.

mechanisms for non-enforcement of environmental laws, with penalties such as monetary assessments rather than trade sanctions. Both refer to an *Environmental Cooperation Agreement* that will be negotiated at a later date between the Parties.

In the FTAs which locate environmental considerations in 'chapters', measures for capacity-building and cooperation on the implementation of environment regulations appear more concrete and detailed. However, both the 'chapter' and the 'side agreement' approaches provide for environmental cooperation and social development through institutional structures such as committees and ongoing cooperation agendas and by encouraging public and civil society engagement in the process.

Specific Operational Provisions

Beyond the exceptions and the parallel side agreement/chapters, a more strategic approach is beginning to evolve which addresses instances where specific provisions related to the same subject matter in the trade agreements and other treaties related to sustainable development might overlap, constraining policy choices and affecting the potential for effective implementation of social and environmental commitments. In one example, the intellectual property rights (IPRs) provisions in the NAFTA, the *Chile–US FTA* and others may overlap with provisions of the 1992 *United Nations Convention on Biological Diversity* (UN CBD),[108] as well as human rights commitments to provide access to essential medicines.[109] Concerns have been raised as to how, under strict IPR disciplines, Parties will have the policy space to fulfill their UN CBD commitments to ensure that local and indigenous communities have control over and can benefit from their biodiversity-related traditional knowledge and 'informal' innovations,[110] and how, in accordance with sovereignty over genetic resources recognized in the UN CBD, countries can decline to patent life-forms, and balance plant breeders' rights with others.[111]

Two innovative approaches are found in the context of the *Peru–US FTA*. At Article 16, this trade agreement contains relatively strict and detailed provisions to protect intellectual property rights, including a commitment that, by 2008, both Parties will be members of the 1991 *International Convention for the Protection of New Varieties of Plants* (UPOV Convention),[112] which has attracted criticism due

108 *UN CBD*, *supra* note 34.

109 See Garforth and Prabhu 2005, 549–573. See also Balasubramaniam 2003, and Zaveri 2003, 135–142, 149–156.

110 UN CBD, *supra* note 34, at 8j and 10. See Lettington 2000.

111 UN CBD, *supra* note 34 at 1. See Vivas Eugui 2003.

112 There have been three versions of the UPOV Convention, two of which are of concern here: *International Convention for the Protection of New Varieties of Plants*, 2 December 1961, as revised on 23 October 1978, U.K.T.S. 74 (1984) (entered into force 8 November 1981); *International Convention for the Protection of New Varieties of Plants*, 2

to its requirements on patenting of plant genetic resources.[113] These commitments may be balanced by an Agreement, included in the *Peru–US FTA* package, titled *Draft Understanding Regarding Biodiversity and Traditional Knowledge*. The Draft Understanding recognizes the importance of obtaining prior informed consent from appropriate authorities, equitably sharing the benefits arising from the use of traditional knowledge and genetic resources, and promoting quality patent examination to ensure that the conditions of patentability are satisfied. It refers to the use of contracts that reflect mutually agreed terms between users and providers of traditional knowledge and genetic resources, and includes an operational commitment to share information through publicly accessible databases and an opportunity to cite, in writing, to the appropriate examining authority prior art that may have a bearing on patentability.[114] Under strong IPR regimes, genetic resources based on traditional knowledge ('prior art') could be patented without benefit sharing. In such situations, biodiversity-rich states can be unwilling to grant strong IPR protections, and may need trade measures to prevent such resources from being patented beyond their control. The Draft Understanding commits to cooperation between the Parties on such issues. It builds on the experience of the Andean Community in Decision 391 on Common Access Regime for Genetic Resources,[115] which responds to CBD Article 15, regulating access to genetic resources and the equitable distribution of benefits derived from their use, and recognizing the contributions of indigenous peoples' traditional knowledge.[116] Such regimes, also found in Central America, guarantee the direct participation of communities and local populations and seek ways to equitably distribute benefits from genetic resources that are identified using traditional knowledge.[117] As such, this aspect of the trade agreement may accommodate the Parties' desire to ensure benefits from traditional knowledge accrue to the originators. For Peru,

December 1961, as revised on 23 October 1978 and 19 March 1991 (entered into force 24 April 1998). The *International Convention for the Protection of New Varieties of Plants*, done in Geneva, adopted at 2 December 1961, revised at 23 October 1978 and 19 March 1991.

113 See Ruiz 2003, 238–245.

114 USTR, *Understanding Regarding Biodiversity and Traditional Knowledge*, As part of the *Peru–US Free Trade Agreement*, DRAFT: 6 January 2006, not yet entered into force, <http://www.ustr.gov/assets/Trade_Agreements/Bilateral/Peru_TPA/Final_Texts/asset_upload_file869_8728.pdf>.

115 Secretariat for the UN CBD, International Regime on Access and Benefit-Sharing: Proposals for an International Regime on Access and Benefit-sharing, UNEP/CBD/MYPOW/6, adopted 7 January 2003, at 6–7. Andean Community, Decision 391, <http://www.sice.oas.org/trade/JUNAC/decisiones/DEC391e.asp>.

116 Secretariat for the UN CBD, International Regime on Access and Benefit-Sharing: Proposals for an International Regime on Access and Benefit-sharing, UNEP/CBD/MYPOW/6, adopted 7 January 2003, at 6–7. Andean Community, Decision 391, <http://www.sice.oas.org/trade/JUNAC/decisiones/DEC391e.asp>.

117 See Medaglia 2003.

this recognition could be helpful to meet their obligations in the UN CBD. Much will depend on how this Draft Understanding is implemented, and if substantive progress is made.

Rules on Relationships between Treaties

Disagreements about the appropriateness of using trade measures to achieve the goals of 'non-trade' regimes are possible and in some cases, well documented. As mentioned above, when trade, environment and social development regimes overlap, there is seldom a direct conflict of positive obligations (i.e., prohibition versus obligation), though some parties may see rights gained in one regime limited by commitments in the *lex posteriori.* However, trade rules may work formally or informally to constrain the use of social or environmental measures, affecting Parties' ability to implement other important social or environmental commitments and frustrating the sustainable development objectives of all. Essentially, the trade agreement limits policy space, constraining the use of economic instruments to achieve the goals of sustainable development treaties. For example, as mentioned above, measures to support emissions reductions and the use of market-based instruments (carbon taxes) to implement the 1997 *Kyoto Protocol* to the 1992 UN *Framework Convention on Climate Change* might be constrained by commitments to reduce subsidies, or to avoid certain types of border adjustments and non-tariff barriers to trade. In another example mentioned above, the 1992 *United Nations Convention on Biological Diversity*[118] and its 2001 *Cartagena Protocol on Biosafety*[119] appear to contain provisions which could overlap with the provisions of several trade agreements. Problems may arise from intersections between the right of Parties under the *Cartagena Protocol* to use precaution in making decisions concerning LMOs, and WTO SPS obligations only to maintain SPS measures that can be justified by scientific methods.[120] Perhaps the most cooperative approach to this issue is adopted in the *Canada–Chile FTA* and the *Canada–Costa Rica FTA*, which establish cooperation mechanisms on SPS measures in the context of the environmental side agreements.[121] However, if it is not the intention of the Parties to the trade agreement that are also Parties

118 United Nations Convention on Biological Diversity ('UNCBD'), adopted 5 June 1992, I.L.M. 31: 822, at 15.

119 See the *Cartagena Protocol on Biological Diversity*, at Cartagena, adopted 29 January 2000, I.L.M. 11: 1416, treaty text available online, <http://www.biodiv.org/default.shtml>.

120 See, e.g. Trudeau and Nègre 2005, 593–630. See also Button 2004.

121 For instance, in order to apply the WTO SPS Agreement, Canada and Costa Rica, at Art. IX.5, inaugurated a Committee for consultation and cooperation purposes, which may consider: ' ... co-operation programs; ... mutual recognition and equivalence agreements, and product control, inspection and approval procedures; ... the identification and resolution of SPS-related problems; ...' etc. See *Agreement on Environmental Cooperation between the Government of Canada and the Government of the Republic of Costa Rica*, adopted

to the *Cartagena Protocol* to permit their measures to be constrained, it could be useful to include provisions in the trade agreements which offer clear guidance to States in the event of overlaps or conflicts between the two sets of rules, rather than simply re-confirming problematic obligations and then providing forums for discussion.

As further examples, measures to develop a multi-lateral system of access and benefit sharing in the 2004 *International Treaty on Plant Genetic Resources for Food and Agriculture* (FAO Seed Treaty) might conceivably be limited by commitments to liberalize agriculture; regional measures to reduce air or water pollution might be found to infringe on the rights of investors and be subject to compensation claims in closed arbitral processes; or other regional or national measures to meet human rights commitments regarding access to water, health care or education might be blocked by the results of services liberalization processes.

Where constraints are not intended by the Parties, provisions can be included in trade agreements which directly address potential overlaps and clarify which regime will have precedence. This approach precludes, in a limited way, measures taken under these accords from the purview of trade disciplines. Such provisions were included in NAFTA, and also appear in the *Canada–Chile FTA* at Articles A-03 and A-04 [122] and the *Canada–Costa Rica FTA* at Articles I.3 and I.4.[123] A useful example is provided by Articles 102 and 104 of NAFTA.[124] Chapter 1 sets forth the Agreement's basic objectives and rules of interpretation. Article 102 states the objectives of NAFTA and agrees that it will be interpreted in accordance with the applicable rules of international law. Article 103 affirms existing rights and obligations under both bilateral and multilateral agreements, including the WTO Agreements, providing that NAFTA prevails in the event of any inconsistency between it and such other international agreements, except as otherwise noted.[125] Finally, Article 104 reverses the general rule of Article 103 in regard to certain international environmental agreements.[126] The 'listed MEAs' were already in force during the negotiation of NAFTA in 1994, and each authorizes the use of trade measures to achieve its objectives. These measures include trade bans against products made with CFCs in non-Parties to discourage 'free-riders', bans on trade in endangered species products to discourage their exploitation and bans on the import/export of hazardous wastes, as well as other restrictions. If not for Article 104, these measures would be disallowed by the former provision.

---

23 April 2001, treaty text available online, <http://www.sice.oas.org/Trade/cancr/English/enve.asp>.

122 *Canada–Chile FTA*, *supra* note 101.

123 *Canada–Costa Rica FTA*, *supra* note 103.

124 NAFTA, *supra* note 79.

125 Organization of American States, *Overview of the North American Free Trade Agreement*, <http://www.sice.oas.org/summary/nafta/nafta1.asp>.

126 NAFTA, *supra* note79, 104.

This NAFTA approach is also found in the *Canada–Chile FTA* and the *Canada–Costa Rica FTA*. It can be compared with a second approach found in the environment chapter of the *Peru–US TPA* at Article 18.10 and the *Chile–US FTA* at Article 19.9. The *Peru–US TPA* commits to 'seek means to enhance the mutual supportiveness of multilateral environmental agreements to which they are all party and trade agreements to which they are all party …' It also commits to 'consult, as appropriate, with respect to negotiations on environmental issues of mutual interest'. And at 3, it states that, 'Each Party recognizes the importance to it of the multilateral environmental agreements to which it is a party'.[127] This provision simply commits the Parties to seeking means to enhance 'mutual supportiveness', and provides that Parties will consult, as appropriate, on 'issues of mutual interest'. It limits the commitment to MEAs to which the TPA Parties are 'all parties', and trade agreements to which they are all Parties. The commitment to mutual supportiveness would not apply to measures taken under environmental agreements to which some Parties are Parties, but others are not. This problem is clearly acknowledged in the final provision that '[e]ach Party recognizes the importance to it' of the MEAs to which it is a party, but not resolved. Perhaps the least problematic approach can be found in the *Chile–US FTA* Environment Chapter at Article 19.9, which simply states: 'The Parties recognize the importance of multilateral environmental agreements, including the appropriate use of trade measures in such agreements to achieve specific environmental goals'.

With regards to social development, the *Peru–US TPA* provides an example of an innovative provision in the body of the text which indicates the relationship of the trade agreement to international social development (labour) treaties and bodies, at Article 17.1 (Statement of Shared Commitments). In particular, this provision states that all Parties 'shall strive to ensure that such labor principles and the internationally recognized labor rights … are recognized and protected by its law' and that the Parties 'reaffirm their full respect for their Constitutions and recognize the right of each Party to adopt or modify its labor laws and standards. Each Party shall strive to ensure that it provides for labor standards consistent with the internationally recognized labor rights …'. This commitment is made operational at Article 17.5 (and following), on the Labor Cooperation and Capacity Building Mechanism, which also states that the mechanism 'shall operate in a manner that respects each Party's law and sovereignty'. The rights protected include:

a) the right of association;
b) the right to organize and bargain collectively;

127 The *Peru–US Free Trade Agreement*, not yet entered into force, <http://www.ustr.gov/assets/Trade_Agreements/Bilateral/Peru_TPA/Final_Texts/asset_upload_file852_8712.pdf>.

c) a prohibition on the use of any form of forced or compulsory labor;
d) labor protections for children and minors, including a minimum age for the employment of children and the prohibition and elimination of the worst forms of child labour; and
e) acceptable conditions of work with respect to minimum wages, hours of work, and occupational safety and health, but not a common minimum wage.

The provision does not commit to precedence for all labour agreements, as such. The ILO enshrines over 190 Conventions, but the TPA only mentions ILA Convention No. 182 *Concerning the Prohibition and Immediate Action for the Elimination of the Worst Forms of Child Labor.*[128] As such, its provisions are still quite limited, as are the similar provisions in the 2003 *Chile–United States Free Trade Agreement.*[129] On contentious social issues, such provisions may hold some potential to become tools for 'reconciliation' of the trade treaty norms with other social norms.[130]

It is not yet clear which of several strategies or instruments will have the most success in helping to integrate social and economic development and environmental protection. It is likely that no one single type of provision has an answer to this problem. Rather, many different provisions and instruments are being developed and tested in the regional context. These provisions alone will not ensure that sustainable development objectives are given more weight. However, they appear likely to contribute to the achievement of a greater degree of balance in the agreements, which is a first step.

Process Innovations Develop More Sustainable Trade Agreements

Effectiveness is not just affected by the rules embodied in substantive treaty provisions. Process changes can also contribute a great deal toward addressing the intersections and uneasy overlaps between treaty regimes in public international law, particularly where States share a common public interest. This is demonstrated by recent attempts to pioneer new trade negotiation and implementation procedures

128 International Labor Organization Convention No. 182 *Concerning the Prohibition and Immediate Action for the Elimination of the Worst Forms of Child Labor*, adopted 17 June 1999, entered into force 10 November 2000, 38 I.L.M. 1207 7.1 and 8.

129 *Chile–US FTA*, *supra* note 93, at 19.3.

130 Additional Protocol to the American Convention on Human Rights in the Area of Economic, Social and Cultural Rights (Protocol of San Salvador), entered into force 16 November 1999, OAS Treaty Series No. 69, reprinted in Basic Documents Pertaining to Human Rights in the Inter-American System OEA/Ser L V/II.82 Doc 6 Rev 1 at 67.

based on impact assessment, openness, consultation, capacity-building and cooperation.

Impact Assessments and Reviews

One particularly important procedural step for sustainable development involves impact assessment of new trade rules. Critics of trade agreements have warned that the economic growth stimulated by a trade agreement may have significant negative impacts on social and environmental sustainability.[131] Partly in response to this pressure, States have begun to seek ways to identify, then prevent or mitigate, environmental and social impacts of new trade rules. Through the use of national and regional environmental impact assessments, potential impacts can be considered, taken into account and even avoided; social or human rights impact assessments can also be conducted, running parallel to environmental impact assessments.[132] Further, social and environmental impacts can be considered together in an assessment, using integrated or 'sustainability impact assessments' that are usually applied to specific chapters of a trade agreement, sector by sector.[133] While not all sustainability impact assessments include a strong social dimension, it is becoming increasingly accepted to do so.[134] At present, several States have committed to perform regular impact assessments of global and regional trade negotiations.[135] Pilot studies have been conducted for the North American Symposium for the Assessment of Trade and Environment policies,[136] and for the United Nations Environment Programme.[137]

131 See, e.g., The Public Citizen, *Global Trade Watch: Promoting Democracy by Challenging Corporate Globalization*, <http://www.citizen.org/trade/nafta/>; Stop CAFTA, <http://www.stopcafta.org/> and Anti-GATT, <http://www.gatt.org/>.

132 United Nations Environment Programme (2001). See also Walker 2005, 217–256.

133 Kirkpatrick et al., WTO New Round: Sustainability Impact Assessment Study (Phase Two Report): Sustainability Impact Assessment, <http://fs2.idpm.man.ac.uk/sia/Phase2/EXSUMFINAL>.

134 Blanco 2003.

135 For example, General Council – Preparations for the 1999 Ministerial Conference – Trade and Sustainable Development – Communication from the United States WT/GC/W/304 99-3364, adopted 6 August 1999 and General Council – Preparations for the 1999 Ministerial Conference – Canadian Approach to Trade and Environment in the New WTO Round – Communication from Canada WT/GC/W/358 99-4298, adopted 12 October 1999.

136 Blanco and Gallagher 2003.

137 Centro de Investigación y Planificación del Medio Ambiente (CIPMA) (1999), Environmental Impacts of Trade Liberalization and Policies for the Sustainable Management of Natural Resources: A Case Study of Chile's Mining Sector (Geneva: UNEP), available online, <http://www.unep.ch/etu/etp/acts/capbld/rdone/chile.htm>.

These commitments are reflected in the side agreements of several trade agreements. For example, the *North American Agreement on Environmental Cooperation* contains the obligation to assess environmental effects of NAFTA. The Commission on Environmental Cooperation is, institutionally, separate from the NAFTA Commission. However, according to Article 10.6(d) of the NAAEC, the Council of Ministers of the CEC is responsible for 'considering on an ongoing basis the environmental effects of the NAFTA' in cooperation with the NAFTA Commission.[138] While seeking broad public participation,[139] the CEC studied methodological approaches[140] and tested them in case studies,[141] leading the CEC Ministerial Council to adopt an *Analytic Framework for Assessing the Environmental Effects of the North American Free Trade Agreement.*[142] The Analytical Framework has since been applied in case studies, examining for instance Mexican corn, beef production in the United States and in Canada and the electricity market in all three countries.[143]

National reviews can also be conducted. For instance, the United States carried out a Final Environmental Review of the *US–Chile FTA.*[144] While the review concluded that 'changes in the pattern and magnitude of trade flows attributable to the FTA will not have any significant environmental impacts in the United States',[145] it noted concerns for the Chilean side with regards to increased resource extraction and pesticide use. It also found that trade in environmental goods is likely to increase and thus could yield positive effects. In another example, the US carried out an Interim Environmental Review of the *US–Andean Free Trade Agreement* (Peru, Ecuador and Colombia).[146] It found that degradation of mahogany forests, marine

138 Barr 2000,100.

139 Barr 2000, iii.

140 CEC (1996), Building a Framework for Assessing NAFTA Environmental Effects – Report of a Workshop held in La Jolla, California, on April 29 and 30, 1996 (Montreal: CEC).

141 CEC (1999), Assessing Environmental Effects of the North American Free Trade Agreement (NAFTA) – An Analytic Framework (Phase II) and Issue Studies (Montreal: CEC).

142 CEC (1999), Analytic Framework for Assessing the Environmental Effects of the North American Free Trade Agreement (Montreal: CEC), available online, <http://www.cec.org/files/pdf/ECONOMY/Frmwrk-e_EN.pdf>.

143 CEC, *supra* note 141, 65.

144 USTR, *Final Environmental Review of the US–Chile Free Trade Agreement*, June 2003, <http://www.ustr.gov/assets/Trade_Agreements/Bilateral/Chile_FTA/asset_upload_file411_5109.pdf>.

145 USTR, *Final Environmental Review of the US–Chile Free Trade Agreement*, June 2003, <http://www.ustr.gov/assets/Trade_Agreements/Bilateral/Chile_FTA/asset_upload_file411_5109.pdf>, 4.

146 USTR, *Interim Environmental Review of the US–Andean Free Trade Agreement*, February 2005, <http://www.ustr.gov/assets/Trade_Agreements/Bilateral/Andean_FTA/asset_upload_file27_7305.pdf>.

resources and marine water quality might be exacerbated by the trade agreement, if environmental laws and standards were not implemented effectively.[147] In 2001, the Canadian Cabinet Decision on Environmental Assessment of Trade Negotiations[148] began to mandate examinations, *ex-ante*, of environmental impacts for new trade agreements. As such, while there are no EAs for either the *Canada–Chile FTA* or the *Canada–Costa Rica FTA*, an Initial Environmental Assessment was carried out for the Canada–Chile Government Procurement Chapter to be added to the *Canada–Chile Free Trade Agreement*.[149] The ministry concluded that there were no significant environmental impacts in Canada, and thus refrained from conducting a draft EA. Such studies provide one procedural mechanism to support the achievement of sustainable development through a trade agreement, as they can both identify and recommend areas for greater social or environmental cooperation between Parties to a trade agreement and also find ways to adjust the drafting of certain provisions in order to minimize their potential impacts on the environment. It is extremely possible that the many reservations taken by Parties to new regional and bi-lateral trade agreements are directly related to the problems identified in such impact assessments.

Other Procedural Innovations Related to Sustainable Development

Recent regional trade agreement negotiations have sought also to promote sustainable development through other procedural innovations. One set of examples can be found in the (stalled) negotiations for a new Free Trade Area of the Americas (FTAA).

First, in the interest of transparency, trade ministries can periodically release draft texts of trade negotiations, inviting public comment. For example, there were consecutive releases of the FTAA Draft Text during the course of FTAA negotiations and Ministers established a Committee of Government Representatives for the Participation of Civil Society to consider comments received.[150] The need to promote openness in order to be consistent with sustainable development was part of the arguments used by States to secure this innovation.[151]

---

147 USTR, *Interim Environmental Review of the US–Andean Free Trade Agreement*, February 2005, <http://www.ustr.gov/assets/Trade_Agreements/Bilateral/Andean_FTA/asset_upload_file27_7305.pdf>, 10.

148 DFAIT, Framework for Conducting Environmental Assessments of Trade Negotiations, <http://www.dfait-maeci.gc.ca/tna-nac/EAF_Sep2000-en.asp>.

149 ITCan, Initial Environmental Assessment of the Canada–Chile Government Procurement Chapter to be added to the Canada–Chile Free Trade Agreement, <http://www.dfait-maeci.gc.ca/tna-nac/RB/report_chile-en.asp>.

150 Rivas 2003; Cabrera and Cordonier Segger 2005.

151 'Hemisphere Ministers Agree To Release FTAA Texts, Set Deadlines', Inside US Trade, 9 April 2001.

Second, civil society organizations, in the context of sustainable development, are often capable of organizing themselves to provide constructive input into trade agreement negotiations. For instance, during the FTAA negotiations civil society organizations prepared an 'Americas Trade and Sustainable Development Forum' parallel to each meeting of the FTAA ministers.[152]

Third, national trade authorities are increasingly consulting with national environment and development authorities on specific issues related to trade agreement negotiations. Such consultations can also be carried out through relevant inter-governmental organizations, which also provide training for such authorities where this is needed to ensure meaningful input.[153]

Finally, State and civil society officials, particularly from smaller economies, can also benefit from commitments for capacity-building in areas of concern in order to build their capacity to respond to requests for participation, requests for information regarding social and environmental measures that might be affected by trade disciplines, and other demands.[154] For instance, upon the request of the smaller economies in the FTAA negotiations, a Hemispheric Cooperation Programme was established and supported capacity building in trade issues, including civil society, environment and development projects.[155]

Conclusions: Processes and Provisions to Reconcile Intersections between Regimes in the Implementation of Trade Law for Sustainable Development

The explicit recognition of the objective of sustainable development in the preamble to a trade agreement has relevance in trade law and can be used to interpret trade measures, shedding light, in particular, on the meaning of exceptions and other aspects of a trade agreement.[156] However, there is no stand-alone strategy to ensure that a trade agreement will be able to promote sustainable development. Rather, many mechanisms are possible. Several are currently being tested in regional trade agreements. These appear to have been influenced by (and to be influencing) recent WTO debates on sustainable development, including negotiations and dispute

152 Ministerial Declaration of Miami, FTAA 8th Ministerial Meeting, done at Miami, adopted 20 November 2003, <http://www.ftaa-alca.org/Ministerials/Miami/Miami_e.asp>: 'We appreciate the recommendations made by the ... Americas Trade and Sustainable Development Forum, organized with a broad representation of civil society, and with whom we met here in Miami, Florida ...'.

153 See references to UNEP and UNDP collaboration in Perez-Esteve 2003.

154 Tripartite Committee of the FTAA – Consultative Group on Smaller Economies, Hemispheric Cooperation Programme, *Summary Matrix of Project Profiles*, FTAA.Sme/Inf/105/Rev.3, adopted 14 July 2003.

155 See also Draft FTAA, Annex III, at <http://www.ftaa-alca.org/FTAADraft03/Index_e.asp>.

156 Gehring and Cordonier Segger 2005, 1–24, 129–186.

settlement decisions, as Parties learn from and are inter-actionally shaped by their participation in the WTO and other international trade regimes.

First, certain substantive provisions can be included in the text of the regional trade agreements. These include provisions which create 'windows' or exemptions from trade rules, where trade obligations might otherwise constrain regulators and policy-makers, mitigating their effects, such as: general exceptions related to the conservation of natural resources, and the use of measures, including environmental measures, necessary to protect human, animal, or plant life or health; specific exceptions in sections of the trade agreement where it is clear that trade rules on, for example, sanitary and phytosanitary standards, technical barriers to trade, intellectual property rights, public procurement, services, or investment, might constrain the use of environmental and social measures (potentially addressing problems identified in *ex-ante* impact assessments); explicit reservations by the Parties of socially or environmentally sensitive sectors (such as nature reserves and parks reserved from investment provisions, or health and education sectors from services disciplines); and general interpretive statements to guide potential areas where trade rules could otherwise constrain the use of measures agreed in other international (or regional) agreements.

They can also include provisions which develop 'value-added' but parallel (non-integrated) social and environmental cooperation strategies, such as: parallel agreements (or chapters) for cooperation on environmental and social matters; the development of institutions for social and environmental cooperation related to trade; common work programmes on specific environmental or social projects, particularly when accompanied by reliable capacity-building, technology transfer and financing commitments (also often in areas identified in impact assessments); and factual report/complaints mechanisms to provide recourse when environmental or social rules are violated.

And Parties can include constructive 'sustainable development' oriented trade rule enhancement initiatives, where a positive 'triple-win' might be achieved within the trade agreement, such as: sanitary and phytosanitary provisions which promote cooperation to improve levels of protection; intellectual property rights provisions which support biodiversity protection, the recognition of traditional knowledge or public access to essential medicines; and liberalization of environmental goods and services (such as biofuels, or solar power equipment).

Second, and perhaps most significantly for this chapter of this volume, States may be able to contribute to more effective implementation of all public interest agreements related to sustainable development through the adoption of certain process innovations. These process innovations, for maximum effectiveness, should be undertaken by the Parties during trade agreement negotiation as well as during implementation. They may assist Parties (and others) in identifying useful innovations for the agreement and in finding ways to address ongoing problems of implementation. They include *ex-ante* (or ongoing) environment, development, human rights or sustainability impact assessments and reviews of trade liberalization policies and draft treaties. They also include the use of consultations between economic, environment and development authorities. States are also adopting new mechanisms to ensure transparency, including in negotiations, and mechanisms to strengthen public participation in trade negotiations and dispute settlement. Finally, States are providing for capacity-building and financing mechanisms for social and environmental cooperation related to negotiation and implementation of new and emerging trade regimes.

In conclusion, though regional trade may have unsustainable impacts, trade rules might also promote development that is – in the public interest – more sustainable. Through innovative procedures and provisions that can integrate economic and social development and environmental protection in a balanced, mutually supportive way, emerging trade regimes could limit recourse to trade-related measures not based on international consensus while demonstrating respect for environmental protection and social development as goals of national and international policy.

It is clear that in the implementation of intersecting legal regimes and systems, neither the 'trade norms always trumps environmental and human rights norms', nor the 'trade norms have no connection to environmental and human rights norms' perspectives in current legal and international relations literature are fully accurate. A third way is possible, based on a rather more complex picture of the situation today.

It may be possible to develop world trade law that deliberately promotes sustainable development. New instruments such as human rights impact assessment of trade agreements, environmental impact assessment of trade policies and the new integrated 'sustainability impact assessment' methods, can assist with this process. It focuses on enhancement of positive effects and mitigation of the negative. Moreover, it seeks 'triple-win' scenarios, where changes in trade law would also deliver direct social and environmental benefits.[157] Such an integrated agenda, premised on a search for new provisions in world trade law to ensure that it can be mutually supportive of social and environmental regimes, contributing to development that is sustainable over the long term, could influence the trade law-making and interpretation forums, including the dispute settlement body of the WTO and its deliberative organs.

At all levels, the emergence of new trade law processes and provisions to coordinate among disparate regimes is worthy of further scholarly scrutiny, debate and analysis. This agenda has the potential to contribute substantively to improvements in the implementation of trade, environment and social regimes, towards more effective achievement of sustainable development in the public interest.

157 Beyond the scope of this chapter, one could also anticipate that similar assessments and searches for 'triple-win' laws and policies would also be sought when changes were sought to social or environmental rules. See, e.g., Hahn and Litan 2005, 473–508; and see Guasch and Hahn 1999, 137–158.

References

Books, Articles and Chapters in Books

Aguilar, G. (2003), 'Access to Genetic Resources and Protection of Traditional Knowledge in Indigenous Territories', in Bellmann et al.

Alanis Ortega, G. (2002), 'Public Participation within NAFTA's Environmental Agreement', in Kirton and Maclaren.

Araya, M. et al. (2003), *ALCA y medio ambiente: Ideas desde Latinoamerica* (Santiago: CIPMA/GETS/CINPE).

Assuncao, L. (2000), 'The Climate Change Convention and Trade Regimes' in Konz et al.

Balasubramaniam, K. (2003), 'Access to Medicines and Public Policy Safeguards under TRIPS', in Bellmann et al.

Banks, K. (2002), 'Civil Society and the North American Agreement on Labor Cooperation', in Kirton and Maclaren.

Barcena, A. et al. (2002), *Financing for Sustainable Development in Latin America and the Caribbean: From Monterrey to Johannesburg* (Santiago: ECLAC and UNDP).

Barria, L. et al. (2003), 'Challenges and Opportunities for Central American and Caribbean Countries', UNCTAD, *Trade and Environment Review* (Paris: UNCTAD/DITC/TED/4).

Bartels, L. and Ortino, F. (2006), *Regional Trade Agreements and the WTO* (Oxford: Oxford University Press).

Bellmann, C. et al. (eds), (2003), *Trading in Knowledge: Development Perspectives on TRIPS, Trade and Sustainability* (London: Earthscan).

Bhala, R. (1998/1999), 'The Myth about *Stare Decisis* and International Trade Law (Part One of a Trilogy)', *American University International Law Review* 14, 845–956.

Bhala, R. (2000/2001), 'The Power of the Past: Towards de Jure Stare Decisis in WTO Adjudication (Part Three of a Trilogy)', *George Washington International Law Review* 33, 873–978.

Biermann, F. (2000), International Law Association's *New Delhi Declaration on Principles of International Law Related to Sustainable Development (2002) International Environmental Agreements: Politics, Law and Economics* (The Hague: Kluwer Academic Publishers).

Blanco, H. (2003), 'Evaluacion de la sustentabilidad de los acuerdos comerciales y su aplicacion en el contexto latinoamericano y del ALCA', in Araya et al.

Boyle, A. and Freestone, D. (1999), *International Law and Sustainable Development: Past Achievements and Future Challenges* (Oxford: Oxford University Press).

Brunnée, J. (2002), 'Coping with Consent: Lawmaking under Multilateral Environmental Agreements', *Leiden Journal of International Law* 15, 1–52.

Brunnée, J. and Toope, S.J. (2000), 'International Law and Constructivism: Elements of an Interactional Theory of International Law', *Columbia Journal of Transnational Law* 39, 19–74.

Brunnée, J. and Toope, S.J. (2002a), 'The Changing Nile Basin Regime: Does Law Matter?', *Harvard International Law Journal* 43:1, 105–159.

Brunnée, J. and Toope, S.J. (2002b), 'Persuasion and Enforcement: Explaining Compliance with International Law', XIII *Finnish Yearbook International Law* 1–23.

Button, C. (2004), *The Power to Protect: Trade, Health and Uncertainty in the WTO* (Oxford: Hart).

Cabrera, J. and Cordonier Segger, M.C. (2005), 'Public Participation in Americas Trade and Environment Regimes', in Cordonier Segger and Leichner Reynal.

Corbin, H. (2003), 'The Proposed United States–Chile Free Trade Agreement: Reconciling Free Trade and Environmental Protection', *Colorado Journal of International Environmental Law and Policy* 14, 119.

Cordonier Segger, M.C. et al. (2002), *Ecological Rules and Sustainability in the Americas* (Winnipeg: IISD/UNEP).

Cordonier Segger, M.C. (2006), 'The WTO, Regional Trade Agreements and Sustainable Development', in Bartels and Ortino.

Cordonier Segger, M.C. and Khalfan, A. (2004), *Sustainable Development Law: Principles, Practices and Prospects* (Oxford: Oxford University Press).

Cordonier Segger, M.C. and Leichner Reynal, M. (eds) (2005), *Beyond the Barricades: The Americas Trade and Sustainability Agenda* (Aldershot: Ashgate).

Deere, C. and Esty, D. (eds) (2002), *Greening the Americas: NAFTA's Lessons for Hemispheric Trade* (Cambridge, MA: MIT Press).

Dhar, B. (2003), 'The Convention on Biological Diversity and the TRIPs Agreement: Compatibility or Conflict?', in Bellmann et al.

Durbin, W. (2000), *A Comparison of the Environmental Provisions of the NAFTA, the Canada–Chile Trade Agreement and the Mexican–European Community Trade Agreement* (New Haven: Yale Centre for Environmental Law and Policy).

Dworkin, R. (1977), *Taking Rights Seriously* (London: Duckworth).

Francioni, F. (ed.) (2001), *Environment, Human Rights and International Trade* (Oxford: Hart Publishing).

French, D. (2005), *International Law and Policy of Sustainable Development* (Manchester: Manchester University Press).

Garforth, K. and Prabhu, M. (2005), 'International Public Health and Trade Law', in Cordonier Segger and Gehring.

Gehring, M. (2004), 'Sustainable International Trade, Investment and Competition Law' in Cordonier Segger and Khalfan.

Gehring, M. and Cordonier Segger, M.C. (eds) (2005), *Sustainable Development in World Trade Law* (The Hague: Kluwer Law International).

Gehring, M., Cordonier Segger, M.C. and Newcombe, A (eds) (2009), *Sustainable Development in World Investment Law* (The Hague: Kluwer Law International).

Gitli, E. and Murillo, C. (2002), 'A Latin American Agenda for a Trade and Environment Link in the FTAA', in Deere and Esty.

Guasch, L. and Hahn, R.W. (1999), 'The Costs and Benefits of Regulation: Implications for Developing Countries', *The World Bank Research Observer* 14:1, 137–158.

Hahn, R.W. and Litan, R.E. (2005), 'Counting Regulatory Benefits and Costs: Lessons for the US and Europe', *Journal of International Economic Law* 8, 473–508.

International Law Association (2002), 'ILA New Delhi Declaration of Principles of International Law Relating to Sustainable Development', *International Environmental Agreements: Politics, Law and Economics* (The Hague: Kluwer Academic Publishers) 2:2, 209–216.

Kelsen, H. (1996), *Theorie Generale des Normes* (Paris: Presses Universitaires de France).

Kirton, J. and Maclaren, V. (eds) (2002), *Linking Trade, Environment and Social Cohesion: NAFTA Experiences, Global Challenges* (Aldershot: Ashgate).

Kiss, A. et al. (eds) (2003), *Economic Globalization and Compliance with International Environmental Agreements*, International Environmental Law and Policy Series 63 (The Hague: Kluwer Law International).

Konz, P. et al. (eds) (2000), *Trade, Environment and Sustainable Development: Views from Sub-Saharan Africa and Latin America* (Geneva: ICTSD and UNU-IAS).

Krasner, S. (ed.) (1983), *International Regimes* (Ithaca, NY: Cornell University Press).

LePrestre, P.G. (ed.) (2002), *Governing Global Biodiversity: The Evolution and Implementation of the Convention on Biological Diversity* (Aldershot: Ashgate).

Lettington, R.J.L. (2000), 'The Biodiversity Convention and TRIPS', in Konz et al.

Lowe, V. (1999), 'Sustainable Development and Unsustainable Arguments', in Boyle and Freestone.

Medaglia, J.C. (2003), 'The Central American Regional Protocol on Access to Genetic and Biochemical Resources', in Bellmann et al.

de Mestral, A. (2003), 'The NAFTA Commission on Environmental Cooperation – Voice for the North American Environment?', in Kiss et al.

Orellana, M. (2001), 'The EU and Chile Suspend the Swordfish Case Proceedings at the WTO and the International Tribunal of the Law of the Sea', *The American Society of International Law* Insights no. 60.

Orellana, M. (2002), 'The Swordfish Dispute between the EU and Chile at the ITLOS and the WTO', *Nordic Journal of International Law* 71, 55.

Pauwelyn, J. (2003), *Conflict of Norms in Public International Law: How WTO Law Relates to Other Rules of International Law* (Cambridge: Cambridge University Press).

Perez-Esteve, M. (2003), 'Oportunidades para reforzar los beneficios resultantes de la globalización en America Latina y el Caribe: Mejoramiento de la Capacidad en Materia de Comercio, Medio Ambiente y Desarrollo', in Araya et al.

Pythoud, F. and Thomas, U.P. (2002), 'The Cartagena Protocol on Biosafety', in LePrestre.

Rivas, M. (2003), 'ALCA y participacion de la sociedad civil', in Araya et al.

Ruggie, J.G. (1983), 'International Regimes, Transactions and Change: Embedded Liberalism in the Postwar Economic Order', in Krasner.

Ruiz, M. (2003), 'The Andean Community Regimes on Access to Genetic Resources, Intellectual Property and Indigenous Peoples' Knowledge', in Bellmann et al.

Singh, S. (2005), 'Environmental Goods Negotiations: Issues and Options for Ensuring Win–Win Outcomes' (Winnipeg: IISD).

Trudeau, H. and Nègre, C. (2005), 'Precaution in Multilateral Environmental Agreements and Its Impact on the World Trading System', in Cordonier Segger and Gehring.

United Nations Environment Programme (2001), *Reference Manual for the Integrated Assessment of Trade-Related Policies* (Geneva: UNEP).

Vivas Eugui, D. (2003), 'Requiring the Disclosure of the Origin of Genetic Resources and Traditional Knowledge: The Current Debate and Possible Legal Alternatives', in Bellmann et al.

Vogler, J. (ed.) (2000), *The Global Commons: Environmental and Technological Governance*, 2nd Edition (Chichester: Wiley).

Walker, S. (2005), 'Human Rights Impact Assessments of Trade-Related Policies', in Cordonier Segger and Gehring.

Wilson, S. (2002), 'Article 14-15 of the North American Agreement on Environmental Cooperation: Intent of the Founders', in Kirton and Maclaren.

WTO (1999), *The Legal Texts – The Results of the Uruguay Round of Multilateral Trade Negotiations* (Cambridge: Cambridge University Press).

Zaveri, N.B. (2003), 'The TRIPS Agreement and Generic Production of HIV/AIDS Drugs', in Bellmann et al.

Official Documents and Others

International Law Commission, Report on the Work of its Fifty-second Session (1 May–9 June and 10 July–18 August 2000), Official Records of the General Assembly, Fifty-Fifth Session, Supplement No. 10 A/55/10 (2000).

Basel Convention on the Control of Transboundary Movements of Hazardous Wastes and Their Disposal, 22 March 1989.

Blanco, H. and Gallagher, K.P. (2003), 'Sustainability Assessments: Tools for Effective Trade Policy in the Hemisphere' (Interhemispheric Resource Center (IRC) Paper, 9 April 2003).

Cartagena Protocol on Biosafety to the United Nations Convention on Biological Diversity (entered into force 29 January 2000).

Convention on International Trade of Endangered Species and Wild Fauna and Flora, 3 March 1973.

Hafner, G. (2000), 'Risks Ensuing from Fragmentation of International Law', UN Doc. ILC(LII)/WG/LT/L.1/Add.1: 24, included as Annex to *International Law Commission, Report on the Work of its Fifty-Second Session (1 May–9 June and 10 July–18 August 2000), Official Records of the General Assembly, Fifty-Fifth Session, Supplement No. 10* A/55/10 (2000).

'Function and Scope of the lex specialis Rule and the Question of "Self-Contained Regimes"', ILC(LVI)/SG/FIL/ CRD.1 (4 May 2004) Add.1.

Gabcikovo-Nagymaros Project (Hungary v Slovakia), [1997] I.C.J. Rep. 7 at 78.

International Experts' Meeting on Sustainability Assessments of Trade Liberalisation – Quito, Ecuador, 6–8 March 2000.

Iron Rhine ('Ijzeren Rijn') Railway Case (Belgium v the Netherlands) (2005), <http://www.pca-cpa.org/ENGLISH/RPC/BENL/BE-NL%20Award%20240505.pdf> at 59, 114 (Permanent Court of Arbitration) (Arbitrators: Judge Rosalyn Higgins, President, Professor Guy Schrans, Judge Bruno Simma, Professor Alfred H.A. Soons, Judge Peter Tomka).

IUCN (2003), *An Explanatory Guide to the Cartagena Protocol on Biosafety* (Cambridge, UK: International Union for Conservation of Nature and Natural Resources and FIELD).

Montreal Protocol on Substances that Deplete the Ozone Layer, 17 September 1987.

Proceedings of the WTO High Level Symposium on Trade and Environment, Geneva, 15–16 March 1999 and WTO High Level Symposium on Trade and Development, Geneva, 17–18 March 1999.

United Nations Convention on Biological Diversity (UNCBD), adopted 5 June 1992.

Vienna Convention on Law of Treaties, May 23, 1969.

World Commission on Environment and Development (1987), *Our Common Future* (Oxford: Oxford University Press).

WTO Agreement on the Application of Sanitary and Phytosanitary Measures (SPS Agreement), 33 I.L.M. 1125 (1994).

WTO Appellate Body in the case of *US–Standards for Reformulated and Conventional Gasoline* (20 May 1996), WTO Doc. WT/DS2/AB/R.

WTO Secretariat (ed.) (2000), *Trade, Development and the Environment* (The Hague: Kluwer Law International).

Internet-based References

2002 Johannesburg Declaration and 2002 Johannesburg Plan of Implementation, Report of the World Summit on Sustainable Development, Johannesburg (South Africa) (4 Sept. 2002), UN Doc. A/CONF.199/20 at 140(c), WSSD, available online at <http://www.un.org/esa/sustdev/documents/WSSD_POI_PD/English/POIToc.htm>.

Agreement on Environmental Cooperation between the Government of Canada and the Republic of Chile, 36 I.L.M. 1196, adopted 6 February 1997, Articles 2 and 10, sections 1 and 2, treaty text available online at <http://www.sice.oas.org/trade/chican_e/chcatoc.asp#environ>.

Agreement on Environmental Cooperation between the Government of Canada and the Government of the Republic of Costa Rica, adopted 23 April 2001, treaty text available online at <http://www.sice.oas.org/Trade/cancr/English/enve.asp>.

Anti-GATT, available online at <http://www.gatt.org/>.

Cabrera, C. and Gehring, M. (2001), 'Sustainable Development Angles to the Swordfish Dispute', Bridges Journal 5:7, 13, available online at Bridges Journal website: <http://www.ictsd.org/monthly/bridges/BRIDGES5-7.pdf>.

Cartagena Protocol on Biological Diversity, at Cartagena, adopted 29 January 2000, I.L.M. 11: 1416, treaty text available online at <http://www.biodiv.org/default.shtml>.

CEC (1999), 'Analytic Framework for Assessing the Environmental Effects of the North American Free Trade Agreement' (Montreal: CEC), available online at <http://www.cec.org/files/pdf/ECONOMY/Frmwrk-e_EN.pdf>.

Centro de Investigación y Planificación del Medio Ambiente (CIPMA) (1999), 'Environmental Impacts of Trade Liberalization and Policies for the Sustainable Management of Natural Resources: A Case Study of Chile's Mining Sector' (Geneva: UNEP), available online at <http://www.unep.ch/etu/etp/acts/capbld/rdone/chile.htm>.

Conservation and Sustainable Exploitation of Swordfish Stocks in the South-Eastern Pacific Ocean v European Communities, ITLOS, available online at <http://www.oceanlaw.net/cases/swordfish1.html>.

DFAIT, 'Framework for Conducting Environmental Assessments of Trade Negotiations', available online at <http://www.dfait-maeci.gc.ca/tna-nac/EAF_Sep2000-en.asp>.

Draft FTAA, Annex III, available online at <http://www.ftaa-alca.org/FTAADraft03/Index_e.asp>.

'EU and Chile Reach an Amicable Settlement to End WTO/ ITLOS Swordfish Dispute' (Brussels), available online at Europa website: <http://europa-eu-un.org/articles/cs/article_2230_cs.htm>.

Fadzil, R. and Rani, M.H.A., 'The Role of the World Trade Organisation (WTO) and its Dispute Settlement Procedure – An Overview', *Malayan Law Journal*, available online at *Malayan Law Journal* website: <http://www.mlj.com.my/free/articles/rozlinda&harris2.htm>.

First Annual Report: *Canada–Chile Agreement on Labour Cooperation* (July 1997–June 1998), available online at <http://www.labour-travail.hrdc-drhc.gc.ca/doc/ialc-cidt/eng/e/backen.htm#background>.

ITCan, 'Initial Environmental Assessment of the Canada–Chile Government Procurement Chapter to be Added to the Canada–Chile Free Trade Agreement', available online at <http://www.dfait-maeci.gc.ca/tna-nac/RB/report_chile-en.asp>.

Kirkpatrick, C. et al., 'WTO New Round: Sustainability Impact Assessment Study (Phase Two Report): Sustainability Impact Assessment', available online at <http://fs2.idpm.man.ac.uk/sia/Phase2/EXSUMFINAL>.

Marrakesh Agreement Establishing the World Trade Organization, 15 April 1994, 1867 U.N.T.S. 154, I.L.M. 33: 1144, Preamble, available online at WTO website: <http://www.wto.org/english/docs_e/legal_e/legal_e.htm>.

Ministerial Council (2000 December), 'Report on the Three-Year Review of the Canada–Chile Agreement on Labour Cooperation', available online at < http://www.labour-travail.hrdc-rhc.gc.ca/psait_spila/aicdt_ialc/2003_2004/report_english.htm>.

Ministerial Declaration of Miami, FTAA 8th Ministerial Meeting, done at Miami, adopted 20 November 2003, available online at <http://www.ftaa-alca.org/Ministerials/Miami/Miami_e.asp>.

NAALC Secretariat, available online at <http://www.naalc.org>.

NAFTA, Human Rights Watch, available online at <http://www.hrw.org/reports/2001/nafta/nafta0401-05.htm>.

North American Agreement for Environmental Cooperation ('NAAEC'), adopted 1 January 1994, I.L.M. 32:1480, treaty text available online at <http://www.cec.org>.

North American Commission for Environment Cooperation, available online at <http://www.cec.org>.

Organization of American States, Overview of the North American Free Trade Agreement, available online at <http://www.sice.oas.org/summary/nafta/nafta1.asp>.

Permanent Court of Arbitration, available online at <http://www.pca-cpa.org/ENGLISH/RPC/BENL/BE-NL%20Award%20240505.pdf>.

Peru–US Free Trade Agreement, not yet entered into force, available online at <http://www.ustr.gov/assets/Trade_Agreements/Bilateral/Peru_TPA/Final_Texts/asset_upload_file852_8712.pdf>.

Preamble: North American Free Trade Agreement (NAFTA), adopted 1 January 1994, I.L.M. 32: 289, 605, treaty text available online at <http://www.sice.oas.org/trade/nafta.asp>.

Public Citizen, 'Global Trade Watch: Promoting Democracy by Challenging Corporate Globalization', available online at < http://www.citizen.org/trade/nafta/>.

'Relationship between WTO Rules and MEAs', available online at WTO <http://www.wto.org/english/tratop_e/envir_e/envir_backgrnd_e/c5s3_e.htm>.

Resolution Adopted by the General Assembly on the Report of the Sixth Committee (A/58/514), *Report of the International Law Commission on the Work of its Fifty-Fifth Session*: ILC, available online at <http://www.un.org/law/ilc/sessions/56/56sess.htm>.

Secretariat for the UN CBD, 'International Regime on Access and Benefit-sharing: Proposals for an International Regime on Access and Benefit-sharing', UNEP/CBD/MYPOW/6, adopted 7 January 2003, at 6–7. Andean Community, Decision 391, available online at <http://www.sice.oas.org/trade/JUNAC/decisiones/DEC391e.asp>.

Stop CAFTA, available online at <http://www.stopcafta.org/>.

WTO, Chile – Measures affecting the Transit and Importing of Swordfish, available online at <http://www.wto.org/english/tratop_e/envir_e/envir_backgrnd_e/c5s1_e.htm>.

USTR, Final Environmental Review of the US–Chile Free Trade Agreement, June 2003, available online at <http://www.ustr.gov/assets/Trade_Agreements/Bilateral/Chile_FTA/asset_upload_file411_5109.pdf>.

USTR, 'Interim Environmental Review of the US–Andean Free Trade Agreement', February 2005, available online at <http://www.ustr.gov/assets/Trade_Agreements/Bilateral/Andean_FTA/asset_upload_file27_7305.pdf>.

USTR, 'Summary of Chile–US Free Trade Agreement', available online at <http://www.ustr.gov/regions/whemisphere/samerica/2002-12-11-chile_summary.pdf>.

USTR, 'Understanding Regarding Biodiversity and Traditional Knowledge, As Part of the Peru–US Free Trade Agreement', DRAFT: 6 January 2006, not yet entered into force, available online at <http://www.ustr.gov/assets/Trade_Agreements/Bilateral/Peru_TPA/Final_Texts/asset_upload_file869_8728.pdf>.

United States–Chile Free Trade Agreement, Chile, United States, 1 January 2004, available online at <http://www.ustr.gov/trade-agreements/free-trade-agreements/chile-fta/final-text >.

World Trade Organization (2004), 'Environment Backgrounder: The Relationship Between MEAs and the WTO' (Geneva: WTO) WTO available online at <http://www.wto.org/english/tratop_e/envir_e/envir_backgrnd_e/c5s1_e.htm>.

World Trade Organization, < http://www.wto.org/english/tratop_e/dispu_e/cases_e/ds193_e.htm>.

Chapter 10

Effective Implementation of International Environmental Agreements: Learning Lessons from the Danube Delta Conflict

Mari Koyano[1]

Introduction

In international environmental law a key question is how to ensure the effective implementation of multilateral environmental agreements (MEAs). In general, the principal factors in the implementation process of MEAs are assumed to include the method of ensuring implementation, involvement of non-State stakeholders, coordination between relevant international agreements or legal systems and coordination with the relevant domestic legal systems of the parties concerned.

In this chapter some hints of an answer to this intractable question are given based on a case study, focusing on the management processes of a particular conflict under several MEAs. This study includes: presenting the overview of a conflict, analyzing the management processes, discussing their characteristics in terms of the principal factors mentioned above and extracting some possible lessons to be learnt.

The Danube Delta conflict is here dealt with. The conflict consists of a series of international disputes concerning the Ukrainian project of opening the Danube–

1 The author is grateful for kind help given by the staff of the following institutions in collecting relevant information. These include: the European Commission, DG Environment, the Secretariats of the *Convention on Access to Information, Public Participation in Decision-making and Access to Justice in Environmental Matters* (Aarhus Convention), the *Convention on the Conservation of European Wildlife and Natural Habitats* (Bern Convention), the *Convention on Environmental Impact Assessment in a Transboundary Context* (Espoo Convention), the *Convention on Wetlands of International Importance especially as Waterfowl Habitat* (Ramsar Convention), the *International Commission for the Protection of Danube River* (ICPDR) and *UNESCO Man and Biosphere* (MAB) *Programme*, the Ministry of Foreign Affairs of Romania, the Ministry of Foreign Affairs of Ukraine, the *Centre for Regional Studies* (CRS), the *Danube Environmental Forum* (DEF), the *Environment-People-Law* (EPL), the *European Eco-Forum,* the *Save the Danube*, the *World Wildlife Fund International* (WWF) *Danube-Carpathian Programme* and the WWF Romania. The views expressed in this chapter are exclusively those of the author and unrelated to the positions taken by these institutions.

Black Sea Navigation Route in the Danube Delta (Bystroe Canal project: BCP).[2] The conflict has been dealt with under five MEAs and the *UNESCO Man and Biosphere* (*MAB*) *Programme*, as well as by the European Commission since the summer of 2003. The conformity of the execution of the BCP has been questioned. In particular, Ukraine's failure to implement various procedures required under the MEAs and the UNESCO MAB Programme have been a source of much controversy.

The view presented in this chapter is based on developments up to March 2009. Therefore, conclusions on the issues raised are not fully determinant due to the fact they are on-going processes. However, lessons learnt at the present stage are valuable, since developments to date have already contained major points concerning the effective implementation of MEAs. Moreover, they could stimulate the future management processes related to the Danube Delta conflict.

Overview of the Danube Delta Conflict

Background

Overview of the Danube Delta The Danube Delta, shared by three countries (Moldova but primarily Ukraine and Romania), is the second largest European delta (about 6,000km^2) created by three arms of the Danube River, the Kiliya, Sulina and Gheorghe arms (see Figure 10.1). This is one of the largest wetland and reed beds in Europe, also forming the largest water purification system in Europe. The Delta is an important wildlife habitat. It has the largest number of birds of any South Eastern European wetland, being a key area for the passage of migrant and wintering birds. Over 320 species of birds can be found in the area, of which 12 are globally threatened. The Delta is also renowned for its fish stocks.[3]

In this Delta local people live in small-scale agriculture, fishing and cattle-breeding communities. In addition to the failure of reclamation projects in the communist era, they are faced with difficulties in the post-Soviet political and economic transition. Living standards are relatively low, and the local economy is declining. In the region the unemployment rate is higher than the average in both Romania and Ukraine. The average age of the local population has also been getting higher as younger people leave the area. Decreased shipping, caused mainly by the destruction of bridges in Yugoslavia during the war in 1990s, has accelerated the decline of the local economy. The shipping industry has been severely destroyed particularly in Ukraine. This is partly due to the lack of proper

2 The project has been given various names, such as the Ukrainian Danube–Black Sea Navigation Route Restoration Project, the Danube–Black Sea Deep Navigation Channel, etc. In this chapter the title of the Bystroe Canal project is adopted following official documents produced under the Espoo Convention. E.g., UNECE, ECE/MP.EIA/2008/6, p. 1.

3 See for instance: Council of Europe (CE), T-PVS/Files(2004)3, 3–4; Espoo Inquiry Commission 2006, 8; Ramsar/UNESCO 2003, para. 2; UNESCO 2004, 12.

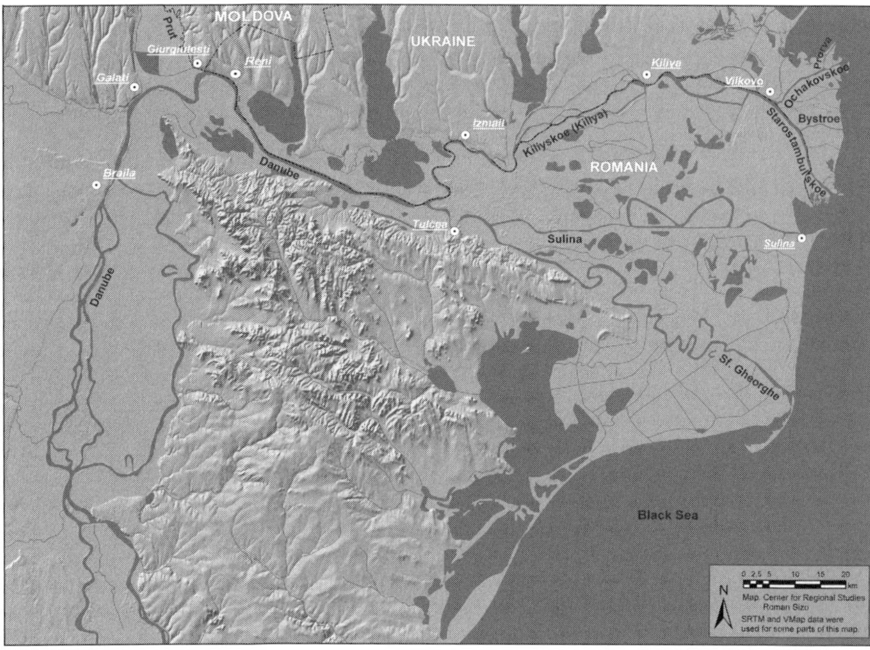

Figure 10.1 The Danube Delta region
Source: © Centre for Regional Studies (Odessa, Ukraine)

maintenance of a formerly navigable waterway, the Prorva Channel, located in the north of the Bystroe Channel, currently being hindered by sediments accumulated in the riverbed, after the collapse of the USSR.[4]

In the Danube Delta the channel cutting across the Romanian territory and passing through the city of Tulcea to Sulina, built along the Sulina arm in 1880, currently provides the only navigable access of a large ship from the Danube River to the Black Sea (see Figure 10.1 above). Consequently, Romania has been in an advantageous position economically with tax income in navigation, as well as strategically as a result of having the waterway in its own territory in the Danube Delta. Ukraine has concerns about the situation.[5]

International Environmental Regulations for the Conservation of the Danube Delta

The ecological and hydrological significance of the Danube Delta has been widely recognized. A large part of the Delta is incorporated into specially protected areas under three MEAs and the UNESCO MAB Programme. First, as Wetlands

4 See for instance: UNESCO 2004, 12–14.

5 See for instance: CE, T-PVS/Files(2004)3, 4–5.

of International Importance under the *Convention on Wetlands of International Importance especially as Waterfowl Habitat* (Ramsar Convention) a Romanian site was designated in 1991, and a Ukrainian site, the Kyliiske Mouth, in 1995, within the Danube Delta. Secondly, the Romanian site was inscribed on the *UNESCO World Heritage List* in 1991. Thirdly, within the framework of the UNESCO MAB Programme the transboundary biosphere reserve (TBR) of the Danube Delta was recognized in 1998. This consists of the Romanian biosphere reserve (BR) and the Ukrainian BR, i.e., the Dunainsky BR, 17 per cent of the whole TBR. Finally, the unity of the Delta has prompted the signing, under the auspices of the Council of Europe (CE), of the *Agreement on the Creation and Management of a Transfrontier Nature Protection Area between Moldova, Romania and Ukraine, in the Natural Reserves of the Danube Delta and Lower Reaches of the Prut*, in 2000.

In addition to these regulations, several other MEAs also apply to the Danube Delta, such as the *Convention on Cooperation for the Protection and Sustainable Use of the Danube River* (Danube River Protection Convention) of 1994 and the Bern Convention of 1979, i.e., the *Convention on the Conservation of European Wildlife and Natural Habitats*.

Furthermore, the Kiliya arm, being a national border between Romania and Ukraine, is regulated by their bilateral border agreement concluded in 2003, *Treaty between Romania and Ukraine on Romanian–Ukrainian State Border Regime, Collaboration and Mutual Assistance on Border Matters*. The *Convention Regarding the Regime of Navigation on the Danube* (Belgrade Convention), signed in 1948, applies to the navigable part of the Danube River between Ulm and the Black Sea through the Sulina channel (art.2).[6]

History Concerning the Danube Delta Conflict

Stage I (2003–April 2004): Decision on Start of the BCP and Rise of International Concern Following Ukrainian consultation with UNESCO on its plan of opening a navigation route in the Danube Delta, a UNESCO/Ramsar Joint Mission was sent to Ukraine in 2003. The BCP, which is to open the Bystroe Channel, a natural stream, as a navigation route, was one of the options suggested. According to Ukraine the BCP consists of two phases.[7] The Bystroe Channel, connecting the

---

6 Ukraine proposed an amendment to the Belgrade Convention in 2007, in which the Kiliya arm was to be included into territorial scope of the Convention, in a process of revising the Convention that has currently been going on. As to the process of revising the Convention, see Dinescu 2006.

7 Phase 1 is to attain a minimum water depth of 7m from the mouth to 165km upstream of the Danube River, and to include deepening of the sandbar section of the Bystroe Channel, dredging of some sills in the river section between Ismail and Vilkovo, and construction of a part of retaining dam into the sea. Phase 2 is to attain a minimum water depth of 8.2m and to include dredging various rifts upstream, locating dump sites

Kiliya arm and the Black Sea, flows across the heart of both the Dunainsky BR and the Kyliiske Mouth as a Ramsar site[8]. The Mission found the BCP to be likely to produce the most adverse effects on the TBR.[9]

In February 2004, however, Ukraine officially approved the BCP principally on the grounds that it was the cheapest option on the table, and immediately issued a Presidential Decree[10] to alter the zoning of the Dunainsky BR.[11] According to Ukraine the project would contribute to the promotion of the shipping industry and economic development in the local community of Vilkovo.[12]

In response to the Ukrainian actions, questions were raised under several MEAs, such as the Danube River Protection (DRP) Convention and the Bern Convention. Under the former, a resolution was adopted by the *International Commission for the Protection of the Danube River* (ICPDR),[13] and, the latter, the on-the-spot appraisal on the BCP, as a part of the case file procedure, was undertaken upon receipt of a complaint by a NGO, the *Danube Environmental Forum* (DEF).[14] Moreover, in Ukraine several lawsuits were brought to domestic courts concerning the BCP. Many of them were challenges by a Ukraine-based NGO, the *Environment-People-Law* (EPL), against measures or decisions taken by the Ukrainian Government.[15] These actions called the attention of the people to the BCP to a certain extent although such legal challenges were not successful.[16]

---

and outbuilding the retaining dam. Espoo Inquiry Commission 2006, 17–21; European Commission 2004, 3–4.

8 The zoning of the Dunainsky BR and the Kyliiske Mouth used to be identical. After the unilateral alternation of the zoning of the Dunainsky BR by Ukraine in 2004, however, only the Kyliiske Mouth is said to be cut across by the Bystroe Channel.

9 Ramsar/UNESCO 2003.

10 'The Presidential Decree, No. 117'.

11 CE, T-PVS/Files (2002)3, 6.

12 See for instance: CE, T-PVS/Files(2004)3, 4–5; European Commission 2004.

13 ICPDR, FINAL IC/078, 13–14.

14 CE, T-PVS (2004)3, 6. The DEF, established in 1999, is a coalition of NGOs which deal with issues on conservation and sustainable development of the Danube River and its basin. As to the DEF, see <http://def.distelverein.at/>.

15 The EPL is a NGO, founded in Lviv, Ukraine in 1994, in order to provide assistance to individuals and legal persons in the protection of environmental rights, to promote the development of the environmental protection, etc. Its legal unit is involved with various legal activities. As to the EPL, see <http://www.epl.org.ua>.

16 In Ukraine there have been five lawsuits concerning the BCP so far. Four of them were brought by the EPL or its members against the Ukrainian Ministry of the Environment or the Ukrainian President, and the other, by the Vilkovo Town Council against the Kiliya Region Council on the withdrawal of straits and internal ponds from the Danube BR. The former include: three suits challenging of the environmental experts' conclusions and one, challenging of the Presidential Decree. Three of the cases by the EPL were closed, and the EPL lost in all the cases except for one decision by a lower court. EPL 2002–2003, 9; Melen (2004). Comment of the staff of the EPL in an interview with the author in November 2007. In terms of the latter case, *Vilkovo Town Council v the Kiliya Region Council*, the Ukrainian

Stage II (May 2004–August 2005): Start of the BCP and Intensification of Criticism under MEAs In May 2004 Ukraine approved a Cabinet Decree on the alternation of the Dunainsky BR, and Phase I of the BCP started immediately. Responding to these actions, international criticisms intensified, in particular, through a series of actions taken by institutions established by the MEAs and under the UNESCO MAB Programme. Such actions included: adopting a resolution respectively by the ICPDR[17] and the UNESCO MAB Council (MAB ICC),[18] sending letters to Ukraine by the Secretary General of the Ramsar Convention[19] and approving non-compliance with the Bern Convention by Ukraine based on findings of the on-the-spot appraisal[20] and adopting a recommendation by the Bern Standing Committee.[21] The European Commission also started communications with Ukraine concerning the BCP upon the receipt of letters from various NGOs.[22] A common element in these actions was a request of submitting sufficient information on the BCP by Ukraine. Moreover, all the institutions concerned successfully constructed mutually co-operative relationships in 2004. Its momentum was the international informal consultation held in Geneva in September in which all the institutions concerned, some NGOs and Romania participated.[23] This was followed by a joint mission of an international expert team organized by the European Commission. Its report pointed out a number of unresolved issues concerning the BCP and included some recommendations.[24]

Romania, as a neighbour State, started to take various actions against Ukraine, expressing its concern regarding the risk of the transboundary effects, submitting non-compliance by Ukraine with the two ECE Conventions, the *Convention on*

Supreme Court annulled the decisions of all the lower commercial courts in November 2007, which allowed withdrawal of the Bystroe Mouth from the territory of the Dunainsky BR, and expedited the case to the court of first instance. In addition to the domestic legal actions, the EPL started to send complaint letters concerning the BCP to secretariats of the MEAs concerned in the autumn of 2003. As to the five lawsuits and international actions taken by the EPL, see <http://www.epl.org.ua/a_cases_Danube_C.htm>.

17 ICPDR, FINAL IC/097, 18–19.

18 UNESCO, SC-04/CONF.204/14, 18–19.

19 The letter dated 3rd May 2004, a copy of which was obtained at the Ramsar Secretariat.

20 CE, T-PVS/Files (2004) 3.

21 'Recommendation No. 111 of the Standing Committee of the proposed navigable waterway through Bystroe Estuary (Danube Delta, Ukraine)', CE, T-PVS (2004)16, 12–16 and 56.

22 NGOs, including the WWF, sent letters to various organs of the EU. Comment of the staff of the European Commission, DG Environment, and the WWF staff, in the interviews held by the author in March 2006.

23 'Moderator's Summary of the Informal International Consultation on the Bystroe Canal, Ukraine'. This consultation, in which Ukraine did not participate in spite of being invited, had been proposed by Romania and organized by the UNEP.

24 European Commission 2004, 1–2.

Access to Information, Public Participation, in Decision-making and Access to Justice in Environmental Matters (Aarhus Convention) and the *Convention on Environmental Impact Assessment in a Transboundary Context* (Espoo Convention). Under the former, a determination of non-compliance by Ukraine was concluded by the 2nd Meeting of the Parties to the Convention (MOP) in May 2005.[25] Under the latter the inquiry procedure was requested by Romania in August 2005.[26]

NGOs, such as the *World Wildlife Fund International (WWF)*, the *Bird Life International*, etc., also became very active, politically and legally, putting pressure on both Ukraine and the institutions concerned.[27] Their coordinated work included a joint meeting of NGOs held in parallel to the joint mission.[28] Non-compliance by Ukraine with the Aarhus Convention was communicated by the EPL and concluded, being examined together with the Romanian complaint mentioned above.[29]

In 2005, the inauguration of the pro-European president, V.A. Juschenko, in Ukraine, as a result of the so-called Orange Revolution, led to the change in its attitude to some extent. Ukraine announced a plan of holding an international conference on the conservation and sustainable development of the Danube Delta for September and implemented preparatory work, such as holding international seminars, etc.[30]

Stage III (September 2005–October 2006): Suspension of the BCP and Emergence of International Co-operation Towards the end of 2005 Ukraine changed its attitude and started to take a more positive response to requests under some MEAs. Consequently, international co-operation on a number of issues developed at various levels.

First, Ukraine reported to the ICPDR in December,[31] as well as the Bern Standing Committee in November,[32] that it was revising the environmental impact assessment (EIA) of Phase 2, suspending the BCP since the September, accelerating its ratification of the 2000 trilateral agreement, and having talks with Romania and consultation with relevant international institutions. Second, the

25 UNECE, ECE/MP.PP/2005/2/Add.8.

26 Consequently, non-compliance procedure was suspended.

27 Among the NGOs involved the WWF was one of the most active in such campaigns. This was based on the deep involvement of the *Danube–Carpathian Programme* with the management of the Danube Delta for the last 15 years in the region. As to the activities of the WWF concerning the Danube Delta, see <http://www.panda.org/about_wwf/where_we_work/eurpe/what_we_do/danube_carpathian/our_work/index.cfm>.

28 'News, WWF Welcomes International Fact-finding Mission to the Ukrainian Danube Delta, 14 Oct 2004'; EPL 2004, 7.

29 UNECE, ECE/MP.PP/2005/2/Add.8.

30 ICPDR, Final, IC/114, 23; Ramsar Convention 2005.

31 ICPDR, Final, IC/114, 23–24.

32 CE, T-PVS (2005)20, 10–11.

Esopoo inquiry procedure was completed in June 2006, funded by both parties and based on their co-operation.[33] In its conclusion the BCP was found to be likely to have significant transboundary adverse impact.[34] Third, Ukraine expressed its intention of submitting strategies, which had been requested, by a particular date to the Aarhus Compliance Committee, in August, 2006.[35]

Finally, the International Conference for the Sustainable Development of the Danube Delta, the so-called Odessa Conference, was hosted by Ukraine with support by and participation of most of the institutions and NGOs concerned in February 2006. Its aim was to generate an overall shared vision under which individual project decisions could be taken to promote the conservation and sustainable development of the Delta in a holistic, co-operative manner. The Conference was judged a success. A follow-up process was expected to produce constructive dialogue for managing the Danube Delta conflict in the wider context by facilitating the sustainable development of the region.[36] Consequently, a framework for preparing a river basin management plan for the Delta was started to be discussed under the ICPDR.[37] The 2000 trilateral agreement entered into force in October, too.[38]

Stage IV (November 2006–April 2008): Resumption of the BCP and Renewed Deadlock Ukraine, however, resumed the BCP in November 2006 without fully responding to the requests by the institutions concerned.[39] The Bystroe Canal was launched, albeit in trial mode, in May 2007,[40] and officially forecasted to be opened as a deep-water shipping canal Danube–Black Sea by 2009 with the final decision on the BCP.[41] Large-scale maintenance work in eliminating sediments is, however, said to be continuously necessary in order to keep it navigable. This has been predicted to cost a great deal.[42]

In response to these actions, the international institutions concerned and NGOs expressed their concern and repeatedly requested Ukraine to respond to requests by the institutions and/or to comply with the MEAs concerned, referring to

33 UNECE, ECE/MP.EIA/WG.1/2007/5, 9.

34 Espoo Inquiry Commission 2006.

35 UNECE, ECE/MP.PP/C.1/2006/6, 6.

36 'Conference Conclusion'.

37 ICPDR, IC/121, Draft 2, 20/12/2006, 15.

38 CE, T-PVS (2006)24, 13.

39 Ukraine has insisted that the work constituted part of Phase 1, but this argument has widely been criticized by Romania and in the institutions concerned based on the blur distinction between Phase 1 and 2. On this point see: CE, T-PVS (2006) 24, 13; CE, T-PVS/Files (2007) 30; CE, T-PVS/Files (2007) 9.

40 'News, Ukraine opens Bystroe Canal through Danube Delta, 16 May 2007'.

41 Ministry of Foreign Affairs of Ukraine (2008), As to a newspaper article on this matter: see 'XVII.) Vinskyi forecasts opening of Danube–Black Sea Canal by 2009'.

42 Considering the large amount of the potential cost, the report of the Bern on-the-spot appraisal questioned the feasibility of the BCP against the views of the Ukrainian Government. CE, T-PVS/Files(2004)3, 6.

findings of the Espoo Inquiry Commission.[43] The European Commission, in their bilateral meetings, also requested Ukraine to take proper procedures in accordance with the two ECE Conventions.[44] Moreover, under the Espoo Convention a non-compliance procedure was initiated upon a new submission by Romania in 2007, and non-compliance by Ukraine was found by the Implementation Committee in February 2008.[45] No agreement was achieved on the issues of the BCP between the two states although they had several bilateral meetings at various levels in 2007.[46]

The follow-up process of the Odessa Conference was much slower than expected, too. No meeting of the joint commission was arranged for the 2000 trilateral agreement although this issue was discussed to a certain extent in the bilateral meetings mentioned above.[47] A follow-up international conference to the Odessa Conference originally planned for the autumn of 2006 was not held.

Under these circumstances some pessimistic views as to a comprehensive solution of the conflict were shared among the institutions concerned. On the other hand, however, the above findings of the Espoo Implementation Committee led to the revival of active co-operation between the relevant institutions. Serious concern with the Ukrainian official announcement on the BCP aforementioned accelerated their mutual communication as well. Its momentum was the informal joint meeting of April 2008 held in Geneva.[48]

Moreover, some new initiatives occurred, particularly facilitated by the ICPDR. One was to prepare and implement the sub-basin management plan of the Danube Delta. A trilateral memorandum of understanding as its framework was signed at the end of 2007.[49] Another was to promote integrated planning of navigation and environmental improvement projects in the Danube River and its basin. This was the first attempt ever to link the two sectors in the region.[50] A joint statement on guiding principles was adopted by the ICPDR, the *Danube Commission* and the *International Sava River Basin Commission*. Parties agreed to pursue co-operative

43 CE, T-PVS (2006)24, 10–11 and 13; CE, T-PVS/Files(2007)30; CE, T-PVS/Files(2007)9; CE, T-PVS (2007)24, 9–10; ICPDR, IC/144, Draft 1, 12/12/2008, 25; ICPDR, IC/125, 24; ICPDR 2007, 29; UNECE, ECE/MP.PP/C.1/2006/8, 4 and UNECE, ECE/MP.PP/C.1/2007/2, 5; UNESCO MAB, SC-05/CONF.204/14,18–19.

44 Comment of the staff of the European Commission, DG Environment, in an interview with the author in March 2007.

45 UNECE, ECE/MP.EIA/WG.1/2007/4, 5; ECE/MP.EIA/2008/6: paras. 1–18; ECE/MP.EIA/10, 83–96.

46 These meetings include those of Ad Hoc Working Group on Navigation, of Presidential Commission, etc. CE, T-PVS/Files (2007)9, 9–10; ICPDR, IC 125, 26–27.

47 CE, T-PVS/Files (2007)9, 9–10; ICPDR, IC 125, 26–27.

48 UNECE 2008.

49 'Towards a River Basin Management Plan for the Danube Delta Supporting Sustainable Development of the Region: Memorandum of Understanding between the Governments of Moldova, Romania and Ukraine'.

50 ICPDR, IC/125, 14–15; ICPDR 2007, 15.

relations between two sectors of navigation and ecology concerning the Danube River.[51] A particular project has been discussed in line with the guiding principles formulated by the joint statement of navigation and ecology of the Danube River and its basin.[52] Neither of these attempts was intended to directly manage the Danube Delta conflict but to promote the sustainable development of the Danube Delta or the Danube River and its basin as a whole. It should, however, be noted that the conflict gave a certain momentum to these developments.

Stage V (May 2008–): Improved International Communication but an Uncertain Future? The momentum for moving into a new stage was provided by the outcome of the MOPs of the two ECE Conventions. Under the Espoo Convention the non-compliance by Ukraine was decided by the 4th MOP in May 2008.[53] The following month the 3rd MOP of the Aarhus Convention also determined that Ukraine was still in non-compliance as the action plan submitted by Ukraine in May 2008 was insufficient.[54] Under both of the Conventions it was decided to issue a caution to Ukraine, to be effective on certain conditions, as one of the measures in response to its non-compliance.[55]

Following the events some positive signs have occurred under all the MEAs concerned, particularly in 2008. This has been appreciated by the international institutions to some extent. First, immediately after the MOPs in June Ukraine decided to repeal the final decision of December 2008 on implementation of Phase

51 'Guiding Principles for the Development of Inland Navigation and Environmental Protection in the Danube River Basin', ICPDR, IC 127. This was a product of three workshops held in 2007. Almost all riparian states and various stakeholders, such as the European Commission, non-state institutions from navigational sector, environmental NGOs, etc., actively participated in the workshop. 'Process: Navigation and Ecology, Joint Statement on Inland Navigation and Environmental Sustainability'.

52 E.g., a navigation project on the Danube between the towns of Calarasi and Braila in Romania to be funded through the EU's ISPA fund, i.e., the ISPA Project. Comment of the Executive Secretary of the ICPDR in the interviews with the author in December 2007 and March 2008. As to the ISPA project, see for instance: 'Factsheet, Bottleneck: Romania, Project: ISPA'; 'News, Growing Concern as Danube Modification Projects move Forward, 04 Jan 2008', 4 Jan 2000.

53 'Decision IV/2: Review of Compliance', UNECE, ECE/MP.EIA/10, paras. 7–14. As to the significance of the Espoo Convention for managing the Danube Delta conflict, see Koyano 2008, 302–311.

54 'Decision III/6f: Compliance by Ukraine with its Obligations under the Convention (Ref. Decision II/5b)', UNECE, ECE/MP.PP/2008/.

55 The Espoo MOP decided to issue a caution to Ukraine, to become effective on 31 October 2008, unless it 'stops the works, repeals the final decision and takes steps to comply with the relevant provisions of the Convention'. UNECE, ECE/MP.EIA/10, para. 10. The Aarhus MOP decided to issue a caution to Ukraine, to become effective on 1 May 2009, unless Ukraine has fully satisfied the conditions indicated in the decision concerning preparing for the action plan. UNECE, ECE/MP.PP/2008/.

II of the BCP following the decision of the Espoo MOP.[56] In October 2008 the Espoo Implementation Committee satisfied all the steps except for construction and maintenance of Phase I of the BCP taken by Ukraine and decided that the caution should not become effective, while it requested Ukraine to stop works on Phase I and to submit a report on the detailed status of the project by February 2009.[57] The process of preparing a strategy by Ukraine has been ongoing with an independent review of legal, administrative and other measures of Ukraine to implement the Convention.[58] Second, under the Aarhus Convention a proper dialogue started between Ukraine and the Compliance Committee for its full implementation of the MOP decision.[59] Third, Ukraine first replied to the Secretary General of the Ramsar Convention.[60] Fourth, in July the second on-the-spot appraisal was carried out with the full co-operation of Ukraine in the framework of the Bern Convention. Secretariats of other relevant MEAs and the institutions, such as the UNESCO and the European Commission, joined the mission.[61] Finally, the ICPDR appreciated initiatives taken by Ukraine following the Espoo MOP.[62] It also re-confirmed the significance of the sub-basin initiatives of the Danube Delta,[63] and works in this direction have started under the ICPDR.[64] In the longer term this may prompt the management processes of the conflict from the substantial point of view, promoting the sustainable development of the Danube Delta.

Since the end of 2008, however, the situation has become strained. International warnings directed towards Ukraine have increased in response to its inadequate implementation of international decisions or recommendations. First, the Bern mission concluded that the situation in Ukraine remained almost the same as before.[65] This led to the request by the Bern Standing Committee that Ukraine

---

56 Government of Ukraine 2008; UNECE, ECE/MP.EIA/IC/2008/2, para. 28.

57 UNECE, ECE/MP.EIA/IC/2008/2, paras. 22–35. The Committee took this position although it decided that Ukraine did not follow the MOP decision which requested to stop 'the works' in terms of Phase 1. This was based on the Committee's perception that the wording of the decision is vague due to the unclear meaning of 'the works'. *Ibid.* This was not clarified in the 4th MOP due to the shortage of time. See Koyano 2008, 305–307.

58 Comment of the staff of the Espoo Secretariat in an interview with the author in March 2009.

59 UNECE, MP/PP/C.1/2008/6, paras. 37–39.

60 Ramsar Convention 2008, 5.

61 Ramsar Convention 2008, 5–6; CE, T-PVS(2008)23, 10; CE, T-PVS/Files(2008)11, 2.

62 ICPDR, IC/144, Draft 1, 12/12/2008, 30–31.

63 ICPDR, IC/144, Draft 1, 12/12/2008, 15–16.

64 A 'bottom-up' approach has been taken, from the technical co-operation to higher political commitments, to produce constructive dialogue between the three basin countries. An international workshop for enhancing information exchange between the Parties was held in March 2009. This succeeded in establishing a working basis for technical co-operation. 'International workshop "Information Assessment Management on Water Resources in the Danube Delta"'.

65 CE, T-PVS(2008)23, 10; CE, T-PVS/Files(2008)11.

fully implement the recommendation of 2004, particularly concerning the need of the EIA, and submit a report in the spring of 2009.[66] Second, under the Ramsar Convention a resolution was adopted by the 10th Conference of the Parties (COP) based on a report of the visit, which was acknowledged by Ukraine, in November 2008. It asked Ukraine to provide full and updated information concerning the BCP and report on progress regarding the transboundary co-operation.[67] Third, the Aarhus Compliance Committee found the action plan submitted by Ukraine in January 2009 unsatisfactory on several issues.[68] Ukraine has not, however, fully responded to these concerns.

Finally, there has been a significant turn under the Espoo Conventions. In March 2009 the Implementation Committee found that a report submitted by Ukraine did not confirm that work had been stopped on Phase I and that steps to apply the Convention to any further works related to Phase I had not been taken. Moreover, a press release by the Ministry of Transport and Communications of Ukraine, dated 7 February 2009, stated that work would be carried out under Phase II. The Committee regarded them as presenting a breach of Ukraine's obligations under the Convention. It also found a summary report on the EIA of the project submitted by Ukraine unsatisfactory on various points.[69] Based on these findings the Executive Secretary of the ECE sent a letter to the Deputy Prime Minister of Ukraine which requested Ukraine to provide confirmation by the middle of April that the conditions imposed in the MOP decision have been met.[70]

Under the circumstances, three trends can be identified in the management processes. First, there exist constant, but sometimes very slow, communications between Ukraine and both the international institutions and Romania at various levels. Such constant communication may be a basis for their co-operation. Second, efforts have been made by Ukraine to some extent to prepare legislation and administrative measures to implement the MEAs concerned and to implement the required procedures on the BCP, such as EIA or transboundary EIA, monitoring, etc., following decisions or recommendations adopted by the relevant institutions. Ukraine has maintained its commitment to these efforts although their processes have been much slower than expected. Finally, provisional suspension of the work on the BCP, which is presumably aimed at ensuring the effectiveness of the procedures required by, or under, the MEAs, has not been taken by Ukraine in spite of repeated requests by the relevant institutions. Presumably this is mainly

66 CE, T-PVS(2008)23, 10.

67 'Resolution X.13: The status of sites in the Ramsar List of Wetlands of International Importance', para. 27.

68 UNECE, ECE/MP.PP/C.1/2008/8, paras. 34–37. Comment of the staff of the Aarhus Secretariat in an interview with the author in March 2009.

69 UNECE, ECE/EHLM/13Z/2009/I.

70 Upon receiving a written statement from Ukraine, the Committee is to decide on the appropriate measures to be taken. UNECE, ECE/EHLM/13Z/2009/I.

because suspension of works may ultimately lead to the termination of the BCP for technical reasons.[71]

Thus, there has been some progress, mainly on procedural aspects, in managing the conflict. However, faced with no suspension of works on the BCP by Ukraine, the management of the Danube Delta conflict has taken on a highly complicated quality.

Furthermore, following a submission by Ukraine a new non-compliance process was started against Romania in March 2009. Ukraine pointed that Romania had implemented a dredging project along the Sulina arm and of dumping dredged materials into the Danube Delta, which had caused a substantial decrease in the water quantity in the Kiliya arm that, in turn, significantly affected the Ukrainian side of the Delta. It was alleged that this occurred without any notification to Ukraine.[72] This may complicate the bilateral relations between the Parties and affect the on-going process continuing in the relevant institutions.

Analysis on the Management Processes of the Danube Delta Conflict

Overview of the Management Processes

Actions Taken under MEAs and the UNESCO MAB Programme As was indicated by the above narrative, various kinds of actions have been taken under the relevant MEAs and the UNESCO MAB Programme since summer 2003. Their formal actions are as follows.

First, under the Espoo Convention, two kinds of institutionalized procedures were undertaken. Ukraine participated in both processes.[73] First of all, inquiry procedure was taken at the request of the Romanian authorities. In its conclusion the project was unanimously found to be likely to have a significant transboundary adverse impact. Recommendations of the Inquiry Commission included the parties' developing joint research programmes, Ukraine taking mitigation measures of transboundary impact, etc. Following the inquiry procedure, a non-compliance procedure was initiated upon the submission of Romania, and non-compliance by Ukraine with arts. 2, 3, 4, 5 and 6 was concluded by the MOP. Ukraine was urged to repeal the final decision and not to implement the BCP without taking

71 Continuous work of dredging the riverbed is needed to maintain the water stream in the Bystroe Canal as a navigable waterway, for an extremely fast water stream naturally brings a lot of sediments into the channel in this region of the Danube Delta. Without such work the canal becomes non-navigable in a relatively short period.

72 Information obtained at the Espoo Secretariat at an interview with the author in March 2009.

73 As to the process taken under the Espoo Convention, see Koyano 2008, 304–307.

procedures required by the Convention[74] and requested to ensure domestic measures sufficient to implement the Convention, to accept an independent view of them, to submit strategy to the Implementation Committee by a certain time, and to enter into negotiation with neighbouring Parties for elaborating a bilateral agreement to implement the Convention. Notably an adversarial measure, namely to issue a caution to Ukraine, to be effective on certain conditions, was adopted as one of several measures to be taken. Interestingly Ukraine has appeared partly to follow up the decision of the MOP. This led to the decision of the Committee not to make the adversarial measure effective. Faced with continuous insufficiency of Ukraine's implementing the MOP decision, however, the Committee is to take appropriate measures to be taken upon receiving a response from Ukraine.[75]

Second, a non-compliance procedure was taken based on the Romanian submission and a Ukrainian NGO's communication under the Aarhus Convention. Ukraine was absent from the whole process. In conclusion, non-compliance by Ukraine with art. 6(1)(a), (2)–(9), art. 4 and art. 3(1) was approved by the 2nd MOP, based on findings of the Compliance Committee, and Ukraine was recommended to submit strategy for implementing the Convention. The 3rd MOP determined that Ukraine still remained in non-compliance and decided to issue a caution to Ukraine on certain conditions. Ukraine has started communication with the Committee and submitted the action plan for preparing its complete strategy. The Committee has, however, not been fully satisfied with the plan, and Ukraine has not responded to it yet.

Third, under the Bern Convention, a case-file procedure, including on-the-spot appraisal, was undertaken as a result of a complaint from an NGO. Based on findings of the on-the-spot appraisal, which pointed out the lack of sufficient consideration of environmental factors, of examination into alternatives and of appropriate consultation with neighbouring States, the Standing Committee approved non-compliance by Ukraine with art. 4 and art. 6 and adopted a number of recommendations, such as Ukrainian suspension of Phase 2 until taking EIA, undertaking ecological compensation for possible environmental damage, co-operation with Romania, etc. The Committee has kept requesting Ukraine to

74 Suspension of the project in question during the period undertaking the procedures is not explicitly required by provisions of the Espoo Convention. There was very limited discussion on its legal grounds concerning the BCP in the fourth MOP. The objects and purposes of the Convention could, however, be used to justify a suspension measure. Moreover, it should be noted that the Implementation Committee took an even stricter approach, a precautionary position, in the interpretation of the Convention, in particular, approving the requirement of suspending the project in question upon the establishment of the Inquiry Commission although the Convention does not refer to the precautionary principle or approach neither in its preamble nor provisions. UNECE, ECE/MP.EIA/2008/6, paras. 48 and 49. On this point, see Koyano 2008, 306.

75 Problems, the Committee has been faced with, are partly rooted in some vagueness of conditions on which the caution should become effective. On this point, see note 55 above.

follow the recommendation. The conclusion of the second on-the-spot appraisal has reinforced the request.

Fourth, the ICPDR has adopted several resolutions under the DRP Convention that requested further information from Ukraine, as well as consultations and the adoption of an appropriate EIA, etc. Also, the President and Executive Secretary of the ICPDR have sent letters to the Ukraine calling for further discussion. Moreover, they have made several visits to Ukraine with the same purposes. Following the actions, Ukraine has been continuing dialogue with the ICPDR.[76] In addition, the ICPDR has facilitated international co-operation for enhancing the sustainable development of the Danube Delta region at various levels.[77]

Fifth, under the UNESCO MAB Programme a joint UNESCO/Ramsar Advisory Mission was sent to Ukraine. Evaluating the potential effects, it recommended Ukraine to undertake a sufficient EIA and to choose an option which was to be likely to have the least impact on the BR. Upon the findings, the MAB ICC has adopted resolutions which requested Ukraine to submit official information on the state of affairs, particularly on its unilaterally altering the zonation of the Dunainsky BR. This was based on a decision of the MAB ICC that altering zonation of BR should be admitted by the MAB ICC Bureau, based on the opinion given by the MAB Advisory Committee, as interpretation of the *Statutory Framework* of the UNESCO MAB Programme.[78] However, Ukraine has not officially responded to the MAB ICC.

Finally, under the Ramsar Convention, in addition to the UNESCO/Ramsar Advisory Mission, the Secretary General sent Ukraine a letter for requesting information. In response to Ukraine's failure to reply, the 9th COP adopted a resolution which recommended Ukraine to suspend the BCP pending the EIA, make compensatory provision for ecological damage of the Ramsar site, ensure appropriate process of information, consultation, etc. in line with art. 5, etc.[79] Upon the start of dialogue between Ukraine and the Secretariat, the 10th COP adopted a resolution which requested Ukraine to provide full and updated relevant information as suggested by the report of the second mission to Ukraine.[80] Ukraine has not, however, replied.

---

76 ICPDR 2007, 29.

77 The ICPDR has recently shifted its emphasis from focusing on the Danube Delta conflict to promoting co-operation between the Parties for achieving the sustainable development of the Danube Delta. This may reflect in its strong commitment to facilitating works on sub-basin management of the Danube Delta.

78 UNESCO, SC-04/CONF.204/14, 18–19.

79 'Resolution IX.15 on the status of sites in the Ramsar List of Wetlands of International Importance', para. 27.

80 'Resolution X.13: The status of sites in the Ramsar List of Wetlands of International Importance', para. 27.

Subject Matter under MEAs and the UNESCO MAB Programme Subject matter under the MEAs and the UNESCO MAB Programme are as follows: under the Espoo Convention, non-compliance by Ukraine with arts. 2, 3, 4, 5 and 6; under the Aarhus Convention, non-compliance by Ukraine with art. 6(1)(a), (2)–(8), (9), art. 4 and art. 3(1); under the Bern Convention, non-compliance with art. 4 and art. 6; under the DRP Convention, non-compliance with art. 10(f) and art. 11 only in the early stage and non-conformity with purposes of the Convention; under the UNESCO MAB Programme, non-fulfillment of procedural requirement in accordance with the Framework Statute; and under the Ramsar Convention, possible non-compliance with art. 3(2). Thus, questions have formally been raised mainly from the procedural point of view under all the relevant MEAs except for the Bern Convention.

Involvement of the European Commission The European Commission has been deeply involved with the management processes since 2004. Upon receiving the NGOs' complaint letters the Commission started ad hoc bilateral talks and exchanged letters with Ukraine. The Commission also initiated a joint mission of an international expert team. Its report pointed out a number of unclear issues on the BCP, criticized the information strategy of Ukraine and recommended that Phase 2 should not be approved before taking sufficient monitoring.[81] Since 2005, the Commission and Ukraine have been continuing discussions in their regular bilateral meetings for implementing the bilateral Partnership and Co-operation Agreement (PCA). This is a rather political dialogue under the Action Programme based on the European Neighbourhood Policy (ENP) under the PCA. The subject matter is taking proper procedures, such as information, consultation, EIA, etc. in accordance with the two ECE Conventions based on art. 63 of the PCA with Ukraine. These actions should be understood in the context of the diplomatic policy of the European Union towards its eastern neighbour States following the extension of its membership to the East.

Characteristics of the Conflict and Management Processes

Multiple Dimensions of the Conflict As was indicated by the above narrative, the Danube Delta conflict has multiple dimensions. First, the conflict is concerned about the common interests of all Contracting Parties to the MEAs, which are dealt with by multilateral mechanisms. Moreover, it also entails a bilateral dispute between Ukraine and Romania as seen under the Espoo Convention. We find these dimensions have two aspects. The BCP may harm both Romanian interests in its territory due to its transboundary adverse effect and the common interests in the conservation or/and the sustainable development of the Danube Delta. Moreover, the execution of the project without proper procedures may impair the procedural interests both of Romania and those common to all the contracting or participating parties to the MEAs or the UNESCO MAB Programme.

81 European Commission 2004.

Second, questions have been, and are likely to be, raised mainly from the procedural point of view under all the MEAs and the UNESCO MAB Programme. Under all these instruments, except for the two ECE Conventions, which aim at the conservation or/and the sustainable development of the Danube Delta, however, the substantial conformity of the BCP with their purposes, that is the appropriateness of the BCP, has directly been a matter of discussion on many occasions. Furthermore, under the Bern Convention the breach of the duty to conserve the habitats of wild fauna and flora (art. 4 and art. 6) was recognized due to the lack of appropriate procedures. Thus, there exist substantial concerns on the basis of the procedural questions except under the two ECE Conventions of which subject matters are solely procedural.

Third, there is the question of the unlawfulness and/or inconformity of the Ukrainian actions that are raised under the MEAs and the UNESCO MAB Programme. Under the MEAs, except for the two ECE Conventions, and the UNESCO MAB Programme, however, the concern about the conformity with their purposes is on the basis of the management of the conflict.

Finally, the dimension of the conflict in the interests of the public can also be seen under some of the MEAs, such as the Aarhus Convention, which require the contracting parties to ensure public participation.

Management Method: Interactive Dialogue Various methods have been used for the management of the Danube Delta conflict as a whole. Under an individual MEA and the UNESCO MAB Programme it depends on their purpose, normative structure, nature, etc, what methods have been adopted.

The main method commonly adopted is, however, the interactive dialogue. This includes: fact-finding as providing the basis of dialogue; persuasion through multilateral consultation and international assistance for facilitating the dialogue process. This aims at managing the conflict by encouraging Ukraine to respond appropriately for achieving the purposes of the MEAs. This is to be distinguished from coercive means, such as sanctions or judicial actions against illegal actions.

First, there were five fact-finding institutions, including the joint UNESCO/Ramsar Advisory Mission (No. 53) of 2003, the two Bern on-the-spot appraisals of 2004 and 2008, the joint mission of an international expert team organized by the European Commission of 2004 and the Espoo inquiry procedure of 2006. Some of them were joined by various institutions involved in this conflict. Their conclusions have often been mutually utilized, as necessary, by the institutions concerned as a basis of their actions.

Second, based on their findings, persuasion of Ukraine has been attempted through multilateral consultation. Three means have been utilized for this: institutionalized non-compliance mechanisms, multilateral consultation in standing forums and direct communication with the Parties. The last method has been complementarily used under almost all MEAs and the UNESCO MAB Programme. These methods succeeded in changing Ukrainian attitudes to a certain extent. This was partly because Ukraine recognized through multilateral consultation that international criticisms were not on the substantial legitimacy of the project, which is a delicate issue, but on its procedural appropriateness.[82] Moreover, continuous pressure, strengthened by the possibility of adversarial measures, appears to have had some effect on the stance of Ukraine.

Finally, attempts at facilitating such persuasion have been made via the provision of international assistance for capacity-building of the parties concerned. There have been two kinds of assistance; support to taking requested procedures, and encouraging finding alternatives by assisting preparation of development programmes of the Danube Delta. The former aims at managing the conflict from the procedural viewpoint, and, the latter, substantial. Under almost all the MEAs the former is given with the assistance of experts. In terms of the latter, the institutions concerned with the conservation and/or the sustainable development of the Delta are involved with the Odessa Conference and its follow-up processes. The recent development on sub-basin initiatives, facilitated by the ICPDR, should particularly be noted in this context.

Involvement of NGOs NGOs, both international and Ukrainian-based, have been involved with the management processes from the early stages. Some of them are in the observer status of some MEAs[83] and/or operating or facilitating programmes or projects on the Danube Delta.[84] Their involvement is part of such continuous commitments.

There are five levels of their involvement. They cover all the three components of the interactive dialogue as a whole.

First, some NGOs have formally initiated and/or participated in institutionalized mechanisms, such as non-compliance procedures, standing institutions, etc. Furthermore, the five fact-finding institutions referred to the information and scientific views given by NGOs as necessary.[85]

Second, their daily activities, such as collecting, analyzing and providing information or technical advice to relevant institutions or Parties, have been useful. Particularly, information on the status of the BCP collected and provided by NGOs has often prompted responses by the institutions under the MEAs and by UNESCO, which can hardly get it for themselves, as the project is solely within the Ukrainian territory. Moreover, frequent communication by NGOs has put pressure on the institutions

82 The bilateral talks between Ukrainian Foreign Minister and the ICPDR President and Executive Secretary held in September 2005 seemed to have prompted this change in Ukrainian perception. Comment of the ICPDR Executive Secretary in an interview with the author in August 2006.

83 E.g., DEF is an observer of the ICPDR, and the WWF, that of the ICPDR, the Bern Standing Committee, etc.

84 See note 27 above.

85 CE, T-PVS/Files(2004)3, 13; CE, T-PVS/Files(2008)11, 6; European Commission 2004, 2–3; Ramsar/UNESCO 2003, 9–10; UNECE, ECE/MP.EIA/WG.1/2007/5, 9.

to urge coordinated action. These information activities are facilitated by networks among NGOs and the informal networks constructed among all the institutions and NGOs.

Third, some NGOs operate or facilitate the management programmes or projects of the Delta.[86] They have deeply been involved with the Odessa Conference, its follow-up processes, works on sub-basin initiatives facilitated by the ICPDR, etc., making use of their local networks and other resources. The WWF, for instance, was engaged in a study for identifying alternatives to the BCP to achieve the sustainable development of the region.[87]

Fourth, NGOs have promoted communications among NGOs and other stakeholders – most obviously, the public – by various activities. They include: adopting and submitting their joint statements to the Parties or the institutions concerned; publishing information and promotion of public consultations; and influencing the public opinion through media.[88] Consequently, the Parties and the institutions concerned are exposed to pressure from the public.

Finally, some internal legal actions were taken by Ukrainian-based NGOs. This has attracted the attention of the people to the BCP although the NGOs have lost almost all the cases. Thus, resort to legal actions by the NGO had certain political implications in the management processes.

Such involvement of NGOs is contributing not only to ensuring the transparency and democracy of the management processes[89] but also enhancing their quality by supplementing limits in the ability or usable resources of the institutions or Parties. Moreover, their involvement with multiple processes has brought about factual coordination between the institutions.

Complex Interaction between Multiple Processes There exists interaction between the multiple processes under the MEAs concerned and the UNESCO MAB Programme. They have contributed to the effective management under the individual MEAs and the UNESCO MAB Programme. Moreover, different approaches taken under each of the MEAs and by the UNESCO, including procedural and substantial approaches, and approaches for ensuring the lawfulness under or the conformity with purposes of the MEA or the UNESCO MAB Programme, have complementarily prompted the management of the conflict.

The complementary interaction is based on the practical co-operation between the institutions concerned. The informal network, established at the 2004 Geneva

86 As to the WWF, for instance, see note 27 above.

87 The study was completed in February 2009, and upon a peer review its outcome is to be made public by the end of April 2009, WWF 2009. Comment of the staff of the WWF Danube-Carpathian Programme in an interview with the author in March 2009.

88 Various Ukrainian NGOs have actively been involved with such activities. Comment of the staff of the EPL in an interview with the author in November 2007.

89 See for instance: Ebbesson 2007, 667–668; Epiney 2006, 338–339.This was also confirmed in Chapter 27 of the Agenda 21 adopted by the Rio Summit in 1992.

consultation meeting and reinforced at the 2008 Geneva meeting, is mainly working as a framework of such co-operation, although the degree of commitment is different among the institutions[90] and from time to time.[91]

There exist three types of co-operation: sharing information on relevant matters; mutual utilization of resources; and joint activities. Their co-operative activities include: provision of relevant information, exchange of views or consultation, mutual reference of results of fact-finding, joint fact-finding, joint preparation of or support to international conferences or seminars. Such co-operation has been developed, either formally through official meetings of the institutions or informally at the practical level between secretariats, at the *ad hoc* or regular basis within the framework of the MEAs and the UNESCO MAB Programme.

The complementary interaction has ensured efficient and consistent management to a certain extent.[92] All the relevant institutions, being aware of the difference in their individual tasks, utilize the co-operative relationships in accordance with their own mandate.[93] Thus, they have made it possible to avoid mutually conflicting actions by paying due regard to others and also saving costs by utilizing resources of one another.

There are several factors underlying such complementary interaction. First, the MEAs and the MAB Programme, of which contracting or participating parties are overlapping with each other to a great extent, do not conflict with each other in their content.[94] Second, the method of interactive dialogue has been utilized under almost all the instruments. This includes flexible and continuous processes where various factors may be regarded and where standing organs, such as MOPs, secretariats, etc., generally take on an important role. These organs provide the framework of practical co-operation. Third, there have been official relations between some of the instruments independently of the conflict. For instance, in addition to the partnership relations between the Ramsar Convention and the UNESCO MAB Programme, European Community ratified the Bern Convention, DRP Convention and the two ECE Conventions. Fourth, there exist institutions that lead, or led, to co-operative

---

90 Secretariats of the two ECE Conventions have been minimally involved with the co-operative actions for the conservation and sustainable development of the Danube Delta, such as the Odessa Conference, etc. This was mainly due to the procedural character in subjects of these conventions. Comments of their staff in an interview with the author in August 2006.

91 Co-operation became less active in the deadlock situations in 2007. However, their coordinated activities have been revived in spring 2008 as aforementioned.

92 For a thorough analysis of distinctive functions of the Espoo Convention in terms of such complementary interaction, see Koyano 2008, 307–311.

93 This was accelerated by communications between the institutions established at an early stage.

94 Almost all the ECE States, except for Russia, ratified the two ECE Conventions; almost all the ECE States, including European CE States and many CIS states apart from Russia joined the Bern Convention; all 13 riparian States ratified the DRP Convention; and most of these States ratified the Ramsar Convention and joined UNESCO MAB Programme.

relationships, such as the ICPDR, the European Commission and the Espoo Secretariat.[95] Fifth, members or staff of the institutions have shared a certain degree of enthusiasm about the issues, so that they spend a certain time to deal with them.[96] Finally, NGOs, formally or informally, urge the institutions concerned to coordinate their works by putting pressure on them.

European Factors There are several European factors underlying the management processes. First, the rapid increase of MEAs among European states, accelerated by initiatives of European regional institutions, such as the CE, EU and UNECE, lies behind the multiple regulations over the BCP and simultaneous discussions under the MEAs or the UNESCO MAB concerned. In the conflict contracting/participating parties of many MEAs also overlap particularly due to European developments, and recently extending membership of the European institutions. These conditions have made it necessary, and also possible, to harmonize the application of overlapping regulations to a certain extent.

Second, the utilization of procedural methods of controlling environmental risk under European MEAs is another key factor. The main subject matter of the conflict is the procedural legitimacy of executing the BCP on account of the emphasis within European MEAs. The significance of procedural regulation by prior notification, consultation, exchange of information, EIA, public participation in environmental processes, etc., has recently been focused at the global level as well. The speed of their institutionalization is, however, much more remarkable in Europe.[97]

Third, the extremely active involvement of NGOs should be understood in the European context. European MEAs tend to allow NGOs to participate in the formal process of their implementation. The Bern and Aahrus Conventions

95 Some changes can be seen as to which institution take such a coordinating role. At Stage I the UNESCO took it by the joint UNESCO/Ramsar Advisory Mission. At Stage II it was the European Commission and the ICPDR that coordinated the co-operation, organizing the joint mission of an international expert team or leading the Geneva joint meeting. At Stage III the ICPDR Secretariat still remains in an important position in the preparation and execution of the Odessa Conference. At Stage V the Espoo Secretariat tends to take an initiative with the momentum of the decision of non-compliance under the Espoo Convention, mainly convening the informal joint meeting of 2008. The second meeting is planned on its initiative for spring 2009 in Geneva. Comment of the staff of the Espoo Secretariat in an interview with the author in March 2009.

96 One factor in the decline of joint/co-operative commitment by the institutions observed in Stage IV might be the lack of time and manpower to be spent for the issue in each of the institutions partly due to the prolonged processes of the management of the conflict.

97 As to the comprehensive assessment of their introduction and functions, see Koyano 2006.

are the most advanced examples under which NGOs can formally initiate non-compliance mechanisms by complaint. This reflects the recent emphasis on public participation in the field of environmental protection in Europe.

Finally, European institutions have taken an important role in the processes. The CE, as a political framework, supports the implementation of the Bern Convention. For instance, political discussions lay behind the activities of the Standing Committee. Furthermore, the role of the EU is remarkable. The political relations between the EU and Ukraine support the bilateral exchange between the European Commission and Ukraine. Following the extension of the EU area to the East after the Cold War era, Ukraine has become geo-politically important for the EU. This prompts the EU to implement the ENP and makes the Commission active in managing the Danube Delta conflict. Simultaneously there are political incentives for Ukraine, who wants to join the EU in the long term,[98] in keeping bilateral talks with the Commission. Such a highly political role for the Commission is becoming more and more expected by the institutions involved.

Has the Conflict Been Effectively Managed?

Has the Danube Delta conflict been effectively managed? Have compliance with, and the effectiveness of, the MEAs and the UNESCO MAB Programme been ensured? Regrettably we cannot provide clear answers to these questions at this stage. Some positive signs have recently appeared on some points after many twists and turns. However, there remain uncertainties regarding the main direction to be taken in finding a comprehensive solution to the conflict.

There are five trends in positions currently taken by Ukraine in the management processes. First, Ukraine has improved international communication, including information provision or exchange, consultation, etc., at various levels under all the relevant MEAs. Second, It has maintained its commitment to preparing legislation and administrative measures generally to implement the MEAs concerned. Third, Ukraine has been preparing full EIA, including transboundary EIA, with advice provided by the relevant international institutions. These three stances are in marked contrast to its positions observed at the beginning of the conflict[99] although their slow process and insufficient substance have been criticized frequently. Fourth, Ukraine has not, however, taken any measures for ecological compensation already occurred in the region following international recommendations. Finally, it has not suspended the work on the BCP which has been repeatedly requested by the relevant institutions. It is the slow pace and inadequate content of the required procedures taken by Ukraine without suspension of the work on the BCP that are currently at the heart of criticisms under the MEAs and the UNESCO MAB Programme.

98 Kuzio 2003a, 18; Kuzio 2003b, 29.

99 Ukraine was not responsive in the beginning. In some instances it was absent from meetings of the institutions under the MEAs concerned, such as the ICPDR.

In general, the main obstacles to ensuring the compliance with and effectiveness of MEAs may include the lack of will of the state/states concerned, the uncertainty of content of MEAs or relevant facts, the shortage of resources and conflict with domestic legal and/or administrative systems of the state/states concerned. In the Danube Delta conflict these obstacles have begun to be overcome to a certain extent after many complications over a period of more than five years.

First, the uncertainty of facts concerning the BCP and their potential impact had been gradually overcome by the four fact-finding institutions by the end of Stage III. At Stage V the second Bern on-the-spot appraisal, joined by other institutions concerned, has given another opportunity for the Parties, the relevant institutions and other stakeholders to acknowledge the situation and facilitated dialogues between each other. Furthermore, uncertainties of the content of the MEAs and the UNESCO MAB Programme, which Ukraine had faced, have presumably been dealt with through dialogue within the institutions concerned.

Second, shortage of resources has been responded by the international community to some extent. International co-operation under the instruments concerned is not only for undertaking of the relevant procedures but also for the sustainable development of the Danube Delta in finding alternatives to the BCP. Such co-operation has been reinforced at various levels from time to time.

Third, at Stage III the necessity of coordination with domestic systems was more or less recognized by Ukraine, for example, through international seminars, on matters of EIA, monitoring, etc., and, in the exchange with the Aarhus Secretariat, upon strategies for implementing the Convention. At Stage V Ukraine has been put under a great deal of pressure to adopt domestic measures to comply with the MEAs concerned mainly by the decisions of the Aarhus and Espoo MOPs. Moreover, animated dialogues with the relevant institutions have enabled Ukraine to more clearly understand what it should do to comply with the MEAs. Furthermore, it may be assumed that coordination between different institutions of Ukraine, mainly the Ministries of Foreign Affairs, the Environment, Transportation and Communication, has gradually been improved at the internal level. The high-level intergovernmental coordination council for implementing the Espoo Convention, of which plan the Deputy Prime Minister of Ukraine addressed to the Secretary of the UNECE,[100] may be one such momentum.

Finally, the will of Ukraine has been a fundamental factor in the whole process. There were, and have been, signs of some change in the two stages, Stage III and V. At Stage III Ukraine showed its positive will towards international criticisms although it kept silence under the Ramsar Convention and the UNESCO MAB Programme. Two factors may be assumed underlying this: the changing Ukrainian perception of the issues and changes within the Ukrainian political situation. In the process of multilateral consultation Ukraine presumably realized that the procedural legitimacy of the BCP, rather than substantial issues, was a matter of concern under the MEAs. It may also be said that there existed some shift

100 Government of Ukraine, 6186/0/2-08.

in policies in the Ukrainian Government in the political changes following the Orange Revolution. The deadlock at Stage IV has been broken to some extent with the momentum of the Espoo and Arhus MOPs. Their decisions, particularly with the possible adversarial measure, namely issuing a caution, have presumably functioned as a significant external pressure on Ukraine. Ukraine indicated its commitment to procedural undertakings concerning the BCP and for preparing domestic measures to implement the relevant MEAs. The pressure on Ukraine has been strengthened by the revival of the co-operative activities between the institutions concerned at the end of Stage IV. Ukraine's policy towards the EU is surely a key factor in this context.

However, there still remain some factors which may hinder ensuing full compliance with, and the effectiveness of, the MEAs concerned and the UNESCO MAB Programme. Factors in the slow pace and inadequate substance of required procedures taken by Ukraine may still include: the shortage of its domestic resources, technical, financial, human, etc., the lack of full and proper coordination between the relevant institutions, i.e. the Ministries of Foreign Affairs, the Environment, and Transportation and Communication on the related matters, the inadequate co-operation between them and other stakeholders, such as project developers, the public, etc., and the lack of transparency in its administration, including decision-making process, at various levels. In this sense there may be no single intentional will of Ukraine in its adequate implementation of the MEAs and the UNESCO MAB Programme.

Nevertheless, no suspension of the work on the BCP may reflect the strong will of Ukraine, or of an internally powerful sector in domestic politics, to pursue the project. This may be based on its economic and strategic incentives for opening a navigable waterway from the Danube River to the Black Sea which may be closely linked to competition for power with Romania in the region. The national pride of the state might reinforce such a firm position of Ukraine. It should, in this context, be noted that there is a view which questions the economic efficiency of the BCP due to its enormous predicted cost to construct and maintain the canal.[101] Moreover, the recent global economic stagnation may be a major obstacle to the completion of the BCP for the same reason.

What may be possible for the better management under these circumstances? From the legal point of view we may first expect positive functions of the Espoo and Aarhus non-compliance processes, to continue, and to which Ukraine has been responding to some extent.[102] Second, strengthened offer and measures of international assistance based on decisions or recommendations adopted under the MEAs may prompt Ukraine to overcome the slow pace and insufficient substance of required procedures for implementing them. Third, for the present it may not be useful to think about coercive measures, such as judicial or arbitral enforcement by Romania or any other contracting parties to the MEAs concerned. Such measures may aggravate the bilateral relations between the Parties which have started to

101 See note 42 above.

102 See Koyano 2008.

be improved under the relevant MEAs. Moreover, this may negatively affect the commitment which Ukraine has recently continued the processes of undertaking the required procedures. However, under the extreme circumstances where deadlock is renewed it may be one option, although their negative effects should be taken into account at the same time.[103] Considering a bilateral element of the conflict, judicial or arbitral means are technically quite possible in the conflict.[104] Nevertheless, there is a jurisdictional issue here. A bilateral agreement between the parties concerned is required under the MEAs, such as the Espoo Convention, which oblige contracting parties to take specific actions, not only to ensure due regards for achieving certain results, and, therefore, of which enforcement appears to be effectively ensured by judicial means. [105]

From the political point of view it may be effective to strengthen the work of the European Commission as complementary to methods of multilateral consultation under the MEAs and the UNESCO MAB Programme for the reasons already mentioned. Integrated action between sectors of the environment and transportation in the EU may be useful in this context due to their financial implications.[106] The continuously enhanced co-operation between the relevant international institutions may also contribute to offsetting institutional weakness of each Convention. Their virtually coordinated supervision may also place more pressure on Ukraine.

Finally, a substantial approach to the issues in the wider context will remain significant in the longer term. This includes facilitating the sustainable development in the region, which may lead to an agreement between Romania and Ukraine and/or to finding alternatives to the BCP or to utilizing the Bystroe Canal with some damage-control measures as a deep-sea waterway. In this context, the on-going sub-basin initiatives of the Danube Delta, facilitated by the ICPDR, may produce some constructive dialogue between the Parties. Moreover, co-operation

---

103 It might be argued that the suspension of rights or privileges referred to under the Aahrus Convention may be useful. However, its effectiveness should be questioned due to the unclear meaning of suspension of privileges and to negative results of suspension of rights, which may in fact result in exempting the party concerned from the regulation by the Convention, etc. See Koester 2007, 211–213.

104 Judicial or arbitral means, which traditionally premise a bilateral relations between the parties concerned, may be useful for settling an environmental dispute, which has a bilateral element, in marked contrast to less-use in that of solely a multilateral character. Bothe 2006, 256–257.

105 Under the Aahrus, Espoo and Ramsar Conventions a bilateral agreement between the parties concerned is required, while, it is not, under the Bern and DRP Convention. Under the latter MEAs, however, general obligations to take due regards tend to be at the central issues of the conflict.

106 It should be noted in this context that the second Bern site-visit of 2008 was joined by both DG Environment and DG Transportation of the European Commission. Ramsar Convention 2008, 6.

with navigation sectors for the sustainable development would be useful.[107] This is a method of making use of positive incentives on issues of high priorities for the parties. In this context international support to the current developments in this direction should be continued and, if possible, extended at various levels. The work of NGOs should also be noted in this regard as a useful means. The WWF, for instance, is opening a dialogue with the Government of Ukraine based on its aforementioned study for identifying alternatives to the BCP.[108]

Lessons Learnt from the Management Processes of the Danube Delta Conflict

Usefulness and Limits of Interactive Dialogue

It should be useful to combine the following methods, depending on the nature of the subject matter and obstacles to implementation.[109]

First, fact-finding mechanisms, which are one of the traditional means for settlement of international disputes,[110] may be useful not only for clarifying relevant facts but also for suggesting measures to be taken by recommendation, provided their structures sufficiently reflect peculiarities of environmental problems, for example, involvement of scientific or technical experts. The latter function is similar to that of mediation, promoting the conformity of the actions in question with the purpose of the relevant MEA.

Second, the method of interactive dialogue, constituted by fact-finding, persuasion through multilateral consultation facilitated by international assistance, may be useful, to a certain extent, under certain specific conditions. This is consistent with current developments in international environmental law. It is argued that traditional methods for implementing international agreements, such as the suspension or termination of treaties in the case of their serious breach, application of law of State responsibility and taking counter-measures, are less useful due to the peculiarities of the contemporary environmental problems. Instead, various institutionalized mechanisms, such as continuous supervision by standing organs

107 There has been significant progress, including an international workshop of January 2009. See 'Proceedings of the Meeting on the Follow-up of the Joint Statement on Inland Navigation and Environmental Sustainability in the Danube River Basin at the Danube Commission, Budapest, 29–30 January 2009'.

108 See note 87 above.

109 In this sense the notion of the compliance continuum suggested by Brunnée provides us with useful tools for analysis. Brunnée 2006, 387–408.

110 Merrills 2005, 45–63.

based on report, monitoring, inspection, non-compliance procedures, etc., tend to be utilized under MEAs[111] These mechanisms aim at ensuring the conformity of an action by contracting parties with MEAs by requesting them to take appropriate measures with assistance, as necessary, for achieving the purposes of the MEA concerned.[112]

Third, under certain circumstances some other supplementary methods, either coercive or non-coercive, may, however, be needed for overcoming the limits of interactive dialogue. It may be useful to make use of negative incentives or positive incentives on issues of high priority for the parties concerned when there is a lack of will on the part of State parties. They typically include: imposing sanctions, taking judicial means, particularly where there exists a bilateral element in the issues, and linking the issue concerned with other matters of high priorities for the Parties concerned.

Active Roles of NGOs

These days NGOs are becoming more and more involved with the implementation of MEAs.[113] Global MEAs tend to institutionalize some kind of public involvement in general,[114] while this tendency is much more noticeable in European MEAs as already mentioned. The Danube Delta conflict suggest three points pertinent to the current increase of such involvement.

First, NGOs may contribute to ensuring the legitimacy and effectiveness of the implementation of MEAs. This is due to their functions already mentioned. Second, such roles may be strengthened by the formal involvement of NGOs with processes of institutionalized mechanisms for ensuring implementation. This is contrasted with their traditional position where they held no legal status under conventions, and, therefore, only concerned themselves with factual assessments regarding their implementation.

Moreover, the active role of NGOs may be realized when the involvement of a particular NGO with the processes is procedurally and substantially legitimate. We may here overcome criticisms that there should be problems of representativeness, systematic control, efficiency, etc. in the active involvement of NGOs.[115] Procedural

111 Bothe 1996, 12–38. This has been emphasized by the so-called managerial school, such as Chayes and Chayes 1995.

112 In these mechanisms, except for non-compliance procedures, the decision on breach of treaty obligations is not always made in each case. The policy-oriented character of these mechanisms, however, may result in decisions or measures adopted of which legal implications are not always very clear. We may find an example in the Espoo process concerning the Danube Delta conflict. See Koyano 2008, 306–307.

113 See for instance Yamin: 2001, 149–153.

114 E.g., art. 3(3) and (6) of the Annex I, Protocol on Environmental Protection to the Antarctic Treaty; Procedures and Mechanisms relating to compliance under the Kyoto Protocol (Decision 27/CMP.1); art. 23 of the Convention on Biodiversity.

115 Epiney 2006, 337.

legitimacy may be ensured where the NGO concerned is subject to appropriate procedural controls by clear rules under the MEA concerned. On the other hand, substantial legitimacy means that the involvement of the particular NGO in question contributes to the effective implementation of the MEA. Two conditions need to be fulfilled. One is the institutionalization of appropriate channels under the MEA, and the other, the goodwill and ability of the NGO in question.

Coordination Between Overlapping or Conflicting MEAs

Problems of overlap or conflict between different international environmental agreements have been raised on various occasions in recent years.[116] Two factors underlie their distinctiveness in the field of the environment. One is the rapid increase of MEAs. Overlap or conflict between them may easily occur unless adequate attention is paid in their preparation or operation. Particularly, overlap tends to increase in terms of procedural requirements, for MEAs introducing procedural regulations have increased significantly in recent times.[117] Another factor is the multi-dimensional character of environmental problems.[118] One environmental problem or environmentally harmful activity may be subject to multiple MEAs from different angles.

Such problems may impede the effective implementation of MEAs. Overlap may obstruct the effective use of limited resources. Moreover, conflicting measures or actions between different MEAs on the same issue may virtually hinder its effective management with each other. In addition, problems of competing decisions may be serious when conflicting decisions are made on the same issue by judicial organs between different MEAs. There may be forum-shopping problems as well.[119] Furthermore, conflict may cause a more serious situation. Conflicting requirements should severely injure the normativity of the MEAs concerned.

Therefore, some kind of coordination is needed. In general two approaches are useful. One is to make use of mechanisms in law of treaties, including application of relevant provisions of the Vienna Convention on the Law of Treaties and the insertion of relevant provisions into MEAs. The other is to utilize mechanisms for co-operation or coordination between MEAs or international institutions.[120]

Management of the Danube Delta conflict provides a precedent for the latter approach. This suggests that problems of overlap may be avoided to a certain

116 As to these problems, see for instance: Romano 2007.

117 Koyano 2006, 51–59, 73–102 and 132–161.

118 Wolfrum and Matz 2003, 4–6.

119 Problems of competing jurisdiction occurred concerning the MOX plant conflict between Ireland and the UK. As to the problems of the conflict, Romano 2007, 1047–1050; Churchill 2004, etc. Also, see the Southern Bluefin Tuna case between Australia and New Zealand and Japan. '*Southern Bluefin Tuna Case, Australia and New Zealand v Japan*, Award on Jurisdiction and Admissibility, 4 August 2000'.

120 On this approach see for instance: Wolfrum and Matz 2003, 119–204.

extent and that overlap may rather produce complementary interaction between multiple processes where co-operative mechanisms well function between MEAs or the institutions concerned. It is also suggested that NGOs may take certain positive roles for promoting the coordination between activities of the institutions. Thus, overlap does not always necessarily impede the effective implementation of MEAs but may contribute to it to some extent on certain conditions.

However, there are limits to such practical coordination. This is no more than factual. Therefore, such coordination is not always initiated nor achieved, or it might not be maintained even if it is once established. It depends on the circumstances. As already mentioned, there should be certain factors underlying the successful coordination, notably non-conflict in contents between the MEAs, the use of interactive dialogue as a common method of ensuring their implementation, the existence of institutions coordinating interaction, etc.[121] Moreover, the difficult problems aforementioned might be caused if a party takes judicial measures, such as bringing the case to court.

Conclusion

MEAs aim at protecting public interests for the international community, and, thus they have a public nature. However, there are two difficult problems in their implementation in the international community constituted by autonomous sovereign States. The first problem is how to ensure the effective implementation of each MEA. We are here confronted with two difficulties. One is how to ensure the compliance with the MEA, and the other comes from the fact that only ensuring compliance with it is not always enough to achieve its purposes.[122] The second problem is how to ensure consistency and integrity in the implementation of MEAs as a whole, i.e. how to manage conflict or overlap between different MEAs with a public nature.

These two problems are interlinked with one another. The more each MEA becomes self-contained with precise and well-elaborated mechanisms for ensuring its implementation, the more the second problems may occur. On the other hand, the more the consistency and integrity between various MEAs are pursued, the less the implementation may be ensured for each of the MEAs, which shall deal with various kinds of multi-dimensional environmental problems, in the decentralized international community. This can be characterized as a dilemma of contemporary MEAs.

Such problems have appeared in the Danube Delta conflict. The coordination between different MEAs has practically been achieved to a certain extent in

121 Such limits can be seen in both the decline of joint/co-operative commitments by the institutions concerned in 2007 and its recent revival already mentioned.

122 As to discussions on the notion of effectiveness in international law, see the Introduction of this book.

the use of the method of interactive dialogue. After many twists and turns, we have seen some provisional signs of enhanced management of the conflict and of ensuring the effectiveness of the MEAs concerned. However, we still find uncertainties in the future direction of the management processes. How can we achieve a comprehensive and lasting solution in a consistent and integrated way? The management of the Danube Delta conflict is certain to be a touchstone in this context.

References

Books, Articles and Chapters in Books

Beyerlin, U., Stoll, P.T. and Wolfrum, R. (eds) (2006), *Ensuring Compliance with Multilateral Environmental Agreements: A Dialogue between Practitioners and Academia* (Leiden: Martinus Nijhoff Publishers).

Bodansky, D., Brunée, J. and Hey, E. (eds) (2007), *The Oxford Handbook of International Environmental Law* (Oxford: Oxford University Press).

Bothe, M. (1996), 'The Evaluation of Enforcement Mechanisms in International Environmental Law: An Overview', in Wolfrum (ed.).

Bothe, M. (2006), 'Ensuring Compliance with Multilateral Agreements: Systems of Inspection and External Monitoring', in Beyerlin, Stoll and Wolfrum (eds).

Brunnée, J. (2006), 'Multilateral Environmental Agreements and the Compliance Continuum', in Winter (ed.).

Chayes, A. and Chayes, A.H. (1995), *The New Sovereignty: Compliance with International Regulatory Agreements* (Cambridge: MIT Press).

Churchill, R. (2004), 'The MOX Plant Litigation: The First Half-Life', *International and Comparative Law Quarterly* 52, 643–676.

Ebbesson, J. (2007), 'Public Participation', in Bodansky, Brunée and Hey (eds).

Dinescu, C. (2006), 'The Process of Revision of the Belgrade Convention of 1948 regarding the Regime of Navigation on the Danube', *Romanian Journal of International Law 3*, 175–179.

Epiney, A. (2006), 'The Role of NGOs in the Process of Ensuring Compliance with MEAs', in Beyerlin, Stoll and Wolfrum (eds).

Koester, V. (2007), 'The Convention on Access to Information, Public Participation in Decision-making and Access to Justice in Environmental Matters (ECE Aarhus Convention)', in Ulfstein (ed.).

Koyano, M. (2006), *Kokusai kankyouho niokeru Jizenkyougiseido: Shikkoushudan toshiteno Kinou no Tenkai* (Prior Consultation Procedures in International Environmental Law: The Evolution as an Implementation Process of Legal Institutions), (Tokyo: Yushindou Koubunsha).

Koyano, M. (2008), 'The Significance of the Convention on Environmental Impact Assessment in a Transboundary Context (Espoo Convention) in International

Environmental Law: Examining the Implications of the Danube Delta Case', *Impact Assessment and Project Appraisal* 26:4, 299–314.

Kuzio, T. (2003a), 'EU and Ukraine: A Turning Point in 2004?', Occasional Papers 47, *European Union Institute for Security Studies* [Website], <http://aei.pitt.edu/1611/01/occ47.pdf> accessed 22 June 2009.

Kuzio, T. (2003b), 'Ukraine's Relations with the West: Disinterest, Partnership, Disillusionment', *European Security* 12:2.

Melen, O (2004), Enforcement of Law in Danube Delta, in Eco-Tiras, *Integrated Management of Natural Resources in the Transboundary Dniester River Basin, Proceedings of the International Conference, Chisinau, Moldova, September 16-17 2004*. (A copy was given by its author.)

Merrills, J.G. (2005), *International Dispute Settlement, 4th ed.* (Cambridge: Cambridge University Press).

Romano, C.P.R. (2007), 'International Dispute Settlement', in Bodansky, Brunée and Hey (eds).

Ulfstein, G. (ed.) (2007), *Making Treaties Work: Human Rights, Environment and Arms Control* (Cambridge: Cambridge University Press).

Winter, G. (ed.) (2006), *Multilateral Governance of Global Environmental Change: Perspectives from Science, Sociology and the Law* (Cambridge: Cambridge University Press).

Wolfrum, R. (ed.) (1996), *Enforcing Environmental Standards: Economic Mechanism as Viable Means?* (Berlin: Springer).

Wolfrum, R. and Matz, N. (2003), *Conflict in International Environmental Law* (Berlin: Springer).

Yamin, F. (2001), 'NGOs and International Environmental Law: A Critical Evaluation of their Roles and Responsibilities', *Review of European Community and International Environmental Law Review* 10:2, 1037–1056.

Official Documents and Others

Documents of inter-governmental institutions referred to in this chapter, such as reports of COPs, MOPs, commissions, etc. of conventions or other international instruments, are not included in the following list, except for those released without official classification number, due to the space constraints. Their official classification number is cited in footnotes.

'Biosphere Reserve Information: Romania/Ukraine: Danube Delta', *UNESCO* [Website],<http://www.unesco.org/mabdb/br/brdir/directory/biores.asp?code=ROM-UKR+01&mode=all>.

'Conference Conclusion', *International Conference, Conservation and Sustainable Development of the Danube Delta* [Website], <http://www.ramsar.org/mtg/mtg_danube_conference2006a.pdf>.

EPL (2002–2003), *Biennial Report 2002–2003*, Lviv: Ukraine.

EPL (2004), *EPL Annual Report 2004*, Lviv: Ukraine.

Espoo Inquiry Commission 2006, *Report on the Likely Significant Adverse Transboundary Impacts of the Danube–Black Sea Navigation Route at the Border of Romania and Ukraine, June, 2006*, UNECE [Website], <http://www.unece.org/env/eia/documents/inquiry/Final%20Report%2010%20July%202006.pdf>.

European Commission (2004), *Joint Mission of the Expert Team of the European Commission and International Conventions to the 'Bystroe project' in the Ukrainian Part of the Danube Delta (6–8 October 2004)*, *European Commission* [Website], <http://ec.europa.eu/environment/enlarg/bystroe_project_en.htm>.

'Factsheet, Bottleneck: Romania, Project: ISPA', WWF [Website], <http://assets.panda.org/downloads/romania_factsheet_en.pdf>.

Government of Ukraine (2008), *Report of the Government of Ukraine on the Implementation of Decision IV/2 of Parties to the Convention on Environmental Impact Assessment in a Transboundary Context (Espoo Convention) Adopted on the 4th Meeting of Parties to the Convention held on 19–21st May, 2008 in Bucharest*, Kyiv: Ukraine, *UNECE* [Website], <http://www.unece.org/env/eia/documents/ImplementationCommittee/Report_of_Ukraine_Danube-Black%20Sea_Oct08_main.pdf>.

'International workshop "Information Assessment Managment on Water Resources in the Danube Delta"', *Centre for Regional Studies* [Website], http://crs.ua/en/events/carrent/izo.html.

Ministry of Foreign Affairs of Ukraine (2008), *Note Verbale Transmitting 'The Final Decision Taken by Ukraine Concerning the Full-scale Implementation of the Danube–Black Sea Navigation Route Project in the Ukrainian Part of the Danube Delta'* (addressed to the Ministry of Foreign Affairs of Romania on 17 January 2008). (A copy was obtained by the author at the WWF).

Moderator's Summary of the Informal International Consultation on the Bystroe Canal, Ukraine, UNEP International Environmental House, Geneva, 21 September 2004. (A copy was given by the staff of the Secretariat of the ECE Aahrus Convention).

'News, WWF Welcomes International Fact-finding Mission to the Ukrainian Danube Delta, 14 Oct 2004', *WWF* [Website], <http://www.panda.org/what_we_do/where_we_work/danube_carpathian/news/?15822>.

'News, Ukraine Opens Bystroye Canal through Danube Delta, 16 May 2007', WWF [Website], <http://www.panda.org/what_we_do/where_we_work/danube_carpathian/news/?102720>.

'News, Growing Concern as Danube Modification Projects Move Forward, 04 Jan 2008', WWF [Website], <http://www.panda.org/what_we_do/where_we_work/danube_carpathian/news/?120860>.

'Proceedings of the Meeting on the Follow-up of the Joint Statement on Inland Navigation and Environmental Sustainability in the Danube River Basin at the Danube Commission, Budapest, January 29–30, 2009'. (A copy was obtained by the author at the ICPDR Secretariat.)

'Process: Navigation and Ecology, Joint Statement on Inland Navigation and Environmental Sustainability', *ICPDR* [Website], <http://www.icpdr.org/icpdr-pages/navigation_and_ecology_process.htm>.

Ramsar Convention (2005), 'Follow Up to Ramsar Advisory Mission 53: Danube Delta/Kyliiske Mouth Ramsar Site, Ukraine, Mission of 26–29 April 2005', *Ramsar Convention* [Website], <http://www,ramsar.org/ram_rpt_53 e_update.htm>.

Ramsar Convention (2008), 'Navigation and Wetlands: Follow Up to Ramsar Advisory Mission 53, Danube Delta/Kyliiske Mouth Ramsar Site, Ukraine, Mission of 28–31 July 2008', *Ramsar Convention* [Website], < http://www.ramsar.org/ram/ram_rpt_53e_update2008.htm >.

Ramsar/UNESCO (2003), 'UNESCO (Man and Biosphere Programme) and Ramsar Convention Mission Report: Danube Biosphere Reserve/Kyliiske Mouth Ramsar Site, Ukraine, 27–31 October 2003', *Ramsar Convention* [Website], <http://www.ramsar.org/ram/ram_rpt_53e.htm>.

'Resolution X.13: The status of sites in the Ramsar List of Wetlands of International Importance', 10th Meeting of the Conference of the Parties to the Convention on Wetlands (Ramsar, Iran, 1971), *Ramsar Convention* [Website], < http://www.ramsar.org/res/key_res_x_13_e.pdf>.

'Resolution IX.15 on the status of sites in the Ramsar List of Wetlands of International Importance', 9th Meeting of the Conference of the Parties to the Convention on Wetlands (Ramsar, Iran, 1971), *Ramsar Convention* [Website], < http://www.ramsar.org/res/key_res_ix_15_e.htm>.

'Southern Bluefin Tuna Case, Australia and New Zealand v. Japan, Award on Jurisdiction and Admissibility, August 4, 2000', *International Legal Materials* 39, 1359.

'The Danube: Facts and Figures', *EC* [Website], <http://ec.europa.eu/environment/enlarg/danubefactsfigures_eu.htm>.

'Towards a River Basin Management Plan for the Danube Delta supporting sustainable development of the region: Memorandum of Understanding between the Governments of Moldova, Romania and Ukraine' (a copy was obtained by the author at the ICPDR Secretariat).

UNESCO (2004), *Five Transboundary Biosphere Reserves in Europe, Biosphere Reserves, Technical Notes* (Paris).

UNECE (2008), *Background Note: Overview of Activities Addressing the Bystroe Canal Project under Multilateral Environmental Agreements and by Intergovernmental Organizations, 9 May 2008* (a copy was delivered by the Espoo Secretariat at the 4th MOP).

WWF (2009), *Information Document: 'Bystroe Canal'/Danube–Black Sea Deep Navigation Channel*, March 2009 (a copy was obtained by the author at the WWF Danube-Carpathian Programme).

'XVII.) Vinskyi forecasts opening of Danube-Black Sea Canal by 2009', *Ukrainian News Agency* (published online 24 January 2008) <http://www.ukranews.com/eng/article/96214.html> (home page).

Chapter 11

The Principle of Complementarity in Reality: Who Actually Applies It and in What Way under the ICC System?

Shuichi Furuya

Introduction

In trying persons responsible for serious violations of international humanitarian law, we may have two options. The first is that any State, in whose territory the violations took place, whose nationality the persons have, or even in whose territory the persons were just found, exercises its own criminal jurisdiction and tries them in accordance with its national legislation. The second is that any international criminal judiciary directly tries the persons with the cooperation of the States concerned relating to the arrest and surrender, taking and production of evidence, execution of searches and seizures, and so on. While the former reflects the decentralized social structure of traditional inter-state relations, the latter embodies a newly born and more centralized mechanism which is intended to realize the interest of the international community as a whole.

However, the experiences of some international criminal judiciaries established after the end of Cold War, like the International Criminal Tribunal for the former Yugoslavia (ICTY), the International Criminal Tribunal for Rwanda (ICTR), and the International Criminal Court (ICC), demonstrate that the emergence of an international judicial mechanism does not necessarily lead to the demise of decentralized adjudication by States. On the contrary, the international criminal judiciaries have been and are developing with the encouragement of trials by national courts. Take the preamble of the Rome Statute of ICC for example. It reads: 'the most serious crimes of concern to the international community as a whole must not go unpunished and [...] their effective prosecution must ensured by taking measures at the national level and by enhancing international cooperation',[1] and it goes on to declare that 'it is the duty of every State to exercise its criminal jurisdiction over those responsible for international crimes'.[2] While it is disputable whether the 'duty' means a legal obligation in a strict sense, it is apparent that the Rome Statute does not deny the exercise by States of their own national

1 Preamble of the Rome Statute, paragraph 5.

2 Preamble, paragraph 7.

jurisdiction over those who may also be subject to the jurisdiction of the ICC, but rather encourages it.

One of the reasons for this is the limited material and human resources of which the international criminal judiciaries can make use. As international criminal trials are more costly and time-consuming than national ones, it is unfavorable and even impossible for the international criminal judiciaries to conduct all the trials of those responsible for international crimes. In light of an effective use of those limited resources, a kind of division of roles between international and national judiciaries is indispensable. This is why the general interest of the international community in not leaving those responsible for international crimes unpunished does not lead directly to the monopoly of jurisdiction by the international criminal judiciaries. Rather, a well-suited cooperation between international and national jurisdictions may realize that general interest more effectively.

The duality of international and national jurisdictions is institutionalized as the system of concurrent jurisdiction,[3] under which an international judiciary and national courts of the States concerned may concomitantly have jurisdiction over a case. Thus essential is a rule that may properly determine which court, international or national, should deal with a case. Otherwise, conflicting exercises of international and national jurisdictions would disturb the proper balance between the general interest that an international criminal judiciary intends to realize on one hand, and effective and efficient use of limited resources of the international community on the other.

This chapter aims to explore the principle of complementarity of the ICC system as one of the rules determining the allocation of cases between international and national jurisdictions. As the preamble and Article 1 of the Rome Statute show, the principle of complementarity is one of the underlying rules governing the relationship of the ICC with national courts. However, it cannot be denied that the research so far on the principle has focused on the interpretation of relevant provisions, particularly the notions of 'unwillingness' and 'inability' in Article 17 which indicate the intent and capability of the State concerned in carrying out an investigation and prosecution instead of the ICC. It is true that the 'unwillingness' and 'inability' of the State concerned are important factors to be taken into account in determining the allocation of cases between the ICC and national courts. It is also true, however, that the research so far has lacked a broader and more dynamic perspective by over-emphasizing these two notions as the admissibility tests.

Past research has been limited in scope in the sense that it has not necessarily paid attention to other notions relevant to the application of complementarity, such as the 'sufficient gravity' of the case (Article 17 (1)(d)) and the 'interest of justice'

3 *Ex.* ICTY Statute Article 9 (1), ICTY Statute Article 8 (1), Statute for the Special Court for Sierra Leone Article 8 (1). In contrast, the Rome Statute does not refer explicitly to the concurrent jurisdiction. However, judging from Article 19 that endows a State having jurisdiction over a case with a right to challenge the jurisdiction of the ICC, it is evident that the ICC is also based on the same system.

(Article 53 (1)(c) and (2)(c)). Even if some research has considered these points, it mainly relied on the interpretation of the Rome Statute and the Rules of Procedure and Evidence (RPE), including the preparatory works for these documents. In this connection, it was also quite static in that it had not considered who actually applies the principle and in what stage of the whole proceedings of the ICC.

However, since the actuality of the complementarity is in the tangible and dynamic process of the ICC, this chapter attempts to explore the ICC's practice on the principle of complementarity, and to illustrate the significance and problems of that principle in reality. For this purpose, this chapter will first consider the principle on the Statute and RPE, which may serve to clarify the dynamism of the principle in reality, which will be dealt with in the later part.

Screening Processes of Complementarity

Three Levels of Screening

Generally the issue of whether a situation or a case can be, or should be, dealt with by an international criminal judiciary is determined through three levels of screening: (1) jurisdiction, (2) admissibility and (3) judicial propriety.

In terms of jurisdiction, it is commonly understood that, in light of its possible caseload, an international criminal judiciary confines its subject-matter jurisdiction to the violations of certain 'seriousness' or 'gravity'. Article 5 of the Rome Statute, for example, limits the jurisdiction of the ICC to 'the most serious crimes of concern to the international community as a whole'. Thus, if a crime does not have the nature of such seriousness, it could be allocated to national courts instead of the ICC. In this regard, the limitations imposed on the jurisdiction constitute screening factors to be evaluated in determining the allocation of cases in light of the principle of complementarity.[4]

At the level of admissibility, a case is screened as to whether the ICC may actually exercise its jurisdiction over a crime which falls under the subject-matter jurisdiction of the ICC. Pursuant to Article 17, the ICC is required to rule a case inadmissible when the case has been or is being appropriately dealt with in national

4 Some point out that the principle does not affect the existence of jurisdiction of the ICC, but regulates when this jurisdiction may be exercised by the ICC (Benzing 2003), 594.). This remark is correct in the sense that the principle works *mainly* at the level of admissibility, which is involved in the exercise of jurisdiction. However, this does not mean that the principle is irrelevant to the existence of jurisdiction at all. In fact, the basic idea of the principle was taken into consideration when the framework of the subject-matter jurisdictions of the ICC were constituted, and the principle itself does and will function when the Prosecutor or Chambers interpret the relevant provisions on the jurisdiction. See also Crawford 2003, 147.

criminal proceedings,[5] or when it is not of sufficient gravity to justify the action by the ICC.

Judicial propriety at the third level of screening concerns the issue of whether it is appropriate for the ICC to deal with a situation or a case in light of its status of international judiciary. If the Prosecutor or a Chamber considers it inappropriate to initiate an investigation or prosecution of a case, that case will be left to the national proceedings of any State. In contrast with the tests of jurisdiction and admissibility, which impose *legal* limitations on the power of the ICC, the decision on judicial propriety belongs to the discretion of the ICC, particularly that of the Prosecutor. At this level, it is most crucial whether the prosecution of the case is in the interest of justice.

While these three levels are independent of each other in theory, the decisions of these levels are made more than once in the multi-stage screening process. In addition, substantive factors to be taken into account at each level are overlapping to a certain extent.

Three Stages of the Screening Process

Pursuant to the relevant provisions of the Rome Statute, the screening process in the ICC can be classified into three stages: the preliminary examination stage, the investigation stage and the post-indictment and trial stage.

Preliminary Examination Stage Preliminary examination occurs prior to an official investigation. At this stage, the Prosecutor explores whether the information made available provides for sufficient factual and legal grounds for initiating an official investigation.[6] In this process, the Prosecutor evaluates the information in the light of factors enumerated in Article 53 (1), and determines whether there is a reasonable basis to proceed with an investigation. Article 53 (1) requests the Prosecutor to consider whether: (a) the information provides a reasonable basis to believe that a crime within the jurisdiction of the ICC has been or is being committed; (b) the case is or would be admissible under Article 17 and (c) taking into account the gravity of the crime and the interest of victims, there are substantial reasons to believe that an investigation would not serve the interests of justice. To be noted here is the fact that, even at this stage, all levels of

5 Schabas 2004, 85.

6 As the term 'preliminary examination' is used only in Article 15 (6), this originally means the pre-stage of the investigation *proprio motu* by the Prosecutor. However, as all kinds of information submitted to the Prosecutor, including that submitted by the Security Council and by the States Parties, is to be evaluated as to whether it can be sufficient grounds for investigation, one can recognize the stage of preliminary examination regardless of the information sources. The Office of the Prosecutor describes the examination at this stage as 'analysis'. See Letter from the Prosecutor 2004; Letter from the Prosecutor 2005.

screening, namely jurisdiction, admissibility and judicial propriety, are required to be conducted by the Prosecutor.

If the Prosecutor concludes, after the preliminary examination, that the information provided does not constitute a reasonable basis for an investigation, he shall inform those who provided the information.[7] Further, the decision of the Prosecutor not to initiate the investigation may be reviewed by the Pre-Trial Chamber, on request of the State Party or the Security Council if they referred the situation under Article 13 (a) or (b) (Article 53(3) (a)). The Pre-Trial Chamber may, on its own initiative, review the decision of the Prosecutor if it is solely based on the factors of 'interest of justice' (Article 53(3) (b)). Accordingly, when the Prosecutor decides not to initiate an investigation in light of the factors set out in Article 53 (1), the Pre-Trial Chamber may be given an opportunity to re-evaluate the information pursuant to the same factors in Article 53 (1). If the Pre-Trial Chamber does not confirm the decision by the Prosecutor, the Prosecutor is obliged to proceed with the investigation in accordance with the decision by the Pre-Trial Chamber (Rule 110 (2)). The possibility of judicial review on the decision by the Prosecutor is intended to reduce as much as possible the risk that an investigation may be unduly omitted, and to avoid arbitrary and non-transparent choices in the prosecutorial determinations on criminal action.[8]

If the Prosecutor decides, on the other hand, that there is a reasonable basis to proceed with an investigation, he may immediately initiate investigation if the situation in question was referred to by the State Party or the Security Council. In the case of investigation *proprio motu*, on the other hand, the Prosecutor shall submit to the Pre-Trial Chamber a request for authorization of an investigation (Article 15 (3)). The Pre-Chamber again have a chance to evaluate the decision by the Prosecutor in light of the factors of Article 53 (1). Without the authorization of the Pre-Trial Chamber, the Prosecutor cannot proceed to an investigation.

Investigation Stage In the investigation stage, the Prosecutor attempts to identify individual cases in the situation referred to him, and to evaluate the information provided or collected in the preliminary examination stage whether there is a sufficient basis to initiate prosecution of alleged perpetrators. In the case of referral by the State Party or an investigation *proprio motu* by the Prosecutor, however, the Prosecutor shall notify all States Parties and other States which would normally exercise jurisdiction over the crimes in question. According to Article 18 (2), a State, within one month of receipt of that notification, may inform that it is investigating

7 Article 15 (6) prescribes merely the information provided for an investigation *proprio motu* by the Prosecutor. Under Rule 105 of the RPE, however, the same rule is applied to the information referred to by the State Party and the Security Council. In addition, while Article 15 (6) requires the Prosecutor to inform just his conclusion not to initiate an investigation, Rule 105 dictates him to notify the reason for the conclusion as well. See, e.g., Iraq Response 2006; Venezuela Response 2006.

8 Turone 2002, 1156–1157.

or has investigated the crimes in question and request that the Prosecutor shall defer to the State's investigation of the crimes[9] unless the Pre-Trial Chamber, on the request of the Prosecutor, decides to authorize the investigation. In deciding this, the Pre-Trial Chamber evaluates whether the State requesting the deferral is willing and able genuinely to carry out the investigation or prosecution on the basis of the parameters of Article 17(2). If the case is found to be inadmissible, it would be deferred to national judicial proceedings of the State concerned.

The Prosecutor proceeds to an investigation, if no request of deferral is made by the State concerned or the Pre-Trail Chamber authorizes the Prosecutor to do it. At the end of investigation, the Prosecutor is obliged to conclude whether there is a sufficient basis for a prosecution. In making this decision, the Prosecutor may evaluate the information gathered by the investigation from the three factors: (a) there is sufficient legal or factual basis to seek a warrant or summons for the alleged perpetrator; (b) the case is admissible under Article 17 and (c) a prosecution is in the interest of justice, taking into account all the circumstances, including the gravity of the crime, the interests of victims and the age or infirmity of the alleged perpetrator, and his or her role in the alleged crime (Article 53 (2)). Accordingly, at this stage again, all levels of screening are to be conducted by the Prosecutor.

If the Prosecutor decides that there is not a sufficient basis for a prosecutor, he shall inform the Pre-Trial Chamber and the State Party or the Security Council, if either making a referral, of his conclusion and the reason of it. This decision may also be subject to the review by the Pre-Trial Chamber, in the process of which the Chamber reevaluates the decision not to proceed with a prosecution in light of the same factors of Article 53 (2). Just as in the preliminary examination stage, if the Pre-Trial Chamber does not confirm the decision by the Prosecutor, the Prosecutor is obliged to proceed with the prosecution (Rule 110 (2)).

Post-indictment and Trial Stage In this stage, a challenge to the jurisdiction and admissibility may be made by: (a) an accused or a person for whom a warrant of arrest or a summons to appear has been issued; (b) a State alleging that it is investigating or prosecuting the case in question or has investigated or prosecuted or (c) a State from which acceptance of jurisdiction is required under Article 12. The challenges may be raised prior to or at the commencement of the trial, but those to the admissibility of a case at the commencement of a trial may be permitted only on the basis of *non bis in idem* under Article 17 (1)(c). Thus, the allocation of cases between the ICC and national courts is to be determined, for the most part, before a trial starts. The challenges shall be referred to the Pre-Trial

9 In this regard, this process substantively constitutes a form of challenge to the admissibility. Holmes 2002, 682. Under the Rome Statute, however, this is not regarded as a challenge to the admissibility which can be raised only once by one State, and the request for deferral in Article 18 (2) does not preclude a future challenge under Article 19 (Article 18 (7)).

Chamber (prior to the confirmation of the charges) or to the Trial Chamber (after confirmation of the charge).

Characteristics of the Screening Process in the ICC

It is sometimes pointed out that the principle of complementarity under the ICC is an exact antithesis of the primacy under the ICTY/ICTR, in that while national jurisdiction prevails over international jurisdiction in the former, international jurisdiction does in the latter.[10] It is true that, under the principle of complementarity, a national court of the State concerned, not the ICC, may exercise its jurisdiction on the case in question, as far as that State is willing and able genuinely to carry out an investigation or prosecution.

As the foregoing analysis indicates, however, it is the organs of the ICC (mostly the Prosecutor and the Pre-Trial Chamber), not a national court, that decides the unwillingness or inability of that State at any stage of screening process. Further, the Prosecutor is endowed with the competence to review the deferral to a State's investigation at any time when there has been a significant change of circumstances based on the State's unwillingness or inability to carry out the investigation (Article 18 (3)), and to request the State concerned to inform him periodically of the progress of its investigation and any subsequent prosecution (Article 18 (5)). Therefore, as the competence of the ICC concerned, the description of complementarity that 'national jurisdiction prevails over international jurisdiction' is simplistic and even misleading.[11]

In addition, even in the ICTY/ICTR, certain criteria have been developing in order to allocate cases between them and national courts, and actually the ICTY/ICTR have decided if they deal with a case or refer to national judicial proceedings by taking into account the situation of national judicial system, the gravity of crimes in question, and so on.[12] In this respect, the framework of complementarity and that of primacy are basically similar with each other.

Of course, this does not necessarily mean that the two systems are completely identical. In the ICTY/ICTR, the allocation of cases is mostly determined at the discretion of the Prosecutor as a matter of judicial propriety. As there are few rules at the levels of jurisdiction and admissibility, the Prosecutor at any stage

10 Bos 1998, 259; Bergsmo and Triffterer 1999, 15.

11 See Olasolo 2005, 137.

12 Rule 11 *bis* of the ICTY's RPE, in determining whether to refer a case to the authorities of the State concerned, requires the Trial Chamber to consider the gravity of the crimes charged and the level of responsibility of the accused (paragraph (C)), and to be satisfied that accused will receive a fair trial and that the death penalty will not be imposed or carried out (paragraph (B)). For the cases that the Trial Chamber has admitted the referral to the national judicial proceedings, see *Prosecutor v Radovan Stankovic* 2005; *Prosecutor v Zeljko Mejakic, Momcilo Gruban, Dusan Fustar, Dusko Knezevic* 2005; *Prosecutor v Gojko Jankovic* 2005.

of the procedure may request the national court of State concerned to defer to the competence of the ICTY/ICTR.[13] On the other hand, the ICC gives greater importance to the allocation at the level of admissibility. Organs of the ICC including the Prosecutor are legally obliged to take into account the factors specified in the Rome Statute, and are not endowed with as wide a discretionary power as the Prosecutors of ICTY/ICTR are. This difference stems from the concern shared by many States at the negotiating process of the Rome Statute that, if the Prosecutor has a wide discretionary power, he might abuse his power and carry out a politically biased investigation and prosecution. This is the reason why the multi-stage screening process is adopted in the Rome Statute and the RPE, in which most of the decisions by the Prosecutor are basically subject to the review by the Pre-Trial Chamber. In other words, this process is intended to balance properly a functional and effective conduct of investigation and prosecution by the Prosecutor on one hand, and a need to restrict an arbitral use of his power on the other.

Substantive Tests under the Rome Statute

In the screening process, Article 53 requires the Prosecutor and the Pre-Trial Chamber, if it reviews the decision by the Prosecutor, to rely on the admissibility tests under Article 17 and the tests of interest of justice.

Tests under Article 17

Article 17 provides that the case is inadmissible where any of the following conditions is met: (a) the case is being investigated or prosecuted by a State which has jurisdiction over it; (b) the case has been investigated by a State which has jurisdiction over it and the State has decide not to prosecute the person concerned; (c) the person concerned has already been tried for conduct which is the subject of

13 The Statute of ICTY has no provision on the conditions for invoking its primacy over national courts, and leaves them to the RPE. Rule 9 of the RPE stipulates that the Prosecutor may propose to the Trial Chamber that a formal request be made that a national court defer to the competence of the ICTY, where it appears to the Prosecutor that in any such investigations or criminal proceedings instituted in the courts of any State: (i) the act being investigated is characterized as an ordinary crime; (ii) there is a lack of impartiality or independence, or the investigation or proceedings are designated to shield the accused from international criminal responsibility or (iii) what is in issue is clearly related to, or otherwise involves, significant factual or legal questions which may have implications for investigations or prosecutions before the Tribunal. All the requests of deferral so far made by the Prosecutor have been based on the condition (iii), which is so ambiguous and general that the Prosecutor substantively can apply it to any cases before national courts. For the application of Rule 9, see Jones and Powles 2003, 379–384.

the complaint, and a trial by the ICC is not permitted under Article 20 (3) or (d) the case is not of sufficient gravity to justify further action by the ICC.

Among these tests, tests (a), (b) and (c) address the national investigation and prosecution, and have common exceptions: the case is admissible if the State concerned is unwilling or unable genuinely to carry out the investigation or prosecution, or the decision not to prosecute or the criminal proceedings in that State resulted from the unwillingness or inability of the State genuinely to prosecute or try the person responsible for the crimes under the jurisdiction of the ICC. In this regard, it is important to clarify two points: (1) what proceedings can be regarded as an investigation, prosecution or trial under Article 17 (formal conditions of national proceedings), and (2) in what situations the investigation, prosecution or trial falls under the exceptions of unwillingness and inability (substantive conditions of national proceedings).

As the formal conditions of national proceedings, a case must at least be or have been subject to an investigation by relevant national authorities. However, it is disputable that the 'inaction' by the State concerned against a case leads automatically to the decision that the case is admissible. The reason why a State does not proceed with an investigation of a case is not necessarily confined to the instances of 'unwillingness' and 'inability'. For example, one can imagine a case where an investigation is interrupted because of a bar under national law, such as a statute of limitations, immunity or a grant of amnesty. Or there may be a case where a State gives up initiating an investigation, because national laws bearing on criminal responsibility define a scope of responsibility narrower that that provided for in the Rome Statute, and the crime in question is obviously outside of this scope.[14] Many scholars maintain that, as far as this 'inaction' does not correspond to the terms of Article 17 (1)(a) or (b), the case in question is to be admissible regardless of the reason for not initiating the investigation. On the other hand, some assert that the Prosecutor and the Pre-Trial Chamber should examine whether the 'inaction' took place because of the 'unwillingness' or 'inability'.[15]

It is true that the decision to give up an investigation because of a bar of national laws, such as the statute of limitations, is not substantively different from the decision of non-prosecution after having conducted the investigation formally. Pursuant to Article 17, however, the former is admissible, while the latter is inadmissible. This difference of result seems unreasonable. On the other hand, if the ICC allows every challenge to admissibility raised by the State concerned who did not initiate an investigation due to its national law, it would not serve an effective and efficient conduct of judicial proceedings. In addition, though the Rome Statute does not oblige the States Parties to ensure that its judicial authorities can investigate and prosecute ICC crimes, it also intends to give impetus for the States to make such changes by appealing to States' desires to protect their interests

14 Broomhall 2003, 91.

15 Benzing 2003, 601, note 50.

of exercising their own criminal jurisdiction.[16] Thus if a State Party fails to change its national law to respond to ICC crimes, this is equivalent to a prior acceptance that the ICC would instead exercise jurisdiction over the crimes. Accordingly, the 'inaction' should be found admissible simply because any investigation required under Article 17 has not taken place.

In terms of the substantive conditions of national proceedings, Article 17 requires the States Parties to ensure a genuine conduct of national proceedings. If a State is unwilling genuinely to carry out an investigation, prosecution and trial, the case could be subject to the proceedings of the ICC as it is admissible. Article 17 (2) provides for three parameters to decide the unwillingness: (a) the proceedings were or are being undertaken or the national decision was made for the purpose of shielding the person concerned from criminal responsibility; (b) there has been an unjustified delay in the proceedings which is inconsistent with an intent to bring the person concerned to justice; (c) the proceedings were not or are not being conducted independently or impartially, and they were or are not being conducted in a manner which is inconsistent with an intent to bring the person concerned to justice.

As to the inability, this is purported to respond to a so-called 'failed State', in which the governmental system has been collapsed, or social order has been in total chaos because of internal armed conflicts or natural disasters.[17] Article 17 (3) assumes the situation that the State is unable to obtain the accused or the necessary evidence and testimony, or otherwise unable to carry out its proceedings, due to a total or substantial collapse or unavailability of its judicial system.

In contrast to the tests set out in Article 17(1) (a), (b) and (c) which involve the nature of national judicial proceedings, the test of subparagraph (d) relates to the gravity of the crimes in question. As an objective test, the gravity test can apply to all cases, whether there have been national proceedings or not.[18] However, it is open to question what the term 'sufficient gravity' exactly means.

Article 5 confines the jurisdiction of the ICC to 'the most serious crimes of concern to the international community as a whole'. For this, a scholar maintains that the gravity test of subparagraph (d) is a logical conclusion from Article 5.[19] Following this view, once a crime is found to be within the jurisdiction of the ICC, it would mean that that crime automatically satisfies the gravity test under Article 17. If so understood, however, the gravity test does not make any sense as an independent test. Accordingly, it would be more rational to understand that the purpose of subparagraph (d) is to narrow down the cases that the ICC actually deals with by applying the gravity test to the situations where the most serious crimes, such as genocide, crimes against humanity and war crimes, have been committed. If following this understanding, the Rome Statute would have double

16 Dembowski 2003, 141–142.
17 Arsanjani 1999, 70.
18 Broomhall 2003, 89.
19 Williams 1999, 393.

filters in the gravity test; one concerns the subject-matter jurisdiction of the ICC, and the other involves admissibility. Even if a case can pass through the first filter, this does not lead to the automatic passing through the second filter. Further, it suggests that the second filter of gravity needs its own substantive parameters to decide whether a case is sufficient grave to be admissible. However, as neither the Rome Statute nor the RPE answers explicitly which view is correct, it is left to the subsequent practice of the ICC, particularly of the Prosecutor, which will be discussed in the next section.

Test of the Interest of Justice

If the Prosecutor decides that an investigation or prosecution of a case is inconsistent with the interest of justice, the case will be allocated to national jurisdiction. Though this decision basically belongs to the discretionary power of the Prosecutor, Article 53 provides for the factors to be taken into account: the gravity of the crimes in question and the interest of victims at the preliminary stage (paragraph 1 (c)); and the gravity of the crimes, the interest of victims and the age or infirmity of the alleged perpetrator, and his or her role in the alleged crime at the investigation stage (paragraph 2 (c)).

Therefore, the gravity of crimes as an element of the interest of justice is overlapped with the gravity test under Article 17. As far as the provisions of Article 53 concerned, the difference between these tests of gravity is not manifest. Theoretically, while the latter is a test for legal evaluation of admissibility to which an accused and a State having jurisdiction over the case concerned can make a challenge, the former is one of the factors for the Prosecutor to take into account in selecting cases suitable for his investigation and prosecution. However, the lines between them may blur at the preliminary examination and the investigation stages. On these stages, it is the Prosecutor that decides the gravity of crimes as an admissibility test and as a factor of the interest of justice. If he does not intend to clearly distinguish between a level of admissibility and that of judicial propriety in practice, no one could do it. This is also left to the practice of the ICC.

Complementarity in Practice

Self-referral and the Screening Process

As of writing this, four situations are under the investigation by the Prosecutor: Uganda, Democratic Republic of Congo (DRC), Central African Republic (CAR) and Darfur in Sudan. What is to be noted here is that all situations except Darfur were referred to the Prosecutor by the States where the alleged crimes were committed. As previously explained, the principle of complementarity assumes that, as the first principle, the State concerned should undertake an investigation and prosecution, and then, as an exception, the ICC may exercise jurisdiction only if that State is unwilling or unable genuinely to carry out its national proceedings. However, the governments of Uganda, DRC and CAR have intended to transfer their situations voluntarily to the ICC, instead of undertaking their own criminal proceedings from the very beginning.

According to the drafter of the Rome Statute, the referral by the State Party under Articles 13 (a) and 14 would be made by any State(s) other than the State where the crimes concerned were committed. On the other hand, there is no provision in the Rome Statute and the RPE which prohibits explicitly the State *locus criminis* from referring its own situation in which one or more of crimes within the jurisdiction of the ICC appears to have been committed. Moreover, as pointed out before, since the 'inaction' of a State which has jurisdiction over a case does not fall in any conditions stipulated in Article 17 (1), then the case is to be regarded admissible irrespective of the reasons for the inaction. Accordingly, there is no question that the self-referral by the State *locus criminis* is to be permitted.[20] However, this 'irregular' referral may make an impact on the screening process, and is likely to change the substance of the principle of complementarity.

Interestingly, before these self-referrals were actually made, the Prosecutor had suggested the possibilities in his so-called 'Policy paper' of 2003 that such a referral would take place. It reads as follows:

> There may be case where inaction by States is the appropriate course of action. For example, the Court and a territorial State incapacitated by mass crimes may agree that a consensual division of labour is the most logical and effective approach. Groups bitterly divided by conflict may oppose prosecutions at each others' hands and yet agree to a prosecution by a Court perceived as neutral and impartial. [...] In such cases there will be no question of 'unwillingness' or 'inability' under article 17.[21]

Presumably, three self-referrals were actual applications of 'a consensual division of labour' envisaged in the 'Policy paper'. However, it is to be noted that the self-referrals did not take place spontaneously due to the domestic circumstances of the States concerned.[22] Behind the referrals by the States, there were positive actions of the Prosecutor. In the Annex to the Policy paper (the Annex), the Prosecutor explained the necessity of his action to the State concerned as follows: In contrast to a national prosecutor who may be seen to prejudice his or her independence if contacts are made with the political authorities of the State, the Prosecutor of the ICC must enter into dialogue with heads of State and government and with other agencies of a State. He may have to have such meetings in order to receive referrals of situations, in order to discuss the modalities of cooperation with the Court, and in order to discuss prospects for a State's own authorities taking

20 Kress 2004, 946.

21 Paper on Some Policy Issues 2003, 4.

22 Gaeta 2004, 949.

proceedings themselves.[23] Later at the second public hearing in 2006, the Office of the Prosecutor explicitly admitted that the Prosecutor had adopted the policy of inviting voluntary referrals by territorial States as a first step.[24]

The policy suggested in these documents illustrates the image of the Prosecutor engaging vigorously in the 'diplomacy' with the States concerned. Being understood from the terms of Articles 14 and 42 (1), the Prosecutor is merely a passive receiver of referrals by the State Party and the Security Council. If he wants to investigate a certain case, they can initiate it *proprio motu* in accordance with Article 15. Then why does the Prosecutor have to contact the authorities of the State concerned? The Annex also explains the reason for this:

> Where the Prosecutor receives a referral from the State in which a crime has been committed, the Prosecutor has the advantage of knowing that that State has the political will to provide his Office with all the cooperation within the country that it is required to give under the Statute. Because the State, of its own volition, has requested the exercise of the Court's jurisdiction, the Prosecutor can be confident that the national authorities will assist the investigation, will accord the privileges and immunities necessary for the investigation, and will be anxious to provide if possible and appropriate the necessary level of protection to investigators and witnesses.[25]

Behind this policy, one can find an intrinsic defect of the complementary function of the ICC. As previously examined, the ICC deals with a case if the State concerned is unwilling or unable to carry out an investigation and prosecution. Once the ICC initiates its judicial proceedings, all the States Parties including that State concerned are obliged to cooperate fully with the ICC in its investigation and prosecution of the crimes in question. From a practical point of view, however, it cannot be easily anticipated that a State party, which is unwilling or unable to initiate its national proceedings of the crimes, would be willing or able to cooperate with the ICC in investigation and prosecution of those crimes. Even if a case is found to be admissible by a Pre-Trial or Trial Chamber, it does not ensure that the Prosecutor could fully enjoy the cooperation of the State concerned in his investigation and prosecution. This stems from an inherent mechanism of the ICC that, while the ICC itself has a centralized competence to conduct a prosecution and trial, it has to rely on the cooperation of the States Parties, particularly of the State *locus criminis*, in order to take measures to the suspects and accused that are not on the premise of the ICC. Without the cooperation of the State *locus criminis*, it would be extremely difficult for the Prosecutor to proceed with a prosecution and trial. This concern has led the Prosecutor to entering into dialogue with the State *locus criminis* in order to receive the referrals of situations.

---

23 Annex to the Paper on Some Policy Issues 2003, subparagraph I. D.

24 Office of the Prosecutor 2006, 3.

25 Annex to the Paper on Some Policy Issues 2003.

This prosecutorial strategy of seeking self-referral changes the substance of the screening process envisaged in the Rome Statute. In the practice of self-referral, it is quite unlikely that the State concerned would challenge the admissibility of a situation or a case in the investigation stage (Article 18 (2)) and the post-indictment and trial stage (Article 19 (2)). Further, the Prosecutor can skip the authorization by the Pre-Trial Chamber of his investigation, as the self-referral is a referral by a State Party, not an investigation *proprio motu*, even though the Prosecutor substantially takes an initiative. Accordingly, if the 'diplomacy' of the Prosecutor succeeds to receive a referral by the State *locus criminis*, he can pass through the tests of complementarity in the preliminary examination and the investigation stages on his own decision without the possible intervention by the Pre-Trial Chamber and the State concerned.

This is also applied to the post-indictment and trial stage, if an accused or a person for whom a warrant of arrest or a summons to appear has been issued does not challenge the admissibility of his or her case. Even if he or she raises a challenge to the admissibility, it is much less likely that his or her case would be found inadmissible, because the self-referring State did not initiate any national proceedings. As previously examined, 'inaction' does not fall in any conditions of Article 17 (1)(a)–(c) under which the ICC shall determine that a case is inadmissible.

As the result of the practice of self-referral, the Prosecutor may seize the initiative in applying the principle of complementarity in whole of the screening process. This overwhelming, if not exclusive, status of the Prosecutor in determining the issue of complementarity may shift a weighted consideration on the complementarity tests from the later stage to the earlier stage of the process, namely to the preliminary examination stage. In the case of self-referral, in fact, most crucial is the decision by the Prosecutor at the earliest stage of preliminary examination whether a situation could be admissible and the investigation of it would serve the interests of justice. From this viewpoint, one may say that it is the Prosecutor, not judges, who actually apply the principle of complementarity in the judicial proceedings of the ICC.

Self-referral and the Substantive Tests

Under the Rome Statute, 'unwillingness' and 'inability' are the main tests to be considered in determining whether the ICC can and should deal with a situation or a case. In self-referral, however, the 'unwillingness' and 'inability' tests may substantially become moot because a self-referring State has not initiated any national proceedings. The increasing practice of self-referral is, therefore, changing the weight of substantive tests in the screening process. In practice, the Prosecutor has been paying more attention to the gravity of crimes and the interests of justice.

As to the gravity test, the Prosecutor has explicitly admitted that this test is independent of the grave nature of the crimes falling within the subject-matter jurisdiction of the ICC. For example, the Prosecutor pointed out in the statement on the Iraq situation that 'while, in general sense, any crime within the jurisdiction of the Court is "grave", the Statute requires an additional threshold of gravity even where the subject-matter jurisdiction is satisfied'.[26] The Pre-Trial Chamber I followed this view in the case of Thomas Lubanga Dyilo.

> Concerning the second part of the admissibility test, the Chamber notes that according to article 17 (1) (d) of the Statute, any case not presenting sufficient gravity to justify further action by the Court shall be declared inadmissible. The Chamber also observes that this gravity threshold is in addition to the drafters' careful selection of the crimes including in articles 6 to 8 of the Statute, a selection based on gravity and directed at confining the material jurisdiction of the Court to 'the most serious crimes of international concern'. Hence, the fact that a case addresses one of the most serious crimes for the international community as a whole is not sufficient for it to be admissible before the Court.[27]

In considering the gravity of crime as an admissibility test, the Prosecutor has attached importance to the number of persons killed, because this tends to be the most reliably reported.[28] Thus, the situation in which the number of victims is reported to be less than 100 is less likely to be dealt with by the Prosecutor than that reportedly involving thousands of victims. In fact, the Prosecutor decided not to proceed with the investigation of Iraq situation by pointing out that the number of potential victims in this situation – 4 to 12 victims of willful killing and a limited number of victims of inhuman treatment – was of a different order than the number of victims found in other situations currently under investigation by the Prosecutor: Northern Uganda, DRC and Darfur, each of which involves thousands of willful killings as well as intentional and large-scale sexual violence and abductions.[29]

As mentioned in the previous section, the tests of the interests of justice also include the gravity of crimes, which is in theory different from the gravity as the admissibility test. In practice, however, the Prosecutor has not considered separately the gravity of crime at the admissibility level and that at the judicial propriety level. This implies that a decision by the Prosecutor on the gravity of crimes entails a nature of policy as well as that of law.

Actually, before the Prosecutor began a preliminary examination of the first situation, he had formulated the prosecutorial strategy concerning the gravity test. In the Policy paper, the Prosecutor declared his position that he 'should focus its investigative and prosecutorial efforts and resources on those who bear the greatest responsibility, such as the leaders of the State or organization allegedly responsible for those crimes'.[30] This policy was actually applied by the Prosecutor

26 Iraq Response 2006, 8.
27 *Prosecutor v Thomas Lubanga Dyilo* 2006, paragraph 41.
28 Statement by Luis Moreno-Ocampo 2005, 6.
29 Iraq Response 2006, 9.
30 Paper on Some Policy Issues 2003, 7.

in order to specify the person to be indicted in the situations of Uganda[31] and Darfur.[32] The Pre-Trial Chamber also followed it in the situation of DRC:

> [T]he Chamber considers that the additional gravity threshold provided for in article 17 (1) (d) of the Statute is intended to ensure that the Court initiates cases only against the most senior leaders suspected of being the most responsible for the crimes within the jurisdiction of the Court allegedly committed in any given situation under investigation. In the Chamber's view, this additional factor comprises three elements. First, the position of the persons against whom the Prosecution requests the initiation of a case through the issuance of a warrant of arrest or a summons to appear (the most senior leaders). Second, the roles such persons play, through acts or omissions, when the State entities, organizations or armed groups to which they belong commit systematic or large-scale crimes within the jurisdiction of the Court. Third, the role played by such State entities, organizations or armed groups in the overall commission of crimes within the jurisdiction of the Court in the relevant situation (those suspected of being most responsible).[33]

In terms of the tests concerning the interests of justice except the gravity of crimes, the Prosecutor does not appear to have paid so much attention to them, or at least to have refrained from revealing them to the public. Only in the situation of CAR, the Prosecutor mentioned as an issue of interests of justice that 'many of the victims in the Central African Republic were awaiting the involvement of the ICC in order to see justice done and to recover their dignity'.[34] In any case, it is certain that, in the practice of self-referral, the interest of justice is also taken into account by the Prosecutor in the earlier stage of screening process, mainly in the preliminary examination stage. If the Prosecutor finds the investigation and prosecution of a targeted situation to serve the interests of justice from his *overall* evaluation of that situation, he will then enter into dialogue with the State *locus criminis* to induce it to refer the situation to him. This might be a reason why the Prosecutor has not so mentioned specific tests concerning the interests of justice.

Conclusion

The foregoing analysis demonstrates the following significance as well as problems in the practical application of the principle of complementarity.

31 Warrant of Arrest for Joseph Kony 2005, paragraph 37; Statement by the Chief Prosecutor 2005, 2.

32 Second Report 2005, 3.

33 *Prosecutor v Thomas Lubanga Dyilo* 2006, paragraphs 50–52.

34 Office of the Prosecutor 2007, 3.

First, it has been commonly believed that the principle of complementarity would be mainly examined in the post-indictment and trial stage by the Pre-Trial or Trial Chamber in response to a challenge to the admissibility raised by an accused or a State having jurisdiction over the case in question. The practice so far reveals, on the contrary, that complementarity has been taken into account chiefly by the Prosecutor in the preliminary examination stage and/or the investigation stage. In this regard, the principle of complementarity works not as a norm of adjudication for Pre-Trail or Trial Chamber, but rather as a code of conduct for the Prosecutor. Actually, the prosecutorial strategies that the Prosecutor has made public clearly indicate this character of the principle. The positive actions taken by the Prosecutor towards the self-referral have made it more obvious.

Second, in deciding on the issue of complementarity, the Prosecutor has keenly taken into account the limited material and human resources that the ICC can make use of. This has inspired the Prosecutor to fix the order of priority among the situations or cases referred to him. The sense of priority brought forth his strategy, which emphasizes the number of victims in a situation and focuses on the leaders most responsible for the crimes. This implies, in practice, that the gravity test prevails over the 'unwillingness' and 'inability' tests. Even when there is a case of which a State concerned is not willing or able to proceed with an investigation and prosecution, the Prosecutor might decide not to deal with it, at least for the time being, because there are other cases to be preferentially investigated and prosecuted in light of the gravity of the crimes. In particular, the Prosecutor is more likely to have such a thought when no referral was made by the State *locus criminis* or by the Security Council. It cannot be denied, in fact, that similar thoughts have induced the Prosecutor to decide not to proceed with an investigation into the Iraq situation, aside from the highly sensitive aspect of that situation as a political matter.

Third, the strategy of the Prosecutor leads us to reconsidering the function of the complementarity. Originally, the principle of complementarity was intended to act as a brake on the excessive interference by the ICC into the sovereign power of a State to exercise its own criminal jurisdiction. Under his current strategy, however, the Prosecutor has attempted, from a very early stage, to confine targeted situations to the limited number in light of the number of victims. Further, he also attempts to conduct 'diplomacy' on the self-referral so that he tries to minimize a political friction which may lead to the uncooperative attitude of the State *locus criminis*. As the result of this strategy, there is concern that the Prosecutor may make the activities of the ICC too self-restrictive.

If the ICC does not deal with a case, we have no other choice but to leave that case to national proceedings. However, for the State which is not able to prosecute the most senior leaders bearing the greatest responsibility, it is quite difficult to prosecute even the middle- or low-ranking perpetrators. The current strategy of restricting the targets from the viewpoint of the political and military ranking of the perpetrator and the gravity of crimes may entail the risk that it would eventually extend the scope of impunity that the drafters of the Rome Statute intended to bring to an end.

References

Books, Articles and Chapters in Books

Arsanjani, M. (1999), 'Reflections on the Jurisdiction and Trigger Mechanism of the International Criminal Court', in von Habel, Lammers and Schukking (eds).

Benzing, M. (2003), 'The Complementarity Regime of the International Criminal Court: International Criminal Justice between State Sovereignty and the Fight against Impunity', *Max Planck Yearbook of United Nations Law* 7, 591–632.

Bergsmo, M. and Triffterer, O. (1999), 'Preamble', in Triffterer (ed.).

Bos, A. (1998), 'The Role of an International Criminal Court in the Light of the Principle of Complementarity', in Denters and Schrijver (eds).

Broomhall, B. (2003), *International Justice and the International Criminal Court: Between Sovereignty and the Rule of Law* (New York: Oxford University Press).

Cassese, A., Gaeta, P. and Jones, J. (eds) (2002), *The Rome Statute of the International Criminal Court: A Commentary*, Vol. II (New York: Oxford University Press).

Crawford, J. (2003), 'The Drafting of the Rome Statute' in Sands (ed.).

Dembowski, L. (2003), 'The International Criminal Court: Complementarity and Its Consequences', in Stromseth (ed.).

Denters, E. and Schrijver, N. (eds) (1998), *Reflections on International Law From the Low Countries: In Honour of Paul de Waart* (The Hague: M. Nijhoff Publishers).

Gaeta, P. (2004), 'Is the Practice of "Self-Referrals" a Sound Start for the ICC?', *Journal of International Criminal Justice* 2:4, 949–952.

Habel, H. von, Lammers, J. and Schukking, J. (eds) (1999), *Reflections on the International Criminal Court: Essays in Honour of Adriaan Bos* (The Hague: T.M.C. AsserPress).

Holmes, J. (2002), 'Complementarity: National Courts versus the ICC', in Cassese, Gaeta and Jones (eds).

Jones, J. and Powles, S. (2003), *International Criminal Practice*, 3rd Edition (Ardsley: Transnational Publishers; Oxford: Oxford University Press).

Kress, C. (2004), '"Self-Referrals" and "Waivers of Complementarity": Some Considerations in Law and Policy', *Journal of International Criminal Justice* 2:4, 944–948.

Olasolo, H. (2005), 'The Trigger Procedure of the International Criminal Court, Procedural Treatment of the Principle of Complementarity, and the Role of Office of the Prosecutor', *International Criminal Law Review* 5:1, 121–146.

Sands, P. (ed.) (2003), *From Nuremberg to The Hague: The Future of International Criminal Justice* (Cambridge: Cambridge University Press).

Schabas, W. (2004), *An Introduction to the International Criminal Court*, 2nd Edition (Cambridge: Cambridge University Press).

Stromseth, J. (ed.) (2003), *Accountability for Atrocities: National and International Responses* (Ardsley: Transnational Publishers).

Triffterer, O. (ed.) (1999), *Commentary on the Rome Statute of the International Criminal Court: Observer's Notes, Article by Article* (Baden-Baden: Nomos Verlagsgesellschaft).

Turone, G. (2002), 'Chapter 29.1: Powers and Duties of the Prosecutor', in Cassese, Gaeta and Jones (eds).

Williams, S. (1999), 'Article 17: Issues of Admissibility', in Triffterer (ed.).

Official Documents and Others

Annex to the Paper on Some Policy Issues (2003), Annex to the 'Paper on Some Policy Issues before the Office of the Prosecutor': Referrals and Communications, <http://www.icc-cpi.int/library/organs/otp/policy_annex_final_210404.pdf>.

Iraq Response (2006), Iraq Response (9 February 2006), <http://www.icc-cpi.int/library/organs/otp/OTP_letter_to_senders_re_Iraq_9_February_2006.pdf>.

Letter from the Prosecutor (2004), Letter from the Prosecutor dated 17 June 2004, annexed to the Decision Assigning the Situation in the Democratic Republic of Congo to Pre-Trial Chamber I, ICC-01/04 (5 July 2004).

Letter from the Prosecutor (2005), Letter from the Prosecutor dated 4 April 2005, OTP/050404/LMO-dr, annexed to the Decision Assigning the Situation in Darfur, Sudan to Pre-Trial Chamber I, ICC-02/05 (21 April 2005).

Office of the Prosecutor (2006), Transcript, Second Public Hearing of the Office of the Prosecutor (25 September 2006), <http://www.icc-cpi.int/library/organs/otp/OTP_PH2_HGSTATES.pdf>.

Office of the Prosecutor (2007), Situation in the Central African Republic, Background (22 May 2007), ICC-OTP-BN-20070522-220-A_EN.

Paper on Some Policy Issues (2003), Paper on Some Policy Issues before the Office of the Prosecutor (September 2003), < http://www.icc-cpi.int/otp/otp_policy.html>.

Prosecutor v Gojko Jankovic (2005), Decision on Referral of Case under Rule 11 *bis*, Case No. IT-96-23/2-PT (22 July 2005).

Prosecutor v Radovan Stankovic (2005), Decision on Referral of Case under Rule 11 *bis*, Case No. IT-96-23/2-PT (17 May 2005).

Prosecutor v Thomas Lubanga Dyilo (2006), Situation in the Democratic Republic of Congo in the Case of the *Prosecutor v Thomas Lubanga Dyilo*, Pre-Trial Chamber I, Decision on the Prosecutor's Application for a Warrant of Arrest, Article 58 (10 February 2006), ICC-01/04-01/06.

Prosecutor v Zeljko Mejakic, Momcilo Gruban, Dusan Fustar, Dusko Knezevic (2005), Decision on Prosecutor's Motion for Referral of Case Pursuant to Rule 11 *bis*, Case No. IT-02-65-PT (20 July 2005).

Second Report (2005), Second Report of the Prosecutor of the International Criminal Court, Mr. Luis Moreno Ocampo, to the Security Council pursuant to UNSC 1593 (2005) (13 December 2005).

Statement by the Chief Prosecutor (2005), Statement by the Chief Prosecutor on the Uganda Arrest Warrants (14 October 2005).

Statement by Luis Moreno-Ocampo (2005), Registration in a Record of Proceedings of Statement by Luis Moreno-Ocampo, Informal Meeting of Legal Advisors of Ministries of Foreign Affairs, New York, 24 October 2005, ICC-02/04-01/05 (2 December 2005).

Venezuela Response (2006), Venezuela Response (9 February 2006), <http://www.icc-cpi.int/library/organs/otp/OTP_letter_to_senders_re_Venezuela_9_February_2006.pdf>.

Warrant of Arrest for Joseph Kony (2005), Situation in Uganda, Warrant of Arrest for Joseph Kony Issued on 8 July 2005 as Amended on 27 September 2005, ICC-02/04-01/05 (27 September 2005).

Chapter 12

Implementation of Article VI of the 1967 Outer Space Treaty: The Responsible State and Appropriate State for Private Space Activities

Akira Sakota

Introduction

While the 1967 Outer Space Treaty (OST) does not prohibit the space activities conducted by private entities, it imposes on a State the responsibility and the obligation for 'national activities', including private activities. Article VI of the Treaty states:

> States Parties to the Treaty shall bear international responsibility for national activities in outer space, including the moon and other celestial bodies, whether such activities are carried on by governmental agencies or by non-governmental entities, and for assuring that national activities are carried out in conformity with the provisions set forth in the present Treaty. The activities of non-governmental entities in outer space, including the moon and other celestial bodies, shall require authorization and continuing supervision by the appropriate State Party to the Treaty.

It might be said that the OST regards the conformity of 'national activities in outer space' with the Treaty provisions as an 'international public interest', thus leaving the realization of that interest to the responsibility of States.

Since the OST does not clarify the extent of 'national activities in outer space', i.e., for what activities of what non-governmental entities States shall bear international responsibility and have the obligation of authorization and continuing supervision, those issues are left to subsequent interpretation and State practice. When the OST was drafted, private space activities were not active and they were present at most only within each given governmental space project. The link between a State and a private activity or enterprise was absolutely clear. It was not questioned in reality which State had the responsibility and the obligation for a given private space activity under Article VI of the OST, although many scholars discussed this issue from the theoretical view.

After a few decades, with the coming of space commercialization and privatization, however, many private companies engaged in a variety of space activities as space businesses with some degree of their own free will. A number of States enacted their national space legislation in regard to those space businesses, whilst keeping a certain distance from those businesses. In these circumstances, the question should be discussed from a more realistic perspective, especially in regards to national implementation, that which State has the responsibility and the obligation under Article VI, i.e., which State is the responsible State and the appropriate State.[1] In other words, the issue in our study is what is to determine the exact meaning of the abstract provisions of Article VI in the reality of the age of space commercialization.

Preliminary Considerations

'International Public Interests' in the 1967 Outer Space Treaty

The OST mentions to the international public interests in the Preamble and Article I:

> 'Recognizing the *common interest of all mankind* in the progress of the exploration and use of outer space for peaceful purposes,' (para. 2 of Preamble)
>
> 'Believing that the exploration and use of outer space should be carried on for the *benefit of all peoples* irrespective of the degree of their economic or scientific development,' (para. 3 of Preamble)
>
> 'Believing that such co-operation will contribute to the development of mutual understanding and to the strengthening of friendly relations between States and peoples,' (para. 5 of Preamble)
>
> 'The exploration and use of outer space, including the moon and other celestial bodies, shall be carried out for *the benefit and in the interests of all countries*, irrespective of their degree of economic or scientific development, and shall be the province of all mankind.' (Article I)
>
> [emphasis added]

There is no doubt that the OST states explicitly some kind of international public interest, while the concrete meanings of these provisions, especially of 'for the benefit and in the interests of all countries' (Article I) are discussed.[2]

1 See COPUOS Secretariat Review 2001.

2 The language in Article I is especially important for the developing countries. See Jasentuliyana 1989, 129 ff. and also see the 1996 United Nations General Assembly Resolution 51/122. This point is, however, not relevant to this chapter.

Principles in the First and Second Sentences of Article VI and the 'International Public Interests'

The provision of the first and second sentences of Article VI are divided into three parts:

1. international responsibility for space activities (the first part of the first sentence)
2. international responsibility for assuring conformity of space activities with space law rules (the second part of the first sentence), and
3. obligation of authorization and continuing supervision to space activities (thc second sentence)

These provisions could be considered also to establish the maintenance of the Treaty regime itself as an international public interest and to leave its realization as it were to the States. It is our task to review how each State takes these provisions and realizes this international public interest.

Meaning of 'International Responsibility' of Article VI

Since the adoption of the 1967 Outer Space Treaty (and also the 1963 'Declaration on Legal Principles of Outer Space' ('Declaration')),[3] there has been a great amount of discussion on the exact meaning of 'International Responsibility'.[4] This provision has been almost universally interpreted as stating that it is the responsibility of the State for any internationally wrongful act and applies the special rule of attribution in the law of State responsibility, i.e., it applies the exceptional rule of attribution of the conduct of private person to the State against the principle in general international law that the conduct of a private person is not attributed to the State.[5] This interpretation, however, could not be supported.

First, many delegates of the member States of the COPUOS (including the Legal Sub-committee) used the word 'responsibility' in the discussion of drafting the OST (and the Declaration) not as 'responsibility for an internationally wrongful act'.[6]

3 The origin of Article VI of the OST is para. 5 of the 1963 Declaration and both provisions are perfectly same, although there are some differences in regards to precise wording. See Sakota 2002b, 392.

4 Lachs 1966, 74–75; Bittlinger 1987, 191–193; Cheng 1998, 14–18. See Sakota 2005, 48–50.

5 Bittlinger 1987, 191; Malanczuk 1997, 294–205. On the comprehensive list of literatures in regards to this view, see Sakota 2005, notes 33, 34, 35 and 48.

6 For example, in the course of drafting the Declaration, US delegate said in his speech in regards to the 1962 Communications Satellites Act that 'Such private agencies would not be free to engage in space programmes without governmental permission and continuing governmental supervision. The principle of national responsibility for national space activities was embodied in the United States Communications Satellite Act of 1962'

Accordingly the word 'responsibility for the activities' in the discussion did not have the meaning of the special attribution rule at all.[7] It should be duly noted that in the discussion no mention was given to the drafts and works for the codification of State responsibility at that time,[8] including the 1961 Amador revised draft in the International Law Commission (ILC),[9] the 1961 Harvard draft[10] and the 1962 Restatement of the Law, 2nd.[11] The meanings of the word 'responsibility' and phrase 'responsibility for the activities' in the COPUOS discussions and literatures of writers at that time seems respectively to mean 'obligation' and 'obligation to regulate the activities'.[12]

The second reason is from the point of view of compatibility of the rule of attribution with the law of State responsibility. The attribution rules regulate the issue of when the conduct of a person or persons is regarded as an act of the State. In principle the conduct of private person is not regarded as an act of the State, but it is known generally that exceptionally the former might be regarded as the latter in the certain circumstances.[13] Generally speaking the conduct of a person or persons is attributed to a State when (1) the nature of the conduct is an exercise of the element of governmental authority and (2) there is the relationship between the person and the State in which the State authorize the person(s) to exercise the element of governmental authority. In short, the conduct through which a State performs a State function to realize its own will is regarded as an act of the State in the law of State responsibility. In this context the formal difference in the position in the State organization (State organ or private person) is not a decisive factor.[14] Considering the argued special attribution rule in Article VI of OST with the attribution rule in general international law, there is some doubt about the compatibility of both rules, especially on the nature of the space activities and

---

(A/AC.105/C.2/SR.20, 12). This US Act did not have any clauses of responsibility for an internationally wrongful act. For almost all the discussions and statements in the COPUOS and literatures on the word 'responsibility' before the time of adoption of the OST, see Sakota 2002a, 232–247 and Sakota 2002b, 385–413.

7 Sakota 2002c, 206–209.

8 Sakota 2002c, 208.

9 YbILC, 1961, vol. II, 46 ff.

10 Sohn/Baxter 1961.

11 American Law Institute 1965, 512 ff.

12 Sakota 2002c, 209. The word 'responsibility' has a number of meanings, including 'obligation', i.e., so-called primary rule. See the sentence of the judgment of 'Trail Smelter case'; 'the Dominion of Canada is responsible in international law for the conduct of the Trail Smelter' (*Reports of International Arbitral Awards*, vol. 3, 1905, 1965). This sentence never had the meaning associated with the special attribution rule.

13 See Art. 8 of 2001 ILC draft on Responsibility of States for Internationally Wrongful Acts. On the analysis of many judgments on such exceptional attribution, including those delivered by ICJ, arbitrations, claims commissions and Iran–United States Claims Tribunal, see Sakota 1996, 4–19.

14 Sakota 1996, 35.

the relationship between the activities and the responsible State. Many writers, as can be seen below, have argued that a State is responsible under Article VI based on the facts without relationship of the will of that State (e.g. the location of the activity; the nationality of the entity, etc.) and that several States might be responsible under Article VI.

Third, the object and purpose of Article VI does not support that interpretation. This provision is the result of compromise between the eastern countries, which suggest the prohibition of private space activities and the western countries, which oppose such prohibition. The object and purpose of this provision is, on the one hand, not to prohibit those private space activities and, on the other hand, to remove or diminish some problems and complications which would occur in the course of private space activities.[15] Many delegates of the COPUOS (and the Legal Sub-committee) and scholars considered that such possible problems and complications would be things such as irresponsible or unregulated private activities[16] and avoidance of States from their responsibility and obligations,[17] as well as harm to mankind, the ignoring of international interests, unamenableness to the control of international law and bankruptcy of private agencies, etc.[18] It seems to be difficult to consider that most of all of such possible problems and complications might be removed or diminished by means of regarding the space activities conducted by private entities as the act of a State. Rather, it would be natural to consider that these might be done so by State regulation. From the point of such considerations, these are not practical reasons to understand the word 'responsibility for the activities' in the context of the special attribution rule.

The fourth and final reason is concerned with the question on what matters Article VI governs as a whole. The second sentence of Article VI covers the space activities of non-governmental entities (private enterprises) and the third sentence covers space activities of international organizations. These two sentences govern exceptional situation that non-State actors engage in space activities. Considering that the first sentence covers State responsibility for internationally wrongful act, which is a very general matter in the eyes of international law, it subsequently sounds quite strange, because Article VI covers both very general matters and exceptional situations in one article. It would be very difficult to explain what this article aims to cover when the first sentence of this article covers the State responsibility for internationally wrongful act. Considering the discussions in the making of OST and

15 Sakota 2004, 159.

16 USSR (A/AC.105/C.2/SR.17, 7); Canada (A/AC.105/C.2/SR.21, 6; A/AC.105/C.2/SR.27, 5); Japan (A/AC.105/C.2/ SR.22, 12); UK (A/AC.105/C.2/SR.24, 11–12). And see Gál 1969, 142; van Bogaert 1986, 44.

17 USSR (A/AC.105/C.2/SR.22, 4). See also Dembling/Arons 1967, 436; Bittlinger 1987, 192.

18 See Sakota 2004, 140–143.

the Declaration, it seems to be more reasonable to understand Article VI as a whole enacts basically the case of the space activity conducted by other than State.[19]

What meanings should this article have? In one's own view the word 'responsibility for activities' in the first part of the first sentence means, as stated above, as an obligation to regulate activities. The word 'responsibility for assuring' in the second part of the first sentence, which some Japanese scholars argue as having the special meanings of 'responsibility to guarantee' with the expression 'responsibility to ensure' in several international instruments including Principle 21 of 1972 Declaration of the Human Environment,[20] should be understood as an obligation to regulate. The second sentence states the obligation to authorize and supervise these space activities. Accordingly the core content of all these three provisions is an obligation to regulate. The meaning of the responsibility for an internationally wrongful act would be, if included in this article, of no great importance. The word 'responsibility' is not, however, same as the expression of mere 'obligation' and seems to include the meaning of some position of States to be complaint when a problem should occur in regards to private space activities.[21]

Relationship among the First Part and the Second Part of the First Sentence and the Second Sentence

There has not been much discussion on the issue of the relationship among the three provisions of the first part and the second part of the first sentence and the second sentence. Especially when the first part of the first sentence is understood as responsibility for an internationally wrongful act and a special attribution rule, it would be almost impossible to explain the relationship with the second part and the second sentence.

Since those three provisions were from the same issue of private space activities in the drafting discussion of the Treaty and the Declaration and, as stated above, these provisions have, at their core, obligation to regulate, they should be understood as essentially having same meaning. Accordingly the responsible State in the first sentence and the appropriate State in the second sentence *is* the same State.[22]

19 Sakota 2002c, 212–213.

20 Yamamoto 1994, 276, 487; Murase 1994, 151–154.

21 Sakota 2004, 160–163.

22 See Sakota 2005, 78, n. 88. In this consideration, the case of the space activities conducted by governmental agency is omitted.

Responsible State and Appropriate State in the Drafting Discussion in COPUOS, Legal Literature and Various National Space Legislation

In this chapter we examine the responsible State and the appropriate State of Article VI with the normal approach; *travaux préparatoires*, legal literature and national space legislation as State practice.

Drafting Discussions in COPUOS

There were no discussions on the issue of which State is the responsible and obligatory State under Article VI, because, as mentioned above, possibly the issue that private spacc activities should be prohibited or not itself was the big issue and at that time it was not practical to consider with concrete precision the scope of private space activities. Based on this fact let us see what they discussed when making the Treaty in COPUOS.

As stated above, in the COPUOS there was mention of possible problems and complications such as irresponsible activities, avoidance of States from responsibility and obligations of States, etc. All such matters except bankruptcy are abstract. There were no concrete discussions on what practical problems might occur nor on which State should regulate such private activities and what regulations would be effective. In the discussion some delegate of eastern countries referred to two examples of Telstar and Comsat. It should be noted that the activities of both were satellite communications.[23] The eastern countries did not point out possible concrete problems resulting from the private space activities. On the other hand, western countries seemed to consider that the possible problems resulting from those activities would be launching activities,[24] but they did not point out any concrete problems. One might even go as far as to imply that in the drafting discussions the private space activities which would possibly raise some problems include satellite communications and launching activities, but no one knows decisively what activities would be covered by the Article VI.

Concerning the responsible State and the State of authorization, while a few delegates mentioned the issue of the State of nationality,[25] there did not seem to be agreement on this issue.

We cannot find much in the way of useful information on the kind of space activities and responsible State in Article VI in the discussions of COPUOS.

23 See Sakota 2002c, 196–197.

24 France (A/AC.105/C.2/SR.9, 3; A/AC.105/PV.13, 17); United States draft Declaration, para. 6 (A/C.1/881). See also India (A/AC.105/SR.22, 9–10).

25 Czechoslovakia (A/AC.105/PV.11, 32); Canada (A/AC.105/C.2/SR.21, 6); India (A/AC.105/C.2/SR. 22, 9–10); UK (A/AC.105/C.2/SR.24, 11–12).

The Responsible State and the Appropriate State Argued by Writers

Since the adoption of the 1963 Declaration many writers have argued about which State is the responsible State and which the appropriate State in Article VI.[26]

The Responsible State Many scholars suggest as one of the responsible States the State of nationality of the entity which conducts the space activities.[27] Some of them base their reasons on the expression 'national' activities in Article VI or in the obligation of State for its nationals in Article IX.

Many writers also support the criterion of the location of space activity. Under this view, the responsible State is the State of territory or territorial jurisdiction,[28] the flag State of the ship when the space activity is conducted on a ship and the State of registration when the activity is conducted in an aircraft.[29]

Some authoritative scholars consider launching activity as a decisive criterion.[30] Under this view, the responsible State is the State of the location of the physical launch, the 'Launching State' defined in the Liability Convention and Registration Convention, the State which has the jurisdiction over the launching activity or the State of nationality of the launching organization.

Some writers regard the State of Registry of the space objects as one of a responsible State based on the fact that only that State has the jurisdiction and control under Article VIII of the 1967 OST and may regulate those activities.[31]

Recently some discuss the 'jurisdiction and/or control' as an important criterion.[32] Under this view the criterion is that the State must have such power but does not necessarily exercise the power to do so in reality.

Some scholars also suggest so-called subjective approach or national approach.[33] In this approach it is the State that decides which State is the responsible State by its own national legislation. Many writers, however, criticize this approach.[34]

Another criteria of the responsible State are suggested includes the finance element of the activity[35] and licensing.[36]

26 On the comprehensive arguments given by lawyers, see Sakota 2006, 37–60.
27 Bittlinger 1987, 192–193; van Traa-Engelman 1993, 63; Cheng 1998, 24–25.
28 Marcoff 1973, 533; Wassenbergh 1991, 23, fn. 5; Cheng 1998, 24–25.
29 Cheng 1998, 24–25.
30 Bittlinger 1987, 192–193; van Traa-Engelman 1993, 62–63.
31 Wassenbergh 1991, 26–27; Cheng 1998, 24–25.
32 Wassenbergh 1991, 23, fn. 5; Cheng 1998, 23–25; Hermida 2004, 9, 17, 27, 35, 68.
33 Csabafi 1971, 122; Wassenbergh 1997, 335.
34 Bittlinger 1987, 192; van Traa-Engelman 1993, 61; Hermida 2004, 8, 70.
35 Jenks 1965, 212; Kerrest 1997, 139.
36 Jenks 1965, 212; Vereshchetin 1983, 264; Wassenbergh 1991, 24–25.

The Appropriate State While the criterion of the appropriate State in the literatures is basically same with that of the responsible State, there are some differences.

As in the argument on the responsible State, many writers support the criterion of nationality in regards to determining the appropriate State.[37] Similarly, many scholars consider launching activities as very important.[38] A number of lawyers regard the State of registry of a space object as the appropriate State.[39]

Separate from the argument on the responsible State, fewer lawyers discuss the appropriate State in the view of the location of activities[40] or jurisdiction and/or control.[41]

Another view supports the criteria of the location of manufacture of the space objects,[42] whilst another views takes a more subjective approach in this matter.[43]

Lack of Positivism Approach in the Literature Many lawyers argue a variety of criteria on both the issue of the responsible State and the appropriate State. One of the serious problems in the literature of space law is that most arguments are abstract with a distinct lack of sound reasoning, i.e. they argue this issue without a view towards the positivism approach. In the face of space commercialization and privatization in which many private companies engage that were not imagined when the 1967 OST was adopted, we should examine how each State responds to this reality from the point of view of the interpretation of Article VI of the Treaty. It should be noted that while, as stated above, the delegates in the COPUOS speak of satellite communication and launching activities as possible private activities, those lawyers dealing in space law do not fully argue the different kind of space activities.

To consider this issue more positively, first of all, we should analyze the national space legislation of each State.

National Space Legislation

Since the 1980s, several States have enacted national space legislation to facilitate and regulate the space activities of private entities in the course of space commercialization. Since these pieces of national legislation have an aspect of national implementation of international obligations of States under Article VI of

37 Dembling 1970, 287; Gorove 1983, 377; Wassenbergh 1991, 23–25.

38 Gorove 1983, 108; van Traa-Engelman 1993, 63.

39 Bourély 1986, 160; Wassenbergh 1991, 26–27, 29; Silvestrov 1991, 327–328.

40 Wassenbergh 1991, 23, fn. 5.

41 Wassenbergh 1991, 23, fn. 5; Meredith/Robinson 1992, 41.

42 Bourély 1986, 159.

43 Aoki 2001, 250.

the OST,[44] they give us some useful information on for which private activities each State considers itself to be responsible and obligatory for.

Now there are different views in the articles and materials on the extent of 'national space legislation' as the national implementation of Article VI of the OST. Following laws are referred usually as national space legislation:

Australia (1998 Space Activities Act)
Russian Federation (1993 Law about Space Activities)
South Africa (1993 Space Affairs Act)
Sweden (1982 Act on Space Activities)
Ukraine (1996 Law on Space Activities)
United Kingdom (1986 Outer Space Act)
United States of America (1984 Commercial Space Launch Act and 1984 Land Remote-sensing Commercialization Act)[45]

Space Activities Covered by Various National Space Legislation Some national space laws have comprehensive definition on 'space activities', such as:

Swedish Act, Article 1: 'activities in outer space (space activities)',
Russian Law, Article 1, para. 1: 'any activity immediately connected with operations to explore and use outer space',
South African Act, Article 1: '(space activities:) the activities directly contributing to the launching of spacecraft and the operation of such craft in outer space' (space-related activities: all activities supporting, or sharing mutual technologies with, space activities),
Ukrainian Law, Article 1: 'scientific space research, the design and application of space technology and the use of outer space'.

These show clearly that the space activities covered under various national space legislation are very different.

Most legislation from the list details the exact form of space activities. First, many national laws regulate launching activity and make it subject to license (Sweden, USA, UK, Russian Federation, South Africa, Ukraine, Australia). Only the UK Act regulates explicitly 'procuring the launch of a space object'.

44 As an excellent analysis, see COPUOS Secretariat Review 2001. The title of this Review implies that the Review considers national space legislation as the implementation of the first and second sentences of Article VI as a whole.

45 Relevant regulations/ordnances and amendments are omitted here. The texts and English translations of non-English texts cited here are from UN/Nigeria Workshop 2005. These are also available at <http://www.unoosa.org/oosaddb/browse_countries.jsp>.

Furthermore only the Australian Act regulates the return of space objects. The States that regulate the operation of launching sites are the USA, Australia, South Africa and Ukraine.

Fewer States regulate the operation of satellites explicitly in their national space law: Sweden, UK and South Africa.

The South African Act regulates the space activities entailing international obligations of that State without making clear the kind of such activities. The 1984 US Land Remote-sensing Commercialization Act is often referred to as national space legislation, which regulates operation of private remote-sensing space system, selling and delivering unenhanced data, etc.

Russian Federation Law lists concretely many kinds of activities such as: (1) space rcsearch, (2) remote sensing of the Earth from outer space, including environmental monitoring and meteorology, (3) use of navigation, topographical and geodesic satellite systems, (4) piloted space missions, (5) manufacturing of materials and other products in outer space, (6) other kinds of activity performed with the aid of space technology and (7) creating as well as using and transferring of space techniques, space technology, other products and services necessary for carrying out space activity.

Some national laws state explicitly that they do not cover some kinds of space activities. For example, the Swedish Act states that 'Merely receiving signals or information in some other form from objects in outer space is not designated as space activities according to this Act. Nor is launching of sounding rockets designated as space activities'.

Relationship between the Activity/the Entity of the Activity and the State The laws which state explicitly their application to the activities conducted by their nationals (natural and legal person) are the UK Act, the Russian Federation Law, the South African Act and the US Commercial Space Launch Act. Considering that the Swedish Act and Australian Act apply to the activities conducted by their nationals outside their territories and that Ukranian Law applies to the activities under its jurisdiction outside its territory, all States regulate the space activities conducted by their nationals inside or outside their territory.

The laws which state explicitly their application to the activities conducted within their territories are the Swedish Act, the Ukranian Law and the Australian Act. The Russian Federation Law applies to the 'space activity of foreign organizations and citizens under the jurisdiction of Russian Federation'.

Concerning these forms of the activities, the US Commercial Space Launch Act and South African Act cover both launching activities in their territories and launching activities by their nationals outside their territories. The US Act extends its application to the launching activities (and operation of a launch site) by a foreign entity of which a controlling interest is held by a US citizen in a certain circumstance (the location of the activity and the existence of international agreement).

On the other hand, the US Land Remote-sensing Commercialization Act states that 'No person who is subject to the jurisdiction or control of the United States may, directly or through any subsidiary or affiliate, operate any private remote-sensing space system without a license'.

Although there are not any common criteria of the relationship between the space activity/entity and the State, all of the national legislation seems to adopt substantially same criteria, i.e., the link of territory/location and nationality.

Evaluation of National Space Legislation by Virtue of Article VI This examination of the various pieces of national space legislation shows that: all States regulate the launching activities conducted in their territories and/or the launching activities conducted by their nationals outside their territories; some States regulate the operation of satellites; and no national space legislation regulates satellite communication by the legislation itself (possibly States regulate it by another means). Moreover it should be emphasized that there appears to be no close relationship between these pieces of national space legislation and the 1967 OST, because (1) one cannot find common features in any national space legislation, (2) the fact that all States enacted their national space legislation after about 15 years after the adoption of the 1967 OST and that not all show that the legislation was made for their own internal necessity.

From this fact it is very difficult to determine which part of the legislation is to implement the responsibility and obligations in the OST and which part is enacted at the discretion of the State by virtue of its policy for space industry. The reason why national space legislation does not have close relevance to the OST seems that, since the words of Article VI are very abstract and ambiguous, the extent of interpretation of this article becomes broad and because private entities began to engage in space activities long after the adoption of the OST. These results are due to the fact that there were not any such discussions in the COPUOS for making the Treaty based on the possible problems that would occur from private space activities. In this situation we should examine other practices in the international law of outer space.

The Link between a Space Object and a State in the Practice of Registering Space Objects

The United Nations system on the registration of space objects consists of two systems: one is the system of 1975 Registration Convention and the other is the 1961 UN General Assembly Resolution 1721 (XVI). Although the State parties to the Registration Convention register their space objects as a conventional obligation and the others register those at its discretion under the 1961 GA Resolution, both systems are conducted together in practice. The practice of registering space objects is an important State practice because a State shows explicitly the relationship with the space object through the registration procedure by the State itself in the norms of international space law. We will examine the registration practices in order to make clear the link with which States register their space objects.[46]

Analysis of the Registration Practice of Space Objects Launched in 2001

Table 12.1 shows the registration practice of space objects launched in 2001. These are 87 functional space objects and 469 non-functional space objects. The analysis is different between the case of functional objects and the one of non-functional objects.[47]

State of Registry of the Functional Space Objects Among 77 registered functional space objects, 76 objects are registered by the State of nationality of the operator/owner the space objects.[48] Among the 77 registered objects, 67 objects are registered by the State of the location of the launching; 53 objects registered by the State of nationality of the manufacturers of the launching vehicles; 72 objects registered by the State of nationality of the manufacturers of the space objects (Table 12.1 doesn't show this information).

The only exception is TURKSAT 2A (2001-002A), which is operated/owned by Eurasiasat Corp. (Monaco) and registered by Turkey. This Monaco corporation is 75 per cent owned by Turk Telecom Corp. (Turkey) and 25 per cent owned by Alcatel Space Corp. (France, the manufacturer of TURKSAT 2 A). This satellite is used for satellite communication in Turkish territory. These facts show that this satellite has a much closer relationship with Turkey than Monaco. Indeed this satellite is considered as a Turkish satellite in the satellite communications industry. This space object has a link with Turkey in financial and operational aspects.

This analysis shows that, first, the decisive factor of the registration of a functional space object is ownership/operation of the object. It should be emphasized that the location of the launch has no relevance to the registration. Second, in most cases the State of nationality of the owner/operator of the space object registers the object, although the State other than that State might register

46 The registration information supplied by States and gathered by COPUOS Secretary are available at <http://www.unoosa.org/oosa/showSearch.do>. The registration documents provided by these States are available at <http://www.unoosa.org/oosa/en/SORegister/index.html>.

47 In this context, 'functional space objects' include satellites, probes, spacecraft and space station components, and 'non-functional space objects' include spent rocket stages and deactivated satellites. See COPUOS Secretary Background Paper 2005, 5, para. 5.

48 Among the 76 objects, two are registered by two States and two are operated by several States. They are all registered by the State of nationality of owner/operator. See Sakota 2007, 195–196.

Table 12.1 Space objects launched in 2001

International Designator	Name of Space Object [1]	State of Registry	Date of Launch	Location of Launch [2]	Nationality of the Owner/Operator of the Object	Result F [3]	Result N [4]	Remarks
2001-001A	SHENZHOU 2	China	09/01/2001	China	China	O		
2001-001B		Non-reg.	09/01/2001	China	Non-functional		-	
2001-001C	SHENZHOU 2 module	Non-reg.	09/01/2001	China	China	-		
2001-002A	TURKSAT 2A	Turkey	10/01/2001	France	Monaco	X		
2001-002B		France	10/01/2001	France	Non-functional		O	
2001-003A	PROGRESS M1-5	Russian Fed.	24/01/2001	Kazakhstan	Russian Fed.	O		
2001-003B		Non-reg.	24/01/2001	Kazakhstan	Non-functional		-	
2001-004A	USA 156 (NAVSTAR GPS-2R-7)	USA	30/01/2001	USA	USA	O		
2001-004B～D		USA	30/01/2001	USA	Non-functional		O	
2001-005A	SICRAL 1	Non-reg.	07/02/2001	France	Italy	-		
2001-005B	SKYNET 4F	UK	07/02/2001	France	UK	O		
2001-005C～D		France	07/02/2001	France	Non-functional		O	
2001-006A	STS 98 (ATLANTIS)	USA	07/02/2001	USA	USA	O		
2001-006B	US LAB (DESTINY)	USA	07/02/2001	USA	USA	O		
2001-007A	ODIN	Sweden	20/02/2001	Russian Fed.	Sweden	O		
2001-007B～J		Non-reg.	20/02/2001	Russian Fed.	Non-functional		-	
2001-008A	PROGRESS M-44	Russian Fed.	26/02/2001	Kazakhstan	Russian Fed.	O		

2001-008B		Non-reg.	26/02/2001	Kazakhstan	Non-functional		-	
2001-009A	USA 157 (MILSTAR 2)	USA	27/02/2001	USA	USA	O		
2001-009B		USA	27/02/2001	USA	Non-functional		O	
2001-010A	STS-102 (DISCOVERY)	USA	08/03/2001	USA	USA	O		
2001-010B		USA	08/03/2001	USA	Non-functional		O	
2001-011A	EUROBIRD	France	08/03/2001	France	EUTELSAT	O		5)
2001-011B	B-SAT 2A	Japan	08/03/2001	France	Japan	O		
2001-011C～D		France	08/03/2001	France	Non-functional		O	
2001-012A	XM 2 ROCK	USA	18/03/2001	On High Sea	USA	O		Launched by Sea Launch
2001-012B		USA	18/03/2001	On High Sea	Non-functional		*	Launched by Sea Launch
2001-013A	MARS ODYSSEY	USA	07/04/2001	USA	USA	O		
2001-013B～C		USA	07/04/2001	USA	Non-functional		O	
2001-014A	EKRAN M	Russian Fed.	07/04/2001	Kazakhstan	Russian Fed.	O		
2001-014B～C		Non-reg.	07/04/2001	Kazakhstan	Non-functional		-	
2001-015A	GSAT 1	India	18/04/2001	India	India	O		
2001-015B		India	18/04/2001	India	Non-functional		O	
2001-016A	STS 100 (ENDEAVOUR)	USA	19/04/2001	USA	USA	O		
—	CANADARM 2	Canada	19/04/2001	USA	Canada	O		
2001-017A	SOYUZ TM-32	Russian Fed.	28/04/2001	Kazakhstan	Russian Fed.	O		
2001-017B		Non-reg.	28/04/2001	Kazakhstan	Non-functional		-	
2001-018A	XM 1 ROLL	USA	08/05/2001	On High Sea	USA	O		Launched by Sea Launch
2001-018B		USA	08/05/2001	On High Sea	Non-functional		*	Launched by Sea Launch

2001-019A	PAS 10	USA	15/05/2001	Kazakhstan	USA	O		
2001-019B～D		Non-reg.	15/05/2001	Kazakhstan	Non-functional		-	
2001-020A	USA 158 (GEOLITE)	USA	18/05/2001	USA	USA	O		
2001-020B～C		USA	18/05/2001	USA	Non-functional		O	
2001-021A	PROGRESS M 1-6	Russian Fed.	21/05/2001	Kazakhstan	Russian Fed.	O		
2001-021B		Non-reg.	21/05/2001	Kazakhstan	Non-functional		-	
2001-022A	COSMOS 2377	Russian Fed.	29/05/2001	Russian Fed.	Russian Fed.	O		
2001-022B		Non-reg.	29/05/2001	Russian Fed.	Non-functional		-	
2001-023A	COSMOS 2378	Russian Fed.	08/06/2001	Russian Fed.	Russian Fed.	O		
2001-023B		Non-reg.	08/06/2001	Russian Fed.	Non-functional		-	
2001-024A	INTELSAT 901	Non-reg.	09/06/2001	France	INTELSAT	-		6)
2001-024B		France	09/06/2001	France	Non-functional		O	
2001-025A	ASTRA 2C	Luxembourg	16/06/2001	Kazakhstan	Luxembourg	O		
2001-025B～D		Non-reg.	16/06/2001	Kazakhstan	Non-functional		-	
2001-026A	ICO F2	UK、USA	19/06/2001	USA	UK	O		Double registration
2001-026B		USA	19/06/2001	USA	Non-functional		O	
2001-027A	MAP	USA	30/06/2001	USA	USA	O		
2001-027B		USA	30/06/2001	USA	Non-functional		O	
2001-028A	STS 104 (ATLANTIS)	USA	12/07/2001	USA	USA	O		
2001-028B	QUEST	Non-reg.	12/07/2001	USA	USA	-		
2001-029A	ARTEMIS	ESA	12/07/2001	France	ESA	O		
2001-029B	BSAT-2B	Non-reg.	12/07/2001	France	Japan (planned)		-	Failure to be placed in orbit
2001-029C～D		France	12/07/2001	France	Non-functional		O	

2001-030A	MOLNIYA 3-K	Russian Fed.	20/07/2001	Russian Fed.	Russian Fed.	O		
2001-030B～E		Non-reg.	20/07/2001	Russian Fed.	Non-functional		-	
2001-031A	GOES M (GOES 12)	USA	23/07/2001	USA	USA	O		
2001-031B		USA	23/07/2001	USA	Non-functional		O	
2001-032A	CORONAS F	Russian Fed.	31/07/2001	Russian Fed.	Russian Fed./ Ukraine	O		For an international project
2001-032B～F		Non-reg.	31/07/2001	Russian Fed.	Non-functional		-	
2001-033A	USA 159 (DSP 21)	USA	06/08/2001	USA	USA	O		
2001-033B～E		USA	06/08/2001	USA	Non-functional		O	
2001-034A	GENESIS	USA	08/08/2001	USA	USA	O		
2001-034B～C		USA	08/08/2001	USA	Non-functional		O	
2001-035A	STS 105 (DISCOVERY)	USA	10/08/2001	USA	USA	O		
2001-035B	SIMPLESAT	USA	21/08/2001	USA	USA	O		
2001-036A	PROGRESS M-45	Russian Fed.	21/08/2001	Kazakhstan	Russian Fed.	O		
2001-036B		Non-reg.	21/08/2001	Kazakhstan	Non-functional		-	
2001-037A	COSMOS 2379	Russian Fed.	24/08/2001	Kazakhstan	Russian Fed.	O		
2001-037B～H		Non-reg.	24/08/2001	Kazakhstan	Non-functional		-	
2001-038A	LRE	Japan	29/08/2001	Japan	Japan	O		
2001-038B	VEP 2 + second stage	Non-reg.	29/08/2001	Japan	Japan	-		
2001-039A	INTELSAT 902	Non-reg.	30/08/2001	France	INTELSAT	-		6)
2001-039B		France	30/08/2001	France	Non-functional		O	
2001-040A	USA 160	USA	08/09/2001	USA	USA	O		
2001-040B～C		USA	08/09/2001	USA	Non-functional		O	

2001-041	PIRS	Non-reg.	14/09/2001	Kazakhstan	Russian Fed.	-		
2001-041A	Progress M-SO1	Russian Fed.	14/09/2001	Kazakhstan	Russian Fed.	O		
2001-041B		Non-reg.	14/09/2001	Kazakhstan	Non-functional		-	
2001-042A	EUTELSAT ATLANTIC BIRD 2	France	25/09/2001	France	EUTELSAT	O		5)
2001-042B		France	25/09/2001	France	Non-functional		O	
2001-043A	STARSHINE 3	USA	30/09/2001	USA	USA	O		
2001-043B	PICOSAT 9	USA	30/09/2001	USA	USA	O		
2001-043C	PCSAT	USA	30/09/2001	USA	USA	O		
2001-043D	SAPPHIRE	USA	30/09/2001	USA	USA	O		
2001-043E		USA	30/09/2001	USA	Non-functional		O	
2001-044A	USA 161	USA	05/10/2001	USA	USA	O		
2001-044B		USA	05/10/2001	USA	Non-functional		O	
2001-045A	RADUGA 1	Russian Fed.	06/10/2001	Kazakhstan	Russian Fed.	O		
2001-045B～H		Non-Reg.	06/10/2001	Kazakhstan	Non-functional		-	
2001-046A	USA 162	USA	11/10/2001	USA	USA	O		
2001-046B		USA	11/10/2001	USA	Non-functional		O	
2001-047A	QUICKBIRD	USA	18/10/2001	USA	USA	O		
2001-047B		USA	18/10/2001	USA	Non-functional		O	
2001-048A	SOYUZ TM-33	Russian Fed.	21/10/2001	Kazakhstan	Russian Fed.	O		
2001-048B		Non-reg.	21/10/2001	Kazakhstan	Non-functional		-	
2001-049A	TES	India	22/10/2001	India	India	O		
2001-049B	PROBA	Non-reg.	22/10/2001	India	ESA	-		
2001-049C	BIRD	Germany	22/10/2001	India	Germany	O		

2001-049D		India	22/10/2001	India	Non-functional		O	
2001-049E~PN		Non-reg.	22/10/2001	India	Non-functional		-	
2001-050A	MOLNIYA 3	Russian Fed.	25/10/2001	Russian Fed.	Russian Fed.	O		
2001-050B~D		Non-reg.	25/10/2001	Russian Fed.	Non-functional		-	
2001-051A	PROGRESS M1-7	Russian Fed.	26/11/2001	Kazakhstan	Russian Fed.	O		
2001-051B		Non-Reg.	26/11/2001	Kazakhstan	Non-functional		-	
2001-051C	KOLIBRI 2000	Russian Fed.	20/03/2002	Kazakhstan	Russian Fed.	O		
2001-052A	DIRECTV 4S	USA	27/11/2001	France	USA	O		
2001-052B		France	27/11/2001	France	Non-functional		O	
2001-053A	COSMOS 2380	Russian Fed.	01/12/2001	Kazakhstan	Russian Fed.	O		
2001-053B	COSMOS 2381	Russian Fed.	01/12/2001	Kazakhstan	Russian Fed.	O		
2001-053C	COSMOS 2382	Russian Fed.	01/12/2001	Kazakhstan	Russian Fed.	O		
2001-053D~H		Non-reg.	01/12/2001	Kazakhstan	Non-functional		-	
2001-054A	STS 108 (ENDEAVOUR)	USA	05/12/2001	USA	USA	O		
2001-054B	STARSHINE 2	USA	05/12/2001	USA	USA	O		
2001-055A	JASON	USA	07/12/2001	USA	France/USA	O		
2001-055B	TIMED	USA	07/12/2001	USA	USA	O		
2001-055C~E		USA	07/12/2001	USA	Non-functional		O	
2001-056A	METEOR 3M-N1	Russian Fed.	10/12/2001	Kazakhstan	Russian Fed.	O		
2001-056B	KOMPASS	Russian Fed.	10/12/2001	Kazakhstan	Russian Fed.	O		
2001-056C	BADR B	Pakistan	10/12/2001	Kazakhstan	Pakistan	O		
2001-056D	MAROC TUBSAT	Non-reg.	10/12/2001	Kazakhstan	Morocco	-		

2001-056E	REFLEKTOR	Russian Fed./ USA	10/12/2001	Kazakhstan	Russian Fed./ USA	O		Double registration
2001-056F~L		Non-reg.	10/12/2001	Kazakhstan	Non-functional		-	
2001-057A	COSMOS 2383	Russian Fed.	21/12/2001	Kazakhstan	Russian Fed.	O		
2001-057B~J		Non-reg.	21/12/2001	Kazakhstan	Non-functional		-	
2001-058A	COSMOS 2384	Russian Fed.	28/12/2001	Russian Fed.	Russian Fed.	O		
2001-058B	COSMOS 2385	Russian Fed.	28/12/2001	Russian Fed.	Russian Fed.	O		
2001-058C	COSMOS 2386	Russian Fed.	28/12/2001	Russian Fed.	Russian Fed.	O		
2001-058D	GONETS D1-7	Russian Fed.	28/12/2001	Russian Fed.	Russian Fed.	O		
2001-058E	GONETS D1M-8	Russian Fed.	28/12/2001	Russian Fed.	Russian Fed.	O		
2001-058F	GONETS D1M-9	Russian Fed.	28/12/2001	Russian Fed.	Russian Fed.	O		
2001-058G		Non-reg.	28/12/2001	Russian Fed.	Non-functional		-	

1) The name of space objects is generally attached only to a functional object.

2) In this Table the Baikonur cosmodrome in Kazakhstan is considered as part of the Russian Federation.

3) 'O': the State of nationality of the owner/operator is the State of registry; 'X': is not; '-': non-registered.

4) 'O': the State of location of launch is the State of registry; 'X': is not; '-': non-registered; '*': is other.

5) Under France and EUTELSAT Agreement, France registers EUTELSAT satellites.

6) In this table the State of nationality of the owner/operator of INTELSAT satellites is INTELSAT.

Source: Some materials and many Internet sites including COPUOS site and JAXA site (see Sakota 2007, 193, fn. 144).

the object on the ground of some facts. This chapter calls this result of analysis as 'Result F' ('F' means functional space objects).[49]

State of Registry on the Non-functional Space Objects Among 28 registered non-functional space objects, 26 objects are registered by the State of the location of launch.

The two exceptions are the objects that were launched by Sea Launch Company on high sea and don't have the State of the location's launching. We will discuss the examples from the Sea Launch Company below.

The analysis shows that the decisive factor of the registration of non-functional space object seems to be the location of the launch when it is launched in the territory of a State. Most of the non-functional objects are, however, not registered (432 among 460). Because of this reason we can only point out a trend which, for the non-functional space objects, the State of the location of launch of the object registers the object. This paper calls this trend as 'Result N' ('N' means non-functional space objects).[50]

Registration Practice Relevant to Japan

Table 12.2 lists 92 space objects which have some relevance to Japan and have launched since 1989 when Japanese private companies began to engage in space activities. Table 12.2 has only functional space objects as the Japanese government doesn't register non-functional objects.

Among 84 registered objects, the State of nationality of the owner/operator is the State of registry for all of them.

Registration Practice of the Objects Launched by Sea Launch Company on the High Sea

The space objects which are launched by Sea Launch Company on the high sea don't have the State of location of the launch. This company is an international joint venture owned by a US company (40 per cent), Russian entity (25 per cent),

---

49 Prof. Aoki has the same view as with 'Result F': Aoki 2002, 82. Ms. Uchitomi points out that 'Generally, the State of the national who owns the launched space object registers it' (Uchitomi 2001, 57). While Uchitomi has almost same with 'Result F', she excludes the factor 'operation'.

50 'COPUOS Secretary Background Paper 2005' is the only literature or report which analyzes the registration practice of non-functional space objects. It says simply 'Registration of non-functional objects resulting from a launch is normally done by the States that provide launch services'. Although this view seems to be in accordance with 'Result N', the words 'the States that provide launch services' is not clear when a launching service is provided by private enterprise.

Table 12.2 Space objects relevant to Japan [1)]

International Designator	Name of Space Object	State of Registry	Date of Launch	Location of Launch [2)]	Nationality of the Owner/ Operator of the Object	Result F [3)]	Remarks
1989-016A	EXOS D	Japan	21/02/1989	Japan	Japan	O	
1989-020A	JCSAT 1	Japan	06/03/1989	France	Japan	O	
1989-041A	SUPERBIRD A-1	Non-reg.	05/06/1989	France	Japan	-	
1989-070A	GMS 4	Japan	05/09/1989	Japan	Japan	O	
1990-001B	JCSAT 2	Japan	01/01/1990	USA	Japan	O	
1990-007A	MUSES A	Japan	24/01/1990	Japan	Japan	O	
1990-007B	HAGOROMO	Non-reg.	24/01/1990	Japan	Japan	-	
1990-013A	MOS IB	Japan	07/02/1990	Japan	Japan	O	
1990-013B	DEBUT	Japan	07/02/1990	Japan	Japan	O	
1990-013C	JAS 1B	Japan	07/02/1990	Japan	Japan	O	
1990-077A	BS 3A	Japan	28/08/1990	Japan	Japan	O	
1990-107A	SOYUZ TM-11	USSR	02/12/1990	USSR	USSR	O	Japanese journalist on board
1991-060A	BS 3B	Japan	25/08/1991	Japan	Japan	O	
1991-062A	SOLAR A	Japan	30/08/1991	Japan	Japan	O	
1992-007A	JERS 1	Japan	11/02/1992	Japan	Japan	O	
1992-010A	SUPERBIRD B	Japan	26/02/1992	France	Japan	O	
1992-044A	GEOTAIL	Japan	24/07/1992	USA	Japan	O	
1992-061A	STS 47 (ENDEAVOUR)	USA	12/09/1992	USA	USA	O	Japanese astronaut on board
1992-084A	SUPERBIRD A1	Japan	01/12/1992	France	Japan	O	
1993-011A	ASTRO D	Japan	20/02/1993	Japan	Japan	O	

1994-007A	OREX	Japan	03/02/1994	Japan	Japan	O	
1994-007B	VEP	Japan	03/02/1994	Japan	Japan	O	
1994-039A	STS 65 (COLUMBIA)	USA	08/07/1994	USA	USA	O	Japanese astronaut on board
1994-040A	PANAMSAT 2 (PAS 2)	Non-reg.	08/07/1994	France	USA	-	Communication satellite for Japanese area
1994-040B	BS 3N	Japan	08/07/1994	France	Japan	O	
1994-056A	ETS 6	Japan	28/08/1994	Japan	Japan	O	
1995-011A	SPACE FLYER UNIT	Japan	18/03/1995	Japan	Japan	O	
1995-011B	GMS 5	Japan	18/03/1995	Japan	Japan	O	
1995-040A	PANAMSAT 4 (PAS 4)	USA	03/08/1995	France	USA	O	Communication satellite for Japanese area
1995-043A	JCSAT 3	Japan	29/08/1995	USA	Japan	O	
1995-044A	N-STAR 1	Japan	29/08/1995	France	Japan	O	
1995-062A	ISO	ESA	17/11/1995	France	ESA	O	
1996-001A	STS 72 (ENDEAVOUR)	USA	11/01/1996	USA	USA	O	Japanese astronaut on board
1996-007A	N-STAR B	Japan	05/02/1996	France	Japan	O	
1996-046A	ADEOS	Japan	17/08/1996	Japan	Japan	O	
1996-046B	JAS 2	Japan	17/08/1996	Japan	Japan	O	
1997-005A	MUSES B/VSOP	Japan	12/02/1997	Japan	Japan	O	
1997-007A	JCSAT 4	Japan	17/02/1997	USA	Japan	O	
1997-016B	BSAT 1A	Japan	16/04/1997	France	Japan	O	
1997-036A	SUPERBIRD C	Japan	28/07/1997	USA	Japan	O	
1997-039A	STS 85 (DISCOVERY)	USA	07/08/1997	USA	USA	O	

1997-073A	STS 87 (COLUMBIA)	USA	19/11/1997	USA	USA	O	Japanese astronaut on board
1997-074A	TRMM	USA	27/11/1997	Japan	USA	O	
1997-074B	ETS 7	Japan	27/11/1997	Japan	Japan	O	
1997-074E	ETS 7 TARGET	Japan	27/11/1997	Japan	Japan	O	
1997-075A	JCSAT 5	Japan	02/12/1997	France	Japan	O	
1998-011A	COMETS	Japan	21/02/1998	Japan	Japan	O	
1998-022A	STS 90 (COLUMBIA)	USA	17/04/1998	USA	USA	O	
1998-024B	BSAT-1B	Japan	28/04/1998	France	Japan	O	
1998-034A	STS 91 (DISCOVERY)	USA	02/06/1998	USA	USA	O	
1998-041A	PLANET B	Japan	03/07/1998	Japan	Japan	O	
1998-064A	STS 95 (DISCOVERY)	USA	29/10/1998	USA	USA	O	Japanese astronaut on board
1998-065A	PANAMSAT 8	Non-reg.	04/11/1998	Kazakhstan	USA	-	Communication satellite for Japanese territory
1999-006A	JCSAT 6	Japan	16/02/1999	USA	Japan	O	
2000-010A	STS 99 (ENDEAVOUR)	USA	11/02/2000	USA	USA	O	Japanese astronaut on board
2000-012A	SUPERBIRD B2	Japan	18/02/2000	France	Japan	O	
2000-017A	IMAGE	USA	25/03/2000	USA	USA	O	
2000-060A	N-SAT-110	Japan	06/10/2000	France	Japan	O	
2000-062A	STS 92 (DISCOVERY)	USA	11/10/2000	USA	USA	O	Japanese astronaut on board
2000-081C	LDREX	Japan	20/12/2000	France	Japan	O	
2001-011B	BSAT 2A	Japan	08/03/2001	France	Japan	O	
2001-029B	BSAT 2B	Non-reg.	12/07/2001	France	Japan (planned)	-	Failure to be placed in orbit

2001-038A	LRE	Japan	29/08/2001	Japan	Japan	O	
2001-038B	VEP 2 + second stage	Non-reg.	29/08/2001	Japan	Japan	-	
2002-003A	MDS-1	Japan	04/02/2002	Japan	Japan	O	
2002-003B	DASH	Japan	04/02/2002	Japan	Japan	O	
2002-003C	VEP 3	Non-reg.	04/02/2002	Japan	Japan	-	
2002-015A	JCSAT 8	Japan	29/03/2002	France	Japan	O	
2002-022A	AQUA	USA	04/05/2002	USA	USA	O	
2002-035B	N-STAR C	Japan	05/07/2002	France	Japan	O	
2002-042A	USERS	Japan	10/09/2002	Japan	Japan	O	
2002-042B	DRTS	Japan	10/09/2002	Japan	Japan	O	
2002-056A	ADEOS II	Japan	14/12/2002	Japan	Japan	O	
2002-056B	FEDSAT 1	Australia	14/12/2002	Japan	Australia	O	
2002-056C	WEOS	Japan	14/12/2002	Japan	Japan	O	
2002-056D	MICRO LABSAT	Japan	14/12/2002	Japan	Japan	O	
2003-009A	IGS 1A	Japan	28/03/2003	Japan	Japan	O	
2003-009B	IGS 1B	Japan	28/03/2003	Japan	Japan	O	
2003-019A	MUSES C	Japan	09/05/2003	Japan	Japan	O	
2003-028A	BSAT 2C	Japan	11/06/2003	France	Japan	O	
2003-031E	CUTE 1	Japan	30/06/2003	Russian Fed.	Japan	O	
2003-031J	XI	Japan	30/06/2003	Russian Fed.	Japan	O	
2003-044A	HORIZONS 1; GALAXY 13	USA	01/10/2003	On high sea	Japan/ USA	O	4)
2003-050A	SERVIS 1	Japan	30/10/2003	Russian Fed.	Japan	O	
2004-007A	MBSAT	Non-reg.	13/03/2004	USA	Japan	-	5)

2004-011A	SUPERBIRD A2	Japan	16/04/2004	USA	Japan	O	
2005-006A	MTSAT 1R	Japan	26/02/2005	Japan	Japan	O	
2005-025A	ASTRO EII	Japan	10/07/2005	Japan	Japan	O	
2005-026A	STS 114 (DISCOVERY)	USA	26/07/2005	USA	USA	O	Japanese astronaut on board
2005-031A	OICETS	Japan	23/08/2005	Kazakhstan	Japan	O	
2005-031B	INDEX	Japan	23/08/2005	Kazakhstan	Japan	O	
2005-043F	CUBESAT XI-V	Japan	27/10/2005	Russian Fed.	Japan	O	

1) 'Space Objects Relevant to Japan' include the objects launched since 1989 (a) of which the State of registry is Japan, (b) launched from, Japanese territory, (c) owned/operated by Japanese organizations, (d) on which Japanese nationals are on board or (e) communication/broadcasting satellites licenced by Japanese government, and exclude non-functional space objects.

2) In this table the Baikonur cosmodrome in Kazakhstan is considered as in Russian Federation.

3) 'O': the State of nationality of the owner/operator is the State of registry; 'X': is not; '-': non-registered.

4) Owned by Horizons Satellite LLC (USA). This corporation is owned equally by PanAmSat (USA) and Jsat International Inc. (USA). Jsat International is a subsidiary of Jsat (Japan).

5) Jointly owned by Mobile Broadcasting Co. (Japan) and SK Telecom (Korea) and operated by SCC (Japan).

Source: See Table 12.1.

Norwegian corporation (20 per cent) and Ukrainian entity (15 per cent). It was incorporated in Cayman Islands (UK) and since 2000 it is a US corporation. Two ships, of Liberian nationality, are used for launching. Since the first launching, this company has obtained licensing by the US government.[51]

Table 12.3 lists all of the space objects launched by Sea Launch Company on the high sea. As shown in the Table 12.3, for all of the 17 registered functional space objects, the States of nationality of the owners/operators of the objects are the States of registry.

There are five registered non-functional space objects, all of which were registered by USA during the period 1999–2002 where the functional space objects launched simultaneously with those non-functional objects were also registered by USA. The link between these non-functional objects and the USA seems to be the US license issued. The USA has not, however, registered non-functional space objects launched by that company since 2003. There are not enough practices to find some result on registration of non-functional space objects launched outside State territories.

Other Registration Practices

There are several interesting registration practices, such as:

1. internal registration criteria of several States (especially USA practice and Russian Federation law),
2. a newly registered space object as transferred of ownership to foreign company,
3. change of the State of registry on 4 satellites on the occasion of transfer of the sovereignty of Hong Kong,
4. actions of UK and Netherlands on several INTELSAT and INMARSAT satellites,
5. determination of the State of registry under the agreements between States or governmental space agencies.

Owing to limited space, we cannot analyze the registration practices in this chapter. These practices also support in main the 'Result F'.[52]

Analysis of Registration Practices and Article VI of the 1967 OST

The analysis of registration practices of space objects shows the following. First, for the functional space objects, the practice is fully established that the State of nationality of the owner/operator of the object registers the object. Second, for the

51 See Sea Launch 2003, 11–6 and see also the Protocol attached to the 1996 US–Ukraine Commercial Space Launch Agreement.

52 In regards to these practices see Sakota 2007, 200–210.

Table 12.3 Space objects launched by Sea Launch Company

International Designator [1]	Name of Space Object	State of Registry	Date of Launch	Nationality of the Owner/ Operator of the Object	Result F [2]	Remarks
1999-014A	DEMOSAT	Non-reg.	28/03/1999	UK	-	
1999-014B		Non-reg.	28/03/1999			
1999-056A	DIRECTV 1-R	USA	10/10/1999	USA	O	
1999-056B		USA	10/10/1999			Registered by USA
2000-043A	PAS 9	USA	28/07/2000	USA	O	
2000-043B		USA	28/07/2000			Registered by USA
2000-066A	THURAYA 1	UAE	21/10/2000	UAE	O	
2000-066B		Non-reg.	21/10/2000			
2001-012A	XM 2 ROCK	USA	18/03/2001	USA	O	
2001-012B		USA	18/03/2001			Registered by USA
2001-018A	XM 1 ROLL	USA	08/05/2001	USA	O	
2001-018B		USA	08/05/2001			Registered by USA
2002-030A	GALAXY 3C	USA	15/06/2002	USA	O	
2002-030B		USA	15/06/2002			Registered by USA
2003-026A	THURAYA 2	UAE	10/06/2003	UAE	O	
2003-026B		Non-reg.	10/06/2003			
2003-034A	ECHOSTAR 9 ; TELSTAR 13	USA	08/08/2003	USA	O	
2003-034B		Non-reg.	08/08/2003			
2003-044A	HORIZONS 1; GALAXY 13	USA	01/10/2003	USA/Japan	O	See note [4] of Table 12.2
2003-044B		Non-reg.	01/10/2003			
2004-001A	ESTRELA DU SOL-TELSTAR14	Non-reg.	11/01/2004	Brazil	-	

2004-001B		Non-reg.	11/01/2004			
2004-016A	DIRECTV 7S	USA	04/05/2004	USA	O	
2004-016B		Non-reg.	04/05/2004			
2004-024A	APSTAR 5 (TELSTAR 18)	Non-reg.	29/06/2004	China/USA	-	
2004-024B		Non-reg.	04/05/2004			
2005-008A	XM 3	USA	01/03/2005	USA	O	
2005-008B		Non-reg.	01/03/2005			
2005-015A	SPACEWAY 1	USA	26/04/2005	USA	O	
2005-015B		Non-reg.	26/04/2005			
2005-022A	INTELSAT AMERICAS 8	Non-reg.	23/06/2005	Intelsat	-	See note [6] of Table 12.1
2005-022B		Non-reg.	23/06/2005			
2005-044A	INMARSAT 4-F2	Non-reg.	08/11/2005	Inmarsat	-	[3]
2006-003A	ECHOSTAR 10	USA	15/02/2006	USA	O	
2006-003B		Non-reg.	15/02/2006			
2006-010A	JCSAT 9	Japan	12/04/2006	Japan	O	
2006-010B		Non-reg.	12/04/2006			
2006-023A	GALAXY 16	USA	18/06/2006	USA	O	
2006-023B		Non-reg.	18/06/2006			
2006-034A	KOREASAT 5	Korea	22/08/2006	Korea	O	
2006-034B		Non-reg.	22/08/2006			
2006-049A	XM 4	USA	30/10/2006	USA	O	
2006-049B		Non-reg.	30/10/2006			

1) The object with 'B' of the last letter of international designators is a non-functional space object. Failure to ascertain the existence of object '2005-044B'.

2) 'O': the State of nationality of the owner/operator is the State of registry; 'X': is not; '-': non-registered.

3) In this table the State of nationality of the owner/operator of INMARST satellites is INMARSAT.

Source: See Table 12.1.

non-functional objects, there seems to be the trend that the State of the location of launching the object registers that object. And third, it might be possible to point out from the registration practice the fact that a State generally considers the relationship with the objects according to the forms of the space activities.

Now one turns back to the problem of Article VI of the Outer Space Treaty. While the registration system of space objects governs the relationship between a State and a space object, Article VI governs the relationship between a State and a space activity. Because both norms govern different matters, the registration practice itself is not necessarily regarded as the practice of Article VI. In the registration practice, however, we find that the activities of operation of the functional space objects and the activities of launching of the non-functional space objects are the decisive factors to connect the State with the space activities. We can find in this case the relationship between a State and a space activity, which is governed by Article VI.

Based on this consideration, we can point out on the interpretation of Article VI as follows. First, as indicated in the registration practices of space objects, States distinguish the forms of space activities operation of space object, etc. in order to link itself with the activities. This fact seems to lead us to the fact that the responsible State/the appropriate State might be different according to the forms of space activities, in that there would be different responsible States/ appropriate States for different forms of activities, such as launching, operation of space object, manufacture of space object and launching vehicle or utilization of satellite for communication or broadcasting, etc. It should be noted, however, that the activities for which State is responsible and obligatory under Article VI are limited to 'activities in outer space' as stated in that clause.

Second concerning the functional space objects, the State considers that the State of nationality of the owner/operator has the closest relationship with the space object. From this fact, we might hypothesize that this State is the responsible State/appropriate State for the operational activity of the objects in Article VI. It is very difficult to consider from this fact that some another State such as the State of location of launch of the object, the State of nationality of the manufacture of the object or the launching vehicle, the State of nationality of the ship where the activity is conducted, etc. is the responsible State/appropriate State in Article VI.

Finally concerning the non-functional space objects, the State seems to consider that the State of the location of the launch of the object has closer relationship with the space object. From this fact and the analysis of national space legislation, we might be able to make another suggestion that this State is the responsible State/ appropriate State for the launching activity of the object, whether the object is functional or non-functional, in Article VI.

Conclusion

Article VI of the 1967 OST is one of most arguable provisions in international space law. Most writers have focused mainly on the argued special attribution rule and absolute liability of State emphasizing the theoretical aspects. It is very important in the light of reality of the age of space commercialization, however, to examine the implementation of Article VI by States. The abstract norm in this article could be seen as having concrete content through State practices in relation to the real space activities conducted by private enterprises, and these practices should be found in the implementation of this article. As we have seen in this chapter, however, States' national space legislation do not provide much in the way of useful information on this point. In such a situation, the registration practices of space objects would provide some useful information on the interpretation of Article VI.

It is the functional space objects that play the most important roles in space activities. The analysis in this chapter shows that the registration practice is established by the State of nationality of the owners/operators of the functional space object. Although this practice itself cannot be identified with the implementation of Article VI, this should be taken as the starting point to interpret this article, because an interpretation which contravenes or neglects this fact is not effective in international space law.

To conclude, mention must be made of the meaning of 'ownership/operation'. The analysis shows that 'ownership/operation' of the functional space objects is decisive factor. Why exactly is that the decisive factor which links the State to the object? Why is the nationality of the entity important? Is the nationality truly an essential element? What is the most reasonable and universal reason to base the relationship between the State and the functional space object with the nationality of owner/operator? It is necessary to solve these questions in order to identify the responsible State and the appropriate State. In this context the meaning of 'ownership/operation' is important. This is a mixed notion of (a) ownership in private law, (b) telemetry, tracking and command (TT&C), and (c) practical utilization, such as communication, broadcasting, etc. One might find in the practices of the ITU system the decisive meaning of 'ownership/operation' in identifying the responsible State and appropriate State in Article VI of the Outer Space Treaty.

References

Books, Articles and Chapters in Books

American Law Institute (1965), *Restatement of the Law, 2nd, Foreign Relations Law of the United States 1962* (St. Paul, Minn.: American Law Institute Publishers).

Aoki, S. (2001), 'Commercial Utilization of Outer Space', in Japanese Association of International Law (ed.), *One Century of Japan and International Law* 2 (Tokyo: Sanseido Publishing) 243–269 [in Japanese].

Aoki, S. (2002), '"Launching States" Concept in the Era of Commercial Space Launching', *Journal of Law, Politics, and Sociology* (Keio University) 75:2, 57–85 [in Japanese].

Bittlinger, H. (1987), 'Private Space Activities: Questions of International Responsibility', *IISL 1987* 30, 191–196.

Bogaert, E. van (1986), *Aspects of Space Law* (Deventer: Kluwer Law and Taxation Publishers).

Bourély, M. (1986), 'Rules of International Law Governing the Commercialization of Space Activities', *IISL 1986* 29, 157–160.

Cheng, B. (1998), 'Article VI of the 1967 Space Treaty Revisited: 'International Responsibility', 'National Activities', and 'The Appropriate State', *Journal of Space Law* 26:1, 7–32.

Csabafi, I. (1971), *The Concept of State Jurisdiction in International Space Law* (The Hague: Nijhoff).

Dembling, Paul G. and Arons, Daniel M. (1967), 'The Evolution of the Outer Space Treaty', *Journal of Air Law and Commerce* 33:3, 419–456.

Dembling, P. (1970), 'Commercial Utilization of Space and the Law', *Yearbook of Air and Space Law 1967* 1, 283–295.

Gál, G. (1969), *Space Law* [translated by Imre Móra] (Leyden: Sijthoff).

Gorove, S. (1983), 'Liability in Space Law: An Overview', *Annals of Air and Space Law* 8, 373–380.

Hermida, J. (2004), *Legal Basis for a National Space Legislation* (Dordrecht: Kluwer Academic).

Jasentuliyana, N. (1989), 'Article I of Outer Space Treaty Revisited', *Journal of Space Law* 17:2, 129–144.

Jenks, C. (1965), *Space Law* (London: Stevens).

Kerrest, A. (1997), 'Remarks on the Responsibility and Liability for Damages Caused by Private Activities in Outer Space', *IISL 1997* 40, 134–140.

Lachs, M. (1966), 'The International Law of Outer Space' *Recueil des cours 1964-III* 113, 1–115.

Malanczuk, P. (1997), *Akehurst's Modern Introduction to International Law*, 7th ed. (London: Routledge).

Marcoff, M. (1973), *Traité de droit international public de l'espace* (Fribourg: Editions Universitaire Fribourg Suisse).

Meredith, P. and Robinson, G. (1992), *Space Law: A Case Study for the Practitioner* (Dordrecht: Nijhoff).

Murase, S. (1994), 'State Responsibility for Corporate Activities in International Environmental Law', *Journal of International Law and Diplomacy* 93:3–4, 130–159 [in Japanese].

Sakota, A. (1996), 'The Criterion of the Attribution to the State of the Conduct of Private Persons', *Waseda Law Journal* 46, 1–43 [in Japanese].

Sakota, A. (2002a), 'Making of the Article 6 of 1967 Outer Space Treaty (1)', *The Economic Review* (Otaru University of Commerce) 52:4, 221–247 [in Japanese].

Sakota, A. (2002b), 'Making of the Article 6 of 1967 Outer Space Treaty (2)', *The Economic Review* (Otaru University of Commerce) 53:1, 385–413 [in Japanese].

Sakota, A. (2002c), 'Making of the Article 6 of 1967 Outer Space Treaty (3)', *The Economic Review* (Otaru University of Commerce) 53:2–3, 187–216 [in Japanese]

Sakota, A. (2004), 'The Object and Purpose of the First Part of the First Sentence of Article VI of 1967 Outer Space Treaty', *The Economic Review* (Otaru University of Commerce) 54:4, 131–163 [in Japanese].

Sakota, A. (2005), 'The Meaning of "International Responsibility" of the First Sentence of Article VI of the 1967 Outer Space Treaty', *Journal of Air Law* 46, 39–78 [in Japanese].

Sakota, A. (2006), 'The Link between a Space Object and a State in the Practice of Registering Space Objects (1)', *The Economic Review* (Otaru University of Commerce) 57:2–3, 33–64 [in Japanese].

Sakota, A. (2007), 'The Link between a Space Object and a State in the Practice of Registering Space Objects (2)', *The Economic Review* (Otaru University of Commerce) 57:4, 183–225 [in Japanese].

Silvestrov, G. (1991), 'On the Notion of the "Appropriate" State in Article VI of the Outer Space', *IISL 1991* 34, 326–330.

Sohn, L. and Baxter, R. (1961), 'Responsibility of States for Injuries to the Economic Interests of Aliens', *American Journal of International Law* 55:3, 545–585.

Traa-Engelman, H. van (1993), *Commercial Utilization of Outer Space* (Dordrecht: Nijhoff).

Uchitomi, M. (2001), 'State Responsibility/Liability for "National" Space Activities: Towards Safe and Fair Competition in Private Space Activities', *IISL 2001* 44, 51–60.

Vereshchetin, V. (1983), 'Space Activities of 'Nongovernmental Entities'', *IISL 1983* 26, 261–266.

Wassenbergh, H. (1991), *Principles of Outer Space Law in Hindsight* (Dordrecht: Nijhoff).

Wassenbergh, H. (1997), 'International Space Law: A Turn of the Tide', *Air and Space Law* 22:6, 334–341.

Yamamoto, Soji (1994), *International Law*, 2nd ed. (Tokyo: Yuhikaku Publishing) [in Japanese].

Official Documents and Others

COPUOS Secretary Background Paper (2005), Secretary of COPUOS, 'Background paper: Practice of States and international organizations in registering space objects' (AC.105/C.2/L.255, 25 January 2005).

COPUOS Secretariat Review (2001), Secretariat of United Nations Committee on the Peaceful Uses of Outer Space (COPUOS), 'Review of existing national space legislation illustrating how States are implementing, as appropriate, their responsibilities to authorize and provide continuing supervision of non-governmental entities in outer space' (A/AC.105/C.2/L.224, 22 January 2001).

IISL 19XX, International Institute of Space Law, *Proceedings of the Colloquium on the Law of Outer Space 19XX.*

Sea Launch (2003), *Sea Launch User's Guide, rev. C* (2003).

UN/Nigeria Workshop (2005), United Nations/Nigeria Workshop on Space Law, *Meeting International Responsibilities and Addressing Domestic Needs: National Legislation and Policy Selected Texts* (2005).

YbILC 1961, vol. II (1961), *Yearbook of the International Law Commission 1961*, vol. II.

Chapter 13
How to Design an International Liability Regime for Public Spaces: The Case of the Antarctic Environment

Akiho Shibata[1]

Introduction

In 2005, at the 28th meeting of the Antarctic Treaty Consultative Parties (ATCM) held in Stockholm, Sweden, a new Annex to the Protocol on Environmental Protection to the Antarctic Treaty (Madrid Protocol) was adopted. This is 'Annex VI on Liability Arising from Environmental Emergencies' (Liability Annex).[2] The Liability Annex could be considered as the first complete legally binding environmental liability regime applicable to cases where both the cause and effect of an environmental incident occur in a public space.[3] The Antarctic Treaty area can be considered as a public space, similar to the high seas and outer space.[4] In public spaces, certain freedoms for all States are recognized and the exercise of territorial jurisdiction is prohibited, restricted or made inopposable to other States by the applicable international law. In Antarctica, the freedom to conduct scientific activities is guaranteed to all nations under Article II of the Antarctic Treaty. According to Article IV of the Treaty, the claims to territorial sovereignty asserted by seven States over Antarctica are not legally opposable to those States that do not recognize such claims.[5]

---

1 The author participated in the negotiation of the Liability Annex as a member of the Japanese delegation. The views expressed in this chapter are the author's personal ones and do not reflect those of the Japanese government.

2 Liability Annex 2005. For a brief analysis of the Liability Annex, see Shibata 2007, 201–232. See also Gautier 2006, 418.

3 See Scott 2006, 87. Philippe Sands wrote in 2003 that one of the issues remaining to be addressed in international law on environmental liability is the liability for damage to the environment in areas beyond national jurisdiction. Sands 2003, 939.

4 Many international lawyers treat Antarctica as a 'common area or space'. Boyle 1997, 83–85; Fitzmaurice 1996, 305; Brunnée 2007, 557–561.

5 Article IV of the Antarctic Treaty provides that, although the Treaty shall not be interpreted as a renunciation by the seven claimant states of previously asserted rights of or claims to territorial sovereignty in Antarctica, the positions of non-claimant not to recognize any of those rights or claims shall not be prejudiced. 'From the jurisdictional point of view the area is treated as res nullis and the nationality principle presumably governs'. Brownlie 2003, 255.

In the high seas, there are some provisions in the existing treaties mandating that the Parties develop such liability regimes,[6] but none has yet actually been successfully negotiated.[7] As will be examined in more detail, the International Maritime Organization's (IMO) oil pollution liability conventions cover, in principle, the pollution damage occurring only in the national jurisdiction, including the Exclusive Economic Zones (EEZ), of coastal states. With regard to the deep seabed and the liability arising from mineral resource activities there, Article 139 of the United Nations Convention on the Law of the Sea (UNCLOS) and Article 22 of Annex III on Basic Conditions of Prospecting, Exploration and Exploitation provide for a skeleton legal framework. In 2000, the International Seabed Authority adopted regulations on prospecting and exploration for polymetallic nodules in the Area.[8] These regulations foresee that the liability of Contractors would be provided in contracts between the Authority and companies. Much of their content, however, still depends on the future practice of the Authority.[9] These liability schemes are either not applicable in public spaces, or are far from complete as a legal design.

A partial liability regime for Antarctica has been negotiated and adopted in the past. Article 8 of the Convention on the Regulation of Antarctic Mineral Resource Activities (CRAMRA)[10] contains certain provisions related to the liability arising from mineral resource activities in Antarctica. First, CRAMRA leaves important details for future elaboration in a separate protocol. Second, it applies only to mineral resource activities in Antarctica, considered by many at the time as environmentally risky, warranting a special legal response. Finally, and significantly, from the view point of this article, CRAMRA is not expected, at least for a few decades, to be a legally binding instrument, requiring the Consultative Parties to implement its provisions into their domestic laws. On the other hand, the Liability Annex applies to all activities, including scientific research programmes, tourism and other governmental and non-governmental activities for which advance notice is required under Article VII (5) of the Treaty, as long as these activities cause environmental emergencies in the Antarctic Treaty area. The Liability Annex intends to be a complete regime enforceable as of today. The

6 Article X of the London Convention on the Prevention of Marine Pollution by Dumping of Wastes and Other Matter, adopted on 29 December 1972. Article 235 (3) of the United Nations Convention on the Law of the Sea, adopted on 10 December 1982.

7 Birnie and Boyle 2002, 383–391, particularly footnote 201. Draft guidelines on liability and compensation for damage resulting from pollution of the marine environment in the Mediterranean Sea Area under the 1976 Barcelona Convention will soon be adopted. But this is a non-binding instrument. See the Council of Europe Civil Liability Convention of 1993, especially Article 3(b), for a unique approach.

8 Decision of the Assembly, ISBA/6/A/18 (4 October 2000), Regulation 30. See also de La Fayette 2005, 199–201.

9 de La Fayette 2007, 122–124.

10 The Convention on the Regulation of Antarctic Mineral Resource Activities, adopted on 2 June 1988, reprinted in ATCM Handbook 2002, 385. See generally Burmester 1989, 621.

Consultative Parties are expected to ratify the Liability Annex as soon as possible to allow this legal instrument to enter into force.[11] The possible ways and means to implement the Annex domestically and its entering into force in timely manner were recognized as major challenges for the Parties during its negotiation.[12] The issue of domestic implementation of the Annex has continued to attract significant interest among the Consultative Parties.[13]

A liability regime in Antarctica would truly be significant if the objective and the actual effect of the Annex were to protect the Antarctic environment, going beyond the traditional tort mechanism of compensating injuries to persons and property.[14] In other words, could the Liability Annex be qualified as an environmental liability regime that intends to protect the Antarctic environment 'in the interest of all mankind'? In essence, the Liability Annex establishes the liability of operators to pay the costs of response action taken by other States to avoid, minimize or contain the impact of environmental emergencies caused by those operators in the Antarctic Treaty area.[15] The Chair of the Legal Experts Group, Professor Rudiger Wolfrum, decided to focus the discussion on the environmental aspect of the liability, setting aside the damage to persons and property.[16] However, nowhere does the phrase 'environmental damage' appear in the Liability Annex. In fact, this phrase, which remained in the preamble of the negotiating text, was deleted at the final Stockholm meeting.[17]

Thus, the Liability Annex adopted in 2005 by the Antarctic Treaty Consultative Parties raises a number of interesting questions. First, is it really an environmental liability regime applicable in Antarctica? Second, how is the design of the Liability Annex different or unique compared with other international environmental liability regimes, and how does that uniqueness relate to its being applicable in public spaces such as Antarctica? Finally, to what extent, if any, would the design and the approach of the Liability Annex influence our understanding of the significance

11 According to Article 9 of the Madrid Protocol and Article IX of the Antarctic Treaty, the Liability Annex shall become effective (enter into force) when approved (ratified) by all the 28 Consultative Parties who were entitled to participate in the 28th ATCM.

12 Johnson 2006, 45–47.

13 Decision 1 2005 on Annex VI on Liability Arising from Environmental Emergencies to the Protocol on Environmental Protection to the Antarctic Treaty, ATCM 29 (2006), 333. During the 29th ATCM in 2006, with the information that Sweden has enacted a Statute to implement the Annex, the Parties both formally and informally exchanged views on the issue and decided to set up an intersessional informal e-mail exchange process led by the United Kingdom. ATCM 29 (2006), paras. 90–93. During the 30th ATCM in 2007, more discussions have been undertaken based on an information paper submitted by the United Kingdom. United Kingdom 2007.

14 Wolfrum 1998, 565–566.

15 Vigni 2005, 217.

16 Wolfrum Third Offering 1995, Notes, para.11. Shibata 2007, 169–200.

17 MacKay's Revised Draft of Annex VI 2005, preambular paragraph 1.

and effectiveness of liability regimes under international law generally?[18] Based on a careful reading of the texts of the Annex in light of the negotiating history and international practice in the field of environmental liability, this chapter argues, first, that the Liability Annex is indeed an environmental liability regime. Second, this chapter demonstrates that, while confining itself to the manageable and practical scope of compensable costs under the regime, the Liability Annex has taken a bold step in recognizing the novel concept of liability for the costs of response action that was not actually undertaken. This chapter explains that the recognition of this novel concept was the consequence of the Annex being applicable in Antarctica, with its unique factual and legal settings. The implementation schemes for this novel liability are also interesting. For the liability of State operators, the Liability Annex provides for an institutionalized mechanism of implementation and compulsory settlement of disputes by arbitration or in the International Court of Justice. For the liability of non-State operators, the Annex provides for enough flexibility in implementing this novel liability domestically, including administrative or penal, rather than civil, approaches. Such a development of domestic practice in implementing international environmental liability regimes is itself a noteworthy phenomenon in understanding future 'public' liability regimes.

A Regime for the Environment?

Article 16 of the Madrid Protocol stipulates that 'the Parties undertake to elaborate rules and procedures relating to liability for damage arising from activities taking place in the Antarctic Treaty area and covered by this Protocol'. This was the enabling provision for the Consultative Parties to commence negotiations on a liability annex. Although Article 16 does not specify what damage the prospective annex will cover, it was expected that this annex would establish liability for damage to the Antarctic environment. This can be assumed from the first part of the first sentence of Article 16, which states that this prospective annex be '[c]onsistent with the objectives of this Protocol for the comprehensive protection of the Antarctic environment and dependent and associated ecosystems'. The vast majority of the Consultative Parties at the early stages of the negotiation took for granted that this annex would establish liability for damage to the Antarctic environment.[19] These assumptions, made in the early 1990s, were also in line with the general trend in liability regimes to expand their scope to include environmental damage, as called for by Principle 13 of the Rio Declaration on Environment and Development. For example, in 1992, a Protocol replacing the 1969 International Convention on Civil Liability for Oil Pollution Damage (CLC) was adopted and the 'compensation for

18 For recent arguments questioning the 'sensibility' of negotiating civil liability regimes and their effectiveness, see Brunnée 2004, 351; Fitzmaurice 2007, 1024–1035.

19 Wolfrum's Questionnaire 1994, 1. Japan 1991; Chile 1992; The Netherlands 1992.

impairment of the environment' was explicitly provided for.[20] Other amendments to existing treaties,[21] as well as new conventions adopted[22] in the field of civil liability in the 1990s, generally followed suit.

It was the United States' proposal in 1996[23] that changed the fundamental approach and design of the prospective liability regime. In essence, the United States tried to limit the scope of the prospective annex to 'provide for compensation for costs arising out of a Party's failure to fulfill its obligations under Article 15 of the Protocol to provide for prompt and effective response action to environmental emergencies'.[24] First, this proposal involved a complete turnaround as to the cause of liability:[25] the Wolfrum approach was predicated on the liability arising from harm caused even by lawful activities, whereas the US proposal was based on the liability arising from internationally wrongful acts. Since it is the States that are legally obliged under the Protocol to take prompt and effective response action, the liability rests with the State that fails to take that response action (State liability). Second, the US proposal effectively limited the scope of 'damage' under the Annex. According to the United States, the damage to be compensated would be the costs of the response action provided for by other Parties, and the obligation to pay those costs was defined as the liability of the wrongdoing State.[26]

The new Chair of the Liability Working Group, Ambassador Don MacKay of New Zealand, in his draft submitted in 2001, reinstated the liability of operators; in other words, the scheme of civil liability was restored.[27] But the US concept of liability arising from failure to take response action and for the costs of response action taken by other Parties was also retained.[28] Consequently, under the Liability

20 See generally Nicholas 2005, 59–66.

21 Protocol to Amend the 1963 Vienna Convention on Civil Liability for Nuclear Damage [hereinafter Nuclear Liability Protocol], adopted 12 September 1997. See Lahorgue 2007, 103.

22 Convention on Civil Liability for Damage resulting from Activities Dangerous to the Environment, adopted on 21 June 1993 within the framework of the Council of Europe [hereinafter Council of Europe Civil Liability Convention 1993]; International Convention on Liability and Compensation for Damage in Connection with the Carriage of Hazardous and Noxious Substances by Sea, adopted on 3 May 1996, within the framework of IMO [hereinafter HNS Convention 1996]; and Protocol on Liability and Compensation for Damage Resulting from Transboundary Movements of Hazardous Wastes and Their Disposal, adopted 10 December 1999, within the framework of the Basel Convention on the Control of Transboundary Movements of Hazardous Wastes and Their Disposal [hereinafter Basel Liability Protocol 1999].

23 United States 1996.

24 United States 1996, Article 1 (Purpose).

25 As to the cause and the form of liability under international law, see Zemanek 1988, 319–332.

26 United States 1996, Article 6(1).

27 Mackay's Draft 2001.

28 Mackay's Draft 2001, Article 6(1).

Annex as finally adopted, the operators are required under the domestic laws of their Parties to take prompt and effective response action to environmental emergencies arising from their activities (Article 5(1)). In the event such response action does not take place, the Parties of the operator and other Parties are encouraged, but not obliged, to take response action (Article 5(2)). Then, Article 6(1) provides:

> An operator that fails to take prompt and effective response action to environmental emergencies arising from its activities shall be liable to pay the costs of response action taken by Parties pursuant to Article 5 (2) to such Parties.

Thus, the Liability Annex is based on a different legal logic from other regular civil liability regimes. Under the Liability Annex, the liability arises not from the fact that the damage was caused by one's activity, but from the fact that the operator, having caused an environmental emergency that may have significant and harmful impact on the Antarctic environment, did not take the required response action to avoid or minimize such impact. In such cases, the operator is liable to pay the cost of response action taken by other Parties. The Liability Annex does not at all use the term 'damage' in its substantive provisions. As noted already, the Consultative Parties deleted the last remaining reference in the preamble to 'damage to the Antarctic environment' during the final negotiations in 2005.

A careful reading of the texts and the negotiating history of the Liability Annex demonstrates, however, that the deletion of the phrase 'damage to the Antarctic environment' was the consequence not of this Annex being indifferent to the Antarctic environment, but of some aspects of the concept of 'damage' that had been controversial. The negotiating Parties had different views as to whether an environmental impact already assessed in accordance with the Protocol as permissible could still be considered as damage subsequently and thereby lead to liability.[29] Also, the Parties could not agree on including the costs of measures to reinstate the impaired environment as part of compensable damage. This last aspect will be discussed later.

The objective of the Liability Annex is indeed to protect the Antarctic environment by preventing, minimizing or containing the significant and harmful impact on the Antarctic environment caused by environmental emergencies. The concept of environmental emergencies is defined in Article 2(b) as 'any accidental event … that results in, or imminently threatens to result in, any significant and harmful impact on the Antarctic environment'. The 'response action' is defined in Article 2(f) as 'reasonable measures … to avoid, minimize or contain the impact of the environmental emergency, which to that end may include clean-up in appropriate circumstances, and includes determining the extent of that emergency and its impact'. By obliging the operators to take prompt and effective response action, and by obliging them to pay the costs of response action taken by the Parties, the Liability Annex effectively established a legal arrangement to promote

29 Germany 1997, 4–6.

the taking of response actions by the operators themselves or by the Party of the operator and other Parties to avoid, minimize or contain the harmful impact on the Antarctic environment resulting from environmental emergencies.[30] This objective of the Annex is not significantly different from the Wolfrum texts, which retained the concept of damage.[31]

The liability established by the Annex for the costs of response action as defined above could even be seen as a partial recognition of liability for environmental damage. Under several environmental liability regimes, the compensable damage usually includes the 'costs of preventive measures' as well as the 'costs of measures of reinstatement of the impaired environment'.[32] For example, under the Basel Liability Protocol 1999, the 'damage' includes, in addition to traditional loss or damage to persons or property, (1) the costs of measures of reinstatement of the impaired environment, limited to the costs of measures actually taken or to be undertaken, and (2) the costs of preventive measures. According to this Protocol, 'measures of reinstatement' means 'any reasonable measures aiming to assess, reinstate or restore damaged or destroyed components of the environment', whereas 'preventive measures' means 'any reasonable measures taken by any person in response to an incident, to prevent, minimize, or mitigate loss or damage, or to effect environmental clean-up'. In other words, the costs of response action that is compensable under the Liability Annex are comparable to the costs of preventive measures recognized as one element of damage under several environmental liability regimes.[33] Moreover, since the response action under the Liability Annex may include measures to determine the extent of the emergency and its impact (Article 2(f)), the Annex may even have expanded its scope of 'damage' to include the costs of measures 'aiming to assess the damage', an element of the costs to reinstate the environment in other environmental liability regimes.

Accordingly, although the Liability Annex does not establish liability for damage as such, it establishes the obligation on the part of the operators to pay the costs of response action, the scope of which is comparable to 'the costs of preventive measures' recognized as one element of environmental damage in

30 Liability Annex 2005, first preambular paragraph.

31 According to Wolfrum Eighth Offering, the purpose of the prospective annex was to 'promote the prevention, minimization and containment of damage to the Antarctic environment' (Article 1 or Preamble). The 'damage' was defined as 'any harmful effect of an impact on the Antarctic environment … which [is significant and lasting]' (Article 3(1)(a)). Wolfrum Eighth Offering 1997, 19–20.

32 CLC 1992: Article 1(6)(a) and (b) and (7); Council of Europe Civil Liability Convention 1993: Article 2(7)(c) and (d), (8) and (9); HNS Convention 1996: Article 1(6)(c) and (d) and (7); Nuclear Liability Protocol: Article 1(1)(k) (iv) and (iv), (m) and (n).

33 Indeed, during the negotiation on the Basel Liability Protocol 1999, a proposal was made to add 'response measures'. See USA proposal for Article 2, UNEP/CHW.1/WG.1/4/CRP.16 (26 June 1996).

many recent environmental liability regimes.[34] In this sense, the Liability Annex is a liability regime for the environment, protecting the public interest for all mankind.

A Liability Regime for Public Spaces

The Liability Annex, if compared with other regular international civil liability regimes, exhibits several unique features, some of which could be considered to be the result of its being applicable in the Antarctic Treaty area, a public space. These features will be examined below.

Compensable Costs: Why Not the Reinstatement Measures?

The Liability Annex established the liability for costs of response action only, excluding explicitly the costs of reinstatement or remedial measures taken by other Parties. This is unique when compared with other international environmental liability regimes as examined above.[35] Let us examine this question in light of the US argument because it was the United States that opposed the inclusion of 'reinstatement measures'.

The Wolfrum draft intended to establish the liability of an operator for the costs of response action that included the costs of measures to clean-up or otherwise 'remedy' the damage.[36] The US opposition to the inclusion of costs of measures to 'clean-up or otherwise remedy the damage' was multifaceted. First, the United States opposed the inclusion of restoration or remedial measures or clean-up operations because these measures are 'clearly not covered under the Protocol'.[37] According to the US, the liability for the costs of remedial measures would only arise if the prospective Annex established anew the obligation to take remedial measures. For the US, this was an unacceptable expansion of the obligations under the Madrid Protocol. However, this objection is not convincing.[38] The liability regime foreseen in Article 16 is not necessarily based on the liability arising out of the breach of international and/or national obligations. On the contrary, a plain reading of Article 16 directs us to the establishment of liability for damage arising from activities or incidents that are not themselves unlawful. If our premise is

34 Although the costs of preventive measures are distinct from the damage to the environment *per se*, their nature as environmental damage is clear from the practice of 1969 CLC and 1971 Fund Convention. See Brans 2001, 323–324.

35 For an emotional criticism, see Bederman and Keskar 2005, 1391. See also Vöneky 2007, 165.

36 See Articles 5 and 4(3) in conjunction with the definition of 'further response measures' in Article 4(2), Wolfrum Eighth Offering 1997, 22–24.

37 United States 1998, 3.

38 '[D]isingenuous', according to Scott 2006, 92.

based on this plain reading of Article 16, the liability for costs of remedial action may be established independently of the existence of the obligation to take such action. Here, the question becomes that of the definition of damage, rather than that of the existence of obligation, already provided in the Protocol or otherwise.

Second, the United States also argued that the inclusion of obligation to take remedial measures and of liability for not taking them would lead to the concept of liability for 'irreparable harm'.[39] According to the United States, to render operators legally responsible for irreparable damage had led to proposals for making such operators amenable to suit in numerous domestic jurisdictions, and in international fora. It had been suggested that plaintiffs could be States, NGOs, or a Secretariat or Fund acting for the Treaty Parties. Indeed, the Wolfrum draft did provide for the liability for irreparable damage and for the Environmental Protection Fund being able to sue the operator in arbitration.[40] For the United States, these proposals were 'inappropriate, undesirable and unmanageable'.[41] The US objection to including liability for irreparable damage is understandable as a policy matter,[42] but the international community has already found a partial answer to this question by defining the damage to the environment as 'the costs of measures of reinstatement of the impaired environment, limited to the costs of measures actually taken or to be undertaken' (Basel Liability Protocol 1999). Thus, accepting the liability for costs of remedial measures does not necessarily lead to the concept of irreparable harm in which no remedial action is possible.

Finally, according to the United States, it is extremely difficult, if not impossible, to 'restore the Antarctic environment in the event of serious harm, given the difficulty of and lack of data for establishing baselines'.[43] It is true that, in order for the liability to be established for the costs of 'restoration' or 'reinstatement' measures for an impaired environment, one would need baselines or benchmarks to assess and evaluate the degree of environmental damage and the appropriateness of measures to reinstate the environment.[44] Under existing international environmental liability regimes, such baselines or benchmarks are often left to the interpretative practice of national legal systems.[45] The national legal system where the damage occurred would be the most appropriate one to evaluate the extent of the damage and the appropriateness of restoration and/or

39 United States 1998, 4.

40 See Wolfrum Eighth Offering 1997, Article 5bis and Articles 10 and 11.

41 United States 1998, 4.

42 Sandvik and Suikkari 1997, 64–69.

43 United States 1998, 4.

44 For example, in order to assess the appropriateness of reinstatement measures, it is necessary to have baselines or benchmarks to evaluate the feasibility of the proposed measures, their prospects of success, the climate and other environmental factors in the affected area, the type of natural resources affected, and the relative scope of recovery by natural processes.

45 Birnie and Bolye 2002, 387–388; de la Rue and Anderson 1998, 384–385.

reinstatement measures taken in order to establish (or refute) the liability for such measures. In other words, the liability for the costs of reinstatement measures for an impaired environment would usually be established by applying the national legal system where the damage occurs. Alternatively, an international instrument must be drafted to provide for a uniform standard of necessary and specific baselines and benchmarks. However, this has proved to be extremely difficult in practice.[46] Thus, the United States' objection effectively said that: (1) in Antarctica, there is no applicable national law to assess the damage occurring there and the appropriateness of reinstatement measures to cope with such damage; and (2) formulating international uniform baselines to make such assessment possible would be extremely difficult in light of the unique environmental conditions in Antarctica and the lack of actual experience there. This objection is both legal and technical.

Applying different national laws, including the baselines for the assessment of environmental damage, based on jurisdiction over its nationals (e.g., the Party of the operator causing the damage) is conceivable. However, unlike the practice in the CLC regime where different liabilities may be established for damage occurring in different States, in Antarctica, the same damage in the same locality may lead to different liabilities depending on who the Party of the operator was. This result is more troublesome from a fairness perspective. The value of the Antarctic environment should be the same for all.

If the Antarctic environment and its protection are in 'the interest of all mankind', theoretically and ideally, the baselines and benchmarks for assessing and evaluating the environmental status of Antarctica should be worked out by the collective exercise of the Parties to the Madrid Protocol. In fact, with regard to deep seabed mining, the environmental baselines are to be established taking into account the recommendations of the Legal and Technical Commission of the International Seabed Authority.[47] Such an institutional approach is theoretically conceivable for the Antarctica, too. For example, the Environmental Protection Fund, with advice from the Committee on Environmental Protection (CEP), establishes the environmental baselines, assesses the degree of damage against such baselines, and decides what reasonable reinstatement measures are in a particular set of circumstances. Such a decision by the Fund is binding on the domestic court where the action for reimbursement is brought. However, in view of the United States and some other Consultative Parties, negotiating such a quixotic and expensive scheme was not practical in the context of Antarctica, where no such serious damage has yet occurred. Nor was it politically feasible in light of the experience in the negotiation of the establishment of the Secretariat

46 See the practice under the CLC 1969 and 1992 on the definition of 'pollution damage' and the role of national laws and courts and the IOPC Fund. Brans 2001, 318–360. See also de la Rue and Anderson 1998, 385–390.

47 Decision of the Assembly, ISBA/6/A/18 (4 October 2000), Regulation 31(4).

of the Antarctic Treaty, in which the proposal to give full-fledged international personality to the Secretariat or to the ATCM was clearly not acceptable.[48]

Excluding the costs of reinstatement measures undertaken in the areas beyond any national jurisdiction from the compensable damage can also be sustained from the precedents of international environmental liability regimes. First, under the still formative stage of the deep seabed liability scheme, the applicable Regulations do not mention restoration or reinstatement measures, whereas they explicitly refer to the payment for damage, including the costs of reasonable preventive (or response) measures.[49]

Second, the marine pollution liability regimes and the Basel Liability Protocol also distinguish between the costs of response (or preventive) actions and those of reinstatement measures, the former being compensable even when undertaken on the high seas, but the latter is restricted to those taken within the limits of national jurisdiction. For example, the Basel Liability Protocol 1999, closely following the relevant provisions of the NHS Convention,[50] provides that the damage includes: '(iv) the costs of measures of reinstatement of the impaired environment, limited to the costs of measures actually taken or to be undertaken, and (v) the costs of preventive measures, defined as any reasonable measures taken in response to an incident, to prevent, minimize, or mitigate loss or damage, or to effect environmental clean-up' (Article 2(2)(c)). As to the geographical scope, Article 3(3)(a) provides that 'the Protocol shall apply only to damage suffered in an area under the national jurisdiction of a Contracting Party'. Notwithstanding this provision, under (c) of the same subparagraph, the Protocol shall apply to the preventive measures taken in areas beyond any national jurisdiction. In other words, just as in the NHS Convention, the compensable costs of reinstatement measures would be limited to those taken in areas under national jurisdiction; while for the costs of preventive measures, such limitation does not apply.

Although the reasons for non-inclusion of the costs of reinstatement measures taken outside the limits of national jurisdiction of States may be different for the deep seabed damage caused by mineral resource activities there and marine pollution caused by oil and other hazardous materials, these instruments suggest

48 Shibata 2004, 533. See also Vigni 2007, 24–25.

49 de La Fayette 2007, 124.

50 See Canadian Proposal on Article 3: Scope of Application, UNEP/CHW.1/WG.1/4/CRP.9 (24 February 1996). The Report of the Fourth Session of the Ad Hoc Working Group, UNEP/CHW.1/WG.1/4/2 (3 July 1996), paras. 33, 43, 50 and 54. Report by the contact group on the geographical scope of the protocol (Article 3, chaired by Belgium), UNEP/CHW.1/WG.1/10/CRP.11 (1 September 1999). During the final negotiations, Japan raised the question on the issue of differentiating the compensable damages in relation to the place those damages occur. The overwhelming Parties were satisfied with the proposed Article 3 because it followed the relevant provision in the NHS Convention. Report of the Tenth Session of the Ad Hoc Working Group, UNEP/CHW/WG.1/10/2 (23 September 1999), 6. New Article 3, paragraph 2(c), Proposal from small group chaired by Norway, UNEP/CHW.1/WG.1/10/CRP.14 (3 September 1999).

at least the difficulty in establishing such liability and the lack of international practice in this field.

An idealist would criticize the Liability Annex for not providing for liability for the costs of reinstatement measures, with possible international institutions and procedures to assess the environmental damage in Antarctica and to determine the reasonableness of such reinstatement measures. Such a regime is legally and theoretically conceivable. But, in the Antarctic context where activities related to mineral resources are prohibited[51] and where the actual experience of significant environmental damage is extremely limited, and in light of the lack of international practice in establishing the liability for the costs of reinstatement measures taken in public spaces, it could be concluded that such a liability was neither necessary nor practical at this time.

Payment of Costs of Response Action that was not Actually Undertaken

Article 6(2)(a) and (b) provide as follows:

> Article 6 (2)
>
> (a) When a State operator should have taken prompt and effective response action but did not, and no response action was taken by any Party, the State operator shall be liable to pay the costs of the response action which should have been undertaken, into the fund referred to in Article 12.
>
> (b) When a non-State operator should have taken prompt and effective response action but did not, and no response action was taken by any Party, the non-State operator shall be liable to pay an amount of money that reflects as much as possible the costs of the response action that should have been taken. Such money is to be paid directly to the fund referred to in Article 12, to the Party of that operator or to the Party that enforces the mechanism referred to in Article 7(3). A Party receiving such money shall make best efforts to make a contribution to the fund referred to in Article 12 which at least equals the money received from the operator.

Both subparagraphs (a) and (b) establish an operator's liability to pay the costs of response action which should have been taken, even when no response action was actually taken by the Parties in accordance with Article 5 of the Liability Annex. Subparagraph (a) relates to State operators for which such costs shall be paid directly to the Fund. It is a straightforward provision. On the other hand, subparagraph (b)

51 It should be noted that, in 1988 under CRAMRA, the Consultative Parties did agree to establish a liability of operators for environmental damage in Antarctica, for which the Antarctic Mineral Resource Commission would have the right to appear as the plaintiff against the liable operator. Article 8, paragraph 10 of CRAMRA.

relates to non-State operators for which, because of the difficulties expressed by some Parties in implementing the idea domestically, a carefully negotiated flexible scheme is established.

The liability to pay the costs of response action that was not actually undertaken is a novel idea, with no international precedents, and perhaps without national precedents either.

The Genesis of this Novel Idea

The US Proposal and the Wolfrum Drafts The genesis of this novel idea was suggested by the US in 1996. Article 3(1)(a)(i) of the 1996 US proposal provided that the Parties are obliged to provide effective response action to environmental emergencies by implementing, with respect to their non-State operators, measures that would ensure that those operators are financially accountable for failing to take response action, in order to allow the Party or the Fund to be compensated. The liability under the original US proposal fell on the Parties, rather than the operators, that failed to fulfill their obligations under Article 3(1)(a) (Article 4). Such a liable Party would be responsible to pay, in addition to the costs of response action actually taken by other Party (Article 6(1)), the costs of response action that should have been undertaken, but was not, to the Fund (Article 6(2)).[52] In other words, the US proposal was based on the administrative intervention of the relevant States in the compensation scheme when non-governmental activities were the cause of environmental emergencies.[53]

The rationale for proposing such a novel liability was not explicitly provided for in the US proposal or in its explanatory notes of 1998.[54] The previous discussions in the Legal Experts Group do shed some light on the circumstances leading to such a proposal. Before the US proposal in 1996, the discussion focused on whether and how to incorporate the idea of 'irreparable damage' into the Annex. This issue had been the thorniest one in the negotiations from the beginning.[55] In 1995, the Chairman reported that 'now the view seems to prevail that a State Party or person having damaged the Antarctic environment with no removal or remedial action being possible should not be in a better position, as far as the obligation to provide for compensation is concerned, than a State Party or a person having

52 United States 1996.

53 In 2001, the US submitted a slightly revised version of the 1996 proposal. One major addition in this 2001 version was that the liability of a non-State operator that failed to take response action could now be pursued in domestic courts of Parties. Here, we can see the US sidled up towards the concept of civil liability as provided in MacKay's draft. United States 2001, Article 9.

54 United States 1998.

55 See Wolfrum First Offering 1994, 7–11.

damaged the Antarctic environment to a lesser degree'.[56] This argument raises a fundamental fairness issue, which relates not only to the situation where remedial actions are impossible but also to the situation where the operator causing the emergency absconded from the scene to avoid liability. In Antarctica, activities are often undertaken in remote areas with no one else in the vicinity. Under Article IV of the Antarctic Treaty, a 'territorial' interest of claiming States cannot be the basis of legal action. It is therefore foreseeable that an operator may decide to abscond from the scene of an environmental emergency it has caused when the likelihood of other Parties taking the response action would be low. For operators, absconding would certainly be cheaper than taking response action by themselves.

The US proposal tried to respond to this fairness question by requiring the Parties to ensure that their operators would be financially accountable to compensate the Fund when they failed to take the necessary response action, and by requiring the Parties to pay the costs of response action that should have been undertaken to the Fund when those Parties failed to fulfill such obligation to ensure. In other words, characterized by Antarctica's unique factual and legal settings, this novel liability could be interpreted as having the intention of reducing the temptation to the operator to abscond and of providing a legal incentive for the operator to take response action. Therefore, its rationale lies more in the incentive to take the necessary response action than in the allocation of costs that a Party would have incurred.[57]

After the US proposal, the Wolfrum drafts underwent a subtle change: the Wolfrum last draft in 1997 provided that 'where an operator has caused damage, *but neither it nor a third party has undertaken response action* or where response action is not possible, feasible or … desirable, the operator shall be under an obligation to provide compensation to the Fund' (Article 5bis(1)). Regarding the valuation of such costs, the Wolfrum draft provided that 'the amount of such contribution *shall reflect the estimated costs of the response action that should have been taken* or, if it is not reasonably possible to estimate such costs, reflect the nature and significance of the damage including the loss of or impairment to potential future uses and the circumstances which gave rise to it' (Article 5bis(2) Alternative A).[58] The emphasized phrases are the additions from the previous drafts and are clearly intended to incorporate the US idea.

56 Wolfrum Third Offering 1995, Explanation by the Chairman regarding Article 5 (liability), 9.

57 It cannot be excluded, however, the US proposal, as a negotiating tactic, might well be a compromise 'give' in order to 'take' the deletion of 'irreparable damage'.

58 Wolfrum Eighth Offering 1997, 24–26. See also Wolfrum Report 1997, 17, para. 47(4).

The MacKay Draft After careful consideration,[59] the new Chairman of the Liability Group submitted his first draft in 2001,[60] which clearly distinguished the two situations. One is when response action should have been undertaken but was not, making the operator liable to pay the costs of the response action which should have been undertaken into the Fund (Article 6(2)); another is when response action was not possible, and the resultant harmful impact on the Antarctic environment is significant and lasting, making the operator liable to make payment to the Fund, and the amount of such payment shall take into account the elements specified in Article 6(3). During the final rounds of negotiations, Article 6(3) on 'irreparable damage' was deleted, whereas Article 6(2) on 'liability for costs of response action that was not actually undertaken' survived.[61]

Thus, a novel liability as provided in Article 6(2) of the Liability Annex is indeed a legal innovation to deal with the special situations present in public spaces, especially where response actions by others could hardly be expected because of factual and legal reasons. The main objective of such liability is to provide a legal incentive for the operator to take the required response action, so that the harmful impact on the environment can be prevented, minimized or contained.

Implementing this Novel Liability with Regard to State Operators

The scheme for implementing and enforcing this novel liability is also distinctively unique. With regard to State operators, the scheme for collective valuation of such costs and for institutional dispute resolution is clearly established in Article 7(5) and (6). First, the costs of the response action which should have been undertaken and was not, to be paid by a State operator into the Fund, shall be approved by means of a Decision of ATCM. In deciding such costs the ATCM should seek the advice of the CEP (Article 7(5) (b)). According to Decision 1 (1995) of ATCM,[62] a Decision of ATCM is an internal organizational matter of the ATCM and will become operative at its adoption. It is therefore internally binding. There is a strong presumption within the Antarctic Treaty culture that such a Decision would be complied with and the payment be made by the liable Party. After all, all Decisions of the ATCM must be adopted by unanimity of all the Consultative Parties present and voting,[63] including the Consultative Party of the State operator.

Second, the liability of a Party as a State operator under Article 6(2)(a) shall be resolved by the ATCM. The questions relating to such liability include: (i) the identification of the State operator that caused the environmental emergency

59 MacKay's Report 1999; MacKay's Draft 2001.

60 MacKay's Draft 2001.

61 Mackay's Draft of Annex VI 2004, 1 and Article 6.

62 For the text of Decision 1 1995, see ATCM Handbook 2002, 130. For a legal analysis of this decision, see Shibata 2004, 548–550.

63 Rule 24 of the Revised Rules of Procedure of the ATCM (2005), Decision 3 (2005): Amendment to the Rules of Procedure, ATCM 28 (2005), 335.

(Article 2(c)), (ii) the identification of the Party of such operator (Article 2(d)), (iii) the evaluation of the emergency as to whether it was of such a nature that triggered the operator's obligation to take response action (Article 2(b)), (iv) the evaluation of the circumstances as to whether the taking of response action was reasonable (Article 2(e) and (f)) and, finally, (v) by taking into account all these examinations, the determination whether, in the particular circumstances of the case, the State operator should have taken the response action, but did not. These questions will be the subject of institutional scrutiny in the ATCM. Considering the still prevalent hesitance regarding the institutionalization of the Antarctic Treaty System, the institutional question-resolving procedure foreseen in Article 7(5)(a) is worth taking note of.

Lastly, should the question remain unresolved in the ATCM, Article 7(5)(a) continues to provide that the liability of a State operator shall be resolved by any enquiry procedure which may be established by the Parties, the provisions of Articles 18, 19 and 20 of the Protocol and, as applicable, the Schedule to the Protocol on arbitration. It is extremely important that Articles 19 and 20 of the Protocol are listed here. Under Article 18 of the Protocol, the Parties shall resolve the disputes by such means to which the disputing Parties agree. However, under Article 19, with regard to disputes concerning the interpretation or application of Articles 7 (prohibition of mineral resource activities), 8 (environmental impact assessment) and 15 (emergency response action) and, except to the extent that an Annex provides otherwise, the provisions of any Annex, the Parties are obliged to resolve these disputes either through the ICJ or the Arbitral Tribunal; in other words by the binding decisions of international courts. Article 20(1) of the Protocol provides that, with regard to disputes relating to those provisions enumerated in Article 19, if the disputing Parties cannot agree on a means for resolving a dispute within 12 months, the dispute shall be referred, at the request of any Party to the dispute, for settlement by the Arbitral Tribunal (19(5)) or in the ICJ under certain circumstances (19(4)). By referring to Articles 19 and 20 of the Protocol, Article 7(5)(a) of the Liability Annex effectively established a compulsory dispute settlement procedure for disputes concerning the liability of a Party as a State operator. They will ultimately be resolved by a binding decision of either the Arbitral Tribunal as constituted in accordance with the Schedule to the Protocol or the ICJ.[64]

Because of the insistence of one Consultative Party, Article 7(6) provides that 'the provisions of Articles 19(4), 19(5) and 20(1) of the Protocol are only applicable for compensation for response action that has been undertaken to an environmental emergency or for payment into the fund'. This is an awkward provision, inconsistent with the overall structure of the Annex. For example, this paragraph is the only provision in the Annex that uses the concept of 'compensation'

64 The same compulsory procedure is provided for the cases of liability of a Party as a State operator under Article 6 (1), namely the cases in which other Parties did take the response action. See Article 7(4) of the Liability Annex.

for response action. According to the Party proposing it, the purpose of this provision was only to reaffirm that the compulsory dispute settlement procedure would apply only to the disputes concerning liability arising from the non-taking of response action, excluding especially those concerning preventive measures as provided in Article 3 of the Liability Annex. Trusting this explanation, Article 7(6) does not affect in anyway the significance of Article 7(5) of the Liability Annex establishing the compulsory dispute settlement procedure for the questions concerning liability of a Party as a State operator. It will be an interesting question for the Arbitral Tribunal or the ICJ whether and how to determine the standing of a particular Party in a dispute requesting payment by the alleged liable Party of money that corresponds to the costs of response action that should have been undertaken into the Fund.

Implementing this Novel Liability with Regard to Non-State Operators: The Flexible Approach

The discussion on how to design a scheme for implementing and enforcing the novel liability established under Article 6(2)(b) in relation to non-State operators became a make-or-break issue in the final rounds of negotiations. As has already been mentioned, the original US proposal regarding this novel liability was predicated on administrative intervention in the implementation of the liability. However, when Chair MacKay tried to combine the US proposal with the Wolfrum draft, his 2001 draft reinstated the traditional concept of civil liability, as the liability squarely rests on the operator causing the environmental emergency and the action for compensation against the operator needs to be brought in the domestic courts. It was not clear, however, who would be the plaintiff and under what cause of action he/she would bring the action in cases coming under Article 6(2).

During the discussion, it became clear that certain Parties are considering the possibility of implementing this novel liability not by civil procedure between the 'injured' person and the liable operator, but by some kind of administrative or even penal procedure. Some Parties envisioned that the Party of the operator might be able to impose a fine on the operator that did not take the required response action. The payment of such a fine could also be enforceable by a court of law. However, depending on the legal system of the Party, and in comparison with other administrative fines imposed for reasons of non-compliance with laws and administrative orders, the amount of the fine set out in the law for not taking the response action might not be as high as the 'costs of response action that should have been taken'. Also, in such an administrative scheme, the fine collected from the operator would be deposited in the National Treasury and, consequently, the money would not automatically be paid to the Fund, as envisioned in MacKay's draft. It became obvious that 'maximum flexibility in the drafting of (the scheme was necessary), given that the mechanism used to implement the obligation would vary significantly amongst States'.[65]

Recognizing the need for such flexibility, the Annex refers to the liability of the non-State operator in Article 6(2) situation as 'the payment of money' (instead of the costs) and such money needs to reflect 'as much as possible' the costs of the response action that should have been taken. It should be remembered that the objective of this provision was to provide a disincentive to abscond from the scene of environmental emergency, and not to allocate the costs. Thus, the administrative fine, even if a small amount, would have a significant impact on the conduct of non-State operators if used in conjunction with the publication of such non-compliance by the operator and the possibility of withholding permits for future activities by the same operator. Also, this money could be paid directly to the Fund, to the Party of that operator (cf. administrative fine), or to the Party that enforces such payment (cf. court orders). Finally, taking into account the possibility of an administrative scheme as described above, the Party receiving such money (as an administrative fine) shall 'make best efforts to make a contribution to the Fund … which at least equals the money received from the operator'. This provision recognizes that the transfer to the Fund of the fine collected from the liable operator is not automatic. This flexibility allows a Party considering an administrative implementation of this Article to collect the fine from the operator in the National Treasury and later to endeavour to make a one-off contribution or several instalments over some years to the Fund, the total amount of which should at least equal the money received from the operator.[66]

Corresponding to this flexibility, Article 7(3) of the Liability Annex provides in part that '[e]ach Party shall ensure that there is a mechanism in place under its domestic law for the enforcement of Article 6(2)(b) with respect to any of its non-State operators within the meaning of Article 2(d), as well as where possible with respect to any non-State operator that is incorporated or has its principal place of business or his or her habitual place of residence in that Party'. The flexibility provided by this provision regarding the various approaches to the concept of liability becomes even more evident if one compares the relevant provision in Article 7(2) in cases where other Parties did take response action. Article 7 (2) provides, very simply, that '[e]ach Party shall ensure that its courts possess the necessary jurisdiction to entertain actions under paragraph 1 (on the liability of non-State operators in cases of Article 6(1))'. This is a standard provision for domestic implementation of civil liability.[67] The Party incurring costs by taking

65 ATCM 28 (2005), 36, para. 108.

66 In this respect, Article 6(2) of the Liability Annex could not be interpreted 'as an acknowledgement that perhaps the State was to blame for not responding to the emergency and should therefore pay into the Fund not only the amount paid by the operator, but also an additional amount'. De La Fayette 2007, 146.

67 See, for example, Article IX (2) of CLC 1992: 'Each Contracting State shall ensure that its Courts possess the necessary jurisdiction to entertain such actions for compensation

the response action which the liable operator should have taken can bring a civil action for the reimbursement of such costs against the operator in the courts where the operator is incorporated or has its principal place of business or his or her habitual place of residence (Article 7(1)).

Thus, while maintaining the 'civil' nature of liability in normal cases of allocation of costs between the Party taking the response action and the liable operator, the Liability Annex reintroduced the possibility of administrative and/or penal approaches to implement the liability for the unique case of environmental emergencies for which no one has taken response action. Although a question can be posed as to whether the administrative fine imposed for reasons of non-compliance with laws or administrative orders can still be termed 'liability' in the strict sense of the word,[68] the Liability Annex established a new design for an international environmental liability regime. If this unique regime had the objective of protecting the environment in a public space such as Antarctica, the design agreed to by the Consultative Parties of the Antarctic Treaty as reflected in the Liability Annex could provide a model for future 'public' liability regimes. The potential for a criminal law approach to the environmental liability regimes applicable in public spaces had already been identified by Alan Boyle in 1997.[69] An administrative approach to environmental liability was exemplified in the elaborate EU Directive adopted in 2004 on environmental liability with regard to the prevention and remedying of environmental damage.[70] The concept of an administrative approach to the liability for damage to the conservation and sustainable use of biological diversity has gained prominence in the negotiations on the elaboration of international rules and procedures on liability and redress under the Cartagena Protocol on Biosafety.[71] Although the last two examples are not within the context of 'spatial' public nature, they nevertheless pertain to 'functional' public nature. The Liability Annex adopted in 2005 could be considered as another small yet important stream that may converge in the near future with a new river called 'international public liability regimes', of which the scholastic examination has just begun.

(for pollution damage caused in its territory)'.

68 De La Fayette 2007, 152.

69 Boyle 1997, 100. It should be noted, however, that, in the context of the Liability Annex, the view was expressed during the negotiation that the payment into the Fund under Article 6(2) of the Annex should not be deemed as having a punitive element. ATCM 28 (2005), 36, para. 108.

70 Directive 2004/35/EC of the European Parliament and of the Council of 21 April 2004 on environmental liability with regard to the prevention and remedying of environmental damage, OJ L 143/56 (30 April 2004). See Brans 2005, 90–109.

71 *Proposed Operational Texts on Liability and Redress in the Context of Article 27 of the Biosafety Protocol*, Decision BS-IV/12 (2008): Liability and Redress under the Cartagena Protocol on Biosafety, UNEP/CBD/BS/COP-MOP/4/18 (25 June 2008), 84–101.

Conclusion: Challenges for Domestic Implementation

Annex VI on Liability arising from Environmental Emergency adopted by consensus of 28 Consultative Parties to the Antarctic Treaty in 2005 is indeed the first complete legally binding international liability regime applicable in a public space, Antarctica. Although the Annex does not contain the phrase 'environmental damage', it establishes the liability of the operators to pay the costs of response action. By obliging the operators to take prompt and effective response action, and by obliging them to pay the costs of response action taken by the Party of the operator and other Parties, the Liability Annex effectively established a legal arrangement to promote the taking of response actions by the operators themselves or by others to avoid, minimize or contain the harmful impact on the Antarctic environment resulting from environmental emergencies. The Liability Annex is, thus, a liability regime for the environment, protecting the public interest for all mankind.

Because the Liability Annex intends to protect the environment of a public space, the Antarctic, it exhibits a number of unique features. First, the compensable costs under the regime are restricted to the costs of response action taken by other Parties, uniquely excluding the costs of measures for reinstatement of an impaired environment, normally recognized under other regular international environmental liability regimes like CLC 1992 and Basel Liability Protocol 1999. This exclusion was based on policy and technical reasons, rather than on legal impossibility. In order for the costs of measures for reinstatement of an impaired environment to be compensated, one would need baselines and benchmarks to assess the environmental damage incurred and the appropriateness of the measures to reinstate the environment. Under other liability regimes, it is the national laws and regulations, including the baselines and benchmarks, of the territorial State where the damage occurs that would be applied to assess the extent of the damage. Alternatively, uniform baselines and benchmarks must be drafted and applied in any of the State's courts. The former option is excluded because there is no territorial State in Antarctica whose national laws and regulations could legitimately be applied to assess the extent of the environmental damage there. The latter option was not practical from policy and technical perspectives in view of the difficulty in other fora in drafting and agreeing to such baselines and in light of the fact that no such serious damage has yet occurred in Antarctica.

Second, the Liability Annex established an innovative liability that allows operators to pay the costs of response action that was not actually undertaken. This unprecedented novel liability as provided in Article 6(2) of the Liability Annex is a legal innovation to deal with the special situations present in public spaces, especially where response actions by others could hardly be expected for factual and legal reasons. In Antarctica, there is a strong incentive for operators to abscond from the scene of the emergency they have caused because, first, there may be no one in the vicinity to take the response action for which the operator must later reimburse the costs, and second, there is no territorial interest that can be legitimately invoked against the operator to pursue the liability. The objective of this novel liability to demand that operators pay the costs of response action that should have been taken, but did not, to the Fund is, therefore, to provide a legal incentive for the operator to take the required response action, so that any harmful impact on the environment is prevented, minimized or contained. The scheme for implementing and enforcing this novel liability is also distinctively unique. The liability of a Party as the Party of a State-operator will be pursued in institutional settings, with the possibility of ultimate binding decisions rendered by the Arbitral Tribunal or the ICJ if the dispute remains unresolved. The public nature of this unique liability will best be implemented and enforced by means of such an institutional procedure. Regarding the scheme of implementing and enforcing the liability of non-State operators in cases of Article 6(2) situations, the Liability Annex came to recognize, after difficult negotiations, 'a maximum flexibility'. Such a scheme clearly includes an administrative or penal approach, in addition to normal civil procedures.

Thus, the Liability Annex established a new design for an international environmental liability regime. Some time is required to digest innovative ideas, especially in the legal field. The Consultative Parties are indeed carefully digesting the novelty of the regime and slowly beginning to consider how actually to implement the Annex in their domestic laws. As succinctly expressed by Philippe Sands, the Liability Annex establishes 'the liability of actors (which could include states) under *rules of national law* adopted pursuant to treaties which aim to harmonise national civil liability rules, or set minimum standards'.[72] In other words, this kind of liability (traditionally called civil, as opposed to State, liability) could be legally imposed only if rules of national law provide for such a liability. The domestic implementation of an international liability regime is a *sine qua non* for its effectiveness.

Recognizing this essential consideration, the negotiators of the Liability Annex took extreme care to identify, and resolve if possible, any element in the Annex that poses constitutional or systemic difficulties in its domestic implementation. The flexibility provided in Article 6(2)(b) and Article 7(3) as examined above was just such an attempt to resolve these difficulties.[73] Also relating to the implementation of Article 6(2) liability, under Article 11(2) of the Liability Annex, the requirement of insurance and other financial security to cover liability under Article 6(2) was made optional, taking into consideration that some Parties may make this liability an administrative fine or penal sanction for breaching the laws or administrative

72 Sands 2003, 869 (emphasis added). It should be noted, however, under the Liability Annex, the liability of a Party as the Party of a State operator could no longer be considered as civil liability under national law.

73 See the non-paper submitted by Japan, and the subsequent negotiations on Article 6(2) and Article 7(3) in the Contact Group during the Stockholm meeting. None of these papers were available as official meeting documents. For discussion during the Cape Town meeting, see ATCM 27 (2004), 19–20, paras. 103 and 111.

orders, which the insurance usually would not cover.[74] The limits of liability as provided in Article 9 of the Liability Annex were also controversial in the light of the lack of sufficient information as to the availability of insurance (or, more correctly, the availability of reasonable insurance for which the premium would not be prohibitively costly),[75] and in the light of the obligation provided in Article 11(1) for the Parties to require their operators to maintain adequate insurance to cover the liability.[76] It is still not at all clear whether these solutions internationally agreed to in 2005, many as compromises, would actually be the solutions for each and every Consultative Party within the context of their concrete attempts to implement them domestically.

A formidable task still confronts many of the Consultative Parties to implement the first international environmental liability regime applicable in a public space domestically. Seemingly non-controversial provisions internationally may require creative thinking domestically. For example, Articles 7(1) and (2) provide the Party's obligation to ensure that its courts possess the necessary jurisdiction to entertain actions involving the liability of non-State operators that cause an environmental emergency in Antarctica for the costs of response action taken by the Parties there (Article 6(1) liability actions). The implementation of this provision involves extraterritorial application of a Party's substantive civil liability laws to events occurring in a place where the exercise of territorial jurisdiction is in dispute. For example, according to Japanese civil law, the liability provided in Article 6(1) would be assimilated to *negotiorum gestio* (jimu-kanri: Minpo Articles 697–702), in which if a person without obligation executes work on behalf of another, that person may redeem the costs incurred in executing such work from the latter. However, according to Japanese private international law, the law that shall be applied for jimu-kanri with foreign elements, in principle, is the law of the place where the execution of the work occurred (Ho-no Tekiyo ni kansuru Tsusoku-ho Article 14).[77] In the Liability Annex context, it will be the law of the place where the response action had taken place: namely the domestic law of Antarctica! The implementation of Article 6(2)(b) liability in the form of an administrative fine would also involve extraterritorial application of a Party's administrative law to Antarctica. As long as the non-State operator is a national of the Party, the jurisdiction

74 ATCM 28 (2005), 38, para. 120.

75 The issue of insurance was extensively discussed during the Madrid meeting in 2003, in which a representative from P&I Club was invited to exchange information with the Consultative Parties. See ATCM 26 (2003), 21–25, paras. 82–98. See also IAATO (2003).

76 See the non-papers submitted by Norway and US, and the subsequent negotiations on Article 9 in the Contact Group during the Stockholm meeting. None of these papers were available as official meeting documents. For discussion during the Cape Town meeting, see ATCM 27 (2004), 17–20, paras. 96–98, 112.

77 See, however, Articles 15 and 16 of the Law that allow for other laws to be applied.

based on nationality may provide the basis for applying its administrative law to operators having its nationality in Antarctica. However, the definition of 'operator of the Party (Party of the operator)' as provided in Article 2 (d) of the Liability Annex does not guarantee that the Party's operator, for which the Party is obliged to take the necessary measures as provided in Article 5 (response action), Article 6(2)(b) (imposition of liability) and Article 7 (3) (establishment of mechanism for enforcement of the liability), will actually have the nationality of that Party. For example, the current Japanese law for the protection of the Antarctic environment which implements the Madrid Protocol and which is most likely to provide the administrative legal framework to implement the Liability Annex for Japan, is based solely on the nationality principle for the exercise of its jurisdiction.

The resolution of these and other points domestically and the ratification of the Liability Annex as a result of such exercise by all the Consultative Parties will undoubtedly provide a firm foundation for the innovative concept and design of liability established in the Liability Annex to be a model for future public liability regimes in international law.

References

Books, Articles and Chapters in Books

Bederman, D. and Keskar, Soniya P. (2005), 'Antarctic Environmental Liability: The Stockholm Annex and Beyond', *Emory International Law Review* 19:3, 1383–1405.

Birnie, P. and Boyle, A. (eds) (2002), *International Law and the Environment*, 2nd edition (Oxford: Oxford University Press).

Bodansky, D., Brunnée, J. and Hey, E. (eds) (2007), *The Oxford Handbook of International Environmental Law* (Oxford: Oxford University Press).

Boyle, A. (1997), 'Remedying Harm to International Common Spaces and Resources: Compensation and Other Approaches', in Wetterstein (ed.).

Brans, E. (2001), *Liability for Damage to Public Natural Resources* (The Hague: Kluwer Law International).

Brans, E. (2005), 'Liability for Damage to Public Natural Resources under the 2004 EC Environmental Liability Directive: Standing and Assessment of Damages', *Environmental Law Review* 7:2, 90–109.

Brownlie, I. (2003), *Principles of Public International Law*, 6th ed. (Oxford: Oxford University Press).

Brunnée, J. (2004), 'Of Sense and Sensibility: Reflections on International Liability Regimes as Tools for Environmental Protection', *International and Comparative Law Quarterly* 53:2, 351–368.

Brunnée, J. (2007), 'Chapter 23 Common Areas, Common Heritage, and Common Concern', in Bodansky, D. et al. (eds).

Burmester, H. (1989), 'Liability for Damage from Antarctic Mineral Resource Activities', *Virginia Journal of International Law* 29:3, 621–660.

Cheng, B. and Brown, E. (eds) (1988), *Contemporary Problems of International Law: Essays in Honour of Georg Schwarzenberger on his Eightieth Birthday* (London: Steven & Sons).

de La Fayette, L. (2005), 'New Approaches for Addressing Damage to the Marine Environment', *International Journal of Marine and Coastal Law* 20:2, 167–224.

de La Fayette, L. (2007), 'Responding to Environmental Damage in Antarctica', in Triggs and Riddell (eds).

Fitzmaurice, M. (1996), 'Liability for Environmental Damage Caused to the Global Commons', *Review of European Community and International Environmental Law* 5:4, 305–311.

Fitzmaurice, M. (2007), 'Chapter 14 International Responsibility and Liability', in Bodansky et al. (eds).

Gautier, P. (2006), 'L'Annex VI au protocole de Madrid relatif à la protection de l'environnment de l'Antartique: <Reponsabilité découlant de situations critiques pour l'environnment>', *Annuaire français de droit international* 52, 418–431.

Johnson, M. (2006), 'Liability for Environmental Damage in Antarctica: The Adoption of Annex VI to the Antarctic Environmental Protocol', *Georgetown International Environmental Law Review* 19:1, 33–55.

König, D., Tobias-Stoll, P., Röben, V. and Matz-Lück, N. (eds) (2007), *International Law Today: New Challenges and the Need for Reform* (Heidelberg: Springer).

Lahorgue, M.B. (2007), 'Vignt ans après Tchenobyl: un nouveau régime international de responsibilité civile nucléaire', *Journal du droit international* 134:1, 103–124.

Maes, F. (ed.) (2005), *Marine Resources Damage Assessment: Liability and Compensation for Environmental Damage* (Heidelberg: Springer).

Nicholas, J. (2005), 'Chapter 4: Scope of Compensation for Environmental Damage under the 1992 Civil Liability Convention and the 1992 Fund Convention', in Maes (ed.).

de la Rue, C. and Anderson, C. (1998), *Shipping and the Environment* (LLP).

Sands, Ph. (2003), *Principles of International Environmental Law*, 2nd Edition (Cambridge: Cambridge University Press).

Sandvik, B. and Suikkari, S. (1997), 'Harm and Reparation in International Treaty Regimes: An Overview', in Wetterstein (ed.).

Scott, K. (2006), 'Liability for Environmental Damage in Antarctica: Annex VI to the Environmental Protocol on Liability arising from Emergencies', *Environmental Liability* 14:3, 87–99.

Shibata, A. (2004), 'The Establishment of the Secretariat of the Antarctic Treaty: A Legal Analysis', *Okayama Law Journal* 53:3–4, 533–596 [in Japanese].

Shibata, A. (ed.) (2007), *Evolution of the Antarctic Treaty System: An Analysis of its Institutional and Environmental Responses* (Final Report of the Grant-in-Aid for Scientific Research) [in Japanese].

Triggs, G. and Riddell, A. (eds) (2007), *Antarctica: Legal and Environmental Challenges for the Future* (British Institute of International and Comparative Law).

Vigni, P. (2005), 'A Liability Regime for Antarctica', *Italian Yearbook of International Law* 15, 217–242.

Vigni, P. (2007), 'The Secretariat of the Antarctic Treaty: Achievements and Weaknesses Three Year After its Establishment', in Triggs and Riddell (eds).

Vöneky, S. (2007), 'The Liability Annex to the Protocol on Environmental Protection to the Antarctic Treat', in König et al. (eds).

Wellens, K. (ed.) (1998), *International Law: Theory and Practice* (The Hague: Kluwer Law International).

Wetterstein, P. (ed.) (1997), *Harm to Environment* (Glouchestershire: Clarendon Press).

Wolfrum, R. (1998), 'Liability for Environmental Damage: A Means to Enforce Environmental Standards', in Wellens (ed.).

Zemanek, K. (1988), 'Causes and Forms of International Liability', in Cheng and Brown (eds).

Official Documents and Others

ATCM 26 (2003), Antarctic Treaty Consultative Meeting, *Final Report of the 26th Antarctic Treaty Consultative Meeting* (2003), http://www.ats.ag.

ATCM 27 (2004), Antarctic Treaty Consultative Meeting, *Final Report of the 27th Antarctic Treaty Consultative Meeting* (2004), http://www.ats.ag.

ATCM 28 (2005), Antarctic Treaty Consultative Meeting, *Final Report of the 28th Antarctic Treaty Consultative Meeting* (2005), http://www.ats.ag.

ATCM 29 (2006), Antarctic Treaty Consultative Meeting, *Final Report of the 29th Antarctic Treaty Consultative Meeting* (2006), http://www.ats.ag.

ATCM Handbook (2002), *Handbook of the Antarctic Treaty System*, 9th Edition (United States Department of State).

Chile (1992), Basic Elements for an Annex on the Liability Envisaged by the Antarctic Treaty Protocol, 17 ATCM/WP.11 (1992), submitted by Chile.

Germany (1997), Liability: Report of the Group of Legal Experts, 22 ATCM/WP.1 (1997), submitted by Germany.

IAATO (2003), Insurance Amount for IAATO Tourist Vessels, 26 ATCM/INF.85 (2003), submitted by IAATO.

Japan (1991), Draft Outline of the Rules and Procedures Relating to Liability for Damage to the Antarctic Environment and Dependent and Associated Ecosystems, 16 ATCM/WP.33 (1991), submitted by Japan.

Liability Annex (2005), Annex VI to the Protocol on Environmental Protection to the Antarctic Treaty: Liability Arising from Environmental Emergencies, adopted as an attachment to Measure 1 (2005), ATCM 28 (2005), 63.

MacKay's Draft (2001), Chairman's Draft of the Annex VI to the Protocol on Environmental Protection to the Antarctic Treaty: Liability arising from Environmental Emergencies, 24 ATCM/WP.17 (2001), submitted by New Zealand.

MacKay's Draft of Annex VI (2004), Chairman's Draft of Annex VI to the Protocol on Environmental Protection to the Antarctic Treaty: 'Liability Arising from Environmental Emergencies', 27 ATCM/WP.6 (2004), submitted by New Zealand.

MacKay's Report (1999), Personal Report of the Chairman of the Liability Discussion in Working Group I, 23 ATCM/WP.1 (1999), submitted by New Zealand.

MacKay's Revised Draft of Annex VI (2005), Revised Chairman's Draft Annex VI to the Protocol on Environmental Protection to the Antarctic Treaty, 28 ATCM/WP.47 Rev.2 (2005), submitted by New Zealand.

Netherlands, The (1992), Liability for Damage Arising from Activities taking place in the Antarctic Treaty Area, 17 ATCM/WP.8 (1992), submitted by the Netherlands.

United Kingdom (2007), Antarctic Liability: Domestic Implementation of Annex VI to the Environmental Protocol: Key Issues and Areas of Difficulty, 30 ATCM /IP.54 (2007), submitted by the United Kingdom.

United States (1996), Annex VI to the Protocol on Environmental Protection to the Antarctic Treaty, 20 ATCM/INF.43 (1996), submitted by the United States.

United States (1998), Negotiating on an Annex or Annexes on Liability, submitted by the USA, 22 ATCM/IP 126 (1998), submitted by the United States.

United States (2001), Annex VI to the Protocol on Environmental Protection to the Antarctic Treaty 'Prevention of damage, contingency planning and liability for failure to provide for emergency response action', 24 ATCM/WP.6 (2001), submitted by the United States.

Wolfrum Eighth Offering (1997), Chairman's Eighth Offering: Annex on Environmental Liability, 22 ATCM/WP.1 (1997), submitted by Germany.

Wolfrum First Offering (1994), Chairman's First Offering, 18 ATCM/WP.2 (1994), submitted by Germany.

Wolfrum's Questionnaire (1994), Answers of the States to Professor Wolfrum's Questionnaire on the Annex on Environmental Liability in Antarctica, in Liability Annex to the Protocol on Environment Protection to the Antarctic Treaty, 18 ATCM/WP.2 (1994), submitted by Germany.

Wolfrum Report (1997), Report of the Group of Legal Experts on the Work undertaken to Elaborate an Annex or Annexes on Liability for environmental damage in Antarctica, 22 ATCM/WP.1 (1997), submitted by Germany.

Wolfrum Third Offering (1995), Chairman's Third Offering: Liability Annex to the Protocol on Environmental Protection to the Antarctic Treaty: Annex 2, 19 ATCM/INF.24 (1995), submitted by Germany.

PART IV
Diversification of Actors in the Implementation of International Public Interests

Chapter 14

International Economic Law and the Basel Committee on Banking Supervision – An Alternative Form of International Law-making?

Kern Alexander[1]

Introduction

The Basel Committee on Banking Supervision is the most influential international financial standard-setting body. It exercises either direct or indirect influence over the development of banking law and regulation for all developed countries and most developing countries. Because of its influence on national regulatory standards and importance as an international norm builder, its governance structure merits close examination regarding its decision-making processes and its role in creating domestic public law standards for banking regulation. The Basel Committee has produced a number of important international agreements that regulate the amount of capital that banks must set aside against their risk-based assets and the allocation of jurisdictional responsibility for bank regulators in overseeing the international operations of banks. Its activities have usually been kept away from the fanfare of high politics, but its recent efforts to amend the 1988 Capital Accord by adopting the Basel II agreement and to extend its application to all countries where international banks operate has attracted significant critical comment and brought its work under close scrutiny by leading policymakers and regulators.

The chapter considers the role of the Basel Committee on Banking Supervision in influencing the development of public international law norms that govern domestic law standards and rules of banking regulation. In doing so, the chapter

1 I would like to thank Professor Teruo Komori for inviting me to participate in his research project. I would also like to thank Professor Karel Wellens, Professor Christine Kaufmann and Professor Rolf Weber for their collaboration, comments and support. Special thanks also to the Swiss National Science Foundation for its financial support on the research project entitled: 'Trade and Finance: The Regulatory Impact of Liberalized Financial Services' and for the research assistance of Laura Paez and Xenia Roduner at the University of Zurich Rechtswissenschaftliches Institut in 2006–2007.

will analyze the Committee's decision-making and its substantial influence on the development of international norms of banking regulation, which has significantly influenced the formation of the domestic public law of banking regulation in most countries. The chapter suggests that the Basel Committee's important role in developing international norms of banking regulation and its impact on general principles of banking law constitutes an alternative form of public international lawmaking. Because the Committee's voluntary, non-legally binding decision-making and standard-setting process has important implications for the development of general principles of banking regulation, it merits closer scrutiny and review regarding its effectiveness, accountability, and legitimacy. Finally, it will suggest that in today's globalized financial markets that a sounder legal basis is needed for the development of efficient and effective international norms of banking regulation and that the loosely structured decision-making process of the Basel Committee explains in part the weaknesses of the Basel II Capital Accord which have put the global financial system at serious risk in the present international credit crisis.

Sources of International Economic Law and Financial Regulation

International economic law has become important for economic policymakers who seek to design legal rules by which to manage the growth of global economic interdependence.[2] In 1965, Vellas defined the foundations of international economic law as 'dynamic and evolutionary', in contrast to the traditional sources of 'general public international law', which he found to be more primitive because they are limited to elementary relationships, such as the concept of state sovereignty, which made gap-filling in international legal rules and principles extremely difficult.[3] Vellas further noted that international economic law is characterized by the specific qualities of a vocation for constituting a supranational legal order, of an empirical and non-formalistic order, of pragmatism, realism, flexibility and mobility.[4]

More recently, Lowenfeld (2003) suggests that international economic law should be considered to be all 'rules ... that have been developed against the backdrop of the theory of international trade, and of the question, sometimes explicit, at other times tacit – how far deviations from the theory should be allowed'.[5] A broader doctrine includes the role of money, exchange rates and the

2 Malanczuk 1997, 222 and fns 2.4–5.

3 Vellas 1965, 21–22. See also the US Restatement (Third) of 1987 defines international economic law as 'all the international law and international agreements governing economic transactions that cross state boundaries or that otherwise have implications for more than one state, such as those involving the movement of goods, funds, persons, intangibles, technology, vessels or aircraft'. Restatement 3d of the Foreign Relations Law of the US, Vol. 2, §261.

4 Vellas 1965, 21–34.

5 Lowenfeld 2003, 8.

balance of payments, and related areas that add international financial issues to the definition of international economic law, such as the Articles of Agreement of the International Monetary Fund (IMF). According to this view, international economic law covers many specialized areas such as trade in the WTO agreements and the UN Commission on International Trade Law[6] (UNCITRAL), and corporate governance, competition, and anti-money laundering and terrorist financing controls as set forth by agreements adopted by the Organisation for Economic Cooperation and Development (OECD), and the regulation of central banking activities under the treaties establishing the Bank for International Settlements (BIS). It has usually been a law of bilateral and multilateral agreements, rather than one based on custom or governed by general principles of law.

International financial law has been defined as 'encompassing both private and public international law, [and including] the private law of international banking relationships, national regulation of financial transactions, and the public international law of money, including the rules of the IMF'.[7] The inclusion of international financial law into the broader regime of international economic law, as well as the emergence of a special field of international law called 'international monetary law', has been largely attributed to the works of the late Sir Joseph Gold, former IMF General Counsel, and the drafter of the First and Second Amendments to the IMF Articles of Agreement.[8] Indeed, Gold defined the purpose of international monetary law as consisting 'of a complex of relationships among countries on matters ... that are governed by rules and understandings that are more extensive than international monetary law as a branch of public international law'.[9]

In contrast, global economic law has been interpreted as a self-replicating process in which legal norms arise from non-state actors, such as associations of private market participants and multi-national corporations that operate on a transnational basis. Teubner and others build on Ehrlich's 'Bukowina' to argue that a modern *lex mercatoria* has emerged outside public law sources and in relative insulation from state institutions to constitute a new 'trans-national law of economic transactions'.[10] This global non-state law governing commercial and economic transactions can be explained by a theory of legal pluralism and has arisen from diverse social systems and is subject to 'a highly asymmetric process of legal self-reproduction'.[11] For example, the model contracts for cross-border investments such as project finance or financial services between wholesale counterparties

6 Cf. Malanczuk 1997, 223.

7 Zamora and Gold 1990, 439 and fn 2.

8 Sir Joseph was the Fund's General Counsel between 1960 and 1979. See 17; and Zamora and Gold 1990, 439.

9 Zamora and Gold 1990, 801, cited in Zamora and Gold, 446. Gold argued that the IMF administered a legal regime.

10 Teubner 1997, 11.

11 Teubner 1997, 11.

often are governed by contractual terms that derive from model contracts that do not have a necessary link to a national legal system.

Moreover, accountants and lawyers have agreed to transnational rule-making processes to govern multinational insolvencies. Similarly, the internal legal regimes of multinational corporations are devised independently of any one country's corporate law and apply *sui generis* to particular areas of corporate activity. This has also been recognized in the area of labour relations where multi-national firms adopt agreements to govern employee relations with transnational labour unions that are outside the laws of any national legal system.[12]

The generation of international economic norms has also been analyzed through various institutional perspectives. For instance, Slaughter (2004) describes the current global order as a world of 'disaggregated states' rather than the traditional realist notion of unitary states. These disaggregated states interact with each other not only through foreign ministries, but also through regulatory, judicial, sub-state and legislative bodies.[13] She views this 'network' system as a novel development that is a response to globalization. Networks involve mainly government officials who create links across national borders and between national and supranational institutions. They perform a variety of functions, including the facilitation of information collection and sharing, technical assistance and coordinating cross-border enforcement. The scope of these networks can be bilateral, plurilateral, regional or global, and they interact with a wide range of international organizations, non-governmental organizations and civil society movements. Upon closer analysis, however, the novelty of the 'network' theory is undermined by the fact that economic, financial and commercial diplomacy has been conducted through inter-state networks since the nineteenth century and therefore is not a new form of international cooperation.[14] Nevertheless, as Howse (2007) observes, Slaughter's theory of networks helps to 'keep in perspective the role of international law and international institutions in contrast to other mechanisms and tools of governance'.[15]

Globalization and International Standard Setting

State borders no longer contain and define economic activity. While sovereign nation states regulate domestic markets, cross-border trade in goods, services, capital and labour are facilitated by advances in transportation and communication

12 See discussion Teubner 1997, above n. 9, at 13–15.

13 Slaughter 2004, 5.

14 Extensive networks of economic, financial and central bank policymakers were involved in the negotiations at the London Conference in 1932 on currency and trade arrangements, as well as in the creation of the Bretton Woods institutions in 1944 and the GATT in 1947.

15 Howse 2007, 232.

links, which require trans-national management and international regulation. The growth of financial markets and cross-border capital flows and financial transactions has led states to create multi-lateral institutions and international standard-setting bodies to attempt to control and regulate the cross-border activities of trans-national corporations and other firms and non-state actors which impact domestic economies and financial systems. It is recognized that the influence of these multi-lateral institutions and standard-setting bodies has grown immensely and that many states have responded to this by building parallel structures to counterbalance the influence of these institutions and bodies.[16] The question arises regarding how state decision-making and standard-setting practices should be regulated in these multi-lateral institutions and what type of legal competency states should exercise when engaged in standard setting and the optimal allocation of competency between international and state-level actors.

Although nation states remain the main actors in public international law, it is widely accepted today that legal personality can also extend to international organizations and in certain circumstances to other non-state actors, such as individuals and juridical or corporate persons.[17] Sovereign states, however, remain the main actors in economic policy and regulation. Insofar as national governments initiate and establish international organizations and institutions, and are members of these organizations, they lay down the initial roles and terms of reference, decide the future membership, finance their activities, and carry out continuing control over the exercise of the assigned functions of international organizations.

States are finding it increasingly difficult to regulate and manage cross-border trading activities and financial transactions given the new modes of production, distribution and consumption, and the rising interconnectedness of governments, societies and private actors in the world economy. Indeed the forces of globalization are changing the structure of the world economy and are posing major regulatory challenges for states.[18] As a response to the growing cross-border flow of goods, services, capital, ideas and people, states have sought to enhance their regulatory control and surveillance of cross-border economic activities by coordinating their economic and financial policies and regulatory practices with other states through international organizations and multilateral bodies and institutions. States have also facilitated the rise and transformation of domestic corporations and firms into multinational enterprises (MNEs), thus creating new and influential entities at the international level. For international financial markets, the process of

16 See LeRoy Bennett 1996, 265; see also Woods 2000, 1.

17 See Higgins 1994, 46–48. See also Seidl-Hohenveldern 1992, 13.

18 See, e.g., Delbrück 2001, 16. For a definition of globalization as '... the process or the processes of denationalization/deterritorialization of politics, markets, and laws or, more specifically, process of denationalization/deterritorialization of clusters of political, economic and social transactions involving national and international actors, public and private, leading to a global interconnectedness of these actors in time and space including individuals'.

globalization has been no different. Expansion, diversification and international coordination of banking activities and operations have alternated with increased 'global competition among bank and non-bank financial intermediaries' and have resulted in the rise of global financial service companies and the consolidation and conglomeration of the banking and financials services industry.[19]

International Standard Setting and the G10 Committees

In contrast to international economic organizations such as the World Trade Organization or the Bank for International Settlements,[20] international standard-setting bodies are not entities created by states with separate legal personality, but rather informal associations of state representatives and/or professionals which meet to address specific problems or to identify issues of concern. In international finance, the globalization of financial services has necessitated that regulators develop cooperative relations to facilitate their oversight and regulation of banking and financial services. Beginning in 1962, the central banks of the ten leading industrialized nations, including the Swiss National Bank, began to meet regularly at the BIS and other venues to coordinate central bank policy and to organize lending to each other through the General Arrangements to Borrow. These ten countries plus the Swiss National Bank became known as the Group of Ten or G10. Goodhart (2008) described the relationship of the G10 committee with one of its standard-setting committees – the Basel Committee on Banking Supervision – as one of delegated authority to engage in regulatory standard setting:

> Having established a standing committee of specialists in this field, the G-10 Governors would find it difficult to reject a proposal from them, especially on a technical matter. The relationships between the G-10 Governors and the BCBS [Basel Committee] emerge from the analysis of what the BCBS actually did and were quite complex. The G-10 Governors set priorities for work, and frequently required papers to be revised and reconsidered. But at the same time they often gave the BCBS considerable freedom to decide its own agenda, and frequently rubber-stamped the papers emerging; basically the Governors did not have the

19 See Norton 1990, 249.

20 The Bank for International Settlement (BIS) is an international organization created under the Hague Agreements of 1930 and the Constituent Charter of the Bank for International Settlements of 1930. It was established in the context of the Young Plan, which dealt with the issue of the reparation payments imposed on Germany by the Treaty of Versailles following the First World War. The BIS served as the payment agent for the European Payments Union (EPU, 1950–1958), which facilitated the restoration of currency convertibility for the western European countries following the Second World War. See Gros and Thygesen 1998, 4–8.

> time or the desire for textual criticism. They had a general oversight role; the detail was to be hammered out in the BCBS.[21]

The G10 established several committees whose secretariats were based at the BIS. These committees were initially the Eurocurrency Standing Committee (the Markets Committee, 1962), which was formed to monitor and assess the operations of the then newly established Euro-currency markets. This committee later became the Committee on the Global Financial System (1971), which deals today with broader issues of systemic risk and financial stability. The best known was the Basel Committee on Banking Regulation and Supervisory Practices (BCBS, 1974), which today is known as the Basel Committee on Banking Supervision. Finally, the Committee on Payment and Settlement Systems (1990) negotiates and sets standards to support the continued functioning of payment and settlement systems.[22]

These committees have examined many important economic policy and financial regulatory issues, and elaborated and promulgated best practices in supervisory and regulatory practices and in the functioning of payment and settlement systems and the overall operation of financial markets. Committees are usually chaired by senior officials of member central banks and are composed of experts from central banks, regulatory authorities and finance ministries. In the case of the Basel Committee on Banking Supervision, members also include non-central bank supervisory authorities and other regulatory and economic policy experts. Committee members have voting power and decision-making authority, while non-G10 country representatives are often consulted for their views on a variety of regulatory and economic issues. Frequently, special initiatives are undertaken to share experience with, and invite the views of, those not directly involved in the work of the committees. In promoting cooperation in their respective areas, the committees determine their own agenda and, within their mandate, operate independently from the BIS itself, which only provides its good offices for meetings and administrative and research support.

In late 1974, the G10 central bank governors decided to form the Basel Committee on Banking Regulation and Supervisory Practices in response to several bank failures in 1974, including the collapse of the German Herstatt Bankhaus, which had led to significant problems with foreign exchange and settlement risk between US and German banks, and the insolvency of the US Franklin National Bank, which posed significant bank counterparty risks, on account of its miscalculations of foreign exchange risk in the wholesale loan market. The systemic impact of these bank failures exposed substantial gaps in the ability of central bankers and national regulators to control and manage a crisis with cross-

---

21 Goodhart, Chapter 14.

22 See Baker 2002, 32. Three other secretariats operate out of the BIS: The Financial Stability Board, the International Association of Deposit Insurers, and the International Association of Insurance Supervisors.

border effects. In response, they adopted a Concordat in 1975 that established principles of information exchange and coordination for the oversight of the cross-border operations of banking institutions.[23] The 1975 Concordat was amended in 1983 in response to the collapse and insolvency of the Italian bank Banco Ambrosiano.[24] The Revised Concordat contained the principle of consolidated supervision that provides that home country regulators shall have responsibility for ensuring that the transnational operations of their home country banks are sound regarding credit risk exposure, quality of assets and the capital adequacy of the banking group's global operations.

Later, following the Latin American debt crisis of the early 1980s and the near collapse of several major US banks, the Basel Committee adopted the 1988 Capital Accord that established for the G10 countries a minimum eight per cent capital adequacy requirement on internationally active banks within their jurisdictions.[25] The Capital Accord was originally calculated based on a bank's credit risk exposure, but was later amended in 1996 to include a bank's market risk exposure (i.e., trading book exposure), which extended the eight per cent capital adequacy requirement to a bank's trading book activities.[26] Between 1999 and 2004, the Committee engaged in a lengthy and radical revision of the Accord known as 'Basel II'. The Committee agreed upon and published a final text of the Basel II Capital Accord in June 2004 with most of its members committing to implement the Accord by December 2007.[27]

23 See Walker 2001, 30–42.

24 See the '1983 Principles for the Supervision of Banks' Foreign Establishments'.

25 The 1988 Capital Accord's original purpose was to prevent the erosion of bank capital ratios resulting from aggressive competition for market share by the leading banks during the 1980s. The Accord also hoped to harmonize the different levels and approaches to capital among the G10 countries. In adopting the 1988 Accord, banking regulators wanted to establish an international minimum standard that would create a level playing field for banks operating in the G10 countries and that banking regulators wanted capital requirements to reflect accurately the true risks facing banks in a deregulated and internationally-competitive market. The 1988 Capital Accord required banks actively engaged in international transactions to hold capital equal to at least 8 per cent of their risk weighted assets. This capital adequacy standard was intended to prevent banks from increasing their exposure to credit risk by imprudently incurring greater leverage. The 1988 Capital Accord was entitled 'International Convergence of Capital Measurement and Capital Standards' and it applied based on the principle of home country control to banks based in G10 countries with international operations (Basel 1988).

26 This was known as the Market Risk Amendment 1996. See Alexander et al. 2006, 38–39.

27 The European Union implemented the Accord with the adoption of the Capital Requirements Directive in 2006, while the United States will not fully implement the Accord for all its banks until 2012–2014.

Although Basel II has attracted much criticism on economic and regulatory grounds,[28] its negotiation and approval has been haled as an example of the benefits of informal and flexible decision-making procedures that work by consensus and do not subject states to the strict procedural rules that often accompany treaty negotiations – especially multilateral agreements that cover sensitive areas of state economic and regulatory policy. Indeed, it has been argued that a particular strength of the Committee's standard-setting process are that they are *legally non-binding* in a public international law sense and place a great deal of emphasis on decentralized implementation and informal monitoring of member compliance.[29] The Committee's informal decision-making process has been viewed as effective for its members because of its absence of formal procedure (Jackson 2000). The Committee has sought to extend its informal network with banking regulators outside the G10 through various consultation groups.[30] Most recently, it has conducted seminars and consultations with banking regulators from over 100 countries as part of the consultation process for adopting Basel II.

Monitoring non-compliance has generally been a decentralized task that is the responsibility of member states themselves, and not international organizations, such as the BIS or other international bodies (Norton 1995). Nonetheless, the Committee monitors and reviews the Basel framework with a view to achieving greater uniformity in its implementation and convergence in substantive standards. Moreover, the Committee aims to apply its standards to all countries which have cross-border and international banking so that all countries – including emerging markets and developing countries – are strongly encouraged to adopt 'strong prudential standards' and 'effective supervisory structures'.[31] To ensure that its standards are adopted, the Committee expects the IMF and World Bank to play a surveillance role in overseeing member state adherence through its various conditionality and economic restructuring programs. The extended application of the Basel Committee's standards to non-G10 countries has raised questions regarding the accountability of its decision-making structure and its suitability for application in developing and emerging market economies. In addition, because most G10 countries are members of the European Union, they are required by EU law to implement the Capital Accord into domestic law. The only G10 countries

28 See Alexander et al. 2007, 2–4.

29 Norton 1990 (cf. Walker 2001, 30–38, arguing for a stronger international legal basis for the Committee's standard setting).

30 The Core Principles Liaison Group remains the most important forum for dialogue between the Committee and systemically relevant non-G10 countries. Moreover, the BIS established the Financial Stability Institute to conduct outreach to non-G10 banking regulators by holding seminars and conferences on implementing international banking and financial standards.

31 This mandate derives from a communiqué issued by the G7 Heads of State in 1997. The Committee has interpreted the G7 communiqué as authority for it to devise global capital standards and other core principles of prudential regulation for all economies where international banks operate.

that are not required by local law to implement the Capital Accord are Canada, Japan and the United States.[32]

The Traditional Sources of Public International Law and International Financial Regulation

An analysis of the international legal relevance of the Basel Committee standards can be done by applying the traditional sources of public international law. There is a growing recognition of the inadequacy of the traditional sources of public international law, as enumerated in Article 38(1)(a)–(d) of the Statute of the International Court of Justice (ICJ),[33] to explain and describe the normative development of many areas of inter-state relations (Wellens and Borchardt 1989). The two most cited sources are treaties and international custom (customary international law). Treaties create legally binding rights and obligations between states and can take the form of multilateral, regional or bilateral agreements. Many treaties (though not all) contain procedures for enforcement or dispute resolution that allow state responsibility to be invoked under a treaty for breach of obligation that may result in liability and/or reparation. In contrast, international custom takes the form of customary rules or principles that must be evidenced by (1) a general or uniform state practice with respect to the particular rule or obligation, and (2) accepted by states as a legal obligation (*opinio juris*).[34] State practice forms the basis of customary international law. It consists of patterns of state behaviour or

---

32 In fact, a major obstacle in negotiations over Basel II had been the initial reluctance of US Congress and refusal of some US bank regulators to apply Basel II to most US banks. The Federal Reserve, which has been an important supporter of Basel II and has authority to apply it to US Financial Holding Companies, has begun applying it to the 12 largest US financial holding companies, while all other US credit institutions will follow a different implementation schedule that may result in Basel II not being fully adopted by US banks until 2013–2015. See 'Risk-based Capital Guidelines; Capital Adequacy Guidelines; Capital Maintenance; Domestic Capital Modifications', Advanced Notice of Proposed Rule-making' 12 CFR part 3 (6 October 2005).

33 See Art. 38(1)(a)–(d), ICJ Statute. The traditional sources of public international law as stated in Article 38(1) are:

> international conventions, whether general or particular, establishing rules expressly recognised by the contesting states; international custom, as evidence of a general practice accepted as law; the general principles of law as recognised by civilised nations; … judicial decisions and the teachings of the most highly qualified publicists of the various nations, as subsidiary means for the determination of rules of law.

34 See Military and Paramilitary Activities in and against Nicaragua (*Nicaragua v United States of America*), ICJ Reports 986, 97, para. 183 (observing that to determine 'rules of customary international law' the court must look 'to the practice and *opinio juris* of states').

conduct that contain both objective and subjective elements that are necessary for a state (or states) to form or maintain legally binding customary rules.[35]

The absence of a binding international legal commitment to implement the Basel Accord and other international financial standards has taken these standards outside the scope of customary international law and treaties. Nevertheless, over 100 countries claim to have implemented the 1988 Capital Accord and are undertaking transition arrangements to implement Basel II. It should not be forgotten that the European Community has implemented the Capital Accord into EU law and has committed itself to implement Basel II as well. The growing consistency of state practice with the Basel Accord and other international financial standards suggest that it is possible to have a uniform practice of states without *opinio juris*, that is, a general practice of states which does not have as its motive the formation of customary rules of international law.[36] In this sense, the subjective element of state practice does not contain the belief that it has a legal obligation. The absence of a legal obligation provides regulators and standard setters with the necessary flexibility to respond rapidly to developments in financial markets and to implement non-binding standards in a particular manner that suits the needs of their jurisdictions. This is why international soft law will remain viable as an instrument for reforming international financial regulation.

Other sources of international law include general principles of law whose validity derives from the world's leading legal systems and subsidiary sources such as judicial decisions and the works of leading publicists. General principles of law have derived mainly from private law principles, such as estoppel and reparation, but the growing importance of public administrative law in most jurisdictions means that commonly accepted principles of public law can potentially qualify as general principles of law and thereby become sources of international law. This appears to be taking place in a number of countries where there is growing convergence in public law principles with respect to banking and financial regulation that has been influenced substantially by international soft law principles. In fact, the standards of the Basel Committee and the core principles of banking supervision

35 The objective element takes the form of actual deeds (e.g., administrative decisions and the adoption of regulatory rules) that are observable and manifest, while the subjective element consists of a state's attitude or intent which may present itself in certain acts or behaviour, such as official statements of heads of state or governments, diplomatic correspondence, or voting at international organizations, that provide evidence of a state believing it has a legal obligation. The actual practice of states is the objective element of state practice, while the subjective element consists in the state's belief that its performance or omission, or that of other states, is required by international law. See discussion in *Tunisia/Libya Continental Shelf case*, ICJ Reports 1982, 18, 44–46, para. 43.

36 *The Lotus case* PCIJ, Ser. A, No. 10 (1927). In fact, the Basel Accord and other international financial standards represent what Mendelson 1995 has called *opinio non-juris*, in which states expressly state that although they may act in a certain way they do not consider their acts to be motivated by any legal obligation or that their behaviour should serve as a precedent to restrict their future conduct.

have directly influenced and shaped the development of national banking law principles, including liability rules for senior officers and directors and even the rules that define the types of regulatory capital which banks are required to hold. This dramatic convergence of domestic banking law principles could arguably constitute a future source of international law based on general principles of public regulatory law. Indeed, this would occur by the formation of international soft law principles and rules at the international level which would then filter down to national legal systems and domestic regulations of the world's leading states and legal systems and thereby germinate into general principles of public law for the regulation of banks that may become legally relevant as sources of public international law.[37]

As a general matter, however, the sources of public international law are increasingly viewed as unsatisfactory for explaining the variety of international obligations and commitments undertaken by states in many areas of international relations. This is especially true in many areas of international finance, the environment, and corporate governance where legally non-binding international standards and codes play a prominent role in governing state regulatory practice and conduct. The enormous expansion of activities by international organizations and standard-setting bodies and the increasing use by states of informal, legally non-binding agreements and instruments to mediate and regulate their foreign relations has marked a dramatic shift away from formal international lawmaking to informal soft law techniques of standard setting and implementation. As a result, state behaviour and conduct has become increasingly influenced in a permissive, prescriptive and prohibitive way by an unprecedented number of international non-conventional or non-treaty agreements, which have been adopted by states acting through a variety of international organizations and standard-setting bodies.

Insofar as these organizations are neither composed of states nor founded upon an international treaty, they do not meet the traditional legal definition of an international organization. Nonetheless, recent scholarship suggests that precisely because these international standard-setting bodies are devoid of legal personality and excluded from the potential discipline of international law, they gain in flexibility and enhanced coordination benefits in devising international norms that turn out to be more effective in influencing state practice than traditional methods of public international lawmaking.[38]

Expanding the Basel Committee's Scope of Application

Although the scope of application of the Basel Committee's capital adequacy standards and rules on consolidated supervision was intended to apply only to

---

37 This means that the institutional structure of decision-making of international soft law bodies, such as the Basel Committee, merit closer examination because of their potential indirect impact on the formation of general principles of public regulatory law.

38 See Alexander et al. 2006, 136–139.

credit institutions based in G10 countries which had cross-border operations, this changed dramatically in 1998 when the Committee stated its intent to amend the Capital Accord and to make it applicable to all countries where banks operate on a cross-border basis. The expansive remit of the Committee's standard-setting operations raised important questions regarding whether the non-G10 countries and jurisdictions now subject to the Accord should have some role in the standard-setting process and a say in the substantive content of the norms adopted. Because Basel II now applies to all countries and jurisdictions where international banks operate, the Committee's decision-making structure has been criticized on the grounds of procedural accountability and broader issues of political legitimacy.

Nevertheless, many non-G10 countries have incorporated the Basel standards into their regulatory framework for a variety of reasons, including to strengthen the soundness of their commercial banks, to raise their credit rating in international financial markets, and to achieve a universally recognized international standard. As discussed below, the International Monetary Fund and World Bank have also required many countries to demonstrate adherence or a realistic effort to implement the Basel Accord in order to qualify for financial assistance and as part of IMF Financial Sector Assessment programs and World Bank Financial Sector Adjustment programs. Also, all G10 countries require foreign banks to demonstrate that their home country regulators have adopted the Capital Accord and other international agreements as a condition for obtaining a bank license. Moreover, international reputation and market signals are also important in creating incentives for non-G10 countries to adopt the Capital Accord. Many non-G10 countries (including developing countries) have found it necessary to require their banks to adopt similar capital adequacy standards in order to attract foreign investment as well as to stand on equal footing with international banks in global financial markets.

Other International Financial Supervisory Bodies

The international standard-setting process of the Basel Committee is not unique, as other international financial supervisory bodies have utilized similar soft law techniques to devise international regulatory standards for others sectors of financial markets. The International Organization of Securities Commissions (IOSCO), comprising most of the world's securities commissioners, have adopted standards with respect to disclosure, insider dealing, and capital adequacy for securities firms that have fostered a type of convergence in standard-setting in the world's leading securities markets. Similarly, the International Association of Insurance Supervisors (IAIS) is a voluntary association of the world's leading insurance commissioners and regulators who meet several times each year to negotiate international standards and best practices for insurance regulation.[39] In

39 See International Association of Insurance Supervisors, 1999 Annual Report 2, 2000.

the area of money laundering and terrorist financing, the OECD's Financial Action Task Force (FATF) has attained a high profile role in setting international standards (so-called Recommendations) of disclosure and transparency for the regulation of banks, financial service providers, and other businesses in order to combat the global problem of financial crime.[40] The FATF and the Basel Committee have each played a much higher profile role in their respective international regulatory standard-setting functions as compared to the IOSCO and IAIS. In recent years, however, IOSCO and IAIS have attracted much more policy attention as their standards and recommendations have been recognized by the IMF and World Bank as international benchmarks against which IMF and Bank member countries are assessed for compliance in their financial sector assessment programmes.

Similarly, the Joint Forum on Financial Conglomerates (Joint Forum) and the Financial Stability Board[41] provide inter-governmental networks for the regulators and supervisors who serve on the international standard-setting bodies. The Joint Forum was established in 1996 under the aegis of the BCBS, IAIS and IOSCO. It is an inter-institutional international financial body, as mentioned above, an international financial entity created by other IFIs. The Joint Forum issues documents, which are considered soft law. In contrast to its constituents, the Joint Forum establishes sets of principles which are designed to assist regulated entities in devising a coherent compliance policy and specific management or other programmes as well as determining the types of issues that should be considered in contracts. The report also contains some broad principles to help supervisors. It develops its principles in conjunction with the IOSCO. The Joint Forum's

40 Other important international standard-setting bodies include the International Accounting Standards Board and the International Federation of Accountants, which are composed of non-state representatives that include professional accountants and academics who devise international accounting standards for the accounting industry. Similarly, the International Auditing and Assurance Standards Board sets standards for international financial reporting.

41 The Financial Stability Board was originally known as the Financial Stability Forum, which was established in 1999 in response to the Asian financial crisis. The FSB is composed of regulatory officials from leading developed countries and some large developing countries. It relies on the work of the other international financial standard-setting bodies and the central banks and the various departments of the OECD. See Financial Stability Board, 'Overview' (online). The FSF compiled a Compendium of Standards (CoS) with a summary and classification of the most significant rules, best practices, principles and guidelines of international financial regulation. They are categorized according to the sector they pertain to, such as government and central bank, banking, securities, and insurance industries, and the corporate sector, and functionally, such as to governance, accounting, disclosure and transparency, capital adequacy, regulation, and supervision, information sharing, risk management, payment and settlement, business ethics etc., and according to their specificity in principles, practices and guidelines. See http://www.fsforum.org/compendium/what_are_standards.html.

principles are in its own words 'high-level and cross-sectoral, designed to provide a minimum benchmark' for all financial institutions.

The Joint Forum coordinates activities relating to issues common to the banking, securities and insurance sectors. The Joint Forum as the common body of three international financial institutions, the BCBS, the IAIS and the IOSCO, sets soft law in the form of guidance (2004 outsourcing guidance), reports (report on financial disclosure 2004) in the form of broad principles which serve to establish a benchmark minimal standard.

The above international bodies and supervisory networks have adopted standards, principles, codes, guidelines, framework and reports that have had a significant impact on the development of domestic public law standards of regulation and supervisory practices. Similar to the Basel standards, the regulations issued by these international financial bodies are not legally binding, as regulators seek to agree regulatory standards that can be flexibly implemented into the regulatory regimes of different jurisdictions. Although these international standards are without legal effect, they provide normative influence on the public lawmaking processes of the countries that have agreed to adopt the standards.

Basel Committee's Decision-making and Implementation Issues

Questioning the Committee's Legitimacy

The Basel Committee is possibly the most effective and well-known international standard-setting body which does not possess any formal supranational authority, and whose agreements do not have any legal force under international law.[42] The Committee's decision-making process, however, has been criticized for serious deficiencies in accountability and legitimacy for those countries and economies subject to its standards. Some of the problems with the existing decision-making process are that its internal operations and deliberations are not disclosed to the public and that the increasing number of countries subject to its standards play no meaningful role in influencing their development. In previous years, when the Basel committee was seeking to address problems that were only of concern to G10 regulators, secrecy and informality were viewed as hallmarks of effective decision-making. Today, however, the global impact of the Committee's standard setting has called into question its legitimacy. Although the Basel Committee has sought

42 The Committee has stated its *raison d'être* as: it formulates broad supervisory standards and guidelines and recommends statements of best practice in the expectation that individual authorities will take steps to implement them through detailed arrangements – statutory or otherwise – which are best suited to their own national systems. In this way, the Committee encourages convergence towards common approaches and common standards without attempting detailed harmonisation of member countries' supervisory techniques. (Bank for International Settlements, 'About the Basel Committee' [online])

to involve policy makers and regulators from non-G10 countries in various aspects of the standard-setting process, the actual decision-making remains controlled by the G10 countries. The Basel II Accord should be of serious concern to all countries and their banking regulators because the Committee's decision-making now exercises substantial influence over the development of international banking norms that apply to all countries. Indeed, the Basel Committee has interpreted its new mandate as providing authority for it to extend the scope of coverage of its international standards and principles to all countries where international banks operate. Its efforts to create common and uniform standards that would apply throughout the global financial system have met with resistance from many large developing countries and emerging economies who believe that they should not have to adopt standards which they played little role in influencing.[43]

The Committee has traditionally represented the world's most systemically important financial markets. But in recent years, in light of the Asia crisis of the late 1990s and the recent international credit crisis which arose from severe weaknesses in the regulatory regimes of the G10 countries (in particular, in the US and UK), there has been a growing recognition that more developing countries and emerging market economies should be represented on the Committee and that alternative regulatory perspectives should be considered. Indeed, the Basel Committee recognized this problem during the deliberations over Basel II by establishing a Core Principles Liaison Group with 13 non-G10 countries, which include Brazil, China, India and Russia, to consult regarding core principles on banking supervision as well as capital adequacy standards. Nevertheless, although these 13 non-G10 countries were often consulted about the possible impact of Basel II in their economies, they had no seat on the Committee and therefore did not exercise a meaningful nor direct influence over the promulgation of Basel II. Most recently, in response to the global credit crisis of 2007–2009 and to serious defects in G10 country regulation, the Committee expanded its membership from 13 to 20 countries in March 2009.[44] Although the expansion of the Basel Committee's membership to 20 countries (including India, Russia, China and Brazil) improves its accountability and political legitimacy, there remain serious concerns regarding the legitimacy of the Committee's mandate because a great number of developing countries and emerging market countries are not on the Committee and have little, if any, influence over its standard-setting.

43 For instance, in 2001, Russia, South Africa and Saudi Arabia proposed an alternative minimum requirement to the Capital Accord of 9 per cent capital to asset charge on all credit and market risk assets.

44 See 'Expansion of membership announced by the Basel Committee' (13 Mar. 2009) http://www.bis.org/press/p090313.htm (Basel Committee decided on 10–11 March 2009 to expand its membership from 13 to 20 countries by adding Australia, Brazil, China, India, South Korea, Mexico, and Russia). The BCBS's expanded membership, however, does not apply to the membership of the G10 central bank governors, which remains the same with the 12 developed countries plus the European Central Bank.

The Committee's Accountability

Regarding implementation, the Committee's decentralized approach to implementation has resulted in uneven implementation and perhaps enforcement of the standards adopted. For instance, throughout the 1990s, Japan suffered from a major banking crisis that derived in part from a collapse of its capital markets. This resulted in the value of Japanese banking assets plummeting, leading Japanese regulators to forbear in ensuring that Japanese banks follow appropriate guidelines for marking down the value of their assets to reflect their true market value. This type of regulatory forbearance is often not available for developing and emerging market economies undergoing transition programs overseen by the IMF and World Bank. Instead, these countries are required, as a condition of financial assistance, to implement stringent banking sector reforms in accordance with the Basel standards and in particular to ensure that the banking sector is well capitalized and that bank assets reflect their true market value. This situation where non-G10 countries are required to implement as part of conditionality or similar programs, or subject to the threat of withdrawal of private investor support, international standards devised by the Basel Committee raises important issues regarding the accountability of the Committee to those countries subject to its standards.

Indeed, there is no clear procedure for how decisions are made in the Basel Committee. Moreover, the decision-making process itself is not disclosed, nor are the minutes of meetings made publicly available. On the other hand, however, it should be recognized that the standard-setting process often involves the exchange of sensitive information and regulators need the flexibility and discretion to give honest and frank assessments of country regulatory policies without having such information released publicly. Full disclosure of all negotiations may deter regulators from making candid assessments of reform proposals and thereby undermine the efficacy of the standard-setting process. Moreover, in times of crisis, effective decision-making may often require regulators and officials to meet at short notice and out of the public eye in order to make emergency decisions that may have a substantial effect in averting a full-blown crisis. Safeguards are necessary therefore to ensure against the unnecessary disclosure of sensitive financial market information during regulatory negotiations and proceedings. Effective standard setting requires a certain level of secrecy and discretion for regulators to make difficult decisions, especially in times of crisis. Nevertheless, accountability requires that the process for such decision-making be made clear in advance and that lines of authority for decision-making are also clear and indicate how states can participate in setting standards, but also understand how their role may be limited in times of emergency.

In addition, the political legitimacy has been called into question. As mentioned above, the Basel Committee is composed of the central bank governors and national bank regulators of the 13 richest developed countries in terms of per-capita income. At the time it was established in 1974, the Committee was only concerned with the regulatory practices of G10 countries because it was only their banks that could have an impact on global financial stability. As more countries began to liberalize their foreign exchange controls in the 1980s and to deregulate their financial sectors, however, the Committee became more concerned with the regulatory and supervisory practices of non-G10 countries. Following the financial crises of the late 1990s, the Committee began to interact more with, and to seek the views of, large and systemically important developing countries in such forums as the G22 and now the G20.[45] Also, during this period, the IMF was making compliance with the Capital Accord and various other principles of prudential supervision mandatory as a condition for financial assistance under IMF conditionality programs, while the World Bank was doing the same with respect to its financial sector adjustment lending programs.

Moreover, these international organizations were able to utilize their technical assistance programs to advise developing and emerging market countries to adopt international financial standards (IFI standards), including the Basel standards. In addition, the effect of increased liberalization of the capital account, combined with pressures from foreign direct and portfolio investors, led many national regulators to adopt Basel standards and other IFI standards in order to prevent foreign capital flows from shifting out of their countries. As a result, by 2008, over 150 countries have claimed either to have adopted the 1988 Basel Accord and/or are in the process of adopting Basel II.

The Capital Accord and other BIS committee standards are undoubtedly perceived today as international standards of best practice with broad adherence by most countries of the world. The real weaknesses with Basel II, however, as demonstrated by the 2007–2009 international credit crisis, is that international financial standards can be bad economic policy not only for the rich G10 countries who adopt them, but also for the great majority of countries who are pressured to adopt them by international economic organizations and by foreign investors. This raises important issues of how these countries were pressured to adopt the Basel standards through conditions imposed by other international economic institutions and by the regulatory practices of other states and by market pressures.[46]

---

45 International financial regulation was the main topic of discussion at the London Summit of the G20 which met in April 2009.

46 The issues of legitimacy in international financial standard setting are discussed in Alexander et al. 2006, 44–47. Indeed, by applying the international political principles of legitimacy to international decision-making, the substantive standards of financial regulation devised by IFIs might be improved significantly in a way that enhances financial stability for both individual countries and the global financial system. Indeed, enhanced legitimacy for the Basel Committee would involve an expansion of its membership to include more non-G10 countries, especially large, systemically relevant developing countries, such as Brazil, India, China and South Africa. It is argued that the principle of legitimacy is a core element of devising an efficient and equitable structure of global financial governance.

Alternative Modes of Implementation and Enforcement of the Basel Accord

To understand the international legal relevance of the Basel Committee standards, it is necessary to extend the analysis beyond traditional sources and principles of public international law by identifying other relevant sources of official sector pressure and market-based pressure. As mentioned above, the Basel Capital Accord and its amended version Basel II are not legally binding in any way for G10 countries or other countries which adhere to it. Nevertheless, the Basel Committee's standards do generate international norms of banking regulation and exercise considerable influence over state regulatory practice in both developed and developing countries.[47] Generally, Basel Committee standards only become legally effective when they are adopted by national authorities into domestic law and regulation. Although there is a tendency to attribute international legal significance to the international standards generated by the Basel Committee and other international committees that meet at the BIS, the overwhelming opinion of experts and policymakers clearly holds that the international standards adopted by the committees are not legally binding in any way. Nevertheless, the Basel standards seem to hold a powerful influence over state banking law and regulation that may arguably be greater than some areas of public international law which are violated frequently without the invocation of state responsibility.

Although the Basel framework is expressly non-binding in a legal sense, its standards are enforced through other mechanisms where the use of less-direct sanctions can be used to achieve compliance. For example, the International Monetary Fund uses the Basel framework as a benchmark of good banking regulation which all member states must strive to achieve as part of their Article IV assessment programmes. The IMF will also deny certain types of financial assistance to members who fail to take the necessary measures to comply with the Basel standards in their respective jurisdictions. Moreover, market forces may impose a sanction in the form of a higher risk premium on capital investment for countries that fail to demonstrate adherence with Basel standards. It is not surprising therefore that over 130 countries claim to have adopted the Basel Accord into their national banking regulations (Hawkins and Turner 2000), even though they exercised little or no influence in its promulgation. The use of sanctions by international organizations and capital cost penalties by financial markets undermines the so-called voluntary nature of the Basel framework. Moreover, the extent to which official and market sanctions are used to pressure states (especially in developing and emerging market economies) to comply with so-called voluntary international agreements raises the important issue of the nature of a state's obligation to implement and comply with international financial standards.

47 See discussion in Alexander et al. 2006 (Chapter 3, discussing international soft law).

Official and Market Incentives to Adopt International Banking Standards

Most countries do not have an international legal obligation to adopt the Basel Accord, yet more than 130 countries have claimed to have done so. Why have so many countries decided to adhere to the Accord? The most important of these reasons can be categorized as follows: official sector discipline, market discipline, market access requirements, reputation, international spillovers, and reduced administrative costs.

Official Sector Discipline

Before agreeing to release funds for structural adjustment programmes, the IMF agrees a reform programme with a recipient country.

The loan financing is therefore conditional, and this is intended to create incentives for the recipient. The World Bank also attaches conditions to its Financial Sector Adjustment Loans. The criteria for a lending decision by the IMF and World Bank emphasize international 'best practice standards' for transparency, disclosure, governance, regulation and supervision. The principles of regulation and supervision fall primarily within the 25 Core Principles for effective Banking Supervision (BCBS 1997), designed by the Basel Committee's Core Principles Liaison Group (CPLG). The IMF and World Bank increasingly conduct Core Principles Assessments during FSAPs, as well as during technical assistance missions. (IMF 2000).

The Sixth Core Principle makes reference to the Capital Accord. It states in relevant part:

> Banking supervisors must set prudent and appropriate minimum capital adequacy standards for all banks. Such requirements should reflect the risks that banks undertake, and must define the components of capital, bearing in mind their ability to absorb losses. At least for internationally active banks, these requirements must not be less than those established in the Basle Capital Accord and its amendments.

In effect, this incorporates the Basel Accord into the Core Principles and renders the sixth principle a highly detailed and prescriptive rule. These few words therefore change the nature of the Core Principles.

Most IMF emergency programmes and many structural adjustment programmes have regard to core principles assessments and so are likely to include conditions that require adherence to certain regulatory benchmarks, such as the core principles. These conditionality and surveillance powers are exercised through a variety of programmes, including the Article IV Financial Sector Assessments, Financial System Stability Assessments, Reports on the Observance of Standards and Codes, Supplementary Reserve Facilities and Contingent Credit Lines. The IMF and World Bank usually assess financial sector vulnerabilities and identify development priorities during FSAPs. They are also conducting core principle assessments as part of their FSAP missions, as well as in technical assistance missions (IMF 2000).

In the future, IMF emergency financial assistance programmes are likely to come with conditions that the member comply with core principles, including the Basel Accord. This was the case with the stand-by facilities for Turkey and Uruguay.[48] The IMF and World Bank may now play a major role in influencing national regulators' choice of policies based on the carrot of emergency financial assistance. IMF and World Bank conditionality programmes have incentive properties, and regulators realize that their choice of policies are likely to influence the availability of finance. This is because the financial sector requirements of IMF and World Bank conditionality programmes often include compliance with the Basel Capital Accord.

Market Discipline

This involves the notion that compliance with international financial standards would lower funding costs for sovereign borrowers, and possibly for their financial institutions as well. This is unlikely to be a strong incentive, however, because market participants, including rating agencies, may evaluate the financial system of the country of incorporation without any reference to compliance with international standards. Indeed, the Financial Stability Forum (FSF) assessed empirical data that showed market participants to be generally unaware of international codes, and ignored them if they were aware. Unlike the IFIs, market participants have little incentive to devote resources to assessing a country's level of implementation.[49] Also, market participants are not allowed to use IFI assessments, because they cannot be published (except when the assessed country requests it). Market discipline will at best encourage countries to state that they have implemented international standards, but not necessarily to have implemented them.

Market Access Requirements

A national authority's decision to restrict market access is likely to influence more countries to adopt international standards. For example, the Basel Concordat recommends that host countries review the supervisory and regulatory regimes of home countries with a view to determining whether the home country regime is adequate. The Core Principles and Capital Accord have defined 'adequate' as

48 In 2002, the Turkish government had a SDR 12.8 billion ($17 billion) standby arrangement with the IMF. In its Letter of Intent of 19 June 2002, Turkey committed itself to recapitalizing its troubled banks in accordance with the Capital Accord and to adhere to other principles of the Core Principles.

49 For example, core principle assessments take up to several weeks, and they are still unable to identify regulatory forbearance.

complying with Basel Committee framework and other relevant international standards. In the European Economic Area (EEA), the Second Banking Coordination Directive requires that standards applied to third country banks (i.e., branches or agencies) outside the EEA be no more favourable than those applied to banks from other EU member states, and this has been interpreted to include capital adequacy standards.

The UK Financial Services Authority, subject to the requirements European Union financial services legislation, bases its decisions on market access on whether the home country regime applies and enforces the Basel Core Principles.[50] Moreover, the EU Financial Conglomerates Directive requires EU state authorities to judge the equivalence of the supervisory regime of a third country (non-EU) state. If the third country regime fails the equivalence test, for example, the UK authorities are required to apply its regime to the global operations of the third country financial firm as a condition for issuing it a licence to operate in the UK market.

The supervisory regimes of developing countries, and other non-G10 states, will be judged adequate if they adopt a regime that is at least as strict as, but not necessarily identical to, the Basel framework and other relevant international standards. As a practical regulatory policy, the best way to gain access would be for them to adopt the international benchmark. In effect, the Basel Accord is a safe harbour. (Recall the fourth characteristic of soft law enumerated by Gold.) In addition, banks in non-G10 countries may have an incentive to lobby their governments to seek adoption of the Basel framework because such a comprehensive regulatory regime may limit entry to, and thus reduce, competition in the banking market. The type of banks that would seek the adoption of Basel regulations would normally be larger, more sophisticated banks with the resources to comply with the requirements. They would thus have a strong market position to limit competition and foreign access to their markets.[51]

The other option for a bank based in a non-G10 jurisdiction to gain access to the G10 markets would be for it to establish a subsidiary in the host state. Indeed, the UK FSA requires the banks from countries whose regulatory regimes are judged by the UK authorities as inadequate to incorporate locally. If the foreign bank already has a branch operation, but its home country regulator is later judged inadequate, it will have to convert to a subsidiary or exit the market. This is a restriction on the mode of access, in WTO terminology.

Reputation

The benefits derived from reputation will encourage banks to adopt the Basel framework and other international standards of accepted regulatory practice. Banks and other financial firms operating outside the G10 will adopt Basel II and

50 Directive 2000/12/EC, Art. 24.

51 This would especially have implications for a state's obligations to liberalize access to its financial markets under the WTO General Agreement on Trade in Services.

other international standards, not necessarily because there will be capital savings nor because it may be more convenient for risk management purposes, but because they will want to signal to the world that they have moved to the latest, most sophisticated models, and have received the approval of the G10 regulators.

Moreover, good regulation attracts financial services firms from overseas. Most states wish to acquire a reputation for good regulation, and even if they are reluctant to implement the Basel framework because of its high costs, they may be induced to do so for signalling reasons. If we assume that here are two types of states, one for whom the adoption of the Capital Accord would be much more costly because its regulatory and financial system is at a lower level of sophistication, and another for whom adoption of the Accord would require relatively lower compliance costs because of thc sophisticated nature of its economy, then both types of countries would be able to signal that they are sophisticated by implementing the model. There are obvious inefficiencies in such an approach that does not allow the less sophisticated jurisdiction to adopt a framework that more adequately suits its stage of economic and financial development.

One solution could be that non-G10 regulators would be allowed for signalling purposes to implement 'a simpler and harsher version' of the Basel framework (Ward 2002) that would not require, for instance, the regulators of less-sophisticated financial systems to implement some of the more complex and technical requirements of Basel II.[52] They would therefore be able to signal to the world that they operate adequate capital adequacy standards without full implementation of some of the more onerous requirements of international bank capital adequacy standards.

International Spillovers

This involves the spillover of negative externalities from one jurisdiction to another. For example, the implementation of a regime that has more relaxed standards than the G10 regimes may lead to banks arbitraging between regimes. Regimes with perceived lower standards will then collect under-priced financial assets. This is a type of adverse selection and it is the historical reason for the creation of the Basel Committee and of the 1988 Accord.

Regulatory Costs

The design of a regulatory regime incurs fixed costs. This is because national regulators must devote skills and staff to design regulatory policy. This can be especially expensive for developing country regulators who have often fewer

52 This would be similar to international anti-money-laundering standards which regulatory authorities from less-developed countries are permitted to adopt less onerous disclosure and transparency standards under the FATF Forty Nine Recommendations based on the level of development and sophistication of their economies.

skilled staff, and suffer from relatively higher regime design costs. A global regime therefore may be viewed as a lower cost option in terms of regime design because it can be taken off the shelf. Nevertheless, there would be implementation and enforcement costs, which could be prohibitive for many countries.

Enforcement also Requires Skills and Other Institutional Costs

The adoption of an international regime may be cheaper to enforce if it involves coordination and collaboration with other authorities. An international regime of more precise rules will require less skills and resources to enforce than a regime of standards, whose more general and vague nature require more skills for interpretation and implementation. More precise rules are easier to copy, and require less interpretation and discretion in implementation than more broadly stated standards. Nevertheless, it may be more efficient for a state to adopt an international regime, rather than devise its own, especially if that regime is based on a prescriptive set of rules that lend themselves to adoption in different jurisdictions, but the introduction of external or international rules will always lead to higher costs of implementation and possibly enforcement.

Assessment of the Basel Committee's Role in the Present International Financial Regulatory Regime

Most national regulators outside the G10 regard the Basel Accord and other international standards as soft law. The operation of official and market incentives outlined above creates pressures that can unduly influence the exercise of regulatory discretion in some jurisdictions. The real incentives and sanctions are determined by the IFIs in their assessments and funding choices, and by the G10 countries in determining market access. IMF and World Bank conditionality is likely to take account of a country's progress, rather than its actual compliance with international standards at any one point in time. By contrast, core principles assessments do take account of actual compliance. US and UK regulatory standards look to the foreign regime's equivalence with either US/UK standards or international standards. Although the IMF/World Bank may allow states to implement standards at a phased pace, market access rules in the European Union and United States encourage foreign regulators to move too fast in implementing standards in a way that may create regulatory risks.

The discussion above suggests that the adoption of the Basel Committee standards may not lead to the most efficient regulation of financial markets in developing country and other non-G10 countries. This international soft law framework also raises issues of accountability and legitimacy. Indeed, the standard-setting process of the Committee can result in a governance gap in international financial regulation. The Committee has attempted to address this in the Core

Principles on Banking Supervision by creating a Core Principles Liaison Group (CPLG) that creates a venue for discussion of these issues with non-G10 regulators. Although this allows some non-G10 countries to influence the development of the core principles, the G10 retains sole authority over developing the Capital Accord. Although a non-G10 country can make comments to the Basel Committee, the Committee has no obligation to take notice. The standard-setting process remains dominated by the G10, even though, as demonstrated above, these standards are increasingly being applied on a global basis.

In summary, many of these defects can be blamed in part on the Committee's composition and decision-making process and structure. As an international body that exercises significant influence over the development of banking regulation, its decision-making procedures fail to conform with accepted principles of accountability and legitimacy. The decision-making process is too secretive and thereby lacks transparency. Moreover, it is subject to disproportionate influence by private sector banks that are based in the countries on the Committee. To date, there are no proposals for reform, although it is becoming increasingly accepted that lack of accountability and legitimacy in the decision-making process has resulted in lower quality standards of banking regulation for most countries. Indeed, by expanding the number of countries involved in the standard-setting process, the quality of the regulatory standards might be improved immeasurably in terms of improving long-term financial development. On the other hand, expanding the number of countries in the decision-making process may create logistical problems and undermine the committee's effectiveness. However, a carefully negotiated multilateral framework to establish a more effective and legitimate decision-making process is not beyond the realm of practical policy.[53]

The substantive content and scope of international financial regulation has been influenced chiefly by the regulators of the world's major financial systems and the standards and rules they have produced do not find their origins in traditional sources of public international law, but rather are a result of bargaining and softer techniques of implementation that seek to utilize indirect forms of pressure on states to adopt these standards. These indirect forms of pressure include a variety of official and market incentives that play a crucial role in shaping the development of state regulatory practice. It is important to note that the present international financial regulatory regime derives primarily from these sources and should be viewed with concern because most countries that are subject to these standards do not play a role in their promulgation and have not consented to their adoption. As evidenced by the aftermath of the Asian financial crisis, these standards often result in poor regulatory and economic policy for many countries and thereby undermine economic growth and development (Stiglitz 2002). Reform efforts should focus on devising decision-making and institutional structures that are more accountable and legitimate and developing a regulatory framework that emphasizes less the role of official and market incentives.

---

53 See discussion in Alexander et al. 2006, 155–173.

Moreover, increased integration and interdependence in international banking markets suggests that the existing international soft law framework is no longer a second best arrangement for generating efficient standards of banking regulation. Indeed, increasing integration and cross-border activity may require further institutional and legal consolidation at the international level to promote more effective and accountable international regulation. This would require states to move forward through the soft law process by building on the collective intent of most states to develop binding international rules of banking regulation. States could potentially delegate the adjudication of violations to an international financial authority, but states would retain ultimate enforcement authority, including sanctions.

Although soft law once served as a useful instrument for developing international standards of banking regulation, globalized financial markets require a more coherent international legal framework that more effectively manages the use of official incentives by international economic organizations and channels the pressures of global financial markets to induce more efficient financial regulation. This will require greater institutional linkages between the IFIs and international economic organizations so that a greater number of countries can participate in international standard setting. Discriminatory trade barriers imposed by G10 countries to restrict market access to banks from jurisdictions that do not follow G10 regulatory standards should be reconsidered in light of different approaches to prudential regulation. Moreover, more empirical data is needed to analyze the extent to which certain prudential regulatory regimes attract foreign investment and foreign entry into the financial sector.

Conclusion

The globalization of financial markets and other areas of economic activity have dramatically changed the structure of international economic decision-making and the formation of international economic norms. Outside the IMF Articles of Agreement, international financial relations between states are generally not encumbered by the strictures of traditional public international law. Yet international soft law as set forth in the Basel Accord and other international financial standards provides more constraints on the behaviour of governments and economic agents than would be expected by international lawyers. International relations has become subject to a large and increasing number of international norms, not binding under international law, to which a growing number of countries and jurisdictions are committed to follow. The Basel standards are an important example of this.

This chapter suggests that the current enthusiasm for international financial soft law standards such as the Basel Capital Accord has two disquieting implications. First, the many governments who are not actively involved in the Basel standard-setting process are suffering an involuntary loss of sovereignty. It is involuntary, as most countries concerned have not been involved in the negotiation and design of the international standards. Putting it more strongly, this is at odds with the general presumption in international law that governments are sovereign unless they decide to cede their sovereignty. Moreover, the growing tendency for states to adopt the Basel standards without representation in the standard-setting process raises important questions about the accountability and legitimacy of the Basel Committee. Perhaps the G10's effective monopoly on decision-making should be ended by allowing other countries that are also representative of the global financial system have a seat at the table. Second, as a matter of economic policy, if those designing the standards maintain the fiction that the standards are voluntary when in fact they are not, the content of the standards is likely to be suboptimal for economic growth and financial development. Future research should elaborate what role international economic law should play in enhancing the institutional structure of decision-making in order to devise more effective international bank regulation standards and to facilitate their implementation into domestic regulatory systems.

References

Books, Articles and Chapters in Books

Akehurst, M. (2000), 'Custom as Source of International Law', in Koskenniemi.

Aleinikoff, A.T. (2004), 'International Law, Sovereignty and American Constitutionalism: Reflections on the Customary International Law Debate', *American Journal of International Law* 98, no. 1 (January 2004), 91–108.

Alexander, K., Dhumale, R. and Eatwell, J. (eds) (2006), *Global Governance of Financial Systems: The International Regulation of Systemic Risk* (Oxford: Oxford University Press).

Alexander, K., Eatwell, J., Persaud, A. and Reoch, R. (2007), 'Financial Supervision and Crisis Management in the EU' (Brussels: EU Parliament), 2–4.

Bagheri, M. and Nakajima, C. (2002), 'Optimal Level of Financial Regulation under the Gats: A Regulatory Competition and Cooperation Framework for Capital Adequacy and Disclosure of Information', *Journal of International Economic Law* 5, no. 2, 507–530.

Bärmann, J. (1961), 'Pacta Sunt Servanda: Considérations Sur L'histoire Du Contrat Consensuel', *Revue Internationale de Droit Comparé*, 18–53.

Bazinas, S.V. (2002), 'Multi-Jurisdictional Receivables Financing: Uncitral's Impact on Securitization and Cross-Border Perfection', *Duke Journal of Comparative and International Law* 12, no. 2, 365–388.

Bennett, A.L. (1996), *International Organizations: Principles and Issues*, 6th ed. (New York: Prentice Hall).

Berger, S., and Dore, R. (1996), *National Diversity and Global Capitalism* (Ithaca, NY: Cornell University Press).

Cranston, R. (2002), *Principles of Banking Law*, 2nd ed. (Oxford: Oxford University Press).

Crockett, A. (2004), 'Progress Towards Greater International Financial Stability', in Vines and Gilbert (eds).

Dam, K.W. (1990), 'Introduction to Festschrift in Honour of Sir Joseph Gold', in Werner and Norton (eds).

Dasgupta, D., Uzan, M. and Wilson, D. (eds) (2001), *Capital Flows without Crisis? Reconciling Capital Mobility and Economic Stability* (London: Routledge).

Delbrück, J. (2001), 'Structural Changes in the International System and Its Legal Order: International Law in the Era of Globalization', *Schweizerische Zeitschrift für internationals und europäisches Recht* 11, 1–36.

Dombrowski, P. (1998), 'Haute Finance and High Theory: Recent Scholarship on Global Financial Relations', *Mershon International Studies Review* 42, 1–28.

Eatwell, J. and Taylor, L. (2000), *Global Finance at Risk: The Case for International Regulation* (New York: The New Press).

Ebert, M.D. (1998), 'The Asian Financial Crisis and the Need for a New Global Financial Architecture', *Butterworths Journal of International Banking and Financial Law* 462.

Ebke, W.F. and Norton, J.J. (1990), *Festschrift in Honor of Sir Joseph Gold* (Heidelberg: Verlag Recht und Wirtschaft).

Fitzgerald, E.V.K., Cubero-Brealey, R. and Lehmann, A. (1998), 'The Development Implications of the Multilateral Agreement on Investment', Report Commissioned by the Department for International Development OECD, 21 March 1998.

Fitzmaurice, G.G. (2000), 'Some Problems Regarding the Formal Sources of International Law', in Koskenniemi.

Foqué, R. (1998), 'Global Governance and the Rule of Law: Human Rights and General Principles of Good Global Governance', in Wellens (ed.).

Geva, B. (2000), 'Forged Check Endorsement Losses under the UCC: The Role of Policy in the Emergence of Law Merchant from Common Law', Winter 2000 Symposium, *Wayne Law Review* 45, 1733.

Giovanoli, M. (2000), 'A New Architecture for the Global Financial Market: Legal Aspects of International Financial Standard Setting', in Giovanoli (ed.).

Giovanoli, M. (ed.) (2000), *International Monetary Law: Issue for the New Millennium* (Oxford: Oxford University Press).

Giovanoli, M. and Heinrich, G. (1999), *International Bank Insolvencies: A Central Bank Perspective* (The Hague: Kluwer Law International).

Gold, J. (1989), *The Fund Agreement in the Courts. Some Problems of the Uniform Interpretation of Multilateral Treaties. Vol. IV* (Washington, DC: International Monetary Fund).

Goodhart, C.A.E. (2008), *A History of the Basel Committee on Banking Supervision* (chapter manuscript on file with author).

Grenville, S. (2001), 'Financial Crisis and Globalisation', in Dasgupta, Uzan and Wilson (eds).

Gros, D. and Thygesen, N. (1998), *European Monetary Integration*, 2nd ed. (London: Longman).

Haller, W. and Kölz, A. (1999), *Allgemeines Staatsrecht*, 2nd ed. (Basel: Helbing & Lichtenhahn).

Held, D. and McGrew, A. (2000), 'Globalization and the Challenge to International Institutions', in Woods (ed.).

Held, D. and McGrew, A. (2002), *Governing Globalization: Power, Authority and Global Governance* (Cambridge: Polity Press).

Higgins, R. (1994), *Problems and Process – International Law and How We Use It* (Oxford: Oxford University Press).

Howse, R. (2007) *American Journal of International Law*, Book Review, 231–234.

International Association of Insurance Supervisors (2000), 1999 Annual Report 2.

Jennings, R.Y. (1981), 'What Is International Law and How Do We Tell When We See It?', *Annuaire Suisse de Droit International* 31, 59–88.

Kapteyn, P.J.G., Verlooren van Themaat, P. and Gormley, L.W. (1998), *Introduction to the Law of the European Communities: From Maastricht to Amsterdam*, 3rd ed. (London: Kluwer Law International).

Kelsen, H. (1967), *Principles of International Law*, edited by Robert W. Tucker, 2nd ed. (New York: Holt, Rinehart and Winston).

Kelsen, H. (1998), 'The Undesirability of Soft Law', *Nordic Journal of International Law* 67, 381–391.

Klabbers, J. (1996), *The Concept of Treaty in International Law. Vol. 22. Developments in International Law* (The Hague: Kluwer Law International).

Knight, M., Schembri, L. and James Powell, J. (2004), 'Reforming the Global Financial Architecture: Just Tinkering around the Edges?', in Vines and Gilbert (eds).

Koenig, C. and Haratsch, A. (2003), *Europarecht*, 4th ed. (Tübingen: Mohr Siebeck).

Koh, H.H. (2004), 'International Law as a Part of Our Law', *American Journal of International Law* 98, no. 4, 43–57.

Kokott, J., Doehring, K. and Buergenthal, T. (2003), *Grundzüge Des Völkerrechts*. 3., neu bearb. Aufl. ed. (Heidelberg: Müller).

Koskenniemi, M. (2000), *Sources of International Law* (Aldershot: Dartmouth/ Ashgate Publishing).

Krueger, A.O. (1998), 'Whither the World Bank and the IMF?', *Journal of Economic Literature* 36, no. 4, 1983–2000.

Lastra, R.M. (2003), 'Cross-Border Bank Insolvency: Legal Implications in the Case of Banks Operating in Different Jurisdictions in Latin America', *Journal of International Economic Law* 6, 79–110.

Lowenfeld, A.F. (2003), *International Economic Law*, International Economic Law Series (Oxford: Oxford University Press).

Ludwigs, M. (2004), 'Die Kompetenzordnung Der Europäischen Union Im Vertragsentwurf Über Eine Verfassung Für Europa', *Zeitschrift für Europarechtliche Studien (ZeuS)* 2, 211–249.

Malanczuk, P. (1997), *Akehurst's Modern Introduction to International Law*, 7th rev. ed. (London: Routledge).

Meyer, L.H., Doyle, B.M., Gagnon, J.E. and Henderson, D.W. (2004), 'International Coordination of Macroeconomic Policies: Still Alive in the New Millennium?', in Vines and Gilbert (eds).

Müller, J.P. and Wildhaber, L. (2000), '*Praxis Des Völkerrechts*. Dritte Auflage, Unter Mitarbeit Von Robert Kolb Und Andrea Binder, Mit Einer Einführung in Das Wirtschaftsvölkerrecht Von Thomas Cottier Und Manfred Wagner' (Berne: Stämpfli Verlag).

Norton, J.J. (1990), 'The Multidimensions of the Convergence Processes Regarding the Prudential Supervision of International Banking Activities: The Impact of the Basel Supervisors Committee's Efforts Upon, within and without the European Community', in Ebke and Norton (eds).

Polk, A. (2002), 'Multilateral Agreement on Investment (MAI): A Critical Assessment from an Industrial Economics Point of View', Socioeconomic Institute, University of Zurich, Working Paper No. 0201, 8 February 2002. Manuscript on file with the author.

Raworth, P. (1995), *Foreign Trade Law of the European Union* (New York: Oceana Publications).

Roberts, A.E. (2001), 'Traditional and Modern Approaches to Customary International Law: Reconciliation', *American Journal of International Law* 95, no. 4, 757–791.

Sautter, H. (2004), *Weltwirtschaftsordnung*. Vahlens Handbücher Der Wirtschafts- Und Sozialwissenschaften. (Munich: Verlag Vahlen).

Schaffner-Matter, E. (2004), 'Andauernde Mängel in Der Finanzarchitektur: Global Tätige Grossbanken Fordern G-7 Zum Handeln Auf', *Neue Zürcher Zeitung*.

Schefer, K.N. (1999), *International Trade in Financial Services: The NAFTA Provisions* (The Hague: Kluwer Law International).

Schermers, H.G., and Blokker, N.M. (1995), *International Institutional Law* (The Hague: Martinus Nijhoff).

Scheurer, C. (1998), 'The Interpretation of ICSID Arbitration Agreements', in Wellens (ed.).

Schwarcz, S.L. (2002), 'International Securitization and Structured Finance: The Universal Language of International Securitization'. Symposium. *Duke Journal of Comparative and International Law* 12, 285.

Seidl-Hohenveldern, I. (1992), *International Economic Law*, 2nd rev. ed. (Dordrecht: Martinus Nijhoff).

Seidl-Hohenveldern, I. and Loibl, G. (1996), *Das Recht Der Internationalen Organisationen Einschliesslich Der Supranationalen Gemeinschaften*, 6th rev. ed. (Cologne: Carl Heymanns Verlag).

Sekolec, J. (1999), 'The Uncitral Model Law on Cross-Border Insolvency', in Giovanoli and Heinrich (eds).

Shihata, I. (2000), 'The Dynamic Evolution of International Organizations: The Case of the World Bank', *Journal of History of International Law* 2, 217–249.

Simma, B. (1999), 'The Work of the International Law Commission at Its Fifty-First Session', *Nordic Journal of International Law* 68, 293–361.

Slaughter, A.-M. (2004), *A New World Order* (Princeton: Princeton University Press).

Slomanson, W.R. (2003), *Fundamental Perspectives on International Law*, 4th ed. (Belmont, CA: Thomson/West).

Stiglitz, J. (2002),*Globalization and its Discontents* (London: Penguin/Allen & Lane).

Taylor, J.L. (2000), 'The Governing Law in Legal Agreements Used by the European Bank for Reconstruction and Development in Its Banking Operations', in Giovanoli (ed.).

Teubner, G. (1997), '"Global Bukowina": Legal Pluralism in the World Society' in Teubner (ed.).

Teubner, G. (ed.) (1997), *Global Law Without a State* (Aldershot: Dartmouth).

Vellas, P. (1965), *Droit International Economique et Social* (Paris: Sirey).

Verdross, A. and Simma, B. (1984), *Universelles Völkerrecht: Theorie Und Praxis* (Berlin: Duncker & Humblot).

Vines, D. and Gilbert, C.L. (2004), *The IMF and Its Critics Reform of Global Financial Architecture* (Cambridge: Cambridge University Press).

Walker, G.A. (2001), *International Banking Regulation – Law, Policy and Practice* (London: Kluwer Law International).

Ward, J. (2002), 'Basel 2 and Developing Countries', Working Paper #4, *The Cambridge Endowment for Research in Finance.*

Weber, R.H. (2003), 'Ethik Im Aussenwirtschaftsrecht: Überlegungen Am Beispiel Der Politik Von Iwf Und Weltbank', *Aktuelle Juristische Praxis* 11, 1338–1352.

Weber, R.H. (2003), *EU- und EG-Vertrag; Kommentar zu dem Vertrag über die Europäische Union und zu dem Vertrag zur Grundung der Europaisen Gemeinschapft, jeweils in der durch den Vertrag von Nizza geanderten Fassung*, 3rd ed, edited by Lenz and Borchardt (Köln: Bundesanzeiger, Helbing & Lichtenhahn, Ueberreuter, Vorb. Art. 56–60, Rn. 4, Rn. 7).

Weissbrodt, D. and Kruger, M. (2003), 'Norms on the Responsibilities of Transnational Corporations and Other Business Enterprises with Regard to Human Rights', *American Journal of International Law* 97, no. 4, 910–922.

Wellens, K.C. (ed.) (1998), *International Law: Theory and Practice; Essays in Honor of Eric Suy* (The Hague: Kluwer Law International).

Werner F.E. and Norton, J.J. (1990), *Festschrift in Honour of Sir Joseph Gold* (Heidelberg: Verlag Recht und Wirtschaft).

Woods, N. (2002), 'Global Governance and the Role of Institutions', in Held and McCrew (eds).

Woods, N. (2000), *The Political Economy of Globalization* (Basingstoke: Macmillan).

Zamora, S. and Gold J. (1990), 'Development of International Monetary Law', in Ebke and Norton (eds).

Internet-based References

Bank for International Settlements, 'About the Basel Committee', http://www.bis.org/bcbs/aboutbcbs.htm.

Financial Stability Board, 'Overview', http://www.fsforum.org/about/who_we_are.html.

Financial Stability Board, 'What are Standards?', http://www.fsforum.org/compendium/what_are_standards.html.

Chapter 15
Corporate Social Responsibility and Its Implications for Public International Law

AGO Shin-ichi

A wide range of recent works has focused on the question of corporate social responsibility (hereinafter referred to as CSR). Research in CSR is booming. Much of it is studies in business administration and management. It will soon become obvious that this chapter does not deal with the question of CSR from the perspective business administration, but instead it looks into the question of CSR from the point of view of public international law.[1]

That is to say, it tries to answer the question to what extent CSR has a proper status in international law. It examines whether CSR is a process that aims to give substantive effective to a legal norm. The legal norm in this chapter is international labour law. This delimitation of the object of analysis has been made because there already exist several international legal instruments, which can be conceived as CSR codes pertaining to international labour law and an analysis thereof may be deemed easier than CSR in general, which involves various legal rules, such as environmental law, economic law and human rights law.

It is widely stated that initiatives undertaken by private enterprises, such as the proclamation of company codes or adherence to other CSR codes administered by non-profit organizations (hereinafter referred to as NPOs), are not subject to legal regulation; Organization for Economic Cooperation and Development (hereinafter referred to as OECD) Guidelines on Multinational Enterprises and other similar guidelines are international instruments without legally binding effects; and that CSR has objectives different from those of law. But, then, why has this concept intrigued so many writers? CSR has a considerable number of legal implications and private enterprises can no more conduct their operations without taking due consideration of CSR. If CSR is conferred with legal validity one day, enterprise management must conduct their operations in accordance with the legal consequences emanating from CSR. At the same time, enterprise management, and legal departments in particular, may stand to gain from the legality of CSR and have an easier task to convince supply-chain enterprises to adhere to the mother enterprise's code. This chapter concludes that CSR is not a valid international rule, at least for the time being, although it may well become one if certain conditions are met. On the other hand, it will be contended that CSR

1 See Zerk 2006.

does already play a significant role as a process to materialize various international legal rules. The chapter aims at explaining the legal implication of CSR from the implementation perspective of public international law. It critically observes the general consensus that international law provides for inter-state relationship on the basis of the principle of equality of states and does not address individuals directly. With the emergence of an international community, which not only consists of sovereign states, a fundamental re-orientation is needed to perceive the scope of public international law and attach a more significant role to the 'operation process' of an international legal rule.

Preliminary Observations: The Position of CSR in Domestic Law and the Legal Status of an Enterprise in International Law

A few words about the relationship of CSR to national law are necessary in order to develop a clearer picture about the issue before discussing its relevance to international law. In addition, the earlier discussion on the position of an enterprise in international law must also be briefly recapitulated before examining the relevance of CSR in international law.

As a recent public announcement by the Nippon Keidanren (Japan Business Federation) shows, the general attitude of most enterprises is that CSR is a private initiative and it should neither be regulated by law nor administered by the government. This is not only the attitude of Japanese business. Employers' associations in many countries have expressed similar positions on various occasions.[2] And yet, the fact that Nippon Keidanren must reiterate this position in its announcement[3] reflects the other side of the coin: CSR does have some legal implications. Furthermore, company codes try to set rules applicable within each corporate entity, often expanding the coverage to affiliated entities as well as supply-chain companies. To that extent, they function as a law *within* the company and its surroundings. When a company code or other private codes drafted by NPOs become widely accepted and a majority of influential enterprises subscribe to the code, they may become *de facto* laws.

As long as principles enshrined in CSR contain a considerable amount of legal norms, it is obvious that there are a number of national laws which are relevant to

---

2 'The employers' position is also clear in what it does not want the International Labour Organization (hereinafter referred to as ILO) to be doing: namely becoming a monitoring or verification organization with respect to voluntary company Corporate Social Responsibility (hereinafter referred to as CSR) initiatives ...' (CSR, An Ongoing Engagement' [online], accessed on 21 June 2009). This position given on the home page of the International Organization of Employers (IOE) is a clear sign that businesses not only like national legal regulation, but also international regulation by the ILO.

3 See Nippon Keizai Dantai Rengoukai [Japan Business Federation] [online news], (home page), accessed on 20 August 2008.

CSR. The notion of 'compliance', an important element of CSR, reveals that CSR precepts are based on existing laws, such as company law, security regulations, criminal law and even constitutional law.

The fact that CSR embodies positive national laws has two implications. First, enumeration of existing national legal rules in a CSR code is simply a restatement of existing law. Therefore, it is a unilateral declaration by the drafter of the code to abide by the rules. Second, it is a matter for public regulation. A declaration to comply with the law presupposes an enterprise's readiness to be regulated. However, whatever the business declares, it cannot deny its subordination to existing legal regulations. For it is not logical to ascertain that enterprises 'voluntarily' accept legal duties under the valid company law, criminal law and other positive laws and they are under legal obligation to observe these laws to the extent they have expressly agreed. However, the very nature of CSR is that it goes a step further. This additional advancement has two features. One is to supplement an abstract content of law by concretely applying certain measures. Suppose a law contains a provision, such as 'with due respect to specific situations' or 'to be implemented by appropriate measures'; a CSR code can substantiate the law. The second role is CSR-particular. CSR codes can supersede the level of protection covered by law. Here lies the inherent meaning of CSR. It is at this level that CSR can be meaningfully said to be outside of legal regulation. Other aspects of CSR are legal and can be considered to be a part of positive law.

The inherent part of CSR is not necessarily positive law. As mentioned above, it can, however, become a *de facto* law, or 'soft law'. Emerging rules (so-called soft law) may not be directly applicable in a court of law today, but they may become hard law in future. If soft law is supplemented by additional legal principles, such as estoppel or good faith, it can play an important legal role, before it may become hard law.[4]

Another issue to be discussed before going into the substance of the international legal implication of CSR concerns the status of individuals, companies and private persons in international law. Many international instruments, discussed below, directly address enterprises (multinational enterprises, in particular). As is well known, since the time of Hugo Grotius, international law has only governed sovereign states. Individuals have been absorbed into a state and they have not been subjects of international law. Diplomatic protection ensures that rights of nationals are not infringed, but individuals have not been able to initiate such international claims. The right of diplomatic protection is vested in a state and not in the individual. This basic principle in public international law has not changed even in our era of globalization. We clearly see it in the dispute settlement system of the World Trade Organization (hereinafter referred to as WTO), which is basically

4 Fikentscher 1982, 577–604.

designed to be a system of inter-state procedure, although private companies' interests are at stake, in practice.[5]

However, a change is occurring to this basic principle of international law. The emergence of the concept of crimes against humanity, the creation of the international criminal court and the establishment of an international system for the protection of human rights, for example, have all introduced change into the traditional principle of international law as merely being inter-state law. Individuals, including business enterprises, are now emerging as subjects of international law. They are no longer simply objects of international law. The new subjects of international law do not remain passively awaiting their national governments to exercise the states' intrinsic rights of diplomatic protection. In certain cases – human rights cases, in particular – individuals cannot expect their home countries to protect them because their own countries perpetrate human rights abuses. Individuals are now claiming their own international legal rights. They do not only claim rights, but also assume international legal duties. The Global Compact initiated by the UN Secretary General is not a private agreement between Mr Kofi Annan and world business leaders, but it is an international commitment between a principal organ of the United Nations, the Secretariat, and private enterprises, the latter having assumed certain international obligations albeit not enforceable by international adjudication. CSR becomes relevant under these circumstances where private enterprises begin to assume legal responsibilities directly under international law. Various international instruments addressing CSR become pertinent. For they directly address private enterprises and request them to take certain positions or to refrain from taking specific actions.

If private enterprises are accountable to international law, CSR norms enshrined in international instruments will also have a legal bearing on them. The instruments, which we will see below, are not international agreements in the sense of the Vienna Convention on the Law of Treaties; they are, however, more than just paper. They are multilateral instruments and definitely not national laws. Here we see some elements of international law, which play a role in the development of CSR at an international level.

5 For example, consider the dispute between United States of America and European Union concerning the subsidies paid to the production of commercial aircraft. This case was actually a dispute between Boeing and Airbus Industries, but for the purpose of the World Trade Organization (hereinafter referred to as WTO) procedure, the interests of the companies were represented by two state members of the WTO.

Existing International CSR Rules and their Implementation

OECD Guidelines for Multinational Enterprises[6]

In 1976, long before the world started talking about CSR, the Organization for Economic Cooperation and Development (hereinafter referred to as OECD) adopted the 'OECD Guidelines for Multinational Enterprises' (hereinafter referred to as OECD Guidelines). They are nothing but CSR in our contemporary usage of the term. They provided voluntary principles and standards for responsible business conduct, in a variety of areas including employment and industrial relations, human rights, environment, information disclosure, competition, taxation, and science and technology. The OECD Guidelines are not an international treaty and, therefore, do not legally bind OECD Member States. Nor do they legally bind the enterprises. However, the unique feature of the Guidelines is that they do not only address entities, which are not nation-states, but also the fact that an implementation mechanism is well established. The Guidelines are not simply words, but are also put into operation. The whole system of 'National Contact Points' has been able to elaborate on the contents of the Guidelines and make them operational. National Contact Points are government offices responsible for encouraging observance of the OECD Guidelines in their national context and for ensuring that the OECD Guidelines are well known and understood by the national business community and by other interested parties. Because of the central role they play, the effectiveness of National Contact Points is a crucial factor in determining how influential the OECD Guidelines are in each national context. The recently concluded review has enhanced the accountability of National Contact Points by calling for an annual report of their activities, which will serve as a basis for exchanges of views on the functioning of the National Contact Points among the OECD Guidelines–adhering governments.

Recently, it has become increasingly common for enterprises to refer to the OECD Guidelines in their own code of conducts. High-level political declarations, such as the Group of Eight's (hereinafter referred to as G8) African Programme of Action 2002 and the Joint Statement by the G8's Finance Ministers of May 2003 make special reference to the OECD Guidelines. Analysis of the outcome of several National Contact Points' activities reveals an important development, namely using the OECD Guidelines as a normative framework for the conduct of multinational enterprises. Among several successful cases recorded, credit is usually given to a case in Myanmar, which came to a conclusion in 2003. Operations of an oil and gas multinational enterprise in Myanmar were alleged to have violated a number of provisions under the OECD Guidelines, including prohibition of the use of forced labour and protection of human rights of the people living in the vicinity of the pipeline. The French National Contact Point took this case seriously and had

6 See Organization for Economic Cooperation and Development (OECD), *The OECD Guidelines for Multinational Enterprises* 2000 (online).

come up with various recommendations, which eventually made the multinational enterprise concerned withdraw its investment from Myanmar.[7] In all other cases the OECD Guidelines have been utilized in a quasi-legal way. As such, the legal relevance of the OECD Guidelines can no longer be underestimated.

The ILO Tripartite Declaration on Multinational Enterprises

In June 1976 the International Labour Organization's (hereinafter referred to as ILO) Tripartite World Employment Conference discussed questions related to multinational enterprises. The Workers' Group, as well as the Group of 77, recommended that a Convention on the social aspects of the activities of multinational enterprises be adopted. The Employers' Group did not share this view but agreed on the usefulness of a tripartite declaration of principles, which would be of a voluntary character. The Governing Body in November of 1977 adopted the 'Tripartite Declaration of Principles concerning Multinational Enterprises and Social Policy'. There are various reasons for the ILO to adopt the CSR code of conduct as a Governing Body Declaration, instead of an ordinary ILO Convention or a Recommendation. First, the target entities are neither states nor ILO constituents, but private enterprises. Multinational enterprises, being by nature multinational and conducting their activities across borders, cannot, in many cases, be regulated by nation states. Even if a country is bound by a treaty and assumes certain duties to control multinational enterprises, the latter frequently bypass national jurisdictions and, therefore, cannot be effectively regulated. Second, the employer group of the ILO, which largely represents the interests of multinational enterprises, was strongly against adopting a legally binding instrument. In this last point, we find a basis for the argument that CSR has a legal effect. If it did not, why should employers object to having it incorporated into an ILO Convention or a Recommendation?

The Tripartite Declaration is a legally non-binding instrument. However, like the OECD Guidelines, it is more than just a policy statement of an inter-governmental institution. It also has a follow-up machinery attached to the substantive provisions. The follow-up is conducted in the form of an 'interpretation by the ILO', a procedure approved by the Governing Body in 1980 and revised in 1986.[8] It provides for the submission of requests for interpretation in cases of a dispute on the meaning and application of its provisions. The importance of this procedure lies in its ability to contribute to the harmonious development of labour

7 Organization for Economic Co-operation and Development, 'Recommendations by the French National Contact Point to Companies on the Issue of Forced Labour in Burma', 28 March 2002, Annex I of the OECD 'Multinational Enterprises Situations of Violent Conflict and Widespread Human Rights Abuses', Working Papers on International Investment, Number 2002/1, 30 May 2002.

8 International Labour Organization (ILO), 'Interpretation Procedure', Multi: Multinational Enterprise and Social Policy (online).

relations, either by its use or by its availability, the latter of which may encourage disputants to confront their difficulties and to gain a perspective capable of mutual accommodation.

Unlike in the case of the OECD Guidelines, the ILO's procedure has not been fully utilized. To date there have only been five cases in which the Governing Body of the ILO issued 'official' interpretations of the relevant provisions of the Declaration. Nonetheless, a 'successful' conclusion was reported in one case, where paragraph 26 of the Declaration was 'interpreted' as to the duties of a multinational enterprise to give reasonable prior notice of changes, which would have major employment effects. The ILO (Governing Body), referring to the Termination of Employment Convention, 1982 (No. 158) as a guide, maintained that paragraph 26 requires reasonable prior notice of intended changes in operations to be given to the workers' representatives and their organizations, where such organizations are identifiable under national law and practice, and if such representatives and organizations exist, it is insufficient to inform the workers affected on an individual basis.[9]

UN Human Rights Instruments

The Sub-Commission for the Promotion and Protection of Human Rights of the United Nations adopted an instrument entitled 'Norms on the Responsibilities of Transnational Corporations and Other Business Enterprises with Regard to Human Rights' in 2003.[10] This document is a product of a Working Group set up under the Sub-Commission in 1998. It has wide coverage, namely, to wit: A. General Obligations; B. Right to Equal Opportunity and Non-discriminatory Treatment; C. Right to Security of Persons; D. Rights of Workers; E. Respect for National Sovereignty and Human Rights; F. Obligations with Respect to Consumer protection; G. Obligations with Respect to Environment Protection; H. General Provisions of Implementation; and I. Definitions.

The remarkable fact regarding these norms is that they not only address member states of the United Nations, but also private enterprises.[11] This fact is by itself an innovative approach from the point of view of traditional international

9 ILO, 'Interpretation Procedure at Work: BIFU Case (1984–1985)', Multi: Multinational Enterprise and Social Policy <http://www.ilo.org/public/english/employment/multi/tripartite/cases.htm>.

10 UN ESCOR, 55th Sess., 22nd mtg. Agenda Item 4, UN Doc. E/CN.4/Sub.2/2003/12/Rev.2 (2003).

11 U.N. ESCOR, 55th Sess., 22nd mtg. Agenda Item 4, U.N. Doc. E/CN.4/Sub.2/2003/12/Rev.2 (2003), par. 1; '... Within their respective spheres of activity and influence, transnational corporations and other business enterprises have the obligation to promote, secure the fulfilment of, respect, ensure respect of and protect human rights recognized in international as well as national law, including the rights and interests of indigenous peoples and other vulnerable groups'.

law theory, but it is more important that a UN body is now taking up CSR in a legal document. It is so innovative that it is obvious that a considerable amount of reservations have been expressed with respect to the legal nature of the document as well as its validity. The parent body, the Commission of Human Rights, in its 2004 Resolution explicitly reserved its position and even mentioned that the Working Group had worked without a clear mandate given by the Commission and, therefore, the document must not be followed up.[12] An up-hill task seems to lie ahead in materializing the body of rules established by the Working Group. On the other hand, if the document received sufficient support, its legal effect would be of a great significance in the future *vis-à-vis* the legal norms of CSR.

GUF Framework Agreements

The foregoing sections dealt with a group of documents that are international legal instruments duly adopted by inter-governmental institutions, even though they cannot qualify as formal positive laws. The next two examples are cases in which private entities formulate the norms with an international application in sight. Therefore, under no circumstances can they be called international law in the traditional sense of the term. However, it is worth discussing them in this context because, depending upon how they are applied, they may, nevertheless, have some legal consequences.

The first type of this kind is that of a Framework Agreement concluded between an international sectoral trade union organization, the global union federation (hereinafter referred to as GUF),[13] and a multinational enterprise. There are currently over 30 of this kind of agreement concluded, for instance, between Volkswagen, Bosch, Renault, etc., and the International Metalworkers' Federation; between Ikea, etc., and International Federation of Building and Woodworkers (hereinafter referred to as IFBWW); between Carrefour, etc., and Union-Network International (hereinafter referred to as UNI); between Club Mediterranée, Chiquita, etc., and International Union of Food, Agricultural, Hotel, Restaurant, Catering, Tobacco and Allied Workers Associations (hereinafter referred to as IUF).[14] When we look at the agreement between Ikea and the IFBWW, for instance, we find that many ILO Conventions are referred to therein. As a company selling furniture, there is an important meaning for Ikea to conclude

12 E.S.C. Dec. 2004/279, UN ESCOR, 49th mtg., Agenda Item 14(g), at 195, U.N. Doc. E/2004/INF/2/Add.2.

13 Education International (EI), International Federation of Chemical, Energy, Mine and General Workers' Union (ICEM), International Federation of Building and Wood Workers (IFBWW), International Federation of Journalists (IFJ), International Metalworkers' Federation (IMF), International Transport Workers' Federation (ITF), International Textile Garment and Leather Workers Federation (ITGLWF).

14 Ohmi 2005, 82–83.

such an agreement with an international trade secretariat organizing workers in the construction, building, wood, forestry and allied trades and industries. For the agreement becomes binding for a business, in which trade unions affiliated to IFBWW are involved. One of the final provisions of the agreement states, 'that in order to achieve the objectives and undertakings given in the agreement, IKEA and the IFBWW will engage in on going dialogue and will meet regularly and as the need arises to examine the implementation of this agreement and any reported breaches of its terms.'[15] Another important feature can be found in agreements reached between Volkswagen and the IMF, in which suppliers and sub-contractors are encouraged to apply the contents of the framework agreement as their own codes. The case of the agreement between Daimler-Chrysler and the IMF goes one step further by not only encouraging the suppliers to adopt their own codes in accordance with the framework agreement, but also to consider their adoption as an important element in order to continue Daimler-Chrysler's business with them. We see from these examples that the scope of the framework agreements has expanded to the supply chain enterprises, some of which may have greater difficulties in applying CSR due to their relative size and economic performance.

When we look at the international legal importance of these framework agreements, the following observations can be made. The Global Union Federations are non-government organizations (hereinafter referred to as NGOs) and they are not subject to international law. Likewise, multinational enterprises, which enter into framework agreements with GUFs, are private persons, deprived of a formal international legal personality. What is, however, interesting here and worthy of comment, is that the agreement is not a simple contract between Company *X* and Organization *Y*, covered by a civil code or a commercial code of a particular country. Both parties to framework agreements of this kind are operating internationally. The GUF, for example, covers over 125 countries and 289 affiliated unions. The effect of the agreements thus immediately spread all over the world and will cover a great many enterprises and workers employed therein. Any multinational enterprises that seek to maximize profits by shifting their production sites across national borders, are now accompanied by CSR. The importance of a framework agreement can be analogously compared with that of collective agreements in a national context. While individual labour contracts have legal effects only on the parties, collective agreements have a wider application and in some countries they are given the status of law. In a similar way, a framework agreement of the kind can perform a quasi-legislative function in the context of a decentralized international legal system.

15 International Federation of Building and Wood Workers (IFBWW), 'IFBWW Model Framework Agreement' (online).

'Standards' Adopted by ISO and other NGOs

International Organization for Standardization (hereinafter referred to as ISO) has started drafting an international standard incorporating social standards. It will be known as ISO26000 and, according to the ISO's home page, it is expected to be adopted in 2009. ISO has been greatly successful in introducing and operating a number of technical standards, mainly in industrial sectors. It therefore provoked attention among many commentators when it announced its intention to draft a standard on CSR. The ILO was one of the entities largely affected by this ISO initiative. It was therefore natural that the ILO was very concerned about such a standard, which involved labour standards. Finally, the ILO agreed to support the ISO's new code by concluding an inter-agency Memorandum of Understanding, which requested that the ISO consult the ILO at all times and that no reference to ILO standards should be made without prior consultation with the ILO.[16] The contents of ISO26000 are not yet known. However, if it were adopted in 2010 and began its operation, it would have a great impact, because the reputation of ISO standards is firmly established and its implementation would presumably be extremely efficient. However, the more the new instrument includes labour rights and human rights, the more difficult it becomes to secure co-ordination with other international bodies working in the field of labour and human rights.

Equally problematic is the relationship between private initiatives of social labelling with the official sources of international law. There are a number of NGOs that provide certification services to private enterprises with their own standards. The most famous NGO in this respect is Social Accountability International (hereinafter referred to as SAI) based in the United States of America. With its Code, that is the Social Accountability 8000 (hereinafter SA8000), SAI has expanded its influence to many parts of the world and most recently in China, the fastest growing economy in the world. The Fair Labor Association (hereinafter referred to as FLA), also based in the United States of America, is another organization of the same nature and it is also expanding its sphere of influence. The codes these organizations apply frequently refer to official international legal sources, such as the ILO Conventions and UN instruments, but the choice of the standards and the degree of importance attached to each of these standards are often arbitrary and involve certain risks. As long as their standards offer a higher level of protection in labour conditions and in other general human rights situations, no significant problem arises. However, if their choice of standards were biased, their interpretation of official international legal sources would be inaccurate and if they competed with other certifying institutions in terms of fees and the level of standards, the outcome would be detrimental in a number of respects: (1) Such bodies may adopt only those standards that please managers of enterprises. To take a simple example, a significant number of managers do not necessarily endorse the

16 *Report of the Subcommittee on Multinational Enterprises*, ILO, Governing Body, 292nd Sess. Agenda Item 24, 24, UN Doc. GB.292/11 (2005).

principle of freedom of association. The certifying institutions may not include trade union rights in the set of standards they provide for in their codes. Even when they are included, they may do so by giving trade union rights a secondary place after equality principles or child labour prohibition. (2) Such bodies may not be equipped with the proper expertise in interpreting international legal instruments. Even if they are, they have no legal authority to interpret international law, such as the ILO Conventions and the International Covenant on Civil and Political Rights. (3) Adoption of voluntary codes, such as SA8000, by large-scale multinational enterprises necessarily forces small- and middle-scale enterprises to follow suit in order to maintain their competitiveness. However, the certification fees to be paid to certifying agencies are not negligible for some of the small companies and some of the standards, which are suited for large-scale multinational enterprises, may not necessarily be appropriate for small businesses. Here, a drive towards market monopolization can be felt.

The above-mentioned potential detrimental effects may not only negatively affect national societies, but also the international society as well. Suppose the child labour provision of SA8000 is interpreted by SAI in a different way from what the Committee of Experts on the Application of Conventions and Recommendations of the ILO has, for many years, been advocating, and if the number of SA8000 adhering enterprises were big and the market dominating power of those enterprises was sufficiently important, there would be a true risk that the internationally recognized authority of the ILO's supervision would be in jeopardy. The ILO's supervisory machinery has itself been cautious in pronouncing its competence to interpret ILO Conventions, because the ILO Constitution provides that only the International Court of Justice can authoritatively interpret ILO Conventions. Now a new NGO comes along and interprets the Convention as it pleases and has that interpretation enforced as a result of the enormous power of multinational enterprises. Who has authorized Company *X* or NGO *Y* to set up a code, which may, in practice, substantially revise a positive law? What will happen, when the code conflicts with existing laws?

Many private initiatives, including rapidly expanding codes proposed by private institutions such as SAI and FLA, refer to international treaties, such as ILO conventions on the prohibition of forced labour and child labour. Consultants hired by the SAI or FLA then inspect a company's adherence to such codes. How can we assume that these consultants know the correct interpretation of ILO Conventions Nos. 29 and 138? Who has given authority to the SAI and FLA, and all other private companies, whose codes refer to ILO Conventions or UN treaties, to interpret the international treaties in this way? The soft law aspect of CSR should, therefore, be carefully observed. Legalization without due process must be avoided and necessary measures must be taken so that globalization does not undermine the traditional law-making and law-interpreting procedures of the international community.

The Expanding Space of the International Legal Community

It is widely accepted that international instruments, such as the OECD Guidelines and the ILO Tripartite Declaration, are not legally binding. At the same time, it is also widely maintained that the so-called 'non-binding' instruments may have some bearing on international law, when they are supported by an established system or machineries to follow-up the original instruments.[17] Some of them may even claim to have accumulated sufficient weight to be called 'law' by virtue of customary rule creation. For instance, the Universal Declaration of Human Rights was adopted in 1948 at the General Assembly of the United Nations as a resolution, but many commentators now view it as a set of customary international rules. The instruments adopted by the OECD and the ILO can, therefore, not be disqualified just because they are *a priori* non-binding. They should be evaluated in the light of various conditions surrounding the original instruments. The existence of a follow-up mechanism plays a crucial role in this regard. The Burmese case, in which a French petroleum company had to withdraw from Myanmar, mentioned above, shows the positive effect of a strong initiative taken by a National Contact Point. The enterprise concerned may not have made its decision to withdraw from Myanmar because it considered the OECD Guidelines to be law, but the accompanying machinery for implementation, the National Contact Point, in particular, was crucial in bringing about that result. The ILO Tripartite Declaration also has a follow-up mechanism in the form of 'interpretation', but it is less efficient as in the case of the OECD Guidelines, partly due to the fact that the degree of consensus was low at the adoption of the instrument. The Global Contact is not equipped with a machinery to implement the provisions of the Compact and, therefore, it is legally speaking less relevant. A proposed instrument made within the context of the United Nations Human Rights framework has the potential of becoming legally important. For the United Nations has a sophisticated mechanism of supervising the implementation of its human rights instruments and once an instrument is put on this track, it will undergo heavy scrutiny by supervisory bodies and the original instrument will have a quasi-legal function. However, as was shown above, the fate of UN instruments is rather weak at this stage.

To sum up the findings so far, the emergence of a new perspective of international law can be ascertained. It should be stressed that this is not new to the contemporary theory of international law. Half a century ago, Phillip C. Jessup introduced the idea of transnational law, and, thereafter, Wolfgang Friedmann came up with the notion of an international law of co-operation contrasted to an international law of co-existence. In the seventies, French scholars strongly propagated the 'droit international du développement' or international law of development. More recently, efforts have been made to reconcile international relations theory with that of law, through what is referred to as the constructivist approach. The notion of global administrative law is the most recent endeavour

17 Ago 1997.

to explain the non-traditional (that is non-Grotian) basis of the international legal system. To this extent, the findings made above are not radically different from that found in a number of other recent scholarly efforts. The present chapter may, however, contribute to strengthening the modern discourse of the changing structure of international law and add another element, which can perhaps throw light on various features of positive law in our era.

CSR may have a bearing on the understanding of the actual status of international law on two levels. First, it is a process by which 'hard' international law is implemented. Second, it will itself become 'hard' law under certain conditions. We shall now turn to an examination of these two levels.

CSR as a Vehicle to Implement Traditional International Law (the Procedural Aspect of Law)

As we have seen, CSR contains two different elements: One is a set of hard rules, which exist as *lex lata* (hard law as opposed to soft law) in the form of company law, criminal code, etc., simply re-stated. Within our delimitation of the analysis, hard law means practically the ILO Conventions.[18] The other, again divisible into two parts, consists of guidelines according to which enterprises direct their own activities: one part that merely supplements existing law and the other part that goes further and develops existing law by giving it new substance.

Firstly, CSR, which merely re-states *lex lata*, functions as supervision or control of a legal norm. The great part of the so-called 'compliance' provisions of a CSR code, such as a declaration to observe accounting regulations, corporate laws, competition laws, intellectual property laws, etc., play a role of governmental advice and instruction to enforce relevant laws effectively. In our context, CSR declaring observance of principles enshrined in ILO Conventions supplements the activities of the ILO's supervisory organs.

For example, ILO Convention Number 138 on the minimum age to enter into employment, in Article 2, paragraph 3, states: '[t]he minimum age specified in pursuance of paragraph 1 of this Article shall not be less than the age of completion of compulsory schooling and, in any case, shall not be less than 15 years'. The Adidas Workplace Standards provides: '[b]usiness partners must not employ children who are less than 15 years old, or less than the age for completing compulsory education in the country of manufacture where such age is higher than 15'.[19]

18 Bilateral treaties entered into by sovereign states to regulate labour-related matters are also hard international labour law. European Community Regulations and Directives, as well as other European regional agreements covering social aspects of life are 'hard' laws too.

19 Adidas Group, 'Our Workplace Standards' (online).

The second supplemental role played by CSR, that is concretely implementing a legal obligation, which has been stated in vague language, functions as implementing regulations, ministerial regulations and administrative rules. In our context, this would be the case, in which CSR gives concrete meanings to some ILO Conventions. For example, the ILO Convention Number 29 (Forced Labour Convention) offers the following definition of the concept of forced labour: '[f]or the purposes of this Convention the term forced or compulsory labour shall mean all work or service which is exacted from any person under the menace of any penalty and for which the said person has not offered himself voluntarily'. The corresponding provision in the Adidas Workplace Standards states: 'Business partners must not use forced labour, whether in the form of prison labour, indentured labour, bonded labour or otherwise …'.[20] While the ILO's supervisory organs, the Committee of Experts on the Application of Conventions and Recommendations, in particular, have long discussed the problem of bonded labour within the scope of the Conventions, this company code now enforces the ILO's interpretation of the Convention clearly bringing bonded labour into the scope of the Convention.

The last case, the unilateral declaration by an enterprise proclaiming its determination to achieve *higher* standards is almost outside the implementation process of the law. It may, in fact, enter into the realm of law-making and, as such, it may not always be in the public interest. The expansion of the scope of coverage can, therefore, be admitted only to the extent that it is in conformity with the relevant legal regulation.

A possible detrimental effect has been shown earlier. One could even add another negative aspect of the element of CSR. That is to say, an enterprise, usually a giant multinational enterprise with considerable power in the international market, may use higher standards to differentiate itself from smaller and weaker enterprises thereby ensuring its dominant status. In other words, CSR would be used as a tool to legally secure a monopoly situation.[21] While making this final reservation, it should be acknowledged that CSR plays a significant role in facilitating an effective implementation of *lex lata*.

An example again taken from the forced labour issue: ILO Convention Number 29 admits forced labour as a 'consequence of a conviction in a court of law, provided that the said work or service is carried out under the supervision and control of a public authority and that the said person is not hired to or placed at the disposal of private individuals, companies or associations'[22] The Adidas Workplace Standards as quoted above do not qualify prison labour in this way. It thus appears as if the company code provides broader protection in the sense that it categorically prohibits the use of convicted prisoners. This may not necessarily be in conformity with the public policy of the country concerned, as well as with the

20 Adidas Group, 'Our Workplace Standards' (online).

21 It is admitted that this is the most controversial aspect of CSR as well as the most crucial point in a debate on the very existence and merits of CSR.

22 ILO Convention No. 29, Art. 2(1)(c).

ILO's practice to allow certain groups of prisoners to work for private companies. The reference cited above on the prohibition of child labour may also give rise to a question in this context. The Adidas Workplace Standards do not appear to allow children under the age of 14 to be employed. However, ILO Convention Number 138 (Minimum Age Convention) in Article 2, paragraph 4, provides that 'a Member whose economy and educational facilities are insufficiently developed may, after consultation with the organizations of employers and workers concerned, where such exist, initially specify a minimum age of 14 years'. When Adidas operates in a country that has availed itself of this provision of the Convention, Adidas may act against the host country's policy, which is in conformity with international labour standards.

CSR as Emerging Law (Operation Processes that Play an Important Role in Law-making)

CSR norms are now emerging and their implication for public international law is significant. Although instruments such as the OECD Guidelines for Multinational Enterprises, the ILO Tripartite Declaration of Principles Concerning Multinational Enterprises and Social Policy, and the United Nations Norms on the Responsibilities of Transnational Corporations and other Business Enterprises with Regard to Human Rights, which is still now in the process of deliberations are 'legally non-binding', they do begin to play a significant role in the actual life of many people and enterprises that operate across national borders. The efforts undertaken by these inter-governmental organizations to regulate multinational enterprises through a set of emerging CSR rules are commendable because they are legally responsible towards the international community and through it to national communities. The framework agreements signed between international trade secretariats and multinational enterprises, too, may have a significant effect on international labour legislation.

We have indicated in the previous section that 'hard' international labour law consists of mainly ILO Conventions. Even ILO Recommendations are not 'hard', to the extent that they do not constitute a treaty.[23] OECD Guidelines and ILO Tripartite Declaration are even less so, because they are neither treaties nor non-binding instruments accompanied by reporting obligations. They do, however, constitute a set of normative guidelines on the part of the Member States as well as private enterprises. They may not be applied in a court of law, but they function as a norm for states, enterprises, workers and employers in their daily activities. It is

23 The International Labour Recommendations, however, are more than simple resolutions of an international organization, because reporting obligations are attached to them under Article 19 of the ILO Constitution. Member states are not legally bound to apply the contents of a Recommendation, but they are legally bound to supply reports to the ILO describing the measures they have taken to give effect to it (Art. 19, par. 5).

widely accepted that an international instrument gains more weight when they are equipped with a machinery to follow it up.[24] When they become legally relevant, that is to say when they are given general acceptance as a code to be adhered to, they will occupy a place in the body of international labour law.

The Framework Agreements of GUFs (international sectoral trade union organizations), referred to in the foregoing section, is more interesting. As we have already mentioned, this type of agreement is not a mere contract between a worker and an enterprise. It can be assimilated to a collective agreement in the international plane. That is to say, if we assume a centralized international legal system,[25] the Agreement will play the same role a collective agreement plays in the national legal system. In other words, it will possess the value of law. Thus a Framework Agreement (a clear case of CSR) will become international law. However, we are not at this stage yet. We still find ourselves in an international society, which consists of sovereign states with their full sovereign power. Individuals and corporate entities have not, for the moment at least, attained full legal personality in the context of the international legal system.

CSR prescribed in other private initiatives, including that of ISO, may contribute to enhancing workers' rights and to the promotion of public welfare, thus playing a role in international labour law, but they may, if wrongly employed, undermine the efforts undertaken by the international community to attain social justice through international co-operation. There is yet no proof that a CSR code that has been established by a private enterprise has attained recognition as a globally accepted norm. Whether a company code or something like SA8000 attains the status of international labour law depends upon whether these codes are given authorization by relevant international bodies, such as the ILO. In this context, a Memorandum of Understanding entered into between the ILO and the ISO in the formulation of the forthcoming ISO26000 on social responsibility shows a possible solution for the legalization of private initiatives.

Conclusion

The discussion about CSR leads us to an important finding that an interesting development is taking place in international law and in international labour law, in particular. Attaching legal importance to a quasi- or para-legal phenomenon of CSR makes us to reconsider the traditional frame of reference, including the basic presumption that the subjects of international law are states. It also foresees

24 For several decades, the legal significance of non-binding United Nations resolutions has been widely studied. Abi-Saab 1981, 1–5; Stern 1984, 43–53.

25 The idea of 'a global legal space', as defined in the study on the Global Administrative Law Project of the Inst. For Intl. Law and Justice of the NYU School of Law (Kingsbury, Krisch and Stewart 2005), appears to point the same direction with the foregoing analysis of the current situation regarding international law.

the trend towards diversifying the international legislative processes. It also strengthens the argument that a 'process-based approach' is required in evaluating the current situation and future trends of international law.

References

Books, Articles and Chapters in Books

Abi-Saab, G. (ed.) (1981), *Concept of International Organization* (Paris: UNESCO), 1–5.

Ago, S. (1997), 'Follow-up of United Nations Resolutions', *Journal of Law and Politics* 61, 3–4.

Fikentscher, W. (1982), 'United Nations Codes of Conduct: New Paths in International Law', *American Journal of Comparative Law* 30, 577–604.

Kingsbury, B., Krisch, N. and Stewart, R.B. (2005), 'The Emergence of Global Administrative Law', *Law & Contemporary Problems* 68, 15–61.

Ohmi, N. (2005), 'Corporate Social Responsibility Dealt with by Trade Unions', *Report of the Japan Institute for Labour Policy and Training* 45, 82–83.

Stern, B. (1984), 'Le Droit international du développement, un droit de finalité', in La Formation des normes en droit international du développement, C.N.R.S., Paris et O.P.U. Alger.

Zerck, J.A. (2006), *Multinationals and Corporate Social Responsibility: Limitations and Opportunities in International Law* (Cambridge: Cambridge University Press).

International Documents and Others

ILO Convention No. 29.

'Recommendations by the French National Contact Point to Companies on the Issue of Forced Labour in Burma', 28 March 2002, Annex I of the OECD 'Multinational Enterprises Situations of Violent Conflict and Widespread Human Rights Abuses', Working Papers on International Investment, Number 2002/1, 30 May 2002.

Report of the Subcommittee on Multinational Enterprises, ILO, Governing Body, UN ESCOR, ILO GB.292/11, March 2005, Geneva, 1.

Internet-based References

Adidas Group, 'Our Workplace Standards', The Adidas Group Supply Chain Code of Conduct, <http://www.adidas-group.com/en/sustainability/Overview/our_standards/standards_of_engagement.asp>.

CSR, 'An Ongoing Engagement', *International Organization of Employers*, <http://www.ioe-emp.org/en/policy-areas/csr/index.html>.

International Federation of Building and Wood Workers (IFBWW), 'IFBWW Model Framework Agreement', <http://www.ifbww.org/index.cfm?n=191&l=2&on=7>.

International Labour Organization (ILO), 'Interpretation Procedure', Multi: Multinational Enterprise and Social Policy, <http://www.ilo.org/public/english/employment/multi/tripartite/interpretation.htm>.

International Labour Organization (ILO), 'Interpretation Procedure at Work: BIFU Case (1984–1985)', Multi: Multinational Enterprise and Social Policy, <http://www.ilo.org/public/english/employment/multi/tripartite/cases.htm>.

International Organization of Employers, 'CSR, An Ongoing Engagement', International Organization of Employers, <http://www.ioe-emp.org/en/policy-areas/csr/index.html>.

Nippon Keizai Dantai Rengoukai [Japan Business Federation] [online news], <http://www.keidanren.or.jp/indexj.html> (home page).

Organization for Economic Cooperation and Development (OECD), *The OECD Guidelines for Multinational Enterprises* (2000), <http://www.oecd.org/dataoecd/56/36/1922428.pdf>.

Chapter 16
Privatization of Childcare as a Way of Implementing Young Children's Rights: The Recommendations of the Committee on the Rights of the Child and Their Implications for Japan

OTA Ikuko

Introduction

The 1989 United Nations Convention on the Rights of the Child (UNCRC) has brought about a historical turnaround for children's legal capacity: now all children under 18 are to be regarded, not as entities to be protected, but as capable of exercising their own rights. This chapter deals with the rights of children, children's human rights as an international public interest. In the context of optimal implementation of young children's rights, it considers the privatization of child welfare as traditional State functions. 'Young children' are defined here as children at birth and throughout infancy – until about three or four years of age, who are inevitably dependent on care by adults, such as parents and caregivers, and unable to fully communicate their own views through language. As a case study of domestic implementation, this chapter examines the ongoing privatization of public day-care centers in Japan and their implication for children's rights in early childhood.

In its original policy designs for implementing children's rights, the UNCRC envisaged the 'parent–child–State' triangular framework. Within such framework, the UNCRC allocated the primary responsibility of upbringing and development of children to parents (or legal guardians), and the supplementary family assistance for child-rearing to States parties.[1] In the light of children as rights-holders, these

1 It might be because of the following two factors that the original policy designs were expected to function well: first, the traditional conception of family autonomy, which has venerated freedom from State control and has outlined domestic family laws in most legal systems, was generally accepted in the drafting process for the UNCRC; second, as part of 'a familiar requirement' for the universal human rights treaties, the UNCRC has stipulated, for the sake of the review and comments by the Convention organ, that States

responsibilities of parents and States parties were to be subject to Article 3 (calling for the best interest of the child to be a primary consideration when taking action involving a child) and Article 12 (the right to express a child's own views freely in all matters affecting him/her).

In attempting to ensure effective implementation of the obligations stipulated by the UNCRC, however, two problems common to industrialized States parties have arisen in the policy designs mentioned above. First, the family's role in raising children have deteriorated because of the rapid changes in economical and societal conditions caused by market globalization. Second, under market-oriented, neoliberal reforms, States parties have increased their reliance on private, for-profit actors in providing the childcare services, which those parties have traditionally financed and delivered under the obligations of the UNCRC. Nonetheless, it has not been clarified yet whether, and in what ways, it is generally considered appropriate, in order to realize 'the best interests of the child', to provide what States parties had been taking as the UNCRC obligations by market-style private-sector provision.

These two problems are related to the changing nature of the two responsible entities, parents and States parties, in the UNCRC triangular framework. Therefore, we are faced with the fundamental issues of whether, and how, the two entities are capable of fulfilling their UNCRC obligations under the unavoidable influence of economic globalization, while paying attention to children's voices and best interests as the primary consideration.

Besides, for young children, the changing nature of parents and States parties may have a direct and profound impact, on the ground that they are 'with particular interests, capacities and vulnerabilities, and of requirements for protection, guidance and support in the exercise of their rights'.[2] In particular, young children's inability to express their own views freely through adequate verbal communication in all matters affecting them (Art. 12) may increase the importance of the responsible authorities considering their best interests (Art. 3). Nevertheless, neither the UNCRC nor the Committee on the Rights of the Child (CRC), a monitoring body for the UNCRC, directly defines 'best interests';[3] the concept of 'best interests' in itself remains indeterminate. This indeterminacy involves a high degree of risk, as it may provide 'a convenient cloak for bias, paternalism and capricious decision-making',[4] especially in the exercise of young children's rights.

In order to address these fundamental issues for securing the best interests of young children under the UNCRC, this chapter focuses on the two documents adopted by the CRC: the recommendations of 2002 regarding the private sector

parties are required to submit, to the Committee on the Rights of the Child (CRC), periodic reports about their domestic implementation of the UNCRC obligations, Steiner and Alston 1996, 505.

2 GC7, para. 2(c).

3 Freeman 2007, 50.

4 Parker 1994, 26.

as service provider and its role in implementing child rights, and the General Comments of 2005 for implementing children's rights in early childhood.

As Gregory Kasza points out,[5] case studies of Japan's welfare policies generally have had a tendency to overstate its difference. By taking up Japan as a case of domestic implementation of the UNCRC, however, it is to be emphasized that Japan's policy-changeover in child and family welfare should be understood within a broader pattern of global policy diffusion and in the light of guaranteeing international human rights standards. Indeed, most of the welfare challenges addressed by Japan in recent years resemble those facing other industrialized societies; and it is so especially in the case of the privatization of public services under the influence of economic globalization.

At the same time, nevertheless, national policies on child and family welfare are likely to reflect the historic, cultural and social contexts of respective countries.[6] Although recent alarming symptoms of 'family dysfunction', such as the dramatically plunging birthrate and rapidly increasing child abuse and domestic violence, can be observed commonly in the industrialized societies, there should be Japan's own source and structure of problems in the sector of child and family welfare. There should be also, accordingly, Japan's specific solution approaches matched to its particular circumstances.

This chapter will help provide some insights into how stakeholders in Japan are endeavoring to realize the best interests of the most vulnerable children in the changing landscape of childcare policies under economic globalization.

The UNCRC and Its Implications for Young Children

The UNCRC and Its Monitoring Body the CRC

The UNCRC was adopted by the General Assembly as a resolution 44/25 of 20 November 1989.[7] On 2 September 1990, with ratifications of 20 members, the UNCRC entered into force in accordance with Article 49. Since then, 193 States parties have ratified and acceded to the UNCRC, making it the most widely accepted multilateral treaty in existence of any kind.

Under the UNCRC, all children under age 18 are holders of autonomy rights as well as protective rights; even infants and toddlers have all the rights enumerated in the Convention. Young children are entitled to 'the progressive exercise of their rights'[8] according to their evolving capacities, with protection, guidance and support of parents or others with legal responsibility for them. The UNCRC

---

5 Kasza 2006, 81–112.

6 See, e.g., Freymond and Cameron 2006, 3–26.

7 Convention on the Rights of the Child, New York, 20 November 1989, 1577 UNTS 3.

8 GC7, para. 3.

includes a wide range of civil, political, economic, social and cultural rights. In its implementation, the CRC, the monitoring body of the UNCRC, classifies the four articles as 'general principles'[9]: Article 2 (non-discrimination), Article 3 (best interest of the child), Article 6 (the right to life, survival and development) and Article 12 (respect for the views of the child).

Created under Article 43, the CRC is the body of 18 independent experts, and its primary mandate is to review progress made by States parties in implementing the UNCRC and its two optional protocols. Pursuant to Article 44, States parties are required to submit a periodic report[10] to the CRC on how it is fulfilling its obligations that are mainly specified in Part One (Arts. 1–41) of the UNCRC. The CRC examines each report and communicates its concerns and recommendations to the State party in the form of 'concluding observations'.

The CRC also publishes its interpretation of the UNCRC provisions, known as 'General Comments'[11] on thematic issues, 'with a view to promoting its further implementation and assisting States parties in fulfilling their reporting obligations'.[12] The CRC as well coordinates periodically 'Day of General Discussion' to a specific article of the UNCRC or to a theme about children's rights, 'in order to enhance a deeper understanding of the content and implications of the Convention'.[13] The discussions are public; those invited to participate in are government representatives, United Nations human rights mechanisms, as well as United Nations bodies and specialized agencies, NGOs and individual experts.[14]

In relation to the topic of this chapter, the CRC has organized following two General Discussion Days, both held at Palais Wilson, Geneva: The Day of General Discussion on the Private Sector as Service Provider and Its Role in Implementing Child Rights in 2002 (DGD 2002),[15] and the Day of General

9 UN Doc. CRC/C/5, para. 13; UN Doc. CRC/C/58, paras. 25–47. See also UN Doc. CRC/GC/2003/5, para. 12.

10 The first report needs to be submitted by the State party two years after acceding to the convention. After that, a progress report is required every five years.

11 Regarding the functions of the General Comments issued by international human rights organs in general, Steiner and Alston points out the following two: aid to states in filing reports under the respective human rights treaties; and restatement, interpretation and elaboration of provisions of the respective human rights treaties, Steiner and Alston 1996, 522–534.

12 CRC 2005, 21, Rule 73. For general information, see http://www2.ohchr.org/english/bodies/crc/comments.htm.

13 CRC 2005, 21, Rule 75. For general information, see http://www2.ohchr.org/english/bodies/crc/discussion2008.htm.

14 Each year, children, NGOs and experts are invited to submit documents to inform the CRC's one-day discussion with stakeholders mentioned in the text. All submitted documents are posted on the Child Rights Information Network (CRIN) website (http://www.crin.org/resources/treaties/discussion.asp).

15 See DGD 2002. For the full text of the outline for this DGD, see UN Doc. CRC/C/114 Annex VIII (187–190).

Discussion on Implementing Child Rights in Early Childhood in 2004 (DGD 2004).[16] Based on the findings of the working groups and the plenary discussion, the CRC adopted the corresponding recommendations. Regarding the theme of DGD 2004, the CRC additionally adopted, in its 40th session of September 2005, a more detailed document as the General Comments No. 7 (GC7).[17] More details on these documents will be provided in the later section.

The Original Policy Designs for Implementation: The Parent–Child–State Tripartite Framework

Parental 'rights', not 'authority', in their own household to direct the upbringing of their children are prescribed in the UNCRC (Arts. 5 and 14(2)). However, parents or guardians now can be considered as fiduciaries[18] in regard to their children's rights, while paying their attention to the best interests of the child as 'their basic concern' (Arts. 18(1) and 27(2)). As such, parents or guardians are obliged to perform their fiduciary responsibilities and duties, and States parties provide appropriate assistance to parents and legal guardians in performing their child-rearing responsibilities (Arts. 3(2), 18(2) and 27(3)). If parents or guardians are not able to discharge their duties of protection and guidance, States parties shall step in a private realm of family life (Arts. 9(1) and 19(1)), in which traditionally the State could not intervene.

The patriarchal concept of family autonomy used to consider the child as merely a recipient of protection under the parental (that is, head of household's) authority.[19] This concept has contributed substantially to shaping the longstanding legal paradigm of competition for control between the private authority of the family and the power of the State. Then the UNCRC introduced the new category of children's rights into the existing realm of international human rights, and formulated the parent–child–State framework for the allocation of decisional power and responsibility among these three parties.

Under the Convention, therefore, the traditional legal paternalism seems to finally end, even though the major human rights documents recognize the right to family life or privacy.[20] From this point of view, the legal paradigm of family–

16 See DGD 2004. For the full text of the outline for this DGD, see UN Doc. CRC/C/137 Annex II (132–135). For its summary record (partial), see UN Doc. CRC/C/SR.979.

17 See GC7.

18 See, e.g., Kandel and Griffiths 2003, 1056; Scott and Scott 1995, 2401.

19 Under the patriarchal model, in which 'the father's power over his household … was absolute[, l]aw employed a property theory of paternal ownership and treated children "as assets of estates in which fathers had a vested right"', Woodhouse 1992, 1037.

20 The States parties shall protect the family and its members, and are not allowed to subject an individual to arbitrary or unlawful interference with his/her family life or privacy, as is recognized in the major human rights documents, such as the 1948 Universal Declaration of Human Rights (UDHR), the 1966 International Covenant on Civil and

State competition is supposed to have already been replaced with a new paradigm of partnership, in which the parents and the State cooperate in ensuring children's healthy development.[21]

However, it would be notable that the UNCRC emphasizes the significance of the family (that is, parents and other primary caregivers) for realizing children's rights. In the Preamble, for instance, States parties consider that the family is 'the fundamental group of society and the natural environment for the growth and well-being of all its members and particularly children' (para. 5), and are aware that 'the child, for the full and harmonious development of his or her personality, should grow up in a family environment, in an atmosphere of happiness, love and understanding' (para. 6).[22] Based on this fundamental philosophy on the gravity of children's upbringing in the family, the UNCRC adopts the stance that States parties, in the first place, play a role of backing and assistance for the family, by monitoring whether children's rights are being respected within the private sphere of family.[23] Worth emphasizing here is the fact that this complementary, supportive positioning of States parties presupposes the sound functioning of the family in rearing their children, and the atmosphere of understanding, instead of the parental authority, should reside at the center of this functioning.

The Impediments to Ensuring Effective Implementation of the UNCRC

Deterioration of Family Role in Raising Children

Growing Economic and Social Uncertainty As stated above, the sound functioning of the family is a precondition for child-rearing, but it is becoming increasingly questionable in many industrialized societies.

The International Labour Organization (ILO), a specialized agency of the United Nations, released its annual Global Employment Trends report in January

---

Political Rights (ICCPR), the 1950 European Convention for the Protection of Human Rights and Fundamental Freedoms (ECHR), and the 1961 European Social Charter (ESC). See, e.g., Article 16(3) of the UDHR, Articles 17 and 23(1) of the ICCPR, Article 16 of the ESC and Article 8 of the ECHR.

21 Woodhouse 2004, 85.

22 Furthermore, Article 7 (name and nationality) defines the rights for the child as 'as far as possible, the right to know and be cared for by his or her parents' and in Article 9 (separation from parents) sets a rule that a child shall not be separated from the parents against his/her will, and even if separated for reasons of abuse or parental divorce, States parties respect the right 'to maintain personal relations and direct contact with both parents on a regular basis'.

23 This formulation of responsibilities for realizing children's rights can be speculated as a reflection of family law outline of most legal systems. For the detailed description of this paragraph, see Ota 2001, 195–199.

2009.[24] Indicating that the global number of unemployed in 2008 is estimated at 190 million, the ILO report estimates the influence of global financial crisis of 2008 as follows:[25]

- In a current worst case scenario, the global unemployment rate could rise to 7.1 per cent and result in an increase in the global number of unemployed of more than 50 million people; and
- The number of working poor – people who are unable to earn enough to lift themselves and their families above the US$2 per person, per day, poverty line, may rise up to 1.4 billion, or 45 per cent of all the world's employed.

Even before the global financial crisis triggered a serious slowdown in world economic growth, economic globalization has been causing rapid changes in economical and societal conditions; a prime example is the impact coming from tough global competition. As a result, most economies, even those with robust economic growth, have failed to turn GDP growth into job creation or wage increases. The ILO pointed out in its 2006 Global Employment Trends report that this failure has hit the world's working poor the hardest, together with successive natural disasters and rising energy prices.[26]

The working poor symbolizes the recent industrialized societies in which the gap between the rich and poor has been growing.[27] In Japan, the term 'working poor' is generally used to describe individuals and families whose annual incomes fall below the poverty line of two million Japanese yen (about US$20,000), despite working two or even three jobs. The number of underclass young adults aged 15–34, working as freelance, part-time or contract workers totaled 2.01 million at the end of 2005.[28] They are regarded as the product of neoliberal economic reforms to reduce the national budget deficit by cutting down on public spending, together with private companies' attempts to squeeze costs.[29] Takanobu Igarashi, chief economist at Mitsubishi UFJ Research and Consulting, commented in 2007

24 See ILO 2009.

25 ILO, 28 January 2009.

26 Japan Economic Newswire, 25 January 2006; ILO 2006.

27 Suvendrini Kakuchi reports that '[w]hile official statistics are not available, figures compiled by Japan's Asahi TV and released in September 2006 showed that in the 1980s the top 20 per cent of the population made 10 times more than the 20 per cent in the low-income bracket. By 2000, the rich were making 168 times more than poor workers' (Kakuchi, 19 October 2006).

28 According to Inata, 6 July 2007, the total of young adults is 2.01 million, comprised of 1.04 million aged 15–24 and 970,000 from 25 to 34 years old. There were another 300,000 working poor aged 35–44, bringing the total number of freelance workers to about 3 per cent of Japan's 66 million workforce in 2005. In addition, as of July 2007, there are 640,000 people aged 15–34 who are in the group called NEET (Not in Education, Employment, or Training).

29 Kakuchi, 19 October 2006.

that '[t]he average working poor in Japan earns only about a quarter of the amount that the average employee with a permanent position can make in his/her lifetime, pays one-third or one-fourth in taxes and will receive less than a half of regular pension payments'.[30] Without a secure foothold in the labor market, these young people will not be able to make future plans, especially those regarding their future dependents; they can rarely save for the future, get no unemployment benefits, and cannot pay for public medical insurance.

Besides, even before the global financial crisis, a survey by the Labour Research Council in Japan found in 2004 that approximately half of young regular employees are worried about getting sick if current working and living conditions continue.[31] The survey was based on the information about the work and life of 5,165 young regular workers of 34 years of age or less, mainly working at large corporations in the Tokyo metropolitan area. The Council sees the results as reflecting the reality that, with the advance of corporate restructuring and changes in working conditions, younger workers are employed mainly for their immediate skills and forced to take on heavy workloads.[32] Therefore, given the current crisis, even in permanent employment, young workers would be confronting a growing deficit of decent work opportunities and higher levels of economic and social uncertainty in Japan.

Increasing Difficulty of the Parents' Growing into 'Caregivers or "Persons Who Raise"' Under market globalization, capitalist logic and practice permeate all places on the globe and all spheres of livelihood unlike ever before. In particular, the notion of private ownership, which composes a vital precondition of modern civil liberties, has been pervasive, even to the extent that 'his/her existence' has become almost equivalent to 'his/her possessions'. For instance, according to *Josei rodo hakusho* [the White Paper on Women and Labor], released by the Japanese Ministry of Health, Labour and Welfare in July 2005, lots of younger Japanese parents regard children more as 'consumer goods' in order to improve the quality of parents' lives than as 'future workers for the community', unlike the previous generations widely viewed their children.[33] For parents or legal guardians, this mind-set preoccupied with the desire of possession to fulfill parents' own lives, may impede their life-course shift to the stage of caregivers or 'persons who raise' who are ready for rearing their children in the 'atmosphere of happiness, love and understanding' (UNCRC, Preamble, para. 6); as described below, this capacity of caregivers is regarded as crucial for the sound functioning of the family in realizing 'the best interests' of young children under the UNCRC.

Developmental psychologist Takashi Kujiraoka argues that, recently, even biological parents are unable to transform themselves into caregivers or *Sodateru*

30 Inata, 6 July 2007.

31 *Nihon Keizai Shinbun*, 7 August 2004.

32 *Nihon Keizai Shinbun*, 7 August 2004.

33 Maeda, 8 August 2005.

mono ['persons who raise'], because the natural transfer of generativity can occur of its own accord less and less.[34] Generativity, the concept introduced by Psychologist Erik Erikson, is defined as follows: 'the concern for and commitment to promoting the next generation, through parenting, teaching, mentoring, and generating products and outcomes that aim to benefit youth and foster the development and well-being of individuals and social systems that will outlive the self'.[35]

In traditional generational change, the transfer of generativity had occurred, in general, unintentionally. Dependent care-receivers had gradually grown out of their self-preoccupation and learned how to provide care through other caregivers and demeanors of caring. However, as capitalist logic and practice came to permeate through market globalization, it has accelerated the tide of commodification of all things human; in consequence, autonomous, non-market values and behaviors through which our needs of daily lives were used to be satisfied have been undermined more and more. Under such circumstances, if parents of young children are preoccupied with their own desires and concerns, such as the desire for children as a possession to fulfill the parents' own lives, it would become extremely difficult for them to transform into 'persons who raise' and cultivate their capability for rearing their children in the 'atmosphere of happiness, love and understanding' (UNCRC, Preamble, para. 6).

Eventually, these factors are make it difficult for parents or guardians to effectively fulfill their responsibilities for raising children while considering 'the best interests of the child' under the UNCRC. Furthermore, such parents or legal guardians may impede children's life-course so that when they become parents, they are unable to rear their own children in the familial atmosphere of understanding, which was originally envisaged in the UNCRC as a crucial precondition for realizing 'the best interests' of young children.

Unproven Appropriateness of Market-Style Private-Sector Provision of Day-Care Services for Young Children

Current Situation of Japan's Privatization of Public Day-Care Centers The deterioration of family roles has resulted in a highly acute growth in demand for State-supported childcare (Arts. 3(2), 3(3), 18(2) and 18(3)), which played a supplementary role in original policy design of the UNCRC. Simultaneously, market-oriented values and ways of thought that come together with globalization have been entering into public policy in a variety of ways worldwide.

Under these circumstances, also in Japan, child support provided by the State, as envisioned in the UNCRC, is also gradually evolving, from a structure planned and run by the State and for which the State is directly responsible, into the one

34 Kujiraoka 2002, specifically Chapter 1 (10–79).

35 McAdams and De St. Aubin 1998, xx. Almost 60 years ago, Erik Erkison introduced this concept in his famous eight-stage model of human development as the seventh stage of the life cycle, *generation vs. stagnation*.

based on private competition in which private service-providers place competitive bids. According to the Ministry of Health, Labour and Welfare, the number of public day-care centers assigned or transferred to private entities in a year increased from 13 in fiscal 2000 to 29 in fiscal 2001 when the Koizumi administration started, and continued to increase to 169 in fiscal 2005 and 132 in fiscal 2006. Also, the number of public day-care centers wholly consigned to private entities in a year increased from 13 in fiscal 2001 to 49 in fiscal 2002, then to 40 in fiscal 2005 and to 61 in fiscal 2006.[36]

Under the *Jido fukushi ho* [Child Welfare Law] (Law No. 164 of 1947), the day-care system in post-war Japan has been operated on the 'principle of providing day-care in kind'. The principle is to provide young children in need of care with day-care in kind of no less than 'the minimum standard' throughout Japan – either in public or private centers – with the use of public resources. This 'minimum standard' is established by the national government for licensing day-care centers and also constitutes requirements to receive grants from the national and local governments. The Japanese public education system and healthcare insurance are typical social security programs offered in kind, along with day-care.

As opposed to this, 'provision of cash' is to provide or supplement with cash the required income for purchasing these social services. The Japanese elderly care insurance system introduced in 2000, based on the Care Insurance Law (Law No. 123 of 1997), is a cash-provision type where 90 per cent of the cash required for elderly people in need of care to purchase care services is provided. Also, the assistance expenditure system introduced in 2006 for the welfare of the handicapped based on the Law to Assist the Handicapped to Become Financially Independent (Law No. 123 of 2005) follows the same approach.

The cash-provision system has two features: first, utilization of social services is decided through 'free contracts between the buyer and the seller' of given social services; and second, public financial resources for social services are used, not for the operation of such services (licensed with 'the minimum standard' satisfied), but are provided in the form of subsidies to users of such services that can be purchased through free contracts. In this context, changing the current 'provision of child welfare in kind' to 'cash-provision for day-care services' can be considered as the essence of Japan's day-care privatization.

In reality, a direct contract between a licensed day-care center and a user (guardian) is not *yet* approved in Japan. However, with the revision of the Child Welfare Law (Art. 24(1)) in 1997, the use of licensed day-care centers was already changed, from the existing measures-based system to a choice-by-guardians-based system.

If we take note of what happened in Japan's care services for the elderly where the principle of cash-provision was introduced ahead of the childcare sector,

36 *Hoiku Hakusho* 2008, 54, *'Zuhyo 1-3K1: Koyu shisetsu wo katsuyo shita hoikusho secchi jokyo no suii'* [Diagram 1-3K1: Status regarding establishment of day-care centers utilizing public facilities].

it is assumed the following five phenomena would occur with the principle's introduction to the field of child welfare:[37]

1. Complete closing of public-built and public-operated day-care centers (model facilities of day-care standard established by local governments and operated by public employees as a general rule);
2. complete elimination of direct public financial resources for operation of day-care centers;
3. increases in cash-provision to parents/guardians due to rising day-care service costs and subsequent cuts in day-care budgets;
4. occurrence of disparities among day-care centers; and
5. lower pay to nurses and destabilization of their employment.

Therefore, the shift from the 'provision of service itself' to the 'benefit of service cost' can conduce to a retreat of public responsibility in the field of child welfare.

Concerns for the Decline in the Quality of Day-Care Services Accompanied with Privatization Even under the existing principle of 'providing day-care in kind', in Japan, there is a general trend for private day-care centers to have lower labor and operating costs than publicly run centers. Also, privately managed facilities offer more flexible services such as extended night and weekend care. Facing tight government budget conditions, many regional governments explain that by privatizing, they are able to respond to diverse childcare needs, achieve zero-waiting, and reinvest operational savings into other forms of child-rearing assistance.

However, there have been many cases in which the overall privatization schedule or selection criteria are not revealed, or the all-important roadmap for improving services is modified in mid-course, the result of which is no shortage of public disapproval and suspicion that the reason for privatization 'might be only to reduce costs'.[38]

Also, in accordance with privatization, the staff of public day-care center, including a director, is to be replaced, because all of them have served as public officials. Due to this replacement of professional caregivers, many parents or guardians worry about various changes in caregiving and the potential negative impacts on their children.[39] Actually, a certain social welfare corporation in eastern Japan which accepted management of the public day-care center admits that 'when existing public day-care centers are privatized, the pre-existing relationships between nurses, parents, and children are broken, so the work has to start, not

37 Ninomiya 2008, 113.

38 *Nihon Keizai Shinbun*, 7 June 2006.

39 Kosaka, 31 May 2006.

at zero, but in negative territory. There are burdens that cannot be quantitatively measured, such as anxieties of parents and laborious burdens of nurses'.[40]

In this kind of environment, parents and day-care staff in various locations in Japan have been waging opposition campaigns against privatization.[41] Besides, there have been several administrative lawsuits demanding a reversal of privatization or restitution for damages filed in cities such as Osaka, Yokohama and Kawasaki.[42] In these cases, it has been argued that privatization caused corresponding decline in the quality of day-care services.

Indeterminacy of the 'Best Interests' Principle and Its Risk for Young Children

The 'Best Interests' Principle of the UNCRC As mentioned above, in the implementation of the UNCRC, the CRC classifies the four Articles as 'general principles'. Children in early childhood are relatively immature and inescapably dependent on responsible authorities that represent their rights. Considering this specific vulnerability of young children, Article 3, 'the best interests of the child' principle, takes on a growing importance in making decisions and taking actions that concern their well-being.

Article 3 of the UNCRC consists of three paragraphs. Article 3(1) articulates the principle of the best interests of the child as follows:

> In all actions concerning children, whether undertaken by public or private social welfare institutions, courts of law, administrative authorities or legislative bodies, the best interests of the child shall be a primary consideration.

Ensuring children's well-being, Article 3(2) places an obligation on States parties to take appropriate measures in the areas of legislation and administration as follows:

> States Parties undertake to ensure the child such protection and care as is necessary for his or her well-being, taking into account the rights and duties of his or her parents, legal guardians, or other individuals legally responsible for him or her, and, to this end, shall take all appropriate legislative and administrative measures.

Lastly, in conformity with Article 3(1), Article 3(3) prescribes States parties' obligation, first, to establish proper standards, in conformity with Article 3(1),[43] for those responsible for caring and protecting children, and second, to ensure that those responsible conform with such standards. It reads as follows:

---

40 Kosaka, 31 May 2006.

41 *Osaka Yomiuri Shinbun*, 27 July 2006; *Tokyo Yomiuri Shinbun*, 15 June 2006.

42 *Asahi Shinbun*, 11 October 2006.

43 Freeman 2007, 71.

> States Parties shall ensure that the institutions, services and facilities responsible for the care or protection of children shall conform with the standards established by competent authorities, particularly in the areas of safety, health, in the number and suitability of their staff, as well as competent supervision.

Seen from the main concern of this chapter, that is, privatization of day-care, Article 3(3) can be considered to be specifically related to Articles 18(2) and (3).[44] Under Article 18(2), States parties 'shall render appropriate assistance to parents and legal guardians in the performance of their child-rearing responsibilities and shall ensure the development of institutions, facilities and services for the care of children'. Article 18(3) imposes States parties an obligation to 'take all appropriate measures to ensure that children of working parents have the right to benefit from childcare services and facilities for which they are eligible'.

As the above overview of the articles shows, this principle can be primarily considered to be 'an aid to construction as well as an element which needs to be taken fully into account in implementing other rights'.[45] This principle also can function 'as a basis for evaluating the laws and practices of States [p]arties where the matter is not governed by positive rights in the Convention'.[46]

The Principle's Indeterminacy and Its Implications for Young Children However, as mentioned above, neither the drafters of Article 3(1) nor the CRC defines the child's 'best interests'. According to Philip Alston, the drafters of Article 3(1) seem to feel 'no need either to defend [the] open-endedness [of the phrase 'the best interests of the child'] or to propose elements which might inject some particular content into it', because of the awareness of 'its extensive usage in the domestic laws of many countries' and the unawareness 'of the controversy over [this] principle in many of these jurisdictions'.[47] Regarding the CRC, it invokes this principle in criticizing domestic laws, policies and practices of States parties that are regarded as incompatible with 'the best interests of the child'; some examples are the lower marriageable age of girls in a number of jurisdictions, laws penalizing children born outside wedlock, the treatment of children from minority cultures, the low legal age of criminal responsibility, corporal punishment, economic difficulties and a concern that the best interest of children are neglected with budgetary constraints.[48] Nevertheless, the CRC has not directly defined the 'best interests' principle in itself.

This indeterminacy of the principle's concept involves a high degree of risk, namely, abuse of discretion by the responsible authorities. As Michael Freeman points out, in upholding the 'best interests' principle, prejudice (for instance,

---

44 Freeman 2007, 71–72. See also Detrick 1999, 94.

45 Alston 1994, 16.

46 This role of the principle was first identified by Stephen Parker. Freeman 2007, 32.

47 Alston 1994, 11.

48 Freeman 2007, 41–44, 51–59.

anti-gay sentiments) and 'dominant meanings' (for instance, dominant ideology, individual arbitrariness, and 'family and more general social policies for which the law serves as an instrument'), can exercise an influence behind the principle's 'smokescreen'.[49]

Even in the case of children endowed with fairly adequate ability for verbal communication, they often cannot speak for their own interests in a world run by adults. And the mentioned risk may increase in the case of young children, for the reason of their apparent cognitive immaturity.

The CRC's Approaches to Re-strengthening the Roles of Parents and States Parties

Based on the considerations in the previous sections, the following sections focus on the CRC's approaches to re-strengthening the roles of parents and States parties, for addressing the impediments to ensuring effective implementation of the UNCRC; the CRC has utilized aforementioned two DGDs (2002 and 2004), their corresponding recommendations and the GC7 to help parents and States parties fulfill the UNCRC obligations in the domain of childcare. The GC7, adopted in 2005, is supposed to be based on the discussion, findings and recommendations of the DGD 2004. The following sections, therefore, mainly deal with the GC7 and the recommendations of the DGD 2002.

Signaling the Significance of Professional Caregivers in Support of Parents/ Guardians

The most remarkable feature of the GC7 may be the emphasis placed on the importance of relationships with 'strong emotional attachments' (para. 6(b)) between young children and their parents or other caregivers in implementing children's rights. The GC7 makes maximum use of research achievements which back up the view that the survival, well-being and development of young children both depend on and evolve around 'close relationships … with a small number of key people' (para. 8). It considers that young children's sound development is 'best provided for within a small number of consistent, caring relationships [that] are with some combination of mother, father, siblings, grandparents and other members of the extended family, along with professional caregivers specialized in childcare and education' (para. 19). In other words, it regards these key caregivers as the 'major conduit' (para. 16) through which even babies can implement their rights.[50]

49 Freeman 2007, 2.

50 The GC7, paragraph 16 explains the way that babies implement their rights as follows: Newborn babies are able to recognize their parents (or other [primary] caregivers) very soon after birth, and they engage actively in non-verbal communication. Under

In this context, the GC7 has three distinctive underpinnings. First, based on the findings on research into early childhood, it enunciates the CRC's unwavering recognition of young children as 'social actors from the beginning of life' (para. 2(c)) with 'evolving capacities' (para. 17) or as 'active social agents' (para. 16), who 'actively make sense of the physical, social and cultural dimensions of the world they inhabit, learning progressively from their activities and their interactions with others, children as well as adults' (para. 6(d)).

Second, the GC7 reflects the CRC's solid conviction and corresponding concern that early childhood[51] is a critical period for achieving children's rights (para. 1) and States parties have not paid adequate attention 'to young children as rights holders and to the laws, policies and programmes required to realize their rights during this distinct phase of their childhood' (para. 3).

Third, the GC7 shows the CRC's willingness to assist 'primary caregivers', such as parents or legal guardians, in realizing young children's rights with particular attention to their best interests (paras. 15, 16). Since the early childhood forms 'the period of most extensive (and intensive) parental responsibilities related to all aspects of children's well-being' under the UNCRC, implementation of young children's rights depends on the 'well-being and resources available to those with responsibility for their care' (para. 20). Therefore, the GC7 relates in detail the significance of carefully crafted assistance to those primary caregivers.

Paragraph 20 exemplifies the necessary assistance as follows:

> (a) An integrated approach would include interventions that impact indirectly on parents' ability to promote the best interests of children (e.g. taxation and benefits, adequate housing, working hours) as well as those that have more immediate consequences (e.g. perinatal health services for mother and baby, parent education, home visitors);
>
> (b) Providing adequate assistance should take account of the new roles and skills required of parents, as well as the ways that demands and pressures shift during early childhood – for example, as children become more mobile, more verbally communicative, more socially competent, and as they begin to participate in programmes of care and education;

---

normal circumstances, young children form strong mutual attachments with their parents or primary caregivers. These relationships offer children physical and emotional security, as well as consistent care and attention. Through these relationships children construct a personal identity and acquire culturally valued skills, knowledge and behaviours.

51 In the GC7, the CRC's working definition of 'early childhood' is all young children below the age of 8 years: at birth and throughout infancy; during the preschool years; as well as during the transition to school (paras. 1, 4).

> (c) Assistance to parents will include provision of parenting education, parent counseling and other quality services for mothers, fathers, siblings, grandparents and others who from time to time may be responsible for promoting the child's best interests;
>
> (d) Assistance also includes offering support to parents and other family members in ways that encourage positive and sensitive relationships with young children and enhance understanding of children's rights and best interests.

As these examples indicate, the CRC realizes the fact that the primary caregivers are expected to perform as 'children's first educators', and therefore, need to learn how to 'provide appropriate direction and guidance to young children in the exercise of their rights, and provide an environment of reliable and affectionate relationships based on respect and understanding (Art. 5)' (para. 29). Although the CRC adopts neither the term 'generativity' nor 'persons who raise', its concern over the deterioration of family roles in raising children may overlap with the one maintained in previous section. Out of this concern, the professional caregivers are marked out by the CRC as the substantive educators of primary caregivers.

Signaling the significance of professional caregivers in support of primary caregivers, paragraph 29 (b) of the GC7 recommends as follows:

> (b) In planning for early childhood, States parties should at all times aim to provide programmes that complement the parents' role and are developed as far as possible in partnership with parents, including through active cooperation between parents, professionals and others in developing 'the child's personality, talents and mental and physical abilities to their fullest potential'. (Art. 29.1 (a))

Furthermore, the CRC deliberately stipulates, in paragraph 23, some quality standards to which the institutions, services and facilities responsible for early childhood should conform. These standards include working conditions as safeguards for professional caregivers, and the CRC confirms that States parties 'must ensure' (para. 23) their observance, regardless of whether those facilities run privately or publicly (para. 32), as discussed in the following section.

Encouraging Public–Private Partnership in Support of States Parties

Regarding legal obligations of States parties in the context of service provision, the CRC has firmly upheld its fundamental principle that the State is the primary duty-bearer even in the case of service delivery by private providers.[52] As pointed out clearly by Professor Paul Hunt, Rapporteur of the UN Committee on Economic, Social and Cultural Rights, in his keynote speech in the opening

52 See DGD 2002, para. 653, sub-paras. 1, 15.

session of the DGD 2002 on 'The Private Sector as Service Provider and Its Role in Implementing Child Rights',[53] 'while a state may privatize health or other services, it cannot privatize its international human rights obligations'.[54] The GC7 also adheres to this principle in paragraph 32 entitled 'the private sector as service provider'. And the DGD 2002 recommendations further confirm this principle in any process of decentralization as well as of privatization.[55] The GC7 also refers to the same point as follows: 'where services are decentralized, this should not be to the disadvantage of young children' (para. 38).

Besides, it is worth noting that the CRC explicitly requires States parties' uncompromised implementation of their obligations under market globalization; the CRC demands it even in the middle of economic or fiscal reform initiated at the national level or by international financial institutions, such as the IMF and the World Bank.[56] Based on the States parties' obligation to devote the maximum amount of available resources to the realization of economic, social and cultural rights of the child (Art. 4), the CRC recommends in the DGD 2002 recommendations that:[57]

> States parties undertake assessments of the potential impact of global trade policies concerning the liberalization of trade in services on the enjoyment of human rights, including children's rights. In particular, the [CRC] recommends that these assessments should be undertaken prior to making commitments to liberalize services within the context of WTO or regional trade agreements. Further, if commitments to liberalize trade in services are made, the effects of those commitments should be monitored on the enjoyment of the rights of children and the results of monitoring should be included in States parties reports to the Committee.

Although the CRC acknowledges that non-State actors (including the private business sector) have responsibilities to respect and ensure children's rights,[58] this does not absolve States parties from 'the paradigm of ultimate State responsibility'.[59] It is States parties that have to make sure that private sector provision of services is consistent with the UNCRC obligations as well as national laws enacted for its implementation at all stages of services provision: 'the process by which the

53 In the context of DGD 2002, the private sector encompasses businesses, non-governmental organizations and other private associations, both for-profit and non-profit (DGD 2002, para. 632, note 1).

54 Hunt, 20 September 2002, para. 14.

55 DGD 2002, para. 653, sub-para. 15.

56 DGD 2002, para. 653, sub-paras. 13, 21.

57 DGD 2002, para. 653, sub-para. 13.

58 DGD 2002, para. 653, sub-paras. 6, 16; GC7, para. 32.

59 Hunt, 20 September 2002, para. 26.

policy [of services provision] is formulated; the content or substance of the policy; and the policy's monitoring and accountability arrangements'.[60]

To this end, the CRC recommends that States parties 'establish a permanent monitoring mechanism aimed at ensuring that non-State service providers respect the relevant principles and provisions of the Convention, especially Article 4 [States parties' obligation to undertake all appropriate measures in implementing the UNCRC]' and the four general principles.[61] In evaluating the service provisions by non-State providers, the CRC gives States parties the clear criteria as follows: availability, accessibility,[62] acceptability, quality, overall compliance with the UNCRC and condition funding on the compliance.[63] Additionally, the GC7 emphasizes non-discriminatory access to services, especially for the most vulnerable groups of young children, such as those living in poverty, with disabilities, from migrant families, and of alcohol- or drug-addicted parents (para. 24).

Together with the above top-down approach, the CRC encourages the bottom-up approach; it recommends self-regulation mechanism to non-State service providers, while exemplifying the detailed criteria to be included, such as indicators/benchmarks for measuring progress and establishing accountability.[64] It further encourages non-State service providers – *inter alia*, for-profit service providers – as well as the media, 'to engage in a continuing process of dialogue and consultation with the communities they serve' and to 'create alliances and partnerships with different stakeholders and beneficiaries' in order to enhance transparency by including grass-roots community groups in the processes of decision-making and service provision where appropriate.[65] For the purpose of financing services and infrastructure on behalf of early childhood, the GC7 also encourages States parties 'to develop strong and equitable partnerships between the Government, public services, non-governmental organizations, the private sector and families' (para. 38).

Therefore, by encouraging public–private partnership in support of States parties, it seems that the CRC, on the one hand, helps expand the States parties' reach into realms that were traditionally considered private, and, on the other

60 Hunt, 20 September 2002, para. 22.

61 DGD 2002, para. 653, sub-para. 8. Regarding the importance of a system of accountability in operating rights and obligations by service providers, see Hunt, 20 September 2002, para. 19.

62 'The CRC defines accessibility in the same manner as the Committee on Economic, Social and Cultural Rights in its General Comments 14, meaning non-discrimination, physical accessibility, economic accessibility and information accessibility' [DGD 2002, Note to para. 653, sub-para. 8].

63 DGD 2002, para. 653, sub-para. 8.

64 DGD 2002, para. 653, sub-para. 17.

65 DGD 2002, para. 653, sub-para. 18.

hand, helps commit for-profit providers to traditionally public goals such as accountability and equality.[66]

Striving for Young Children's Best Interests in Day-Care Privatization in Japan

With the ongoing privatization of public day-care centers, parents and veteran nurses have shared a deep concern for the decline in the quality of childcare services. The following sections examine the actual examples of opposition campaigns and administrative litigation cases in Japan's day-care privatization. These two examples of the UNCRC's domestic implementation may help clarify the validity of the CRC's re-strengthening approaches in the context of securing 'the best interests of the child', especially in the following two points: To what extent the stakeholders have valued the close relationships with strong emotional attachments between young children and professional caregivers in day-care services; and to what extent the stakeholders have facilitated the public-private partnerships to ensure the above-mentioned relationships in the process of day-care privatization.

Example One: An Opposition Campaign in Nerima Ward, Tokyo

Hikariga-oka No. 8 Public Day-Care Center in Tokyo's Nerima ward shows a typical example of the confusion that has occurred in regional government concerning privatizing day-care facilities. Operation of this Center was transferred from direct ward management to a for-profit corporation (a childcare-goods manufacturer Pigeon Corporation) in December 2005. In the summer of 2004, the ward suddenly announced that it planned to privatize operations beginning from April 2005, but was forced to delay implementation by half a year (September 2005) in the face of heavy parental opposition.

As part of the opposition campaign, the parents, guardians, nurses and other ward residents invited Professor Lothar Krappmann, a member of the CRC, for a visit in October 2005. They succeeded at informing Mr. and Mrs. Krappmann of the 'best practice of high quality'[67] of care that publicly run ward day-care centers have provided on the basis of accumulated experience and knowledge of professional day-care staff. Presumably based on the GC7 and the DGD 2002,[68]

66 Jody Freeman deals with the similar issues, arguing that privatization can be a means of 'publication', and it might extend public law norms – such as accountability, due process, equality and rationality – to private actors through vehicles such as budgeting, regulation, and contract. See Freeman 2003.

67 Discussion Forum with the CRC Member Mr. Krappman [Translation of Japanese appellation of the committee as an editor] (Discussion Forum 2006), 29.

68 GC7, para. 38 and DGD 2002, para. 653, sub-para. 15.

Mr. and Mrs. Krappmann remarked in the lecture meeting that where day-care services are decentralized, the local government has the burden of proof that any change of day-care policies does not put young children at a disadvantage.[69] Therefore, they expressed deep concern about the unwillingness of Nerima ward to 'engage in a continuing process of dialogue and consultation' (GC7, para. 18) with the parents, guardians, nurses and residents, while praising the grass-roots partnerships among privatization-opponents as a glimpse of 'strong civil society'.[70] To end the stalemate with Nerima ward, Mr. Krappmann suggested the parents and other opponents submit a counter-report to the CRC, by the time the CRC reviews the third periodic report from the Japanese government (submitted in April 2008).

On the other hand, unable to complete preparations for privatization due to a sudden transfer in the middle of the year, eight of 26 nurses hired by Pigeon quit between December 2005 and March 2006, citing 'health reasons' (another six quit by the end of May, for a total of 14). In March 2006, the ward admonished Pigeon to improve the situation, but at the same time signed a one-year outsourcing contract with the company dated 1 April 2006. Ward residents demanded that the contract be canceled and submitted an audit request to freeze 222 million yen (about US$2.22 million) of outsourcing payments, but the ward audit committee dismissed the request in May 2006, finding 'no contract illegalities and insufficient grounds for the complain'. The committee ruled that the residents' claim of 'no improvement in sight' was groundless since Pigeon was striving to resolve the ward's original admonishment and nurses who had quit were being replaced. However, it made no reference to the quality of care.[71]

Even under such confrontational circumstances, new signs are emerging that the grassroots partnerships among parents, guardians and nurses are beginning to oversee the responsibilities of public authorities and to facilitate continuing processes of dialogue and consultation, among the national and regional governments, NPOs, private service-providers and families, in Japan's day-care privatization.

In the Nerima ward case, the parents and guardians have been making steady efforts in introducing the systems of third-party evaluation that are to be applied to some welfare-services under the control of the Tokyo Metropolitan Government. The evaluation has been carried out twice, before (in 2005) and after (in 2006) the private consignment of Hikariga-oka No. 8 Day-Care Center.[72] Therefore, it can be said that the campaign members succeeded in following up and supervising the quality of day-care even after the privatization of their center.

Furthermore, the Nerima ward's campaign members linked arms with those of other opposition campaigns throughout the country, and established *Houn-*

69 Discussion Forum 2006, 34.

70 Discussion Forum 2006, 12.

71 *Tokyo Yomiuri Shinbun*, 31 May 2006; *Tokyo Yomiuri Shinbun*, 15 June 2006.

72 *Houn-Net* 2007.

Netto (The Network of Parents Thinking about Privatization of Public Nurseries)[73] in March 2007, for exchanging diverse information and knowledge on Japan's day-care privatization and building mutually supportive relationships among the members of the Network.

In addition, it is particularly worth noting that such grassroots groups have become to have an appreciable effect on the decision-making of the local governments in the ongoing changeover of public day-care centers to private consignment.

A good example can be found in the case of *Hoikuen wo kangaeru oya no kai* (Parents Concerned with Day-Care Centers), a network formed by day-care center users, represented by freelance writer Aki Fukouin. Based on her own children's experiences of day-care centers and the results of numerous questionnaires by the users' network, Fukouin has spoken for the majority of parents and guardians facing the privatization of public day-care centers as follows: 'What parents really want is for day-care centers to not bring instability into their lives. However, considering social conditions, one option is to work with private operators with a clearer vision for childcare provision. The bottom line is in the method. Parents want to be deeply involved, from selection of provider to transfer procedures, to ensure that day-care quality is not worsened'.[74]

Striving to be an information resource for parents, day-care staff and administrative officials, the group has published on its website the following '10 Minimum Rules for Private Outsourcing or Privatization':[75]

1. Ensure that necessary 'quality' is achieved;
2. Redirect cost savings into care;
3. Disclose planning at an early stage, and hold information sessions that can calm users, and listen to their opinions;
4. Remember that excessive labor reductions lead to reduction in quality;
5. Ensure that the outsourcing provider is sensibly selected;
6. Strive to minimize the impact on children and parents;
7. Clearly define lines of responsibility;
8. Retain the public nature of day-care centers;
9. Verify the role fulfilled by directly managed centers and keep a long-term outlook in investigating the impact of sudden changes; and
10. Disclose post-handover information and promote equal relations with users.

Then, Fukouin herself has brought into practice these 10 Rules as a committee member for the privatization of Hashimoto day-care center in Sagamihara-City

73 See http://www.houn-net.org/.

74 Kosaka, 31 May 2006.

75 *'Minkan itaku, mineika ni motomerareru saitei joken 10-ka-jo'*, http://www.eqg.org/oyanokai/opinion_10kajo.html.

(Kanagawa, Japan); the City explicitly prioritized 'the best interests of the child' in the process of privatization, facilitated partnerships with different stakeholders in the process of decision-making for enhancing transparency and accountability, scheduled more than three years for the privatization program.[76]

Example Two: Administrative Lawsuits of Yokohama City and Daito City

Yokohama City Case In May 2006, in response to a claim filed by 67 parents and guardians of children attending four city-owned day-care centers privatized in April 2004, the Yokohama District Court announced its ruling that privatization 'affected development of attending children' and demanding reversal of privatization and damages of 200,000 yen (about US$2,000) per person.[77] According to plaintiff attorneys, the court ruling that ending public day-care centers by shifting to privatization is illegal was the very first case nationwide.[78]

In relation to the UNCRC, the plaintiff utilized Article 3 as well as provisions of Japanese domestic laws in arguing the children's right to continue to receive day-care from the same day-care facility. On the basis of the evidence offered by several nurses, the plaintiff's argument emphasized the significance of the specific day-care quality that the professional day-care staff at the specific center can continuously provide, to children as caregivers, and to parents or guardians as educators. Although the court did not admit that Article 3 as well as domestic provisions directly supports the above-mentioned 'right', it agreed that the children themselves as well as parents or guardians have a 'legal interest', as distinguished from a 'reflex interest',[79] to choose day-care facilities and to continue to receive day-care from the same facility, based on Articles 1 and 3 of the Child Welfare Law.[80] The court further examined the necessary quality of day-care in the process

76 Shiomi et al. (2005), 43–51. Regarding the privatization plan by Sagamihara-city, see http://city.sagamihara.org/kodomo/ko-ikusei/keikaku_sonota/pdf/mineika_keikaku.pdf.

77 *Yokohama Chiho Saibansho* [Yokohama District Court] 2006; *Asahi Shinbun*, 23 May 2006; *Nihon Keizai Shinbun*, 23 May 2006; *Asahi Shinbun*, 25 May 2006; *Tokyo Yomiuri Shinbun*, 25 May 2006.

78 *Nihon Keizai Shinbun*, 22 May 2006.

79 'To bring a case under the [Japanese Administrative Case Litigation Act (ACLA)], a plaintiff must have standing to sue. … To have standing a plaintiff in an ACLA suit must have a "legal interest" as distinguished from a "reflex interest". The requirement for a legal interest comes from the ACLA itself, which requires that a plaintiff have a 'legal interest' that is injured in order to proceed'. Goodman 2003, 328.

80 Article 1 of the Child Welfare Law provides that 'all people shall strive to ensure the sound birth and growth of children, both in mind and body. The livelihood of each and every child shall equally be guaranteed and protected'. Article 3 of the said Law stipulates that 'the principles stipulated in the preceding two articles guarantee the welfare of children and shall be observed at all times in the enforcement of all laws and ordinances concerning children'. (Article 2 explicitly defines the duty of the State and local public entities for child welfare.)

of privatization, from the perspective of the importance of 'deliberate nursing provision based on a continuous, long-term perspective',[81] so as to protect the stable day-care environment.

In April 2004, Yokohama Kakinoki-dai Public Day-Care Center, attended by the five-year-old daughter of Toshiki Kanemichi, the representative for the plaintiff in the Yokohama case, was privatized. Every single nurse was replaced, and incidents of injuries, crying at night, bedwetting, and re-emergence of other infantile activities increased among the children. The confusion continued for two years. In December 2005, Kanemichi's daughter ran into a tricycle in the playground and suffered an injury to her lip requiring 20 stitches. Saying that he could 'no longer send her there because it is too dangerous', he moved her to a nearby city-run day-care center in January 2006. As Kanemichi's experience has already shown, the plaintiff argued that the December 2003 revision of City day-care center ordinance to facilitate privatization, have encroached on the children's right to continue receiving day-care from the same facilities, on the basis of the UNCRC Article 3 as well as Articles 13 (the right to pursuit happiness), 25 (the right to life), 26 (the right to education) of the Japanese Constitution and Chapter 1 (General Provisions, including the mentioned Articles 1–3) of the Child Welfare Law.

The following were the main points of contention in the court: (1) Were the procedures leading to privatization appropriate?; and (2) Did privatization negatively affect the children attending said public day-care center?

Regarding (1), like many other local governments, Yokohama's day-care center privatization was carried out by announcing privatization plans six months to one year in advance and transferring operation to private management over a three-month period. With regard to joint management for three months in which City day-care staff would work together with the new company's nurses to transfer operations for privatization, the court noted the 'confusion that occurred in Takaishi City and Daito City (Osaka) in which privatization handovers occurred over a period of three months', and found 'no grounds' to Yokohama's claim that it had based its privatization plans on those of the experiences of other cities that had privatized their day-care centers. Furthermore, while noting that 'privatization itself is not illegal', finding that 'it is clear that there were budgetary issues behind the decision to privatize' and that there were 'insufficient grounds to legitimize the need to quickly privatize when considering the potential detriment to children', the presiding judge Yoshiaki Kawamura ruled that the city's plans to privatize its day-care centers by April 2004 was an abuse and misuse of discretionary powers, and therefore illegal.

Concerning (2), while the court decision noted that privatization does not necessarily mean care quality would deteriorate, Judge Kawamura offered the opinion that 'it is easily imaginable that a complete change of nurses could trigger massive confusion', and found that there was a possibility that privatization

81 *Yokohama Chiho Saibansho* 2006, 87.

activities negatively affected the children attending said day-care center. On that basis, stating that 'children, parents and guardians have the legal interest to choose day-care facilities as well as the one to continue to receive day-care from the same facility', he ruled that the revisions to the city day-care center ordinance for the purposes of facilitating privatization contained irregularities in the explanations to citizens and the privatization procedures, since the revisions were made in December 2003 without consent from parents and guardians.

Consequently, the court ordered 100,000 yen (about US$1000) to be paid to the household of each child, for a total of 2.8 million yen (about US$28,000). However, it dismissed the residents' request to reverse day-care center privatization, finding that 'at this stage, reversal could potentially cause additional unnecessary disruption'. It also dismissed the suits filed by the parents or guardians of children who had already graduated from the day-care centers.

Mayor Hiroshi Nakada, however, responded that 'privatization is impossible if parents do not attend information sessions and then complain that explanations are insufficient and premature', revealing his view that the city did nothing wrong,[82] and appealed in June 2006.

On 29 January 2009, Tokyo High Court (the court of second instance) overruled the original decision,[83] and the parents (plaintiffs of the original instance) appealed against this ruling to the Supreme Court on 9 February 2009.[84]

Daito City Case Despite this overturning of the lower court decision, the parents of Yokohama still have some possibility to win the case at the Supreme Court. The reason for this is that in a similar lawsuit relating to the closing and privatization of a public day-care center in Daito City of Osaka Prefecture, the first petty bench of the Supreme Court dismissed in November 2006 the appeal of said City and upheld the ruling of the court of second instance (The Osaka High Court) that ordered consolation money be paid to the parents. Incidentally, some of the parents sought for the City's decision to close said day-care center to be invalidated, but their demand was denied as had been done in the court of second instance.[85]

In November 2001, Daito City decided to privatize the City's public day-care centers due to budgetary difficulties. The Kamisanga Day-Care Center was also privatized in April 2003, and run by a social welfare corporation after three months of joint operation for work-transfer. In November 2002, the parents and guardians of children attending said Day-Care Center filed suit in the Osaka District Court, claiming that 'the City's explanation was insufficient'. The Osaka District Court

82 *Tokyo Yomiuri Shinbun*, 1 June 2006.

83 *Asahi Shinbun*, 30 January 2009; *Mainichi Shinbun*, 30 January 2009. The contents of this judgment are not released yet as of February 2009.

84 *Asahi Shinbun*, 10 February 2009.

85 *Osaka Yomiuri Shinbun*, 17 November 2007; *Sankei Shinbun*, 18 November 2007.

originally denied and dismissed the claim that was then appealed to the Osaka High Court.

In these lawsuits filed in Daito City, the parents did not refer to the UNCRC. However, in the appeals court,[86] the presiding Judge Youichiro Yamato confirmed such facts admitted in the original ruling as 'based on the day-care usage contract entered into between the appellants (parents) and the appellee (Daito City), children supervised by the appellee had the right to be nursed at said facility until they reached the age to enter school, so long as the facility existed'; 'while human environment has substantial influence on the growth of children, and trust between nurses, children and parents is very important in nursing children, it was deemed difficult to build such trust if just a few nurses participated in the work-transfer program that lasted for three months'; and nurses themselves expressed concerns that 'if nurses who had worked at the facility left due to hasty privatization, no matter how much work-transfer was practiced, nursing continuity, including safety of the children, could not be ensured'.

In view of these facts and the intent of the day-care usage contract, it was acknowledged by the appeals court that the appellee, in executing 'the decision to close and privatize said Day-Care Center involving, among other things, the replacement of the entire day-care staff, and having tremendous affects on the rights of children and appellants' had due fiduciary obligations (associated with a contract finalized under the public law), to give 'specific and sufficient considerations based on the exchanges of old and new nurses', which encompassed setting aside at least a year or so of work-transfer period and keeping the children concerned from becoming mentally unstable at the new privatized day-care facility; and alleviating 'to the extent practicable concerns and anxieties of the appellants'. With the foregoing taken into account, the court ruled that the actual work-transfer implemented by the defendant lacked sufficient consideration, was in breach of the above obligations, and should be held liable to pay compensation to the appellants due to default. Consequently, the original decision of the Osaka District Court was overruled and an order issued to pay 51 appellants (31 households) 330,000 yen (about US$3,300) per household (10.23 million yen in total; about US$102,300) of consolation money.

Overall Evaluation: The Acknowledged Importance of Close and Continuous Relationships in Day-Care Services

These two examples regarding the privatization of Japanese public day-care centers indicate that parents, guardians, and day-care staff as public employees generally recognize the paramount importance of close and continuous relationships in day-care services between young children and professional caregivers; thus, these

86 *Osaka Koto Saibansho* [Osaka High Court] 2006.

stakeholders will be able to form a united front against the mounting dominance of market rules govern childcare services provision.

Japanese courts also have regarded, as the quintessential factor in childcare services provided by the day-care centers, the close relationships between young children and professional caregivers in the stable day-care environment; the courts have recognized generally the paramount importance of the mentioned relationships, indicating that young children and their parents have a 'right' or a 'legal interest' not only to choose day-care facilities, but also to continue to receive the comparable quality of day-care from the same facilities even after their consignment to private sectors.

Therefore, the two examples in this chapter would enable us to gain a clearer understanding of what is critical in interpreting 'the best interests' for, at least, the confined group of young children in day-care facilities; that is, the close and continuous relationships between young children and professional caregivers are to be considered a primary standard or concern among other elements of interpretation. And in order to realize the mentioned relationships, it would be also indispensable for young children's parents and day-care staff to engage in mutual cooperation for child-rearing based on the relations of trust.

As Philip Alston points out, the UNCRC (and also the CRC) should not seek 'to provide any definitive statement of how an individual child's interests would best be served in a given situation', as 'any such pretension would obviously be misplaced'.[87] However, the above-mentioned standard or concern for the relationships between young children and day-care staff can be a '[signpost] capable of guiding those seeking to identify what is in the best interests of the child, and excludes from the equation, by implication, various other elements';[88] this means that the mentioned standard or concern may serve to confine the pool of possible interpretations of the best interest principle, at all stages of the private sector provision of day-care services.

The CRC's Contribution to Ensuring Effective Implementation of Young Children's Best Interests

This chapter started out with the question of how the optimal implementation of young children's rights should be secured in privatization of welfare services as traditional State functions. Two examples of Japan's day-care privatization show that, as long as the public–private partnerships among stakeholders are possible and can ensure close and continuous relationships in day-care services between young children and professional caregivers, the commodification of childcare (specifically, in the context of privatization of traditional State functions, nursery

87 Alston 1994, 19.

88 Alston 1994, 19.

labor performed for compensation by private, for-profit providers) would be acceptable and feasible without incurring destructive consequences.

Now, how has the CRC, through the two documents of GC7 and DGD 2002 recommendations, contributed to ensuring the public–private partnerships among stakeholders for securing the above-mentioned close and continuous relationships in the privatization of day-care services?

First, the CRC has complemented the original design of implementation by assisting parents and State parties in fulfilling their UNCRC obligations. This complementation has been envisaged by signaling the significance of professional caregivers in support of parents, and by encouraging public–private partnerships among all stakeholders in providing day-care services.

Second, the CRC has implicitly helped clarify the interpretation of primary rule Article 3 (the best interests of the child), regarding, at least, the best interests of young children in general. The CRC's documents examined in this chapter recognized explicitly that the foundation for exercising young children's rights resides in close relationships with strong emotional attachments between young children and their caregivers (both professional and primary). Due to such clarification, it has become possible, at all stages of the private sector provision of day-care services, to reduce the well-known indeterminacy of the concept of 'best interests' by giving greater weight to the securing of the above-mentioned relationships than to other considerations.

In securing and facilitating the public–private partnerships, indispensable are the understanding and cooperation on equal footing from responsible public authorities as well as for-profit providers of day-care services. The aforementioned two examples, however, show that the traditional motivation, behavior and practices of for-profit providers tend to thrive even in the provision of human services; mainly as a result of political reform pressures, public agencies themselves seem to go along with management systems of private providers in reducing costs and improving efficiency.

As Mary Sanger asserts, it is the responsibility and capacity of public agencies 'to select competent and responsible providers, to manage them and ensure accountability, and to design contract systems to reward them without creating perverse incentives or distortions in their disposition to serve the public interest'.[89] As a State party of the UNCRC, the Japanese government cannot privatize its international human rights obligations; it is the government that must ensure that the privatized day-care services in Japan be consistent with the UNCRC obligations, and especially with 'the best interests of the child'.

89 Sanger 2003, ix.

References

Books, Articles and Chapters in Books

Alen, A. et al. (eds) (2007), *A Commentary on the United Nations Convention on the Rights of the Child* (Leiden: Martinus Nijhoff Publishers).

Alston, P. (1994), 'The Best Interests Principle: Towards a Reconciliation of Culture and Human Rights', International Journal of Law and the Family 8, 1–25.

Detrick, S. (1999), A Commentary on the United Nations Convention on the Rights of the Child (The Hague: Martinus Nijhoff Publishers).

Discussion Forum (ed.) (2006), *Kokuren 'kodomo no kenri iinkai'iin Krappman-san to kataru kai jikko iinkai* [Discussion Forum with the CRC Member Mr. Krappman] (ed.), *Kodomo no kenri joyaku kara hoiku no minkan itaku wo kangaeru* [Considering Private Consignment of Day-Care from the Perspective of the UNCRC], (Tokyo: Tokyo Jichi Mondai Kenkyusho).

Freeman, J. (2003), 'Symposium: Public Values in an Era of Privatization: Extending Public Law Norms through Privatization', Harvard Law Review 116, 1285–1352.

Freeman, M. (2007), 'Article 3. The Best Interests of the Child', in Alen (eds).

Freymond, N. and Cameron, G. (2006), Towards Positive Systems of Child and Family Welfare: International Comparisons of Child Protection, Family Service, and Community Caring System (Toronto: University of Toronto Press).

Goodman, C. (2003), *The Rule of Law in Japan: A Comparative Analysis* (New York: Kluwer Law International).

Kandel, R. and Griffiths, A. (2003), 'Reconfiguring Personhood: From Ungovernability to Parent Adolescent Autonomy Conflict Actions', Syracuse Law Review 53, 995–1065.

Kasza, G. (2006), *One World of Welfare: Japan in Comparative Perspective* (Ithaca: Cornell University Press).

Kujiraoka, T. (2002), *'Sodaterareru mono' kara 'sodateru mono' he* [From 'Persons to be Raised' to 'Persons Who Raise'], (Tokyo: NHK books).

McAdams, D. and De St. Aubin, E. (eds) (1998), *Generativity and Adult Development* (Washington: American Psychological Association).

Ninomiya, A. (2008), *'Shin taiki jido zero sakusen to hoiku seido kaikaku no gen dankai'* [Operation zero children on the waiting list for admission into day-care centers and the current status of the day-care system reform], in *Hoiku Hakusho* 2008: 110–113.

Ota, I. (2001), *'Kodomo no jinken'* [Children's Human Rights], in *Nihon kokusaiho gakkai* [The Japan Society of International Law] (ed.), *Nihon to kokusaiho no hyakunen*: vol. 4, *jinken* [Japan and International Law Over the Last Hundred Years: vol. 4, Human Rights] (Tokyo: Sanseido).

Parker, S. (1994), 'The Best Interests of the Child – Principles and Problems', International Journal of Law and the Family 8, 26–41.

Sanger, M. (2003), *The Welfare Market Place: Privatization and Welfare Reform* (Washington: Brookings Institution Press).

Scott, E. and Scott, R. (1995), 'Parents as Fiduciaries' (1995), *Virginia Law Review* 81, 2401–2476.

Shiomi, T. et al. (2005), *Hoikuen no mineika wo kangaeru* [Considering the Privatization of Day-Care Centers], Iwanami Booklet No. 651 (Tokyo: Iwanami Shoten).

Steiner, H. and Alston, P. (1996), *International Human Rights in Context* (Oxford: Oxford University Press).

Woodhouse, B. (1992), '"Who Owns the Child?": Meyer and Pierce and the Child as Property', *William and Mary Law Review* 33, 995–1122.

Woodhouse, B. (2004), 'Reframing the Debate about the Socialization of Children: An Environmentalist Paradigm', *The University of Chicago Legal Forum* 2004, 85–166.

Official Documents and Others

Asahi Shinbun [Asahi Newspaper] (23 May 2006), *'Hoikuen mineika "Isogi sugi", Yokohama Chi-sai, Shi ni baisho meirei'* [Yokohama District Court Rules Day-Care Center Privatization 'Too Fast', Orders City to Pay Damages], Morning edition <http://telecom21.nikkei.co.jp/nt21/service/>.

Asahi Shinbun (25 May 2006), *'Gyosei, fubo to mukiatte, Yokohama-shi no hoikusho mineika ni "Iho" hanketsu'* [Government Needs to Face Parents, Yokohama City Day-Care Privatization Plan Ruled 'Illegal'], Morning edition <http://telecom21.nikkei.co.jp/nt21/service/>.

Asahi Shinbun (11 October 2006), *'Hoikuen no mineika, torikeshi motomeru, Kawasaki, hogoshara ga teiso'* [Parents and Guardians Sue Kawasaki City to Demand Reversal of Day-Care Center Privatization], Morning edition <http://telecom21.nikkei.co.jp/nt21/service/>.

Asahi Shinbun (30 January 2009), *'Hogosha-gawa, nishin wa haiso, Yokohama-shi no hoikusho mineika meguru sosho'* [Parents Lost in Appeal Trial, Yokohama City Day-Care Center Privatization Case], Morning edition <http://telecom21.nikkei.co.jp/nt21/service/>.

Asahi Shinbun (9 February 2009), *'Jumin-gawa ga jokoku, hoikuen mineika sosho'* [Parents Appeal to Supreme Court in Yokohama Day-Care Center Privatization Case], Morning edition <http://telecom21.nikkei.co.jp/nt21/service/>.

CRC (2005), Committee on the Rights of the Child, *Provisional Rules of Procedure* (Adopted by the Committee at its first session, 1991, and revised by the Committee at its 33rd session, 2005), UN Doc. CRC/C/4/Rev.1.

DGD 2002, Committee on the Rights of the Child, *Day of General Discussion: The Private Sector as Service Provider and Its Role in Implementing Child Rights* (Held at the Palais Wilson, Geneva, on 20 September 2002), 31st session, UN Doc. CRC/C/121, 145–158, paras. 630–653.

DGD 2004, Committee on the Rights of the Child, *Day of General Discussion: Implementing Child Rights in Early Childhood* (Held at the Palais Wilson, Geneva, on 17 September 2004), 37th session, UN Doc. CRC/C/143, 108–116, paras. 532–563.

GC7, Committee on the Rights of the Child, *General Comment No.7 (2005), Implementing Child Rights in Early Childhood*, 40th session, UN Doc. CRC/C/GC/7/Rev.1.

Hoiku Hakusho (2008), [White Paper on Childcare 2008], *Zenkoku Hoiku Dantai Renrakukai & Hoiku Kenkyusho* (eds) (Tokyo: Hitonaru Shobo).

Houn-Net (2007), *'Hoikuen no daisansha hyoka'* [The Third-party Evaluation for Day-Care Centers] (updated 11 May 2007) <http://www.houn-net.org/modules/tinyd0/index.php?id=2>.

Hunt, P. (20 September 2002), 'The International Human Rights Treaty Obligations of States Parties in the Context of Service Provision' [Text of the presentation given by Professor Hunt in the opening session of the General Day of Discussion, 20 September 2002, Office of the High Commissioner for Human Rights, Palais Wilson, Geneva] <http://www.crin.org/docs/resources/treaties/crc.31/Paul_Hunt-Legal-Obligations.doc>.

ILO (2006), *Global Employment Trends Brief January 2006* (Released 24 January 2006) <http://www.ilo.org/public/english/employment/strat/download/getb06en.pdf>.

ILO (2009), *Global Employment Trends January 2009* (Geneva: International Labour Office) <http://www.ilo.org/global/What_we_do/Publications/lang--en/docName--WCMS_101461/index.htm>.

ILO (28 January 2009), 'Unemployment, working poor and vulnerable employment to increase dramatically due to global economic crisis', [Press release, ILO/09/2], *ILO* <http://www.ilo.org/global/About_the_ILO/Media_and_public_information/Press_releases/lang--en/index.htm>.

Inata, Y. (6 July 2007), 'Reality Check: Japan's Working Poor Become Entrenched', *The Main Wire* <http://www.lexis.com>.

Japan Economic Newswire (25 January 2006), 'Youth make up 50% of world's unemployed, ILO report says' <http://www.lexis.com>.

Kakuchi, S. (19 October 2006), 'Japan: Number of Working Poor Balloons as Income Gap Grows', *Inter Press Service/Global Information Network* <http://www.lexis.com>.

Kosaka, K. (31 May 2006), *'Susumu hoikuen mineika, oya mo ko mo fuan, shitsu no kakuho kadai'* [Day-Care Center Privatization Continuing, Parents and Children Worry about Maintaining Quality], *Tokyo Yomiuri Shinbun* [Tokyo Yomiuri Newspaper], Morning edition <http://telecom21.nikkei.co.jp/nt21/service/>.

Maeda, M. (8 August 2005), 'Working Women Deserve Support in Child Rearing', *Nikkei Weekly* <http://www.nni.nikkei.co.jp/AC/TNW/Search/Nni20050808OP5CC555.htm>.

Mainichi Shinbun [Mainichi Newspaper] (30 January 2009), *'Yokohama-shi hoikuen mineika sosho: jumin ga gyakuten haiso, Tokyo Ko-sai'* [Yokohama-City Day-Care Center Privatization Case: Parents Overruled the Original Decision by Tokyo High Court], Morning edition <http://telecom21.nikkei.co.jp/nt21/service/>.

Nihon Keizai Shinbun [Nihon Keizai Newspaper] (7 August 2004), *'Wakate shain no hansu, ima no hatarakikata dato byoki ni, Rodo Chosa Kyo'* [Half of Young Employees Worry about 'Getting Sick If Continuing to Work Like This', Labour Research Council], Web edition <http://www.nikkei.co.jp/news/main/20040807AT1G2803907082004.html>.

Nihon Keizai Shinbun (22 May 2006), *'Hoikuen mineika, Yokohama-shi ni baisho meirei, Chi-sai "Sairyo-ken wo ranyo"'* [Court Orders Yokohama City to Pay Damages in Day-Care Center Privatization Case – 'Abuse of Discretionary Power'], Web edition <http://www.nikkei.co.jp/news/main/20060522AT1G2203P22052006.html>.

Nihon Keizai Shinbun (23 May 2006), *'Hoikuen no mineika iho, Chi-sai hanketsu, Yokohama-shi ni baisho meirei, "Isogu beki riyu nashi"'* [Day-Care Center Privatization Ruled Illegal, District Court Orders Yokohama City to Pay Damages 'No Reason to Hurry Privatization'], Morning edition <http://telecom21.nikkei.co.jp/nt21/service/>.

Nihon Keizai Shinbun (7 June 2006), *'Hoikuen no mineika, nanchakuriku he mosaku tsuzuku'* [Continuing Plans for a Day-Care Privatization Soft-landing], Evening edition <http://telecom21.nikkei.co.jp/nt21/service/>.

Osaka Koto Saibansho [Osaka High Court] (2006), Case No. Heisei-17-Gyo-Ko-13 et al., 20 April 2006 <http://www.courts.go.jp/hanrei/pdf/20061023154241.pdf>.

Osaka Yomiuri Shinbun [Osaka Yomiuri Newspaper] (27 July 2006), *'Takamatsu-shi, hoikuen mineika wo ichi-nen enki, hogosha hantai, Yokohama hanketsu eikyo mo'* [Takamatsu City: Day-Care Center Privatization Plans Delayed One Year, Objections by Parents and Guardians, Yokohama Court Decision Also Had an Effect], Morning edition <http://telecom21.nikkei.co.jp/nt21/service/>.

Osaka Yomiuri Shinbun (17 November 2007), *'Hoikusho haishi de baisho meirei, Saiko-sai jokoku kikyaku, Daito-shi, hogosha ni 1,000 man-en'* [Supreme Court Dismisses Final Appeal on Closing of Day-Care Center, Daito City Ordered to Pay Damages 10 million yen to Parents], Morning edition <http://telecom21.nikkei.co.jp/nt21/service/>.

Sankei Shinbun [Sankei Newspaper] (18 November 2007), *'Daito no hoikuen haishi sosho, Saiko-sai, Shi no sekinin mitomeru'* [Supreme Court Admits Daito City's Responsibilities in Day-Care Center Closing Case], Morning edition <http://telecom21.nikkei.co.jp/nt21/service/>.

Tokyo Yomiuri Shinbun [Tokyo Yomiuri Newspaper] (25 May 2006), *'Hoikuen mineika de Yokohama-shi ni baisho meirei, sessoku gyosei no ihosei nintei'* [Yokohama City Ordered to Pay Damages in Day-Care Center Privatization

Case, Quick and Sloppy Administration Deemed Illegal], Commentary, Morning edition <http://telecom21.nikkei.co.jp/nt21/service/>.

Tokyo Yomiuri Shinbun (31 May 2006), *'Tokyo, Nerima no hoikuen, ku kansa iin, itaku chushi seikyu wo kikyaku'* [Tokyo Nerima Ward Audit Committee Dismisses Request to Halt Day-Care Center Outsourcing], Morning edition <http://telecom21.nikkei.co.jp/nt21/service/>.

Tokyo Yomiuri Shinbun (1 June 2006), *'Shiritsu hoikuen mineika sosho, Yokohama shigikai ga "Koso" kaketsu'* [Yokohama City Council Votes to Appeal City Day-Care Center Privatization Case], Morning edition. <http://telecom21.nikkei.co.jp/nt21/service/>.

Tokyo Yomiuri Shinbun (15 June 2006), *'Kisarazu-shi, yon-hoikuen mineika wo enki, Hogosha kara hantai iken ooku'* [Kisarazu City: Privatization of Four Day-Care Centers Delayed – Many Opposing Viewpoints from Parents and Guardians], Morning edition <http://telecom21.nikkei.co.jp/nt21/service/>.

Yokohama Chiho Saibansho [Yokohama District Court] (2006), Case No. Heisei-16-Gyo-U-4, 22 May 2006 <http://www.courts.go.jp/hanrei/pdf/20060525130611.pdf>.

Concluding Remarks

Karel Wellens

The main purpose of our research project was to analyze the structures of the complex processes of implementation of rules protecting public interests of the international community and to identify the factors that are concerned with the diversification of those processes. It also attempted to grasp the character of those diversified processes by analyzing the functioning of such processes in particular cases and areas of international law.

Relevant questions were approached from a constitutional perspective in Chapters 1 and 3, whereas a more functional approach was called for when an analysis had to be made of the diversity and complexity of institutionalized processes (Part II), of the challenge of coordination of legal regimes (Part III) and of the diversification of actors taking part in the process (Part IV).

The duality of perspectives appears to have been fortuitous.

Two categories of factors have an impact on the effectiveness of the implementation process. There are factors internal to the institution mandated to secure the implementation of public interest rules such as the available resources, both domestic and international, governmental and non-governmental, and the methods used (*de facto* or *de jure*, soft or hard approach).

External factors are reflected in intentional or capacity-based non-compliance.

The preceding chapters have identified impediments and obstacles that have hindered implementation of public interest rules. They have also shown how various actors and regimes have found mechanisms to enhance the effectiveness of the process.

Time has come now to make a modest attempt to formulate some tentative concluding remarks based upon the wealth of information and analysis in the preceding chapters of this book.

The Instrumental Role of Interpretation in the Process

The object and purpose of the primary public interest rule play a decisive role in the shaping and reshaping of the process of implementation and enforcement. Hence the multiple faces of the concept of effectiveness.

Continuing opposition between groups of States Parties about the interpretation of the very object of the treaty, such as within the International Whaling

Commission, substantially undermines both the effectiveness and the legitimacy of the whole process.

An 'interpretation resulting in an escape route from the obligations defined cannot be easily reconciled' with the object and purpose of public interest rule.[1]

While object and purpose of a public interest rule *sensu lato* may change over time, it is only the interpretation of a public interest rule *sensu stricto* that may develop to better protect and enforce the values guarded by the rule in the first place.[2]

The quality and the legitimacy of the public interest rule are also important for the effectiveness of its implementation process.

The difficulties surrounding the interpretation of Article VI of the Outer Space Treaty have confirmed the great importance of precise rule-setting for the effectiveness of its implementation.

The degree of clarity of public interest rules and the margin of appreciation left to States will determine the role subsequent practice is called to play in their interpretation.

Monitoring bodies have helped to clarify the interpretation of rules that possessed a certain 'indeterminacy': the Committee on the Rights of the Child stepped in with regard to the notion 'best interests of the child' of Article 3 of the UN Convention on the Rights of the Child to assist the parties to fulfil their international obligations.

However, interpretation of public interest rules in the field of human rights or labour law by powerful non-State actors may result in a lower degree of protection than the one traditionally provided by bodies entrusted by the international community with delivering an authentic and authoritative interpretation. Professor Ago has aptly illustrated how the ILO as the monitoring body has then established a mechanism of prior consultation by concluding a Memorandum of Understanding with the International Organization for Standardization.

The Flexibility of the Process to Adapt to Changing Circumstances Reflects Its Effectiveness

Consistency in decision-making contributes to the effectiveness of the process of implementation. However, as is the case with ordinary primary rules of public international law, the implementation process of some public interest rules needs to be more frequently adapted to (ever) changing situations and conditions in order

1 The ICSID Tribunal in the *Enron Corporation and Ponderosa Assets L.P. v Argentine Republic* case, (ICSID Case No. ARB/01/3, Award of 22 May 2007, para. 331, as reproduced by Oleson 2007, 172.

2 The object and purpose of a public interest rule will inevitably also have to be taken into account when applying the principle of mutual supportiveness: Boisson de Chazournes and Moise Mbengue 2007, 829–862, at 836.

to maintain or to improve the level of effectiveness. Multilateral environmental agreements (MEAs) and rules protecting the maintenance of international peace and security clearly belong to this category.

Such adaptation may take place by way of evolutive interpretation and/or by changing the procedures of implementation.

Professor Sakai has skilfully analyzed how – through an innovative use of Chapter VII with regard to UN Peacekeeping – a rearrangement of fundamental principles took place in order to enhance both the effectiveness and the legitimacy of a mechanism mandated to ensure the compliance with the public interest rules regarding international peace and security. The trinity principles of consent, impartiality and self-defence have been adapted accordingly to secure the performance of the mandate of those operations, including the implementation of peace agreements.

The international financial standards set by the Basel Committee on Banking Supervision and aimed at governing national banking laws and regulations may be considered to be public interest rules *sensu lato*. The legally non-binding nature of the Committee's decisions carries with it the required flexibility to adapt to changing circumstances.

Restatement and elaboration of provisions by monitoring bodies through expansive interpretation may not always provide an effective response to new challenges.

Sometimes measures of a more continuous nature have to be considered. The adoption by the Security Council of Resolution 1540 in the fight against terrorism is a case in point, although the follow-up record of the resolution is not particularly impressive.

An example of an institution adapting its structures to the changing circumstances of the twenty-first century is the United Nations and its 2005 reform package analyzed by Professor Muntarbhorn: its aim was to enhance the effectiveness of the organization to monitor compliance with public interest rules.

The privatization of certain public services may require adapting the process of implementation. However, as Professor Ota has reported, the Committee on the Rights of the Child had no difficulty in emphasizing that this does not diminish the required degree of uncompromised implementation by States parties.

In both situations of expansive interpretation or of exploring new ways to adapt the process to changing circumstances, providing and maintaining legitimacy is of utmost importance given the public interest nature of the rules at stake and in order not to affect the effectiveness of the implementation process.

The Link Between Procedural and Substantive Aspects of the Process

The effectiveness of the process is also dependent on respect for the inherent link between the procedural and substantive aspects of the process.

The examples of the rearrangement of the fundamental principles with regard to peacekeeping, resulting from the innovative use of Chapter VII of the Charter, and the change of the very concept of sovereignty through the introduction of the responsibility to protect – in the process of the 2005 UN institutional reform package – illustrate once more the importance of this inherent link.

In some situations States are forced to choose between measures based on procedural legitimacy or on substantive legitimacy.[3]

In some cases procedural equity may require the participation in the decision-making process by non-members in order to enhance the legitimacy of the rules envisaged. Kern Alexander described the need for this with regard to the Basel Committee while for the same reason, prior to the adoption of resolution 1540, the Security Council provided an opportunity to non-members to express their views as noted by Professor Asada. He also made clear that sharing sensitive information with a wider membership than the Nuclear Suppliers Group may carry serious risks; procedural equity is thus not unlimited.

Lessons may be learned, however, when in the future monitoring bodies would be tempted to pay more attention to procedural over substantial intentional non-compliance, dissociating to some extent the inherent link.

The meticulous analysis by Professor Koyano of the Danube Delta Conflict has made it clear that although the subject-matter of the various procedures under the MEAs were both mainly non-fulfilment of procedural requirements and substantial conformity with the purposes of the agreements, the procedural approach was dominant; the main focus was on the procedural appropriateness of the Ukrainian project and not on its substantial legitimacy, considered to be a 'delicate' issue. Partly as a result of this more procedural approach there had been a temporary change in the Ukrainian attitude.

The Role of the Domestic Systems

The role of domestic systems in the process of implementation and enforcement of public interest rules is paramount for reasons set out by Professor Komori in Chapter 2.

The multiplicity of reasons why States are implementing public interest rules *sensu lato* is amply reflected for instance in the processes regarding the implementation of the Basel Committee's standards.

Professor Asada has demonstrated how the adoption of Security Council resolution 1540 was an alternative method for the Council to reaffirm the public interest rules contained in the Chemical Weapons Convention in the face of the poor record of adoption of domestic legislation to implement it. This may have been the result of the margin of discretion left to States Parties to choose

3 See the example of Kosovo given by Komori in Chapter 2, 67–88.

the necessary measures. On that occasion, the Security Council dealt with both intentional and capacity based non-compliance.

Flexible implementation of public interest rules *sensu lato* in the various jurisdictions has been found in the processes concerning space activities and with regard to the Annex on Liability arising from Environmental Emergencies on Antarctica.

Common but differentiated responsibilities – perhaps also in the phased implementation of public interest rules *sensu lato* – could, at least in the long term, increase the effectiveness of the whole process. Implementation by non-G10 regulators of the Basel Committee's banking and financial regulations adapted to their degree of development and the state of their economies, as suggested by Kern Alexander, could be a case in point.

On the other hand, extraterritorial application of domestic civil liability or administrative fine laws to ensure compliance by non-State operators with the public interest rule of the protection of the environment in an international public space like Antarctica may not be straightforward due to the absence of a nationality link, as Professor Shibata pointed out.

The Need to Establish Benchmarks to Asses the Performance by States

Effectiveness has many faces, as Oran Young has argued,[4] and the way it is measured varies between different public interest rules given the dominant role of the object and purpose of those rules in the process.

In Chapter 1 it was already pointed out that attempts to measure the effectiveness of processes of implementation of public interest rules are facing problems of a methodological nature.

Once the effectiveness of a particular institutionalized mechanism of implementation is being questioned, such as with regard to HR bodies, then the search for alternative routes is inevitable as the renewed attention for diplomatic protection demonstrates.

But then it is remarkable that in turn any attempt to assess the respective effectiveness of human rights protection through the established mechanisms and of diplomatic protection 'raises a series of methodological questions and insurmountable problems with regard to the comparability and representativeness of collected materials'.[5] Moreover, the 'often quiet diplomacy' *modus operandi* of diplomatic protection makes it 'impossible to answer the questions of effectiveness based on empirical data'.[6]

A two-fold conclusion seems to present itself here.

4 Referred to by Komori in Chapter 2, 73.

5 Vermeer-Kûnzli 2007, 213.

6 Vermeer-Kûnzli 2007, 213.

A thorough and painstaking analysis of one particular case, such as the Danube Delta Conflict, based on accessible and reliable information may lead to a well-reasoned assessment of the effectiveness of the process.

On the other hand, it seems clear that further research is needed to asses the relative or comparable effectiveness between various mechanisms to ensure compliance with public interest rules.

The perennial debate about the effectiveness of hard enforcement of public interest rules through the imposition of sanctions by the Security Council is a constant reminder of the difficulties lying ahead.

The object and purpose of the public interest rule provide the ultimate, decisive benchmark against which to assess the adequateness of the domestic process of implementation and enforcement, but this does not solve all the problems.

Even when a treaty considers conformity of national activities with its provisions a matter of international public interest, identification of the State responsible to regulate such activities is not always an easy exercise as both the cases of the Outer Space Treaty and of the Antarctica Liability Annex illustrate.

Pursuant to MEAs States Parties may be under an obligation to put in place a domestic framework and review mechanisms. In the Mox plant case the Tribunal made it clear that a State Party 'remains responsible to those other States for the adequacy of this framework and the conduct of its competent authorities who, in the exercise of their executive functions, engage the domestic system'.[7]

Under the Convention on the Rights of the Child, States Parties have an obligation to establish proper standards for those responsible for caring and protecting children and to ensure that for instance private operators conform to such standards. This obligation still stands, but the Committee on the Rights of the Child has stipulated quality standards for child care: in doing so it stepped in, in order to reach more uniformity in the implementation process, as Professor Ota made clear.

Benchmarks against which to assess the adequacy of the domestic process of implementation and enforcement of public interest rules are sometimes difficult to establish. This may be due to a variety of factors, such as the complexity of the activities the rules are trying to govern and, as with Antarctica's environmental liability regime, the absence of applicable national legislation to assess damage occurring. The unique features of the overall Antarctica regime made it rather unlikely to establish appropriate institutions to carry out that task, as Professor Shibata pointed out.

---

7 *Dispute concerning Access to Information Under Article 9 of the OSPAR Convention* (*Ireland v United Kingdom*), Final Award of 2 July 2003, para.144, as reproduced by Oleson 2007, 59.

The Principle of Complementarity as Traditionally Defined

In addition to what has been said about the principle of complementarity in Chapter 1, the following observations could be made.

Utilization of the principle of complementarity presents itself in various ways and modalities.

Actors involved in the implementation process may intentionally turn to the principle in order to enhance the effectiveness of a process. Indeed, as Professor Sakai has demonstrated, parties to peace agreements gave their consent on the modalities for their implementation, whereas the Security Council turned to an innovative invocation of Chapter VII to ensure the effectiveness of the mandate of the troops entrusted with overseeing and monitoring, if need be with the use of force, those peace agreements.

The principle of complementarity may also perform its role in an incremental but no less decisive way. That is what happened with diplomatic protection.

Perhaps also because the ILC was not successful in agreeing on an article providing for the enforcement of public interest rules, diplomatic protection could assume, as also shown by Professor Kato, the complementary and even remedial role, *vis à vis* the deficient functioning of mechanisms that are at a State's disposal under existing treaties, to ensure effective respect for the public interest rules protecting human rights.

With regard to the respective, complementary role of diplomatic protection and the use of Article 48 of the ILC Articles on state responsibility in the enforcement of public interest rules *sensu stricto* Kûnzli has pointed out that 'responsibility for non-serious instances of breaches of peremptory norms may be invoked through diplomatic protection but not through an appeal to Article 48, whereas breaches that do not cause injuries to individuals, even if they are indirect, can result in invocation under Article 48 but not in the exercise of diplomatic protection'.[8] And she convincingly added that both 'diplomatic protection and invocation of state responsibility erga omnes can and should be used for the protection of individuals'.[9]

The *obligation* to exercise diplomatic protection 'if the injury (to its national) results from a grave breach of a ius cogens norm' did not survive the first reading of ILC Draft Article 4 but it is clear that – when formulating the recommended practice in Article 19 to give due consideration to the possibility of exercising diplomatic protection especially when significant injury has occurred – the ILC had 'serious breaches of fundamental human rights norms, if not breaches of peremptory norms' in mind.[10]

8 Vermeer-Kûnzli 2007a, 553–582, at 556–557.

9 Vermeer-Kûnzli 2007a, 554.

10 Vermeer-Kûnzli 2007a, 563.

In exercising diplomatic protection as a response to a violation of a public interest rule sensu *stricto*, the State also ensures respect for the public interest rule of the international community at large.

Principal actors may also re-direct the route the principle of complementarity would normally take in the process of implementation of public interest rules *sensu stricto*, as Professor Furuya has skilfully shown us. Self-referral triggered by the 'diplomacy' of the Prosecutor may very well change the substance of the principle of complementarity; in those cases, it does not work anymore as a norm of adjudication for the Chambers, but as code of conduct for the Prosecutor. In the end, however, this prosecutorial strategy may in fact enhance the effectiveness of the enforcement process as the co-operation by the referring State seems guaranteed.

But there are also actions by States aimed to have a negative impact on the role envisaged for the principle of complementarity. The successive adoption of Security Council Resolutions 1422 and 1487 is a case in point.

Allegedly adopted to protect the effectiveness of peacekeeping operations, they have in fact undermined the effectiveness of the institutionalized process to enforce public interest rules *sensu stricto* of international humanitarian law.[11]

Conversely, a State may also be tempted to undermine the effectiveness of peacekeeping operations as a process to implement and enforce the public interest rule on international peace and security if it is convinced that impunity agreements to 'circumvent' the effectiveness of the ICC institutionalized process to implement other public interest rules would not be forthcoming.[12]

These agreements aim 'to protect *an individual interest of states* [my italics]: the right to exercise the criminal jurisdiction over its nationals preferably'.[13]

As Professor Furuya has pointed out, an intentional failure of a State to change its national laws to respond to ICC crimes in order to protect its state interest of exercising its own criminal jurisdiction, is tantamount to prior acceptance that the ICC would instead exercise jurisdiction over the crimes.[14]

Sometimes there is room for more than a complementary role *vis à vis* legally binding norms. Professor Ago has rightly stressed that corporate social responsibility can, in certain circumstances, supersede the level of protection covered by law.

---

11 Quesada-Alcala 2006, 295–314, at 301.

12 Quesada-Alcala 2006, 311, referring to the US threat to reject the renewal of the UN Peacekeeping Operations in Bosnia-Herzegovina.

13 Quesada-Alcala 2006, 303. It is difficult not to agree with Quesada that the 'policy of State sovereignty adopted by the US has prevailed over the protection of certain fundamental interests of the International Community that are the basis of International Humanitarian Law', Quesada-Alcala 2006, 313.

14 See also in this regard Wayde Pittman and Heaphy 2008, 165–183.

The (Emerging) Principle of Mutual Supportiveness

The principle of complementarity definitely contributes to the effectiveness of the process of implementation, but '(il) vise une neutralité active devant permettre à chacun des corps de normes … de concourir à un objectif similaire tel le développement durable mais sans qu'il n'y ait d'interpénétration juridiques entre les différents régimes'.[15]

The principle of mutual supportiveness (*soutien mutuel*) transcends the principle of complementarity as traditionally defined.[16] It is:

> [U]n principe de cohérence et de coexistence entre les instruments juridiques internationaux. En tant que principe de cohérence, il dicte une lecture harmonieuse des différents corps de règles internationales afin de garantir à chacun de ceux-ci la pleine réalisation des droits et obligations qui y sont attachés. En tant que principe de coexistence, le soutien mutuel commande une lecture intégrative des divers instruments juridiques internationaux dans l'optique de la préservation de leur intégrité et de la non modification des droits et obligations y afférents et négociées au sein de fora internationaux distincts.[17]

In contrast with the neutrality of the principle of complementarity, the principle of mutual supportiveness puts forward 'la cohérence consubstantielle' for instance of international trade relations and the protection of the environment, through a 'process' of 'accrétion et de cumul'.[18]

As a principle of interpretation, mutual supportiveness aims at a harmonious interpretation of various sets of rules.[19]

As a principle of direction, it guides the parties towards an harmonious implementation of their rights and obligations.[20]

That the principle of mutual supportiveness works both within a set of treaties such as MEAs themselves and between MEAs and the WTO,[21] and social regimes, has been aptly demonstrated by Cordonnier Segger. She has convincingly shown the importance of inserting into international agreements substantive 'interlocking provisions', by way of coordination *ex ante*.[22]

Such interlocking provisions give expression to and largely contribute to the effectiveness of the principle of systemic integration of Article 31(3)(c) of the

15 Boisson de Chazournes and Moise Mbengue 2007, 832.
16 Boisson de Chazournes and Moise Mbengue 2007, at 832.
17 Boisson de Chazournes and Moise Mbengue 2007, at 830.
18 Boisson de Chazournes and Moise Mbengue 2007, at 832–833.
19 Boisson de Chazournes and Moise Mbengue 2007, at 834.
20 Boisson de Chazournes and Moise Mbengue 2007, at 834.
21 Boisson de Chazournes and Moise Mbengue 2007, 831.
22 Boisson de Chazournes and Moise Mbengue 2007, 860.

Vienna Convention, thereby satisfying 'the need to take into account the normative environment more widely'.[23]

Professor Horiguchi has given us the example of how the principle of mutual supportiveness may be instrumental in enhancing the effectiveness of implementation He has amply analyzed the interaction between the normative principle of precaution and the principle of proportionality, where the latter mitigates excessive application of the former, and between the principle of precaution and the principle of sustainable development.

Throughout the process of implementation of various sets of public interest rules, and in order to increase their effectiveness, there is every need for States and other actors involved to carry out a 'systemic impact assessment' exercise on social, human rights, environmental and developmental aspects and issues, as proposed by both Professors Cordonnier Segger and Ota. This is not surprising as sustainable development is forming part of the object and purpose of a growing number of treaties as argued by Marie-Claire Cordonnier Segger.

The need for such an exercise is even more pressing when public interest rules *sensu stricto* are at stake. The principle of 'mutual supportiveness' may be considered inherent to the very concept of public interest rules *sensu stricto*.

The potential role of the principle of mutual supportiveness may be frustrated when states are trying to limit measures that are effective to achieve the objective of one set of public interest rules such as international environment law by invoking, using international trade rules as Professor Cordonnier Segger has analyzed, or when non-authentic and sub-standard interpretation of international labour law is given by non-State actors as indicated by Professor Ago.

Even bringing a case before a regional international court has been considered by States Parties as a method that could undermine the effectiveness of peacekeeping operations as another mechanisms aimed at enforcing public interest rules of a different nature.[24]

The Role of Non-State Actors

The effectiveness of the process of implementation by states of public interest rules may benefit from various kinds of involvement by non-State actors.

We will review briefly the role courts and tribunals, international organizations, NGOs and other private actors could play in this regard.

23 See Chapter 1, 34.

24 *Agim Behrami and Bekir Behrami against France and Ruzhdi Samarati against France, Germany and Norway* (Application no. 71412/01 and Application no. 78166/01), Decision as to the Admissibility of 2 May 2007, paras. 81, 90, 94, 101, 108, 111 and 115.

Courts and Tribunals

The role of courts and tribunals in the process of implementation has recently been poignantly been described by Judge Abraham when he wrote:' … les procédures de règlement judiciaire sont destinées à permettre aux traités ou accords en vigueur entre les parties de produire leurs pleins effets … et non d'empêcher leur mise en oeuvre'.[25] With regard to the public interest rules of international humanitarian law, Daniel Thurer rightly observed that the main factor in the improvement of compliance is the increasing role played by the courts.[26]

Professor Ota has confirmed the instrumental role of the performance by domestic courts towards effective implementation of the rights of the child.

Judicial deference by (some) international courts and tribunals contrasts sharply with the judicial activism of (some) domestic systems to exercise extraterritorial jurisdiction to ensure enforcement of public interest rules.

Judicial deference may present itself in various forms and shapes.

Judicial deference to domestic courts may be institutionalized, as Professor Furuya pointed out with regard to Article 18(2) of the ICC Statute.

Judicial deference may also result from the suspension of a pending procedure; the *Chile Swordfish* case and the WTO Burma case of *United States – Measure Affecting Government Procurement, request for Consultation by the European Communities*, both referred to by Professor Cordonnier Segger, come to mind as good examples.

From the perspective of the effectiveness of the process of implementation of public interest rules the assessment of judicial deference may vary.

Sending the Parties back to the negotiating table may ultimately result in more effective implementation, even if the referral is limited to a good faith attempt to negotiate a solution as the *US – Import Prohibition of Certain Shrimp and Shrimp Products* case has demonstrated.

However, one would prefer a court then to provide Parties with specific and concrete guidance on the direction and scope of the negotiations they have to conduct.[27]

The possibility for a State Party also to act on behalf of the collective interest of the Parties if not of the international community at large as a way to enforce the effective implementation of a public interest rule would face a serious procedural obstacle of *locus standi* as professor Shibata observed with regard to the Antarctic Environmental Liability regime.

In this regard it has to be noted that an applicant in a case before the ICJ does not disqualify itself from also acting in the interest of the international community.

---

25 *Territorial and Maritime dispute (Nicaragua v Colombia), Preliminary Objections*, Judgment of 13 December 2007, Individual Opinion of Judge Abraham, para. 8.

26 Thurer 2007, 157–164, at 161.

27 As the ICJ did in the *Gabcikovo/Nagymaros* case: Koojmans 2007, 741–754, at 749.

In the *Bosnia Genocide* case the Court saw no need to address questions about the legal interest or standing of the applicant and the significance of the norms and *erga omnes* character of the relevant obligations – questions that could be raised by alleged violations of public interest rules *sensu stricto* outside the Applicant's territory – only 'because the applicant has not established to the satisfaction of the Court any facts in support of that allegation'.[28]

In the same case the Court said that it had no jurisdiction 'to rule on alleged breaches of other obligations of public international law, not amounting to genocide', particularly of international humanitarian law', even if the alleged breaches are of obligations under peremptory norms or of obligations which protect essential humanitarian values, and which may be owed *erga omnes*.[29]

Kern Alexander's suggestion of a delegation of adjudicatory powers over violations of future binding international rules of banking regulation to an international financial authority, while the states themselves would retain the ultimate enforcement authority, may provide only a long-term perspective, but it also is a good example of the combination of formal and informal enforcement as outlined in Chapter 1.

International Organizations

Theodore Meron once wrote that 'insisting exclusively on institutional mechanisms of enforcement for the most serious breaches of international law would "deprive the erga omnes concept of much of its practical utility"'.[30]

The effectiveness of institutionalized mechanisms to ensure compliance with public interest rules – what we called *systemic enforcement* – became most questioned with regard to conventional human rights bodies; hence, as indicated earlier, the focus of attention is nowadays more on diplomatic protection and the taking of countermeasures as complementary, or rather corrective ways to remedy the structural deficiencies in the process of implementation of that particular branch of public international law.

At some time in the past, the effective performance of a public interest regime even required the devolution from one international organization to another as was the case with the Mandate system between the League of Nations and the United Nations.[31]

---

28 *Application of the Convention on the Prevention and Punishment of the Crime of Genocide (Bosnia and Herzegovina v Serbia and Montenegro)*, Judgment of 26 February 2007, paras. 185 and 368.

29 *Application of the Convention on the Prevention and Punishment of the Crime of Genocide (Bosnia and Herzegovina v Serbia and Montenegro)*, Judgment of 26 February 2007, para. 147.

30 Dawidowicz 2006, 333–418, at 343.

31 *International Status of South West Africa*, Advisory Opinion: ICJ Reports 1950, 128, at 136–138.

'Quasi-systemic enforcement' of the Basel Committee's legally non-binding international financial standard on banking supervisions takes place by the World Bank and the IMF through their conditionality and restructuring programs. Multinational forces such as SFOR and KFOR are also examples of quasi-systemic enforcement of peace agreements.

The Danube Delta Conflict involved of a multiplicity of international organizations and organs. It is not only an example of 'justificatory discourse' referred to in Chapter 1, but also of what recent doctrine has called *ex post coordination* based on 'l'établissement de passerelles institutionelles (coopération interinstitutionelle)'.[32]

Professor Koyano's case study showed us how the interaction between multiple parallel processes contributed to the effective management of the conflict.

However, the same analysis has shown that time may take its toll when there is a prolonged process of management of the conflict, resulting in a temporary decline in the joint co-operative commitment by the institutions involved.

International organizations are well aware of their important role in the effectiveness of the process of implementation of public interest rules. This explains the determination of the ILO to safeguard and preserve its position as the first authentic interpreter of international labour law *vis à vis* other emerging players in the field.

Other Non-governmental Actors

Various contributors to this research project have sufficiently explored the different *modi operandi* of other non-governmental actors – as representatives of the 'public interest' in the ordinary sense of the word – in the process of implementation of both categories of public interest rules. It may be recalled that greater participatory rights for non-governmental actors in the negotiating process may have an impact on their significant involvement in a treaty's monitoring and implementation process as the example of the Ottawa Anti-personnel Mines Convention illustrates.[33]

Professor Ago has warned us that certification services non-governmental actors provide to enterprises based upon their own interpretation of international labour law standard set by the ILO carry the risk of lower levels of protection, thus affecting the effectiveness of the enforcement process.

Professor Ota has provided us with a fine example of privatization of public services under market globalization, without the State's obligations under the public interest rules being affected in any way.

32 Boisson de Chazournes and Moise Mbengue 2007, 860.

33 Lawand 2007, 324–347, at 324–327.

Professor Koyano-Ike has demonstrated how through the integrated and institutionalized management of the Danube Delta Conflict both the legitimacy and the effectiveness of the process have benefited from the participation by NGOs.

The Variety of Methods Used to Enhance the Effectiveness of the Process

Defects or problems arisen in the process of implementation may in the course of time be remedied or solved by expansive interpretation of the rules or of the competence of the monitoring bodies.

While applying the stipulated procedures to protect the public interests, institutions have also been looking for ways and methods to remedy detected defects.

Efforts to harmonize the interpretation of applicable rules and standards are an obvious method to increase the effectiveness of the implementation process, as automatic and autonomous compliance by states with public interest rules can only be a long-term perspective.

The 2005 Annex VI to the Madrid Protocol on Environmental Protection to the Antarctic Treaty, dealing with Liability Arising from Environmental Emergencies contains the indirect and unusual but potentially rather effective mechanism to enforce the compliance with the primary rules protecting the Antarctic environment in the interest of the international community: liability for costs of response action that was not actually undertaken.

Whether this unique liability regime could provide a model for future liability regimes in other public spaces remains to be seen.

Professor Koyano has given us a fascinating picture of the variety of methods used over the years of the Danube Delta Conflict: request for relevant information, request to suspend further operation, on-the-spot appraisal, expert missions, unilateral submission of non-compliance by other States, inquiry procedure, and the issuance of a caution.

Her analysis has also shown the limited effectiveness of years of NCPs and other procedures of enforcement even in case of parallel proceedings under various MEAs.

The lack of effectiveness of the management approach in this conflict during a prolonged period of time may at first glance appear to be attractive to potential unwilling parties under these or other MEAs.

However, the cautions issued under both conventions had a decisive impact on Ukraine's willingness to corporate and to reconsider the project. As uncertainties remain and renewed deadlock is possible, judicial or arbitral enforcement may still be an option.[34]

The negative outcome, at least for the time being, of the Danube Delta Conflict, due to the persistent unwillingness of the State Party, however does not take away

34 Koyano, Chapter 10, at 283.

the intrinsic value and potential of the various methods used during the relevant period. Notwithstanding its recent but selective resumption of co-operation and/or dialogue with some of the international institutions involved, and it spite of the various cautions issued, the Ukraine has not yet decided to provisionally suspend the controversial works. On the contrary, it has officially announced that it would complete the Bystroe Canal Project.

Although the assessment of the effectiveness of judicial enforcement is generally regarded as high, the recent drop in the implementation rate of WTO rulings should be noted together with an ensuing call for an enhanced system of retaliation to increase the effectiveness of the enforcement process.[35]

With regard to the financial standards set by the Basel committee we find a combination of 'informal' monitoring and enforcement of members compliance and 'quasi-systemic enforcement' through the World Bank and the IMF.

Normative principles may be used in the process of implementation as benchmarks to assess the adequateness of state compliance with public interest rules.

If such principles then are being institutionalized in the process of implementation in the actual decision-making process of for instance precautionary measures, this could enhance the effectiveness of the precautionary regime established under the OSPAR convention, as Professor Komori has rightly observed.[36]

Impact of the Process of Implementation of Public Interest Rules on Some Issues of General International Law

As to the changes brought to the traditional framework of international law by the functioning of institutions monitoring the implementation process of public interest rules, the preceding chapters have shown that distinctions such as the one between law-making and the application of the law, and between compliance procedures and enforcement have become less clear.

Precise rule setting is of great importance for the effectiveness of the process of implementation and enforcement.

When drafting public interest rules, States should not only pay attention to the principle of mutual supportiveness but they should also look carefully at the potential effectiveness of the process of implementation and enforcement they want to put in place: neglecting the inherent link between the procedural and substantive aspects of such interlocking provisions is detrimental for the effectiveness of any enforcement process.

Is there a general duty to prevent the commission of any violation of a public interest rule *sensu stricto*?

---

35 Choi 2007, 1043–1071.

36 Komori in Introduction, at 8, referring to Horiguchi's contribution.

That the Court in the *Bosnia Genocide* case merely hinted at the existence of such an overall obligation can be seen as part of the process of emergence of such a duty.

In the Court's view the duty to prevent genocide is an obligation of conduct: the state should use all means reasonably available to it, given its capacity to influence and within the limits of public international law.[37]

However, Judge Kreca convincingly considers the obligation to prevent genocide to be an obligation of result because of the link between the peremptory nature of the norm and the ensuing 'absolute obligatory force' of the duty to prevent.[38]

Moreover, a recent study, when commenting on the *Bosnia Genocide* case, correctly pointed out that the obligation to prevent genocide 'subsists from the moment that the convention enters into force for any State and does not "arise" at a later date upon the State's knowledge of an impending genocide or of a risk that genocide may take place. Up to that point, the obligation is undoubtedly binding on the State, even if does not require any particular action by the State (apart, perhaps, from a continuing duty of vigilance)'.[39]

This observation certainly applies to any conventional duty to prevent all violations of public interest rules such as within MEAs.

The customary duty to prevent violations of public interest rules comes into being simultaneously with the creation of the rules themselves.

Giorgio Gaja recently noted that the ILC's new formulation in Article 25 on necessity appears to suggest the existence of the possibility to invoke the state of necessity in a case when an interest of the international community is at stake.[40]

In various awards dealing with Argentina ICSID Tribunals, although not faced with a claim exclusively based on the interest of the international community, in applying Article 25 were also assessing whether 'the essential interest of the international community as a whole was affected in any relevant way'.[41]

---

37 *Application of the Convention on the Prevention and Punishment of the Crime of Genocide* (*Bosnia and Herzegovina v Serbia and Montenegro*), Judgment of 26 February 2007, para. 430.

38 *Application of the Convention on the Prevention and Punishment of the Crime of Genocide* (*Bosnia and Herzegovina v Serbia and Montenegro*), Judgment of 26 February 2007, Separate Opinion of Judge *ad hoc* Kreca, paras. 117 and 119.

39 Oleson 2007, 116.

40 Gaja 2007, 417–424, at 424.

41 See for instance *CMS Gas Transmission Company v Argentine Republic* (ICSID Case No. ARB/O1/O8), Award of 12 May 2005, para. 325 and the *Enron Corporation and Ponderosa Assets L.P. v Argentine Republic* (ICSID Case No. ARB/01/3), Award of 22 May 2007, para. 310, as reproduced by Oleson 2007, 163 and 171.

(Potential) Impact of General International Law on the Process of Implementation of Public Interest Rules

The irreversible humanization of international law is bound to have an impact on the process of implementation and enforcement of public interest rules.

Thanks to their constitutional character human rights 'can provide any standard to judge various international interests',[42] and as a consequence the human rights approach to compliance and observance stretches well beyond the impact of the principle of mutual supportiveness.

A change of paradigm takes place; for instance, the prohibition of genocide may be approached under the traditional perspective – in terms of state conduct being prohibited – whereas under the human rights approach the prohibition of genocide starts from the right of individuals to be free from acts of genocide.

The general duty upon States to enforce public interest rules *sensu stricto* flows from the public interest nature of those rules, although it may also have been explicitly laid down in a conventional provision such as in the Genocide Convention.[43]

Dawidowicz's recent analysis of state practice of third-party countermeasures in response to serious breaches of public interest rules has confirmed the conclusion reached earlier by Tams that the ILC's arguments on the limited, embryonic, Western-dominated State practice and the absence of *opinio juris* are not convincing.[44]

There is thus 'strong support in international practice for the view that States are entitled to take third-party countermeasures in order to protect community interest'.[45]

Although it could be argued that in many instances this non-systemic method of enforcement has turned out to be more effective than the systemic or conventional ones, the jury is still out on the question raised in Chapter 1 whether conventional enforcement regimes are more effective if they are exclusive *vis à vis* extra-conventional means of enforcement.

---

42 Teraya, Chapter 3.

43 As to the duty to enforce public interest rules, a WTO Panel recently noted that the ILC articles 'do not speak of *enforcement* [my italics] when addressing the use of countermeasures': WTO Panel Report, *Mexico – Tax Measures on Soft Drinks and Other Beverages*, WT/DS308/R, 7 October 2005, para. 8.180 as reproduced in *Report of the Secretary-General. Responsibility of States for internationally wrongful acts. Compilation of decisions of international courts, tribunals and other bodies*, A/62/62, 1 February 2007, at 81, para. 127. The same Panel also held that the phrase 'to secure compliance' in article XX(d) 'was to be interpreted as meaning 'to enforce compliance' and that therefore the said provision was concerned with action at a domestic rather than international level', as reproduced *ibid.*, at 81, para. 127.

44 Dawidowicz 2006, 408–415.

45 Dawidowicz 2006, 418.

The Question Raised by Carol Harlow

Has the research undertaken provide indications as to how to meet the challenge posed by Carol Harlow and referred to in Chapter 1? Should the process of implementation of public interest rules be free 'to develop on its own, possibly subject to a process of cross fertilisation' or alternatively 'should conscious efforts be made to stimulate a process of harmonization?'

Unsurprisingly the picture is a mixed one.

The diversification of the implementation process, whether institutionalized or not, as analyzed in Part II, is undeniable and could be (seen as) an indication that the process is developing on its own.

While, on the one hand, object and purpose of a particular public interest rule may be fuelling this diversification, the principle of mutual supportiveness has the potential of producing cross-fertilization and of bringing more consistency in the process.

As to 'conscious efforts' made 'to stimulate a process of harmonization', coordination of legal regimes and systems in the implementation process as described in Part III will certainly continue to play an important role in this regard, while the diversification of actors addressed in Part IV inevitably requires 'conscious efforts' in order to reduce disharmony in the process.

The incremental or more advanced stage of harmonization reaches its limits however, when the object and purpose of the public interest rule, in order to maintain its effectiveness calls for common but differentiated responsibilities as pointed out in Chapter 1.

Even the most effective judicial system for enforcement of human rights is in need of a framework to clarify the way domestic courts apply the European Convention on Human Rights and the European Court's case law and how they apply domestic law in harmonization with the European body of human rights law.[46]

Efforts have been undertaken by monitoring bodies such as the Committee on the Rights of the Child to harmonize within a particular regime the interpretation of applicable rules by States and other actors; as a result the effectiveness of the process was improved.

In the area of international labour law the ILO is anxious to maintain and guarantee the pre-existing level of protection by carefully guarding the 'acquis' of its interpretation and implementation.

In the Danube Delta Conflict, the existence of similar regulations in parallel regarding the project did call for harmonized application of these regulations.

Also the process of implementation of public interest rules through the use of third-party countermeasures could develop on its own and will be subject to a certain process of cross-fertilization, but one has to agree with Dawodowicz that 'the emerging constitutionalisation of the enforcement function under general

46 Wildhaber 2007, 217–232, at 219.

international law has not been matched by a corresponding development of institutional safeguards against the exercise of improper or arbitrary use of third-party countermeasures'.[47]

The picture presented in the preceding chapter of this book indicates that both development on its own with cross-fertilization and conscious efforts of harmonization are taking place. Object and purpose of the public interest rule once again appears to be among the decisive factors in this regard. That is another reason – apart from the methodological obstacles referred to earlier – why measuring the effectiveness of the process cannot be uniform.[48]

The principle of mutual supportiveness undoubtedly provides us with the best chance to meet the main challenge faced by the school of constitutionalism, namely to turn the interconnection, as a matter of fact, of cross-sectorial issues relating to armed conflict, the environment, development and human rights, into a matter of law.

More frequent utilization of the principle of mutual supportiveness both *ex ante* and *ex post*, could certainly improve the degree of effectiveness required by the public interest nature of the rules we have analyzed.

Finally, we should be aware that a number of current devices and mechanisms to implement those rules are only of a temporary nature, to remedy the structural deficiencies of the international legal system until the establishment of more effective machinery.

References

Books, Articles and Chapters in Books

Boisson de Chazournes, L. and Moise Mbengue, M. (2007), 'A Propos du Principe du Soutien Mutuel – Les Relations entre le Protocole de Cartagena et les Accords de l'OMC', *Revue Générale de Droit International Public* 111, 829–862.

Choi, W.M. (2007), 'To Comply or Not to Comply? – Non-implementation Problems in the WTO Dispute Settlement', *Journal of World Trade Law* 41, 1043–1071.

Dawidowicz, M. (2006), 'Public Law Enforcement without Public Law Safeguards? An Analysis of State Practice on Third-Party Countermeasures and Their Relationship to the UN Security Council', *British Yearbook of International Law* 77, 333–418.

Fernandez-Sanchez, P.A. (eds) (2006), *The New Challenges of Humanitarian Law in Armed Conflict. Essays in Honour of Professor Juan Antonio Carillo-Salcedo* (Leyden: M. Nijhoff Publishers).

47 Dawidowicz 2006, 418.

48 Komori, Chapter 2, at 73.

Gaja, G. (2007), 'La possibilité d'invoquer l'état de nécessité pour protéger les intérêts de la communauté internationale', in *Droit du Pouvoir, Pouvoir du Droit. Mélanges offerts à Jean Salmon.*

Koojmans, P. (2007), 'The ICJ in the 21st Century: Judicial Restraint, Judicial Activism, or Proactive Judicial Policy', *International & Comparative Law Quarterly* 56, 741–754.

Lawand, K. (2007), 'The Convention on the Prohibition of the Use, Stockpiling, Production and Transfer of Anti-personnel Mines and on the Destruction (Ottawa Convention)', in Ulfstein, Marauhn and Zimmerman (eds).

Oleson, S. (2007), *The Impact of the ILC's Articles on Responsibility of States for Internationally Wrongful Acts* (London: British Institute of International and Comparative Law).

Quesada-Alcala, C. (2006), 'The Obstacles to the International Criminal Court: Impediments to the Enforcement of International Humanitarian Law', in Fernandez-Sanchez (ed.).

Thürer, D. (2007), 'International Humanitarian Law: Essence and Perspectives', *Revue Suisse de Droit international et européen* 17, 157–164.

Ulfstein, G., Marauhn, T. and Zimmermann, A. (eds) (2007), *Making Treaties Work. Human Rights, Environment and Arms Control* (Cambridge: Cambridge University Press).

Vermeer-Kûnzli, A. (2007), 'A Matter of Interest: Diplomatic Protection and State Responsibility *Erga Omnes*', *International & Comparative Law Quarterly* 56, 553–582.

Vermeer-Kûnzli, A. (2007), *The Protection of Individuals by Means of Diplomatic Protection. Diplomatic Protection as a Human Rights Instrument* (Leyden: Phd).

Wayde Pittman, T. and Heaphy, M. (2008), 'Does the United States Really Prosecute Its Service Members for War Crimes? Implications for Complementarity before the International Criminal Court?', *Leiden Journal of International Law* 21, 165–183.

Wildhaber, L. (2007), 'The European Convention on Human Rights and International Law', *International & Comparative Law Quarterly* 56, 217–232.

Official Documents and Others

Agim Behrami and Bekir Behrami against France and Ruzhdi Samarati against France, Germany and Norway (Application No. 71412/01 and Application No. 78166/01), Decision as to the Admissibility of 2 May 2007.

CMS Gas Transmission Company v Argentine Republic (ICSID Case No. ARB/O1/O8), Award of 12 May 2005.

Dispute concerning Access to Information Under Article 9 of the OSPAR Convention (*Ireland v United Kingdom*), Final Award of 2 July 2003.

Enron Corporation and Ponderosa Assets L.P. v Argentine Republic (ICSID Case No. ARB/01/3), Award of 22 May 2007.

WTO Panel Report, Mexico – Tax Measures on Soft Drinks and Other Beverages, WT/DS308/R, 7 October 2005.

Index